MAUGHAM

Ted Morgan

A TOUCHSTONE BOOK
Published by Simon & Schuster, Inc.
NEW YORK

Designed by Eve Metz

Photo Editor—Vincent Virga

Manufactured in the United States of America

1 3 5 7 9 10 8 6 4 2
1 3 5 7 9 10 8 6 4 2 Pbk.

Library of Congress Cataloging in Publication Data

MORGAN, TED, DATE.
MAUGHAM.
(A TOUCHSTONE BOOK)
INCLUDES BIBLIOGRAPHICAL REFERENCES AND INDEX.
1. MAUGHAM, WILLIAM SOMERSET, 1874–1965—BIOGRAPHY.
2. AUTHORS, ENGLISH—20TH CENTURY—BIOGRAPHY.
PR6025.A86Z765   1981   823'.914   80–26890

ISBN 0-671-50581-5 Pbk.

PERMISSIONS

The author is grateful for the permission of the following publishers, authors, and literary agents to quote copyrighted material from the following works:

A Case of Human Bondage, Beverley Nichols, by permission of Secker & Warburg, and Eric Glass Ltd.

A Child of the Jago, Arthur Morrison, by permission of A. P. Watt & Son.

"A Cool Hand," Morton Zabel, *The Nation,* May 3, 1941, by permission of *The Nation.*

A Writer's Notebook, W. Somerset Maugham, copyright 1949 by W. Somerset Maugham, by permission of Doubleday & Co., Inc., and A. P. Watt & Son.

As We Were, E. F. Benson, by permission of A. P. Watt & Son.

The Barrymores, Hollis Alpert, copyright 1964 by Hollis Alpert, reprinted by permission of The Dial Press.

Between the Thunder and the Sun, Vincent Sheean, by permission of Brandt & Brandt.

Cakes and Ale, W. Somerset Maugham, copyright 1930 by Doubleday & Co., Inc., by permission of Doubleday and A. P. Watt & Son.

Classics and Commercials, Edmund Wilson, copyright 1950 by Edmund Wilson, renewed 1977 by Elena Wilson. From

(Continued page 673)

This book is dedicated to the memory of
S. N. Behrman.

PERSONAL NOTE BY THE LITERARY EXECUTOR TO THE LATE W. SOMERSET MAUGHAM

When W. Somerset Maugham was making his will he asked me to come to his villa to discuss the clause instructing me not to authorize any biography nor "to assist any person who wishes or attempts any such publication." I was therefore fully aware of his wishes. But no literary executor can prevent anyone from writing about a testator—though he can of course prevent the inclusion of any copyrighted material either from his work or from his letters.

However, when Maugham made this stipulation and when I accepted it, neither of us could foresee how many books would be written about him. Some of these books were written with great responsibility, some with an apparent lack of it. But even the most conscientious had been unable, for lack of access to the material, to give a true picture of his final tragic years—the years in which he wrote the autobiography that aroused much adverse comment but from which Maugham did not benefit financially at all; the years in which he tried to adopt Alan Searle as his son; the years when he sold his pictures, many of which belonged to his daughter; the years when a trusted influence was constantly brought to bear on a mind definitely unhinged and on a pathetic (he would not have liked the word) character.

Accordingly, when Ted Morgan sent me his first draft, and I was struck not merely by his scrupulous research but by the fact that he had not attempted to pass any moral judgment on any character concerned, I decided that, lest the flood of gossip, or, at best, incomplete record, should build up for the future a false myth about Maugham's life and character, I would arrange for Mr. Morgan to have access to those facts, based either on written evidence or corroborated by several witnesses, that are for the first time made available to the public in this book.

That I have departed from the explicit letter of my instructions, by "assisting" Mr. Morgan I am well aware, and I take full responsibility, since no urging was at any time put on me by Mr. Morgan or by any other person. But I have always held that a large part of the duty of a literary executor (and I have been asked to fill that difficult position by authors as wildly different from Mr. Maugham, both in their writing and their personalities, as A. A. Milne and Elizabeth Bowen) lay in preventing distortion of an author's reputation either by ill-chosen presentation of his work or by misrepresentation, however innocently intended, of his actions and character. I am also aware, though I have not consulted her, that the truth may help to provide some justice for Mr. Maugham's daughter, who, with her husband, has suffered much but said nothing.

Many people may think that I have acted wrongly. Only one man could have given me a clear decision, and he was the man who had sufficient confidence in me to place his reputation in my hands.

SPENCER CURTIS BROWN

CONTENTS

MAUGHAM

PREFACE

In November 1957, when he was eighty-three, William Somerset Maugham sent his friends a note that said: "Don't please, think me ungracious, but I hate having my letters published. Indeed in my will I have expressly directed my executors to prevent their publication, and I have begged any persons who may have in their possession any to destroy them."[1]

Maugham's plea was reproduced in a number of newspapers, along with editorials to the effect that when a writer as celebrated as Somerset Maugham asked his correspondents to destroy his letters, he would undoubtedly achieve the opposite result. The *Philadelphia Inquirer* wrote on November 17, 1957: "Somerset Maugham . . . has taken the most effective step possible to assure that his letters will be preserved for posterity; he has publicly urged that those letters be destroyed . . . We do not think Mr. Maugham is 'ungracious.' We think he is smart. From now on the burning of a Maugham letter will be 'news.' And the unburned letters will long be talked about when tomorrow's Cakes and Ale are being passed around."

Maugham was not being smart. He honestly wanted his letters destroyed. They were a threat to the benign image of himself he had been working on for years and wanted to perpetuate beyond the grave. Destroying adverse evidence was his way of influencing the opinion of posterity. With the letters gone, no evidence would remain that could be used to judge him *in absentia*. His last will, dated July 9, 1964, made it official:

> I direct that there shall be no biography or publication of my letters and that my literary executor and my trustees are to refuse permission for any such publication and any assistance to any person who wishes

or attempts any such publication. Further, I earnestly request anyone who possesses any of my letters to destroy them.[2]

Maugham then went about destroying the letters in his possession from such correspondents as Lytton Strachey and Winston Churchill. He and his secretary, Alan Searle, held a series of "bonfire nights" in the large stone fireplace in the drawing room of the Villa Mauresque in 1958. Piles of letters were thrown in, as well as some of Maugham's manuscripts. Searle—horrified to see so much valuable material go up in smoke—tried to rescue choice items. Coming down to breakfast after a bonfire night, Maugham would rub his hands and tell Searle: "That was a good night's work. Now we'll burn everything you've hidden under the sofa."[3]

Maugham, who had spent most of his long life prying into the affairs of humankind, did not want his own affairs pried into. What did he have to hide? Why did he go to such lengths to cover his tracks? Most writers, after all, want to be remembered, and biographies help keep their works in print. Maugham, who had a passion for detective stories, turned his own life into one, complete with false clues and surprise ending—but why? Such were the questions that led me to write the present book.

There were several biographical efforts during his lifetime. Bennett Cerf, then editor in chief at Random House, wanted S. N. Behrman to write a book on his friend Maugham, confident that it would be as popular as his book on the art dealer Duveen. On June 2, 1952, Behrman wrote Maugham in a bantering tone that made it easy for Maugham to refuse and easier still for Behrman to face rejection:

> The other day, as I was reading your amended version of "Don Fernando," I came upon a remark which although written by you, seemed to be profound: that if the whole truth were told about any human being, he would inevitably emerge as the most depraved of criminals. I believe this and therefore will not make any attempt to write your life, even if you should consent to let me do so. On the other hand, of course, I could agreeably lie . . . and if the task would permit me to spend six months or a year with Edward [one of Maugham's servants], I might consider it if you would consider it.[4]

Maugham replied that he would not consider it because the truth could not be told in any case.[5]

Ten years later Behrman told William A. Jackson, curator of the

Houghton Library at Harvard, that he was still thinking of doing a Maugham book. Jackson replied: "If you can tell the whole truth it would be more appalling than one of his own stories."[6]

But Behrman decided against it and wrote Jackson on September 4, 1963: "I have already decided, largely on the advice of William Shawn [editor of *The New Yorker*], not to do the Maugham book. The whole story, as you yourself suggest, is appalling and pitiful, and Shawn said why devote two years of time to it?"[7]

To another friend Behrman wrote, on January 7, 1963: "This whole thing—this Maugham nexus—is one of the most bizarre, grotesque, fantastic, and in some respects, farcically funny situations I have ever known about. If I could write it to the full it would be some story! But of course it cannot be considered while this very complicated and ancient creature still lives."[8]

Writing his biography was considered by two men while Maugham was alive. The first was Richard A. Cordell, a professor of English (now retired) at Purdue University, who began corresponding with Maugham in 1928, and published his first book, a critical work on Maugham's writing, with an introductory biographical chapter, in 1937. Maugham approved of the project and offered to read it in proof in order to correct or confirm statements of fact. In this manner he was able to mislead Cordell by feeding him false information about matters that he wanted to cover up. Maugham approved of the book because he controlled its contents.[9] Cordell, for instance, never suspected that Maugham was a homosexual. "I was just a country boy," he later explained.

When Cordell in 1954 told Maugham that he wanted to write a fuller biography, Maugham replied on May 7:

> There are in the United States and England 11 people altogether who are anxious to write my biography. Several have applied to me for sanction. I have invariably refused to have anything to do with any such schemes . . . I know quite well that I cannot prevent anyone from writing a biography, but as he will never have more than such data as he can acquire from my books and from the reminiscences of people who have known me, why should I care? I am all against a biography being written for a variety of reasons. I would not in the least mind the whole truth being written about me, but it would be gravely embarrassing to other persons.[10]

Cordell went ahead, publishing his *Somerset Maugham: A Biographical and Critical Study* in 1959. He sent a copy to the master, who wrote

he had nothing graceful to say about it because he had not read
nfessed to a pathological defect, which was that he was unable
.nything about himself, not even a newspaper cutting.[11]

professed indifference to Cordell's book turned to rage in the
case oi Karl G. Pfeiffer, an English professor at New York University,
who in 1959 published *W. Somerset Maugham: A Candid Portrait*. Pfeiffer had first met Maugham across a bridge table in 1923 when Maugham
was transiting through America on one of his journeys to Asia to collect
material. When Maugham spent the World War II years in America,
Pfeiffer saw him often and wrote several magazine articles about him.
In 1946 he first broached the idea of writing a book. Go right ahead,
Maugham said, but warned him that he would have a good deal of
competition, as he knew three people who were anxiously awaiting his
death to write books about him. Pfeiffer believed that he had Maugham's
imprimatur. He felt betrayed when six years later Maugham wrote him
that since he had turned down requests from Patrick Kinross and S. N.
Behrman, he could not give him any assistance. Maugham repeated his
reason that in any case the truth could not be told.[12]

Pfeiffer forged ahead, against Maugham's increasingly strenuous objections. On March 28, 1958, Maugham wrote him that he had set
himself against a biography as strongly as he could, and that biographies
written when a person was still alive were often inaccurate and disgust-
ingly fulsome. The book was scheduled for publication by Norton in
1959, and on October 16, 1958, George Brockway, an editor at Norton,
wrote Maugham asking for his permission to use a photograph of him
on the jacket. Maugham cabled back on October 20 from the Dorchester
Hotel in London: STRONGLY OBJECT TO PUBLICATION OF BIOGRAPHY IN
MY LIFETIME.[13]

Brockway replied on December 3: "I think I can appreciate your feelings about the publication of a biography about you. On the other hand,
as I am sure you are aware, the life of a man of your distinction has a
significance and an interest beyond his control. At any rate, we are not
using your picture on the dust jacket of the book, but we are publishing
the book. I am sending a copy of it herewith, with the compliments of
the author, who would have written you himself, except that he has just
undergone a serious operation for cancer."[14]

When Maugham received the copy he wrote Cordell, on January 25,
1959, that he had broken his rule never to read anything about himself:
"I was pressed to read Karl Pfeiffer's book. It is full of absurd inaccuracies
—for instance he makes me have an interview with Gandhi who had

died long before I went to India—and vulgar into the bargain. He uses words of which he doesn't know the meaning and he has an unfortunate knack of repeating a sentence of mine so as to kill its point."[15]

What really rankled, however, far beyond inaccuracy and vulgarity, was that Pfeiffer, after worshiping at the Maugham shrine for thirty years, had now written that "He is, in my opinion, a good writer of the second rank." The book was strewn with barbs:

> Maugham couldn't write another *Of Human Bondage* because there is no warmth in the man he made himself into.
>
> . . . . .
>
> Much of his criticism is a thinly disguised justification of his own practice as a writer.
>
> . . . . .
>
> The few Americans in Maugham's novels and short stories lay bare their essential Americanism by saying "Gee" at frequent intervals.
>
> . . . . .
>
> *The Razor's Edge* marks his decline as a novelist . . .
>
> . . . . .
>
> When the critics of the future make up their minds about him, what will be Maugham's rating in the world of letters? Will he be a good writer of the second rank or will he become a footnote in the histories of literature? He has great prestige but no solid reputation.[16]

Pfeiffer later complained to his editor that after thirty years of letters signed "Willie" he was now receiving letters signed "W. S. Maugham."[17]

Throughout his life Maugham's attitude toward biographers was filled with distrust. He saw them bearing not frankincense and myrrh but wormwood and hemlock. He was able to keep them at bay during his lifetime, but after his death in 1965, books by friends and relatives began appearing and told of a tormented personal life. Maugham's nephew Robin, whom he had treated like a son, to the point of settling a $25,000 trust fund on him in 1939, came out in 1966 with *Somerset and All the Maughams*, in which he reported that his uncle had told him his greatest mistake had been that "I tried to persuade myself that I was three quarters normal and that only a quarter of me was queer—whereas really it was the other way around."[18] Simon Raven, in the London *Spectator*, wrote on April 8, 1966, that Robin Maugham's essential aim had been to cash in on his uncle before anyone else could. In 1978 Robin brought out a sequel called *Conversations with Willie*—much of it a rehash of the material in *Somerset and All the Maughams*—which he said was based on a "treasure trove" of notes he had taken about his famous uncle; the notes had been kept in storage and forgotten. Anyone who has seen Maugham's letters to Robin at the Humanities Research Center in Texas will conclude that the origin of some of Robin's "conversations with Willie" were in epistolary form.

Beverley Nichols, a journalist whom Maugham had befriended, wrote a gossipy account of Maugham's marriage called *A Case of Human Bondage*. It was intended as a defense of Maugham's ex-wife, Syrie, whom Maugham had pilloried in a series of autobiographical articles published in the *Sunday Express* in England and in *Show* magazine in the United States. The articles, entitled *Looking Back*, shocked many of Maugham's friends and admirers. Noel Coward said he would no longer have anything to do with Maugham. Graham Greene, in a letter to the *Daily Telegraph* published on June 10, 1966, referred to *Looking Back* as "the sick Maugham's senile and scandalous work." The point of Greene's letter was to express his dismay that Heinemann, Maugham's publisher for more than half a century, should publish Beverley Nichols' attack on him. He congratulated himself on having left Heinemann, thereby protecting himself from the experience of having "one of the lesser hyenas of the group wet its teeth in my dead bowels." (*A Case of Human Bondage* was published by Secker and Warburg, a member of the Heinemann group.)

Also in 1966 there appeared Garson Kanin's memoir, *Remembering Mr. Maugham*. Kanin and his wife, Ruth Gordon, had seen Maugham on and off since the thirties, and Kanin became a sort of Boswell, jotting down their conversations. The result was an amusing and sympathetic treatment, mainly anecdotal. Kanin too judiciously waited until Maugham's death to publish his reminiscences, even though he tiptoed past the topic of Maugham's homosexuality.

Before and after Maugham's death there appeared a number of other critical and biographical studies. Klaus Jonas, a German-born scholar who now teaches at the University of Pittsburgh, founded the Center for Maugham Studies, which compiled Maugham material for about fifteen years. The material is now in the Humanities Research Center in Austin, Texas. Jonas also published three collections of articles and miscellanea concerning Maugham: *The Maugham Enigma* in 1954, *The Gentleman from Cap Ferrat* in 1956, and *The World of Somerset Maugham* in 1959.

In 1965 Wilmon Menard, a South Pacific buff and resident of Hawaii, published *The Two Worlds of Somerset Maugham*, retracing

Maugham's steps in the South Seas and filling in several blank years of his Pacific travels. Anthony Curtis, literary editor of the *Financial Times*, published an interesting critical study called *The Pattern of Maugham* in 1974, and a picture book with a brief text in 1977. He also organized a centenary broadcast on the BBC in January 1974, in which he brought together a number of persons who had known Maugham, such as Terence Rattigan, Fay Compton, Lord Boothby, Lord Clark, Frank Swinnerton, John Gielgud, and A. S. Frere. The result was a good example of oral biography. Frederic Raphael published another picture book with text in 1976.

In 1972 a young Canadian scholar, Robert Lorin Calder, came out with a critical study called *W. Somerset Maugham & the Quest for Freedom*, which made two important biographical contributions. Calder conclusively identified the character of Rosie in *Cakes and Ale*. He also gave a full account of Maugham's role as a British spy in Russia in 1917, based on the papers of Sir William Wiseman, the head of the British secret service in the United States during World War I.

Other interesting findings were made by Joseph Dobrinsky, a professor at the University of Montpellier, who published *La Jeunesse de Somerset Maugham* in 1975. This book takes Maugham up to the age of thirty, in 1903, and gives detailed psychoanalytical readings of all his works up to that time.

While these books were being written, the letters—all those thousands of letters that Maugham had begged their recipients to destroy (for he was an indefatigable correspondent)—began turning up at auction sales and in the shops of rare-book dealers and eventually made their way into the great research libraries of the United States. They turned up piecemeal, some here and some there, and they are still turning up. To give one example: Maugham's letters to his first literary agent, Morris Colles, are scattered among five libraries—the Humanities Research Center in Austin, Texas, the Lilly Library in Bloomington, Indiana, the Fales Collection at New York University, the Houghton Library at Harvard, and the Beinecke Library at Yale.

Besides the letters and those persons still alive who knew Maugham, a third important source was Maugham's own writing. He wrote two explicitly autobiographical works, *The Summing Up* and *Strictly Personal*, and compiled a third, *A Writer's Notebook*, from notes taken from the age of eighteen. But significantly, when *The Summing Up* and *A Writer's Notebook* were published in one volume, the title he chose was *The Partial View*. In addition, he sprinkled fragments of autobiography in prefaces and introductions. He also introduced himself as the narrator in several novels, first under the name Ashenden, and then, in *The Razor's Edge*, under his own name. Finally, three years before his death, he published the brutally candid series of autobiographical articles.

As valuable as an author's account of himself may be, it is subject to distortion, inaccuracy, and in Maugham's case, deliberate falsehood. When the narrator describes himself in such a novel as *The Moon and Sixpence* or a series of stories such as *Ashenden*, is it proper to infer that what he says applies to the author? In such a novel as *Of Human Bondage*, of which Maugham said "my childhood is there word for word," can we attribute everything that occurs in the novel to the author's life? This is terra incognita, and it must be carefully navigated. There are dangers in taking what Maugham wrote about himself at face value. In *A Writer's Notebook*, for instance, he describes under the year 1892 his feelings when Santo Jeronimo Caserio, the assassin of French President Sadi Carnot, was executed. But this event took place two years later, in 1894. In *Cakes and Ale*, to give another example, Maugham wrote, "A little while ago I read in the *Evening Standard* an article by Mr. Evelyn Waugh in the course of which he remarked that to write novels in the first person was a contemptible practice." When Alec Waugh visited Maugham in the summer of 1931, he pointed out that his brother had never written such an article. Maugham shrugged.

It is a curious experience to spend three years trying to get inside another man's skin. Over those years I developed an unnatural passion for postmarks and spent hours correlating dates and tracking down bits of minute information. When I slept, armies of footnotes marched across my dreams in close-order drill. The man's productivity was enormous, and all those novels and plays and stories had to be fitted into the narrative, for one of the ways into the inner life of an important writer is through what he wrote. When I came to the end I was sorry I had to leave Maugham and continue my own life without him. The biographer becomes attached to his subject in a way that cannot be duplicated in other relationships. In many cases he knows a great deal about someone he has never met. Upon his work depends the way that person will be remembered. I can only agree with Maugham:

> It is distressing to think that the composer of the quintet in the *Meistersinger* was dishonest in money matters and treacherous to those who had benefited him. But it may be that he could not have had great

qualities if he had not also had great failings. I do not believe they are right who say that the defects of famous men should be ignored. I think it is better that we should know them. Then, though we are conscious of having faults as glaring as theirs, we can believe that that is no hindrance to our achieving also something of their virtues.

This is the biography of a man whose defects were glaring, but they should not be used to diminish his accomplishments.

ERRATUM
The story on pages 397–98 concerning Cyril Connolly's magazine,
Horizon, is out of chronology. Horizon did not
publish its first issue until 1939. The story
takes place in October 1940.

PART I

1874-1897

Chapter One

The sort of books an author writes depends on the sort of man he is and so it is well to know what is relevant in his personal history.

Maugham, *Ten Novels and Their Authors*

IN ENGLAND in 1874, Queen Victoria had been on the throne for thirty-seven years and showed no inclination to leave. Elections were held that year, and Disraeli, the most enigmatic of British statesmen, became Prime Minister. In the furthest reaches of empire there was a famine in Bengal, and a Zulu revolt in South Africa. At home the Irish revolutionaries, or Fenians, brought terrorism to London, but seven thousand persons attended a demonstration in Hyde Park in favor of amnesty for Fenian prisoners.

In the shadow of these great events life went on as usual. The Thames reached a record high tide of four feet three and a half inches above Trinity high-water mark. Bishops quarreled with urbanists over plans to restore St. Paul's Cathedral. Fifty-one men and boys lost their lives in a colliery explosion at the Astley Deep pit, near Manchester. The celebrated Derby winner Voltigeur had to be shot after his leg was broken from a mare's kick. An elderly gentleman in Barnstable died from the bite of a rat. In the House of Commons a new air machine for better ventilation went into operation but did not affect the rhetoric. Lady Dickes, a leader of London society, was cremated in Dresden, to the consternation of her friends, cremation being practically unknown in England. Seventy-five minutes after the introduction of the coffin into the furnace all that remained of her was six pounds of dust.

In literature Browning and Tennyson were the giants, with Carlyle and Ruskin not far behind. Among the 3,351 books published in England that year was the final tome of a three-volume biography of Dickens by John Forster. Dickens, who had died in 1870, was beyond all comparison the most popular author who ever wrote English. He had been paid a thousand pounds a story. Other notable books that

3

year were Thomas Hardy's *Far from the Madding Crowd*, Aubrey de Vere's *Alexander the Great*, and Swinburne's long poem, *Bothwell*.[1]

France under the Third Republic was still recovering from the Franco-Prussian War and the Commune. Entire neighborhoods of Paris had been reduced to rubble. On January 25, inside the British Embassy on the Faubourg Saint Honoré, Edith Maugham gave birth to her fourth son, William Somerset. In later years it would be said of him that he was the most popular author writing in English since Dickens, and that he was paid a thousand pounds for a story.

Somerset Maugham would live to the age of ninety-one, far beyond the life expectancy of a baby born in 1874. His life spanned two centuries. He was born more or less in the middle of the Victorian era. When he was twenty-one he had friends who were killed in the Boer War. He was too old for active service in World War I. By the time World War II was over he was past seventy. The year he died, 1965, was the year Lyndon Johnson committed half a million American troops to the war in Vietnam.

Maugham's birth in an embassy rather than a hospital was the result of France's defeat in 1870. Concern about manpower led to the proposal of a law that would give all children born on French soil automatic French citizenship, so that they might be conscripted in the next war. The embassy, a mansion with gardens on the Champs-Elysées which had once been the residence of Napoleon's sister, Pauline Borghese, was British soil, and the ambassador, Lord Lyons, had turned the second floor into a maternity ward. Although the law was never passed, three children were born in the embassy during its imminence, all in 1874: Violet Williams-Freeman, daughter of the second secretary; Emily Lytton, daughter of the first secretary, the Earl of Lytton; and William Somerset Maugham.[2]

William Somerset's father, Robert Ormond Maugham, born in 1823, was a lawyer in England who had gone into partnership with a friend named William Dixon. In 1848 they established an office in Paris at 12 rue Royale. Robert Ormond Maugham took over the Paris office and was appointed to handle the British Embassy's legal affairs. In 1863 the office was moved to 54 Faubourg Saint Honoré, almost directly across the street from the embassy.[3]

Also in 1863, on October 1, Robert Ormond Maugham married Edith Mary Snell, a twenty-three-year-old English girl who had been brought up in France by her widowed mother. There was an age difference of seventeen years between Edith and her husband. She was small-boned and delicately featured, with large brown eyes and reddish-gold hair. She was considered beautiful. Robert Ormond had a high-domed forehead, muttonchop whiskers, and a face like a Toby jug. He was considered ugly. Edith's closest friend in Paris was Lady Anglesey, the American-born wife of Henry Paget, fourth Marquess of Anglesey, a descendant of the general who lost a leg at Waterloo. "You're so beautiful and there are so many people in love with you, why are you faithful to that ugly little man you've married?" Lady Anglesey asked Edith Maugham, who replied, "He never hurt my feelings."[4]

In terms of background, there was nothing very grand to report on Maugham's father's side. According to legend, the Maughams originally came from Ireland, where the name is more common than in England. The family settled in Westmorland, the picturesque Lake District near the Scottish border. Maugham said his ancestors were statesmen, which did not mean that they were concerned with politics but that they owned and farmed their own land. When his great-grandfather was ruined in the Napoleonic wars, he sent his son to London, and the family of farmers became a family of lawyers.[5] His grandfather Robert, a lawyer of some prominence, was cofounder of the Law Society, the second most important legal association in England. There is a long list of his legal works in the British Museum, and his achievements merited an article in the Dictionary of National Biography.[6]

On Maugham's mother's side there were hints of grandeur. His grandfather Charles Snell was the son of a sailmaker who enlisted in the service of the East India Company. He married Anne Alicia Todd, the daughter of a Falmouth squire, in whose veins royal blood may have coursed. At least that was the thesis of an article by Patrick Montague-Smith that appeared in the Genealogists' Magazine in June 1952. Entitled "Two Royal Descendants of Viscount Maugham, Lord Chancellor 1938-1939, and Mr. Somerset Maugham," the article traced the Maugham line through Anne Alicia Todd to King Edward I of England and his wife Eleanor of Castile. Anne Todd's mother was a Brereton, a famous family of warriors who went back to the Crusades, and it was through the Brereton line that blue blood is supposed to have mingled with the Maugham "statesman" blood.

When the article appeared Maugham wrote his older brother Frederic Herbert that he was much impressed to learn how nobly he was descended in the female line. He wondered, however, about the

Maughams—were they so obscure that it was better to know nothing about them? He reminded his brother that there had been a prebendary, which was quite a respectable thing to be.[7]

Charles Snell and his bride went to India, where Maugham's mother was born in 1840. A sister, Rose Ellen, was born in 1841, and that same year Charles Snell died. Mrs. Snell settled in France with her two daughters and wrote children's books, edifying tales about orphans and selfish little rich girls who learn humility.[8]

It is important to remember that Maugham was born in France, of a mother who had herself been raised in France from infancy, and that he lived in Paris the first ten years of his life. Until he was twelve he spoke English much less well than French. His first brush with literature was reading the fables of La Fontaine, which his mother called upon him to recite at teatime in front of her friends. Later, when he read Flaubert and Maupassant, they described the Normandy he knew from having spent summer vacations at Deauville. He bought a Boudin seascape in 1945 because he recognized the beach where it had been painted.

Before Maugham was born his mother had given birth to four other sons, of whom three survived. She was consumptive, an ailment that the doctors of the period thought could be treated by bearing children. In 1864 she gave birth to Robert Cleveland Maugham, who died an infant. Charles Ormond was born in 1865, Frederic Herbert in 1866, and Henry Neville in 1868. Thus William Somerset had three older brothers, the youngest of whom was six years his senior. When he was three they went away to boarding school in England, and his days were warmed by an exclusive maternal love.

The Maughams lived on the third floor at 25 avenue d'Antin, today avenue Franklin D. Roosevelt, which runs into the *rond-point* of the Champs-Elysées. It was a spacious apartment that included a billiard room lined with the Tauchnitz Edition novels that his mother liked to read. Engravings by Gustave Doré decorated the drawing room, as well as Tanagra statuettes and Turkish daggers that his father had brought back from his travels.

In 1870, at the start of the Franco-Prussian War, a large map of France was pinned up in the billiard room, with little flags representing troop concentrations, which were moved according to the news of battle. The Maughams had decided that when the flags came within a certain distance of Paris they would leave for London. That day was not long in coming. They returned from England after the horror of the

Commune (17,000 executions when Paris was recaptured by Mac-Mahon and Galliffet), in August 1871, to find their apartment exactly as they had left it. But life was not the same. Robert Ormond Maugham's practice had declined—many of his English clients had remained in their own country—but the Maughams kept up appearances. They had French servants and an English governess. Strings of donkeys stopped at their door to provide the consumptive Mrs. Maugham with asses' milk.[9]

For a child it was a pleasant life, not unlike the life that Marcel Proust described in *Within a Budding Grove*. The Champs-Elysées was still lined with private homes, each of which had its stable. Below the *rond-point* there were walks with open boutiques that sold sweets and toys. You could see the Guignol for nothing outside the ropes or pay 10 centimes for a seat. The pound was then worth 25 francs. Near the *rond-point* was the Cirque d'Eté and a panorama of the siege of Paris.[10] One of young Willie Maugham's playmates was Violet Williams-Freeman, who had been born in the embassy maternity ward the same year as he (although she later became several years younger).

Maugham was a highly imaginative boy who did not stammer, and when he went to the Champs-Elysées, he and Violet and other children formed themselves into clans and played such French children's games as Les Barres and La Tour Prend Garde. Willie fascinated his playmates by passing off imitation sous at the kiosques where paper windmills and colored balloons were sold, along with patterned pieces of gingerbread. Violet's older sister was shocked at his dishonesty, but Violet thought it was clever that shopkeepers could be gulled by an innocent-looking boy.[11]

In the summers, after the Fourteenth of July celebration, the Maughams moved to Deauville, then known as a *plage de famille*. Robert Ormond Maugham rented a house so that his family could benefit from the sea air, and came by train on Saturday, returning to Paris on Sunday night. Willie was looked after by his nurse. His mother chatted with her summer friends and kept an eye on her sons, paddling on the water's edge. Willie took part in the children's pony races.

One day at Deauville, when his mother was walking with two of her sons along the promenade, she saw a glamorous woman approaching. As they passed, Mrs. Maugham and the other woman looked each other up and down. "Who is that lady, Mamma?" one of her sons asked. "Nobody," Mrs. Maugham replied. "Mrs. Langtry." The "Jersey Lily" was the most famous courtesan of her time. She had been the mistress of Edward VII when he was Prince of Wales. Crown Prince Rudolf, the Austrian archduke, was another of her lovers. Millais and Burne-Jones had painted her. Oscar Wilde had written *Lady Windermere's Fan* for her. But to the proper Mrs. Maugham she was "nobody."[12]

In Paris, Willie was the charge of his nurse, with whom he shared a bedroom, and who took him to the Champs-Elysées morning and afternoon to play with his friends. His ritual visits to his mother took place in the morning, when she was resting after her bath, and at tea, for the time of a glamorous woman was carefully measured. Mrs. Maugham was one of the few foreigners listed in the annual directory of Parisians who mattered, *La Société et le High Life*. She had a sort of salon, where political figures met artists.

Maugham grew up speaking fractured French. Seeing a horse from a railway-carriage window, he said, *"Regardez, maman, voila un 'orse."* As soon as he was old enough he attended a school for French children. On his seventh birthday, in January 1881, Lady Anglesey gave him a twenty-franc piece and asked him how he intended to spend it. He said he wanted to see Sarah Bernhardt, an unusual request for a seven-year old boy. One of his brothers took the future playwright to see his first play, a bad melodrama that he found thrilling.[13]

This carefree childhood period was drawing to a close. There was no cure for Edith Maugham's consumption. Her sister, Rose Ellen, had died of it in 1869, at the age of twenty-eight. When Willie was about five his mother had another stillborn child. After that she spent part of each winter at Pau, in the hope that the air of the Pyrénées would help her. In 1881, pregnant again, she was confined to her bed. One day she rose (the scene is described in *Of Human Bondage*) and put on a black skirt and the white damask bodice of her favorite evening dress. If she did not recover from her confinement, how would her son, who was not yet eight, remember her? She went to see a photographer and had her picture taken.

Soon after, on January 24, 1882, Edith Maugham gave birth to a boy, who was baptized Edward Alan and died the next day, January 25, Willie's eighth birthday. Six days later, on January 31, his mother died. She was forty-one years old. Her obituary in *Le Gaulois* on February 1 described her as a woman *"dont la beauté éblouissante rayonnait naguère dans nos plus élégants salons"* ("whose startling beauty once lit up our most elegant salons").[14]

His mother's death when he was eight was the tragedy of Maugham's life. If in some lives there is an original sin, in Maugham's there was an original wound, from which, by his own admission, he never recovered. In many of his photographs one sees, in the wrinkles and the downward-turning mouth and the eyes that give away very little, the face of a permanently deprived child, robbed "of the only love in the world that is quite unselfish."[15]

With his brothers away at school, Maugham was left alone with his ailing sixty-year-old father. Robert Ormond was in fact so ill that an associate had to be brought into the firm. Willie was taken out of the French school and tutored by a clergyman, who made him read aloud the police-court news in the London newspapers. His father was building a country house, which he had designed, on top of a hill in Suresnes, overlooking the Seine. Every Sunday he and Willie would go down the Seine in the *bateau-mouche* to follow the progress in construction. The house was white with red shutters and somewhat resembled a Swiss chalet. One of its distinctive features was a Moorish symbol, which his father had brought back from a trip to North Africa and which he had engraved on the windows.[16]

On June 24, 1884, two years after the death of his wife, Robert Ormond Maugham died of cancer of the stomach at the age of sixty-one. He left less than was expected. His estate had been depleted by summers in Deauville, winters in Pau, and the extravagance of a wife nearly half his age. Willie's beloved mother had a passion for keeping up with the affluent embassy officials and their wives. She was idealized by her son, but not all sides of her character were commendable, and in *Of Human Bondage* he repeated stories that he had heard: "she dressed more magnificently than became the wife of a hardworking surgeon" (in the novel his father is a surgeon rather than a lawyer); "the flowers among which she lived even in winter suggested an extravagance which he deplored. . . . He had seen grapes in the dining-room that must have cost at least eight shillings a pound; and at luncheon he had been given asparagus two months before it was ready in the vicarage garden. . . . She had no more idea of money than a child."

When all Robert Ormond Maugham's possessions had been sold, including the Doré engravings, the Tanagra statuettes, the Turkish daggers, and the house in Suresnes, there was a total of 4,690 pounds to be divided among four sons, which left each one with an income of about 150 pounds a year.[17] Willie also inherited his father's short stature and what he felt was physical ugliness. "The world is an entirely different place to the man of five foot seven from what it is to the man of six foot two," he said in *A Writer's Notebook*. From his mother he inherited weak lungs and a liking for society.

It was decided that Willie would go to England to live with his father's only living brother, Henry MacDonald Maugham, a Church of England clergyman. In one stroke he was orphaned and uprooted from the country where he had spent the first ten years of his life. Henry Maugham was vicar of the parish of All Saints in Whitstable, a town on the coast of Kent, six miles from Canterbury. He and his German-born wife Sophie had been there thirteen years. They were childless and in their fifties.

And so it was that a small ten-year-old boy, like one of Dickens' youthful heroes who are tempered by misfortune at an early age, orphaned like Oliver Twist, living with an aunt like David Copperfield, crossed the English Channel in the summer of 1884 to start a new life. Clutching the hand of his French nurse, he stood at the steamer's rail and watched the beach at Calais fade out of sight. Several hours later he saw the shore of England for the first time, the shore where his future waited. He landed at Dover, and in the excitement of the moment, when he saw the gang of porters and the rank of horse-drawn carriages, he shouted: "Porteur! Cabriolet!"[18]

Chapter Two

Now, although the room grows chilly,
I haven't the heart to poke poor Willie.
"Ruthless Rhymes for Heartless Homes,"
by Harry Graham

THE FIRST THING Maugham's uncle did was dismiss the French nurse who had delivered him to Whitstable. Willie shed bitter tears over the departure of the last remaining link to his Paris childhood. He would remain under his uncle's roof for seven years, but during most of that time he would be at school in nearby Canterbury, returning to the vicarage on holidays. Whitstable (the Blackstable of *Cakes and Ale* and *Of Human Bondage*), in those days a prosperous town of eight to ten thousand, was a world-famous oyster fishery with 190 oyster boats. It had a thriving harbor, which could hold 300 brigantines, and was mainly engaged in unloading Newcastle colliers. As a boy Maugham spent hours wandering around the harbor and watching the men in their grimy jerseys carrying bags of coal. He walked down the High Street, the long, winding main street that led to the sea, past the Railway Inn, the Duke of Kent, and the Bear and Key, listening to the Kentish speech of the townspeople, and reaching the small stretch of beach, looked for flat stones to play ducks and drakes with. In the summer he swam in the cold English Channel.

Whitstable was a class-conscious Victorian town where a few families ruled the roost. The most prominent was a shipping family called Gann. In the days of Maugham's boyhood Henry Gann, known locally as Lord Stallion, was a landlord who offered to overlook the rent in hard winters if he lay with a tenant's wife. She would send a note saying "My husband will be away today," and Henry Gann would arrive and collect his due.[1]

The thing to have in Whitstable was "county status." The vicar had county status and lived in some style in a large ivy-covered vicarage, with a garden and stables and a coach house and servants, at the opposite end of town from the harbor. The gardener, who was paid a pound a week, looked after the chickens and saw to it that the stoves were kept going in the winter. The two maids were paid twelve pounds a year and were given new dresses at Christmas. Bathrooms were considered an ostentatious novelty and the vicarage did not have one. At the time of Maugham's boyhood England still warmed itself with coal fires and lit itself with gaslight. The bicycle was just coming in, equipped with Dr. Dunlop's pneumatic tires, and would change the courtship patterns in rural England, allowing young men to marry outside their villages. The well-to-do drove landaus, while the middle class used four-wheelers, popularly known as "growlers." On Sunday, Maugham's uncle hired a landau from the Bear and Key to take him the two miles from the vicarage to the church for the morning service. Every morning he walked to the fisheries before lunch and bought a dozen oysters for a shilling.[2]

Willie was a little snob who would have nothing to do with children who went to the grammar school at Faversham. Nor would he mix with the summer visitors from London, who were thought vulgar. In July and August his aunt and uncle went abroad to such German spas as Baden-Baden and Ems. The aunt was a Fraulein von Scheidlin, the daughter of Nuremberg merchants, conscious of her noble birth, and had brought as her dowry a rolltop marquetry desk, some Nymphenburg china, and four tumblers engraved with the sixteen quarterings of her family, which she explained to her nephew. "I was a very respectable youth," Maugham wrote of himself in *Cakes and Ale*. "I accepted the conventions of my class as if they were the laws of Nature."

All in all, it cannot have been such a bad life. He was living in a seaside resort, the ward of a local dignitary. The air was clean and the food was good. He did not have to compete with other children for the affection of his aunt and uncle. And yet he was miserable. Whitstable represented social obligation and conformity, the narrow-minded provincialism of nineteenth-century small-town English life. In addition, he took a violent dislike to his uncle, whose faults he listed at length in *Of Human Bondage* and *Cakes and Ale*.

If we go by these two books and by additional remarks in Maugham's autobiographical works, Henry Maugham deserves to join the ranks of villainous clergymen in English fiction, alongside Theobald Pontifex in Samuel Butler's *The Way of All Flesh*. The failings of Rev. William Carey read like an anticlerical pamphlet. Physically unattractive, he wears his hair long to disguise his baldness. He expects his nephew, with his clubfoot, to walk from the station to the vicarage to save the price of a cab. The stove in the hall is lit only when he has a cold, not when his wife has one. His salary does not permit him to take his wife on holidays abroad, so he goes alone. When she dies he hopes that her grave will be adorned with more floral tributes than that of a neighboring vicar's wife, but when the church warden discusses the matter of the tombstone, he argues for economy. He is a mean-minded hypocrite, bigot, and skinflint.

There are a number of set pieces in the portrait. One shows the vicar saying grace at tea, cutting off the top of his boiled egg and handing it to his young ward, who would have liked an egg to himself but took what was offered. Maugham interpreted the egg top as a symbol of parsimony and greed, whereas most small boys in Victorian times thought of it as a welcome bonus. Another was learning the collect. The vicar placed a prayerbook in front of his nephew, open at the proper place, and asked him to learn the collect of the day by heart. His aunt found the boy an hour later crying because he could not learn it. This made his uncle very cross.

Maugham jotted down some of his uncle's maxims in his notebook, such as: "Only ask those people to stay with you or dine with you, who can ask you in return." The vicar kept himself well supplied with whiskey, which he locked in the sideboard, saying: "It is not good for all people to drink spirits, in fact it is a sin to put temptation in their way; and besides, they would not appreciate them at their true value." At the same time the vicar would not let Willie play or read books on Sunday. Reading became an illicit pleasure, one to which he became addicted. He had read all of Walter Scott by the time he was twelve. The vicar was so stingy that he shared *The Times* with two neighbors. In addition, Maugham wrote in *The Summing Up*, "he was incredibly idle and left the work of his parish to his curate and his church-wardens."

The unflattering portrait that Maugham left of his uncle was corroborated by his brother Frederic, who described the vicar as "a very narrow-minded and far from intelligent cleric."[3] But if we look at the situation from the vicar's point of view, it appears that Maugham blackened him for the purposes of fiction. Here was a man in his fifties, a creature of habit looked after by a classic German hausfrau, whose routine was shattered by the arrival of a ten-year-old boy. True, the vicar was not out of pocket, since Willie's 150 pounds a year were sufficient for his upkeep, but he had to learn to be a father overnight. It cannot have been easy, and he made some of the necessary compromises. When Willie wanted a bicycle, he got one.

It seems that Maugham, uprooted from his childhood surroundings, was determined to be miserable. His aunt and uncle could never become substitutes for his dead parents. There is a scene in *Of Human Bondage* in which Philip/Willie is sulking and his aunt asks him what she can do. The boy says he wants to be left alone.

> "Philip, how can you say anything so unkind? Don't you know that your uncle and I only want your good? Don't you love me at all?"
>
> "I hate you. I wish you was dead."
>
> . . . Philip realised that she was crying because of what he had said, and he was sorry. He went up to her silently and kissed her. It was the first kiss he had ever given her without being asked. . . . [She] took the little boy on her lap and put her arms around him and wept as though her heart would break. But her tears were partly tears of happiness, for she felt that the strangeness between them was gone. She loved him now with a new love because he had made her suffer.

Here Maugham established the crucial link between love and suffering. The death of his mother had forged it, and it would appear not only in his work but in all of his important relationships.

He found relief from loneliness in books. He read E. W. Lane's *Arabian Nights,* and *Alice in Wonderland.* He found in their pages a refuge from distress. For this he could thank his uncle, who collected books, and never returned from Canterbury without bringing back three or four. The love of books is an amiable trait, which Maugham would one day share, and surely the vicar might be given some credit for it. Several other items can be found to add to the plus column: the vicar cannot, for instance, have been as lazy as all that, for when he arrived in Whitstable the church was in ruins. He had it completely rebuilt, and it was inaugurated in 1886 by no less a personage than the Archbishop of Canterbury.[4]

Nor can he have been a complete miser. When his wife Sophie died in 1892 she died in Ems, for he did take her on holidays abroad. Instead of arguing for an inexpensive tombstone, he donated to the church a costly stone-and-marble pulpit in her memory. He cannot have been quite as disagreeable as Maugham makes him, for two years after Sophie's death he married the forty-nine-year-old daughter of a general, Ellen Mary Matthew, who was known to be very jocular and

merry and not the sort to marry a grouch. It appears that Henry
Maugham had a sense of humor and that many of the pious remarks
that his nephew jotted down in his notebook were made with tongue in
cheek. Maugham later wondered whether "he was exercising at my
expense a humour which I never suspected him of possessing."[5]

Moreover, the vicar was popular in Whitstable, for when he died, on
September 18, 1897, a Tuesday, most of the places of business in town
closed from one to three, the time of the funeral. For a Kentish store-
keeper to lose business to honor the memory of a dead vicar was a true
mark of respect.

Willie spent the summer of 1884 getting acquainted with his new
home. In the fall he was sent to class at the home of a local physician,
Dr. Etheridge, whose wife conducted a small school. He attended
dressed in a velvet knickerbocker suit with a white lace collar, and he
spoke with a stammer.[6]

In the spring of 1885, however, when Willie was eleven, the vicar
decided that he had outgrown the Etheridge school and should go to the
King's School in Canterbury. It was where the other clergy in the area
sent their sons, it was united by long tradition to Canterbury Cathedral,
its headmaster was an honorary canon, and the boys were encouraged
to aspire to Holy Orders. In addition, it was a twenty-minute train ride
from Whitstable on the branch line. Willie would go to the Junior
School, for boys eight to thirteen, and then to the Senior School. The
idea was that eventually he would be ordained, following in his uncle's
footsteps.

On a day in May 1885 Willie and his uncle went to Canterbury and
waited in a parlor to talk to the headmaster. Willie said, "Tell him I
stammer, Uncle."[7] Afraid, he wanted the headmaster to be warned of
the flaw that set him apart, the stammer.

Maugham was not a stutterer. He did not repeat the same consonant
over and over, he got stuck, like a typewriter key. It is a speech defect
that cannot be imitated in type, and its origins are still unknown. In
Victorian times doctors sometimes cut pieces out of stammerers'
tongues on the theory that they were too long. In recent times theories
on the causes of stuttering and stammering have proliferated. Some
theories now point to organic defects, such as a flaw in the muscles of
the middle ear or a lack of synchronization in the muscles on both sides
of the jaw. But Maugham had not stammered while he lived in France.
He began to stammer only at the age of ten, when he came to England.
He was in an unfamiliar country, speaking a language of which he was

unsure, living with an uncle who to him seemed distant and censorious. The stammer was an expression of juvenile insecurity, of his first stumbling efforts in a new environment. It may also have been the expression of a conflict between giving of himself and holding back. But although many childhood stutterers, like Winston Churchill, overcome their handicap, Maugham's remained with him to the end of his long life, an ever-present reminder of his apartness from others.

Unless it results from a physical defect, which in Maugham's case it apparently did not, a stammer would appear to be self-inflicted. The stammerer has some quarrel with himself, he sets up his own roadblocks. Stammering becomes a self-fulfilling prophecy. The stammerer knows he will be made fun of, and he is. Stammering is a way of guaranteeing the situation that you foresee. It is possible that in stammering, Maugham found a way of punishing himself for the obscure guilt he felt in connection with his mother's death. The stammer was a way of telling the world that he was not like others, a way of expressing his singularity. The stammerer is ambivalent about communicating with others—he desperately wants to communicate, but is afraid of revealing himself.

One may ask why Maugham replaced the stammer with a clubfoot in *Of Human Bondage*. The answer is that a clubfoot is something you are born with, while a stammer is something you do to yourself. A boy with a clubfoot is a more convincing object of pity. He has a crippling handicap that prevents him from joining in games. A stammer can be overcome and is essentially a form of self-hindrance. In *Of Human Bondage* Philip/Willie pretends that a penholder broken by a classmate was a gift from his dead mother. He simulates distress to obtain sympathy. There was also that side to the stammer. It was an appeal for sympathy that backfired.

As Maugham told one of his biographers, "The first thing you should know is that my life and my production have been greatly influenced by my stammer."[8] Without the stammer there would have been no analogous clubfoot and no *Of Human Bondage*. The stammer helped decide his career. He could not be a clergyman or a politician or a lawyer, since he could not deliver a sermon or a speech or a courtroom oration. He once said, with regard to speechmaking, "That is one of the things I *cannot* do."[9] One of the reasons he needed a secretary was his fear of stammering on the telephone.

In a preface for *The Old Wives' Tale* Maugham described the predicament of his fellow stammerer Arnold Bennett in words that applied in part to himself:

> Everyone knew that Arnold was afflicted with a very bad stammer; it was painful to watch the struggle he had sometimes to get the words out. It was torture to him. Few realized the exhaustion it caused him to speak. What to most men was as easy as breathing, to him was a constant strain. It tore his nerves to pieces. Few knew the humiliation it exposed him to, the ridicule it excited in many, the impatience it aroused . . . the minor exasperation of thinking of a good, amusing, or apt remark and not venturing to say it in case the stammer ruined it. Few knew the distressing sense it gave rise to of a bar to complete contact with other men. It may be that except for the stammer which forced him to introspection, Arnold would never have become a writer.

For Maugham, however, the stammer was not completely inhibiting, for it seems to have been sporadic and subject to mood and circumstance. Unlike Bennett, Maugham was not prevented from making amusing remarks, the basis for his reputation as a wit. If the stammer was such a grave handicap, one may ask why he did not make an effort to have it cured until he was in his sixties. Because, perhaps, in certain ways he found it useful. Balzac's Père Grandet, that rich provincial miser, admitted to his daughter Eugénie that he sometimes *faked* a stammer in the middle of a business deal, to gain the upper hand.

His three brothers, who were in their teens when their mother died, and who did well in school, did not stammer. They went to Dover, which had been started in 1871 on the site of the twelfth-century monastery, Dover Priory. Dover had about two hundred boys, one-third of whom were the sons of army officers. At first Frederic, who was eight years older than Willie, admitted that he was unhappy. He had a French accent, and the other boys called him "froggie." All his life he would continue to give the French pronunciation to such words as "liqueur" and "blouse." But Frederic was good at games and played rugby and cricket, and rowed Number 7 on the crew when he went on to Cambridge. He wrote a poem called "Cricket," of which this is the envoi:

> *Life is only a match*
> *With a bat and a ball,*

> *We may make a few runs,*
> *And that's nearly all.*[10]

Frederic was also head prefect and editor of the school magazine. Willie's other brothers did well too. Charles (nine years older than Willie) was head prefect, and Henry (six years older than Willie) played on the rugby team. They were well rounded and well adjusted, quickly fitting into the school mold, with its strenuous emphasis on sports and respect for Victorian institutions.

Willie, many years their junior and in a different school, did not fit in. He was small and frail and in poor health, was no good at games, and, inhibited by his stammer, he shrank from his fellow students. He is recorded in the King's School entry-book as arriving in May 1885. He remained in the school, with interruptions due to illness, until July 1889, when he left for good. The King's School calls itself the oldest school in England, dating its foundation back to Saint Augustine in the fifth century, and is thus listed in the Guinness Book of World Records. Augustine monks were the teachers until the dissolution of the monasteries, when it was reorganized by officers of Henry VIII, thus acquiring its name. One of its illustrious alumni was Christopher Marlowe, but in Maugham's time it was known mainly for turning out men of the cloth.

The school is built on the grounds of Canterbury Cathedral. Its low buildings stand in the shadow of the great central tower, around green courts planted with old elms. Canterbury, the capital of Kent, is because of its cathedral a world center of pilgrimage, and the destination in Chaucer's tales. The cathedral is the mother church of the Anglican faith and stands on a spot where Christian worship has been offered continuously for 1,350 years. The present cathedral was built between 1175 and 1180. Its stained-glass windows were used for teaching at a time when few could read, and its bells rang the hours in days when there were no clocks. When I visited Canterbury in June 1977, a poster outside the cathedral said:

> *St. Augustine founded it.*
> *Becket died for it.*
> *Chaucer wrote about it.*
> *Cromwell shot at it.*
> *Hitler bombed it.*
> *Time is destroying it.*
> *Will you give to save it?*

It was in this school, with its accent on tradition and religion, that Maugham would spend the next four years. The boys wore straw boaters and black uniforms and wing-tip collars. The masters wore mortarboards and gowns.

The account of the King's School that Maugham gave in *Of Human Bondage* was so precise that Canon F. J. Shirley, who was headmaster from 1935 to 1962, recalled that "the trouble with 'Of Human Bondage' was that it was factual—there was hardly a thin disguise: men and buildings, the author 'photographed' them all."[11]

When Willie arrived with his tin trunk, he thought the high brick wall that faces on Palace Street made the school look like a prison. The master of the Junior School was a large, jovial, red-bearded man whom Maugham calls Watson and whose real name was Hodgson. An ordained minister like the other masters, Hodgson read prayers and a chapter from the Bible at breakfast. The physical descriptions of the masters are so accurate that they have all been identified. His teacher in the Junior School, Mr. Rice in the novel, was in reality Dublin-born Pat Price.[12] From the start Willie was cruelly teased because of his stammer. He hated the school. His most persistent dream was that he would awake to find himself at home with his mother.[13]

The stress in studies was on Greek and Latin. He did well, making up in his schoolwork for his poorness in sports. In 1886 he was first in his class for the year, and in 1887 he went into the Senior School on a scholarship (which meant that he wore a black gown) and won the music prize. In 1888 he won prizes in divinity, history, and French. As he wrote in *Of Human Bondage*: "He had quite a collection of prizes, worthless books on bad paper, but in gorgeous bindings decorated with the arms of the school: his position had freed him from bullying and he was not unhappy. His fellows forgave him his success because of his deformity."

The year that he went into the Senior School was the year that England celebrated Queen Victoria's Royal Jubilee. She had been on the throne for fifty years. On June 21 the small figure in black drove out of the stable gate at Buckingham Palace, and bowed slightly to her assembled subjects as the royal cortège wound its way to Westminster Abbey. The guard of honor included sixteen princes related to the queen, three of whom were her own sons. Members of European royal families filled fifteen closed carriages. One discarded suggestion for underlining the importance of the occasion was that each one of her 372 million subjects should send her a congratulatory telegram. On that day the high-water mark of the British Empire was reached. On maps, half the earth's surface was colored a British pink. Peace reigned, except for an occasional punitive expedition in places with strange names like Benin and Ashanti. The British Army and Navy were supreme, and British merchants and bankers were equally unrivaled. The virtues that had created from so small an island so great an empire were cultivated in such schools as the one Willie attended.

In 1887 a new headmaster had just been named, whom Maugham called Mr. Perkins and whose real name was Thomas Field. His appointment showed that upward mobility was possible in Victorian times, for Field was the son of a Whitstable linendraper. A brilliant classical scholar, he had won a scholarship to King's and gone on to win three firsts at Oxford. He became a master at Harrow, and served as headmaster of King's from 1886 to 1896. Field was an intelligent, sensitive man, whose methods of teaching struck the other masters as unorthodox. Willie felt a "dog-like adoration" for the new headmaster, who showed him kindness on more than one occasion. The other masters were middle-aged bachelors, narrow-minded and set in their ways.

In the Senior School he was no longer bullied. He had developed a barbed wit as a defense—which helped to alienate the sympathies of his classmates—while longing for the popularity that seemed to come to others so effortlessly. "He took to a singular habit. He would imagine that he was some boy whom he had a particular fancy for; he would throw his soul, as it were, into the other's body, talk with his voice and laugh with his heart . . . in this way, he enjoyed many intervals of fantastic happiness."[14]

Philip/Willie progresses from an imagined identification with the kind of boy he would like to be to a real friendship with a classmate named Rose. What draws him to Rose is not that he is good-looking but that he is outgoing and popular, the opposite of himself. Rose is an uncomplicated, naturally gregarious boy whose kindness to Philip/Willie leads to friendship. As they become inseparable, and walk into chapel arm in arm, his friendship with Rose brings him "a wild happiness." Philip/Willie and Rose arrange to meet at the station after the holidays so that they can have tea before returning to school. Philip/Willie takes an early train, but Rose stands him up. He grows possessive, resenting Rose's "universal amiability," and wants "an exclusive attachment." Then he is forced to leave school because of illness, and when he returns, Rose has made friends with another boy. Philip/Willie has been jilted. He provokes a scene that uses the vocabulary of a lovers' quarrel:

> "I say, why have you been so rotten to me since I came back?"
> "Oh, don't be an ass," said Rose.
> "I don't know what you see in Hunter."
> "That's my business."
> Philip looked down. He could not bring himself to say what was in his heart. He was afraid of humiliating himself. Rose got up. "I've got to go to the Gym," he said.
> When he was at the door, Philip forced himself to speak.
> "I say, Rose, don't be a perfect beast."
> "Oh, go to hell."

When Rose tries to effect a reconciliation Philip/Willie brushes him off, even though it makes him sick with misery. The cycle of love is complete—he has willed suffering upon himself. A study of the King's School entry records shows that there were no Roses in Maugham's class, but there were two Rosses. Another name of some interest in the records, however, is the name Ashenden, belonging to a classmate with whom Willie shared a prize. Ashenden was the name Maugham gave his autobiographical narrator in three books, *The Moon and Sixpence, Ashenden,* and *Cakes and Ale.* Since we know that he fantasized being another boy, and since he later borrowed the name of a classmate to portray himself, the conclusion might be drawn that Leonard Ashenden was a boy for whom he had formed a romantic attachment. It should be noted that in the first version of *Of Human Bondage,* which Maugham called "The Artistic Temperament of Stephen Carey," the woman Stephen has a passion for is called Rose Cameron. When the name Rose turns up again in *Bondage,* it is no longer the first name of a woman but the last name of a boy. Rose has changed sex between versions. If homosexuality was to be implanted at an early age, no ground was more fruitful than the English public schools. At Harrow pretty boys were made the "bitches" of older boys and given feminine names.[15]

By June 1888 Willie had been moved into a form whose master, a Scot named Gordon, was a violent bully. On the first day of the summer term Gordon asked him to translate a passage in Latin. He knew the passage, but the master's fierce presence made him nervous and he began to stammer. This prompted a fit of mirth among his classmates.

Gordon, shouting to make himself heard in the uproar, banged on his desk and said: "Sit down, you fool. I don't know why they put you in this form." He sat down, enraged but helpless. Gordon listed Maugham in the Black Book, a volume in which the names of boys were written with their misdeeds. If a boy's name was in the Black Book three times in one term, he was caned by the headmaster. The Black Book in which Maugham is mentioned rests in the archives of the King's School. In the margin next to the names of three-time losers one can see in red ink the word "caned," followed by the initials T.F. (Thomas Field). Running down the list of trangressions—such as "robbing fruit orchard," "immoral conduct," "destroying school desk," "muttering impertinently," "throwing snowballs in the grange," "disgraceful work in French," "bringing insects into school"—one comes to an entry dated Friday, June 8, 1888: "Maugham—Gross Inattention." In *Of Human Bondage* he escalated the offense to "Gross Impertinence."[16]

That winter, when Maugham was almost fifteen, he came down with pleurisy and was sent to spend the winter in Hyères, a medieval town on the French Riviera—once famous for its salt pans—where an English tutor took boys recovering from illnesses. He seems to have made up his mind in Hyères to leave Canterbury, its cruel masters and its mocking boys. When he returned to the King's School in the spring of 1889 his work suffered. He gave up Greek and did poorly in mathematics, a subject in which he had previously done well. He told his uncle that he wanted to leave the school. His uncle objected that his tuition had been paid and that he expected him to go on to Oxford and be ordained. Maugham said he had no wish to do either. His uncle asked the school for a remittance of tuition, and had returned to him six pounds, fifteen shillings, and ten pence. Maugham left Canterbury for good.[17]

The next winter he returned to Hyères and came back to the vicarage in the spring of 1890, a sixteen-year-old at loose ends. When his aunt suggested he spend a year in Germany, and asked her relatives in Munich to recommend a family, they proposed the wife of a Heidelberg professor, *geborene* von Grabau, who took boarders. A date was set, and he left for Heidelberg. He later wondered what turn his life would have taken had he remained at the King's School. He knew he was capable of winning a scholarship to Cambridge or Oxford. He might have remained at the university on a fellowship, producing at discreet intervals dull and learned books on French literature. "I never went to Cambridge as my brothers did," the narrator in *The Razor's Edge*, who calls himself Somerset Maugham, says. "I had the chance but I refused it. I wanted to get out into the world. I've always regretted it. I think it would have saved me a lot of mistakes." He also wondered why his uncle had allowed him to leave school and go to Germany. He decided that it was because of his poor health. The vicar, believing that Maugham would die of tuberculosis like his mother, attached little importance to what he did, or where.[18]

He moved into his room at the pension, whose other guests were a French student, a Chinese, and a tall New Englander who taught Greek at Harvard. For the first time in his life since leaving France he was happy. He was freed from the tensions of the King's School, had escaped from the provincial smugness of Whitstable, and realized that acquiring knowledge could be an adventure rather than a duty. It was in Heidelberg that he first knew the delights of conversation, with interminable talks about art and literature, and free will and determinism, and discovered the commonplaces that each teenage boy discovers as if for the first time.

Maugham made friends with the tall New Englander from Harvard, and they went on walks together in the fir-clad hills, to the top of the Königstühl, where he saw stretching below him the plain of the Neckar, and took notice for the first time of the beauty that surrounded him. When the Harvard professor left for Berlin his place was taken by a twenty-six-year-old Englishman named John Ellingham Brooks, who had gone to Cambridge, read for the bar, and then decided to devote himself to literature.

Ellingham Brooks was a homosexual esthete, short like Maugham but with a noble Byronic forehead, curly chestnut hair, sensual lips, and enough money to travel and cultivate his tastes. He and Maugham talked of art and literature and of Italy and Greece. He fired the younger man's imagination and became the arbiter of his tastes. When he found Maugham reading *Tom Jones*, he said that although there was no harm in it, he would do better to read Meredith's *Diana of the Crossways*. He talked of Swinburne and Omar Khayyám, whose works he recited aloud. Maugham was torn between enthusiasm and embarrassment, for Brooks "recited poetry like a high-church curate intoning the Litany in an ill-lit crypt."[19] It was necessary, according to Brooks, to admire George Meredith and Walter Pater, so Maugham dutifully read *The Egoist* and *The Shaving of Shagpat*. Brooks was studying the works of the nineteenth-century Italian poet Leopardi with a view to translating them, but had not yet set pen to paper.

In *Looking Back* Maugham writes that both the Harvard professor and Brooks had been drawn to him not out of kindness for a lonely sixteen-year-old boy or because he listened to their conversation entranced but because they desired him physically. Maugham says he was too innocent to realize that they wanted anything more than his company. In fact, he is covering up his first homosexual experience, for it was Brooks who took his virginity. He kept this first love affair a secret all his life, but admitted it to his close friend Glenway Wescott.[20]

Maugham's homosexual inclinations had begun to show themselves at the King's School when his avoidance of participation in competitive games isolated him from his peer group. He saw the other boys as having a valued alliance which he was prevented from sharing, and admired their attainments. He formed strong passions for boys who had the qualities he lacked. The friend, representing the missing perfection of self, was idealized and eroticized. When Maugham imagined that he was inhabiting the body of another boy, he was saying: "I love what I would like to be."

After the ambiguous attachments of the King's School came his first full sexual experience, with a man ten years his senior. Maugham was drawn to Brooks not only physically but also by his shunning of convention, his pose as a man of letters, and his intention of devoting himself to beauty.

He caught Brooks's love of literature, and he also took German lessons and attended lectures at Heidelberg University. That first winter he went to hear a renowned authority on Schopenhauer, Kuno Fischer, whose lectures were enormously popular.[21] Inspired by the lectures, he began to read Schopenhauer, whose philosophical pessimism fitted his own life experience. Schopenhauer saw a universe whose reason for being is unknown to us; human beings are victims of their instincts, free will is a mirage, and the afterlife is an illusion to help us bear the pain of existence. This was exactly what Maugham wanted to hear after his mother's death, his miserable childhood, and his inability to believe in God. Schopenhauer relieved him of the obscure guilt he had felt over his mother's death, for there was no ordering reason in the universe and no explanation for human tragedy. Maugham accepted as his personal faith Schopenhauer's thesis that only exceptional beings such as artists could free themselves from the human condition.

Heidelberg meant emancipation and new ideas. There was an avant-garde theater that performed the plays of Ibsen, the half-Norwegian and half-German playwright, who had moved to Germany in 1868.

One day in Munich (probably while visiting his aunt Sophie's Bavarian relatives) Maugham spotted Ibsen drinking beer and scowling as he read his newspaper at the Maximilianerhof. Seeing Ibsen was a memorable occasion,[22] for to Maugham he was the most exciting playwright of the age. He had scratched the surface of convention to reveal dark undercurrents of passion and self-interest. He had declared war on society, and discussed taboo subjects such as alcoholism and syphilis. In England his plays had shocked the Victorians. In Germany, too, right-thinking people were violently anti-Ibsen. When *The Doll's House* was shown in Heidelberg, Philip/Willie's German teacher in *Of Human Bondage*, Professor Erlin, calls it obscene nonsense, the ruin of the family, the uprooting of morals, the destruction of Germany. "I would sooner my daughters were lying dead at my feet than see them listening to the garbage of that shameless fellow," he says. But it was Ibsen, along with Schopenhauer, who became a major influence on Maugham.

Heidelberg was an escape from Victorian England, where new ideas seemed to be a mark of disrespect to the old bones that occupied the throne. In 1885 the House of Lords had given a second reading to a bill to make further provisions for the protection of women, the suppression of brothels, and the general defense of morality. The bill came before a committee in the House of Commons, where a maverick MP from Northhampton named Henry Labouchère moved that a clause be inserted to create a new offense of indecency between males, in public or private. The clause became Section XI of the Criminal Law Amendment Act of January 1886, and remained in effect until 1967.[23]

The amendment read: "Any male person who, in public or private, commits, or is a party to the commission of, or procures or attempts to procure the commission by any male person, shall be guilty of a misdemeanor, and being convicted thereof shall be liable at the discretion of the court to be imprisoned for any term not exceeding two years, with or without hard labour." Labouchère had asked for a seven-year maximum sentence, but the government, arguing that such cases were difficult enough to prosecute, reduced it to two. Originally the wording had been "Any male or female person," but when the text was shown to Queen Victoria no one had the nerve to answer her query of "why women were included in the act as surely it was impossible for them." The mention of women was deleted. The new law was soon dubbed "the blackmailer's charter."

Everything, however, was not what it seemed. Homosexuality, although severely punished, was nonetheless widely practiced. In 1889 a male brothel that recruited working-class teenage boys for wealthy and prominent men was discovered in Cleveland Street. The scandal involved several members of the royal household, most notably Lord Arthur Somerset, the son of the eighth Duke of Beaufort and an intimate of the royal family, with the title of Superintendent of the Stables and Extra Equerry. Thanks to the efforts of the Tory Prime Minister Lord Salisbury and the Prince of Wales himself, the scandal was quietly buried, and Somerset was sent abroad.[24]

In the spring of 1892, after a carefree year and a half in Heidelberg, Maugham returned to an England of scandals simmering under the lid of official morality. Now, however, he was armed with the discovery of Schopenhauer's wisdom and Ibsen's daring and a working knowledge of German. In addition, he had experimented with a form of love that in England could fetch him two years at hard labor. In the words of his alter ego, Philip Carey, he had formed this theory of conduct: "Follow your inclinations with due regard to the policeman round the corner."[25]

Maugham was unsure of what he should do, and his aunt and uncle were pressuring him to go to Oxford; it was that or earn a living. He did not dare tell the vicar that his secret ambition was to write. While in Heidelberg he had finished his first written work, a biography of the German composer Meyerbeer, a precursor of Wagner, born in 1791. Maugham knew little about music and had heard none of his operas. Perhaps he thought the subject was topical because 1891 was the date of Meyerbeer's centenary. When this early work was turned down he threw the manuscript into the fire.[26]

The vicar asked an Oxford friend with an eminent position in the civil service whether that would be a suitable career for young Maugham. In 1870 Gladstone had set up a competitive civil service exam, so that it was no longer restricted to gentlemen. The friend wrote back that owing to monstrous changes enforced by a liberal government, the civil service would be no place for Maugham. The vicar then wrote an old friend of the family, Albert Dixon, a lawyer, who had started out as a clerk for Maugham's grandfather. It was Dixon who found Maugham his first job, in an accountant's office in Chancery Lane.[27] Maugham left a description of that ordeal in *Of Human Bondage*. He went to the office in a tailcoat and tall hat, and knowing no one but his fellow clerks, was lonely and depressed. He loathed the work, loathed the office, and loathed London. "Late in the evening [he] wandered through the West End till he found some house at which there was a party. He stood among the little group of shabby people, behind the footmen, watching the guests arrive, and he listened to the music that floated through the window."[28]

After a month, disgusted with accounting, he returned to Whitstable. His uncle was not pleased to see him. He thought Maugham incompetent and lazy and was wondering what to do with him when the local doctor solved the problem by suggesting the profession of medicine. Maugham did not want to be a doctor, for he was now quite sure of his vocation as a writer. As he explained, "I wrote steadily from the time I was 15. I became a medical student because I could not announce to my guardian that I wished to be a writer."[29] It was unheard of at that time that a boy of eighteen from a respectable family should adopt literature as a profession. The notion was so preposterous that he never dreamed of discussing it with anyone. He did think of becoming a lawyer, but since his three older brothers had entered the law he felt there would be no room for him. He was also reluctant to give up the freedom that he had known at Heidelberg and could not bear the thought of going to Cambridge and being subjected to restraint. Medical school gave him the chance of living in his own lodgings in London, gaining the life experience he wanted, and reading and writing in his spare time. He agreed to go, and spent some time at a crammer's so that he might pass the entrance examination.[30]

It seems odd that of all professions Maugham should have chosen medicine. In the drama of his mother's death, doctors were the villains. They had prescribed the perilous remedy of childbirth to treat her tuberculosis. It had killed her. Why should Maugham want to join the very profession that was responsible for his mother's death? It was partly a delaying tactic, for he had no intention of practicing. But the study of medicine did satisfy his obsession with women who, like his mother, died in childbirth or whose children were stillborn. As a medical student Maugham had three months of duty as an obstetric clerk in the midwifery department of his hospital, followed by three weeks "on the district," during which it was compulsory to attend a minimum of twenty confinements. Maugham attended sixty-three, most of them in the slum of Lambeth.

That August his uncle and aunt went on their annual holiday to Germany, where his aunt Sophie died. On September 27, 1892, eighteen-year-old William Somerset Maugham registered at the medical school at St. Thomas's Hospital in London, where he would spend the next five years.[31]

Chapter Three

By some happy chance, what interests me seems to interest a great many other people.

Maugham, *A Writer's Notebook*

ST. THOMAS'S was a teaching hospital with a medical school attached to it. It was founded in the twelfth century in Southwark, a borough at the south end of London Bridge, and in 1551 it was reorganized by royal charter as a hospital for the poor. In 1868 the hospital had to move from Southwark because part of its site was needed for the London Bridge and Charing Cross Railway. It was relocated in Lambeth Palace Road, on the south bank of the Thames, directly across from the Houses of Parliament and Big Ben. On May 13, 1868, Queen Victoria laid the foundation.[1]

Victorian medicine was primitive: the death rate on the operating table was high. Surgeons generally operated bare-handed, in shirt sleeves, and many wounds turned septic despite the fact that antiseptics had been introduced in the 1870s by Joseph Lister and hospitals had begun to use his carbolic-acid spray. Also thanks to Lister, surgeons had begun to sterilize their equipment and wear rubber gloves. At St. Thomas's hospital a gynecology department was established in 1888, and the students took three months of practical instruction in midwifery. If they knew nothing else when they graduated, they knew how to deliver babies.

In the year that Maugham registered, 1892, electric lights replaced gas burners and candles. The first-year students read Ward's *Bones*, and Ellis' *Demonstrations in Anatomy*. There were prizes for best student, and other rewards in the form of clinical clerkships and dresserships. Of the two hundred students, most were Maugham's age, except for some who had spent a couple of years at Oxford or Cambridge and thought of themselves as the elect.[2]

Maugham found rooms at 11 Vincent Square, a modest three-story house, surrounded by a hedge, that looked out at the Westminster School playing field. In the ten-minute walk to the hospital each day he took Aunsel Street, Horseferry Road to Lambeth Bridge, and crossed the Thames. He had a ground-floor bedroom-sitting room, for which he paid 18 shillings a week. Breakfast and an evening meal cost an additional 12 shillings a week. With lunch at the hospital—a scone and a glass of milk—costing only fourpence, Maugham found that he could live quite comfortably on 14 pounds a month during the nine months of the school year. His annuity of 150 pounds was enough to cover his tuition, books, and room and board, with something left over for holidays abroad. In a pinch he could pawn his microscope for 3 pounds. The bedroom was furnished with a narrow iron bed, a chest of drawers, and a washstand. His sitting room he decorated with green serge curtains, a Moorish rug over the chimney-piece, and a large colored reproduction cut out from the Christmas issue of the *Illustrated London News*, later to be replaced by mezzotints purchased from a shop in Soho.[3]

His landlady, Mrs. Foreman, whom he immortalized in *Cakes and Ale*, was a Cockney with a picturesque manner of speech, whose husband worked as a verger in a neighborhood church. Maugham jotted down her conversation: "Oh, it'll all come right in the end when we get four balls of worsted for a penny," and "I should've liked to have a little girl, and I should have taught her scrubbin' and the pianoforte and black-leadin' grates and I don't know what-all." In the mornings she banged on his door if he was late and lit the fire in his sitting room and that of her other lodger, a master at Westminster School.[4]

On his first visit to the hospital Maugham was greeted by a long, dark corridor, the walls painted two shades of red, which led to a door marked Anatomy Theatre. He was given a locker and an instrument case, and it was suggested that he buy a skeleton. Most of the students took the five-year curriculum of the Conjoint Board of the College of Surgeons and the College of Physicians, but the more ambitious added longer studies that gave them a degree from the University of London.[5]

There were about sixty young men in his year, most of them as shy and confused as he was. At first they were like shadows passing across a white sheet. In the first year some dropped out, and it was only in the second year that he discerned in those remaining the outlines of personality, by virtue of the lectures he had attended with them, the scones and coffee he had taken with them at lunch, the dissection he had done at the same board, and such attractions as *The Belle of New York* that he had seen with one or the other from the pit of the Shaftesbury Theatre.[6]

The anatomy course, each morning at nine, was held in the dissecting room, a large apartment also painted two shades of red, with iron slabs at right angles to the wall, grooved like meat platters, on each of which lay a body. The corpses had skins like dark leather from the preservatives in which they were kept. On one occasion Maugham shared a leg with another student because the hospital was short on corpses. The other student said they were lucky it was a man. Maugham asked why. "They generally always like a male better," an attendant said. "A female's liable to have a lot of fat about her."[7] On another occasion, while dissecting a thigh, Maugham looked in vain for a certain nerve that was not where it should have been. Seeing his dismay, the demonstrator came to his side and found the nerve. Maugham was upset because the textbook had misled him. The demonstrator smiled and said: "You see, the normal is the rarest thing in the world." Maugham was struck by the wisdom in this observation about the human species and he resolved to be on the lookout from then on for the hidden oddity in man.[8]

He was a young man of regular habits. He spent the day at the hospital, walked back to Vincent Square around six, bought his copy of the *Star* at Lambeth Bridge, read it until dinner was served, read books for an hour or two, and then wrote until bedtime. He discovered the best fish-and-chips shops in Westminster. On Sundays the muffin man came round ringing his bell, and once a week he went to the theater. He saw Henry Irving and Ellen Terry, Mrs. Patrick Campbell in *The Second Mrs. Tanqueray*, and George Alexander in *The Importance of Being Earnest*. On Saturday afternoons he went to the Tivoli music hall and applauded such now forgotten vaudeville stars as Bessie Bellwood and Vesta Tilley. While his fellow students bragged about their sexual exploits, Maugham was ashamed that he had never had a woman. One Saturday evening he summoned up his courage, went to Piccadilly, and paid a girl a pound to spend the night with him. The result, he said, was gonorrhea, which he shyly asked one of the doctors at St. Thomas's how to treat. Undeterred by this mishap, he said that he persevered in "sexual congress" with a member of the opposite sex whenever he could afford it.[9]

But it was his writing that mattered more to him than social life, anatomy lectures, or biology exams. It was as if he had intuitively understood that going to medical school rather than Cambridge or

Oxford was the proper training for a writer. The classics he could read on his own, whereas medical school brought him what he could not have obtained elsewhere: a direct experience of human suffering and a professional familiarity with the defective organization of the mind and body. He saw at first hand the pathology of human beings. He saw "life in the raw" and would join the ranks of writer-doctors—Anton Chekhov, Louis-Ferdinand Céline, A. Conan Doyle, Frank Slaughter, William Carlos Williams, and Walker Percy. (Keats was apprenticed to a surgeon but left because he could not stomach dissection, while Francis Thompson, the author of *The Hound of Heaven,* went to medical school in Manchester but dropped out after a quarrel with his father.) As Walker Percy has said: "If you want to be a novelist, work in the wards."

In his first years at the hospital Maugham wrote plays in the manner of Ibsen. They delved into the secrets of the human soul. The characters suffered from fatal diseases, concealed guilty secrets, and bore hereditary taints. When the plays were rejected, he despaired of the ignorance of managers and the low tastes of the public and turned to fiction. "It occurred to me," he wrote, "that my best plan was to write two or three novels that would give me sufficient reputation to induce the managers to look on my plays with favor."[10]

Whatever the genre, he had made the crucial decision of his life. It did not matter whether he had talent. He would *will* himself to be a writer. The study of Goethe in Heidleberg had provided a possible model of what could be accomplished. Like Goethe's *Wilhelm Meister,* he wanted to "become what he was." The example of Brooks, who had given up a legal career to pursue beauty, showed him that it was simply a matter of going ahead and doing it. A natural sense of tidyness made him want to design a pattern for his life, and being a writer suited his circumstances. A writer was an outsider, an artistic orphan, an enemy of society, like Ibsen. He could free himself from the confining influence of his family and deal with the secret problems of his life, his mother's death, and his feelings of alienation.

The year that he entered medical school, 1892, he began keeping a notebook in which he jotted down snatches of dialogue and ideas for stories. He already saw his friends and the people he worked with as *characters* and recognized life as something not only to be lived but to be drawn on for material. In his notebooks he adopts the stance of a detached narrator, viewing life with a clinical eye and sparing no one. He took down such hypocritical maxims of his uncle the vicar as "A parson is paid to preach, not to practice." He etched an acid portrait of his first lover, Ellingham Brooks: "He can see beauty only if it is pointed out to him. He can discover nothing for himself. He intends to write, but for that he has neither energy, imagination, nor will. He is mechanically industrious, but intellectually lazy. . . . He has a craving for admiration. He is weak, vain, and profoundly selfish. . . . He has never had an original idea in his life, but he is a sensitive and keen-sighted observer of the obvious."[11] In this eighteen-year-old boy, Maugham the harsh observer of mankind was already at work.

At the hospital, Maugham was considered a shy, retiring, aloof, and almost forbidding individual, who was always seen with but one friend.[12] In fact, he had several friends outside the school. One was Wentworth Huyshe, who was older than Maugham and acted as a sort of artistic mentor. Huyshe took him around London to galleries and museums, and the two of them often went to the British Museum reading room together. When Maugham published *Liza of Lambeth*, in 1897, he would acknowledge his debt to Wentworth Huyshe in a letter that accompanied a copy of the book. "I can never forget how kind you were to me when I was a stupid boy," he wrote. ". . . I can honestly say that I owe a great deal to you, and now it is a pleasure to be able to send you my first-born. . . . I do feel quite confident that you will give me the helping hand."[13] Years later Maugham recalled receiving his first free copies of *Liza of Lambeth* from his publisher: "It was with pride that in the first one I put the name of a friend who had been the dear companion of my lonely youth." It may be that Wentworth Huyshe was that companion.

Huyshe was also a friend of Maugham's brother Henry Neville (Harry). Two of Maugham's brothers, Charles and Harry, had gone to France after graduating from the university, to help run the legal office founded by their father. Harry, however, was a *fin-de-siècle* esthete with a literary bent and did not like legal work. He finally went to live in Italy, settled in Assisi, and wrote a play in blank verse called *The Husband of Poverty: A Drama of the Life of St. Francis of Assisi*. Harry was known in his family as sensitive, charming, and secretive, a young man who yearned for affection but was afraid of marriage. When his will, which was written in 1895, was read, Wentworth Huyshe was among the beneficiaries, all of whom were young men with whom Harry had shared bohemian (and presumably homosexual) adventures.[14]

"The dear companion of my lonely youth" could also have been

Adney Walter Payne. Born in London, the son of theatrical manager George Adney Payne, Walter was educated at the City of London School and then went to Heidelberg, where he met Maugham. They struck up a friendship that lasted until Payne died in 1949, his health broken as the result of injuries received in the 1940 London blitz. Payne and Maugham were roommates for twenty years, between 1898 and 1917, and occupied five different sets of rooms. It was a convenient arrangement. Payne had graduated in 1897 from the Royal Institute of Chartered Accountants and was called to the bar by the Middle Temple in 1899. He was away all day, and Maugham had the flat to himself to work in. He was very good-looking, and Maugham claimed that when Payne was through with his girl friends he passed them on to him. He wrote that one evening a week Payne would manage to be out so that Maugham could engage in "sexual congress" with one or the other of Payne's former girl friends.[15]

In 1910 Walter Payne took over his father's music-hall interests, and in 1924 he became president of the Society of West End Theatre Managers. From 1937 to 1945 he was chairman of the Theatre Royal in Drury Lane. "In spite of a steely precision of mind and an unalterable determination to obtain his objectives, he was one of the most likeable of men and in manner suggested the country gentleman rather than the theatre manager," said his obituary in the London *Times*.[16]

In 1933, years after Maugham had left England, Payne married the blonde and beautiful Claire Beatrice Wisinger, who came from a wealthy Hungarian family and had already been married three times. The Paynes lived at 15 York Terrace, where Maugham sometimes stayed when he came to London, but he did not get along with Mrs. Payne, and soon after the marriage he moved his things out. Payne was a kind, generous, uncomplicated man, and he and Maugham remained friends. The years of close friendship during Maugham's literary apprenticeship, when Payne read his early efforts and occasionally loaned him money, had formed too strong a connection to be easily dissolved by a hostile wife. When success came to Maugham, Payne helped him with his play contracts and tax problems, and Maugham dedicated the first edition of *Liza of Lambeth* "To my good friend, Adney Payne." After Payne's death Maugham pressed his widow to return his letters, which she did. The letters, an inestimable source for Maugham's early years, were destroyed.[17]

In the spring of 1894 Maugham left London during the medical school Easter break for a six-week vacation in Italy. This was the beginning of his nomadic life-style, to which he would remain faithful. He was footloose, he could not stay in one place, he had an urge to put the Channel between himself and England and depart on a *grand* or *petit* European tour. He also saw travel as a necessary part of his apprenticeship. That spring he left for Genoa with twenty pounds in his pocket and a Gladstone bag. In Pisa he sat in the pinewood in which Shelley had read Sophocles and written verses on a guitar. In Florence he took a room in the home of a widow, on the via Laura, with a view of the cathedral dome. He visited Florence with a copy of Ruskin in hand and admired what Ruskin told him to admire. He took Italian lessons from the widow's daughter, Ersilia, with whom he read the *Purgatorio*. In the evening he went out looking for adventure but was too shy to find it. At the end of the holiday he returned to St. Thomas's via Venice, Verona, and Milan.[18]

Having completed the first two years of medical school in the fall of 1894, he realized that the ranks of his class had thinned. Some students had been "ploughed" (flunked out), others had drifted away. One student, who pawned the goods he bought on credit, turned up in the police-court proceedings in the newspapers and went overseas to take up the white man's burden. Meanwhile Maugham learned how to use a stethoscope, dispense mixtures, make ointments. When he passed his exam in materia medica he was ready to work in the wards. It was dangerous work, and as a result of it he caught septic tonsilitis while doing a postmortem on a corpse that was in an advanced state of decomposition. But Maugham was too impatient to be sick, and he quickly resumed his duties.[19]

He signed on as a clerk to one of the three assistant physicians who took outpatients. The hospital's 1551 charter had not changed: it was still a hospital for those who could not pay and was patronized by the poor from the adjacent slum of Lambeth. The outpatient department consisted of three salmon-colored rooms and a large waiting room with massive pillars of masonry and long benches where the patients sat after being given their "letters" at midday. The scene reminded Maugham of a Daumier drawing. A clerk took the "book" for the day, writing in a large volume the name, age, sex, and profession of the patient and the diagnosis of his or her disease. At half past one the house physician arrived, rang the bell, and told the porter to send in the old patients. Most of them suffered from chronic bronchitis. If they were doing well, "Rep 14" was written on their letters, and they went to the dispensary with their bottles or gallipots to get their prescriptions refilled for fourteen days. Then the assistant physician arrived with his clerk to examine the cases that needed more than Rep 14, including many women who suffered from malnutrition. As the afternoon wore on in the crowded waiting room, the odor of disinfectant mingled with the stench of humanity.[20]

It seemed to Philip Carey, the clubfooted, medical-student hero of *Of Human Bondage,* who so closely resembles the novel's author,

> that he alone of the clerks saw the dramatic interest of those afternoons. To the others men and women were only cases, good if they were complicated, tiresome if obvious; they heard murmurs and were astonished at abnormal livers; an unexpected sound in the lungs gave them something to talk about. But to Philip there was much more. He found an interest in just looking at them, in the shape of their heads and their hands, in the look of their eyes and the length of their noses. You saw in that room human nature taken by surprise, and often the mask of custom was torn off rudely, showing you the soul all raw. . . . There was neither good nor bad there. There were just facts. It was life.[21]

Maugham took his tour of duty as a dresser in the surgical wards. Wounds had to be dressed, stitches taken out, and bandages replaced. Sometimes there were operations, and he stood in the well of the theater in a white jacket ready to hand the surgeon the instrument he wanted or sponge the blood so he could see what he was doing. He saw a great many appendixes removed. The surgeon for whom he dressed was in competition with a colleague as to who could remove an appendix more quickly and with the smallest incision.[22]

For three days he was on accident duty, giving first aid to urgent cases. During that time he lived in the hospital and took his meals in the common room. He had a room, with a fold-out bed, on the ground floor near the casualty ward. At night a bell rang to announce the casualties. The worst night was Saturday, when the drunks and abused wives were brought in. The cases ranged from a cut finger to a cut throat. There were attempted suicides, and men who had been knocked down by a cab, and boys who had hurt themselves playing.[23]

One day a man brought his son whose leg had been broken when another boy climbing a wall had fallen on him. Maugham returned him, duly bandaged, to his father's arms, and the boy bent toward him and puckered his lips for a kiss. The father and the nurse laughed, and Maugham blushed a deep red, and later wondered whether the pretty child remembered kissing a weary medical student who had not slept much in several days.[24]

Later he took a six-month appointment as an inpatient clerk. He spent the morning in the wards with the house physician, writing up cases and making tests. He found that the male patients were easier to get along with than the females, who were often querulous and ill-tempered, and complained to the hard-worked nurses. This at least is the way he saw it, for already he was displaying a tendency toward misogyny. Women, going back to his mother, were a disappointment, an unreliable species. They never lived up to one's expectations. He rarely missed a chance to make unpleasant remarks about them and he admired the remark with which his professor of gynecology began his first lecture: "Gentlemen, woman is an animal that micturates once a day, defecates once a week, menstruates once a month, parturates once a year, and copulates whenever she has the opportunity."[25]

When Maugham was in his third year a scandal erupted in England that terrified him and gave him all the more reason to keep his homosexuality a secret. Oscar Wilde was arrested and imprisoned. The year was 1895, and in all of Victoria's long reign there was no greater uproar. It was as much of a turning point in England as the Dreyfus case was in France. In Victorian times homosexuality was the great clandestine subject, and to admit that you were a practicing homosexual was to confess to a criminal offense that could send you to jail. Homosexuals were members of a secret fraternity who could not openly express their views or display their inclinations. To be open and forthright was to expose oneself to prosecution. John Addington Symonds, who came closest to being a crusading Victorian homosexual, had lost the chair of poetry at Oxford in 1877 because he was unreserved about his fondness for boys. He left England and wrote two privately printed pamphlets defending his preference, A Problem in Greek Ethics (1883) and A Problem in Modern Ethics (1891). He died in 1893 and so was unable to write any defense of Wilde when he was arrested.[26]

English literature at the time had its share of secret homosexuals. Edmund Gosse, the very model of an establishment writer, Henry James's best friend in London and librarian of the House of Lords from 1904 to 1914, was one, and wrote Symonds in response to his pamphlets, "I entirely and deeply sympathize with you."[27] Walter Pater was another. He described an idealized friendship between men in

Marius the Epicurean, and gave a more candid account of a homo-erotic friendship in the book he was writing when he died in 1894, *Gaston de Latour.* A. E. Housman was one, and sent a copy of *A Shropshire Lad* to Wilde in prison as an expression of sympathy for the one writer who had had to bite the bullet.[28]

Wilde, however, was not a crusader in the manner of Symonds. He had alluded to homosexual activities in *Dorian Gray,* but in vague enough a manner to avoid prosecution. He ended up in prison not because he admitted to being a homosexual but because he took the trouble to deny it. He was not a martyr for a cause but the victim of an ingrained Victorian reflex. Even though he was a homosexual, when he was accused of it, he felt the need to publicly proclaim that he was not, for the core of the Victorian sensibility was that the accusation of a crime was worse than the crime itself.

The Wilde scandal, unfolding daily in the press, was a saga of great personal relevance to Maugham, whose own homosexual inclinations were becoming increasingly apparent. In 1891 Wilde had met Alfred Douglas, who was still at Oxford. Douglas belonged to a family that took up several pages in *Burke's Peerage.* His father, John Sholto Douglas, the Marquess of Queensberry, had been a gentleman jockey in the Grand National and an amateur lightweight boxer, author of the rules that bear his name, and did not look kindly on behavior that he considered unvirile. It was Douglas—nicknamed Bosie—who sent Wilde the poem "Two Loves," which includes the famous lines:

> *"I am true Love, I fill*
> *The hearts of boy and girl with mutual flame."*
> *Then sighing said the other, "Have thy will,*
> *I am the love that dare not speak its name."*

The scandal began on the afternoon of February 28, 1895, when Wilde dropped in at his club, the Albermarle. The hall porter handed him a card from the Marquess of Queensberry that said: "To Oscar Wilde, posing as a somdomite." In rage or ignorance the marquess had misspelled the key word. Wilde should have torn up the card and thrown it away, but instead he charged Queensberry with making and publishing a criminal libel against him. At the trial Queensberry produced male prostitutes and blackmailers who incriminated Wilde, and was found not guilty. If Queensberry was innocent, Wilde was indeed a sodomite, and he was tried as such in April, under the 1885 La-bouchère amendment, on charges of gross indecency. His first trial ended with a hung jury, but he was found guilty on all counts at his second trial in May and was sentenced to two years' hard labor.[29]

Wilde's conviction had a chastening influence on others of his per-suasion, who feared that his case was but the first of many. The boat train to Calais was packed with homosexual émigrés. They left for Paris and Nice, Naples and Capri, Palermo and Seville, anyplace where they felt safe from prosecution.

Henry Paget, the Earl of Uxbridge, settled in Monte Carlo. Maugham's friend Ellingham Brooks left for Capri, where he remained until his death. The House of Lords was depleted. Newspaper editori-als clamored for "the heads of the 500 noblemen and men of the world who share his turpitude and corrupt youth."[30] The scandal had be-come international in scope. Europeans asked, "Is this how you behave with your poets?" and Americans asked, "Is this how your poets be-have?"

The Oscar Wilde trial had a profound effect on Maugham. He was twenty-one when it took place, an aspiring writer who believed himself to be a homosexual. He sympathized not only with Wilde but with the posture of the artist who challenges conventional attitudes. But Wilde was punished, and for the rest of his life Maugham would associate homosexuality with the threat of punishment. He did his best to conceal his true nature. Glenway Wescott, a close friend and confidant of Maugham's, many years later explained: "What is very hard for your generation to appreciate is that Willie's generation lived in mortal ter-ror of the Oscar Wilde trial."[31]

Maugham never lived to see the decriminalization of homosexuality in England. It was two years after his death, in 1967, that the Sexual Offences Act made homosexuality between consenting adults legal. He never spoke up in favor of homosexuals, because he feared that doing so would be an admission that he was one. At the time that decriminali-zation was in the news he went to a dinner party at the home of Arthur Jeffress, the millionaire homosexual son of the head of the British-American Tobacco Company, who had contributed to a fund to help the defendants in the Montagu-Pitt-Rivers trial, a homosexual scan-dal of the fifties. At the dinner Jeffress pleaded with Maugham to make a gesture—anything—perhaps send a discreet letter to *The Times*. Pale with anger, Maugham pushed aside his snifter of brandy, threw his cigarette in the fireplace and left. He never spoke to Jeffress again.[32]

Maugham did, however, express his sympathy with Wilde in a circuitous and private manner: he sought out and became friendly with persons who had been close to Wilde. It was as if by cultivating them he could establish a link with a writer whose life-style he admired but dared not emulate.

Among the members of Wilde's circle with whom Maugham made friends were Robert Ross, the Canadian-born art critic, who claimed he was the first boy Wilde ever had; Laurence Housman, the brother of A. E. Housman and a close friend of Wilde's; Robert Hichens, a confidant of Wilde who had written the much-discussed book *The Green Carnation*, a humorous account of the Wilde-Douglas ménage; Reggie Turner, the wit and raconteur who had lived with Wilde in exile after his release from prison; Mabel Beardsley, the beautiful sister of the illustrator Aubrey Beardsley, who was part of the *Yellow Book* set that included Wilde and who said she felt at home with sexual misfits; and Ada Leverson, probably Wilde's closest woman friend, whom he dubbed "The Sphinx."

Maugham started publishing as a late Victorian, but as he grew older he found himself writing in a period in which homosexuality could be discussed less guardedly. Books were still banned, but their authors were no longer imprisoned. In spite of changing attitudes, he avoided dealing with homosexuality in his work, with two exceptions. There were no allusions to prohibited pleasures, as in the works of Oscar Wilde. There were no Gide-like confessions about the delights of North African boys. There was in his fiction no major (or minor) homosexual character, such as Proust's Baron de Charlus. There was no homosexual novel that could not be published during his lifetime, such as E. M. Forster's *Maurice*. All that remains in his eighty books as a clue to his real nature is the possibility that Mildred in *Of Human Bondage* was based on a young man (just as Proust's Albertine was based on his chauffeur Albert), several ambiguous scenes in his novels, and two explicit passages in his essays, one concerning El Greco, the other Melville.

In *The Razor's Edge*, for example, the wayward Chicago girl, Sophie MacDonald, introduces a French sailor to Maugham the narrator in Toulon. Maugham is asked to admire the sailor's physique and feel his biceps. "He's strong," says Sophie MacDonald. "He has the muscles of a boxer. Feel them."

... The sailor ... with a complacent smile flexed his arm so that the biceps stood out.

"I did so," says the narrator, "and expressed a proper admiration."

This sounds like the transposed version of a homosexual scene between Maugham and his long-time secretary and lover, Gerald Haxton, who also acted as procurer and went hunting for sailors in Villefranche once they had settled in the south of France.

In his handling of El Greco and Melville, Maugham revealed himself more than perhaps he meant to. He sees them both as homosexuals. In the case of El Greco he is writing from the viewpoint of a heterosexual author who belittles homosexuality. He argues that homosexuality kept El Greco from greatness; because the homosexual has a narrower outlook on the world than the normal man, he cannot see it as a whole, and thus a number of typical human emotions are denied him. He says that homosexuals can never reach the supreme heights of genius, the one exception being Shakespeare, who may have been homosexual, if we go by the sonnets.

Maugham sees El Greco's "work of tortured fantasy and sinister strangeness" as a result of "a sexual abnormality." He then goes on to describe the homosexual temperament:

I should say that a distinctive trait of the homosexual is a lack of deep seriousness over certain things that normal men take seriously. This ranged from an inane flippancy to a sardonic humor. He has a wilfulness that attaches importance to things that most men find trivial and on the other hand regards cynically the subjects which the common opinion of mankind has held essential to its spiritual welfare. He has a lively sense of beauty, but is apt to see beauty especially in decoration. He loves luxury and attaches peculiar value to elegance. He is emotional, but fantastic. He is vain, loquacious, witty and theatrical. With his keen insight and quick sensibility he can pierce the depths, but in his innate frivolity he fetches up from them not a priceless jewel but a tinsel ornament. He has small power of invention, but a wonderful gift for delightful embroidery. He has vitality, brilliance, but seldom strength. He stands on the bank, aloof and ironical, and watches the river of life flow on. He is persuaded that opinion is no more than prejudice. In short he has many of the characteristics that surprise us in El Greco.[33]

He also has many of the characteristics that surprise us in Maugham, such as sardonic humor, a cynical view of subjects most men take seriously, a love of luxury and elegance, and keen insight coupled with small powers of invention (Maugham more than once acknowledged that his own powers of invention were slight). It must have amused him to be thus disparaging his fellow constituents in such sweeping terms. But at the same time the passage is a declaration of failure. Maugham is saying that homosexuality has kept him from the first rank, just as it kept El Greco. All his life he would suffer from the gnawing sense that he was cut off from genius, that he stood on a hillock in the lowlands and would never go higher.

"The sexual proclivities of an author are no business of his readers," he wrote in the passage on Melville, "except insofar as they influence his work, as is the case with André Gide and Marcel Proust; when they do, and the facts are put before you, much that was obscure or even incredible may be made plain."[34] Again he could have been writing about himself.

In the passage on Melville, Maugham, instead of condemning homosexuality, identifies with certain traits in Melville's character which he has uncovered. He bases his argument on the way Melville dwells on the physical perfection of young men, who are presented far more vividly than the girls. He quotes Melville's description of Harry Bolton in *Redburn*: "He was one of those small, but perfectly formed beings with curling hair, and silken muscles, who seem to have been born in cocoons. His complexion was a mantling brunette, feminine as a girl's; his feet were small, his hands very white; and his eyes were large, black and womanly." Maugham argues from this description that "it seems fairly evident that Melville was a repressed homosexual, a type that, if we may believe what we read, was more common in the United States of his time than it is today."[35]

There is in one of Maugham's short stories a description of a young man which is curiously similar to Melville's and which, by the same reasoning, might be used to demonstrate Maugham's homosexuality. Here is the way the narrator, "himself an ugly man, insignificant in appearance, [who] prized very highly comeliness in others," describes Red, the American sailor:

> The most comely thing you ever saw . . . The first time you saw him beauty just took your breath away . . . He was made like a Greek god,

broad in the shoulders and thin in the flanks; he was like Apollo, with just that soft roundness which Praxiteles gave him, and that suave, feminine grace which has something troubling and mysterious. His skin was dazzling white, milky, like satin; his skin was like a woman's . . . And his face was just as beautiful as his body. He had large blue eyes, very dark, so that some say they were black, and unlike most red-haired people he had dark eyebrows and long dark lashes. His features were perfectly regular and his mouth was like a scarlet wound.[36]

If lingering over the hermaphroditic desirability of young men was a proof of homosexuality, Maugham could certainly match Melville.

He goes on to speculate that Melville's repressed homosexuality may have been responsible for his disaffection with married life, which is all the more interesting when we know that his own homosexuality was one of the reasons for the break-up of his marriage. And he concludes by arguing that repressed homosexuality, even though it may never have been yielded to, may have had an overwhelming effect on Melville's disposition. The same might be said of Maugham, although in his case there was no question but that he yielded.

Aside from these two passages in which he dropped his guard, Maugham took care all his long life to keep up the pretense that he was not homosexual. But he admired men who, unlike himself, were able to drop the mask. Jean-Jacques Rousseau's *Confessions* was one of his favorite books because Rousseau "does not hesitate to show himself ungrateful, unscrupulous, dishonest, base and mean. . . . I don't know who, if he is completely honest with himself, can read the confessions of this weak-willed, petulant, vain and miserable creature without saying to himself: 'After all, is there so much to choose between him and me? If the whole truth were known about me, should I, who turn away shocked from these revelations, cut so pretty a figure'?"[37] This was as close to a confession as Maugham could come.

One of the by-products of the Oscar Wilde scandal was that Maugham discovered the island of Capri. Ellingham Brooks had fled there after Wilde's imprisonment, and Maugham joined him during one of his 1895 medical-school holidays, when he was twenty-one. Capri was a quiet, sparsely populated place, not yet overrun with tourists or a sanctuary for the third sex; the funicular from the beach to the town had not even been thought of. Maugham took the boat from Naples and saw a gaunt rock of austere outline dotted with green vineyards and floating on a deep blue sea. It was a place rich in historical associations, and he thought of the homosexual emperor Tiberius, who had retired there in A.D. 26 and ruled Rome by correspondence. There were small hotels where room and board, with wine and a view of Vesuvius thrown in, could be had for five shillings a day.

Maugham found Brooks unchanged from their Heidelberg days; he was still passionately involved with literature, still quoting Pater and Meredith, still studying Dante, still intending to translate Leopardi. Before such fiery intensity, such total commitment to art for art's sake, Maugham did not dare mention that he was working on several stories and a novel. Brooks took him to Morgano's, a wineshop off the piazza, where he met some of the other expatriates: a poet, a painter or two, a Belgian composer, a sculptor named Harvard Thomas, and a Confederate Civil War colonel. Art was discussed with solemnity. What did politics or commerce or the professions matter when set beside the absolute? They might argue about a sonnet or a Greek bas-relief, but they all "burned with a hard, gemlike flame." Maugham also burned with a hard, gemlike flame, but because he was a medical student he was treated, he said, like a philistine, "who cared for nothing but dissecting dead bodies and would seize an unguarded moment to give his best friend an enema."[38]

Despite his long hours in the wards and intermittent holidays, Maugham kept to his schedule of writing at night, and in early 1896 he finished his first two stories and sent them to the publisher T. Fisher Unwin.[39] The stories, "A Bad Example" and "Daisy," were written under the influence of Ibsen, showing nonconformists struggling against an intolerant society. In "A Bad Example" James Clinton, a clerk in the City, is serving on a jury in coroner's court and sits through three cases of suicide caused by social exploitation. (Maugham had seen several attempted suicides fished out of the Thames and brought to St. Thomas's.) He is so shattered by the experience that he decides to devote his life to the service of the poor. His friends and family think he has gone mad. His wife consults a psychiatrist, who has him committed. The moral of course is that society cannot tolerate good men. Maugham would return often to this theme, and James Clinton is the first of a gallery of good men, such as Athelny in *Of Human Bondage* and Erik Christessen in *The Narrow Corner*, who is so Christlike he dies for the sins of others. Dr. Saunders, the spokesman for Maugham in *The Narrow Corner*, says: "Goodness, I know, it's shattering. One doesn't know what to do about it. It knocks human relations endways. Damned shame, isn't it?"

The second story, "Daisy," has the distinction of being the first fiction in which Maugham used the landscape of his youth. It was based on the true story of a Whitstable girl who eloped with an army officer. Maugham calls the town Blackstable, as he does in his later works. Daisy Griffith is banished by her family when she follows a married man to London. After an interim period as a streetwalker she marries a wealthy baronet, which makes her parents eager for reconciliation. In this rather heavy-handed indictment of the hypocrisy of families Maugham used as his main character a heroine to whom he would return: the beautiful, sensual girl of loose morals and cheerful disposition.

Fisher Unwin returned these two stories, and thus Maugham's literary career was launched with a rejection slip. The reader's report for "A Bad Example," dated July 20, 1896, said: "There is some ability in this, but not very much. Mr. Maugham has imagination and he can write prettily, but his satire against society is not deep enough or humorous enough to command attention. He should be advised to try the humbler magazines for a time, and if he tries anything more important to send it to us."[40] The report was signed E.G., for Edward Garnett, a distinguished editor who was credited with discovering Joseph Conrad, whose first novel, *Almayer's Folly*, Fisher Unwin had published the year before.

Of course Maugham was not shown the report. He was simply told that his stories were too short and that he should send Unwin something longer. There is nothing for an aspiring writer like a little encouragement, and Maugham sat down and began a novel based on his experiences in the obstetric ward at St. Thomas's. Medical school had provided him not only with much of what he knew about human nature but with the subject matter of his first book and the clinical attitude required to write it.

It was in his fourth year at the hospital, in 1896, that Maugham, having finished in the other wards, served his three weeks' duty as an obstetric clerk. One day he went into the operating theater to observe a Caesarean birth. The theater was crowded, for they were seldom done, and the doctor explained that the operation was rarely a success. The woman on the operating table had been twice aborted. She had her heart set on a child and was pregnant again. The doctor had told her there was a fifty-fifty chance of survival, but she and her husband wanted to take the risk. The operation seemed to go smoothly, and the doctor, his face beaming, finally lifted the baby from the womb. A few days later Maugham was in the ward and asked one of the nurses how the woman was getting on. He was told that she had died in the night but the baby was doing well. He frowned to keep himself from crying. What had touched him, he said, was the woman's passion to have her baby.[41]

Perhaps there was a connection between Maugham's decision to be a writer and the death of his mother after giving birth to a stillborn child. It seems clear that in his story about the Caesarean he was identifying with his mother and reliving her death. According to psychiatric literature, the creative urge can originate with unconscious reproductive fantasies—an identification with the fertile mother, or in Maugham's case, with the mother who dies giving birth. Creative work can be seen as the transfer of the pre-Oedipal wish to bear children, as the mother does.

There is also evidence for this connection in Maugham's obsession with women whose children are stillborn or die young. In his first novel, *Liza of Lambeth* (1897), Liza has an affair with a married man, becomes pregnant, and miscarries. The doctor arrives too late, and she dies. In *A Man of Honour*, the first Maugham play to be produced in England (1903), Basil Kent is the fellow referred to in the title. He gets a barmaid "in trouble" and marries her, but her baby is stillborn. Basil Kent turns up in the novel *The Merry-Go-Round* (1904), still in the same fix. In *Mrs. Craddock* (1904) there are emotional pages on Bertha Craddock's confinement. After a difficult labor her baby is stillborn. When Bertha finds out "she burst into passionate weeping. Her sobs were terrible, unbridled, it was her life that she was weeping away, her hope of happiness, all her desires and dreams." *Of Human Bondage* opens with the autobiographical scene of Mrs. Carey giving birth to a stillborn child ("Another boy," says the nurse) and then dying a few days later. ("Your mama's in heaven," the nurse tells Philip.) In *Cakes and Ale* (1930) Rosie Driffield has a daughter who dies of meningitis at the age of six. On the night after her daughter's death Rosie goes out on the town, spends the night with an actor friend, and returns to her husband in the morning. This leads us to a secondary theme often found in Maugham, that of the mother who betrays and disappoints.

Maugham's childbirth scenes were grounded in his hospital experience. As an obstetric clerk he worked in the "district," the slum of Lambeth, and delivered an average of three babies a day. He was on call day and night, and so, for convenience, he took a room across from the hospital to which the porter had a key. Pregnant women were given cards, and when their time came, a messenger brought the card to the porter, who went to get the clerk. On his first case he went with the senior obstetric clerk, and then he managed on his own.[42]

Often there was a mile or more to walk, during which he chatted with the messenger about conditions in Lambeth, and picked up the intonations of Cockney speech. He walked up narrow streets into filthy courts and houses without light or air, and entered stuffy rooms lit with kerosene lamps, where the air was so foul he had to light his pipe. The little black bag was his passport in this neighborhood, where outsiders were unwelcome. Often the babies were unwelcome too—another mouth to feed—and two or three women stood around the patient shaking their heads as the obstetric clerk came in. The hospital insisted that the mothers stay in bed for ten days, and the greatest tragedy was loss of work. Maugham spent long hours talking to the midwives and the patient's relatives, chatting with the husbands while he drank their tea. In three weeks he delivered sixty-three babies.[43] In later life he liked to tell his friends that he was a qualified midwife.

Liza of Lambeth, the novel that launched Maugham's sixty-five-year writing career in 1897, was late-Victorian in period. Indeed, the publication date was held up to give the reading public a chance to recover from the excitement of the Diamond Jubilee, marking Queen Victoria's sixty years on the throne, which was celebrated in June throughout the empire. In England the troops of the garrison at Windsor inaugurated the jubilee celebration with a military tattoo in the Grand Quadrangle of the castle. Two thousand five hundred beacon fires were lit on elevated spots between Cornwall and Caithness. A jubilee dinner was given to 310,000 loyal subjects in fifty-six districts.

In 1897 the women's suffrage bill went before the House of Commons for the second time. The miners' eight-hours bill was rejected. Oscar Wilde was released from prison on May 19. Young men took fencing lessons at Angelo's in St. James's Street. John Sargent, at the height of his fame, with more commissions than he could handle, was elected to the Royal Academy. The Tate Gallery was formally opened by the Prince of Wales.[44]

New editions of Meredith and Robert Louis Stevenson were published. Francis Thompson's *New Poems* came out. Arthur Symons, the leading English symbolist, published a collection of sonnets. Edmund Gosse edited *Literature of the World*. Herbert Horne was in the midst of years of fastidious research for a biography of Botticelli, about which Reggie Turner said: "Dear Herbert Horne! Poring over Botticelli's washing bills—and always a shirt missing!"[45]

In literature, Victorian orthodoxy was being challenged from all points of the compass. New ideas were in the air and on the printed page, and were bound to influence young writers like Maugham. Darwin's *On the Origin of Species* had been published in 1859, undermining the Victorian credo of a harmonious, God-inspired universe. To some young writers, including Maugham, Victorian order was a myth. The universe looked like a colossal blunder, the planet was inhospitable, and human life was an accident.[46]

The keeper of Victorian orthodoxy for many years had been the circulating library. The two biggest, Mudie's and Smith's, were institutions powerful enough to determine what the British public read. In the Victorian era the main form of popular entertainment was the novel, and Mudie's and Smith's promoted the three-decker novel, with rivers of type and meadows of margin, which was too expensive for most people to buy, so that they subscribed to a circulating library. Borrowing books from Mudie's was as ingrained a Victorian habit as watching television is to us. The library establishment could make or break a book. In most cases, if Mudie's did not stock a novel, it was stillborn. Publishers catered to their preference for three-deckers, for if Mudie's and Smith's thought a book suited their public, they bought out the entire first printing. Because the triple-decker was such a confirmed convention of Victorian fiction, it was unheard of for a first novel to be published in one volume. Even such established novelists as Meredith and Hardy and Henry James conformed to the rule. Dickens avoided the library circuit by serializing his novels, but wrote *Great Expectations* as a three-decker, after changing the ending to make it less gloomy, on the advice of the three-decker veteran Edward Bulwer-Lytton.

By insisting on the three-decker, the circulating libraries encouraged the windy writing, prolix meditation, and dull moralizing that stamp a great deal of Victorian fiction. Books were padded and distended to go the distance. At the same time the circulating libraries acted as censors by ignoring books that they felt would offend their readers. When the Bishop of Wakefield announced in the pulpit that he had burned his copy of Thomas Hardy's *Jude the Obscure*, Smith's withdrew it from circulation. When George Moore's *Esther Waters* was banned by

Smith's, he complained to the head of the library department, who told him: "You see, we are a circulating library and our subscribers are not used to detailed descriptions of a lying-in hospital."

Eventually Moore and Hardy and other banned authors challenged the system. Moore had his books published in six-shilling, one-volume editions. Such up-and-coming young writers as Kipling and Stevenson shunned the three-decker, and soon the tyranny of the circulating libraries began to crack under increasing attacks in the press. But in the end it was the libraries themselves that decided to scuttle the three-decker, for economic reasons. Mudie's had to choose between raising the steadfast one-guinea-a-year subscription rate and lowering the expenses for fiction by killing off the three-decker. In 1894 Mudie's and Smith's made a joint decision to stock one-volume novels only, and the three-decker sank into extinction.[47] By 1900, new publishers such as Heinemann and Fisher Unwin were printing six-shilling novels, and there was a growing market for short stories in London magazines. Mudie's and Smith's, however, continued to prosper. Here is an entry in Virginia Woolf's diary for October 1917: "First I stood at Mudie's counter while a stout widow chose ten novels; taking them from the hand of the Mudie's man, like a lapdog, only stipulating that she wanted no vulgarity, not much description, but plenty of incident."[48]

Maugham began to publish three years after the stranglehold of the circulating libraries on fiction had been relaxed. It was also a time when English literature was breaking out of the insularity that had shaped it since Chaucer. It was Gertrude Stein, in her lecture "What Is English Literature," who made the point that a large part of its glory was the steady description of the daily island life. The English were shut up with their complete island life, and it sustained them. They had "their daily life as they lived it every day on their island and which made their real solid body of writing."[49] But all this was changing in the last years of Victoria's reign. Anthony Trollope, the chronicler of country life set in Barsetshire, had died in 1882, and Tennyson's death in 1892 marked the passing of the Victorian order in literature. His burial in Westminster Abbey was a state occasion. As his poem "The Silent Voice" was sung, the laureled coffin advanced beneath the soaring arches to its place of rest near Chaucer, in the corner set aside for England's greatest poets.

When Maugham first published, there were a number of literary trends under whose influence he might have come. There was the belle-lettrist trend, as exemplified by Meredith, whose convoluted writing in such novels as *Diana of the Crossways* (1885) and *Lord Ormont and His Aminta* (1894) had won him a small but ardent following. Meredith said he wanted to appeal to "the acute but honorable minority." Fashionable ladies in London drawing rooms confessed to being "whole-hearted Meredithians." It was a coterie thing. When the reading public said he was obscure, his followers said "not to us." Maugham thought this sort of writing was "tiresome acrobatics."

Allied with and overlapping the belle-lettrists were the decadents, disciples of Oscar Wilde. They were the apostles of the bizarre, the esthetic, and art for art's sake. Their house organ was the *Yellow Book*, which published between 1894 and 1897, and among whose contributors were Wilde, Max Beerbohm, and Ada Leverson. Victorian critics called it poisonous. Maugham would be influenced by Wilde in his plays, but in his prose, after a brief flirtation with the ornate, he opted for simplicity.

Then there were the novelists who shocked readers because they dealt with subjects that the Victorians considered improper. Eminent among these were Thomas Hardy and George Moore. When *Jude the Obscure* was denounced and banned in 1897, Hardy's disgust was such that he wrote no more novels. George Moore, the son of an Irish landed gentleman, wrote novels that tried to tell his readers something about direct experience. In 1885 he published *The Mummer's Wife*, about the downward path of a young woman who married an actor and took to drink. It was considered a shocking book. In 1894 he came out with *Esther Waters*, the drama of a maid who is exploited because of her station in life. Captain Oswald Ames, the tallest man in the British Army, who led the Diamond Jubilee procession, and who spoke for the England of iron-clad class-consciousness, summed up its attitude in one sentence: "I am not interested in reading about servants."

With the improvement of primary and secondary education, culture was spreading among the middle class and literacy among the working class. The 1870 Education Act had broken the monopoly of the Church in primary education and had helped supply England with a population that could read and write.[50] This explained the success of Mudie's circulating library and the Victorian three-decker novel. It also helped to form a new class of reader, state-educated. There were now two distinct publics—mass and quality. The masses were reading Hall Caine and Marie Corelli, the Harold Robbins and Jacqueline Susann of their day, in their edifying Victorian incarnations, without the mandatory orgasm every ten pages. Both Caine and Corelli were fiercely moral, for they knew their audience. While Meredith and Hardy had a small public, Caine and Corelli had a vast one. Hall Caine wrote grotesque, violent novels, such as *Shadow of a Crime* (1885) and *The Manxman* (1894). He lived and wrote in a machicolated castle on the Isle of Man, and he died in 1931, leaving an estate of a quarter of a millon pounds. Marie Corelli appealed not only to the masses but to the Crown. Queen Victoria, who had let the literary currents of the age flow past her unnoticed, praised *The Sorrows of Satan* (1895). The Prince of Wales, who seldom read a book, thrilled at *Barrabas* (1893) and invited its author to dinner. Several of her books sold over 100,000 copies, which was phenomenal in those days.[51]

There were also at this time young writers who wrote novels and plays in order to change the world. "Message writers" they would be called today, although the term at the time was "propagagartism." Among these were H. G. Wells, George Bernard Shaw, and John Galsworthy. Wells had begun publishing his books, which combined science fiction and philosophical treatise, in 1895. His first, *The Time Machine*, was followed by *The Island of Dr. Moreau* in 1896 and *The Invisible Man* in 1897. Shaw, the Fabian socialist, had written *Mrs. Warren's Profession* in 1893, but it was banned because the leading character was a procuress. Galsworthy, a lawyer turned writer, wrote plays that were dramatizations of social problems, such as *Strife* (1909) and *Justice* (1910). Maugham looked askance at "message writing," insisting that he was a storyteller and nothing more.

Closer to his heart but as yet removed from his inspiration was the trend of the far-flung, noninsular writer. Robert Louis Stevenson, Maugham's predecessor in the South Seas, had died in Samoa in 1894, but Kipling was at the height of his popularity, having published *The Jungle Book* in 1894 and *Captains Courageous* in 1897. Maugham was a lifelong admirer of Kipling, whom he called "our greatest story writer." Conrad had also, in 1895, begun to write novels that were far removed from the recitation of the daily island life.

There was yet another literary trend at the time, one to which Maugham attached himself when he wrote *Liza of Lambeth*. In the last two decades of the century there had been a general awakening to the living conditions of the working class, to the urban slums, and to the wretchedness of the poor in "the richest country in the world." This mood of social reform took many shapes. There was church work, and General Booth and the Salvation Army, and Henry George's *Progress and Poverty*, and trade-union activity, which produced the dockers' strike of 1889.[52] In literature, social awareness took the form of the slum novel. It became fashionable to mine the poor for literary material.

Other writers had better qualifications than Maugham for writing about slum life, from having known it firsthand—George Gissing for one. After a boyhood in Yorkshire, Gissing was expelled from college in 1877 for stealing money from a cloakroom to give to a prostitute, and he became a social outcast. He married the prostitute and lived through years of bitter poverty in the London slums. The death of his wife reawakened his disgust with working-class life and inspired him to write a sustained study of slum conditions which appeared in 1889, *The Nether World*. Gissing opposed the high-minded presentation of lower-class characters as virtuous and noble, as they were found in Dickens: "the decent poor are the salt of the earth." Gissing presented slum life as a trap from which there was no escape. The true state of the poor was not virtue but hopelessness. Gissing was proprietary about his suffering. When told of a rising young star in literature, he would listen and ask: "But has he starved?"[53]

Another writer who wrote about slum life from the inside was Arthur Morrison, the son of an engine fitter, who was brought up in Kent and obtained his East End experience as a fieldworker for the Charity Commission. With *Tales of Mean Streets* Morrison established the tone of slum fiction in the nineties. The book appeared in 1894 and would not have been published without the support of W. E. Henley, the editor of the *National Observer*. Critical attention focused on one story, "Lizerunt," which told about the early marriage and motherhood of a factory girl. Her brutal husband throws her out of the house to earn money as a streetwalker. Morrison was one of the first writers to attempt to phonetically reproduce Cockney speech—with its dropped aitches, uneven flow, and glottal stop—eighteen years before Shaw did it in *Pygmalion*.[54] A copy of *Tales of Mean Streets* was found in the library of H.M.S. *Ophir*, the yacht in which the future King George V sailed round the world. On the flyleaf was written: "This is very powerful. George."[55]

After the publication of *Tales of Mean Streets* a reform-minded clergyman, Rev. A. Osborne Jay, invited Morrison to visit his parish of Shoreditch, on the edge of a slum called The Old Nichol. From this experience Morrison derived the material for another book, *A Child of the Jago*, which came out in 1896, the year that Maugham was writing *Liza*. The Jago was Morrison's name for The Old Nichol, an area that bred thieves and muggers armed with coshes, foot lengths of iron rod with a knob at one end and a ring at the other. Dicky Perrott is a boy growing up in the Jago. His mother is dying. A doctor is summoned. The doctor is asked if all is well. "People would call it so," he says. "The boy's alive and so is his mother. But you and I may say the truth. You know the Jago far better than I. Is there a child in all this place that wouldn't be better off dead—still better unborn? . . . Here lies the Jago, a nest of rats, breeding, breeding, as only rats can; and we say it is well . . ." Morrison wrote out of moral indignation and his book is an emotional broadside. Dicky's father is in jail, and with his mother's illness the situation is hopeless. In the end Dicky is stabbed in a street brawl and dies. As a social pamphlet *A Child of the Jago* was a success, for the notoriety surrounding its publication led to the demolition of The Old Nichol; a housing project went up in its place.[56]

It was this school of "new realism" that Maugham chose to join. Since Garnett's report on "A Bad Example" was dated July 20, 1896, Maugham must have received the rejection of his stories, with the encouragement to try something longer, shortly after that. He began to work on *Liza of Lambeth* in the summer of 1896. He had already taken copious notes on his weeks in Lambeth, on the way people lived and how they spoke. What he wrote amounted to a verbatim report, a piece of reportage presented as a novel. The book was written in longhand on three schoolboys' notebooks, purchased at the Papèterie F. Brocchi, *spécialité pour cours*, 30 Faubourg Saint Honoré, a few doors down from the Maugham legal office, which had been taken over by his brother Charles. The manuscript, owned today by the King's School, has this note added in Maugham's hand: "The last few pages of this ms. written on loose sheets have vanished in the course of the years. So to complete it I have rewritten them. 15 July 1931. P.S.—This novel, my first, was written in 1895 at 11 Vincent Square." But Maugham is often vague about dates, and it seems more likely that he wrote the novel after he had received the rejection from Fisher Unwin—that is, in 1896.

He was heavily in debt to the more experienced slum writers, Gissing and Morrison. Like Gissing's *The Nether World*, *Liza of Lambeth* showed a funeral among the poor and a fight between two women and devoted a chapter to the amusements of the slum dwellers. Like Morrison's "Lizerunt," his novel described the courting days of a girl in the slums and reproduced Cockney speech patterns. Maugham changed the setting from East London to Lambeth but relied on Morrison for his philosophy of working-class life: infant mortality was the only form of population control and important issues were decided by violence.

Maugham went a bit further than his predecessors in that he introduced the theme of working-class adultery. Liza Kemp is a high-spirited eighteen-year-old girl who lives with her mother in Vere Street, Lambeth. The mother has had thirteen children and explains: "We come from a very prodigal family, we do, we've all gone in ter double figures, except your Aunt Mary, who only 'as three—but then she wasn't married, so it didn't count, like." Liza has an affair with a married man on the block, Jim Blakeston, whose wife is expecting her tenth child. Maugham shows that Liza's behavior makes her an outcast on Vere Street. She is a threat to the married women and a subject of bawdy jokes by the men. She has lost respectability, just as she would have in a middle-class setting. Blakeston's wife confronts Liza in the street and they go at it like prizefighters. By this time Liza is pregnant, and she miscarries as a result of the brawl. The final episode shows Liza dying from puerperal septicemia brought on by the miscarriage, the midwife wiping her feverish forehead with one hand while drinking from a tumbler of gin in the other, and Liza's mother, at the foot of the bed, providing a running commentary on her own twelve confinements. The scene is undeniably powerful.

On the whole, however, *Liza of Lambeth* is a well observed but rather thin slice of life in which Maugham showed a talent for the exact reproduction of what he saw and heard. "I was forced to stick to the truth," he wrote, "by the miserable poverty of my imagination."[57] In this portrait of the Cockney slum, which the Luftwaffe and the welfare state would eventually combine to erase, people say "mikes" instead of "makes," "blime" instead of "blame," and "'oo" instead of "whom." They are given to picturesque expressions, such as "Ain't she got up dossy," "swop me bob," "you ain't shirty," and "barmy on the crumpet." Very little is imagined. Maugham did not write out of indignation, like Gissing and Morrison; he wrote like the intern he was, examining protozoa under a microscope. He was also under the influence of Guy de Maupassant, whom he had begun to read at the age of fifteen, when he browsed over a copy of his stories in one of the bookstores under the arcade of the Odéon theater, near the Luxembourg Gardens. "Though I was not aware of it at the time," he wrote, "I know now that when I came to write *Liza of Lambeth* I wrote it as I thought Maupassant would have written it."[58]

On January 14, 1897, less than six months after he had begun and eleven days before his twenty-third birthday, Maugham submitted his manuscript to Thomas Fisher Unwin, a tall, bearded, nervous man with a reputation for being innovative. The son of a printer, Unwin had founded his own firm and published early work by Conrad, Galsworthy, Yeats, and Ford Madox Ford. He was an idealist in social reform, stingy in money matters, and a tyrant in the office. His spirit of economy expressed itself in the leading of type and the width of margins, and he drove hard bargains with his authors, the best of whom left him. Slow to reach a decision and jealous of his coworkers, he had a knack for antagonizing people. "As an employer," wrote his nephew Stanley Unwin, "he was as jumpy as a cat on hot bricks and wandered about the office tapping every desk or obstacle he passed with a long pencil, and singing 'yes' in a deep voice and repeating it immediately an octave higher. This would continue until he finally came to a halt at someone's desk, when with a quick movement he would lean over the unfortunate individual and mutter quickly, 'Anything for me?' "[59] He was known to his employees as "Fishy Onions."

Unwin had been successful with series such as the Independent Novel Series, the Mermaid Series, and the Story of the Nation Series. In the nineties he made a stir with a series of inexpensive paperbound novels, the Pseudonym Library, which were published under pen names. Part of the fun was guessing who the author was. It was for this series that *Liza of Lambeth* was at first intended, and Maugham signed the book "William Somerset."

He accompanied the manuscript with a letter and a summary. "In the early part of last year," the letter said, "I sent you two little stories, and you in returning them for their excessive shortness suggested that I send you something longer. Herewith I send you a novel which you may think suitable for publication. It has nearly forty-two thousand words, so I imagine it would not be too short. I do not know whether it has 'the greater literary interest' which you mention in your letter."[60]

Maugham's original title was "A Lambeth Idyll." His summary was as follows: "This is the story of a nine-day wonder in a Lambeth slum. It shows that those queer folk the poor live and love and die in very much the same way as their neighbors of Brixton and Belgravia, and that hatred, malice, and all uncharitableness are not the peculiar attributes of the glorious British Middle Class, and finally it shows that in this world nothing much matters, and that in Vere Street, Lambeth, nothing matters at all."[61]

Fisher Unwin first showed the manuscript to one of his regular readers, Vaughan Nash, who took a violent dislike to it. "The author shows considerable acquaintance with the speech and the customs of a certain class of the London poor," he wrote in a report dated January 21, "and if he knew how to use his materials his work might possess a certain value. But this story shows no trace of any such power. . . . Its details, some of which are revolting, and, I should suppose, unsuitable for publication, are strung together loosely, and there is no touch of romance . . . the author's capacity for vulgarity on his own account is considerable."[62]

Unwin decided to get second and third opinions from other readers, the aforementioned Edward Garnett, and W. H. Chesson. They rescued the book. Garnett's report, dated January 25, called it "a very clever realistic study of factory girls and cosher life. . . . The study is a dismal one in its ending, but the temper and tone of the book is wholesome and by no means morbid." It was not so forceful a work as *The Jago*, Garnett said, but it would appeal "to the Arthur Morrison public. . . . If Fisher Unwin does not publish A Lambeth Idyll somebody else certainly will. . . . We should say Publish—but . . . Mr. Maugham has insight and humour and will probably be heard of again."[63] Later, when he got to know Maugham, Garnett said that he had a mind like a pair of scissors.[64] W. H. Chesson was even more enthusiastic:

> This is interesting, impressive, and truthful [he wrote on February 2]. . . . Mr Maugham's quality is clearness, and a sense of proportion. . . . Time was when a story of working-class adultery such as this would have been voted impossible, but the way has now been paved . . . Both from the moral and artistic point of view we should advise the publication of this story. . . . If people don't like to read of a love that takes the form of "a swinging blow in the belly" they don't and if they won't read of it, they won't. Yet one feels that Mr. Maugham knows his people.[65]

The contract was signed in April 1897 between W. Somerset Maugham of St. Thomas's Hospital and Thomas Fisher Unwin of 11 Paternoster Buildings. These may have been "good old days" for publishers, but not for writers. Maugham got no advance, and no royalty on the first 750 copies. Thereafter he got a royalty of 10 percent up to 2,000; 12½ percent up to 4,000; 15 percent up to 6,000; and 20 percent after that. The price of the book was three shillings sixpence. Maugham would get six presentation copies, and Fisher Unwin had an option on his next two books. *Liza* would be published in September, in a first edition of 2,000 copies, and not in the Pseudonym Library. Maugham could use his full name.[66] "My publisher warned me that the book might be violently attacked," he said in *A Writer's Notebook*, "and I did not wish to hide myself under a made-up name."

This was not an unusual first-novel contract for the times. Advances were small and royalties were deferred until production costs were recovered. Two years earlier Unwin had paid Joseph Conrad a twenty-pound advance for *Almayer's Folly*, which he had signed with the pseudonym "Kamundi," the Malayan word for rudder. "Slave traffic, on my word of honor," Conrad remarked. Maugham also felt that he had been taken advantage of because he was an unpublished writer, and complained bitterly about Unwin's closefistedness. He later wrote his agent that with *Liza of Lambeth* Unwin "did me thoroughly in the eye."[67]

Unwin, however, was promoting *Liza*, and tried to sell the American rights to Charles Scribner, who came to England on his annual buying trip in July. (The Copyright Act of 1886 had made it possible for English authors to earn royalties on their American editions.) On July 14 Scribner wrote one of his editors, L. W. Bangs: "Unwin is indeed a most troublesome person and I am glad I escaped him in London until the last day. Of the projects submitted to us by him, I myself declined the slum story . . . it has some merit though its character was not one to tempt me to publish."[68] There would be no American edition of *Liza of Lambeth* until 1921.

In late August, Maugham experienced the thrill of his life when the six presentation copies arrived and he handled the first copy of his first book. It gave him a feeling of exultation to see the neat little books in their pale-green bindings, with his name stretching across the jacket. He inscribed and sent them to his nearest and dearest. One copy went to Wentworth Huyshe, to whom he wrote that Unwin was placing the book in the hands of reviewers and editors.[69] Another copy went to Walter Payne, to whom *Liza* was dedicated. A third copy in all likelihood went to his sister-in-law Helen Mary Maugham, to whom he sent all his books. His brother Frederic Herbert, having graduated from Cambridge and become a lawyer, had married the sister of his lifelong friend, Mark Romer. Maugham liked her, for she was affectionate and demonstrative, the opposite of his frosty brother. But she was not prepared for *Liza* and wrote in her diary: "Willie's book came out, *Liza of Lambeth*, a most unpleasant book." In later years Helen Mary

Maugham's daughter, Kate Mary Bruce, who had become Maugham's favorite niece, reminded her uncle that her mother had disapproved of *Liza*. Maugham replied on February 23, 1956: "Your mother shared her opinion of *Liza of Lambeth* with many other people. My brother Charles advised Mrs. Chempole, an old friend of the family's, not to read it. Why claim that your mother was not Victorian? Of course she was. She was brought up in a rigorously Victorian fashion. Didn't you know how she refused to meet an old friend because she was your uncle Frank's mistress?"[70]

A fourth presentation copy was sent to his uncle Henry, the vicar of Whitstable, on September 2, inscribed: "To the Vicar and Aunt Ellen, with the author's love." On September 18 the vicar died, and his opinion of the book, if he read it, was unrecorded. He was sixty-nine and had been in poor health for some time. Maugham and his brother Henry, the author of blank-verse plays, attended the funeral on September 21.[71]

Unwin did a good job of promotion, and thanks to the press attention it received, the first edition of *Liza of Lambeth* was sold out in a matter of weeks. Reviewers were shocked but recognized the author's talent. The *Daily Mail* wrote on September 7: "The whole book reeks of the pot-house and is uncompromisingly depressing; but it is powerfully and even cleverly written and must be recognized as a true and vivid picture of the life which it depicts." The *Spectator* on November 13, 1897, wrote that "the squalor of this little book is often positively nauseating." *The Athenaeum* wrote on September 11: "Readers who prefer not to be brought into contact with some of the ugliest words and phrases in the language should be warned that Mr. Maugham's book is not for them. On the other hand, those who wish to read of life as it is, without exaggeration and without modification, will have little difficulty in recognizing the merits of the volume."[72]

There was worse to come, when *The Academy*, in its Fiction Supplement on September 11, accused Maugham of plagiarism:

> The successes of one season may be known by the imitations of the next, and Mr. Arthur Morrison may afford to smile at the sincere flatteries of *Liza of Lambeth*. The mimicry, indeed, is deliberate and unashamed. The brutal fight between two women, the talk of plumes around a deathbed, are faithfully reproduced. Unfortunately the qualities which touch Mr. Morrison's work with something akin to genius are precisely the qualities which are here omitted; the directness, the

restraint, the dominance of artistic purpose. What should have been a tragedy becomes a sordid story of vulgar seduction. . . . I quit him [Maugham] with a grimy feeling, as if I had a mud-bath in all the filth of a London street.

In later years Maugham would make it a rule to ignore unfriendly reviews. To defend his first-born, however, he exercised his right of reply and wrote *The Academy* on September 13: "It is perhaps a little annoying to be charged with plagiarism, when my book was finished three months before *The Child of the Jago* appeared" (in October 1896). He was being disingenuous, for he had borrowed most obviously from the story "Lizerunt" in *Tales of Mean Streets,* published three years before *Liza.* If, as he claimed, he finished *Liza* in July 1896 (three months before the appearance of Morrison's book), why did he, eager as he was to be published, wait until January 1897 to send it to Unwin? Maugham went on to say that he had not read Morrison's books, whereas he later admitted that they had inspired him to write *Liza.* At the same time, when it served his purpose, he perpetuated the myth that *Liza of Lambeth* was "the first of the realistic descriptions of the London slums that the English public had had a chance of reading."[73]

In his letter to *The Academy* Maugham presented himself as a defender of the downtrodden, who had written *Liza* so that "it might induce the Philistine to look a little less self-righteously at the poor, and even to pity their unhappiness." He expressed the hope that the offending reviewer, the next time he passed through slums and saw a tear-stained woman with a black eye, would, thanks to having read his book, "not look upon her entirely with contempt." This too was self-serving, for his interest in the poor abated after he had finished capitalizing on them.

He did his best to squirm out of an unpleasant situation, for to be accused of plagiarism with one's first book was tantamount to giving birth to a deformed child. Maugham was filled with uncertainty about his worth as a writer, his position in society, and his sexuality. The foundation that he would build on over the years was his literary reputation, which was undermined at the very start.

Voices rose in defense of *Liza.* Basil Orme Wilberforce, who became Archdeacon of Westminster Abbey, made the book the subject of one of his Sunday sermons.[74] Edmund Gosse, the essential turn-of-the-century man of letters, praised it. This was surprising, for Gosse was not receptive to writing that departed from Victorian canons of taste and would later refer to James Joyce's *Ulysses* as one of "the nasty fads of the hour."[75] In ensuing years, each time they met, Gosse would say: "Oh, my dear Maugham, I liked your *Liza of Lambeth* so much. How wise you are never to have written anything else."[76]

In June 1898 a review appeared in the *St. Thomas's Hospital Gazette* that said:

> Within the last year several works have emanated from St. Thomas', among which we may mention Dr. Brodie's *Experimental Physiology*, with its beautiful tracings, and Mr. Anderson's *Deformities of Fingers and Toes*. A work of a very different character to all the above by Mr. Maugham—*Eliza of Lambeth* [sic], has achieved a great and well-deserved success. It deals with one aspect of Lambeth life in a powerful and perhaps lurid way: the uncompromising vigor of both plot and style will appeal strongly to all lovers of realism.

By the time this review appeared Maugham had said goodbye to medicine. He passed his exams in October 1897 and was awarded his diplomas as a licensed physician and surgeon.[77] The senior obstetric physician at St. Thomas's offered him a minor appointment, which he turned down. In later years one of the eminent surgeons with whom he had worked as a dresser was asked if he remembered him. "I remember him quite well," the surgeon said. "Very sad. Very sad. One of our failures, I'm afraid."[78]

It should be said to Maugham's credit that he had spent a fruitful five years. He completed his medical training and passed all his exams, an arduous enough achievement. At the same time he laid the foundation for his career as a writer by finishing two short stories and two novels, one of which was published just before he qualified, the other just after. He traveled to Italy and got to know something of its manifold pleasures, grave and gay. To have done all this while still a very young man was not far short of amazing.

Equally amazing was his decision to write fiction with no outside means of support. True, Maugham had his 150 pounds a year, but that was not enough to live on. To be a writer of fiction at the end of the nineteenth century was to stare oblivion in the face. It was customary for novelists to do other work. Trollope worked for the post office all his life as an inspector of rural mail delivery. Among Maugham's contemporaries, Arnold Bennett worked as a clerk in a lawyer's office and as the editor of a magazine called *Woman*. H. G. Wells was a teacher and journalist, whose first published work was a biology textbook. Edmund Gosse was librarian of the House of Lords. Hugh Walpole started out as a teacher at the public school of Epsom. Once out of medical school, Maugham did nothing but write. He was never a teacher or a journalist. He did not supplement his income with book reviews. He did not take odd jobs, although a cigar firm in Havana once asked him to write five short stories, each two hundred words in length, using cigar smoke as a theme. "All my lady friends tell me that virginity is a pearl beyond price," he replied, "so I am sure you will appreciate that even for me the price must be high." He asked for an exorbitant sum and heard no more about it.[79]

The success of *Liza of Lambeth*, the fact that the first edition was sold out and that it was talked about, fueled his ambition. "I was determined," he wrote, "to stamp myself upon the age." He announced to Unwin his intention of becoming a full-time writer. "It's very hard to earn a living by writing," Unwin warned. "Writing is a very good staff, but a very bad crutch."[80] With the kind of advances Unwin was paying, that is not surprising. The situation, however, was general throughout English publishing. Walter Besant, a widely read novelist and a one-man Authors' Guild of his day, who devoted himself to the improvement of the copyright laws, wrote in an 1892 essay, "Literature as a Career," that there were perhaps fifty novelists in Britain who earned one thousand pounds a year. Maugham was not one of them. And yet "literature as a career" was what he had embarked upon. As Cyril Connolly once said: "Whom the gods wish to destroy they first call promising." Maugham would have ten lean years before success beckoned again.

PART II

1897-1907

Chapter Four

There are few authors who earn their living by their pen, who are not obliged now and then to write things they wish later they had not written, and I am unfortunately not of those few . . . I have written one or two books because I was too inexperienced to write them better, but they are forgotten, and I can forget them too. It seems to me that every writer can claim to be judged by his best work, and even of his best work there is, Heaven knows, much that the world can spare.

Maugham, in a letter to the French critic Paul Dottin

WRITING WAS the only profession Maugham ever practiced. He was concerned with its every aspect, including business details: he studied the small print in his contracts, was notoriously attentive to money matters, and agreed to the textual changes his publishers required for reasons of good taste. In the manuscript of *Liza of Lambeth* the word "belly" was found to be offensive by Fisher Unwin. Maugham, without a murmur, agreed to its deletion in proof.[1] In a dedicated copy of the novel to one Robert Partridge he wrote: "On page 124 I have restored the word which was changed from the MS on the urgent request of the prudish publisher.—W. Somerset Maugham." On that page he had crossed out the word "stomach" and written "belly" in the margin.[2] James Joyce, by comparison, fought for years against the deletion of the word "bloody" in "Grace," one of the stories in *Dubliners*. Grant Richards wrote him in 1906 that it would have to be changed, for the printer refused to set the book in type. Joyce wrote back from Trieste on May 5: "I cannot alter what I have written. . . . I can plainly see that there are two sides to the matter but unfortunately I can occupy only one of them."[3] As a result *Dubliners* was not published until 1914. Perhaps one of the things that separates genius from talent is this kind of unshakable obstinacy.

In his pursuit of professionalism Maugham was fortunate to have started writing in a period when the relationship between those natural enemies, authors and publishers, underwent a fundamental change, thanks to the emergence of the literary agent. Authors had previously acted on their own behalf, and were not very good at it. They did not like to taint their artistic souls by bargaining and were easily flattered into accepting less advantageous terms. They were notoriously fuzzy about business matters. Publishers had it all their own way. The term "Grub Street" summed up the unequal combat between the all-powerful publisher and the wretched author. But in the 1890s a small number of men pioneered a new profession by placing themselves between author and publisher, with a contract in one hand and an advance in the other.

Publishers were not pleased by the appearance of agents and at first refused to deal with them. William Heinemann, a native of Hanover, who had started a firm in 1890 in two rooms in Covent Garden, and who would eventually publish H. G. Wells, Henry James, Joseph Conrad, and Maugham, wrote in *The Athenaeum* in 1893: "This is the age of the middleman. He is generally a parasite. He always flourishes. I have been forced to give him some little attention lately in my particular business. In it he calls himself the literary agent."[4] Heinemann felt that agents contaminated writers. "Once an author gets into the claws of a typical agent," he wrote a fellow publisher, "he is lost to decency. He generally adopts the moral outlook of a trickster, which the agent inoculates with all rapidity, and that virus is so poisonous that the publisher had better disinfect himself and avoid contagion."[5]

Among the men who made this new profession respectable were two intrepid Scotsmen, Alexander Pollock Watt and James Brand Pinker. Watt, who by 1893 had a modest office at 2 Paternoster Square, approached authors with the following proposition: They had brokers in financial matters, why not have an agent in professional matters, who could apply expertise to the marketing of their product? It was Watt who adopted the 10 percent fee still in use. His success was rapid, and he remained at the top of his profession for a quarter of a century before leaving the business to his three sons. Watt numbered among his clients Arthur Conan Doyle, Rider Haggard, Thomas Hardy, Bret Harte, and Rudyard Kipling. In 1896 he printed a promotional brochure consisting of letters from grateful authors who had been saved from "the many humiliating torments of negotiating with publishers."[6]

Watt moved to more impressive offices in the Strand. A bemedaled sergeant took one's card, inquired with whom one wished an audience, and ushered one silently into the office, where tin boxes labeled "Kipling" and "Hardy" stood on open shelves.

Pinker, who had worked as a magazine editor and publisher's reader, set up offices in Arundel Street, off the Strand, in 1896. He was a short, pink-cheeked man with a pronounced burr whom his authors called "Jy Bee." He was successful because he knew how to make himself indispensable to writers. He mothered them, worried about their work, and on occasion advanced them money. H. G. Wells became one of his first clients. Henry James left Watt to come to him, and on his advice left Heinemann, whom James called "the most swindling of publishers," and went to Methuen. Arnold Bennett followed, and Pinker advanced him fifty pounds a month when he went to Paris to write *The Old Wives' Tale*. Stephen Crane sought him out in London. Ford Madox Ford called him "the most remarkable literary agent on whose lips hung half the young writers of that day."[7] Joseph Conrad said that his books owed their existence "to Mr. Pinker as much as to me. For fifteen years of my writing life he has seen me through periods of unproductiveness, through illness, through all sorts of troubles."[8] Pinker invested heavily in Conrad, keeping this slowest of writers going with advances against future work. He had the agent's greatest strength, a feeling of absolute moral authority. Once, going over a contract that one of his clients had made directly with the publisher, Pinker exclaimed: "But this is swindling!" "Oh," protested the publisher, "that's a very strong word." Pinker stared down the publisher and asked, "What other do you suggest?" "Well," said the publisher, "I admit it was sharp practice." The contract was destroyed.[9]

When he did not admire an author, however, he showed it. D. H. Lawrence, furious because Pinker would not help him as he helped Conrad, called him "that little parvenu snob of a procurer of books."[10] The snob part had to do with Pinker's passion for riding to hounds and driving a four-in-hand.

Pinker and Watt were each at one time Maugham's agents, but his first agent was an Irish barrister named William Morris Colles. Born in 1855, Colles went to Cambridge, was admitted to the bar in 1880, and launched the Authors' Syndicate in 1889, with offices at 4 Portugal Street. He was "a big, burly, bearded lawyer, with a wheezy infectious laugh—a sort of well-spoken, decent-minded, entirely reputable, 19th century Falstaff."[11] He was for many years George Gissing's agent, but he had trouble with his writers, notably Arnold Bennett, who left him in 1902, and Maugham, who left him in 1905.

Colles started representing Maugham in 1897, and their early correspondence illustrates the concerns of a young writer trying to follow up an early success. Maugham complained about the sales of *Liza* and asked Colles to approach Unwin about bringing out a cheap edition, in view of the success of sixpenny books (a sixpenny edition eventually came out in 1904).[12] He complained to Colles about Unwin's stinginess. He said Unwin was so hard up that he had replaced *The Times* in his waiting room with the *Daily News* in order to save threepence a day.[13] He wrote Colles about works in progress and asked him to find magazine commissions. The air of lofty detachment that came with success was not yet in evidence. Maugham was hungry to be published and make enough to live on. He complained bitterly about nonpayment.

Determined to make a career of writing, Maugham prepared an ambitious program of travel, in order to gather the necessary life experience. His plan was to spend a year in Spain and learn Spanish, then go to Rome and learn Italian, then to Greece to learn Greek, and on to Cairo to learn Arabic. It was his intention to become the most polyglot of authors, but as it turned out, he went no farther than Spain, with a side trip to Italy.[14]

Before leaving for Spain toward the end of 1897 he had a surprise for Unwin—a second novel. Unwin had been after him to continue in the same vein with another slum book, but Maugham had lost interest in the slums. He had read some articles by the Scottish man of letters Andrew Lang advising young authors to write historical novels. Lang argued that young men did not have enough life experience to treat the contemporary scene and should apply themselves to the past. Maugham was swayed by this advice. Also, with one eye on what was selling, he may have been influenced by the enormous success of Anthony Hope's *The Prisoner of Zenda*, published in 1894. In any case, he decided to write a historical novel set in Italy at the end of the fifteenth century, based on a story in Machiavelli's *History of Florence*, the Forlì insurrection of 1487. He read works on medieval Italy in the British Museum to get the period right and spent the summer of 1897 in Capri, awakening each morning to write it, like *Liza of Lambeth*, at breakneck speed. It was called *The Making of a Saint*.

On the strength of a favorable report by Edward Garnett, who called it "very strong, fresh and good . . . and continues Maugham's reputation as a clever writer," Fisher Unwin took it, this time at slightly better terms, with Maugham getting a fifty-pound advance on publication.[15] Unwin also managed to sell it to the American publisher L. C. Page, who was on his second visit to London in 1897. "I did not make the deal with Mr. T. Fisher Unwin," Page recalled in a memo, "an elderly man who was little at his office (although I dined with him at his London club). The deal was made with his manager, a fair practical man who was dissatisfied with Unwin. . . . He, the manager, Benn, informed me that the *Saint* was a first novel and was purchased outright by Unwin who yearly ran a First Novel competition." Page went on to say that he had bought the American rights for forty pounds. It was, of course, not a first novel, but it was the first Maugham book to be published in America, in May 1898 (2,000 copies at $1.50). The English edition came out a month later (2,000 copies at 6 shillings).[16] It was not one of Maugham's favorite books. In his nephew Robin's copy he wrote: "A very poor novel by W. Somerset Maugham." When Farrar Straus acquired L. C. Page in 1957 and found that they were in possession of the rights to an out-of-print Maugham novel, he acted to stop its publication. Farrar Straus did not reissue *The Making of a Saint* until 1966, after Maugham's death.

The Making of a Saint purports to be the memoirs of a fifteenth-century Italian soldier of fortune turned monk. In the introduction, supposedly written by the monk's descendant, Maugham alludes to the reception of *Liza of Lambeth*: "I have a friend who lately wrote a story of the London poor, and his critics were properly disgusted because his characters dropped their aitches and often used bad language, and did not behave as elegantly as might be expected from the example they were continually receiving from their betters; while some of his readers were shocked to find that people existed in this world who did not possess the delicacy and refinement which they felt palpitating in their own bosoms."[17]

Having got that off his chest, Maugham starts the pot boiling. A group of conspirators, including the narrator, assassinate the ruler of Forlì and try to take over the city, which is rescued by outside forces. The book is full of swordplay and battle and looting and the detailed description of public executions. Maugham takes a positive delight in the bloodletting. A dagger is plunged into one man's neck, and another is stabbed in the back. The conspirators are hanged and their bodies are torn limb from limb. One of them is pulled apart by horses. In the love interest, the theme of bondage makes its appearance in Renaissance costume. The narrator, Filippo Brandolini, falls in love with Giulia dall'Aste, who betrays him. "I despised myself for having loved her," he writes. Like other Maugham heroines, she is immoral and untrustworthy. But even when Brandolini discovers her true nature he cannot leave her.

The book shows Maugham in the grip of an aphoristic style: "I am too proud to struggle for favors, I would rather dispense with them," and "You professional sentimentalists will never let anyone sentimentalize but yourselves." If he had wanted to write a romantic adventure novel in the manner of *The Prisoner of Zenda,* he was prevented by his own nature from doing so. His pessimistic view of the human condition and his connection of love with suffering cast their shadows over the contrived dialogue and the hackneyed plot.

The Making of a Saint attracted less critical attention than *Liza of Lambeth.* In September 1898 the *Bookman* wrote: "Many will be altogether repelled by the book. It is one for the seasoned novel-reader, who is not easily shocked nor very impressionable." Maugham was maintaining his reputation as a rather scandalous young writer whose works should be barred from proper Victorian homes. Indeed, one reviewer argued that his Cockneys and his Renaissance Italians were brothers under the skin. *The Academy* on September 17 said: "We seem to discern in the persons of the play an incredible kinship to the Bills and Dicks who swear the Cockney oaths and brag the easy amours of the Cockney slums."[18] The book did not, like *Liza,* go into a second printing.

When *The Making of a Saint* was published Maugham was in Spain. He had arrived in Seville on the eve of the Immaculate Conception (early December 1897), and did not get back to England until April 1899. After five years of study in a London hospital he was glad to be his own master. He had no ties and no responsibilities. He was excited and moved by what he saw, and his feelings brimmed over with the highly colored sensations of a land that was in many ways in direct contrast to England.

For a young man enjoying his first taste of freedom he was surprisingly productive. He finished four stories, which, with the two previously turned down, would make up a volume called *Orientations.* One of these, "The Punctiliousness of Don Sebastian," was his first published short story. It appeared in the October 1898 issue of *Cosmopolis,* a magazine that followed the peculiar practice of printing its texts one-third in English, one-third in French, and one-third in Spanish. "The idea was that it would thus find readers in all three countries," Maugham said. "Unfortunately it found readers in none." He was never paid and wrote Morris Colles that the editor, a man named Otmans, was "nothing more than a seedy adventurer."[19] He finished a novel called "The Artistic Temperament of Stephen Carey" and wrote Colles on November 10, 1898, that although "Stephen" was finished, "as it is a little strong I particularly wish to publish something milder first, so that I may not be known as a writer of the George Moore type"[20] (that is, a writer of shocking books like Liza of Lambeth). He finished his first full-length play, A Man of Honour. He worked on a book on Spain to be called The Land of the Blessed Virgin.

In later years Maugham liked to give the impression that his work had never been turned down. "I have never had to suffer," he wrote, "the heartbreak that many authors have to endure of sending a manuscript to publisher after publisher and having it returned time and time again with a curt note of rejection." And yet this is precisely what he endured with The Land of the Blessed Virgin, which was finished in June 1899. He was hoping to get it serialized, with sketches by a Spanish illustrator.[21] But no publisher would touch it. In 1902 he rewrote it completely. It languished for six years before Heinemann brought it out in 1905. The same was true of A Man of Honour, which Maugham sent to Johnstone Forbes-Robertson, a popular actor of the time with the reputation of having artistic inclinations. When he turned it down, Maugham sent it to the impresario Charles Frohman, who also rejected it. The truth is that this most popular of writers had ten hard years, between the publication of Liza of Lambeth in 1897 and the production of Lady Frederick, his first successful play, in 1907. During that time he published seven novels, one volume of short stories, and one travel book, but they all fell like seeds on stony ground.

"The Englishman," Maugham wrote in The Land of the Blessed Virgin, "ever somewhat sententiously inclined, asks what a place can teach him. The churchwarden in his bosom gives no constant enduring peace; and after all, though he may be often ridiculous, it is the churchwarden who has made a good part of England's greatness." There was something of the churchwarden in Maugham. He was an assiduous sightseer, he smoked Filipino cigars, strummed the guitar, and bought a broad-brimmed hat with a flat crown. He lived at calle Guzman el

Bueno, No. 2, in the district of Santa Cruz, the most elegant in Seville, as the guest of the British vice-consul, E. F. Johnson, to whose wife he dedicated his book of short stories *Orientations*.

In the evening he strolled in the calle de las Sierpes, Seville's meeting place. It was crowded with cigarette girls, newspaper boys, and lottery ticket sellers, each offering the grand prize:—*¿Quién quiere el premio gordo?*[22] He stopped for a glass of *manzanilla* in one of those taverns with wine barrels stacked against the wall and bunches of Spanish onions, strings of sausages, and Granada hams hung from the ceiling. Coming home after midnight, he clapped for the *guardia*, a bibulous round man with gray hair, who fumbled with his keys and said:— *Buenas noches, descanse usted bien*. He visited the cathedral, the hospital, and the jail, where the fat, red-faced prison doctor served as his guide. The prison was a former convent and the convicts stood in the patio where nuns had once strolled on summer evenings. The doctor was told that one of the women prisoners had given birth, and Maugham noted the conversation that ensued.

"What a nuisance these women are," the doctor said. "Why can't they wait till they get out of prison? How is it?" he asked.

"It was stillborn."

"*Pero, hombre*, why didn't you tell me that before? Now I shall have to write another certificate. This one's no good."

Maugham attended a bullfight. The great matadors were Mazzantini and Guerrita. They strolled in the Sierpes on the day before the fight. Everyone went down to the Tablada, an open space on the riverbank outside town, to see the bulls, who had been brought from their respective farms. He watched the *encierro*, when the bulls were driven in the dark by oxen to the ring and shut in their boxes. In the morning he went to the Plaza San Fernando to buy a ticket. In the afternoon the fight began. He observed that bullfighting was the only punctual thing in Spain. "It is doubtless vicious and degrading," he wrote, "but with the constant danger, the skill displayed, the courage, the hair-breadth escapes, the catastrophes, it is foolish to deny that any pastime can be more exciting."[23]

Maugham liked the Spanish. He liked their courtesy and their pride, the muted passion that lay beneath the surface of most relationships, and their code of honor, more demanding than that of an English gentleman. He had a fling with "a young thing with green eyes and a gay smile." He "made light love to pretty little creatures whose demands on me were no more than my exiguous means could satisfy."[24] One of the objects of his affection was called Rosarito, of whom he says: "It was not love for you I felt, Rosarito; I wish it had been . . . but perhaps I am just faintly enamored of your recollection."[25] In his later book on Spain, however, published in 1935, Maugham recalls his first stay in Seville and says: "I fell very pleasantly in love while I was in Seville. . . . Even then, not slow to see my own absurdity, I was conscious that I had been made a very pretty fool of."[26]

He went to Ronda and admired the churches and saw Córdoba from the bell tower of its cathedral. The canons walking in the Court of Oranges seemed models of serenity, but three months later he read that one had shot himself. In his pocket were found a letter, a pawn ticket, a woman's bracelet, and some peppermint lozenges (the right mix for a Maugham short story). An English engineer approached him at the hotel and said: "Down here there are a good sight more beer and skittles in life than up in Sheffield." He struck out on horseback to towns that could not be reached by road, such as Carmona and Ecija. Spain was at war with Cuba, and he talked to women who complained that their sons were away fighting the rebels. He met a skinner who showed him the way and said, "My good sir, you must have come on some errand." "Oh yes," replied Maugham, "on the search for emotion."[27]

Much taken with the *Spiritual Exercises* of Saint Ignatius of Loyola, the founder of the Jesuits, he visited the cave in Manresa where the saint was said to have composed these rules of conduct, of which the full title is: *Spiritual Exercises for overcoming oneself and for regulating one's life without being swayed by any inordinate attachment.* Maugham considered the suppression of feeling a noble aim. Perhaps this was the rule of life he had been searching for. He was interested enough to try one of the meditation exercises himself, but found that he could not concentrate properly.

On his first visit to Granada, too excited to stay indoors after dinner, he went down to the town and found a brothel. He picked out a pale girl with large eyes, but when she stripped he saw that she was still a child.

"You look very young to be in a place like this," he said. "How old are you?"

"Thirteen," the girl said.

"What made you come here?"

"Hambre," the girl said. "Hunger."

Maugham gave her some money, told her to get dressed, climbed back up the hill, and went to bed.[28]

He visited Jerez, with its bottle and cask factories, and drank wine that was more than a century old. From Jerez he went to Cádiz, in March 1899. According to his own account, he sailed from Cádiz to Tangier. This trip may have taken place only in his imagination, however, for in 1906 he wrote his friend Violet Hunt during a trip to Egypt that it was the first time he had found himself in a country where he did not understand the language. This would not have been true if he had gone to Tangier in 1899. In any case, he says that he rose at five to catch his boat. A gray mist hung over the city. Fishing boats rolled on the water and fishermen stood in small groups on the docks blowing on their fingers. Soon he was at sea, and the shores of Spain sank out of sight.[29]

By April 1899 Maugham was back in London, staying with his friend Walter Payne in a flat at Albany Chambers, now demolished, near the St. James's Park underground station. Waiting for him was his first royalty statement for *Liza of Lambeth*. He was shocked to find that it came to only twenty pounds, and wrote Colles that, like a certain Mr. Sala who never tipped more or less than one shilling, he suspected that Unwin invariably made his accounts come to twenty pounds. He went to Unwin's office to discuss the publication of *Orientations*, his collection of short stories, which included the two originally rejected.[30] Edward Garnett, in a report dated January 18, 1899, had said that all the stories were "a little flat, a little heavy . . . we feel that Maugham's reputation will suffer if he publishes the present collection." But Unwin decided to go ahead with this third book by a young author with a growing reputation and brought out an edition of 2,000 copies that June.

In addition to "Daisy" and "A Bad Example" the volume included three stories with Spanish settings and a story called "De Amicitia." These early stories were garnets rather than rubies, and Maugham later repudiated them. But several are interesting because they show him coming to grips with themes to which he would often return. In "The Choice of Amyntas" the son of an English schoolmaster goes to Cádiz, where a young woman relieves him of his virginity and his purse. In spite of this misadventure he decides to stay. Leaving one's family to pursue a quixotic ideal was a favorite Maugham theme—it was what Charles Strickland would do in *The Moon and Sixpence*. In "Faith" a monk is whipped after confessing his loss of faith. The healing of his wounds is seen as miraculous and evidence of renewed faith, whereas the man retains his doubt. The illusion that inspires faith would also be the subject of Maugham's last novel, *Catalina*. *Orientations*, which, he explained, was an attempt to find his literary self, did little to enhance his reputation. In July, *Bookman* called it "an average book, fairly readable, but with no serious interest or promise about it." *The Academy* on July 1 said that it was better than his two previous books, but "the more fantastic tales lack point." When Maugham reread them in 1935 he said they gave him so many cold shivers he thought he was coming down with malaria.

After the publication of the stories Maugham began rewriting "The Artistic Temperament of Stephen Carey." In August he sent Colles a revised version, with a request for an advance of a hundred pounds to see him through the year, but Unwin would not pay it, nor would any other publisher. He was shattered to have a book he had been working on for two years turned down, but later came to see it as a blessing in disguise. For "Stephen Carey" was the gauche and immature first draft of *Of Human Bondage*. "If one of them [publishers] had taken my book . . . I should have lost a subject which I was too young to make proper use of," he wrote. "I was not far enough away from the events I described to use them properly and I had not had a number of experiences which later went to enrich the book I finally wrote."[31]

In this early version, with its title proclaiming that the main character was a sensitive bohemian, Maugham was unable to transform his experience into convincing fiction. The novel, about 90,000 words written in two notebooks, was autobiographical, but its looseness of construction, self-indulgence, and lack of attention to the social background of the characters made it weak and ineffective. As in the later version, Stephen is orphaned when his mother dies, and he goes to live with an uncle, who is not in this case a clergyman but the owner of a large property and the father of a girl four years Stephen's junior. Stephen is sent to the Regis School (a Latinization of King's), where he is cruelly teased. But the point of his unhappiness is missed in the earlier draft, for Stephen does not have a clubfoot. As Kingsley Amis would later note: "*Of Human Bondage* shows how one barrier, in the shape of lameness, loneliness, puritanism or stupidity, will set up others: suspicion, over-exclusive affection, vindictiveness, exhibitionism, obstinacy, intolerance, self-torture—the state of what a later generation has learned to call the injustice collector."[32] In the early version Stephen does not have a disability.

At the age of sixteen Stephen is taken out of school and sent to Rouen to learn French. Maugham was somehow reluctant to rely on his own stay in Heidelberg and chose a setting that he knew only slightly. In Rouen, Stephen meets an American older than himself, Francis House, with whom he has philosophical conversations that lead to his loss of faith. Stephen is a romantic young man who plays Wagner on the piano and is given to Byronic reveries. Returning to England, he becomes an articled clerk and has an affair with his cousin's governess, Miss Wilkinson. Learning that Miss Wilkinson is forty, he says: "What a situation for a young man with an artistic temperament."

Stephen falls under the influence of his coworker Greene, an esthete who is just back from Germany and admires Pater. Greene, obviously based on Ellingham Brooks, initiates Stephen into the bohemian life. Stephen meets Rose Cameron, a waitress in a tea shop, and falls in love with her. When he learns that Rose is pregnant by another man, Stephen, like a character in a Victorian melodrama, confronts the philanderer and beats him up, calling him "you cad" and "you cur." Stephen decides to marry his cousin May, who has become "a Greek goddess," but he sleeps with Rose one last time, leaving her a banknote in lieu of a farewell note. Maugham's theme in *Of Human Bondage*, that we are the slaves of our instincts, is already present in the early work. The book ends with Stephen marrying May, and projecting his future as a landowner, social figure, and member of Parliament.

After its initial rejection Maugham prudently let "The Artistic Temperament of Stephen Carey" sit for fifteen years before attempting to improve on it.

It was through the notoriety that *Liza of Lambeth* had brought him that Maugham met one of the most curious figures of the age, Augustus Hare, "the last Victorian." Hare's life covered the entire Victorian reign (1837–1901), for he was born in 1834 and died in 1903. He lived a life of travel, house parties, and dining out. An admitted snob, he was happy only in the company of the upper classes. He left England periodically for the Continent, where he wrote guidebooks that made him known to generations of travelers in Europe. *Walks in Rome* and *Wanderings in Spain* were classics of meticulous observation and went into many editions. He also worked on his autobiography, which he said he was writing for a private, inner circle.[33] In the friendship between Hare and Maugham there was something of the old order passing the torch to the new. Maugham was a young man who would make his mark in the twentieth century. Hare was a man in his late sixties clinging to the values of the nineteenth century.

Hare admired *Liza of Lambeth* and met its author through Rev. Basil Wilberforce, the clergyman who had given a sermon about the book. He advised Maugham that "the only people worth writing about are the lower classes." Maugham became a frequent weekend guest at Hare's country house, Holmhurst, where Hare continued to live the Victorian life, impervious to change. At eight o'clock in the morning a maid in a rustling print dress and a cap with streamers came into Maugham's room with a cup of tea and two slices of bread. Another maid, called a tweeny, brought in a sitz bath, a large round tub with a high back. One's legs dangled outside and it was not easy to wash one's feet. The breakfast bell rang at nine. Hare read a prayer and a passage from the Bible and then said "Let us pray," and all the guests fell to their knees around the table and recited the Lord's Prayer. Hare had crossed out all the passages in glorification of God, saying: "God is certainly a gentleman, and no gentleman cares to be praised to his face." Hare did not allow smoking in the house. He kept a cottage on the grounds for gentlewomen of reduced means (a form of philanthropy among the Victorian landed gentry). At dinner the maids wore black uniforms with white caps and aprons. At ten the guests retired with candles.[34]

Hare complained that conversation was not what it had been and that dinners were no longer worth recording. The old men with beautiful manners were gone, and so were the great ladies, like the Duchess of Cleveland, "the last woman who ever smacked her footman's face in Bond Street." Few young men knew how to behave in polite society and there was no one left to teach them. Hare did his best to teach Maugham. He chided him for saying "bus" instead of "omnibus." After one weekend Maugham received this note from Hare: "My dear Willie, yesterday when we came in from our walk you said you were thirsty and asked for a drink. I have never heard you vulgar before. A gentleman does not ask for a drink, he asks for something to drink."[35]

On December 8, 1902, shortly before his death, Hare was dining at the Wilberforces', and Maugham's new novel, *Mrs. Craddock*, came up in the conversation. "Both the Archdeacon and I much regretted the author's Zola-like realism and that his great talent was not devoted to nobler aims," Hare wrote in his diary. " 'What old maids you both are,' said a lady present, and I believe that would be the prevailing feeling now. How society has changed!"[36]

Indeed it had. The century was ending, and as if on cue, Queen Victoria would survive it by less than a month. In 1899 the Boer War made the British question their assumptions about imperial destiny. When the Transvaal and the Orange Free State declared war on England, their early victories put an end to boastful imperialism. The siege of the British forces at Ladysmith was known in London as the "black week." The mightiest army in the world could not defeat a bunch of Dutch farmers. Eventually the British reversed the situation and made peace with the Boers in 1902, but the war proved that they were fallible.

Maugham saw the Boer War as the start of the collapse of the British Empire. He made it and its effects on English life the subject of his novel *The Hero*. The Boer War, he felt, was a discreditable little affair upon which future historians would look as one of the most important events in the history of England. To Maugham's mind it broke the nerve of the English and the power of the aristocracy and the landed gentry.[37]

On December 31, 1900, the last day of the century, the nation stayed up until midnight, when fires were lit on every hilltop in England, from the South Downs to the Scottish border, and in every belfry bell ringers pulled on their ropes. In Westminster Abbey a future bishop of Oxford, Charles Gore, declared: "Our present-day literature is singularly without inspiration. There is no Carlyle to whom all men naturally turn to find some answer to their chaotic yearnings; there is no Tennyson . . . there is no prophet of the people."[38]

On January 19, 1901, Queen Victoria died, after a reign of more than sixty-three years. The coincidence of the end of the century with the death of the queen seemed like a foreboding. Lady St. Helier, a prominent Victorian hostess, wrote: "Nothing ever impressed me more than the day—a fortnight before the Queen died—when no 'Court Circular' appeared in the morning papers. All through the Queen's long reign a daily notice of her movements had been published, and when I opened the Times on that particular morning, I felt that a great misfortune was impending."[39]

The day came when the queen's body was taken from Osborne to Windsor in great solemnity. In the winter sunset of a January evening her people watched Victoria's last journey, escorted by her fleet from Cowes to Portsmouth. The last two decades of her reign had been a time of peace, prosperity, moral rigor, and social certainty. The first two decades of the new century would see the greatest catastrophe of modern times, the rearrangement of Europe, and the rise of new ideologies.

The death of Queen Victoria, H. G. Wells remarked, removed a great paperweight that had sat on men's minds for half a century. England in 1900 was still in many respects the England of Augustus Hare. There were more than a million men and women in domestic service. The Duke and Duchess of Portland had 15 stable hands, 100 gardeners and a roadman, a head laundress with 12 assistants, and 3 full-time window cleaners. Persons of noble birth were supposed to be without ambition. The Duke of Devonshire said that the happiest moment of his life was when his pig took first prize at the agricultural show. The three-month London season was immutable. The daughters of the well-born were presented at court; unmarried ladies wore two white ostrich feathers in their hair, and married ladies three. After Christmas there were house parties in the country, where the men went shooting and the ladies visited points of interest.

The Edwardian era, from 1901 to the death of King Edward VII in 1910, was a hinge between two centuries, a brief intermission between the age of reason and the age of anxiety. Standards of propriety were still observed, not because they were believed in, as they had been under Victoria, but because a façade had to be kept up. Victoria had lived her moral righteousness. King Edward was a model for the double standard. He scolded his grandson for wearing the uniform of one regiment of Foot Guards with the spurs of another, then went to Paris to patronize its brothels. The Victorian motto was: Is it right? The Edwardian motto was: *Cache ton jeu.* Appearances had to be kept up. King Edward's affairs were numerous, but his standards of public morality remained severe. The Duke and Duchess of Marlborough were excluded from royal functions because they were separating.

But a reaction against hypocritical propriety was also a part of the Edwardian era. Arnold Bennett in 1906 wrote the first novel entirely about divorce, *Whom God Hath Joined.* Havelock Ellis, that tireless discusser of sex, was as much a part of the period as King Edward. The ego was freeing itself from social restraint, and in literature it was the start of modernism. The young writers were James Joyce and D. H. Lawrence, who explained modernism as a situation "wherein each separate little ego is an independent little principality by itself." This would have been unthinkable under Victoria, when energies were pooled in the service of the state. So would the modernist idea, expressed in Ibsen's plays, that it might be morally right to behave in a way that society condemned, because self-fulfillment was more important than duty.

In the Edwardian era there were identifiable vanguards and rear guards. In 1904 the National Gallery refused the gift of a Degas painting. But in 1905 the Paris art dealer Durand-Ruel brought a large collection of Impressionists to London. Joyce wrote *Dubliners*, but its publication was held up for years because of the indignation of Edwardian printers. The Edwardian decade pretended to be a continuation of the Victorian era but in fact was a break from it.[40]

Knowing the rules was the key to social life. "It doesn't matter what you do, so long as you don't frighten the horses," King Edward was quoted as saying. Knowing the rules extended from the proper period of mourning for one's mother-in-law to the country weekend where lovers and mistresses were thoughtfully assigned adjoining rooms. A woman had to know how to enter a room, how to faint, and how to hold her partner in the quadrille. A man had to know how to use a pocket handkerchief, how to remove his cigar when passing a lady, and where to have his suits made and his hair cut. Compton Mackenzie's tailor, Forster, made him an overcoat that he still had thirty years later. When he took it to be let out, the cutter said, "We shall never see cloth like that again, sir." At Burgess', a barbershop going back to the Regency, the brushes had bristles that had come from a Siberian hog, and one was shaved in a Regency chair with one's feet on a Regency stool.[41] Woe to the man who ignored propriety. "How could I ever love that man?" a woman asked. "Why, he takes his salt with a knife." Smartness was crucial—in dress, in manner, in conversation, in all the details of daily life, from where one got one's tobacco to whom one had tea with.

Maugham was Edwardian in the deepest sense. This was the period of history that put its stamp on him. Throughout his life he maintained an Edwardian set of assumptions. He was a façade person. Propriety was all-important. He went to the right tailor, belonged to a club, and was scrupulously courteous. In his writing he often used such Edwardian expressions as "sexual congress" and "unmitigated scoundrel." In one of his best known stories, "The Letter," he used the Edwardian convention of the compromising document.

His belief in a society governed by principles of decorum comes out in stories such as "The Treasure," where a bachelor, a perfect gentleman who has a perfect servant, sleeps with her in a moment of weakness. They then revert to their previous relationship. "He knew that never by word or gesture would she ever refer to the fact that for a moment their relations had been other than master and servant." This was the Edwardian sensibility in full flower.

In the first years of the Edwardian era, from 1901 until 1905, when he went to live in Paris, Maugham was a young man-about-town. He was presentable and well mannered, and the publication of *Liza of Lambeth* a few years earlier had brought him to the attention of London hostesses. Augustus Hare introduced him to titled ladies, and he was invited to luncheons and dinner parties and dances and weekends in country houses. He was so poor that he traveled by bus in white tie and tails. When he went away on weekends he was aware that his worn pajamas and modest toilet articles made an unfavorable impression on the footman who unpacked his Gladstone bag. An added trial was the tips he had to hand out to footmen and butlers.[42]

Through Augustus Hare he met Lady St. Helier, the model of the late-Victorian hostess. The former Mary Mackenzie of Scotland, briefly married to Colonel Stanley of the Coldstream Guards, she had taken as her second husband Francis Jeune, who became the first Baron St. Helier. She decided to experiment with mixing people, and invited together cabinet ministers and sportsmen, poets and politicians. The lions who gained admittance to her drawing room purred contentedly in her presence. Alfred Lord Tennyson had liked to sit by her fireside while she sang his favorite Scotch airs. Her dinners combined relics with monuments in the making, and everyone who was anyone went to her house in Portland Place. The story was told about an explorer who was caught in darkest Africa by a tribe of cannibals. They had him in the pot when the cannibal king arrived. No sooner did he lay eyes on his captive than the gourmet gave way to the man of the world. "Surely we met at Lady St. Helier's," he said. "I owe you an apology for the inconvenience. How is her ladyship?"[43]

At a dinner for twenty-four at Lady St. Helier's to which Maugham was invited the men were in tails and the women in satins and velvets, richly jeweled. The guests assembled in the drawing room and the men were told which ladies they were to take down to dinner. The table blazed with cut glass, old silver, and flowers out of season. The men ate prodigious amounts and later on went to German spas to lose weight. At the dinner Maugham met a man who went to Carlsbad every year with before-and-after sets of clothes. After dinner the ladies went up to the drawing room, leaving the men with coffee and liqueurs. On one such occasion Maugham found himself sitting next to the Duke of Abercorn, who asked his name, and upon hearing it said, "I hear you're a very clever young man." He took a cigar case from his back pocket. "Do you like cigars?" he asked, displaying some long Havanas. "Very much," Maugham said. "So do I," said the duke, "and when I come to dinner with a widow lady I always bring my own. I advise you to do the same." He chose one, rolled it near his ear, and snapped the case shut.[44]

Maugham was ill at ease in society and dressed carefully as a way of compensating for the feeling that he did not belong. In a frock coat and pepper-and-salt trousers, patent-leather button boots with gray spats, top hat, and a stick, he would pay a thank-you call on his hostess, hoping that she was not home. In that case he left two cards, one for her and one for her husband. He went to dances in tails and white waistcoat, and danced polkas and lancers and waltzes (it was considered bad form to reverse).

He also attended the homes of the literary. The world of letters in London was then centered in Hampstead, Notting Hill Gate, and High Street, Kensington. Maugham, who lived near Victoria Station, took long bus rides to reach these neighborhoods, where he was introduced to celebrated men of letters. The kind words they said about his books made him uncomfortable, for he was shy and felt that he should say clever things, but he could never think of any until the party was over.

One of the literary figures he met was Edmund Gosse, who knew everyone. Gosse was the principal literary careerist of his day, as Hugh Walpole would be for the post-World War I generation. White-haired and bespectacled, with hair parted in the middle and a drooping mustache, he presided with donnish fastidiousness over literary London. His work was not of the first order, but he managed to keep himself at the top of the cloistered late-Victorian literary heap with his reputation for clever conversation. Maugham found him "on the whole the most interesting and consistently amusing talker I ever knew."[45] The Gosses were at home at 17 Hanover Terrace on Sundays at four, and among the regulars were Henry James, Thomas Hardy, George Moore, Max Beerbohm, and Edward Marsh, a young patron of the arts who would one day serve as Maugham's proofreader.[46]

An evening at the Gosses' was no less a period piece than a weekend at Augustus Hare's. Gosse guided the conversation along suitable literary lines and filled the intervals with semiprecious bons mots. Discussing a new play, he said, "We were as nearly bored as enthusiasm would permit." Sometimes there was entertainment, and once Gosse hired a conjurer, taking great pains to find one who was a gentleman. At a New Year's dinner in 1898 there was a performance of marionettes. Henry James was there, sitting next to young Eddie Marsh, in whose ear he whispered: "Economy of means—and—economy of *effect*." Marsh told James that he was going to visit Paris. "Do not allow yourself," said James, "to be put off by the superficial and external aspect of Paris; or rather (for the *true* superficial and external aspect of Paris has a considerable fascination) by what I may call the superficial and external aspect OF the superficial and external aspect of Paris."

"Surely, Mr. James," Marsh replied, "that's carrying lucidity to a *dazzling* point."[47]

Gosse's position, H. G. Wells said, was that of "official man of British letters." He was a leading critic, whose column in the *Sunday Times* provided a powerful platform. He wrote biographies of other English writers, and his poem "Tusitala" was much anthologized. *Father and Son*, the story of growing up with a religious crank, was hailed as a masterpiece and crowned by the Académie Française, for reasons which today seem puzzling. He dispensed patronage in the form of chairs of English literature in foreign universities. In 1904 he was appointed librarian of the House of Lords, and from then on he conducted his correspondence on its cream-colored notepaper embossed with the royal arms. When he gave a lecture the front row was solid with duchesses. He called Ezra Pound "that preposterous American filibuster and Provençal charlatan," and said that E. M. Forster's *Howards End* was "coarse in morals."[48] Although he lived until 1928, he remained a late-Victorian in taste and sensibility, and represented what Maugham was breaking away from. Like Maugham, he was a secret homosexual. When André Gide confessed his homosexuality in *Corydon* in 1924, Gosse wrote him: "No doubt, in fifty years, this particular subject will cease to surprise anyone, and how many people in the past might wish to have lived in 1974."[49]

Edmund Gosse's closest literary friend was Henry James, who had been living in England for a quarter of a century and would become a British subject in 1915. Maugham did not meet James at Gosse's, however, but at a matinee of *The Cherry Orchard* given by an experimental theater called the Stage Society. He found himself sitting with James and Mrs. Clifford, the wife of a renowned mathematician. The play disconcerted James, who set out to explain how foreign to his French sympathies all this Russian incoherence was. He hesitated now and then in search of the right word to express his dismay, and Mrs. Clifford would supply it before he thought of it. James was too polite to protest, but his face betrayed his irritation. Stubbornly refusing the word she offered, he sought another. Finally they began to discuss the actress who played the lead, Ethel Irving. James wanted to know to what class she belonged and wrapped his question in a tortuous flow of circumlocutions until Mrs. Clifford blurted out: "Do you mean, is she a lady?" A pained look crossed James's face. The directness of the question had a vulgarity that offended him. Pretending not to hear, he shrugged and asked: "Is she, *enfin*, what you'd call, if you were asked point-blank, if you were put with your back to the wall, is she a *femme du monde?*"[50]

Maugham saw James again, but they never became friends. Their routes were too dissimilar. Maugham was working toward a plain style and stories based on direct experience. James, he felt, observed life from a window. He was amused but also put off by James's mannerisms and pomposity. In his mature years, when he began writing essays, he never lost the opportunity to disparage James's work. In a lecture on the short story before the Royal Society of Literature he said of James: "He was like a man who should provide himself with all the paraphernalia necessary to the ascent of Mount Everest—in order to climb Primrose Hill."

In *Points of View* he wrote: "I don't think Henry James knew how ordinary people behave. His characters have neither bowels nor sexual organs. He wrote a number of stories about men of letters, and it is told that when someone protested that literary men were not like that, he retorted 'so much the worse for them.'" In *Books and You* he wrote that in James's books, "people do not go away, they depart, they do not go home, but repair to their domiciles, and they do not go to bed, they retire." In *Some Novelists I Have Known* he wrote that "Henry James' fictions are like the cobwebs which a spider may spin in the attic of some old house, intricate, delicate and even beautiful, but which at any moment the housemaid's broom with brutal common sense may sweep away." Then, as if realizing that he was assigning to himself the housemaid's job, he added: "The fact remains that those last novels of his, notwithstanding their unreality, make all other novels, except the very best, unreadable."

The part of envy in Maugham's sniping at James is obvious. It was Maugham who spread the story that Hugh Walpole, who had a disciple-master relationship with James, had once tried to consummate it. Walpole is supposed to have approached James, who recoiled and shouted, "I can't, I can't." But since Maugham was unkindly disposed to both Walpole and James, this is a grain-of-salt story. It is true that James felt love for a man, Hendrik Andersen, a Nordic sculptor thirty years his junior, but James's biographer Leon Edel doubts that their intimacy was ever consummated, particularly in the light of James's puritan background, long habit of self-denial, and sublimation of sexual energy into writing.[51]

In 1900 Maugham was twenty-six and had published two novels and a volume of short stories. He was dapper, nice-looking, and was getting out in the world. He lived in bachelor quarters with his friend Payne, and was a member of the Bath Club, which had been founded at 34 Dover Street in 1896, with an emphasis on swimming. The ballroom in the clubhouse had been turned into a pool and the annual swimming contests between Oxford and Cambridge took place there. It was also a club for bridge enthusiasts, who had improved the rules of this new game and added a fourth hand.[52] Maugham had a publisher and an agent and the attention of reviewers but was still rowing against the current: two of his books had recently been turned down and he was having trouble finding commissions. His letters to Morris Colles reflect this time of struggle. When Augustus Hare ignored an offer to write travel sketches for the *Daily Mail*, Maugham jumped into the breach and asked Colles to send the paper his still unpublished book on Spain.[53] In another letter of that time Maugham asked Colles "if you could get me an *Arrowsmith Annual* to do. [The *Arrowsmith Annual* was a collection of short stories.] I have sketched out a rather sensational murder story (quite proper!) somewhat in the manner of Edgar Allan Poe which would run to about the required length."[54] Royalty checks were modest and infrequent. On October 14, 1903, for instance, the Authors' Syndicate sent him eighteen pounds and eighteen shillings.[55] Clearly, he was not getting rich on his writing.

At twenty-six Maugham was like the man in Max Beerbohm's story "The Happy Hypocrite," who has worn a mask so long it becomes his face. He was poised and worldly, and his writer's notebook for the period is studded with epigrams: "At a dinner party one should eat wisely but not too well, and talk well but not too wisely." He had acquired the defenses of an eligible young man-about-town: "When a woman of forty tells a man that she's old enough to be his mother, his only safety is in immediate flight." He takes a mistress, against his inclinations, for it was the fashionable thing for an Edwardian gentleman to do, and breaks with her: "My heart was sad for her sake, and though I had ceased to love her, I found no consolation." His atheism, the result of his years at Heidelberg, was full-formed: "I'm glad I don't believe in God. When I look at the misery of the world and its bitterness I think that no belief can be more ignoble." He gives full vent to his caustic streak, particularly in his appraisal of friends: "K. likes the precious. Of course, he's rather an ass; an intelligent, well-read ass."

Behind the mask of the Edwardian gentleman there hid the alienated, mother-deprived outsider who lacked a secure grip on his identity. As he said, "The accident of my birth in France . . . instilled into me two modes of life, two liberties, two points of view [and] prevented me from ever identifying myself completely with the instincts and prejudices of one people or the other."[56] He pretended to be heterosexual, whereas his deepest sympathies lay elsewhere. He was not what he seemed, and it is no wonder that many of the characters in his short stories are not what they seem.

In "The Lion's Skin" a perfect English gentleman married to an American heiress and living on the Riviera is found out to be the son of a waiter. When his house catches fire he goes in to save his wife's Sealyham, as a gentleman would, and is killed: "Bob Forestier had pretended for so many years to be a gentleman that in the end, forgetting that it was all a fake, he had found himself driven to act as in that stupid, conventional brain of his he thought a gentleman must act." In "Mr. Know-All" a vulgar Levantine turns out to be a gentleman, who saves a lady's reputation at the expense of his own. In "The Yellow Streak" a half-caste tries to hide his background:

"By God, Izzart, you're looking green about the gills. I never saw such a filthy color."

"You see, I had a Spanish grandmother," he answered, "and when I'm under the weather it always comes out. I remember at Harrow I fought a boy and licked him because he called me a damn half-caste."

"You are dark," said Hutchinson. "Do Malays ever ask you if you have any native blood in you?"

"Yes, damn their impudence."

Like Izzart and a whole gallery of his characters, Maugham's life was one of partial concealment.

In terms of his career, things began to look up in 1900, when *Punch* asked him to contribute short stories, and published two, one of which, "Lady Habart," was serialized in three issues. "Lady Habart" is a Maugham woman—pretty, vain, frivolous, lying, dishonest, and unscrupulous. She is in the grip of a moneylender, whom she is able to settle with by maneuvering a former suitor into marriage. Maugham converted "Lady Habart" into *Lady Frederick*, his first successful play. The other *Punch* story, "Cupid and the Vicar of Swale," was the genesis for a novel, *The Bishop's Apron*, and a play, *Loaves and Fishes*. It was Maugham's frugal habit to recycle his material whenever possible.

In 1900 Maugham was also at work on another novel. His first, *Liza of Lambeth*, owed something to luck; he had stumbled upon his material as an obstetric clerk. His second, *The Making of a Saint*, had been a wooden exercise in historical reconstruction. Naturally wishing to reproduce the success of *Liza*, he tried to catch the mood of the moment, as he had done with his slum novel, and chose the timely subject of the Boer War. *The Hero*, which he wrote with his customary dispatch from October 8, 1900, to January 14, 1901, deals with the theme of the returning veteran.[57]

James Parsons has won the Victoria Cross in the Transvaal for saving a subaltern, who, as he is being carried back to his lines, says he thinks he can stand, rises, and is shot and killed. So much for the uses of heroism. Parsons returns to the village of Little Primpton, to his parents and to his fiancée, Mary Clibborn. But he is not the same person and can no longer tolerate the limited vision of those around him. He has learned to think for himself, to doubt, to accept nothing on authority. He is "horrified at the pettiness and prejudice which he found in his home." His parents, "flattering themselves on their ideals and their high principles, vegetated in stupid sloth and in a less than animal vacuity."[58] He shocks them by saying that if he had been a Cape Dutchman he would have fought against the British. He is equally dissatisfied with his fiancée, an overwhelmingly cheerful do-gooder whose acts of charity conceal the will to have her way, as when she rearranges a sick man's pillows to her liking and his discomfort. James can no longer conform, but he cannot escape. He is bound by the

Edwardian mandate to do the right thing. Finding no way out of his dilemma, he shoots himself. This seems a rather extreme method of emancipation, but Maugham's concern is to show the inadequacy of the prevailing code as well as the individual's inability to challenge it. His attack on British provincial society was not for the readers of Mudie's. *The Hero* was an honest attempt at serious social criticism, and perhaps that is why it failed, commercially and critically. But *The Hero* was also clumsy, observed from the outside, much too long, and marred by such ripe descriptive passages as: "And the earth seemed languid and weary, accepting the moisture with little shuddering gasps of relief."[59]

With *The Hero* Maugham parted company with Fisher Unwin, who continued to be annoyed with him because he had taken an agent.[60] Maugham, who felt he had been "done in the eye" with *Liza of Lambeth*, was glad to be out of Unwin's clutches after the expiration of his three-volume contract. *The Hero*, published by Hutchinson, was the first Maugham book to feature his father's Moorish symbol, printed upside down, which may help explain why it did not bring him luck. He used it (right side up) in all his subsequent books, and it was used as a watermark on each page of his collected works. He also used it at the entrance to his house in Cap Ferrat, on his letterhead, on the radiator grille of his cars, on his cigarette cases, and on his matchbooks. In 1935 Robin Maugham, then at Cambridge, asked his uncle if he could use the trademark. Maugham replied that it had been discovered by his father and that Robin had as much right to it as he had.[61] The symbol has variously been interpreted as representing a stylized human hand and fingers, an upright sword covered by the arch of the sky, the wishbone of a chicken, and an upside-down cross of Lorraine. To readers who wrote asking what it was he replied that it served to ward off the evil eye and had succeeded beyond his expectations. Hutchinson printed 1,500 copies of *The Hero* at six shillings, and did not go into a second edition, nor did the book find an American publisher.

Maugham spent part of the summer of 1901 on the Kentish coast, and while there wrote one of the few book reviews of his long career. It was a review of George Gissing's travel book, *By the Ionian Sea*, and it appeared in the *Sunday Sun* on August 11, 1901. It took up three columns and was less a critical appreciation than an expression of longing for southern Italy and admiration for Gissing. "I took it with me to the Kentish coast," he wrote, "and read it in the evenings within sight and hearing of the grey sea, my limbs happily tired after the day's golf. . . . It is good to read sometimes books which are so entirely restful, just as after the turmoil of London, with its unceasing roar, which seems to thunder away even through one's sleep, it is comforting to come to the barren, marshy coast of North Kent, peaceful in its unbroken monotony."[62]

Maugham did not like reviewing. He felt it was soul-destroying and interfered with trying to preserve one's freshness. Moreover, it did not pay:

> We know that he [the reviewer] is paid less well than a skilled artisan in a factory. Of all the forms of literary activity this is the most miserably rewarded. I have reviewed but three books in my life. For the first (it is true my review took up three columns of a now defunct Sunday paper) I was paid two pounds ten; for the second I was paid twenty-five shillings; and for the third twelve and six. I could not but perceive that at that rate I should soon be paying the proprietors of papers for the privilege of writing reviews for them, and being a poor man ceased to look for such unprofitable employment.[63]

He became practiced in refusing to review books, sometimes pretending that he had never done it. In 1944, when he was seventy, Robert van Gelder of *The New York Times* asked him to review a book by Vita Sackville-West. "I am very old," he replied, "too old a dog to learn new tricks, and reviewing would be a new trick to me, and I think it only common sense to confine myself to writing such things as I would like to get written in the short time that in all probability remains to me. I should waste my energy and waste my time if I wrote reviews."[64] Only once after that did he depart from this stated principle, and that was in 1956, when he was over eighty. He was somehow persuaded to review Kingsley Amis' *Lucky Jim* in the *Sunday Times*. Perhaps he did it because it gave him a chance to vent some unfashionable prejudices:

> *Lucky Jim* is a remarkable novel. It has been greatly praised and widely read, but I have not noticed that any of the reviewers have remarked on its ominous significance. I am told that today rather more than sixty per cent of the men who go to the universities go on a government grant. They are the white-collar proletariat. They do not go to the university to acquire culture, but to get a job, and when they have got one, scamp it. They have no manners and are woefully unable to deal with any social predicament. Their idea of a celebration is to go to a public house and drink six beers. They are mean, malicious, and envious. They will write anonymous letters to harass a fellow under-

graduate and listen in to a telephone conversation that is no business of theirs. Charity, kindness, generosity are qualities which they hold in contempt. They are scum. Mr. Amis is so talented, his observation is so keen, his sympathies are so evident that you can hardly fail to be convinced of the truth of what he tells.

This was a singular attack on working-class students, coming from the author of *Liza of Lambeth*, who had made much of his compassion for the underprivileged. Maugham was cranky in his old age and still felt deprived at not having attended a university himself. The review brought a response from C. P. Snow, who sensibly asked, in the London *Times* of January 8, 1956: "Why is it so contemptible to go to a university on a government grant? Why is it so bestial to celebrate by drinking pints of beer?"

The Gissing review was a break in Maugham's serious work. He still thought of himself as an apprentice writer, who could learn his trade by emulating the masters. Under the influence of Brooks he had copied the florid prose of Pater and thought that he should write as the Pre-Raphaelites painted. In 1901, after reading Oscar Wilde's *Salomé*, he went to the British Museum and visited the gem exhibit, making notes to help him achieve a richness of style: "the foliage of the elm trees more somber than jade"; "the ploughed fields gaining in the sunshine the manifold colors of the jasper."[65]

Outgrowing the convolutions of Pater, he worked at developing a style that was direct and precise. He found his models in Swift, Dryden, Addison, and Cardinal Newman. As he told Louise Morgan in a 1931 interview: "I set myself to learn how to write by taking passages from the English classics, copying them out, and then reproducing them from memory. It's not an amusing thing to do. It takes a lot of patience and determination. . . . For a half-hour every day I practiced writing English as they wrote it. Otherwise, a writer has to learn his business at the expense of the public."[66]

Maugham was productive, turning out plays and novels, but theater managers and publishers did not beat a path to his door. In 1899 he had written a novel called *Mrs. Craddock*, which was turned down as improper by most of the leading publishers in London, including Heinemann.[67] It was eventually read by Robertson Nicoll, a partner in the firm of Hodder and Stoughton, who did not think it was for him but urged Heinemann to reconsider. Heinemann agreed to publish *Mrs. Craddock* on condition that Maugham delete offensive passages. This he agreed to do, being always willing to compromise in the interest of publication. The excisions have to do with a love scene between Mrs. Craddock and a young man, and the deleted sentences are: "Her flesh cried out to his flesh, and the desire was irresistible," and "Flesh called to flesh, and there was no force on earth more powerful. Her whole frame was quivering with passion." In a 1955 edition Maugham restored the original text and wrote in a preface that, read half a century later, "the propriety of the book seems almost painful."

Heinemann brought out *Mrs. Craddock* in November 1902. It was the start of a relationship that would last for more than sixty years. William Heinemann was not known for his munificence, but Maugham liked him. "Heinemann made a hard bargain with the young authors," he said. "But if the young authors stood up to him and wrung better terms out of him, he would laugh heartily and say 'Well, you're not a bad businessman.'" Maugham saw quite a bit of Heinemann, a mercurial little man with bright, dark eyes. Once when he dropped by his office he saw a book in Braille. "Oh yes," Heinemann said, "I'm studying it; you know, the oculists tell me I'm going blind and I want to learn it while I have the chance." Maugham thought that showed a fine and courageous spirit. In fact, Heinemann died in 1920 before going blind.[68]

Mrs. Craddock was the most fully realized of his works to date, but when he read it again in 1955 he dismissed it as a period piece. In the preface he wrote:

> It is as a genre picture that I regard it. I smile and blush at its absurdities, but leave them because they belong to the period; and if the novel has any merit (and that the reader must decide for himself), it is because it is a picture, faithful I believe, of life in a corner of England during the last years of the nineteenth century. . . . It was the end of an era, but the landed gentry, who were soon to lose the power they had so long enjoyed, were the last to have a suspicion of it. . . . For the most part, they were narrow, stupid and intolerant; prudish, formal, and punctilious. But they had their points, and I do not think the author was quite fair to them. . . . The landed gentry were on the whole decent, honorable, and upright. They were devoid of envy. They had good manners and were kindly and hospitable. But they had outworn their use, and perhaps it was inevitable that the course of events should sweep them away.

Mrs. Craddock is more than a period piece, however, for it is one of the novels in which Maugham reveals himself through his characters. Set in the last decade of the nineteenth century, near Whitstable, in the Kentish countryside that he knew well, *Mrs. Craddock* tells the story of Bertha Ley, a sensitive and well educated middle-class woman who develops a burning passion for a handsome farmer and marries him despite the difference in their stations. Edward Craddock turns out to be a complacent male chauvinist: "The fact that Edward ate, drank, slept and ate again as regularly as the oxen on his farm sufficiently proved that he enjoyed a happiness equal to theirs." Craddock's view of women is that they are "like chickens. Give 'em a good run, properly closed in with stout wire-netting so that they can't get into mischief, and when they cluck and cackle just sit tight and take no notice."

Not surprisingly, problems develop in the marriage. There are no common interests, and Craddock is unable to reciprocate Bertha's passion. When she becomes pregnant, and then loses the child, she sees Craddock for what he is and falls out of love. Visiting her aunt in London, she falls in love with Gerard Vaudrey, a nineteen-year-old boy, but their affair is not consummated. She returns to her husband, who is killed in a fall from a horse. Instead of feeling grief, Bertha feels that at last she is free.

On one level the novel is a study of the stifling provincial society Maugham has already described in *The Hero*, in which "each set thinks itself quite as good as the set above it and has a profound contempt for the set below it," and in which "if the food was not heavy, the conversation was."

On a second level it is the study of a woman who marries beneath her. Maugham brought to the theme of marriage between those of different classes a candid handling of Bertha's sexual passion. Several critics have referred to *Mrs. Craddock* as an "English Bovary," but Bertha is more of a transitional figure between Madame Bovary and Lady Chatterley. Her pursuit of Edward Craddock must have shocked Edwardian sensibilities. But whereas with Lawrence passion enriches, with Maugham it is disabling and painful. In *Mrs. Craddock* he first fully develops the theme of love as bondage. Bertha's passion is repeatedly described as a physically painful transformation: "her breathing was strangely oppressive, and her heart beat almost painfully." Bertha's passion is masochistic, she abandons herself completely. "She followed him like a dog, with a subjection that was really touching. . . . She wanted to abase herself before the strong man, to be low and humble before him. She would have been his handmaiden, and nothing could have satisfied her so much as to perform for him menial services."

When she falls out of love she is still trapped, and Maugham uses the vocabulary of bondage to describe her situation. Bertha tells Dr. Ramsay, the vicar: "Oh, when I think that I'm shackled to him for the rest of my life, I feel I could kill myself." Suicide was the way to freedom for James Parsons in *The Hero*, but in *Mrs. Craddock* freedom is won by her husband's accidental death.

On a third level *Mrs. Craddock* is a novel in which we see Maugham working out his familiar obsessions—the mother endangered in pregnancy, the stillborn child, the pain of love, and the quest for freedom. Just as Maugham identified with his mother, he makes Bertha Craddock his alter ego. Maugham could say, paraphrasing Flaubert: "Mrs. Craddock, *c'est moi.*"

Bertha is fascinated by Edward's hands. "She looked up at him and then down at the strong hands she was still holding. . . . They were large and roughly made. She felt them firm and intensely masculine. . . . She stretched out the long, strong fingers. . . . She bent down to kiss the upturned palms." She squeezed his hands, "the visible signs of his powerful manhood." She caresses and kisses the palms. Thinking of her husband "gave a tautness to her own muscles." Bertha's finger fetishism begins to seem like an unconscious homosexual fantasy of the author's.

Bertha's infatuation with Gerard Vaudrey may be seen as another such fantasy. Vaudrey is one of Maugham's pretty androgynous boys, like Red in the story of that name. "He was quite a boy, very slight . . . with a small girlish face . . . his cheek soft as a girl's." At nineteen he has been expelled from Rugby and sent out of his home for philandering with a forty-year-old maid. Maugham had a weakness for charming scoundrels, who appear often in his work. He later said that Gerald Vaudrey was one of his favorite characters because he is "gay, amusing, and unscrupulous." There seems to be a double process of identification at work here. Bertha represents both Maugham's mother and Maugham. She is the maternal, nourishing figure, and she is the unconsciously disguised homosexual lover. Although there is only a difference of seven years between them, Bertha keeps reminding Gerald that "I'm old enough to be your mother," and "people will think you're my son." Finally Vaudrey leaves for America, but their physical intimacy has not gone beyond kissing and "her flesh crying out to his flesh"—the phrase that Heinemann cut.

Maugham's grief over the death of his mother is reenacted in the long and harrowing account of Bertha's pregnancy. Bertha's thoughts dwell morbidly on her own death. But one day there is a transference and she has fantasies of Edward's death. In a bizarre necrophilic day-dream she kisses his dead body, his hands, his lips, and his closed eyes. She undresses him and sponges his limbs. "The touch of the cold flesh made her shudder voluptuously." Again she is both mistress and mother. She wants to possess her husband like a mother possessing a son, and she wants to make love to the dead body. One is reminded of Maugham's frustrated desire to be possessed by his mother, and his obsession with her after her death. Perhaps he saw himself in the dead Edward, for when his mother died, Maugham also died in a way, since he did not understand why he had been allowed to survive.

At the end of the book Bertha's fantasy comes true and Edward does die. She is relieved from bondage, and burns his photographs and letters. One remembers Maugham being given the photograph that his mother had taken when she knew she was dying, and which he kept for the rest of his life. There was no relief for him.[69]

Mrs. Craddock had a modest success, winning Maugham higher praise than he had thus far received. *T.P.'s Weekly*, on November 28, 1902, called it "both powerful and true." A. St. John Adcock, an influential critic, writing in the *Bookman* in December 1902, said it was "a subtle and masterly study of a certain female temperament that is probably not so uncommon as we would like to believe. . . .The book as a whole . . . makes a distinct advance on what Mr. Maugham had previously accomplished."[70]

Also in 1902, one of Maugham's plays was performed for the first time, not in London but in Berlin. He had been writing somber, Ibsen-esque plays since medical school, and during the next two or three years he finished several curtain raisers and sent them to various managers. One or two were never returned and, since he had no copies, were lost; he got discouraged over the others and they were put away or destroyed. One such curtain raiser, however, was accepted by an avant-garde cabaret theater in Berlin, where the young Max Reinhardt was a producer. This was called the Café Theatre Society, and it presented evenings of music, farce, satire, and short plays. In October 1901 the Café Theatre Society found new premises in Unter den Linden and changed its name to Schall und Rauch (after Goethe: Gretchen asks Faust if he believes in God, and Faust replies that a name is only rumor and smoke). Schall und Rauch produced Maugham's one-acter, for which he wrote the German adaptation. Unable to have his plays performed in his own country, he was thus associated with the dawn of the new German theater.[71]

The English title was *Marriages Are Made in Heaven*, but the play was performed on January 3, 1902, under its German title, *Schiffbrüchig (Shipwrecked)*. It ran for eight performances and must have met with some success, for it was revived for five more in April and May. This was one of Maugham's earliest dramatic efforts, written in 1896. It combined one of the most durable plot devices of the late-Victorian theater, the woman with a past, with an Ibsenesque flaunting of social convention. The woman with a past, used by such leading turn-of-the-century dramatists as Oscar Wilde in *Lady Windermere's Fan*, and Arthur Wing Pinero in *The Second Mrs. Tanqueray*, is in this case Mrs. Vivyan, whose income of 1,200 pounds a year is a settlement from a former lover, Lord Feaverham. (Another convention of late-Victorian theater was that you had to have a title in the cast.) Mrs. Vivyan is about to be married to Jack Rayner, whose best man reveals her checkered past and asks them not to go through with a socially ruinous wedding. Jack replies that he knows where Mrs. Vivyan's money comes from and has no intention of giving her up. "And the price you pay is dishonor," the best man says. "Respectability and virtue have turned their backs on us," Mrs. Vivyan says. "Give them time and they'll come around," Jack replies. "They only want feeding. You can get a bishop to dine with you if you give good enough dinners."[72]

It is amusing to consider that this banal plot seemed bold at the time. We should remember what sheltered lives English theater audiences had been allowed to lead. When Ibsen's *Ghosts* was produced in 1891 at the Independent Theatre, it had the dean of London theater critics, Clement Scott of the *Daily Telegraph*, foaming at the mouth. He called the play "an open drain," "a loathsome sore unbandaged," and "a dirty act done publicly," and its author "a muck-ferreting dog." English audiences were still shocked at seeing an adulterous woman like Paula Tanqueray onstage.[73] It was in this climate that Maugham wrote *Marriages Are Made in Heaven*, borrowing his moral from Ibsen (that one must go one's own way and make one's own mistakes), his dialogue from Wilde (a stream of epigrams, such as "Illusions are like umbrellas, you no sooner get them than you lose them"), and his plot from Pinero.

Marriages Are Made in Heaven was never performed in England, but it was published in a literary magazine, *The Venture*, that Maugham coedited with Laurence Housman, Oscar Wilde's friend.

This expensively printed annual of art and literature came out in the fall of 1903. It was published as a successor to the *Yellow Book* and cost five shillings. Its unpaid contributors included Thomas Hardy, G. K. Chesterton, A. E. Housman, John Masefield, Havelock Ellis, E. F. Benson, Francis Thompson, and Violet Hunt. *Punch* welcomed it as "a magazine that promises to set a high standard in the field of belles lettres. Bona ventura to *The Venture*." But it was too highbrow to be popular and fizzled out after a second and last issue in 1904.[74]

It was probably through editing *The Venture* that Maugham met Violet Hunt, a turn-of-the-century feminist and writer who scandalized her generation and became known as "Violent" Hunt. She was one of the three daughters of Alfred Hunt, an Oxford don who had, under the influence of Ruskin, become a landscape painter. Her mother was the original of Tennyson's "Margaret," and wrote popular novels. The family lived in a house on Camden Hill called Tor Villa and moved in Pre-Raphaelite circles. Born in 1862, Violet grew up among literary men—her father's friends were Tennyson, Ruskin, and Browning. The Hunts were bohemians who dressed for dinner.

Violet blossomed into a bright-eyed Edwardian beauty who loved writers, married men, and sexual intrigue. She was auburn-haired, with large dark eyes and an expressive mouth, and applied herself to flouting the conventions of her time. When she was twenty-one her mother's friends complained that her décolletage was too low for a maiden. Her first serious lover was the painter George Boughton, who was fifty-one to her twenty-two when their affair began in 1884. She wrote in her diary that Boughton "initiated me into the secret of what I could feel and has not left me—*inassouvie*." Her next lover was Oswald Crawfurd, a former consular official, who had become chairman of the London publishing house of Chapman and Hall, which put out a fiction magazine to which Violet contributed. When they met in 1890 Violet was twenty-eight and Crawfurd was a fifty-six-year-old married man with an invalid wife. His affair with Violet lasted from 1892 until 1898. It was Crawfurd who gave Violet syphilis, according to her friend Douglas Goldring, who wrote in his book *Life Interests* that Crawfurd "did her an injury from which she suffered until the end of her life."[75]

Violet began writing novels in 1898. Her early books had a vein of French realism, à la Colette, and were considered daring. She flirted with H. G. Wells, Henry James, and Arnold Bennett. Of Bennett she wrote after dining with him at the Victorian Club: "He finds me just clever and modern without much knowledge or interest in any traditional matters—my walk of life being too purely sexual for him."[76]

At the same time she was a dedicated suffragette, and belonged to the Committee of Women Writers. She ran a magazine called *The Freewoman* and wrote editorials about the "slave minds" of women. She attended meetings at which Mrs. Pankhurst spoke, and was concerned about conditions in the slums. At one suffrage meeting she heard the story of a slum child who was given sixpence in the street and said: "We are sad at home and not enough to eat and it makes mother so unhappy and if I get her 6d. worth of rum with this she can go and lie down on the bed and not think of things for 24 hours." Violet reported at the meeting that once in Durham she had seen a big child of two still at the breast race up to its mother and say, "Come on, ye' bitch, give me ma' tittie." After the meeting she went to dine at Romano's, a fashionable restaurant. She represented the radical chic of her time, which may have been what drew her to Maugham, who not only had written a slum novel but also knew the right people.[77]

Her first diary entry mentioning Maugham was January 8, 1903. She was then forty-one, and he was twenty-nine. Maugham did considerable boasting about having sex with women in medical school and taking over his friend Walter Payne's mistresses, but this is one of the few documented instances of an affair with a woman. Rebecca West heard "the painful tale" from Violet Hunt herself.[78] She took the role of the older woman seducing the younger man. After the brief affair ended they remained friends, exchanged letters, and dedicated books to each other. Violet dedicated her novel *White Rose of Weary Leaf* to Maugham, and to her annoyance, he dedicated to her his travel book on Spain. He later wrote Edward Marsh that Violet was put out, "chiefly, I think, because it is called *The Land of the Blessed Virgin* and she could not imagine what the hell would be her business in such a country."[79]

Maugham was in a position to know whereof he spoke. At the time of their affair Violet had already contracted syphilis from Oswald Crawfurd, but did not know it, and would not realize what she had until 1906. Her diary for May first of that year reads:

On May Day, through the rain all the smart folk fare to the private view of the Royal Academy . . . there was a day when poor dear Cholmeley [Dr. Albermarle Cholmeley, a friend and longtime suitor] came to the club at ten Adelphi Terrace and with tears in his eyes told me to my face I had a disgraceful illness, in fact Tertiaries, only he did not name it or do more than hint. But I had had warning. Archie Propert [another suitor] looked at me at the Monds [Alfred and Angela Monds, fashionable hosts who gave weekend parties] and my spots on my forehead and said "You ought not to go out." He said—"You ought to be in bed," actually. Then Cholmeley clinched it and sent me to a very distinguished doctor, Dr. Stephen Paget. Paget looked at me and spoke to me as to something unclean. I never went again. . . . It was the most inglorious moment of my life. And of course Archie Propert did not propose, as everyone thought he would.

To this typed entry she had added in her own hand: "Now I know what fallen women feel."[80]

If Maugham suffered any mishap in his "sexual congress" with Violet Hunt, there is no sign of it in their correspondence, which is invariably affectionate. In 1904 she brought out *Sooner or Later*, a fictionalized account of her affair with Crawfurd, which was a great success. Maugham wrote her:

I liked your novel because it explored undiscovered country; I do not think, in English at least, that the relationship between a married man and his mistress, a *jeune fille*, has ever been analyzed before. I think you have done it with very great skill. I confess I should have liked a little more "obscenity," because Appleton's charm is obviously sexual, but I recognize that this was impossible . . . of course the work has an autobiographical ring about it and you must expect to hear a good deal of disagreeable things—however what does it matter? My own impression is that most of what one writes is to a greater or lesser degree autobiographical, not the actual incidents always, but always the emotions. Anyhow we are able to *fouter* ourselves of the world at large—when one has to suffer so much it is only fair that one should have the consolation of writing books about it.[81]

In another letter, written from Tunbridge Wells in Kent, Maugham congratulated Violet on her notices and said that his own book (*Mrs. Craddock*) had cleaned him out and he did not want to write another. "But I suppose I shall. I have got a sort of sneaking desire to do a minor Comédie Humaine for England" (this would be *The Merry-Go-Round*). "Come back soon," he went on, "I have nowhere to go on Thursdays. . . . My 'affair' is over, THANK GOD!"[82] Violet had graduated from mistress to confidante, although whom Maugham's affair was with has remained her secret.

On one occasion Violet invited Maugham to a club for writers she belonged to, and when he went he found the place filled with women, but no Violet.

> It flashed across me that I had come on the wrong day [he wrote her], but since 53 eyes were fixed steadily upon me (I counted them: the odd one is because the lady sitting in a corner could only see me out of one eye) I dared not go away at once. So to keep myself in countenance I began to eat cucumber sandwiches till I had demolished all there were. . . . My retreat was disturbed by a woman of ample proportions and commanding mien, who waylaid me and asked me who I was, what I wanted, and tried to make me sit down. But I put her off with specious words and made a bolt for the stairs. . . . I write you this account so that if you hear that a wild-eyed lunatic with disheveled hair came asking for you at 10 Norfolk Street—you may know that I am he.[83]

Violet had gone to Maugham's publisher, Heinemann, who made her change the ending of one of her books, telling her that the British public would not tolerate a woman being killed while she carried an unborn child. When *White Rose of Weary Leaf* established Violet in the first rank of women writers, admired by Henry James and D. H. Lawrence, Maugham wrote her: "It is much better composed than is usual with you. . . . [There are] slovenly sentences which you want to correct in the proofs. I don't think you should attempt long sentences. Your style is always better when they are short. The full stop does away with any number of obscurities and makes the dragging subsidiary clause which is apparently so dear to you impossible." At the same time, when she wrote about one of his books, he replied: "I wish I had not the uneasy temperament which leads me to accept your strictures without question but to doubt the sincerity of your praise."[84]

In 1902 Violet and her mother took a lease on a house called South Lodge at 80 Camden Hill Road. Violet became a fashionable hostess and gave garden parties where one drank tea and iced coffee and exchanged gossip. Hers was one of the houses where Maugham could hobnob with the literary set. He liked Violet, liked to be invited to her parties, and kept up with her over the years. In 1908 she had an affair with Ford Madox Ford (who was still Ford Madox Hueffer), the editor of the *English Review*. Violet was then forty-six, eleven years older than Ford. In 1911 he left his wife Elsie and moved into South Lodge. Henry James, whom Violet had known since 1890 and thought of as "rather a tedious gentleman [who] repeats himself, and is overelaborate in describing and allowing for sensations and impressions," was shocked and broke off with her.[85] It was then that Violet took up the writers called Les Jeunes—Ezra Pound, Wyndham Lewis, Rebecca West, and Compton Mackenzie.

In 1912 she coauthored a novel with her mother. A notice in the April 3, 1912, issue of a magazine called *The Throne* said:

> Messrs. Chatto and Windus have in the press a book which forms an interesting link between the modern school of fiction and that of a generation or so ago, in the waning days of the three-volume novel— those good old days as they are now remembered, had just as many critics in its own time as the six-shilling novel of today. The forthcoming book is a romance entitled "The Governess," by Mrs. Alfred Hunt, one of the popular novelists of the old days, and her daughter, Miss Violet Hunt (now Mrs. Ford Madox Hueffer), one of the most successful of the modern school.

With Violet claiming to be Ford's wife, his real wife petitioned the court for the restitution of conjugal rights. When the case came up before the divorce division of the High Court, Ford was ordered to return to his wife within fourteen days, and was imprisoned for contempt of court when he refused to comply. Ford's wife also sued *The Throne* for libel and won three hundred pounds in damages. Henry James, seeking a reconciliation with Violet, wrote her: "Well, patch with purple if you must, so long as the piece holds."[86]

The piece held for eight years. Violet and Ford went to Germany and claimed they had been married by a priest. They returned to England and remained together until 1919, when Ford left her for Stella Bowen. He went into hiding to escape Violet's wrath, but after Ford left her Violet Hunt began her downward spiral. She lost her looks to the unforgiving combination of age and disease, and she ceased to be a writer who counted. But Maugham remained a loyal friend and correspondent. When in the spring of 1922 the editor of a volume of "Georgian" stories, a man named Arnold Lunn, organized a lunch for contributors in the St. Pancras Station hotel, Maugham sat next to Violet Hunt and devoted his attention to her as if she was the one person in the room who mattered. Only once did he interrupt his conversation with Violet, when Lunn, at the head of the table, said, "We don't seem to have decided what is a Georgian story." Maugham spoke up: "A story written since George Fifth's accession that we want to read today." Each participant paid for his own lunch, and Maugham paid for Violet, saying, "I think I can stand you a lunch."[87] In the twenties he saw less of Violet, who was settling into quiet old age. In spite of her reckless existence she lived to the age of eighty, and died in 1942 during the bombing of London.

At the time he first met Violet Hunt, Maugham was having no success in placing his plays. It was hard in those days for a young playwright to break through, for the London theater was in the hands of the actor-managers. Sir Herbert Beerbohm Tree, Max Beerbohm's half brother, ran His Majesty's Theatre and did a repertoire of Shakespeare and adaptations from the French. Some actor-managers had house playwrights who wrote parts for them. George Alexander of the St. James's Theatre had Pinero, while his rival Charles Wyndham at the Criterion had Henry Arthur Jones. Gerald du Maurier, son of the author of *Trilby* and father of Daphne, managed Wyndham's Theatre and played swash-buckling roles. Expenses were low and runs were long. Pinero and Jones were society playwrights who presented upper-class characters speaking drawing-room dialogue. Playgoing was restricted to the leisure class, hence the matinee, and the expensive stalls absorbing the cheaper pit seats. The scene was set in what Pinero called "our little parish of St. James," whose inhabitants saw themselves mirrored on the stage and felt at home. The actor-managers guaranteed the style and standard of the product, much as Mudie's had for novels. Some of them, such as Lewis Waller, whose fans wore KOW (Keen on Waller) badges, were immensely popular.

Such avant-garde playwrights as Ibsen were produced outside the actor-manager system, thanks to the efforts of sponsors such as the critic J. T. Grein, who helped found the Independent Theatre in 1891.[88] There was also the Stage Society, where Maugham had met Henry James. It had been founded in 1899 to produce plays of power and merit which could not be presented under the conditions then prevalent on the London stage. The Stage Society would take over a West End theater for a Sunday evening and a Monday matinee and invite the leading critics. It was an early form of Off-Broadway, and presented some of Shaw's first work.

Maugham had written *A Man of Honour* in Rome in 1898 and sent it to several managers, who turned it down. After the success of *Mrs. Craddock*, when he began to be looked upon as a promising novelist, he rewrote it and sent it to the Stage Society. W. L. Courtney, an

Oxford don and keen Ibsenite, was a member of the selection committee, and championed the play. *A Man of Honour* was performed at the Imperial Theatre in Westminster on the evening of February 22 and at the matinee of February 23. In addition Courtney was the editor of an influential highbrow magazine called the *Fortnightly Review*, with a circulation of 5,000, and liked Maugham's play well enough to print it as a supplement to his March issue. Maugham was delighted to see his first play in print and asked Courtney to run off some copies to be sold on opening night. Courtney obliged, and 150 copies in pale printed wrappers were on sale at the theater on February 22.[89]

A Man of Honour is another variation on the Maugham theme that "doing the right thing" can have calamitous results. *In Marriages Are Made in Heaven* "the right thing" was to avoid marrying a woman with a tainted past. In *A Man of Honour* Basil Kent, a decorated veteran of the Boer War (like James Parsons in *The Hero*), marries beneath him (like Bertha Craddock). His pregnant mistress, Jennie Bush, is a barmaid (a lower-class young woman, like Mildred in *Of Human Bondage*), whom he marries out of a sense of duty. But marriage—and this is another favorite Maugham theme—is a trap and a humiliation. The child is stillborn; Basil finds that he has nothing in common with Jennie and is in love with a woman of his own class. He quarrels with Jennie, tells her he wants a divorce, and goes to see the other woman. Jennie follows him. In the fourth act a friend of Basil's informs him that Jennie has drowned herself in the Thames. Basil, like Bertha Craddock, quickly recovers from his grief and decides "to take life by both hands and enjoy it." He concludes that "it's because I tried to do my duty and act like a gentleman and a man of honour that all this misery has come about." As in *The Hero* and *Mrs. Craddock*, freedom requires a death, in *Mrs. Craddock's* case a husband, in this case a wife. In the last scene Basil's new love arrives, and they are in each other's arms when the coroner is announced.

In the Stage Society production Basil Kent was played by Harley Granville-Barker, a rising young actor who would make his mark producing Shaw, and who was three years younger than Maugham. "He had charm and gaiety and coltish grace," Maugham wrote in *The Summing Up*. "He was brimming over with other people's ideas. But I felt in him a fear of life which he sought to cheat by contempt of the common herd." He had written a play, *The Marrying of Ann Leete*, of which Maugham said: "It might really have been written by Meredith, if you can imagine a Meredith who had neither wit, English, nor sense."[90] In a letter to his agent Morris Colles he wrote that Granville-Barker was "a difficult person to deal with, very vain and full of self-conceit."[91]

For the premiere of his first London production, on the evening of February 22, 1903, Maugham invited his barrister brother Frederic and his wife Helen Mary, and his bohemian brother Henry Neville (Harry). An entry in Helen Mary Maugham's diary says: "Went to the first night of Willie's play *A Man of Honour*. Very enthusiastic audience, and it was quite well acted. Willie was pale with terror!" Harry came to the party at the Bath Club after the play. With his unproduced plays in blank verse, he had been the first writer in the family. An esthete, he refused to compromise his artistic standards to the demands of the marketplace. In 1901 he had written a column called "The Amiable Egoist" in *Black and White* magazine. His writing was low-keyed, conventional, a bit anemic. He had none of his younger brother's bite or avant-garde ideas. He traveled to Italy and Egypt but was never found guilty of an original thought or an amusing remark. His comment on the death of Queen Victoria was typical: "That a virile race should have been ruled for two thirds of a century by a gentle lady is a tribute to the people, and also to British womanhood." He had once advised Willie not to be a writer, but now he must have sensed that his younger brother was the real writer in the family. At the party everyone was in evening dress, and Maugham was surrounded by the cast when Harry appeared in a shabby blue suit, under the influence of drink, and said in an unnaturally loud voice, "I'm glad to hear that my little brother has had some success at last."[92]

But Maugham did not feel successful. The first night of *A Man of Honour* was also its last. After two performances and the press notices the play was as dead as mutton. The author looked reflectively into the Thames and was conscious that he had not set it on fire.[93] The press notices chided him for his obsessions with the seamy side of life, and the London *Times* on February 24 wrote that the play was "ugly in subject and . . . dismal in tone." The *Graphic* on February 28 said the play belonged to "the new dramatic school, which takes a pleasure in depressing the spirits of the spectator with sordid and gloomy pictures of Society." The *Athenaeum* critic, picking up the influence of Ibsen, wrote on February 28 that the play reminded him of "a long Scandinavian night." Several critics, however, came to Maugham's defense, among them the Ibsenite J. T. Grein, who in the *Sunday Special* for March 1 said that "the author promises to become, in our stageland, a man of destiny." When the critic of the *Star* called the play a penetrating study of real human beings, Mr. William G. Muir of Fulham wrote the editor on February 24: "May I be allowed to protest against this debased and distorted view of human nature . . . The author I can make certain allowances for as he evidently affects the methods of the Decadents and writes for their edification, but I cannot so easily forgive the critic who finds truth in a monster such as Basil Kent, who is utterly devoid of even the smallest touch of human nature."[94]

One of the critics who reviewed *A Man of Honour*, Max Beerbohm, was to become Maugham's lifelong friend. "The incomparable" Max, wit, writer, and caricaturist, was the son of a German corn merchant named Julius Beerbohm who had come to London in 1830. He married an Englishwoman, Constantia Draper, and had three sons, one of whom was the actor-manager Sir Herbert Beerbohm Tree. (He took the "Tree" from the original "Baum" of "Beerbaum.") When his wife died he married her sister Eliza and had four more children—Max and three daughters. His father was sixty-one when Max was born, in 1872, two years before Maugham: he was an *enfant de vieux*. Oscar Wilde said that by the time Max was twenty he had mastered the secret of perpetual old age. Already at Oxford, where he became Reggie Turner's best friend, Max had a reputation for brilliance, and his caricatures of Oxford celebrities were displayed in Shrimpton's window in the Broad. He contributed to the *Yellow Book*, and soon had made a name for himself, at an exceptionally early age. His second book had an impressive title for a twenty-four-year-old: *The Works of Max Beerbohm*.[95]

By 1903 Max had suucceeded Shaw as theater critic for the *Saturday Review*, and wrote on February 28 that he found *A Man of Honour* "admirably conceived and written; and the third act is a fine piece of emotional drama. The rest of the play falls to pieces. Mr. Maugham becomes too bitter. . . . A weak and well-meaning young man . . . suddenly . . . becomes a monster."

Maugham and Max often met at the home of yet another London hostess whom Maugham cultivated. This was Mrs. George Steevens, the widow of a celebrated foreign correspondent for the *Daily Mail*, who had written the best sellers *With Kitchener to Khartoum*, *From Capetown to Ladysmith*, and *Unfinished Record of the South African War*, and had been killed at the siege of Ladysmith in 1900. Mrs. Steevens was an eccentric Scotswoman, née Christina Stewart, who, as one of his mistresses, was mixed up in the divorce proceedings that cost the Liberal party leader Sir Charles Dilke the premiership. The doors of Mayfair were closed to her. She threw herself into philanthropy, and at various times ran a soup kitchen in Marylebone, a day nursery for the poor, and an orphanage for thirty children. Later she bought Merton Abbey, a house beyond Clapham Common, where Nelson had lived with Lady Hamilton before Trafalgar. She liked to entertain artists, writers, and theater folk, to whom she served champagne in jugs with a hollow receptacle for ice in the center. She once hinted to Henry James that she had poisoned her first husband, a man named Rogerson, and James claimed that "if she had been beautiful and sane, she would have been one of the world's great wicked women." She was once caught cheating at a spiritualist séance she had organized, and was suspected of having set fire to her own home to collect the insurance. By the time Maugham knew her she was in her seventies, with bright eyes and short, curly gray hair. She always wore a linen shirt with starched collar and cuffs, a black leather belt, a black tie in a sailor's knot, a dark-gray skirt, and square-toed Highland shoes with silver buckles. It was said that she was the original for the main character in his first successful play, *Lady Frederick*.[96]

Merton Abbey was about eight miles from London, near enough so that her friends could come by carriage. Maugham, by now nearly thirty, was one of the Sunday callers. He also went there on Tuesday nights, when Mrs. Steevens had what she called her private philanthropy, dinners for hard-up writers. The regulars—Maugham, Max Beerbohm, and Reggie Turner—looked forward to Tuesdays, when they could count on a substantial meal. Mrs. Steevens' servants were recruited from the ranks of orphans whom she had known since infancy. It was disconcerting to hear her say to the butler, "Dearest, will you bring in the cocktails?" or "Darling, will you give Mr. Beerbohm one of those nice little cakes?"[97]

It was at Mrs. Steevens', one sunny afternoon on the pleasant lawn of Merton Abbey, that Max and Maugham had it out about *A Man of Honour*, which Max thought was too grim. Maugham said he was set on writing more plays. Max told him to stick to novels. Drama was a damnable business, he said, the plots were arbitrary, the characters were obvious. In writing a novel one did not have to make these wholesale surrenders. One could be as subtle as life itself. Max said he was talking to him as a father (he was two years older than Maugham). His talent was too subtle. It was easy for people to make money in the theater. Pausing, he tapped Maugham on the chest and said, "But you, my boy, are not one of those people." Maugham seemed to agree, but looked downcast. Max, convinced that he had done his good deed for the day, changed the subject.[98]

But Maugham liked writing plays and had no intention of stopping. He agreed with Dr. Johnson that it was much easier to form dialogues than to contrive adventures. He was not satisfied with the approval of the small band of intellectuals in the Stage Society, nor did he aspire to starving in a garret. He wanted a wider audience and popular success. He had discovered that "money was like a sixth sense without which you could not make the most of the other five."[99]

During the rehearsals of *A Man of Honour* Maugham saw that some scenes of badinage in the first act came off well. He decided he could write a comedy, which he promptly did, finishing it by June 30, 1903. Its hero was a worldly parson who intrigues to get a bishopric and capture a pretty heiress. Leaving all notions of Ibsen and private obsessions aside, the play, *Loaves and Fishes*, was written with commercial success in mind. But no manager would touch a comedy that ridiculed a member of the clergy. Maugham had thought that his earlier Stage Society production would bring managers knocking on his door, but the truth was it made them think of him as an avant-garde dramatist who could write only gloomy and unprofitable plays. By November 1903 another play, *The Explorer*, had been turned down by the actor-manager Charles Wyndham. Maugham then showed it to George Alexander, and wrote Colles that Alexander had expressed himself favorably, "but shows no more than platonic interest." The critic and by now friend J. T. Grein advised a trial run in the provinces.[100] Writing at top speed, Maugham finished another comedy, *Lady Frederick*, and sent it to Colles, but again found no takers.

There was, however, one bright piece of news. The actress Muriel Wylford wanted to revive *A Man of Honour* in a commercial theater. Maugham, who was usually demanding in money matters, was so eager for the production that he waived his fee. "I know you will thoroughly disapprove of this," he wrote Colles, "but I think it is worth my while as an advertisement and there are other reasons as well why I should do my best for Miss Wylford, which it is needless to go into."[101] Maugham changed the ending, omitting the crude announcement in the last act that the coroner's officer wants to see Basil in connection with his wife's death. Critics revised their opinions and said the play did not have the vulgarity of the Stage Society version. Maugham also supplied a curtain raiser, *Mademoiselle Zampa*, a one-act farce with a music-hall setting, which was so lackluster that it was withdrawn for the last week of the run. *A Man of Honour* opened at the Avenue Theatre on February 18, 1904, and had a commercial run of twenty-eight performances, for which critics praised Miss Wylford as a first-rate character actress.[102]

Basil Kent was played by Ben Webster, a fine classical actor, who liked the challenge the part presented. His next role was in a costume drama, which he compared unfavorably to Maugham's play: "Funny, wearing the garments of my manager of 16 years ago! . . . It's such a leap from the realism and humanity of *A Man of Honour* to this inhuman drivel with its inverted sentences to represent period—'To my mother's house I dared not go!' is a specimen—it makes me feel like an amateur."[103] Another tribute came from the Cambridge undergraduate and future writer Louis Wilkinson when *A Man of Honour* was performed at Cambridge, with Maugham in attendance. Wilkinson found Maugham unobtrusive and wary but was impressed with the play. "I remember how in those days," he wrote, "by comparison with Maugham, Shaw seemed to me a writer of pseudo-plays, a freak, Galsworthy a mediocrity, and Barrie a mess."[104]

After the opening of *A Man of Honour* Maugham's bohemian brother Harry decided to stay in London rather than return abroad, and he took rooms at 9 Cadogan Street. He continued to write unproduced plays in blank verse, and also wrote a lyric poem that was included in anthologies, beginning "There was a Knight of Bethlehem."[105] Maugham saw him from time to time, but Harry had grown increasingly quirky. He would not take trains, so when he went to the country he rode a bicycle. He often complained of vertigo. When the brothers met, Harry told Willie his work was trivial and shallow. Harry saw himself as the starving artist of integrity and was full of scorn for his socially ambitious brother who went to smart parties in Mayfair.

When Maugham went to call on him on July 27, 1904, a fine summer day, he found Harry lying fully dressed on his bed. On the table by the bed stood an empty bottle of nitric acid. Maugham put him in a cab and drove him to the hospital of his student days, St. Thomas's, through the Westminster traffic, past the Houses of Parliament, and over the Lambeth bridge. Harry died later that day. He had been lying in agony for three days when Maugham found him. The death certificate, issued by the Lambeth District, County of London, on July 28, said that Henry Neville Maugham, a thirty-six-year-old male of no occupation, had died of "collapse following poisoning by nitric acid. Suicide while of unsound mind." His younger brother's success and his own bitter frustration may have been factors in Harry's death. "I'm sure it wasn't only failure that made him kill himself," Maugham said. "It was the life he led."[106]

Depression was a trait common to all the Maugham brothers. The gentle Charles had terrible bouts of melancholy. The successful Frederic, who would one day become Lord Chancellor, suffered from a general lowness of spirits. Willie was plagued by depression in later life, and Harry became so depressed that he killed himself. In the eyes of some, his writing was far from worthless. The writer and critic E. V. Lucas called him "the real writer in the family."[107]

1

2

W. Somerset Maugham's grandfather, Robert Maugham (1), was a London solicitor who produced a weekly newspaper, *The Legal Observer*.

Maugham's beloved mother, Edith Mary (2), died of consumption when Maugham was eight.

The British Embassy in Paris (3), where the future writer was born on January 25, 1874.

3

5

Orphaned at the age of ten, Maugham (4) went to England to live with his uncle, the Reverend Henry MacDonald Maugham (5), vicar of Whitstable, and model for the miserly priest in *Of Human Bondage.*

4

The vicarage (6), a spacious, ivy-covered house, where Maugham found little joy.　　6

7

Maugham, in chair second from right, was teased because of his stammer when he attended the King's School in Canterbury (7). Although a good student, he made appearances in the Black Book (8). Three mentions resulted in a caning.

8

Two men who influenced his early life were Oscar Wilde (9), imprisoned as a homosexual in 1895, and John Ellingham Brooks (10), an esthete who spent most of his life in Capri, and who was Maugham's first lover.

11

At the age of 18, Maugham enrolled as a medical student (11) in St. Thomas's Hospital, where he could observe "life in the raw."

12   13

Friends of Maugham's early years included Adney Walter Payne (12), his roommate for more than ten years; Aleister Crowley (13), "The Beast," on whom he modeled the main character in his 1908 novel *The Magician;* Hugh Walpole (14), whom he savagely parodied in *Cakes and Ale;* Ada Leverson (15), who had been Oscar Wilde's "Sphinx";

14   15

6   17

Violet Hunt (16), whose novels he admired, and with whom he had an affair; Henry James (17), whose writing he thought mannered; H. G. Wells (18), who eventually became his neighbor in the South of France; and Arnold Bennett (19), who once asked Maugham to share a mistress.

18   19

20

Ethel Irving (20) starred in Maugham's first hit play, *Lady Frederick,* in 1907; Fay Compton and C. Aubrey Smith (21) were in *Caesar's Wife* in 1919; Irene Vanbrugh (22) did the revival of *Caroline* in 1926; and Marie Tempest and Graham Browne (23) appeared in *Penelope* at the Comedy Theatre in 1908.

23

21

22

24

25

Maugham (24), the successful young play-wright in his thirties, asked the beautiful young actress Ethelwyn Sylvia Jones (25)—here shown playing the maid in Maugham's *Penelope*—to marry him, but she turned him down.

Gerald Kelly (26), who later became President of the Royal Academy, painted about 30 portraits of Maugham.

27

The best-known of Kelly's portraits (27) is called "The Jester."

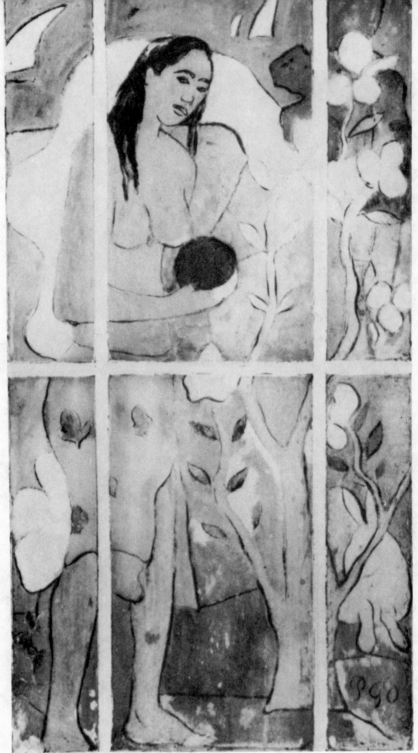

29 The three first American editions (29) of Maugham's best-known novels were all published by Doubleday & Company, which remained his American publisher until his death.

Maugham began collecting modern art when he bought this Gauguin-on-glass (28) in 1916 for $200, while on a trip to Tahiti to research *The Moon and Sixpence.*

30

Bette Davis and Leslie
Howard (30) in the
movie version of
Of Human Bondage.

Greta Garbo and
George Brent (31) in
the movie made from
Maugham's 1925
novel, *The Painted
Veil.*

31

Gwendolen Maud Syrie Barnardo (32), daughter of the founder of the famous Barnardo's homes for boys.

Syrie Barnardo became Mrs. Henry Wellcome (33), wife of a wealthy Wisconsin-born drug manufacturer . . .

32

33

34   . . . and, after her divorce (34), Mrs. W. Somerset Maugham.

Chapter Five

*A fit scene for a group by Watteau; and standing on
the lawn one thought to see Gilles, habited in white,
with pink bows on his dainty shoes, looking at one
with tired and mocking eyes, his lips trembling. But
whether with a sob repressed or with a gibe, who can
tell?*

Maugham, *A Writer's Notebook*

MAUGHAM LEFT for France after Harry's funeral to see his brother
Charles, who had taken over the Maugham legal office in Paris and
was spending the summer in a rented house in suburban Meudon. On
black-bordered stationery Maugham communicated from Meudon with
his agent, Morris Colles, asking if Colles could get him a commission
for the Christmas number of a magazine. From Paris he complained
that Colles had charged him fifteen shillings for postage. He had finished another novel, *The Merry-Go-Round*, which Heinemann was
bringing out in September, and he urged Colles "to impress upon Heinemann the necessity of advertising it well."[1]

At his brother's summer house he met Gerald Kelly, an engaging and
talkative Irishman; it was the start of a sixty-year friendship. Like
Maugham, Kelly had been raised in a vicarage. His father was vicar of
Camberwell, and his mother was independently wealthy. Kelly went to
Eton, and started painting watercolors while in South Africa convales-
cing after an illness. He then went to Trinity College, Cambridge, where
he did no work and had a thoroughly good time. At Cambridge he
made friends with Aleister Crowley, the self-described religious
prophet, whom newspaper headlines called "The Beast" and "The
Wickedest Man in the World," and whose motto was: Do what thou
wilt shall be the whole of law. Crowley eventually married Kelly's sister
Rose.

After Cambridge, in 1901, Kelly went to Paris to study art and develop his taste for pretty girls and fine Bordeaux. He took a studio on the rue Campagne-Première, a cul-de-sac off the boulevard Montparnasse. It was the Paris of the Impressionists, and Kelly was convinced that Manet's "Olympia" was the greatest picture ever painted. He had an introduction to the art dealer Paul Durand-Ruel, thanks to whom he met some of the painters and sculptors whose names are now legendary. He went to see Monet in Giverny, and met Degas, Rodin, and Maillol, who told him: *"Quelquefois je me perds—qu'est-ce que je fais? Je vais à la porte, je l'ouvre, et j'appelle Clothilde. Elle vient, qu'est-ce que je fais? Je lève sa jupe, je vois ses jambes admirables, et ses cuisses splendides, et je retrouve le marbre."* ("Sometimes I lose my way—what do I do? I go to the door, open it, and call Clothilde. She comes, what do I do? I raise her skirt, I see her admirable legs and her splendid thighs, and I find my way back to the marble.")[2]

Kelly made friends with Marcel Schwob, an essayist and short-story writer who was married to the actress Marguerite Moréno. Schwob, who had written French adaptations of *Hamlet* and *Macbeth* for Sarah Bernhardt, was said to be a morphine addict and to have sexual relations with his Chinese butler. Through Schwob, Kelly met Paul Léautaud, an eccentric writer whose *Journal Littéraire* Maugham admired. Léautaud gave Kelly French lessons, in exchange for which Kelly painted Léautaud's portrait.[3]

Crowley came to Paris at about the same time and stayed with Kelly, thus enlarging this bohemian group. Crowley had inherited a fortune when he came of age, and spent much of it on research into the occult and the publication of his poetry. He found Kelly in his Whistler-Velázquez period, darkening his palette to obtain Whistler's "low tone," which struck Crowley as the work of a hack. "He would use paint the color of Thames mud for the highlight on the cheek of a blonde," he said. Kelly talked about art a great deal and "laid down the law with unction," Crowley said. At his art classes Kelly found that the women students of Paris wanted to be treated like men, and he obliged, calling them *"mon vieux"* and when he went to the toilet, announcing: *"Je vais pisser."*[4]

When Kelly met Maugham in August 1904, the promising young writer and the promising young painter five years his junior took to each other at once. They both thought of themselves as cosmopolitan and unconventional English gentlemen turned artists. And they were both short, which has its importance, for Maugham was extremely conscious of his height and instinctively sought out persons who were no taller than himself. Kelly agreed with Maugham that Pater was over-rated. Maugham agreed with Kelly that the new painting eclipsed all else. The basis for a friendship was established.

After he went back to London, Maugham wrote Kelly asking if he could find him a flat in Paris.[5] He had just turned thirty and felt that he was in a rut. He wanted to get out of London and back to the bohemian life in Paris, where he could join the circle of expatriates devoted to the arts. There would be no language problem, for French had been his first language. While watching for an answer from Kelly about the flat he was awaiting the publication of a new novel, *The Merry-Go-Round*, which was to come out in September. The book consisted of three independent stories linked by one character, Miss Ley, a hardheaded spinster, who had already appeared as Bertha's aunt in *Mrs. Craddock*. As Maugham said in *The Summing Up*, "I was myself living in several sets that had no connection with one another, and it occurred to me that it might give a truer picture of life if one could carry on at the same time the various stories, of equal importance, that were enacted during a certain period in different circles." He wanted the book to be like "one of those huge frescos in an Italian cloister in which all manner of people are engaged in all manner of activities, but which the eye embraces in a single look."[6] He later conceded that the experiment had failed because "it lacks the continuous line that directs the reader's interest."[7] The three stories in *The Merry-Go-Round* were those of Basil Kent and Jennie Bush, which he had already used in *A Man of Honour*; the daughter of the Dean of Tercanbury, who falls in love with a young poet dying of tuberculosis; and a married woman who commits adultery with a young rogue but redeems herself by becoming a better wife.

In the novel Maugham further refined Basil Kent's hapless marriage by making him a writer who is working on a historical novel set in Italy, as he himself had been several years earlier. Publication is a disappointment to Basil: "It appeared that this book, which he had imagined would raise him at once to a literary position of some emi-nence, was no more than prentice work, showing more promise than performance." Maugham examined more carefully in the novel than in the play the theme of the destructiveness of virtue. "Society has made its own decalogue," he wrote. "A code just fit for middling people, who are neither very good nor very bad; but the odd thing is it punishes you as severely if you act above its codes as if you act below." He again employed the vocabulary of bondage to describe Basil's marriage: "He realized that he was manacled hand and foot with fetters that were only more intolerable because they consisted of nothing more substantial than the dread of causing pain." With Lady Vizard, Basil's mother, he returned to the theme of the mother who disappoints. Basil discovers through newspaper accounts of a divorce trial that his mother is no better than a harlot. Lady Vizard, another in Maugham's repertoire of disreputable women, is labeled by her name. A vizard is a visor or mask, and by extension a person who wears such a mask, such as the seventeenth-century Venetian whores who wore masks in public.

The other stories were also peopled with familiar Maugham types: the maternal older woman caring for a younger man, as in *Mrs. Craddock*, and the charming scoundrel who has an affair with a married woman. Maugham also introduced a doctor, a friend of Miss Ley's, who wants to give up medicine and travel because he sees life only as sickness. In his longing for exotic places the doctor speaks for the author: "My whole soul aches for the East, for Egypt and India and Japan; I want to know the corrupt, eager life of the Malays and the violent adventures of South Sea Islands. I may not get an answer to the riddle of life out in the open world, but I shall get nearer to it than here; I can get nothing more out of books and civilization."

Heinemann printed 3,000 copies of *The Merry-Go-Round*, and the reviews were good. *The Athenaeum* on October 29 said the three plots were developed with "considerable power" and the characterization was remarkable for its "depth and width of range." *The Academy* on October 15 commented on the character of the doctor and said the merry-go-round was a hospital "with its wards filled to choking with victims of a fantastic passion . . . there is no dull page, no prosy line, no coarseness, no offense in working out the problem which he has set himself to expound."[8]

Maugham was, however, disappointed. He thought Heinemann was not pushing the book, and wrote Colles with heavy irony on December 3, 1904: "I should like you to observe with what energy Heinemann is making the public see what an excellent book *The Merry-Go-Round* is."[9] When sales continued to drag he blamed Colles for not pressing Heinemann to advertise and decided to break with him. In a letter from Capri, where Maugham was spending the month of July 1905, he wrote Colles: "I think I should tell you that owing to the lamentable failure of *The Merry-Go-Round*, I propose to make my own arrangements with regard to my next novel. Under these circumstances I daresay you will prefer to return to me such manuscripts of mine as you have . . . In thus terminating the connection between us I should like to express my thanks for your efforts on my behalf, and my regret that they have not been more profitable to both of us."[10]

Colles protested that the fault was not his, which led to further reproach from Maugham on July 29: "With regard to *The Merry-Go-Round* I think we must agree to differ: I do not wish to enter into recriminations; but I cannot help thinking that what is obvious to me now, your experience might have suggested to you then, namely that when a publisher does not like a book and has made up his mind that it will not sell, one might just as well throw it in the Thames as let him publish it."[11]

Maugham fired his agent but heard from him again four years later. Colles sued him in the High Court in December 1909. He claimed that he had sent Maugham's play *The Explorer* to the actor-manager Lewis Waller, who produced the play in 1908. He wanted his commission. Maugham argued that Colles had had nothing to do with placing the play. "After Mr. Colles had the play in his possession for a year and a half," he testified, "I sent it to two other agents. They did not have any success with it, and I then tried to place it myself. I practically rewrote it, and after many years, I succeeded." The judge summed up in Maugham's favor, but the jury ruled in favor of Colles, who was awarded twenty-one pounds ten shillings.[12]

As disappointed as Maugham was with Heinemann, he remained tied to him, for Heinemann had finally agreed to publish *The Land of the Blessed Virgin*. It had languished since 1899, and Maugham had rewritten it in 1903, making a quick trip to Seville in April to freshen his impressions. It came out in January 1905, in an edition of 1,250 copies, half of which were remaindered. Maugham's impressions of Andalusia were patterned after George Borrow's *The Bible in Spain* and Richard Ford's *Gatherings from Spain*. The reviews were lukewarm, except for one in *The Times Literary Supplement,* which said; "He has his pen well under control . . . he has a sincere desire to find the right word for the beauty which he genuinely loves. . . . His book thus, even when the desire is beyond his power of satisfying it, has a value of its own." The reviewer was Virginia Stephen, then twenty-three, who later became known under her married name, Virginia Woolf.[13] Eventually she and Maugham met and became friends, and she continued to regard his work with sympathy.

Maugham had returned to the London flat he shared with Walter Payne. In 1900 they had moved to 27 Carlisle Mansions, a block of orange brick apartment houses in a somewhat seedy section of West-minster, patronized by clergymen and retired army officers. Maugham told Payne that he felt like a tramcar running on its line from terminus to terminus and needed to get away. Payne could not keep the flat by himself, and so the furniture was sold for what it could fetch, and within a month Maugham was in Paris.[14]

He did not, however, go alone. Several years earlier he had met a young Oxford undergraduate named Harry Philips and they had become friends. Maugham had once spent the weekend with Philips and his parents at their home in Staffordshire, where Maugham shocked them with his views on religion, and was not asked again. When Philips failed his exams Maugham asked him to come to Paris as his secretary-companion. It seems rather pretentious for a not very successful writer to have needed a secretary, but Philips went along mainly as a friend, and there is no evidence that he ever typed any of Maugham's correspondence. Philips is a sketchy figure in Maugham's life, who was never mentioned by Gerald Kelly, and it is only through his letters to the French Maugham expert Joseph Dobrinsky that his role in Maugham's life became known. Their friendship sounds as if it might have developed into a love affair. Philips worried that Maugham would grow tired of him, for he sometimes behaved badly. "One incident in the book *Of Human Bondage*," he wrote, "was undoubtedly an episode in our friendship not very creditable to me which he attributed to her [Mildred]. . . . At the time, I was somewhat ashamed as I realized that I had hurt his feelings more than I thought."[15] It was Harry Philips who said that Mildred was based on a young man when he wrote Dobrinsky: "Mildred was a composite figure and certain episodes connected with incidents in his life. The real Mildred was a youth."[16] Philips soon had enough of Maugham, went back to London late in 1905, and married the daughter of a wealthy family, the Montefiores. "His cynicism distressed me," he said of Maugham, "and being a person who has always acted on impulse, I found it difficult to live with someone who believed that no one did anything without a motive."[17]

In February 1905 Maugham and Philips moved into the fifth-floor flat Kelly had found at 3 rue Victor-Considérant, near the Lion de Belfort, with a *vue imprenable* on the Montparnasse cemetery. Kelly and Maugham shared a *femme de ménage*. It was the Paris of *La Belle Epoque*, of small crafts, good living and low prices, of silk-blouse shops, goat-milking in the streets, Caran d'Ache cartoons, and gas lamps. The English pound yielded 25 francs, and a good dinner cost 2 francs 50. It was the Paris of music halls and *café chantants*, Lautrec's Paris, Degas' Paris. You went to the Concert Rouge to hear a chamber music quartet and ordered *cerises au cognac*. There were still horse-drawn buses, and yellow fiacres whose drivers wore shiny white top hats and would take you anywhere within the city limits for a franc and a half. A cab with a green light meant that the horse's stable was in Montparnasse.[18]

But 1905 was also the year of the automobile exposition at the Grand Palais. The first line of the Métro, Nation-Porte Dauphine, had been completed in 1901. There were electric lights, and in phonograph booths one could listen to Caruso records. Maugham's routine, which he would follow to the end of his life, was to write in the morning until about 12:30. He was working on *The Bishop's Apron*, a novelized version of his unproduced play *Loaves and Fishes*, which he would finish in Paris and dedicate to Harry Philips. After lunch he went out, often to museums. Kelly took him to see the Impressionists, whose pictures had recently been accepted by the Luxembourg. Maugham, who would one day own an important collection of Impressionists, admitted, to his shame, that he could not make head or tail of them.[19] On Sundays he and Philips went to the Café de la Paix and drank grenadine. In the evening Maugham often went to the theater (he admired the actress Dorziat). He particularly liked the Grand Guignol and his favorite sketch was a graphic display of sadomasochism called "*La Dernière Torture.*"[20]

In March, Kelly introduced Maugham to Arnold Bennett, who had been in Paris since 1903. Bennett had a flat in Montmartre, at 4 rue de Calais, and was working on what would be his finest novel, *The Old Wives' Tale*. At that time he still called himself Enoch Arnold Bennett, and the slightly ridiculous, provincial patina of "Enoch" clung to him. Born in 1867 in the grim industrial Midlands region known as the Five Towns, Bennett was the son of a potter who had made himself into a solicitor. He worked as a shorthand clerk in his father's office, and came to London from the provinces, like Shaw and Wells, to make a name for himself. He published a story in the *Yellow Book* and became editor of the magazine *Woman*. His first novel, *A Man from the North*, was published in 1898. Bennett kept the pot boiling to make ends meet and wrote such books as *Journalism for Women* and *What the Public Wants*. He also wrote literary causeries under the name Jacob Tonson, reviewed a book a day, and from Paris wrote an advice column under the name Sarah Volatile. Bennett was the authentic writing machine and he kept a careful count of his daily production. In 1900 he wrote 196 articles, 6 short stories, a one-act play, 2 full-length plays, and a novel. Far more than Maugham, he was a businessman of letters, who once wrote five letters in a single day to his agent, J. B. Pinker. His total surviving correspondence to Pinker consists of 2,600 letters.[21] Henry James said that Bennett regarded life as a gigantic orange to be squeezed indefinitely for the juice of fiction. The charge was: no art. Bennett returned the compliment, saying of James: "I feel bogged down in his books—those awful involved sentences. They've as many folds as a box-pleat kilt."[22] Bennett, like Maugham, had nothing in common with James. He was a hard worker who had raised himself from lower-middle-class origins. His abilities were a plodding honesty and a supreme matter-of-factness.

Bennett was thirty-eight when he met Maugham, who was seven years his junior. His tilted nose, receding chin, bright, inquiring eyes, and tuft of upstanding hair made him look like one of those provincials in Balzac who have come to the capital to make good. Clive Bell, the art historian and Bloomsbury figure, who was in Paris at the time, described him as "an insignificant little man and ridiculous to boot." His upper teeth stuck out, he talked through his nose, and his thumbs were usually hooked in the armholes of his waistcoat.[23]

Bennett and Maugham had several things in common: a concern for the business side of publishing, more tenacity than natural ability, and a stammer. Bennett's stammer, which had developed when he was a child, was worse than Maugham's, it was outrageous, and it retained the broad flat Midlands *a*. His mother thought the stammer had been caused by a fall from his high chair when he was three and was scolded by his father. H. G. Wells thought it was connected with a sexual shock in infancy. Bennett tried hypnotism and went to Scotland to see a speech therapist, but nothing worked.[24]

Arriving in Paris two years before Maugham, Bennett had thrown himself into the expatriate life. He visited Gerald Kelly's studio and thought his work was good and original. Kelly said that painters were afraid of making mistakes, afraid of being vulgar, they all painted the same things. He said that academic artists had admitted to him, "We paint like governesses." Kelly took Bennett to dinner at the Chat Blanc, a hangout for English and American artists on the rue d'Odessa, where Bennett was shocked to see an American girl and an illustrator throwing bread at each other and singing American songs at the top of their lungs. He thought that was the sort of thing that spoiled Montparnasse.[25]

On March 3, 1905, Bennett invited Maugham to tea at his Mont-martre flat. Bennett found his guest calm, almost lethargic.

> He took two cups of tea with pleasure and absolutely refused a third; one knew instantly from his tone that nothing would induce him to take a third. He ate biscuits and *gaufrettes* very quickly, almost greedily, one after the other, without a pause, and then suddenly stopped. He smoked two cigarettes furiously, in less time than I smoked one, and solidly declined a third. I liked him. He said he had sold a play to Liebler through Fred Kerr [an actor and onetime manager of the Court Theatre], on the terms of £300 down, and £100 every quarter until they produced it—in advance of royalties. I asked him if he liked the Quartier Montparnasse and he said, "Yes; the atmosphere of it is rather like Oxford."[26]

Bennett's account of the sale of *Lady Frederick* was not quite ac-curate. Fred Kerr had mentioned the play to George C. Tyler, who was on his annual swing through Europe looking for properties. Tyler, born in Chillicothe, Ohio, was the Broadway producer who had made half a million dollars with Hall Caine's *The Christian* and brought Eleonora Duse and Mrs. Patrick Campbell to America. (Mrs. Campbell was one of the first stars to get a three-dollar top.) Tyler went to see Maugham in Paris and liked *Lady Frederick* well enough to give him a thousand dollars for a year's option. He said the play needed gingering up, and Maugham promised to write two dozen more epigrams. He also bought Maugham his first two cocktails, then a novelty on the Continent, start-ing him on a life-long habit of a dry martini before lunch and dinner. "Maugham told me afterward," Tyler recalled "that when he left me that afternoon with his check for a thousand in his pocket, he was stepping on his left ear with his right hind foot."[27]

Tyler liked *Lady Frederick* because it was built around a star part. "With his usual canniness," he wrote, "Maugham was figuring that a nice fat part that some actress would take a shine to would be good medicine for sales purposes—and I thought I knew just where to go for the person to play it." But no actress would touch it because of the dressing-table scene, in which Lady Frederick, to discourage a young suitor, lets him watch as she makes up her face and dresses her hair, so that he can see how artificial her beauty is.

When I'd bought it [Tyler wrote], I'd had Ellis Jeffreys in mind . . . but she wouldn't touch it with a ten-foot pole. I gave it to Mrs. Campbell to read and, with her usual talent for coming straight to the point, she asked if I meant to insult her. . . . By that time my year's option had run out, so I gave it up as a bad job, feeling pretty melancholy on Maugham's account and pretty sore on my own. . . . All I ever got out of it . . . was the privilege of giving Maugham his first cocktail and paying him a thousand good dollars when he needed them in the worst way.

Maugham thought Bennett "looked like the managing clerk in a city office." His flat, with its piano and fake Empire furniture, gave him the impression of a man "who saw himself in a certain role, which he was playing carefully, but into the skin of which he had not quite got." Kelly said that Maugham was Bennett's exact opposite in everything—dapper, neat, cultivated and urbane—and that they disliked each other instantly. Once when the three of them went to dinner, Maugham told the waiter in his impeccable French, *"Vous me donnerez un anneau."* "You know, Maugham," Bennett said with his Midlands drawl, "the French don't call it an 'anno,'" they call it a 'rong' [*rond*]." Maugham became gray with rage. He had given an overdressed, provincial mountebank an opportunity to show off in public at his expense.[28]

And yet, even though he found Bennett bumptious and common, they continued to dine together in Montmartre or Montparnasse, after which Bennett would play Beethoven on the piano in his flat. One evening Bennett said: "Look here, I have a proposal to make to you."

"Oh," Maugham said.

"I have a mistress with whom I spend two nights a week. She has another gentleman with whom she spends two other nights. She likes to have her Sundays to herself and she's looking for someone who'll take her the two nights that she's free. I've told her about you. She likes writers. I'd like to see her nicely fixed up and I thought it would be a good plan if you took her the two nights that she has vacant."

"It sounds rather cold-blooded to me," Maugham said.

"She's not an ignorant woman, you know," Bennett said. "Not by any manner of means. She reads a great deal, Madame de Sévigné and all that, and she can talk very intelligently."

Maugham was not tempted.[29]

The two writers also discussed agents, and Maugham confessed that he was down on Colles, who had been Bennett's first agent. Bennett had found that Colles did not acknowledge receipt of stories and was not much good at placing them. In 1902 Bennett had switched to Pinker, of whom he thought highly. Pinker was lending him fifty pounds a month while he wrote the Great English Novel in Paris. "There is no other really good agent in England," Bennett said. "The difference between a good and a bad agent might mean a difference of a thousand a year to me." On June 11 Bennett wrote Pinker: "I think I have got you a new client in the person of W. Somerset Maugham. At any rate, after some weeks of my discourses on agents, he demanded from me your address yesterday and said he meant to write you. I have lately got to know him quite well. He seems to me a man who will make his way."[30]

Maugham wrote Pinker on June 26, 1905, before informing Colles that he wanted to drop him: "My friend Arnold Bennett has given me your address. Would you like to place my new novel for me? It is very different in style from my previous work; it is very light and is supposed to be humorous. It is quite moral. Heinemann has published my last three books but I am tired of him."[31] Maugham was concerned that his reputation for writing scandalous books would prejudice Pinker against him and took pains to assure him that he had turned over a new leaf. With the new novel Pinker became Maugham's agent.

Maugham was also introduced by Gerald Kelly to the Chat Blanc, near the Gare Montparnasse. There was a narrow upstairs room, with three tables arranged in a horseshoe, which were reserved for English and American artists. The *prix fixe* was 2 francs 50, served by a motherly waitress named Marie, who wore a black dress and a white cap. The atmosphere was boisterous. Arguments about painting and literature went on until the *patron* started stacking the chairs on top of tables. Among the regulars, besides Kelly, were two painters whom Maugham used as characters in his books: James Wilson Morrice and Roderic O'Conor. Morrice was a Canadian, whom he called Warren in his novel *The Magician* and described as "a small person, with a pate as shining as a billiard-ball, and a pointed beard. He had protruding, brilliant eyes." He was usually so drunk his hand could hardly hold a brush. Morrice recognized the doctor in Maugham, and his standing joke was to look up with grave importance from his *crème de menthe* and *oeufs sur le plat* and consult Maugham "on a matter concerning the welfare of art and artists. What would you do if . . . ," and then, with tedious elaboration, he would describe the symptoms of a repulsive disease.[32]

Roderic O'Conor, the other painter, was influenced by Cézanne and exhibited at the Salon d'Automne and the Indépendants. "His pictures," Clive Bell wrote, "were full of austere intentions unrealized." O'Conor had a gruff and disobliging manner, and disparaged the numerous painters he did not approve of.[33] Maugham called him O'Brien in *The Magician*, describing him as a tall, dark fellow with strong features, untidy hair, and a ragged black mustache. O'Brien, he wrote, was "an example of the fact that strength of will and an earnest purpose cannot make a painter. He's a failure, and he knows it, and the bitterness has warped his soul. If you listen to him, you'll hear every painter of eminence come under his lash. He can forgive nobody who's successful, and he never acknowledges merit in anyone till he's safely dead and buried."[34] In fact, Maugham owed a considerable debt to O'Conor for getting him interested in Gauguin and suggesting the theme of *The Moon and Sixpence*. O'Conor had made friends with Gauguin in Pont-Aven and had loaned Gauguin his studio in the rue du Cherche-Midi. He had paintings by Gauguin and drawings bearing humorous inscriptions. Maugham pumped him for information about Gauguin, went to his studio, and even bought several of his works to encourage him to talk.

The Magician himself was of course the noted Satanist Aleister Crowley, whom Maugham had also met at the Chat Blanc. Maugham was fascinated by Crowley, who was his direct opposite. Maugham was measured and tidy. Crowley practiced the cult of excess, and spoke in mumbo jumbo, which he said was the language of the angels. He talked of reincarnation. When someone called him a magician, he replied solemnly: "I would rather be known as the Brother of the Shadow."[35]

Extracts from his unpublished diary for 1907, some of which is written in strange symbols, give an idea of the man. He practiced yoga, alluded to occult rituals, and smoked hashish. He made a vow to refuse to answer questions: "A slip is to be punished with a razor-cut."

"Messing about with chemicals all day."

"I l——d Rose and slept like a dog."

"Looking back on the year, it seems one continued ecstasy. . . . Not since my Attainment in October has there been any falling away whatever. I am able to do automatic writing at will. . . . At last I've got to a stage where desire has utterly failed. I want nothing."[36]

The other side of Crowley was his wit. Once when Theodore Dreiser was hunting for the word for a young swan, he appealed to Crowley: "What is it? What would you call a young swan?"

"Why not call him Alfred?" Crowley asked.

Another time, when a woman asked him what American women's college would be suitable for her young daughter, Crowley said, "Radclyffe Hall" (the lesbian author of *The Well of Loneliness*).[37]

Maugham thought Crowley "was a fake, but not entirely a fake . . . the odd thing was that he had actually done some of the things he boasted of. As a mountaineer, he had made an ascent of K.2 in the Hindu Kush, the second highest mountain in India, and he made it without the elaborate equipment, the cylinders of oxygen and so forth, which render the endeavors of the mountaineers of the present day more likely to succeed. He did not reach the top, but got nearer to it than anyone had done before."[38]

Other than changing his name to Oliver Haddo, Maugham made no attempt to disguise Crowley in *The Magician*. Haddo was described as a tall, fleshy man given to flamboyant bragging and orotund phrases. Making his entrance at the Chat Blanc, which has become the Chien Noir, Haddo calls the waitress: "Marie, disembarrass me of this coat of frieze. Hang my sombrero upon a convenient peg." Spotting Warren, he says: "I grieve to see, O most excellent Warren, that the ripe juice of the *apéritif* has glazed your sparkling eye."

The comic tone changes when Maugham gets into the plot, which is best summed up briefly: Haddo is spurned by a young woman, and he takes his revenge by seducing her with magic spells and making her a sacrifice in one of his experiments, which include the manufacture of homunculi in test tubes. (Crowley was rumored to have driven women to madness and death.)

When *The Magician* appeared in 1908 Crowley was not amused.

Who would have believed! [he wrote] . . . *The Magician*, Oliver Haddo, was Aleister Crowley; his house, "Skene," was Boleskine [Crowley's home]. The hero's witty remarks were, many of them, my own. He

> [Maugham] had, like Arnold Bennett, not spared his shirt cuff. . . . I found phrase after phrase, paragraph after paragraph, page after page, bewilderingly familiar: and then I remembered that in my early days of the G. [olden] D. [awn] I had introduced Gerald Kelly to the Order and reflected that Maugham had become a great friend of Kelly's, and stayed with him at the Camberwell Vicarage. Maugham had taken some of the most private and personal incidents of my life, my marriage, my exploration, my adventures with big game, my magical opinions, ambitions and exploits and so on. He had added a number of the many absurd legends of which I was the central figure. He had patched all these together by innumerable strips of paper clipped from the books which I had told Gerald to buy. I had never supposed that plagiarism could have been so varied, extensive, and shameless.[39]

Crowley recalled that at the Chat Blanc, Maugham had "suffered terribly under the lash of universal contempt." When they met in London shortly after the book's publication Crowley told him: "I almost wish that you were an important writer."[40] Crowley took his revenge, not with a magic spell but in the December 30, 1908, issue of *Vanity Fair*. In an article signed "Oliver Haddo" he convincingly made the case that Maugham had plagiarized a number of books, by arranging in parallel columns the passage in *The Magician* and the passage it had been lifted from. The books that Crowley singled out were Mac-Gregor Mather's *Kabbalah Unveiled* (1897), Franz Hartmann's *The Life of Paracelsus* (1896), Eliphaz Levi's *Rituel et Dogme de la Haute Magie*, Mabel Collins' *The Blossom and the Fruit* (1888), Dumas's *Memoirs of a Physician*, and H. G. Wells's *The Island of Doctor Moreau* (1896). Maugham's method, Crowley wrote, was to "find a few books dealing with our subject and copy them wholesale into our books; sometimes verbatim, sometimes altering words here and there— for in the case of well-known authors it is best to make a pretense of not having copied verbatim."

This was not the first or the last time that Maugham would be accused of borrowing from other writers, and in a foreword to the 1933 edition of *The Moon and Sixpence* he defended himself by saying that "to make a fuss because one writer uses an incident that he has found in another's book is nonsense. By turning it to good account he makes it sufficiently his own. . . . I would say that any writer is justified in taking from another whatever can profit him." When he reread *The Magician* in later years he said: "I wondered how on earth I could have come by all the material concerning the black ends which I wrote of. I must have spent days and days reading in the library of the British Museum."[41]

In the summer of 1905, when Maugham was writing *The Magician*, he took Harry Philips to Capri, where they spent July and August in the Villa Valentino. Since his first visit Capri had become a refuge for homosexuals and lesbians. There was a colony of expatriates who had fled scandal, including the former vicar of Sandringham, who had been forced to leave England because of his devotion to choirboys. When one such expatriate was asked why he was in Capri, he replied: "A cloud—a cloud no bigger than a boy's hand." The Italians were tolerant, up to a point. Once when an English visitor was being too familiar with a young Caprese, a member of the *guardia* tapped him on the shoulder and said:—*Queste cose, signore, si fanno in casa privata.*[42]

Maugham felt comfortable there. He wrote Violet Hunt on August 25:

> One does nothing from morning till night, yet the day is so short that it seems impossible to find a moment. . . . Capri is as charming as ever it was, the people as odd: everybody is very immoral, but fortunately not so dull as those who kick over the traces often are. Each foreigner has his little scabrous history, which far from being whispered into the willing ear, is shouted from the rooftops. . . . All the morning I bathe; after luncheon I sleep till tea-time, then wander among the interminable vineyards, in the evening read or look at the moon. . . . In January I set out for the East.[43]

The most curious bit of Capri news was that his first lover, Ellingham Brooks, had married an heiress from Pennsylvania. This was Romaine Brooks, who would become well known as a painter and a lesbian. She was born Beatrice Romaine Goddard in 1874 (the same year as Maugham), and her mother, a Waterman, inherited a coal-mining fortune. Romaine first came to Capri in 1899, saw the shimmering island rising through the mist, tasted the wine in jars, smelled the pomegranates in bloom, and fell in love with the place. She met Brooks, who was captivated by her charm and boyishness. Returning in 1901, she found him despondent and contemplating suicide. His small annuity had dwindled and he was unable to support himself in lotus land. In 1902 Romaine's mother died and she came into money. She went back to Capri in 1903 and found Brooks selling his possessions to buy food.

She decided to marry him, hoping that "a pleasant unity through isolation might be achieved."[44]

The wedding, which Brooks's friend E. F. Benson called "a fit of aberration on the part of the bride and the bridegroom alike,"[45] took place on June 13, 1903. But this presumably platonic match between a homosexual and a lesbian did not work out. Brooks insisted on retaining a semblance of Edwardian decorum. Romaine wanted to dress like a boy, but her husband would not permit it. He intended to spend his wife's money to construct an impressive façade—a house in London and social position. Romaine disapproved of his pipe, his British gentleman exterior, and his talk about "our" money. By September 1904 they had broken up. Romaine went to London, with Brooks hurrying after to try to save the marriage. She bought him off with an allowance of three hundred pounds a year. Brooks remained in Capri the rest of his life, saved from insolvency by his wife, an early model of the independent woman, who said: "One should be a slave to nothing but one's toothbrush."

Romaine came regularly to Capri, where she was queen of the lesbian hive, and eventually she made her home in France, where she lived the painter's life. Her works, among them portraits of Cocteau and D'Annunzio, have a quality of brooding elegance, and hang in the Luxembourg. Maugham got to know her in the twenties, in the south of France, where she came with her great love, Natalie Barney, the *doyenne* of lesbians. They spent the summers in a villa near Beauvallon, called the *Trait d'Union* (Hyphen) because it consisted of two separate bungalows joined by a common dining room. Maugham called her "the Romantic Romaine."[46]

While on his holiday in Capri he heard that Gerald Kelly, still in Paris, had fallen ill because he was working and playing too hard. He wrote Kelly the first of a series of tutorial letters of advice on July 24. "By the stupidest carelessness (and I daresay at the bottom of your heart the feeling that it's very romantic and picturesque to cultivate a fine frenzy which ignores the matter of fact)," he said, "you are throwing away all your chances of becoming a better painter than Tom, Dick, or Harry. For the work you do when you're not well is rotten and you know as well as I do that no one has ever done valuable stuff unless he was backed by a vigorous physique. Do not take this lecture in bad part, but devise means whereby you may work well and keep healthy."[47] His advice applied to himself as well, for he believed in the need for physical health in order to work well, and considered a serene personal

life as necessary to the artist. He was resolutely opposed to the bohemian credo of burning the candle at both ends.

A teacher-pupil tone crept into his friendship with Kelly. When, in
1905, Kelly moved into new lodgings with a young dancer, Maugham
warned him that his new arrangement would be expensive and rejoiced
that he was uninvolved. Paul Léautaud ran into Kelly near the Odéon
on November 20, 1906, and reported that "he now lives on rue Tour-
laque, behind the Montmartre cemetery. . . . He is still living with his
dancer and seems happy! He never stops congratulating himself. I
asked him when I would see my portrait, while showering him with
compliments, with praise, both he and his painting. Boastful and vain
as he is, he was delighted. He used to be clean-shaven, à l'anglaise, but
has let his mustache grow. That's what love does to you."[48]

When Kelly's dancer left him, he was disheartened, and at Maugham's
suggestion he went on holiday to Burma. On March 1, 1909,
Maugham, who thought Kelly had stayed away too long, because he
had five commissions which would not wait indefinitely, sent another of
his little lectures:

> Many people have just as much talent as you and it does not avail them
> for want of character, and I know many people who have infinitely
> more strength of character than you. But that too does not avail them
> because they lack the talent: genius is a combination of talent and
> character, but character to a certain extent—I do not know how much,
> but I believe enormously—can be acquired; but you cannot acquire it
> without a certain effort. You seem to have hereditarily more against you
> than most people, but that does not matter if you only see the facts
> clearly and arm yourself against them.[49]

This letter again reflected his convictions about himself, for he felt that
he had acquired character and combined it with talent. So, apparently,
had Kelly, who eventually became a highly successful portrait painter.
Maugham gave a prophetic description of him in Of Human Bondage
as the character Lawson: "Lawson's all right," says another character.
"He'll go back to England, become a fashionable portrait painter, earn
ten thousand a year, and be an A.R.A. before he's forty." Kelly not
only became an A.R.A. but president of the Royal Academy, in 1949.
Clive Bell said he was the best president since Joshua Reynolds.[50]

It was at this time, from Capri, that Maugham sent his letter of
dismissal to his agent, Morris Colles, who had taken Maugham on

when he was a young unknown. He signed on with Pinker, telling him he did not want his new novel, *Loaves and Fishes*, to go to Heinemann, who he thought "had gone slack of late," and had sold only 2,000 of the 3,000 printed copies of *The Merry-Go-Round*. He suggested Chapman and Hall, who he said were "very anxious to have a book of mine, and I imagine they will give an advance of 150 pounds and a good royalty."[51] He also warned Pinker that he was considered something of an enfant terrible in America. "My novels have apparently been too shocking for the American public [but] . . . I don't think there is in *Loaves and Fishes* anything that would bring a blush to the cheek of an American matron."[52]

The chairman of Chapman and Hall was Arthur Waugh, a distinguished editor and the father of Alec and Evelyn. He was, in fact, less than anxious to publish Maugham, and wrote Pinker: "As a rule I have not cared for his stories, as I think they are too gloomy and pessimistic for the general public to take to them. However, I should be very glad to see the M.S. [of *Loaves and Fishes*, later retitled *The Bishop's Apron*] and perhaps you will let us know at the same time what sort of ideas Mr. Maugham has about terms."[53] Six days later Waugh offered an advance of 75 pounds and added: "I believe I am right in saying that 75 pounds is as large an advance as he has ever had for a six-shilling novel."[54]

Maugham, who was back in Paris, was hoping for twice that, but agreed to the terms, telling Pinker: "I rather fancy Chapman and Hall because they have no one of any particular importance and it would be worth while for them to boom me. I am sick of playing third fiddle to Hall Caine" (the best-selling author of *The Manxman*).[55] He was leaving for Greece and Egypt and asked Pinker to find him some commissions for travel articles. He also asked Pinker to place a posthumous novel by his brother Harry, *Richard Hawkblood*, an Italian romance in the Maurice Hewlett style.

Tying up his unfinished business with Colles before his departure, he complained that a check he had received was "so small." He had published a sketch in the *Lady's Field*, and wondered why they had not paid. "Will you press them," he asked Colles, "and suggest that if the money is not forthcoming, I must put the matter in the hands of the Authors' Society?"[56] He was aware of every penny owed to him, and intended to get his hands on it. To Pinker, when one of his stories was rejected by the *Bystander*, he fumed that the editor was "a blithering idiot." However, the *Bystander* did publish "The Fortunate Painter and the Honest Jew," a story with a Paris setting, the following year. He had also been published in the *Strand* magazine, the *Sketch*, and the *Daily Mail*. Again he insisted to Pinker that he would write nothing shocking. "If you can get me anything by the way of a commission for any short stories I can be trusted to be suitably moral," he wrote. "The prices I have been getting lately have been four or five guineas a thousand."[57] Maugham arranged for his earnings to be deposited at the London City Midland Bank at 50 Shaftesbury Avenue while he was traveling.

This concern with living down his reputation as a shocking writer was the sign of a transformation that had come over Maugham. With the possible exception of his cardboard Renaissance novel *The Making of a Saint*, he had written honest books, based on his experience and feelings, set in places he knew firsthand. He had gotten nowhere, and was now bent on success. He could not see why Hall Caine made thousands of pounds while he, Maugham, could barely pay his tailor. He was tired of being called gloomy and pessimistic. For the next ten years, from 1905 until 1915, Maugham wrote for the marketplace. Between 1905 and 1907 he wrote three out-and-out potboilers; his first stage success in 1907 saved him from hatching any more. He was too busy after that writing plays.

The Bishop's Apron was a rewrite of his unproduced play. He wrote it because he already had the dialogue and the plot and was able to turn it out in a few weeks. It described Canon Spratte's campaign to wed a beer heiress and obtain a bishopric. The tone was farcical, the dialogue epigrammatic. This insipid period piece, dedicated to Harry Philips and published in February 1906, while he was in Egypt, found favor with reviewers. The *Bookman* in its April issue said "the whole book is an admirable blend of cynical gaiety and broadly farcical comedy; it is the smartest and most genuinely humorous novel that the season has yet given us." The *Punch* reviewer, who called himself the Baron de B(ook) W(orms) said on February 21 that it was "the best clerical novel since *Barchester Towers*." Maugham's opinion of it, in a letter to Violet Hunt, was: "It seems to me that parts of it are good, but like all my work it is very uneven."[58]

His next effort, *The Explorer*, came out in December 1907 and was the occasion of his return to Heinemann, from whose fold he would not again stray. The attitudes of jingoism and racial superiority, which he had ridiculed in *The Hero* and *Mrs. Craddock* he now made his own in this Kiplingesque tale of a rugged and patriotic explorer, "an ancient

Roman who buys his clothes in Savile Row," who sets out to stop the slave trade in East Africa. This too was the fictionalized adaptation of an unproduced play, the one that was the cause of litigation by his first agent, Morris Colles. Maugham had shifted from the slum novel to the escapist fiction the British needed in order to forget their domestic problems. He pandered to the public mood by celebrating imperialism, and in the figure of his protagonist, Alec Mackenzie, who was based on Henry Morton Stanley, he played to the popular admiration for the empire builder who went to Africa to take up the white man's burden. Again the reviewers liked it. *The Athenaeum* on January 4, 1908, wrote that "the hero represents what is, perhaps, the finest type of man that these islands produce." The book left a bad taste in Maugham's mouth. "I have a great dislike for it," he wrote, "and if it were possible would willingly suppress it. At one time it irked my conscience like the recollection of a discreditable action."[59] *The Explorer*, written in a month, was dedicated to Mrs. G. W. Steevens, the generous hostess of Merton Abbey, whose husband had died in Africa.

The Magician was an attempt to cash in on a novel of the occult at a time when a wave of occultism was sweeping England and when other books with a similar subject, such as E. F. Benson's *Image in the Sand*, had done well. *The Nation* on March 11, 1909, pointed out Maugham's "quickness to seize the theme of the moment," and *The Athenaeum* on December 5, 1908, said that he "alternately plays the parts of the Balzac of *Peau de Chagrin*, of the Du Maurier who created Svengali, and of an H. G. Wells consistently logical in his most fantastic moments."[60]

Maugham did not like *The Magician* much better than *The Explorer*. He took great pains over it, but there was no conviction in the writing. "To me it was all moonshine," he wrote. "I did not believe a word of it. It was a game I was playing. A book written under these conditions can have no life in it."[61] When he sent the manuscript to Pinker in October 1906 he wrote: "Here is the book. I have come to the conclusion it is very dull and stupid; and I wish I were an outside Broker, or Hall Caine, or something equally despicable."[62] The reason *The Magician* was not published until two years after Pinker received the manuscript was that once again Maugham was having publisher problems. Disgruntled with the poor sales of *The Bishop's Apron*, he told Pinker that Arthur Waugh should "bury his head in a bag."[63] Methuen wanted to sign him to a three-novel contract, and took *The Magician* as the first, paying him a seventy-five-pound advance. When it was set in type, one of the partners who read it was so shocked that he stopped publication. Maugham was furious. "What pigs they are," he wrote Pinker. Eventually Heinemann took it, and Maugham became embroiled in a tedious quarrel with Methuen over the three novels he owed them.[64]

Maugham's three potboilers represent the low point of his career. As an admirer of Goethe, he must have realized that he had made a Faustian pact to win success. The progression was from honesty to dishonesty and from writing what he knew to writing fabrications. When he wrote out of his experience, his work was authentic. When he did not, it was contrived and false. The best scenes in *The Magician* are those in the *Chien Noir (Chat Blanc)*, which are pure reportage. Later, in his short stories, he returned to the colonial themes of *The Explorer*, but this time he wrote about places he had been to and people he had met.

The first three months of 1906 found Maugham on a trip to Greece and Egypt. He had long wanted to visit exotic lands and could now afford it thanks to the thousand dollars George Tyler had paid for *Lady Frederick*.

By January 22 he was in Alexandria, having taken a boat from Venice to Port Said. He had found the sea "indescribably dull," he wrote Violet Hunt. "The people whom it excites to poetic effusions take care to know it only from the beach." In Port Said he stayed with a friend from medical school, a Dr. Ron, who worked in the sanitary department there. He was going up the Nile, spending a month in Cairo, and planning to learn Arabic, for this was the first time he had found himself in a country where he was entirely ignorant of the language. "I cannot tell you how awkward I find it," he told Violet Hunt. "It is insufferable not to be able to ask your way in the street, or to tell a cabman where to drive."[65]

Back in London in April, he found a single room in the same building in which his old friend Walter Payne was living, at 56A Pall Mall, between St. James's Palace and Trafalgar Square. During the day he used Payne's sitting room as a study, and there he wrote Pinker harassing letters about money. "Has the *Ladies' Realm* or whatever it is coughed up yet?" he asked. "This is the season when my tailor and hatter send me bills."[66] To raise money he contributed to a number of long-forgotten publications, such as *Windsor Magazine* and *Printers' Pie Annual*.

Despite his note to Pinker, Maugham's money demands were less sartorial than romantic. He was infatuated with a young woman of

extravagant tastes who had rich admirers. He could not afford the luxu-
ries that other men gave her, and thus he was determined to write a
book that would earn him the three or four hundred pounds to enable
him to hold his own with his rivals. He hoped the publication of *The
Bishop's Apron* would give him an edge, but by the time it appeared in
1906, Maugham had lost interest in the young woman.[67] There is no
way of knowing who this young woman was. And if indeed it was a
woman, it shows that he was still trying to deny his homosexuality by
forming romantic attachments with the opposite sex.

It was in April of that year, 1906, that Maugham met the one great
female love of his life. In his memoir *A Writer's Notebook* he described
her as "a woman of ripe and abundant charms, rosy of cheek and fair
of hair, with eyes as blue as the summer sea, with rounded lines and full
breasts. She leaned somewhat to that type of woman that Rubens has
set down forever in the ravishing person of Helena Fourment." The
entry is dated 1904, but Maugham often misdated his entries, and since
there is a jump in the published notebooks from 1904 to 1908, it is
likely that he inserted comments from that period under another year.
It is hard to accept the version that he met his "Helena Fourment" in
1904 for two reasons. Having fallen in love, would he then have gone
to Paris in February 1905 to spend most of the year there? Also, in
Looking Back, where he goes into the love affair in detail, he specifies
that the first time he slept with her he took her back to his single room
in Pall Mall. It was not until his return from his Middle East trip, in
April 1906, that he moved into the Pall Mall room.

Maugham made his lady love the model for the lighthearted and
promiscuous Rosie Driffield in *Cakes and Ale*. In reality Rosie was
Ethelwyn Sylvia Jones, the daughter of the society dramatist Henry
Arthur Jones, who had written such hits as *Whitewashing Julia, The
Case of Rebellious Susan,* and *Dolly Reforming Herself.*

Jones had a family of three boys and four girls and was a friend of
Mrs. Steevens. It was at Merton Abbey, during one of her summer
afternoon parties, that Maugham met Ethelwyn, who was known as
Sue; she came with her father and her teenaged sister Doris. Born in
1883 at Lothian Lodge, New Hampton, Sue Jones was an actress who
had begun her stage career at the age of fourteen in *The Manoeuvres of
Jane*, one of her father's plays. She also played Shakespeare under
Herbert Beerbohm Tree. In 1906 she would have been twenty-three. In
1902 she had married a producer named Montague Vivian Leveaux, but
the marriage was unhappy and ended in divorce.[68]

Sue Jones was wearing a shirt and boater the afternoon she met Maugham. She had pale gold hair, blue eyes, a lovely figure, and the most beautiful smile Maugham had ever seen on a human being. He was smitten. From that day on he saw her often, and one evening, after dinner, he took her back to his room in Pall Mall and became her lover. This is the scene he describes in *Cakes and Ale*, when he cries and she buries his face in her breasts. She wore corsets, and when he touched her he felt the ribbing of the skin from the pressure of the corsets. When he took her home in a hansom, she asked how long he thought their affair would last. "Six weeks," he answered flippantly. It lasted, he said, eight years.[69]

Maugham did more than become her lover, he helped to find her parts. She played Peyton, the maid, in his 1909 comedy, *Penelope*. His friend the drama critic J. T. Grein wrote in the *Sunday Times and Special*, on January 10, of "the stoic and impeccable maid of Miss Ethelwynn [sic] Arthur Jones, who 'buttled' as well as the most time-honored butler." By this time she had divorced Leveaux, and Maugham sensed that he could have married her, but he was put off by her promiscuity. He knew that all his friends had been to bed with her. She was not a wanton but simply enjoyed sex, he thought, and took it for granted that when a man took her to dinner, bed would follow.[70]

In the Modern Library edition of *Cakes and Ale* Maugham wrote in a preface: "In my youth I had been closely connected with the young woman whom in this book I have called Rosie. She had grave and maddening faults, but she was beautiful and honest. The connection came to an end as such connections do, but the memory of her lingered on in my mind year after year. I knew that one day I should bring her into a novel."

In *Cakes and Ale*, published in 1930, Rosie is the first wife of the grand old man of English letters, Edward Driffield. After Driffield's death the narrator visits the second Mrs. Driffield, who has nothing good to say about Rosie.

> "She was a terrible slattern" [the second Mrs. Driffield says]. "Her house was always a mess. . . ."
> "She didn't bother about things like that" [says the narrator]. "They didn't make her any the less beautiful. And she was as good as she was beautiful."
> "Oh, come, Mr. Ashenden, that's really going too far. After all, let's face it, she was a nymphomaniac."

"I think that's a very silly word . . . She was naturally affectionate. When she liked anyone it was quite natural for her to go to bed with him. She never thought twice about it. It was not vice; it wasn't lasciviousness; it was her nature. She gave herself as naturally as the sun gives heat or the flowers their perfume. It was a pleasure to her and she liked to give pleasure to others. It had no effect on her character; she remained sincere, unspoiled, and artless."[71]

All his life Maugham kept Rosie's identity secret. It was Gerald Kelly who first disclosed it to the writer Richard Cordell, on condition that Cordell keep the secret. Kelly wrote Cordell: "All I know is that they had a very happy love affair together and then after a while I think Maugham became aware of her promiscuous nature. Whether they just quarreled and quarreled, or whether he left her, or she left him, I neither know nor care. She was one of the most delightful women I have ever known. I thought her wonderfully beautiful, but she had one failing."[72] Kelly painted and sketched her often, and one of his paintings, "Mrs. L. [Leveaux] in White, 1907," is the portrait of Rosie described in Cakes and Ale, in a white silk dress, with a black velvet bow in her hair.

Maugham was able to find parts for the actress whom he loved but could find no one to produce his own plays. Four years earlier he had taken on a dramatic agent in the person of R. Golding Bright, a former civil servant and drama critic who had joined his brother Addison's firm. In 1901 Bright had married a friend of Maugham's, a talented woman writer named Chavalita Dunne, whose feminist novel, written under the pseudonym George Egerton, had caused a scandal in 1893. Maugham wrote her at the time of the marriage: "Of course no nice-minded person can fail to see that you took an unfair advantage over me in marrying your dramatic agent. I see that the only thing for me to do is to marry Miss Marbury [Bright's partner] and I am starting for Paris at once."[73] In 1906 Golding Bright's brother Addison committed suicide in the wake of a financial scandal, and Golding became head of the firm, inheriting his brother's Broadway contacts. Maugham had by then written five full-length comedies—Loaves and Fishes, The Explorer, Lady Frederick, Mrs. Dot, and Jack Straw—which Golding Bright persistently kept sending to managers.

By this time Maugham was back in the London social swim. In February 1907 he lunched at the Writer's Club with Violet Hunt and Prevost Battersby, a former war correspondent for the Morning Post.

Violet chatted aimlessly about a dinner party at which she had sat next to a surgeon who told her that eating salad was the cause of cancer. She had also heard that Joseph Conrad's wife had written a cookbook. In March, Maugham saw Violet at a fancy-dress ball at Covent Garden.[74]

In April, Violet had Maugham to tea with a young actress named Nancy Price. Violet, although a feminist, was often hard on her sisters. She found Nancy Price "impressive, theatrical, of course, and anxious to show there is something in her. There isn't—but great beauty outside . . . she wants to act Lady Macbeth but Tree says 'she is not ripe enough.'" Again in April, she invited Maugham and Melton Fisher, a fashionable pastelist. "I know exactly where to put myself now, to dominate a room," she commented. In May she invited Maugham again. He must have shown her his plays, for she referred to him as a "dramatic genius." She was annoyed that he was "making *les yeux doux* at Beatrice Lewis, whom I know as a vulgar South Kensington art student, because she happens to be the sister of Lewis Waller [which] shows up the necessary degrading practices demanded by the exigencies of the trade."

She was probably right about Maugham turning on the charm, for it was Lewis Waller who finally produced *The Explorer* in June 1908. On the same day Violet saw H. G. Wells, whom she found stout and out of condition as the result of a sprained ankle, which kept him from his favorite exercise, badminton. "He says times are so bad for novelists that we shall all have to be content to write shorter novels and be published at 2/6," she wrote.[75] But for Maugham times were about to improve.

PART III

1907-1917

Chapter Six

I don't believe it [success] had any effect on me. For one thing I always expected it, and when it came I accepted it as so natural that I didn't see anything to make a fuss about. Its only net value to me is that it has freed me from financial uncertainties that were never quite absent from my thoughts. I hated poverty. I hated having to scrape and scrimp to make both ends meet.

Maugham, *A Writer's Notebook*

By 1907 *Lady Frederick* had been in and out of the offices of seventeen London managers. The objection was always the same: no actress would agree to play the dressing-table scene. The stage directions for the scene, which opens the third act, were: "[Lady Frederick] comes through the curtains. She wears a kimono, her hair is all dishevelled, hanging about her head in a tangled mop. She is not made up and looks haggard and yellow and lined."

> Lady Frederick (to young Lord Mereston): Just at present I can make a decent enough show by taking infinite pains; and my hand is not so heavy that the innocent eyes of your sex can discover how much of me is due to art. But in ten years you'll only be thirty-two, and then, if I married you, my whole life would be a mortal struggle to preserve some semblance of youth. . . . But if I don't marry you, I can look forward to the white hairs fairly happily. The first I shall pluck out, and the second I shall pluck out. But when the third comes I'll give in, and I'll throw my rouge and my *poudre de riz* and my pencils into the fire. . . .
> Mereston: But you break my heart.
> Lady Frederick: My dear, men have said that to me ever since I was fifteen, but I've never noticed that in consequence they ate their dinner less heartily.[1]

Dejected by his inability to gain a foothold on the London stage, Maugham told Harley Granville-Barker as they strolled through St. James's Park that it was useless to try to be a playwright. One manager who looked at *Jack Straw*, a farce about an archduke impersonating a headwaiter, said there was not enough action and suggested he put in a burglary. Maugham had already dipped into capital to support his lifestyle and was reaching the end of his inheritance. He was ready to go back to the hospital, take a refresher course, and apply for a post as ship's surgeon, which few doctors with London degrees wanted.[2]

Before making such a difficult decision, and despite his complaints about impending poverty, he went on a trip to Sicily to see the Greek temples. In the meantime Otho Stuart, the manager of the Royal Court Theatre, who was known for liking idea plays of the Shaw and Granville-Barker sort, had a surprise failure and needed a stopgap play to run six weeks. Golding Bright sold him on *Lady Frederick*, and Ethel Irving, one of the finest actresses on the London stage, had the courage to play the part. When the news reached him in Messina in September, Maugham quickly lost his interest in Greek temples and wrote Golding Bright: "Your letter filled me with exultation, and now the likelihood of an early production makes me realize that the world is not hollow and foolish. . . . It will take me three days to get back and I want to be on hand before Otho the Great scuttles the cast, since all managers are born idiots."[3]

He jumped into a train for Palermo and caught the packet to Naples. When the agent at Cook's would not take his personal check for a boat ticket to Marseilles, he went to another steamship office, asked haughtily for a first-class ticket, and played his role so convincingly that the clerk did not dare refuse. On the boat to Marseilles he gambled his last half crown on the ship's sweepstakes and won, which gave him enough to reach London. He strode into the Royal Court Theatre one September morning feeling like Phileas Fogg entering the Reform Club as the clock struck eight.[4] At last, after years of failure, one of his plays was being produced in a leading West End theater, with a star of the London stage in the title role. One can imagine with what excitement Maugham attended rehearsals.

Lady Frederick opened on October 26. Helen Mary Maugham, his brother Frederic's wife, noted in her diary that she had shared the playwright's box at the premiere: "Willie was very pale and silent. He sat at the back of the box. The play . . . is very witty and interesting. I believe it will prove a success with the public."[5] Prove a success it did. Scheduled as a stopgap, it ran for 422 performances in five West End theaters. The reviews were studded with phrases that could be excerpted in notices, such as "exhilarating entertainment" and "thoroughly enjoyable." For the two hundred and fiftieth performance at the Criterion, on June 3, 1908, a souvenir was presented to the audience in the form of a copy of F. Howard Michael's portrait of Ethel Irving as Lady Frederick. When it had run a year, there was a birthday party, and Maugham resisted the impulse to invite the seventeen managers who had turned it down. *Lady Frederick* launched him on an uninterrupted twenty-six-year career as a dramatist, during which he had twenty-nine plays produced.[6]

It was thanks to *Lady Frederick* that Maugham made friends with Oscar Wilde's companion, Reggie Turner, of whom it was said that he was "the essence of the nineties." Reggie was rumored to be the illegitimate son of Lionel Lawson (originally Levy), whose older brother, Joseph Moses Levy, had taken over the *Daily Telegraph* from its founder.[7] After graduating from Oxford, Reggie wrote a gossip column for the *Telegraph* called "London Day by Day." He got to know Wilde, who called him the boy snatcher of Clement's Inn, where he had rooms. When Wilde was released from prison in 1897 and went to live in exile in Dieppe as Sebastian Melmoth, Reggie joined him. One morning Oscar said: "Last night I dreamed that I was at the banquet of the dead." "I'm sure you were the life and soul of the party," Reggie replied. "That's the wittiest thing I have ever had said to me," Oscar said. Reggie was with him when he died shortly afterward.[8] Maugham called Reggie "on the whole the most amusing man I have known . . . he would take a theme, and embroider upon it with such drollery that he made your sides so ache with laughter that at last you had to beg him to stop."[9]

In 1907 Reggie was drama critic for *The Academy*, and called *Lady Frederick* "a perfect piece of work, because what the author did he did deliberately . . . and he got the greatest possible effect out of his efforts. He was completely, splendidly successful . . . [This is] a witty, original and exquisitely-wrought study of a fascinating personality."

Maugham gave Reggie a first edition of *Lady Frederick*, inscribed "To a wit from an admirer." He would drop in at his flat near Berkeley Square, where on one occasion he was slightly disconcerted to find the already famous H. G. Wells. This led to another friendship, even though Maugham thought that Wells was too busy reconstructing the world according to his own notions to pay much attention to anyone who did not share his sense of mission.

Lady Frederick was an expanded version of the *Punch* short story "Lady Habart," about a widow with money problems who is rescued by a former suitor. Nine pages in *Punch* became three acts, thanks to subplots and subsidiary characters. The play was set in the Hotel Splendide in Monte Carlo, to show that life is a gamble. All Lady Frederick has to do to break the bank is marry young Lord Mereston. She nobly declines to rob the cradle, disenchants the young lord by having him call at 10 in the morning, and ends up marrying his uncle. The play conforms to such Edwardian conventions as titled characters, compromising documents, and epigrams. Maugham, like Oscar Wilde, contributed to the decline of the British aristocracy by making his ladies and duchesses witty, which gave the real ladies and duchesses a gnawing sense of their inadequacy.

The play turns, as many of his plays do, upon marriage and money problems. One almost needs a calculator to follow the financial intricacies. Will Lady Frederick pay her debts? Will her brother pay the nine hundred pounds he owes a moneylender? Will Lady Frederick succumb to the moneylender because of his financial hold over her? It is with money that Maugham creates whatever suspense *Lady Frederick* has. As for marriage, it is seen both as a solution and a trap. It is a trap for a young man to marry an older woman. It is a solution for a debt-ridden woman to marry a wealthy man. In nearly all of Maugham's plays marriage is the key transaction. It is the means society has to curtail individual freedom, a test of conformity, and a problem-solving device.

Maugham's preoccupation with money was as constant in his life as in his plays. As he once told Clare Boothe Luce, "Love may make the world go round but money greases the axle."[10] He never starved, but as a young man he had to scrimp. He did not have a fashionable address. He traveled, but not in style. He saw money as a condition of freedom, and once he had it, he used it to shield him from all in life that was unpleasant. As Malcolm Muggeridge wrote, "Like all timid, lonely people, money seemed to him a protection. It set up a buffer between him and a largely alien and hostile world. To this end he sought it, first diligently and ardently, and finally as an addiction."[11]

It may have become an addiction, but it was based on the commonsense premise that money confers independence—so long, as he put it, as one does not pay more than twenty shillings for the pound one earns.

When Maugham read a story in which a young couple drove off into the sunset in a new red roadster, he wanted to know how they could afford the roadster. He wrote a preface to Louis Marlow's novel *Two Made Their Beds* because he liked the way "money matters vitally affect the persons of this story. . . . The point is the great, the insinuating, and the overwhelming significance of money in the affairs of life. It is the string with which a sardonic destiny directs the motions of its puppets."[12]

Maugham's great care in money matters gave him a reputation for stinginess. "He could be pretty mean about a penny a hundred at bridge," Clare Boothe Luce said.[13] His nephew Robin recalls that in 1944, when he had just made half a million dollars with *The Razor's Edge*, he took a bus rather than a taxi from his doctor's to the Ritz-Carlton Hotel on a cold winter day with snow in the streets.[14] Maugham did not like to spend money he did not have to spend. When he had to spend it, he did not complain. The upkeep of the Riviera home, the Mauresque, with its servants and gardeners, amounted to more than $20,000 a year, but he considered that a necessary expense. Taking a taxi when you could take a bus was not. He may have been niggardly with sums that came out of his pocket, but he was generous with large sums that required only a signature. He gave close to 15,000 pounds to his old school, and far more if one counts the value of his library and manuscripts. In 1947 he established an annual Maugham prize of 500 pounds to allow a young English writer to travel. He sent cash gifts, often anonymously, to many a hard-up writer. He liked to do kindness by stealth. He did not, however, like to be asked for loans. His niece Kate Mary once said to him: "Willie, I adore you. Would it be of any use if I asked you to lend me some money?" "None whatever," he replied. "Uncle Willie, I'm your widowed niece." "May I congratulate you on your happy state," he said.[15]

The oddest thing about his handling of money was his habit of leaving cash in bank accounts and safe deposit boxes all over the world. He squirreled money away, as if fearing that it would be taken from him. In July 1966, the year after his death, the Crocker Citizens National Bank petitioned the state of California to appoint an appraiser to determine what should be done with the $35,000 that he had left in his account and apparently forgotten.[16] The same man who balked at taking a cab forgot $35,000 in a distant bank account.

Besides his treatment of money and marriage in the play, *Lady Frederick* is interesting because it introduces a caricatural Jewish character, the moneylender Captain Montgomerie, who is in reality the son of a

Polish Jew named Aaron Levitsky. Captain Montgomerie wants to marry Lady Frederick so as to climb in society. When she turns him down he produces two bills and demands immediate payment. Conscious that Montgomerie was a burlesque figure, Maugham wrote Golding Bright to make sure that Otho Stuart did "not give the part of the rich Jew to a vulgar man since if it is exaggerated it will be grotesque."[17]

There was in Maugham an ambivalence toward Jews. Writing to his New York literary agent Charles Hanson Towne in 1924 in response to a suggestion that Towne and Oliver Herford should dramatize his short story "The Letter," he said: "Nor have either of you that Semitic air with a dash of Czecho-Slovakia thrown in which I always thought was essential for success on Broadway."[18] Writing to his nephew Robin in 1946 about his ocean crossing from the United States to France, he said: " . . . the passengers were for the most part children of Israel returning to Asia Minor . . . some of them seemed determined to inspire the rest of us with anti-Semitism."[19]

In his work, Jews are usually crude and unscrupulous stereotypes in the tradition of Shylock and Fagin. In "Lady Habart" there occurs the line: "Once upon a time moneylenders were unwashed Hebrews in shabby clothes, malodorous, speaking English with an abominable accent." In "The Fortunate Painter and the Honest Jew," a story published in the *Bystander* on March 7, 1906, a Jewish art dealer drops by the studio of a young English painter living in Paris and spots a copy of a Watteau. He says his son-in-law in New York can sell it and asks the painter to sign it. He then alerts New York customs that an original Watteau is being smuggled in. The customs official has the signature erased, and the publicity surrounding the incident brings a buyer to the son-in-law. The dealer gives the painter the money he needs to marry his fiancée, whose name is Rosie (the first Rosie in Maugham's oeuvre).

The theme of his letter to Robin, that Jews invite anti-Semitism by their behavior, is repeated in a passage from *The Gentleman in the Parlor*, an account of a journey to the Far East. On the steamer from Haiphong to Hong Kong the narrator meets an American Jew, Elfenbein, who is in the hosiery business. He is loud and irascible and vulgar. "He was odious," says the narrator, "but I admit that he was often amusing; he would tell damaging stories about his fellow Jews in a racy idiom that made them very entertaining. . . . He trod heavily on your corns and if you kicked your feet out of the way thought you insulted him. . . . He was the kind of Jew who made you understand the pogrom."

In his 1909 comedy *Smith*, one of the characters is married to a "fat old German-Jew." The critic J. T. Grien, a friend and admirer of Maugham's, noted that "a discordant note in this comedy is the repeated references to Jews in terms of ungraciousness . . . the impression remains that the Jews are considered, not as ordinary members of the community, but as something exotic, akin to freakishness."[20]

Another, much later, short story dealing with Jews, *The Alien Corn*, was used by a Third Reich literary critic to bolster Nazi race theories. The story is about a Jew who becomes an English gentleman. His son, however, rebels against upper-middle-class English life and goes to the Continent to become a pianist, reverting to his origins. When he learns that he does not have the talent to be a first-class concert pianist he kills himself. This story is less about being a Jew than about the dilemma of not being able to achieve one's aims. But in a 1939 German brochure, *A Contribution on Interpreting School Literature*, Hans Kruschwitz wrote an article, "The Race Question in W. S. Maugham's The Alien Corn," in which he argued that his unbiased account proved the Nazi thesis that racial barriers are natural ones and that the Jews will always remain the alien corn in any country they live in.[21]

Maugham would have been shocked to read this distorted interpretation. The year it appeared he was living in the south of France. At the outbreak of World War II, German exiles on the Riviera were interned, on the theory that Nazi agents had been planted among them. One of the interned exiles was Lion Feuchtwanger, author of *Jud Süss*, who was sufficently anti-Nazi to have been stripped of his German nationality. Maugham sent the French dramatist Jean Giraudoux, head of the wartime Bureau of Information in Paris, a telegram on behalf of Feuchtwanger, who was released.[22]

In addition, Maugham's oldest American friend was Bert Alanson, a Jewish stockbroker. His friendships with the Jewish writers S. N. Behrman and Jerome Weidman, and with Jerome Zipkin, a Jewish real estate heir and bon vivant, were warm and enduring. And finally, Mrs. Syrie Wellcome, whom he later married, was a woman he believed to be Jewish. Thus one can argue both sides about Maugham and anti-Semitism. He made unpleasant cracks about Jews in his letters and depicted them in an unfavorable light in his work. He saved Feuchtwanger from internment and had many close friendships with Jews. In

May 1946 Bert Alanson sent Maugham two pamphlets by a rabbi friend of his charging him with anti-Semitism. Maugham replied:

> I do not know what your rabbi means. . . . I gather that he looks upon me as anti-Semitic. God knows I have never been that; some of my best friends both in England and America are Jews and there is one, long known as the best-dressed man in San Francisco, to whom I owe more than to almost anyone in the world. I happen to think that the Zionists are mistaken in their efforts to found a Jewish state in Palestine, but that is an opinion I share with a good many Jews and I have every right to hold it.[23]

Success in the theater, Maugham soon learned, had a tendency to snowball. With *Lady Frederick* settling into a long run, there was an instant demand for more of the same. Rejected for years, he now dug down into his trunkful of unproduced plays. In November he summarily dismissed Pinker. "I have come to the conclusion it is needless for me in the future to have an agent after all," he said. "I do not propose to write any more short stories. I have so many commissions for plays that I would not have time even if I had inclination."[24] He ended the letter with the same phrase he had used in dismissing Colles: "I fear that you have had more trouble than profit in your dealings with me." Pinker was not so easily put off and convinced Maugham to keep him for future stories and novels.

Success crossed the Atlantic when Ethel Barrymore decided she wanted to do *Lady Frederick* in New York. Charles Frohman, the son of a German Jewish cigar maker, who was credited with inventing the star system by pairing Maude Adams and John Drew, produced the play. In 1908, when he started doing Maugham's plays, Frohman was, with David Belasco, one of the two leading producers for the English-speaking stage. The American-based international wheeler-dealer was replacing the London actor-manager. A round ball of a man with protruding lower lip and seal-colored eyes, Frohman put stars under contract and found vehicles for them. In America he owned a string of theaters, and someone once said that if his legs had been a little longer, he could have walked across America on the theaters he controlled. In 1897 he invaded the London stage, leasing the Duke of York in St. Martin's Lane, the heart of the theater district. His name was over the doorway for nineteen years. He hired one of the best known producers, Dion Boucicault (known as Dot), son of the playwright of the same name, and husband of Irene Vanbrugh, one of the best comediennes of the day. In 1904 Frohman produced *Peter Pan* and made James Barrie a millionaire. If he ever had a failure, he forgot it. "Don't revive the past," he said, "pulverize the future."[25]

Frohman spun like a top from continent to continent, jabbing a pudgy forefinger at everything that stood in his way. He never carried a watch or wore shoes that had to be laced. He hated Christmas; he never said "Good morning"—when someone said it to him, he replied, "I doubt it." He never read books, and when a reporter asked him what his favorite book was, he replied: "Roland Strong's The Best Restaurants of Paris." One of his rules for what worked onstage was: Americans love to see women triumph over men. When he offered a suggestion to Mrs. Patrick Campbell, she said: "Pardon me, Mr. Frohman, but you forget that I am an artist." "I'll keep your secret," Frohman said. He produced between five hundred and six hundred plays, and was known as the man who never broke his word.[26]

Ethel Barrymore was a hit in New York with *Lady Frederick*, which ran for 96 performances. One New York critic described the play as "a brilliant, somewhat metallic, but exceedingly entertaining comedy of manners in which an Irish widow makes all the men she meets fall in love with her, then makes some of them fall out again." Maugham was compared to Clyde Fitch, then the most successful American dramatist, who usually had several plays running on Broadway. Miss Barrymore played the dressing-table scene to the hilt, coming on in dressing gown and slippers, her hair frowsy. She let the young lord see how many of her glorious locks had to be pinned to her head, and produced before him a bloom of youth with rouge and powder. Maugham thought it was a tribute to her gifts that, although in the prime of her youth and beauty, she was able to convince the audience that she had seen her best days.[27]

By 1908 Maugham was famous. Having decided to give the public what it wanted, he found London at his feet. Managers who had ignored him now besieged him. He had been industrious in his years of failure and was able to provide them with three vehicles for popular actors of the day: *Jack Straw*, for Charles Hawtrey, which opened on March 26 and ran for 321 performances; *Mrs. Dot*, for Marie Tempest, which opened on April 27 and ran for 272 performances; and *The Explorer*, for Lewis Waller, the only one that was not a hit, which opened on June 13 and closed after 48 performances.[28]

With *Lady Frederick* he had four plays running in West End theaters by mid-June 1908. "Have you seen Somerset Maugham's quartet?" was one of the topical questions of the season. One had to go back to the early days of Sardou, said the critic J. T. Grien, to find a popularity so overwhelming. Maugham's name, on programs, billboards, and buses, was impossible to avoid. On June 24 *Punch* came out with a Bernard Partridge cartoon in which Shakespeare was shown biting his nails in front of the boards advertising Maugham's four plays. This was accompanied by a mock interview with a multiplicity of Maughams, such as Maugham in the street, Mrs. Mahamistion Chant (after Mrs. Ormiston Chant, a social reformer), Maugham Sahib of Nawanagar (after a famous Indian cricketer), and Father Bernard Maugham (after Father Bernard Vaughan, a popular Catholic preacher).

Maugham was interviewed and photographed, and distinguished persons sought his acquaintance. The actor Arthur Bourchier put him up for the Garrick Club, to which he was elected in January 1909. Arnold Bennett wrote in his diary for April 29, 1908: "Noticed in myself: A distinct feeling of jealousy on reading yesterday and today accounts of another very successful production of a play by Somerset Maugham— the third now running."[29] Bennett's feelings of jealousy must have been short-lived, for in 1908 he published *The Old Wives' Tale*, which made his reputation. Maugham told his old friend Gerald Kelly: "Arnold has written a masterpiece." The fortunes of the two struggling Paris writers rose in the same year. Bennett was called the heir to Dickens, bragged about his rate per word, and bought himself a yacht "just to show these rich chaps that a writer can make money too."[30]

Maugham's stagecraft, delicacy of style, and lightning-quick humor were praised and praised again. It was enough to go to his head. One night he was dining alone at the Bath Club and overheard two members who were going to one of his plays. One mentioned that he was a member of the club. "D'you know him at all?" the other asked. "I supposed he's as swollen-headed as he can be." "Oh yes," the first one replied, "I know him well. He can't get a hat big enough to fit him."[31]

Maugham would never be poor again. He could now, if he wanted to squander money, hail a cab on rainy London nights. The money was rolling in like waves, and for the rest of his life he would hear the comforting sound of that green surf. It came from all directions. *Mrs. Dot* was produced in Berlin, Copenhagen, and Petrograd. Metro made a film of *Lady Frederick* in 1919 starring Ethel Barrymore. Famous Players-Lasky made *Jack Straw* in 1920, with Cecil B. De Mille directing. Lasky had also made *The Explorer* in 1915. While Maugham was discovering the pleasant surprises of ancillary rights, he was still careful with his money; he never again wanted to be in a position of not having enough. His one expenditure was for a flat in Mayfair, which he took in 1908 and shared with Walter Payne until 1911. It was at 23 Mount Street, close to Berkeley Square, in a Dutch-style red brick building, which today has an antique shop on the ground floor. Payne, a member of the Institute of Chartered Accountants, handled his financial affairs.

Maugham moved in theatrical circles. His friends were actors and managers, such as Charles Hawtrey, a mainstay of the West End, who produced and acted in more than eighty plays between 1883 and 1923. Hawtrey was a portly man with brown eyes, whose naturalism and timing made him excel in comic parts, and whose acceptance of a play insured its box-office success. It was said that he looked as though he had wandered onstage after leaving his club. His one fault was gambling, and he was always in debt. In *Jack Straw*, which starred Hawtrey, Maugham reached back to Molière and Marivaux for the stock figure of the stage impostor—in this case a man masquerading as himself. Jack Straw, a waiter working in the Grand Babylon Hotel, is presented as the Archduke Sebastian of Pomerania to the daughter of a family of *nouveaux riches*. When they learn that he is a waiter they shun him, but it develops that he is in fact the archduke, and he marries the girl. Maugham's novel solution to the in-law problem is that they will be beheaded if they ever visit Pomerania.

When Hawtrey came onstage in the first act as a bearded waiter he took his fans by surprise. When they recognized him they applauded. Hawtrey was a huge success, while the play was described as "light as a feather and saucy as a sparrow." *Jack Straw* stopped running only because Hawtrey had appendicitis. At one performance an old family friend of Hawtrey's was in the audience. The old lady was charmed when Lady Wanly, a character in the play, spoke of sending her sons to Eton. After the play she told Hawtrey, "Lady Wanly is just the kind of mother who would send her sons to Eton; in fact, she would never think of sending them anywhere else."[32] While *Jack Straw* was on, Maugham was already working on another vehicle for Hawtrey, an adaptation of Ernest Grenet-Dancourt's farce, *Les Gaietés du Veuvage*. One day Hawtrey asked him to come to the Royalty Theatre, on Dean Street, to look at an actress he might cast in the farce.

"Darling," Hawtrey said when he arrived, "this is Mr. Maugham. I've just been telling him you're the most beautiful girl in the world."

Maugham noted with a clinical eye that the young woman had delicate features, a healthy skin, and a virginal air, but when Hawtrey asked "How's the baby?" notions of virginity were dispelled.

"She's married to Buck," Hawtrey explained. Buck was Herbert Buckmaster, a wealthy man-about-town.

When she had left, Hawtrey asked Maugham what he thought. "She's the loveliest thing I've ever seen in my life," he said. "But can she act?"

"It's not a difficult part and I can teach her," Hawtrey said.

"All right then. By the way, what's her name?"

"Didn't I mention it? Cooper, Gladys Cooper."

Gladys Cooper became the most popular actress of her day, exemplifying wholesome English beauty. Her manager at the Gaiety, George Edwards, said he would injunct her if she acted in the Hawtrey farce, but she later played in Maugham's *Home and Beauty* and in the dramatization of *The Letter*. Ernest Thesiger, who had scored a triumph as the dauphin in Shaw's *Saint Joan* and who had a gift for female impersonation, once asked Maugham why he never wrote a part for him. "I do," he said, "but Gladys Cooper always plays them."[33]

As a young actress Gladys Cooper worshiped Marie Tempest, who had starred in the second Maugham play to be produced that year, *Mrs. Dot*. This was Charles Frohman's first London production of a Maugham play. When he asked to read it, Maugham said, "It must be decided tonight." "Give me three hours," Frohman said. At one in the morning he took it.[34] With *Mrs. Dot* Maugham continued his study of the marital dilemmas of the upper classes, where everyone had plenty of time, money, and servants. Mrs. Dot is the wealthy widow of a brewery magnate, who weaves her way through plot devices to disentangle the man she loves from an unsuitable engagement. She is another stock figure, in a category that ranges from *Madame Sans-Gêne* to *Hello, Dolly!* As usual, the dialogue was leavened with epigrams: "You married for love, Lady Sellenger." "I'm anxious that my daughter shouldn't make the same mistake."[35]

One of the characters, Blenkinsop, seems to speak for the author when he says: "When I was young it occurred to someone that I was a cynic, and since then I've never been able to remark that it was a fine day without being accused of odious cynicism."

Marie Tempest, who was short and plump, with reddish-gold hair, had made her debut in 1885, and was on the light musical stage for fifteen years before turning to comedy. Maugham thought she was the greatest comedienne in England. But when he first went to rehearsals he did so with some misgivings. He expected her to be willful, exacting, petulant, and tiresome, as he assumed all leading ladies were. He also expected her to insist on having her own way, and if she did not get it, to fly into a tantrum. Dion Boucicault was directing *Mrs. Dot*, and his method was to work on the first act thoroughly in order to impress the mood of the play on the cast, so that when they got to the second and third acts they would have nothing to do but learn their lines. They worked on the first act for two solid weeks. Maugham was astonished at Marie Tempest's patience. She repeated scenes with good humor; she was punctual, word perfect, and tireless. She listened to Boucicault and did what he asked without question. It warmed Maugham's heart to see what she made of his lines, and he realized that being a star meant more than talent; it meant patience, industry, and discipline. He also learned how complicated was the process by which a play is set before an audience. He grew to respect actors and to realize that their virtues were more solid than they pretended and that their failings were incidental to the exacting profession they followed.[36]

In the dramatic version of *The Explorer* Maugham tugged at the heartstrings of empire-lovers when Alec Mackenzie leaves the drawing rooms of Mayfair for a perilous mission in East Africa. This was the most patently false of Maugham's plays, for he did not believe a word of it. But Lewis Waller, the critics said, made a splendid picture of virility and domination by strength of character, and the public seemed to enjoy the purple patches about the sun never setting.[37]

With four plays running, Maugham felt that he had earned a rest, and spent September and October of 1908 in Italy. But, as usual, it was a working holiday. He had been commissioned by Frohman to write another vehicle for Marie Tempest, which he called "Man and Wife." He wrote Golding Bright from Lake Como: "I have got it pretty shipshape and I do not think there will be any difficulty about it. I am hoping it will turn out far and away the best thing I have done."[38] On October 16, from Varenna, he thanked Bright for sending him notices from Berlin and America. There was a problem with the title of his new play and he had to change it; he decided to call it *Penelope*. Back at Mount Street in November, he was relieved to hear that Frohman liked *Penelope* but indignant that the producer had said it was the slightest of all his plays. "It has got far more in it than any of the others," he angrily wrote Bright. "However, I have long been aware that he knows far less about a play than the youngest call-boy at the most insignificant of his theaters."[39]

Fame's water wings placed Maugham more securely than ever in the London social swim. He made friends with Ada Leverson, Oscar Wilde's Sphinx. When she had first met Wilde at a party in 1892 he boasted about an apache in Paris who had become so attached to him that he followed him about with a knife in one hand. Ada said, "I'm sure he had a fork in the other." Wilde was won over and admitted her into his inner circle. It was at Ada Leverson's that he found refuge between his trials.

Born Beddington, circa 1870, Ada was the daughter of a Jewish wool merchant who had bought a property by that name. She married Ernest Leverson, a diamond merchant and chronic gambler, twelve years her senior, who eventually went broke, left her, and emigrated to Canada. Ada had frizzy hair, a retroussé nose, and looked like Ellen Terry. The charm of her manner, it was said, lay in saying unpredictable things in a low voice.[40]

"An introduction to Mrs. Ernest Leverson," wrote Grant Richards, "was one of the most important things that could happen to a young man at that time." On one occasion, sitting next to Henry James, she expressed her admiration for his work. He turned his melancholy gaze upon her and said: "Can it be—it must be—that you are the embodiment of the incorporeal, that elusive yet ineluctable being to whom through the generations novelists have so unavailingly made invocation; in short, the Gentle Reader? I have often wondered in what guise you would appear, or, as it were, what incarnation you would assume."[41]

Ada Leverson paid Maugham the highest compliment: she told him he was like Oscar Wilde. "I am so much inclined to believe the disagreeable things that people say to me and to ascribe the agreeable things to their good nature," he replied. "And whenever people praise me to my face I am always tortured by the idea that they are laughing at me up their sleeves. I am an excellent example of the difference between conceit and self-satisfaction."[42]

Between 1907 and 1916 Ada Leverson published six light novels. In one called *The Limit* Maugham made a cameo appearance as the successful dramatist Gilbert Hereford Vaughan, known to his friends as Gillie:

> To have eleven plays, all written out of one's head, and all being performed simultaneously in American, in Eskimo, and even in Turkish, besides in every known European language; to have money rolling

in, and the strange world of agents and managers pursuing you by every post and imploring for more contracts by every Marconigram; and these triumphs to have come about quite suddenly, was really enough to have turned the head of any young man; yet Hereford Vaughan . . . had remained remarkably calm. He was not even embittered by success . . . He was rather secretive and mysterious than blatant and dashing, and this, of course, made him, on the whole, more interesting to women.[43]

He was certainly interesting to Ada, an unattached woman several years his senior, for in 1909 she gave him one of her most cherished possessions, a first edition of Wilde's poem *The Sphinx*, published in 1894, illustrated by Charles Ricketts, and limited to two hundred copies. It had been inscribed to her by Vyvyan Holland, Wilde's son: "For the Gilded Sphinx with Love from Vyvyan." When giving it to Maugham she added an inscription of her own: "Oh dark tormenting face of beauty, love."[44] This was as close as Maugham would come to Wilde: he was loved by a woman who had loved Oscar.

Maugham's friendship with Ada Leverson lasted from 1908 to 1911. Like Wilde, he called her The Sphinx, and she teased him because he spelled it with a *y*. He praised her books and she praised his plays. When her novel *The Twelfth Hour* came out he wrote: "It delights me, but it tantalizes me as well because I cannot skip anything; I come upon a description of the weather or the crops, the kind of passage ordinarily I feel by instinct I can miss, and lurking in the middle of it, like a boy lurking round a corner, is a remark so witty that it sends little thrills of satisfaction all through me."[45]

Another novel, which she dedicated to Maugham, caused him to ask: "Why on earth don't you try your hand at a play—it is the easiest thing in the world (if you can do it at all), mere child's play besides writing a novel; it is only to scare away intruders that dramatists shake their heads and talk of the sweat of their brow and the divine fire and the praying and fasting which have gone to create their masterpieces."[46]

After 1911 the friendship faded, although Ada kept Maugham's photograph on her mantlepiece until her death in 1933. She aged fast, grew deaf, and was seen always in a black coat and black picture hat. In the last years before her death she dyed her hair pale yellow, and her face was so heavily powdered that flecks fell onto her bodice.[47]

Maugham was again invited to Lady St. Helier's in Portland Place. It was there that he met Thomas Hardy, who was already settling onto the pedestal of Grand Old Man of English Letters. Maugham observed that even in his boiled shirt and high collar Hardy retained a look of the soil. He was an odd mixture of shyness and self-assurance. The two men talked for three-quarters of an hour, and Hardy then paid Maugham a great compliment. Not having caught his name, he asked him what his profession was.[48]

It was at Lady St. Helier's, in November 1908, that Maugham met Edith Wharton, who had won fame in 1905 with *The House of Mirth* and was now having her first deep immersion in English social and literary life, with Henry James as cicerone. She was taken to Box Hill to meet Meredith, and to the House of Lords to have lunch with its librarian, Edmund Gosse. Lady St. Helier, with whom she was staying, gave a lunch for her and invited Maugham. Mrs. Wharton was small and elegantly dressed, with fine eyes and pale, clear skin. "She was seated in the middle of a small French sofa in such a way as to give it the appearance of a throne," he recalled, "and since she gave no indication that she wished to share it with me I took a chair and sat down in front of her." She talked for twenty minutes and said all the right things about what was currently fashionable in the arts. Maugham, exasperated by the rightness and exactness of everything she said, asked, "And what do you think of Edgar Wallace?"

"Who is Edgar Wallace?" Edith Wharton asked.

"Do you never read thrillers?"

"No," said Edith Wharton, a forced smile curling her lip. Maugham had never heard a more frigid syllable of disapproval. "Her manner," he said, "was that of a woman to whom a man has made proposals offensive to her modesty, but which good breeding tells her it will be more dignified to ignore than to make a scene about."

"I'm afraid it's getting very late," Edith Wharton said. Maugham left Lady St. Helier's thinking that she was an admirable creature but difficult to like.[49] He never saw her again, although their paths must have crossed in London and in the south of France. In the twenties, when he moved to Cap Ferrat, Maugham and Mrs. Wharton were remote neighbors, for she had settled in a chateau in Hyères. They never met, despite the fact that she was particularly fond of his story "Rain"[50] and Maugham's own acknowledgment that "she deserves a place, even though a minor one, in American literature."

Maugham also made friends with Lady St. Helier's daughter Dorothy, from her first marriage with Colonel Stanley. Dorothy had married Henry Allhusen, a wealthy member of Parliament, and was an up-and-coming lion huntress in her own right. Seven years older than Maugham, Dorothy Allhusen was gray-haired but pretty enough to persuade Sargent to paint her after he had said he would take no more commissions. Violet Hunt described her in her diary as "the silliest worldliest nice woman I know [who] collects what she calls with a sensuous inexpressibly gloating tone 'attractive' [persons]."[51]

Success mellowed Maugham, and he made efforts to be charming to hostesses who invited him to parties. For a man who was later feared for his barbed remarks, he was then positively kittenish. The ingratiating tone of his letters to such society women as Ada Leverson and Dorothy Allhusen was one he soon outgrew. He wrote Mrs. Allhusen on one occasion:

> I think it is fearfully rash of you to ask me to come to both your parties. What would you do supposing by next Monday you came to the conclusion that you never wanted to see me again? It would be very awkward for you. You think you would have the courage to say: I've changed my mind and I don't want you to come for next week-end; but you wouldn't, you know. . . . I will forget your extraordinary rashness, so that you should not feel any unpleasantness in the matter. Or is it politeness and not rashness on your part, as overwhelms me even to think of, like the sweets handed round at a party, an ice and a hot one; you've offered both, but it's rather greedy to take more than one.[52]

The Allhusens had a large house at Stoke Poges, near Windsor, and gave weekend parties in the summer. Like her mother, Dorothy Allhusen was attentive to the mix of lords, politicians, and authors. Maugham heard powerful men talk as if running the British Empire was their private business. He was amused to hear it discussed, when a general election was in the air, whether Tom should have the Home Office and whether Dick would be satisfied with Ireland. Not discerning any marked capacity in most of the men he met, he concluded that no great degree of intelligence was needed to rule a nation.[53]

The one exception among the politicians he observed at Stoke Poges was Winston Churchill, who had recently married the beautiful Clementine Hozier, and was swiftly climbing the rungs of government: he was president of the Board of Trade from 1908 to 1910, Home Secretary in 1910 and 1911, and First Lord of the Admiralty from 1911 until 1915. Churchill and Maugham played golf at Stoke Poges. One Sunday afternoon they were behind a very slow couple. "Would you mind letting us through?" Churchill asked. "I have a Cabinet meeting at six o'clock and I've got to get back to London." The slow couple let them through, and mercifully they both hit good straight drives. They drove back to the Allhusens', and Churchill napped until it was time to dress for dinner.[54]

On another evening, when the men had assembled in the smoking room after dinner, a smug naval officer monopolized the conversation. Churchill seemed impressed by his views. Maugham, who thought he was talking dangerous nonsense, interrupted with a single word, which made everyone roar with laughter. The naval officer was silenced. Next morning, when he was alone in the smoking room with the Sunday papers, Churchill came up to him and said: "I want to make a compact with you. If you will promise never to be funny at my expense, I will promise never to be funny at yours."

"You're joking," Maugham said.

"I'm quite serious," Churchill said. "I want you to promise me that."

Maugham promised, amazed that a cabinet minister felt he had anything to fear from a writer of light comedies.[55]

Maugham and Churchill became lifelong friends. They recognized each other as survivors and were comfortable in each other's company because they were both prominent in their respective fields but never competed. Maugham admired the absence of cant in Churchill, and Churchill liked Maugham's wit and urbanity. They were born within months of each other, and died within months of each other. Winston was fond of saying to Maugham, "I'm sure you're right, you're so much older than me."

Maugham got to be on close enough terms with Churchill to once ask: "Winston, your mother often indicated that you had affairs in your youth with men."

"Not true!" Churchill replied. "But I once went to bed with a man to see what it was like."

"Who was it?"

"Ivor Novello."

"And what was it like?"

"Musical."[56]

Ivor Novello, a young man from Cardiff whose real name was David Davies, was the most popular figure in the British musical theater in the twenties. He wrote the World War I marching song "Keep the Home Fires Burning" when he was twenty, and became an idol overnight. He was a beautiful young man, with delicately chiseled features and long-lashed brown eyes. Novello was the protégé of Eddie Marsh, the man-about-town, who had become Churchill's private secretary. In 1911 Marsh brought him to Lady Randolph Churchill's for dinner. Winston was there and asked him to sing the music-hall ditties of his Sandhurst days. "Do you know 'You'd Be Far Better Off in a Home'?" Churchill asked. Novello wondered what he had done to make Churchill think he was crazy.[57]

In December 1908 Maugham went to a dinner at the Ritz in honor of Robert Ross, the Canadian-born art critic and journalist who claimed to have been "the first boy Oscar ever had." When Wilde went into exile Ross had become his chief friend, and when he died Ross became the administrator of his estate and the editor of his collected works. The dinner was a gesture of appreciation for his untiring loyalty to Wilde. Maugham, who was fascinated by everything connected with Wilde, was one of the two hundred guests and wrote Ross the next day: "My dear Ross, I want to tell you how glad I am that your party was such a success last night. It must have been a pleasure to you. I hated most of the speeches, but I was charmed with yours. . . . You are a perfect dear and I'm so glad to have known you. Yours ever."[58] Maugham kept up with Ross until his death in 1918.

Established as a writer of light comedies, Maugham kept at it. In 1909 he matched his previous year's record with four new productions. *Penelope*, starring Marie Tempest, opened in January and ran for 246 performances. In March the French farce for Hawtrey, *The Noble Spaniard*, opened and ran a disappointing 55 performances. In May, Lewis Waller revived *The Explorer* in a revised version, but it closed after seven performances. In September, *Smith* opened with Marie Lohr and Robert Loraine and ran for 168 performances.[59] Maugham was living "on top of happy hours," but was blamed for his facility. He always had half a dozen plays in his head, and when he thought of a theme, it naturally divided itself into scenes and acts and curtains. As soon as he finished one he was ready to start another. There are 20,000 words in a three-act play, and Maugham estimated that he could have written six a year if he had wanted to. A play never took him more than three or four weeks, and he had written *Jack Straw* in two weeks. He once remarked ruefully that it was a pity fertility was a merit only in the dead.[60] At the same time he was relieved that he no longer had to write fiction. One evening as he was walking along Panton Street he passed the Comedy Theatre, where *Mrs. Dot* was playing, and looking up at the sunset, he said to himself: "Thank God I can look at a sunset now without having to think how to describe it."[61]

Several years before, Maugham had sternly lectured Gerald Kelly for burning the candle at both ends. Now he may have been guilty of the same offense. The burdens of work and social life began to affect his health, and he spent the first month of 1909 in a nursing home at 12 Hinde Street, Manchester Square. His room was adorned with fifteen vases of flowers from well-wishers, which made him feel like a prima donna who was expected at any moment to burst out with a high C. He spent such restless nights that he felt sometimes that he was crossing backward and forward between Dieppe and Newhaven on a rough day. By February he was back at Mount Street, feeling wan and weak but again immersed in social London.[62] Ada Leverson relayed a dinner invitation from a friend who wanted to meet him, and his reply shows what a priggish Edwardian gentleman he had become:

> Pray thank your friend for the kind invitation. I will not accept it. I do not suppose people mean it impertinently, but it is a very impertinent thing to invite a total stranger to dine with you. There are certain recognized methods of making the acquaintance of anyone one wants to know and I do not see why they should be neglected because I happen to be a writer. Your friend would not dream of asking the wretchedest lordling to dine with her unless she knew him, but quite a number of rich people think that writers and such like occupy the place of the old buffoons and may be used with as scant ceremony. They think we're cheaper, for a dinner is the only fee, there is not the old risk that they may have to pay for their amusement with the home butter they richly deserve. Not for mine![63]

Although he was collecting royalties on eight productions, Maugham was still no less concerned about money. He inquired regularly about box office returns and worried about the weather, which might discourage theatergoers. In January, *People's Magazine* in New York asked him to make a novel out of *Lady Frederick*, but he decided that the terms were not worth considering and could only damage his reputation. It had not been so long ago that he had pestered his agents for commissions at any price. For the first time in his life he was in a position to turn down offers, and he told Pinker that in negotiating terms with *People's Magazine* he should remember "that I have made something of a success in America and my name is worth a good deal."[64] He wrote Golding Bright that an offer a producer had made was "impertinent," and that the producer "could certainly not get Shaw for those terms."[65] He was comparing himself to Shaw, with whom he shared Ibsenite origins, but privately he criticized Shaw, saying that his kind of plays "have certainly queered the pitch for the rest of us."[66] But it was Shaw, not Maugham, who freed the British stage from the nineteenth century.

Penelope, he said, was written to consolidate his hold on the public. The theme—similar to Barrie's *What Every Woman Knows* (produced in 1908) and to Sardou's *Divorçons*—had to do with a woman who throws her husband into his mistress' arms in order to save her marriage. Maugham was writing in the context of English civil law, which until 1923 accepted a wife's adultery as a ground for divorce, but required additional proof of desertion or cruelty in the case of the husband's adultery. He endorsed the Edwardian assumption that a woman with an unfaithful husband should use her wits rather than retaliate. This theme had already been handled by Henry Arthur Jones in *The Case of Rebellious Susan*, in which a woman stung by her husband's infidelities encourages the attentions of a young man, but is eventually persuaded that paying him back won't work. Susan's uncle tells her: "My dear Sue, believe me, what is sauce for the goose will never be sauce for the gander. In fact, there is no gander sauce."[67]

Marie Tempest had her second Maugham hit with *Penelope*, and Maugham wrote Frohman to tell him how glad he was that it was a success. "It is always rather nervous work to accept a commission," he said. ". . . I feel a much greater responsibility in respect to a play written under those conditions than when a play already written is accepted on its merits."[68]

Penelope offered another opportunity to work with one of the leading directors of the London stage (they were then called producers), Dion (Dot) Boucicault. Pleased with the result, he wrote Dot in January 1909: "You have the added merit of at least pretending not to think the author a driveling idiot who has provided 'words,' but you give him every consideration that he can wish for.[69]

The Noble Spaniard, which opened in March 1909, had Hawtrey playing a burlesqued Spanish duke, in cape and sombrero and black whiskers, who is courting a young widow. To put him off she tells him she is married, and he stalks around for three acts trying to challenge her nonexistent husband to a duel. Max Beerbohm, in the *Saturday Review* of March 20, found this period piece, set in Boulogne in 1850, thin and hackneyed. Other critics said that Hawtrey had not yet recovered full strength after his appendicitis attack and was not his usual volcanic self.

In April 1909 Maugham left for what was becoming his annual trip to Italy, and worked on his new play, *Smith*. He wrote Golding Bright from Lake Como that it would turn out to be the best thing he had done. He corresponded with Dion Boucicault, the director, about the cast, and suggested Marie Lohr and Robert Loraine. Maugham was in Florence in May when Lewis Waller revived *The Explorer*. It annoyed him to read in the papers that Waller had rewritten the last act in accordance with the views of the critics. He asked Golding Bright to insert a correction saying that Waller had, on the contrary, reverted to the version that was in existence when he accepted the play. He felt that it was very stupid and undignified to crawl before the critics, and that if Waller had wanted to prostrate himself before them he should have done it himself instead of presenting Maugham in that attitude.[70] But the play closed before any insert could be made.

In Florence, Maugham saw Reggie Turner and Louis Umfreville Wilkinson, the young man he had met when *A Man of Honour* was performed at Cambridge. Reggie's envy of Maugham's growing fame was "agreeably jesting, never malicious," according to Wilkinson, who wrote under the pseudonym Louis Marlow. Reggie's only complaint was that Maugham was "a little arid and careful about tips." Reggie said of Maugham: "Ah, yes, yes, I know. He's very good, I know. And good to be with. But not as good as Oscar. Not like Oscar. Oh, no, he'd never be like Oscar."[71]

In June, Maugham saw Boucicault in Paris and gave him the first two acts of *Smith* to help him cast and plan the sets. Boucicault was so enthusiastic that Maugham thought something must be seriously wrong, for in the past he had always been sniffy about his work.[72] He spent the month of August recovering from his European travels in a cottage he took with Walter Payne at the Rectory Farm, Taplow, in Buckinghamshire. "I have been living the virtuous life of a bishop's unmarried sister," he wrote Ada Leverson, "and I am wondering if the exercize of virtue for six weeks renders me more capable of debauchery than the exercize of virtue for one. . . . I should be distressed to think that I had only been wasting my time."[73]

Smith, which opened on September 30, was his strongest attack on society since *A Man of Honour*. Giving full rein to his misogyny, he showed four upper-class women addicted to bridge, neglecting their homes, and ignoring their husbands and children. In contrast to these women of fashion who shirk their duties, there was Smith the parlor-maid, hardworking, sensible, and decent. Smith works for Mrs. Dallas-

Baker, who is expecting her brother back from Rhodesia after eight years. The brother is an uptight "backwoodsman" type à la Rousseau, who is looking for a wife to take back to the colonies. Shocked by his sister and their friends, he marries Smith.[74]

Smith was the first play in the history of the theater to open with a game of bridge. One of the players, Mrs. Rosenberg, has left her sick child at home, and in the third act they are playing bridge again when Mrs. Rosenberg's husband calls to tell his wife that the child is dead. The other women express annoyance at this interruption of their bridge party. This was Maugham's rather heavy-handed way of showing his characters' callousness, but in his heart he must have been on the side of the bridge players, for from the time he had started playing at the Bath Club, bridge developed into a passion. He said it was "the most interesting game that the art of man has ever devised." He considered the bridge table a school for the study of mankind, and claimed that he knew the essential facts about a man after a few rubbers. Bridge turns up in many of his books and stories. In *Christmas Holiday*, for instance, there is this conversation:

> "Why didn't you return me a diamond, you fool?" cried Patsy.
> "Why should I return you a diamond?"
> "Didn't you see me play a nine and then a six?"
> "No, I didn't."
> "Gosh, that I should be condemned to play all my life with people who don't know the ace of spades from a cow's tail."
> "It only made the difference of a trick."
> "A trick? A trick? A trick can make all the difference in the world."[75]

Smith was a hit. At the premiere there was an insistent demand for the author, who did not appear. The play ran for 112 performances in New York, with John Drew, and was made into a film in 1917. Back in Italy in October, Maugham approved the replacement of Marie Lohr as Smith by Irene Vanbrugh. "Although somewhat long in the tooth she will play the part beautifully," he wrote Golding Bright, "and if she has any following it should be useful to the play." He worried about receipts. "Why should it rain cats and dogs," he asked, "just when people are wanting to go and see *Smith*?" He confessed that he was "tired and bored. After this I am going to give play-writing a rest for some time. Four plays in the last two years and eight productions!"[76]

This fit of apathy did not last long, however, and he was soon hard at work, loath to see a London theatrical season go by without him. His contribution to the 1910 season was a modest two plays, *The Tenth Man* and *Grace*, both of them flops. *The Tenth Man* opened in February and closed after 65 performances. Maugham had made the mistake of giving up comedy and going back to "serious" dramas. He felt that he was typecast and taken for granted as a writer of frothy comedies. He was furious when Frohman said he wanted another "light play" and wrote Golding Bright: "I am sick of the whole theatrical business. It is all hideous and revolting. Why does Frohman want me to do a 'light play'? Does he think I care to go on repeating myself? . . . If he thinks I am only good enough to provide comic relief from the serious work of Granville-Barker and Galsworthy, he can keep his commissions to himself."[77]

In 1909 Frohman had launched a repertory season at the Duke of York's Theatre. He had invited Henry James, Shaw, Galsworthy, Granville-Barker, and James Barrie to submit plays. Maugham was miffed that he was not asked to contribute and that Frohman seemed to consider his work secondary to those who were. Hence came the urge to return to serious themes, which he later admitted "fell between two schools. . . . One portrayed the narrow, hidebound life of country gentlefolk; the other, the political and financial world; with both of which I had some acquaintance. I knew that I must interest, move and amuse, and I heightened the note. They were neither frankly realistic nor frankly theatrical. My indecision was fatal. The audience found them rather disagreeable and not quite real."[78]

In December he wrote Ada Leverson that he had finished *The Tenth Man*, "and now, I am in that depressed, wretched state of not having the least idea if it is any good or not."[79] *The Tenth Man* had to do with an unscrupulous entrepreneur who uses fraud and blackmail to get what he wants. Because a divorce would ruin his political career, he blackmails his unhappy wife into staying by his side. He floats worthless bonds, and bribes and manipulates his way to power. He says: "I think nine men out of ten are rogues or fools. That's why I make money." His wife tells him to beware of the tenth man, who is neither a rogue nor a fool. The tenth man shows up in the last act, exposes the bond scheme, and the entrepreneur throws himself out a window.[80]

Critics were quick to note Maugham's debt to the French playwright Henri Bernstein, whose great success *Le Voleur* had come out in 1906. He borrowed from Bernstein the character of the crooked financier and copied his method of depending on a violent central character and violent situations. His normally admiring critic J. T. Grien called *The Tenth Man* his first blunder, and *The Times* said on February 25, 1910: "It is not one of Mr. Maugham's happiest efforts. The sentimental business is very stale, the financial intrigue is a little bewildering, and some of the politics not a little absurd." Maugham feigned indifference. He wrote to Ada Leverson, his "Dear Sphinx," that the play had fallen flat on the first night and the critics had been unduly severe. *"Je m'en fouts, je m'en fouts, je m'en triple fouts,"* he said.[81]

But Maugham had high hopes for *Grace*, his other play of the 1910 season, which starred the popular Irene Vanbrugh. He went to every rehearsal, and his distant and immaculate presence made her nervous. She took his diffidence for disapproval and was surprised when he expressed a word of appreciation. Maugham told her that in Berlin leading ladies addressed playwrights as "Great and Highly Honored Master." She took the hint and thereafter always called him "Dear Master."[82]

Grace ran for a disappointing 72 performances. It was a return to the Edwardian theme that you can do what you like so long as you don't frighten the horses. As in *Smith*, Maugham drew the contrast between upstairs and downstairs. Peggy Gann, the gamekeeper's daughter, has been seduced, and according to the principles of the rural gentry, the squire must dismiss the gamekeeper unless he turns his daughter out. In the meantime Grace, the squire's wife, is quietly having an affair. Her lover states the Edwardian code when he says of Peggy Gann: "In point of fact she's done a good deal more than you have. She's been found out." The squire insists that Peggy must go, because he cannot bear the thought of Grace being in contact with a fallen woman. In the end Peggy Gann kills herself to save her father's job. The play was notable for the performance of Edmund Gwenn as the gamekeeper. It was also Maugham's first use of the old Whitstable name of Gann, which he would borrow again in *Cakes and Ale*. But as several critics pointed out, he dealt with one of those "county families" whose manners and customs were known only on the stage.[83]

Chapter Seven

> *It's awful, love, isn't it? Fancy anyone wanting to be in love.*
>
> Philip Carey in *Of Human Bondage*

MAUGHAM HAD reverted to Edwardian drama in the very year when the Edwardian era was drawing to a close. Edward VII died in May 1910. Nine monarchs attended the funeral procession on May 20. There was, however, one major difference between it and Queen Victoria's funeral procession nine years before. This time there were bomb threats, and the titled ladies watching the procession told one another that a bomb would be in very poor taste.[1] The mourning period lasted through June, and Maugham, vacationing in Italy, was glad to have been out of England during that dreary time.[2]

In 1910 Great Britain, held up by other engagements, entered the twentieth century. Virginia Woolf noted that "human character changed in 1910." Ortega y Gasset identified the year as the turning point between the age of reason and the age of existentialism. In 1910 Freud treated Mahler. In 1910 *Der Sturm* printed Kokoschka's drawings. In 1910 Braque and Picasso were painting and Stravinsky was composing. In 1910 James Joyce was working on *Dubliners* and D. H. Lawrence published *The White Peacock*. In 1910 Joseph Conrad had a mental breakdown and H. G. Wells openly took a mistress. The Marchioness of Ripon, commenting on the changes in society, said: "In our day women hid their lovers' photographs, and put their husbands' on the mantelpiece. Nowadays they display their lovers' pictures and bury their husbands' in the bottom of their boxes."[3]

The name of one of England's prominent intellectual journals was *The Egoist*. Vera Brittain wrote in *Testament of Youth*: "The age is intensely introspective, and the younger generation is beginning to protest that supreme interest in oneself is not a sin or self-conscious weakness to be overcome, but the essence of progress." In November, Roger

Fry exhibited Postimpressionist painters at the Grafton Gallery. E. M. Forster, then thirty-one and considered avant-garde, said that "Gauguin and Van Gogh were too much for me."[4] One gentleman laughed so hard at the portrait of Cézanne's wife that he had to be led outside.

In politics 1910 was a year of suffragette agitation, and in June a bill to give women the vote was brought before the House of Commons. Hilaire Belloc declared in the debate that he was glad the argument of the intellectual inferiority of women had not been raised. "As we grow older," he said, "we come to look on the intelligence of women first with reverence, then with stupor, then with *terror*."[5] Churchill, then Home Secretary, had been spurred by Galsworthy's *Justice* to advocate prison reforms. A dinner was arranged so that the two men could meet. Eddie Marsh, who was Churchill's secretary, asked Galsworthy: "If the Archangel Gabriel came down from heaven and gave you your choice: that your play should transform the prison system and be forgotten, or have no practical effect whatever and be a classic a hundred years hence, which would you choose?" Galsworthy thought it over and opted for the classic.[6]

Maugham was unaffected by the spirit of reform. If Galsworthy wanted to reform the prison system and Shaw wanted to reform the divorce laws, those were their concerns; his plays would continue to revolve around the marriage contract. As Ronald E. Barnes has noted in his *The Dramatic Comedy of William Somerset Maugham*, Maugham's plays fall into three periods. The early plays, such as *Lady Frederick* and *Mrs. Dot*, have to do with the conclusion of a marriage contract. The middle-period plays, such as *Grace* and *The Tenth Man*, have to do with the preservation of the marriage contract (will Grace confess her adultery and ruin her marriage?). And the final, postwar group, such as *The Circle* and *The Constant Wife*, have to do with the breaking of the marriage contract. Although his plays reflected the state of English society by examining the institution of marriage, Maugham remained loyal to the Ibsenite influence of his younger days by continuing to explore the difference between moral duty and social duty.

Here was a man in his mid-thirties whose subject was marriage and who remained unmarried. He was rich and famous and eligible, a condition that a number of women tried to change.

A wealthy American woman, Marie Lewis Fleming, known as Dillie, was very interested in Maugham. She had married a titled Englishman named Kent, but the marriage was turbulent and Kent had once tied her to a chair to keep her from going to a garden party. Maugham had met her at a London party, where he mistook her for Marie Tempest. She had auburn hair and wonderful coloring and was of the Rubens mold, which he seemed to like. He signed his letters to her, "Yours always, Billie," a name he rarely used except with the close friends of his youth. As to all his friends, he dispensed advice. Dillie was careless about money, giving it to all sorts of worthless people. She must hang onto it and not dip into capital, and if necessary have the interest paid quarterly. When Dillie became involved with a man named Roland Stuart, who borrowed from her, Maugham was shocked. No decent man, he said, would ask her for money. "I am afraid you will not get your money back again," he wrote her, "and I hope you will not be a silly fool any more. DO NOT LEND MONEY TO ANYONE, MALE OR FEMALE, WHO ASKS YOU."[7]

When Dillie told Maugham she had found just the wife for him, he wrote her: "I shall be interested to see her. But what makes you think she will want to marry me? I think it is very unlikely. When she sees me she will probably say: take him away—I wouldn't have anything to do with him at any price. I expect also she is thin and peaky, with a narrow sunken chest and bent shoulders."[8]

In the summer of 1910 Maugham met a twenty-six-year-old novelist named Hugh Walpole, who soon became a good friend. The two men had a great deal in common. Like Maugham, Hugh Walpole was raised in a clerical family; his father was a clergyman who taught theology in New York for three years and eventually became Bishop of Edinburgh. Like Maugham, he went to the King's School in Canterbury and was miserable there. On one occasion he was forced by his schoolmates to stand naked while they stuck pins in him.[9] Like Maugham, he left the school, but in later years became its benefactor. When Walpole got into *Who's Who* in 1913, he entered himself as having been educated at the King's School and Cambridge, omitting the fact that he had left the King's School to attend Durham Grammar School. Like Maugham, he was social and knew the right people. They had many friends and acquaintances in common—Violet Hunt, Henry James, Robert Ross, and Elizabeth Russell, a first cousin of Katherine Mansfield and the witty author of *Elizabeth and Her German Garden*. Like Maugham, he was painted by Gerald Kelly. Like Maugham, who used his experiences as a medical student in a novel about the slums of Lambeth, Walpole used his experiences as a young schoolteacher at Epsom in a novel called *Mr. Perrin and Mr. Traill*. And also like Maugham, he was a homosexual.

The darling of the women's magazines, Walpole never married. The great loves of his life were the Danish tenor Lauritz Melchior and a broad-shouldered Cornish constable named Harold Cheevers, who was married, had two sons, and had once been revolver champion of the British Isles. Just as Maugham had male secretaries who were more than secretaries, Walpole made Cheevers into a secretary-chauffeur-friend.[10] Walpole hero-worshipped Henry James, whom he had met when he was twenty-four. James was then in his mid-sixties and ill. Walpole called him "my very dear Master," and James responded with "darling Hugh" and "belovedest little Hugh."

Walpole was the essential literary careerist. He wrote the Cornish novelist Charles Marriott in 1906: "I hope you won't think this cheek. I suppose you get any number of these kinds of letters—but I really do want to thank you for the pleasure your books have given me. I've only just come down from Cambridge so it is rather impertinent my writing at all."[11] Doubtless his admiration was sincere. It was also useful, for he soon had Marriott sponsoring his work.

Walpole played leapfrog with people. Having won Marriott's friendship, he stood him up in 1909 to dine with the Countess of Lovelace, who was more useful to his social future. He edged himself into such establishment institutions and publications as the Athenaeum, the Reform, Who's Who, Companion of the British Empire; he won the James Tait Black prize and became chairman of the Book Society. He was adept at coaxing blurbs from his colleagues and giving dinner parties for better known writers. When he had an unfavorable review, he consorted with the enemy, inviting the hostile critic to lunch. When Katherine Mansfield panned his novel Jeremy, in 1919, he wrote her a long conciliatory letter and softened her disapproval. In his diary he listed his friends in order of merit: there were two groups, "First Fifteen" and "Second Thirty."[12] The good side of this shameless climbing was his readiness to assist young writers once he was established. He collaborated with the young J. B. Priestley on an epistolary novel called Farthing Hall. His name guaranteed its success, which gave Priestley the financial security to write his own long novel. He was always ready with a blurb and a letter of introduction. V. S. Pritchett said of him: "The son of a bishop, he bounded around literature as if it were his diocese."[13]

By the 1930s he truly was a bishop of English letters, a figure of power and patronage. His weekly column in the Daily Express made and broke reputations, and his lecture tours made him immensely popular in the United States. His novels, in their discreetly elegant green-and-gold bindings, seemed as safely destined for immortality as Bennett's and Galsworthy's.

But when Maugham met him in the summer of 1910 at a literary garden party given by Violet Hunt in her Camden retreat, Walpole had just set up as a full-time writer in London. In 1909 his first book, *The Wooden Horse*, had been published to little acclaim and (according to the contract) no royalty on the first 800 copies. In the buzz of garden-party conversation (Had May Sinclair showed more than reverence for Henry James in her novel *The Creators*? What was Frank Harris writing about Shakespeare? How shocking were the audacities of the Vedrenne-Barker management at the Court Theatre!) Walpole noticed a gray top hat that sat "audaciously, cynically, with humor and with quite a definite pose of dandyism in which the wearer obviously did not believe."[14] The hat belonged, Walpole later decided, to a man who was determined to make money and had put behind him the unproductive austerities of *A Man of Honour* and *Liza of Lambeth*. Walpole cultivated the successful playwright and sent him a wire on his next first night, to which Maugham replied: "You are a kind old thing."

When Walpole was listed in the 1917 New Year's Honours as a Companion of the British Empire, Maugham wrote him in December, "so that, perhaps for the last time, I may address you as an equal."[15] When Walpole's novel based on his Russian adventures appeared, Maugham wrote him rather fulsomely that "each one of your books is a little better than the last; and this quality of advancing you have alone among your contemporaries. I lay my trembling hands upon your young, unruly locks."[16] Walpole praised Maugham's works with equal ardor. When Gerald Kelly painted Walpole's portrait in 1921, Maugham dropped by his studio for tea. Walpole recorded in his diary that he "warmed my heart by speaking well of my work, especially *The Captives*, and actually praising my 'urbane humor,' which everyone always denies me."[17] But in fact, as he was later to admit, Maugham detested Walpole. The warm notes and the praise were a measure only of his talent for dissembling.

In the fall of 1910 Maugham made his first trip to America. He said he was going like Christopher Columbus, to discover a new continent.[18] It was a continent that had already discovered him and where he would become something of a legend. All his plays from *Lady Frederick* on had been produced there. He sailed on the *Caronia* on October 22, arriving in New York on the twenty-eighth. Frohman was on hand to help him settle in his suite at the St. Regis and show him around. The city's tallest building was the Metropolitan Tower. Sherry's and Delmonico's were the fashionable restaurants. One went to Shanley's to see the Vernon Castles. The only two places where women could smoke in public (between four and six) were Rector's downtown and the Plaza Hotel. On Broadway the first neon signs were going up. Fifth Avenue was lined with great houses staffed by footmen. Buses and streetcars were horse-drawn. Maugham wondered why Americans always had longer names for things: "locomotive" for "engine" and "elevator" for "lift." ("Truck" for "lorry" was an exception that did not occur to him.)

He complained to Frohman about an actor named Desborough, who he said had ruined the American production of *Penelope*, and told Frohman that Desborough should either be killed, maimed, or thrown in the Hudson.[19] He met Billie Burke, the Ohio-born daughter of Billy Burke, a clown for Barnum & Bailey. Under contract to Frohman—she played *Mrs. Dot* for more than two years—Billie Burke was quite taken with Maugham, who seemed to her Parisian rather than Bond Street in elegance, with his swallowtails and striped trousers, piping on his coat, smart gloves and stick, beautifully made shoes, gray top hat with black band, and clipped mustache. "He had great smouldering brown eyes," she recalled. "Ah, yes, Mr. Maugham, so you had, and I was a little in love with you, sir."[20]

It was on this trip that Maugham made friends with a young man who was on his way to becoming the leading American playwright of his day, Edward (Ned) Sheldon, who would play an important part in Maugham's life. Sheldon, the son of a wealthy Chicago real estate dealer, wrote *Salvation Nell* and *The Nigger* (the first play about a black man passing for white), both Broadway sensations. Sheldon was twenty-four and Maugham was thirty-six; both were successful playwrights who knew how to milk a topical theme. They had a high regard for each other's craftsmanship, and recognized in each other a fastidiousness and lack of ease in their relationships with women. Sheldon had an apartment at 8 Gramercy Park, furnished with thick black rugs, gunmetal mirrors, and live macaws on perches. Maugham was a frequent guest there; they also went to the Hamptons together on weekends.[21]

Like Philip Carey in *Of Human Bondage*, Sheldon was a man in doubt about his manhood who had been shabbily treated by a woman unworthy of him. He had fallen in love with Doris Keane, who starred in his biggest hit, *Romance*. They became engaged, but when he found out that she was sleeping with her leading man on tour, he broke off the engagement, saying, "I would make a very poor sort of husband for you, Doris."

Shortly afterward he developed a crippling arthritislike disease that spread from joint to joint until he was almost totally paralyzed. This was a form of physical bondage that, had it been used in a novel, would have seemed farfetched. No organic cause for the illness could be found, and so Sheldon was treated by Dr. Carl Binger of the Rockefeller Institute, a pioneer in psychosomatic illness. Binger could do nothing; he speculated that Sheldon's paralysis was a subconscious withdrawal from life, somehow connected to his unhappy love affair with Doris Keane.[22]

Sheldon was looked after by his mother, who surrounded him with orderlies, masseurs, and attendants to read aloud to him and give him high irrigation. The disease spread until he could move only his lips, but somehow he remained cheerful before the constant stream of visitors from the theatrical world who came to his door. The only time anyone ever saw him cry was when he heard that Doris Keane was dying of cancer of the liver. The illness spread to the eye cartilage, and when he had lost his sight he wore a narrow black-silk mask across his eyes as he continued to welcome his friends. When he died in 1946, at the age of sixty, the illness was attacking his larynx and his ears.[23] He was paralyzed, blind, deaf, and mute. Maugham, who saw his friend on many of his trips to America, may well have pondered a destiny that combined slow self-destruction with an iron will to live.

Maugham experienced the fervor with which America clasps celebrities to its bosom, and he delighted in seeing his name in lights on Broadway. But the high point of his trip was a visit to the Morgan Library. He had a letter of introduction to the formidable curator of that establishment, Belle Green. As a special favor for a visiting British author of note she brought the manuscript of Keats's *Endymion* out of the vault and let Maugham hold it. He took the manuscript, written in Keats's bold, round hand, and was overcome with emotion. He thought of the young poet, who like him had started in life as a medical student, like him had loved Italy, and who had died there at the age of twenty-six. He remembered his own first visit to Italy when he was twenty. He had gone to Rome and had seen the plain stone under which Keats was buried in the Protestant cemetery. On the stone this line was inscribed: "Here lies one whose name was writ in water." When he handed the manuscript back to Belle Green he felt an uncomfortable choking in his throat.[24]

Toward the end of November he went to Boston for a week and stayed at the Hotel Touraine. He did not like Boston as much as New York, and could not help feeling that cultivated Bostonians looked upon writers who had not taken the precaution of dying a hundred years ago as guilty of bad taste.[25] He had a letter of introduction to Charles Eliot Norton and his sister Grace, who were childhood friends of Henry James. When he went to call on them James was there. His brother William had recently died and James had come back to Cambridge to console his sister-in-law. Maugham was asked to dinner at the Jameses's on Irving Street, and it turned out to be a gloomy evening. William James's widow had promised her husband that she would try to communicate with him beyond the grave, and Henry James had promised his brother to remain in Cambridge six months after his death so that there would be two sympathetic witnesses on the spot ready to receive any spirit messages. When Maugham dined with the Jameses the six months were drawing to a close, and no message had come. As Maugham rose to leave, James insisted on walking him to the corner, where he could catch a streetcar back to Boston. This was more than courtesy on the part of James, he thought, for "America seemed to him a strange and terrifying labyrinth in which without his guidance I was bound to get hopelessly lost." As they strolled James confessed that he was counting the days until he could sail for the blessed shores of England. He felt forlorn in Cambridge, and vowed never again to set foot in America, which he found bewildering. "I wander about those great empty streets of Boston," he said, "and I never see a living creature. I could not be more alone in the Sahara." As Maugham reflected on the oddness of that remark the streetcar came into view. Afraid it would not stop, James began waving frantically when it was still a quarter of a mile away. He urged Maugham to jump on with the greatest agility of which he was capable, and warned him that if he were not careful he would be dragged along, and if not killed, at least mangled and dismembered. Maugham informed him that he was quite accustomed to boarding streetcars. Not American streetcars, James said. They were of a savagery and ruthlessness beyond conception. James's anxiety was contagious, and when the car pulled up Maugham jumped on, and felt that he had miraculously escaped serious injury. He looked back and saw James standing on his short legs in the middle of the road, still watching the streetcar, until he faded out of sight.[26]

Back in New York, Maugham discovered that there was an American branch of his family living in New Jersey. A young man named J. Beaumont Maugham invited him to come and meet the American Maughams in Tenafly. Maugham agreed, and Joseph Beaumont came to get him at the St. Regis.[27] He was eighteen, with dark, curly hair, brown eyes, and a stammer, which convinced Maugham that they were related. They crossed the Hudson on the ferry and took the trolley to Tenafly, where Maugham found the coloring of the autumn landscape lovely. He met Joseph Beaumont's father, Ralph S. Maugham, a schoolteacher. Ralph's father, Joseph Beaumont senior, had come to the United States in the 1850s and settled in Passaic. At the outbreak of the Civil War he enlisted in a New Jersey regiment. After the war he became a teacher and edited a local newspaper, the *Tuckerton Beacon*.[28] Maugham kept up with his American "cousins" although he usually professed indifference to family matters.

His first visit to America ended with two newspaper interviews. Janet Vale of the *Morning Telegraph* found him prickly. When she asked how he wrote plays, he replied: "I find out what I have to say and I say it." Sensing that he disliked her, she asked if it was because he thought she was a suffragette. No, Maugham replied, adding: "As to suffrage, I see no reason why women shouldn't vote if they care to, but I can't see why they want to. Voting is not interesting. I don't vote. I don't want to. I can't see why women want to bother about it."[29] Chauncey L. Parsons of the *Dramatic Mirror* saw Maugham as a typical Englishman. In the middle of the interview he rose to open a window, explaining: "I can't get used to the American temperature. While wintry blasts are raging around corners outside, I am wilting in tropic heat. In England we keep our rooms much cooler." Mr. Parsons ended the interview by expressing the hope that someday a sane American might appear as a character in English literature.[30]

Maugham told Janet Vale that he did not vote, but in a thank-you note to his Boston host Eliot Norton he explained that he was cutting his visit short because of the general election in England.[31] In any case, he was back in London in December 1910, in time not only for the election but for the rehearsals of *Loaves and Fishes*, the play about a hypocritical clergyman which he had written in 1903 but had never been able to place and had rewritten as the novel *The Bishop's Apron*. Now Frohman was doing it, but there were casting problems. An actor named Aynesworth, engaged to play the lead, had left the cast after several rehearsals. Maugham wrote Frohman on February 2, 1911, that "his action seems to have been caused by the most childish vanity and he has acted without any regard to the convenience of the other people concerned."[32] A substitute was found in Robert Loraine, and *Loaves and Fishes* premiered on February 24.

It was Maugham's third flop in as many plays. It ran for 48 performances and was not produced in America. Critics found it feeble and distasteful and pointed out that Maugham had already used the material as a novel. Several reviewers said that in satirizing clergymen he was copying Trollope but without Trollope's grasp of clerical background. He was stigmatized as a playwright who would use any means to get a laugh. One of the play's only supporters was A. A. Milne, who was the assistant editor of *Punch*, who reviewed it on March 8, calling it "truly funny," with a moral lesson lacking in Maugham's previous plays.[33]

Maugham believed that the real reason for the play's failure was the British public's refusal to see a clergyman made fun of. He wrote Ada Leverson that he was receiving fifty angry letters a day, mostly anonymous, "and you know, answering anonymous letters is the very devil of a job."[34] He had been told that two lords in the first-night audience had decided that the references to the Holy Sacrament were not only in bad taste but blasphemous. "It is rather a nuisance," he wrote Dorothy Allhusen, "for all the people who have asked me to dine and to stay on the strength of a success and who will now have to put up with me as a failure."[35] On March 6 he wrote his American friend Dillie Fleming that "my play was received with roars of laughter, but unfortunately the public are shocked because ridicule is cast on the cloth and they will not go. It is a great disappointment, especially now that I am moving into a new house."[36]

The new house—along with membership in the Garrick Club and the right tailor—was further proof that Maugham had arrived. It was at 6 Chesterfield Street, in the heart of Mayfair, and established him as a member of a privileged minority. His address made him a part of the leisurely horse-drawn life of the upper classes, with their clubs in Pall Mall, their "at home" teas, afternoon calls, and flourishing salons. Lady Ottoline Morrell was "at home" on Thursdays. The Duchess of Sutherland was "at home" on Fridays. Hostesses spent their mornings writing notes and invitations that went out by hand to people they wanted to meet. Among them was Maugham, who no longer had to take a bus to reach the right neighborhood.

The Georgian house he bought had been built in 1734, and had an eight-hundred-year leasehold at a nominal ground rent, which amounted to a freehold. It was due to go up for auction on May 20, but Maugham bought it by private treaty for eight thousand pounds, and according to the rate books, owned it from April 1911 until March 1919.[37] On a one-block-long street behind Park Lane, it gave him the social cachet of Mayfair. His old and loyal friend Walter Payne moved in with him.

After fifteen years of struggle Maugham could bask in the last rays of the golden Edwardian summer, which would continue until 1914. He was not only famous, he was as respectable as his lawyer brother Frederic, who belonged to the Savile Club.[38] Once the Chesterfield Street house was remodeled, his first dinner guest was Charles Frohman. The invitation said: "Will you come and see the house that Frohman built?"[39] Another guest was Billie Burke, to whom he showed a small framed picture, a portrait of her as Mrs. Dot, and said: "Do you know who that interesting young woman is? Well, let me tell you. That is the woman who bought me this house."[40]

One day when Maugham was reading in his new sitting room the art dealer and critic Hugh Lane dropped by and said he had seen a theatrical picture by Samuel De Wilde in a shop in Pimlico. "They're asking forty-five pounds for it," he said. "You're a dramatist, you ought to buy it." Maugham, aware of the bareness of his walls, went to see the picture, which showed two actors in a scene from an eighteenth-century play. He bought it—the first of what would become the finest collection of theatrical paintings outside the Garrick Club. He soon began to haunt junk shops and those of frame makers in Soho and Chelsea. Frugal as always, his single figures were invariably men, for pretty actresses were more expensive. He bought a full-length portrait of an actor in costume for a pound, and watercolors of actors for five shillings each. He prowled the salesrooms of Sotheby's and Christie's, and bought Zoffany's portrait of Garrick, which had belonged to Henry Irving. Once at Christie's, when he bid on a Zoffany representing Garrick as Macbeth, a dealer bid against him. Maugham, well over his usual limit, went up to two hundred fifty pounds. The dealer sent him a note saying that he was acting for the Maharajah of Baroda and was under instructions to buy at any price. Maugham bowed before superior wealth.[41] Eventually he acquired a collection of 40 oils, including 8 Zoffanys and 15 De Wildes. In the twenties Zoffany came back into fashion, and Maugham had the satisfaction of being offered two thousand pounds for one of his portraits of Garrick.

The same year that Maugham became a collector he also sat for his best known portrait by Gerald Kelly. Maugham had stopped by his studio, at 7 William Street, one day in the summer of 1911 to show Kelly a new top hat. Struck by his dapper appearance, Kelly decided to paint him. Maugham sat between thirty and forty times for the portrait, which Kelly called "The Jester." He is shown in spats and white gloves, with cane and top hat, his mustache carefully brushed, his brown eyes diffident. He looks like the best man at a wedding. In the background Kelly painted a Burmese cabinet and a high lacquered Coromandel screen, which suggests the Oriental intricacy of his character. Kelly later dismissed the portrait as "just done casually. It amused me to paint the cabinet and the screen, and Maugham was introduced as a diversion in the foreground. It is so perfunctory in characterisation as to be quite valueless."[42] In 1933, however, the Tate Gallery bought "The Jester," and Maugham wrote Kelly that he had received as many letters of congratulation as if he "had just been delivered of a son and heir."[43]

By the time Kelly had immortalized him as "The Jester," the debonair playwright who kept West End audiences laughing, Maugham had outgrown the part. He was happy, he was prosperous, he was busy, and his head was full of plays that managers were eager for him to write despite the failure of his last three productions, but the magnet of the past pulled him in another direction. Behind the dapper London man-about-town, behind the author of hit comedies, there lurked the boy who had lost his mother, the stammerer who was teased at school, the London medical student who saw suffering at first hand. Wherever Maugham was, at parties, or rehearsals, or asleep, memories crowded his mind. The past began to reclaim him with such urgency that he felt he could regain his peace only by writing about it. He refused all contracts for new plays and retired from the stage for two years. He took the manuscript that had been turned down by Fisher Unwin, "The Artistic Temperament of Stephen Carey," and in 1911 began rewriting it, hoping that in this way he might exorcise his unhappy past.[44] He was already working on the book that would become *Of Human Bondage* at the time that he was sitting for "The Jester."

He had not published a novel since *The Magician* in 1908, which had been bought by Methuen as part of a three-novel contract, but was eventually published by Heinemann. Now, in November 1911, Methuen suddenly remembered that Maugham owed them three novels. "We have an agreement with you for three new novels," they wrote, "and we should be very pleased to hear that you are likely to deliver the first of these within a moderate time. We admire your brilliant talent, and are looking forward with impatience to the publication of one of your books."[45]

Maugham was incensed. He wrote Pinker, whom he had wisely retained as his literary agent, that the Methuen agreement was

> directly contrary to the views I have from the very beginning stated most clearly to you. I have invariably answered your question whether I would give a book to Methuen with a decided negative. When I consented to withdraw *The Magician* it was clearly understood on both sides that the agreement should be canceled, and on that account I returned the 75 pounds. . . . When Methuen later attempted to get money for the setting up of the book in type, I refused to pay and you upheld me in my refusal. We both agreed that the claim was monstrous. . . . I am determined not to allow Methuen to impose on me in this matter.[46]

He threatened to take the matter to court, and Methuen dropped their claim.

The year ended on a more pleasant note. One evening Maugham was reading in his study when Mrs. Charles Carstairs, the wife of the Knoedler's representative in London, who lived a few doors down at 13 Chesterfield Street, called. She had asked two friends to dinner and the theater (the curtain in those days rose at 9 P.M.), one of whom had let her down. Would Maugham, as a favor to a neighbor, fill in at the last minute? Since he was not busy and wanted to see the play, he accepted. He dressed and walked the short distance to the Carstairs', and was introduced to the other guest, Mrs. Syrie Wellcome, whom he had already met at a luncheon in 1910.[47]

In the account he gave of this first meeting in *Looking Back* he dated it 1913, but in his library there was a book inscribed "Xmas 1911— much love from Syrie."[48] It was a volume of three of George Bernard Shaw's plays, *The Doctor's Dilemma, Getting Married,* and *The Shewing-up of Blanco Posnet.* In the choice of her Christmas gift, as early as 1911, Mrs. Wellcome seemed to be endorsing the Shavian view of marriage as a contract between two intelligent people and announcing her intention of sharing that view with Maugham. A diminutive and pretty woman of thirty-two with close-set brown eyes, lovely magnolia skin, and a gift for flattery, she was the daughter of a remarkable man, and the wife of a remarkable man, from whom she was separated.

Gwendolen Maud Syrie (a compression of Sarah Louise) Barnardo was born in 1879, the daughter of Dr. Thomas John Barnardo. Maugham said the Barnardos were German Jews who had fled Hamburg in 1846 after a wave of anti-Semitism, had settled in Dublin, and converted to Christianity. The official version is that they were a Venetian family—their name originally spelled Bernardo—who had converted to Lutheran Protestantism in the sixteenth century and fled to Hamburg to escape the Inquisition. They set up a banking firm but lost everything in the Napoleonic wars. Thomas John Barnardo's father, John Michaelis Barnardo, emigrated to Ireland and became a fur merchant. He married twice and had seventeen children, one of whom was the tiny, frail Thomas John, who went to London to study medicine with the intention of becoming a missionary doctor in China. But when he saw the cholera epidemics in the East End, he decided that England needed missionary doctors as badly as China. Pursuing his medical studies at London Hospital in 1866, he discovered that Victorian London was populated with thousands of homeless children. They stole and begged and died in the streets. It was far worse than anything Dickens imagined. Dr. Barnardo made up his mind to devote himself to the neglected children of the poor. With the financial help of Lord Shaftesbury, he founded orphanages called Barnardo Homes. He was a driven, round-the-clock worker, himself no bigger than a boy, and almost totally deaf. He became a controversial figure among right-thinking Victorians, who did not want to be reminded of the horrifying conditions that prevailed at the heart of their splendid empire.

On one occasion Barnardo was unable to admit a child for lack of space; the child was later found in a barrel in the Borough Market, frozen to death. His motto thereafter, nailed over the door of every Barnardo Home, was: No destitute child ever refused admission. The homes proliferated until there were twenty-seven in London and sixteen in the rest of England. The orphans were known as Barnardo boys and Barnardo girls, and every home had its Barnardo Musical Boys, who toured the empire and made records. General Booth once said to him: "You look after the children and I'll look after the adults; then together we'll convert the world."[49]

In 1873 Barnardo met Sarah Louise (Syrie) Elmslie, the daughter of a Lloyd's underwriter, who had taken up charity work and invited him to visit a home that she had founded for poor boys in Richmond. Barnardo married her that June, and they had seven children, four of whom survived early childhood, and one of whom was a mentally retarded dwarf. Syrie was born in 1879. A generous supporter named

John Sands had given Barnardo a house in Essex called Mossford Lodge as a wedding present. Barnardo turned the adjoining coach house into a home for orphaned girls. As their number increased he built cottages in the neighborhood, until there were sixty-five cottages scattered over sixty acres of land. Syrie grew up as a member of what was called "the largest family in the world." As the daughter of the best known do-gooder in England, she was raised in an atmosphere of pious philanthropy. She played the organ at her father's fund-raisers in London churches. Smoking and drinking were not allowed at home, and they read the Bible on Sundays. This would have been good training for the nunnery, but Syrie grew up to be a bright and vivacious young lady, who was nicknamed Queenie because of her striking looks and figure. Mrs. Barnardo convinced her husband that she would never find a suitor if they continued to live in Essex among the orphans. Dr. Barnardo rented a house in Surbiton. In 1901, when Syrie was twenty-two and still unmarried, her parents allowed her to travel to Egypt with a group of English tourists. They took a boat up the Nile to Khartoum, where she met Henry Wellcome, the Wisconsin-born founder of a successful pharmaceutical firm, who was in the Sudan to found a tropical research institute. Wellcome, much taken with the seductive Queenie, informed her parents that he wished to marry her. The wedding took place on June 25, 1901, at St. Mark's Church, Surbiton, but the honeymoon was delayed until September to allow Wellcome to tie up some business. At forty-eight, he was more than twice Syrie's age. She may have seen marriage with a middle-aged man as a means of escaping from the orphanage.[50]

Henry Wellcome was a self-made American frontiersman who had turned himself into a prosperous English gentleman. Born in Almond, Wisconsin, the son of an Adventist minister who moved to Minnesota when he was a child, he went to a log cabin school and grew up among the Dakota Indians. Henry was interested in chemistry and attended the Chicago and Philadelphia colleges of pharmacy. In 1880 he went to England and founded a drug company with a Philadelphia friend, Silas M. Burroughs. Prosperity smiled upon them when they began to dispense drugs in a compressed form under the name of "tabloids"; the term soon entered the language to denote anything compressed and condensed, including newspapers.[51]

Wellcome was a complicated man, shy and reserved, with few friends, but he had an adventurous streak and organized several African expeditions. Strange tales were told of his behavior on these trips and found their way into the pages of a scandal sheet of the day called *John Bull*. It was said that his greatest pleasure was flogging the natives.[52] At home, however, he was a pillar of the community who spent millions on research and charity. He became a British subject, was knighted, and when he died in 1936 left an estate of three million pounds.

Syrie settled into domesticity in a house in Kent appropriately called The Nest. In 1903 she gave birth to a son, who was named after his father. He grew up mentally ill and was later sent to live with a family of dairy farmers near London. Over the years the marriage deteriorated. The age difference was too great, and Wellcome was a jealous and domineering husband, who expected his home to be organized as if it were a branch of his business. In addition they were sexually incompatible. Syrie told a friend that her husband would barge into her bedroom wearing only a raincoat, which he would remove before entering her bed. Syrie was gay and fun-loving; she wanted a life as far removed as possible from the Barnardo homes. Instead she seemed to have exchanged one form of sequestration for another.

In 1909, while on a trip to America, Wellcome told his wife he knew she had a lover. A deed of separation was signed in September 1910, and Wellcome settled 2,400 pounds a year on Syrie—a generous sum, about equal to $50,000 in today's currency. He took custody of their son, who was allowed to visit his mother in the summers, and Wellcome never saw Syrie again.[53] She lived in London, a fashionable single woman, with a house in exclusive Regent's Park, who moved in the Mayfair set and was interested in decoration.

When Maugham met her in 1911 the most prominent of her lovers was Gordon Selfridge, the owner of the world-famous store that bore his name. Selfridge, like Henry Wellcome, was a Wisconsin-born American who found fame in England. He was born in Ripon, Wisconsin, in 1856, and his merchandising career began when he was a twelve-year-old errand boy in a department store. He worked his way up to a junior partnership at Marshall Field's, and came to conquer London in 1906. He leased 42,000 square feet in Oxford Street and built a Roman temple of a store, with a long line of Corinthian columns that rose several stories, and an entrance that might have come from the Baths of Caracalla. When Selfridge's opened in March 1909 it had 130 departments, a roof garden, and a bargain basement that covered three and a half acres. The staff of 1,800 had been on the payroll for three months, rehearsing the premiere. Selfridge's was a sensation, and its owner became an instant celebrity.[54]

In his later years Selfridge the hardworking Wisconsin puritan was transformed into Selfridge the high-rolling pleasure-seeker. On weekends he crossed the Channel on the *Golden Arrow* train-ship service and lost thousands of pounds at the Deauville casino. In London his Rolls Royce was often parked near the stage entrance of theaters. He fell for Gaby Deslys, a *"grande horizontale,"* who was credited with the abdication of King Manuel II of Portugal, and set her up in a flat in Kensington. It was said that she sold her favors for fifty pounds. Not the least advantage of being Selfridge's mistress was having a charge account at his store. Selfridge spent money so compulsively that his fortune evaporated and he had to borrow from the banks. In 1940 the board removed him from control and gave him two thousand pounds a year and the empty title of president. He died in 1947 at the age of ninety-one.[55]

One of the women who shopped at Selfridge's on Sunday in the company of the owner was Syrie Wellcome. She later described him to Maugham, who turned him into the character of Arthur Fenwick in a play called *Our Betters*, written in 1915 but not produced in London until 1923. Arthur Fenwick is a red-faced, gray-haired, cigar-smoking, poker-playing American who runs a London department store. He calls a woman "girlie," and can work fourteen hours on end and feel "fresh as a daisy." He admires his mistress, Lady Grayston, an American who has made it in London society, as Selfridge must have admired Syrie for the same reason, and tells her: "You've got there, girlie, you've got there." When Lady Grayston asks him how business is doing he says: "Fine! I'm opening two new branches next week. They laughed at me when I first came over here. They said I'd go bankrupt. I've turned their silly old methods upside down. He laughs longest who laughs last."

When he met Syrie at the Carstairs' on that evening toward the end of 1911, Maugham found her attractive. During dinner both Mr. and Mrs. Carstairs were called to the telephone, and Syrie, radiant-eyed and low-voiced, said, "I wish we didn't have to go to this play, I'd like to listen to you talking all night." After the play they had supper at the Savoy. When they dropped Syrie off she said to Maugham, "We must meet again soon." On the following day he told Mrs. Carstairs that he thought her friend was charming and pretty, an appraisal that Mrs. Carstairs probably lost no time in relaying to the interested party.[56]

Maugham saw Syrie again, and soon they were on first-name terms, but at this time he was still seeing the Rubens-like Sue Jones, still put off by her promiscuity, and still sharing her with his friends.

He was also deep into a novel in which fact and fiction were mingled, in which he was setting down on paper emotions long suppressed and reviving a past that would not lie still. He had put aside all other work, despite his promise to Charles Frohman earlier that year to write a new play based on *The Taming of the Shrew*. The play did not get written, and in September 1911 Frohman wrote: "I am still down with rheumatism—partly on account of the weather, but more especially because you are not doing any work."[57] Although Maugham was working, on a book more difficult and painful than any he had yet written, he did find the time, in 1912, to write an adaptation of Molière's *Le Bourgeois Gentilhomme* for Herbert Beerbohm Tree, which was produced in 1913, ran for eight performances and seemed to many critics conclusive evidence that Molière cannot be done in English.

In December 1912 Maugham interrupted his novel to work on the play that Frohman wanted. He recalled an aunt of his whose companion had left her to live with her brother on a farm in Canada. The former companion eventually wrote the aunt that she had married one of the hired men. The aunt was shocked. This, he thought, was a story to fit his theme, and he made plans to go to Canada.[58]

Maugham found life on a Canadian farm in winter harsh and depressing, as he wrote to his friend Mabel Beardsley, Aubrey's sister, who was dying of cancer.

I have just come back from savage parts and I wish to say that I much prefer civilization. . . . I have been staying on a Canadian farm and have gathered all sorts of material for a dreary, sordid tragedy after the manner of Tolstoi, and this is rather unfortunate since I have been commissioned to write a really pleasant play which shall make people feel better and happier. My God, what a life they lead, at least in the winter, surrounded by the snowy prairie, cut off from their neighbors and absorbed with the struggle of getting three meals a day. Husbands and wives get to such a pitch of irritability that they will pass weeks without speaking to one another. In one house in which I stayed the wife had killed herself, in another there hung a strange gloom of impending madness. I was glad to get away. But it was an interesting experience, and the prairie, even under the snow, had a curious fascination which lingers in my memory now that I am returned to New York.[59]

He was in New York by December 29, and stayed there about a month before returning to London. H. E. Stearns of the *Dramatic Mirror* interviewed him at the St. Regis. His reputation as a clever and epigrammatic writer puzzled Stearns, who saw Maugham as reminiscent of "a young instructor in French in a big university—a trifle short, clear and smooth complexioned, with dark eyes that scrutinize one carefully. His speech is slow and thoughtful, sometimes even hesitant. A certain refinement and delicacy of manner suggests once or twice the esthete."

Stearns was struck by his relativism. There seemed to be no absolute values for him; everything was the expression of an individual personality. "To the thoughtful observer," Maugham said, "praise and blame, except as practical expedients of discourse, are ridiculous. No man is really 'strong'—it is an illusion or perspective of human viewpoints."[60]

Perhaps he was reflecting his own indecision on the problem he now had to face. His attachment to Sue Jones had not faded, and in fact he had recently, through his friendship with Ned Sheldon, helped her get a part in the Chicago production of *Romance*, which was opening in September 1913, starring Doris Keane. Maugham was now approaching forty; he had money, fame, and a house in Mayfair, big enough for two. He decided that the time had come to settle down. He knew in his heart that he was homosexual, but he was not yet willing to surrender to that side of his nature. He felt he was still capable of loving women and of having a satisfactory sexual life with them. Sue Jones was a warm-hearted, unjudging woman who understood his physical needs and whose sunny disposition balanced his tendency to brood. Since Maugham remained an Edwardian gentleman, marriage was in the scheme of things and would also act as a cover for his true inclinations. Sue's promiscuity was not that important, he decided. He had been promiscuous himself.

Sue was going to America in September 1913, and Maugham was in London finishing his Canadian play, *The Land of Promise*. It was due to open in New Haven on November 26, with Billie Burke, and he was going to have to cross the Atlantic for rehearsals. He decided that when he got to New York he would ask Sue to marry him. He went to a jeweler's and bought an engagement ring. Having arrived ahead of her, he met her boat, and spotted her on deck talking gaily to a dashing young man. She told him that she was going straight to Chicago and would not even be able to spend the day with him in New York, where he was kept by rehearsals. It was not until three or four weeks later that

Maugham was able to get to Chicago. Sue seemed delighted to see him, pleased with her part and her success. They had supper in her small suite after the performance. Maugham rang for the waiter, and after some small talk came to the point:

"Sue, I've come to Chicago to ask you to marry me. What do you say to it?" He smiled with the assurance of a man who knows what the answer will be.

"I don't want to marry you," Sue said.

Maugham was astonished. "Why not?" he asked.

"I just don't want to," Sue said.

He thought she wanted to be coaxed. "I thought you could give a fortnight's notice, which would give them time to find someone to take your place," he said, "and we'd get married at once and take a train to San Francisco. Then we'll get on a ship and go to Tahiti."

"It sounds lovely," Sue said. "I don't want to give up my part."

"That's absurd," Maugham said.

"I've had wonderful notices," Sue said.

He handed her the engagement ring, two large pearls set in a small ring of diamonds.

"It's very pretty," Sue said, and handed it back.

"Keep it," he said.

"No, I won't do that," Sue said.

"Are you serious?" he asked.

"If you want to go to bed with me, you may," Sue said, "but I won't marry you."

Maugham did not want to go to bed with her. They sat in silence for a while, then he asked: "Well, there's nothing more to be said, is there?"

"No," Sue replied.

He got up, kissed her, put the ring back in his pocket, and left.[61]

Rejected, Maugham went back to New York and buried himself in rehearsals for The Land of Promise. After a November tryout in New Haven, the play was due to open in New York on Christmas day. One day, shortly before the opening, as he walked down the street, he saw a newspaper headline: ACTRESS MARRIES EARL'S SON. He had a hunch he knew who the actress was and bought a paper. Sue Jones had married Angus McDonnell, the second son of the sixth Earl of Antrim, in Chicago on December 13. He was convinced that McDonnell was the dashing young man he had seen on the boat, and that Sue had gone to bed with him and gotten pregnant. But this was only an excuse to soothe his injured pride, for Sue had no children by McDonnell. When the Chicago run of *Romance* was over, on January 3, 1914, she retired from the stage and spent the rest of her life as the dutiful wife of a country gentleman. McDonnell was an engineer working for the Southern Railway (in the U.S.) when he met Sue Jones and married her. A year later World War I broke out, and he joined the Canadian Railway Troops and was credited with an outstanding job building the railway network behind the western front. He ended the war as a full colonel.

Angus and Sue lived in Five Ashes, a village in Kent. In 1924 he ran for Parliament as a Conservative and won, but he did not like politics and did not run again. McDonnell was a cousin of Lord Halifax, British ambassador to Washington during World War II. Since Angus knew the United States, where he had worked in a variety of jobs, from cowhand to engine driver, and knew all sorts of people, Halifax recruited him as his public relations man, with the title of Honorary Attaché. Halifax gave him high marks for breaking the ice wherever they went. He had the reputation of being irresistible. By this time Sue was an invalid. A member of the British Embassy staff remembers parties and dinners that Angus attended without his wife. Maugham was in the United States too during the war, doing official work for the British government, and had occasion to deal with the embassy. He knew the McDonnells were there but made no attempt to see the woman to whom he had once proposed. Sue died in 1948, at the age of sixty-five, but lives on as Maugham's most fully realized woman character, Rosie, in *Cakes and Ale*. Angus McDonnell spent his last years crippled by illness and died in 1966.[62]

Maugham took the engagement ring back to the jeweler and got a refund less 10 percent. *The Land of Promise* opened in New York to mixed reviews, and ran for 76 performances. Billie Burke played the companion to an elderly lady. Left without a job, the companion seeks employment in Canada and marries a hired man, who tames her into submission and whom, as the curtain falls, she decides she loves. If only life could have imitated art, matters might have worked out differently with Sue Jones.

Maugham forgot his disappointment by taking out Billie Burke. One night they went out dancing, and Miss Burke complimented Maugham on his expert fox-trot. She was again on his arm for New Year's Eve, when they went to the costume ball at the Hotel Astor. It was there that Billie met Florenz Ziegfeld, whom she married in 1914 despite objections from Frohman that Ziegfeld had left a line of broken hearts in his wake.[63]

Maugham was back in London in January 1914 for rehearsals of *The Land of Promise*, which starred Irene Vanbrugh. She had a scene in which conversations are going on while she is ironing, and she got so interested in heating the iron, touching it with her finger to see if it was hot enough, and getting to work, that Maugham complained, "Irene seems quite admirable as a laundress, but while she is ironing, the dialogue rather goes by the board and the play itself loses interest."[64]

Having been spurned by one woman, Maugham was all the more vulnerable to the attentions of another. One day he ran into Syrie Wellcome at the opera. Pleased to see him, she invited him to a house-warming party she was giving for her new house in Regent's Park. Maugham gave her two seats for the opening night of *The Land of Promise*, February 26. She arrived at the theater after the curtain had gone up. Maugham was so annoyed that he decided not to go to her party. But since he did not want to go home alone after a first night, he went. He was congratulated by everyone, and Syrie, who had hired an orchestra, danced with him into the small hours. From that evening on, he saw her almost every day. On the rebound from Sue Jones, he had found a woman who appeared to worship every word that dropped from his lips. Syrie invited him to Paris, where she had an apartment on the quai d'Orsay, and he accepted. One evening after dinner at a restaurant they went back to her apartment and made love for the first time. When they returned to London he had dinner with her every night in her new house and then took her to bed. Apparently things went well. Syrie said she was madly in love, and Maugham was flattered and thought it might be true. He believed that he was more glamorous than the elderly men-about-town who took her to Ciro's and the Four Hundred.[65]

It soon became accepted in the circles they moved in that Maugham was Syrie's lover. He was clearly proud to be seen with a woman who was pretty, well dressed, and socially accepted. The affair escalated when Syrie suggested one day that they should have a baby. Having lost the custody of her son by Wellcome, she wanted a child of her own. She had a married younger brother who was childless, she said, and she was sure he would be glad to keep the baby at first. After three or four years she would adopt it, and no one would know she was its real mother. Oddly enough, Maugham was tempted by this offer of paternity. But in the final analysis he told Syrie he was against the idea. In the spring they went to Biarritz together and then to Spain, in her car, with her maid in attendance. On the trip to Spain Syrie again brought up the subject of having a baby, this time so persuasively that Maugham yielded. Driving to Paris, they spent a night in Bordeaux, and it was there, for the first time, that Maugham slept with Syrie without using a condom. It gave him a peculiar feeling to realize that he was engaging not only in a pleasant physical act but in a solemn one.[66] But when Syrie started talking about getting a divorce from Wellcome, Maugham became alarmed. He confided to Dillie: "Her husband has gone to Bermuda, and there is no talk of getting rid of him, so I breathe again."[67]

Back in London, he was pleased that *The Land of Promise* had settled into a long run. Syrie told him that she was pregnant, but there was no talk of marriage, and the subject of divorcing Wellcome had not been discussed for some time. Several weeks later she called and asked to see him. In bed, pale and worn, she told him she had had a miscarriage. Maugham said he was sorry. Syrie, weak and dispirited, asked if he wanted to end their liaison. Maugham, partly because he was growing attached to her and partly because he hated to see anyone in a vulnerable position suffer, said that he did not.[68]

Chapter Eight

*Sometimes people carry to such perfection the mask
they have assumed that in due course they actually
become the person they seem. But in his book or his
picture the real man delivers himself defenseless . . .
To the acute observer no one can produce the most
casual work without disclosing the innermost secrets
of his soul.*

Maugham, *Ten Novels and Their Authors*

THE SUMMER was approaching, when Syrie had custody of her eleven-
year-old son and took him to the country. Rather than join her in this
domestic situation, Maugham decided to spend July and August in
Capri.[1] He rented a villa with Ellingham Brooks and E. F. Benson,
another curious Edwardian figure. Benson was one of the four sons of
Edward White Benson, who became Archbishop of Canterbury in
1882. Born in 1867, he made a stir at the age of twenty-six with his first
novel, *Dodo*, a *roman à clef* about high society whose main character
was based on Margot Tennant, who became the Countess of Oxford
and Asquith. He was accused of betraying his class. He was among the
most prolific authors of his time, writing one hundred and one books,
although he thought of himself as a failure and said that his works
"lacked the red corpuscle." When his first novel was published Edmund
Gosse told him he would set his mark on English fiction—and in a way
he did, with a series of period novels that have become minor classics.
These were the campy Lucia comedies, written between 1920 and 1939
but Edwardian in spirit.

Maugham was friendly with Benson, who, like one of the characters
in Lucia, was "not an obtrusively masculine sort of person." Brooks
found them a villa for the summer, called Cercola, covered with morning glory and plumbago and set a little above the town, as far inland as
you can get in Capri. It had a terraced garden, six white-walled bedrooms, and a long studio with a view of the Bay of Naples. Maugham

and Benson, who usually came to the villa at different times, were to share the rent, while Brooks, who looked after the Cercola when they were away, stayed there rent-free.[2]

Capri continued to attract expatriates, and among the recent arrivals were Count Fersen, a Swedish nobleman who was rumored to have been jailed in France for an offense against minors, Norman Douglas, who was writing *South Wind*, and Compton Mackenzie. Son of the Scottish actor Edward Compton and brother of the actress Fay Compton, who would later star in several Maugham plays, Compton Mackenzie had written a much-discussed novel called *Sinister Street*. He was cheerful and brisk, small, wiry, full of energy, and pleased with himself. F. Scott Fitzgerald was one of his fans, and Edmund Wilson, in a 1949 letter to Arthur Mizener, wrote: "His career has been disappointing, but I would rather read him than Somerset Maugham, for he seems to me a real and rather remarkably gifted writer." Mackenzie wrote a *roman à clef* about the Capri expatriate colony, called *Vestal Fire*, which he dedicated to Ellingham Brooks, who had supplied most of the material. The homosexual contingent had now completely taken over Capri, and when a young Dutchman named Van Decker gave a party in his villa and danced a *pas seul* wearing nothing but a little bunch of roses, the local priest urged Mackenzie, as a good Catholic, to use his influence to discourage these shameful orgies.[3]

Brooks had not changed at all since Maugham had first met him in Heidelberg. He was translating the sonnets of the French symbolist poet José María de Heredia, and saw this work as his masterpiece, his *Rubáiyát*, slender but immortal, of which every syllable was a tessera in a polished and perfect mosaic. While he would call Benson's attention to an ambiguity in a sonnet that he had beautifully rendered, he thought Maugham's books were coarse. "He turned the pages," Benson said, "and grunted a little, and shut them up." The summer drifted by with long mornings of swimming, walks to the top of Monte Solaro, dinner under a vine pergola, and games of piquet in Morgano's café. Brooks translated, played the piano, and went for walks with his fox terrier.

Partly from laziness, partly from a flawless mental fastidiousness [Benson wrote of Brooks], he made less of fine abilities and highly educated tastes than anyone I have ever known. He was short in stature and clumsy in movement, but his face was very handsome. His mouth had a thin fine upper lip, priestlike and ascetic in character, but below was a full loose lower lip, as if the calls of the flesh had not yet been subdued. . . . In the process of making a complete failure of his life as far as achievement of any sort went, he made himself for many years very happy.[4]

Each day the excursion steamer from Naples landed at the Grande Marina with hordes of tourists and mail and newspapers. One afternoon Brooks brought back a copy of *The Times* dated June 29, 1914. "Hullo," he said after unfolding it, "an archduke's been assassinated. Franz Ferdinand."

"What an awful thing," Benson said. "Who is he? And where did it happen?"

"He's the Emperor of Austria's heir," Brooks said. "He was attending maneuvers at Sarajevo."

"Never heard of it," Benson said. "I want to go up to Monte Solaro after tea. Do come. The tawny lilies should be in flower."

"Too hot," Brooks said. "Besides I must water the garden."[5]

Benson looked up Sarajevo in *The Times* atlas and found that it was in Bosnia. It all seemed very far away and had nothing to do with Morgano's or the Bagno Timberino or the sunset over the Monte Solaro.

When Maugham arrived in July with Gerald Kelly, they joined in the leisurely routine and swam and played tennis. On August 4, a little more than a month after Sarajevo, World War I broke out, but Maugham saw no reason to change his plans, and remained in Capri. One day a wire arrived from Syrie saying she was in Rome, pregnant again by Maugham, and on her way to Capri. Maugham wired back immediately asking her not to come, since he was about to leave. Compton Mackenzie ran into Brooks, who was in a great flutter of excitement and told him that Maugham was involved with a married woman and would have to marry her. "I don't know what I shall do if Maugham brings a wife to the Cercola," he said. "I don't think Benson will like it at all either."[6]

Syrie ignored Maugham's wire and arrived. Three or four days later they left for an England that was at war. From the backs of London buses the brooding mustached face of Lord Kitchener, newly appointed Minister of War, stared out at the populace as he pointed his finger over a caption that said "Your King and Country Need You Now."[7] There was no conscription, however; the British, it was said, wanted to show the Germans that the amateur was better than the professional. Maugham, forty and five foot six, was too old and too short to enlist. At the start of the war a volunteer had to stand five foot eight, but by October the standard had been dropped to five five. And after the 30,000 casualties of October it was dropped again, to five three.[8]

Maugham wanted to do his bit. He could have stayed in England, like Lytton Strachey, six years his junior, who knitted mufflers "for the soldier and sailor lads," or like Shaw and H. G. Wells, his elders, who wrote letters to editors about the end of Prussian militarism. Instead he wrote to his friend Winston Churchill, who was First Lord of the Admiralty, asking to be made use of. While waiting for Churchill's reply he heard that the Red Cross was sending Ford ambulances to France, and applied as an interpreter. Another writer who joined the Red Cross was E. M. Forster, a pacifist by instinct, who went to Egypt as a "searcher" in 1915. In October, Maugham, in uniform, crossed the Channel with the ambulances. He left London with a play still running in the West End, *The Land of Promise*, and with his long autobiographical novel in the hands of his publisher. He did not volunteer as a doctor, never having practiced since his graduation from medical school seventeen years earlier.

By the time his ambulance unit arrived in Boulogne in October 1914 the British Expeditionary Force had sent 213,000 men to France. The first three months of the war had been disastrous for the allies. The French had lost more than half a million men, and in August the Germans had crossed the Meuse and were advancing toward Brussels. The British moved into Belgium to counter the offensive, but were beaten in their first contact with the Germans at Mons on August 23, and retreated to Meaux, thirty miles from Paris. The Germans had conquered Belgium by the end of August, and the road to France was clear. The French government, under President Poincaré, fled to Bordeaux. General Galliéni was named military governor of Paris. Café terraces were closed and bands were forbidden in restaurants. The great hotels were converted into hospitals. Casualties poured in from Orléans and Tours. On the last day of August a German plane flew over Paris and dropped leaflets saying the Germans would be there in three days.

And then there took place what Churchill called the greatest battle ever fought in the history of the world. On September 5, 1914, Joffre issued his celebrated order for the start of the battle of the Marne: "The hour has come to advance at all costs and to die where you stand rather than give way." On a two hundred-mile front along the Marne River, the French and the British pushed the Germans back. Paris' two thousand taxis drove troops to the front. The French took back Rheims, and a new front formed along the Aisne River. In England, hopes that the war would be over by Christmas had vanished. In the music halls a Union Jack backcloth would drop and an actor in naval officer's uniform would come onstage carrying a cricket bat and say: "Cricket for the time must end. This is the wicket we must defend." The British held the Belgian front, moving their headquarters to Ypres, a town famous for its wool and linen manufactures, which the British soldiers called "Wipers." Some of the most savage fighting of the war took place there in the last three months of 1914. Fifty thousand lives were lost to save Ypres. Maugham at this time was in the midst of that strange nightmare world that the British at home called "somewhere in France." He was in the battle of Ypres.[9]

His ambulance unit had been sent to France in mid-October to help cope with the first wave of casualties after Ypres. The British Red Cross Society was headquartered in Boulogne's Hotel de Paris. Maugham saw that drivers were needed more than interpreters, and so he took a fortnight's leave and returned to England to learn to drive an ambulance. When he got back he was attached to the French Army and moved near the front. He wrote his friend Dillie Fleming: "It is bitterly cold here now, and one day there is fog and the next rain—we are either rushed off our feet or bored and idle."[10] It was dangerous work. The ambulances went out at night, and the drivers had to avoid shell holes. The sky was lit by German flares and the flash of guns. Stretcher-bearers loaded the wounded, whom the drivers thought of as parcels marked "fragile." They tried to get back to the hospital without a single groan.[11]

One of Maugham's fellow drivers was Desmond MacCarthy, by profession a literary critic, by nature the proverbial Irishman, born without a rudder, missing trains, hoping and planning, and paying his way with charm. He succeeded Edmund Gosse as the leading critic on the *Sunday Times* and was a member of the Bloomsbury group. A great work was expected of him, but it never materialized. For MacCarthy, talking about it was like having done it. He had the floating element of something brilliant, and a morbid habit of self-deprecation. MacCarthy admired Maugham, who possessed the qualities of tenacity and self-confidence that he lacked. They took their meals together and shared a billet.

They moved around a lot, depending on the fighting. On one occasion, after having been very hardworked for some days, they had lunch in Montdidier, near the Flanders front. Maugham, flushed with wine and a good meal, confessed to MacCarthy that he had more character than brains and more brains than specific gifts. He was surprised, and not pleasantly, some years later to read his self-analysis in the columns of the *Sunday Times*.[12]

On another occasion they were sharing a small bedroom in Saint-Malo, near Dunkirk, when a thick package of proofs arrived. Maugham spread the long strips on the bed, and MacCarthy noticed how few corrections he made. When he commented on it, Maugham replied that he always went over his work carefully before sending it to the printer. "Ah," MacCarthy thought, "he's as business-like as a novelist as he is as a playwright. The itch for perfection doesn't trouble him; the adequate will do. I suppose the book will sell." Maugham was correcting the proofs for *Of Human Bondage*. Later, when he had read it, MacCarthy revised his opinion and called it "a novel which, together with *The Old Wives' Tale*, *A Farewell to Arms*, *Kipps*, *Babbitt*, and a few others, will float on the stream of time when the mass of modern realistic fiction is sediment at the bottom." MacCarthy became one of Maugham's most reliable admirers among English critics. It was he who dubbed Maugham "the English Maupassant."[13]

From Montdidier, Maugham was moved to Amiens, halfway between the Belgian border and Paris, where society ladies helped the wounded. He was told about one woman who wanted to give hot soup to a man shot through the lungs. The doctor in charge told her that she would drown him. "What nonsense," the woman said, holding a cup to the man's lips. He tried to swallow, and died. The woman was furious. "You've killed that man," she told the doctor. "Pardon me," the doctor replied, "you killed him. I told you what would happen."[14]

Maugham moved closer to the fighting, from Amiens to Doullens, where he helped evacuate a hundred wounded so that the temporary hospitals would be ready to receive the many casualties they expected after the big battle. When the evacuation had begun, a fat priest in a cassock and short surplice came into the street, preceded by a blind beadle led by a little boy, and followed by men carrying coffins. They chanted the service for the dead and proceeded slowly to the cemetery as civilians removed their hats and the military saluted. Maugham wondered how the dying men in the hospital felt at seeing this procession.[15]

Another hospital to which he was attached was in a white stone chateau with the date 1726 over the door. The furniture had been pushed against the walls. Drugs and bandages were piled on a grand piano. The French had suffered a defeat and there were hundreds of wounded, lying on straw mattresses on the floor. The circular lawn in front of the chateau, chopped up by ambulances and stretcher-bearers, was as muddy as a football field. The dead were stacked in an outhouse. He saw men with wounds that medical school had not prepared him for, "great wounds of the shoulder, the bone all shattered, running with pus, stinking gaping wounds in the back; wounds where a bullet had passed through the lungs; shattered feet so that you wonder if the limb can possibly be saved."

One soldier kept repeating he was going to die, while another soldier said, "*Mais non, mon vieux, tu guériras.*" He talked to a German prisoner who was convinced that had he been French his leg would not have been amputated. The dresser, seeing that Maugham spoke German, asked him to explain that he would have died had his leg not been removed. The German was sullen and silent. A French amputee was placed beside him to show him that such treatment was not given only to prisoners. Maugham's medical training came in handy, and he cleaned wounds and applied bandages.[16]

He was sent to Flanders, to Steenvoorde and Poperinge, within miles of the front lines. One afternoon when he was not busy he and a doctor friend went to visit the thirteenth-century Cloth Hall in Ypres, a magnificent building, 1,500 feet long, with forty-four statues of the counts of Flanders. Maugham parked the ambulance near a brick wall and stood and gazed at this splendid monument to the medieval wool and linen trades. As they walked down to the other end a shell burst against the wall they had just left. "Rather a near thing," said Maugham's friend.[17]

Winter came, with the armies frozen into place face to face. Instead of positional warfare, there was the grim immobility of the trenches. By the end of the year the permanent trench line with the Ypres salient had been dug. In London, at Christmastime, Norfolk turkeys were tenpence a pound, and *Peter Pan* was in its eleventh year at the Duke of York's. In the *Edinburgh Review* Edmund Gosse predicted that publishing would come to a standstill as soon as the books commissioned before the war had been disposed of.[18]

Maugham saw his quota of action in the great war but remembered his ambulance days fondly. As he wrote Violet Hunt: "What was so pleasant in the Red Cross was that you did what you were told and had no responsibility. I suppose just that is the attractiveness of the monastic life. And your work done, you can idle for the rest of the day."[19] In

Maugham the artist, with his strong sense of responsibility to his gifts, there was the occasional yearning for an institutionalized life, a setting in which he could be rid of the ideas in his head and the desire to express them. Other writers, such as T. E. Lawrence, found refuge from their obsessions in the sort of life in which one is told what to do, and having done it, can claim one's time as one's own.

But there was more to it than that. Maugham found himself in an all-male society, uncomplicated by women. In wartime it was natural to form male friendships, to care about other men, and sometimes to proceed from caring to intimacy. As Paul Fussell pointed out in *The Great War and Modern Memory*, there was a flowering of homosexual activity behind British lines.[20] It was sung in the homoerotic poetry of Rupert Brooke and Wilfred Owen. War was a situation in which two illegal activities, killing and loving men, were sanctioned. It was a situation in which Maugham, in the course of his duties, could admire the physical attractiveness of young soldiers. When men were thrown together in extreme situations, far from the restraints of Edwardian society and with women largely unavailable (Kitchener's Order to the Troops, which was to be kept at all times in the soldier's paybook, said: "While treating all women with perfect courtesy, you should avoid any intimacy"), passions were kindled.

It was on the Flanders front that Maugham met the love of his life, Gerald Haxton, who became his secretary-companion-lover. Haxton, born on October 6, 1892, in San Francisco, was a member of Maugham's ambulance unit. Maugham was forty when they met, and Gerald was twenty-two. His father, George, was American, and his mother, Sarah, was English.[21] They had separated when Gerald was a child and he had been brought up by his mother in England. Haxton was a young man of middle height, with a mustache, brown hair brushed back, and a pleasant but pockmarked face, on which he sometimes wore makeup to cover the scars. Alexander Frere, Maugham's editor at Heinemann, remembers Maugham telling Gerald: "Go and remove your slap."[22] Robin Maugham recalled that "He did not have a single feature that you could call good. He had white teeth, but they were not very even; he had a fresh color, but not a very clear skin; he had a good head of hair, but it was a vague brown between dark and fair; his eyes were fairly large, but they were of that pallid blue that is generally described as grey. He had an air of dissipation and people who didn't like him said he looked shifty."[23]

What Haxton lacked in conventional good looks he made up for in animal magnetism. Maugham was attracted by his immense vitality and adventurous spirit. Haxton cultivated a gregarious manner, which Maugham, who had such trouble approaching his fellow humans, much admired. S. N. Behrman, who saw them often in later years, believed that Gerald's hail-fellow-well-met approach was "an easy routine, a patter he had developed to use on outsiders like myself. There was never anything genuinely personal. It was like a document prepared by a cunning enemy in a war, a document intended to be captured."[24]

Since his early days at the King's School, Maugham had been drawn to men who had the qualities he lacked. Haxton was a reasonable facsimile of the athletic, outgoing, popular boys whom he had desperately envied in Canterbury. He was one of those unself-conscious, social animals whom Maugham had "fancied," throwing his soul into the other's body and enjoying "intervals of fantastic happiness." With Gerald, Maugham's childhood fantasy was made flesh. When he began to travel to far-flung lands in search of material, he and Gerald made a good team. Maugham was the reserved, rather stiff man of letters, and Gerald was his intermediary with the outside world. "I am shy of making acquaintance with strangers," Maugham wrote in *The Summing Up*, "but I was fortunate enough to have on my journeys a companion who had an inestimable social gift. He had an amiability of disposition that enabled him in a very short time to make friends with people in ships, clubs, barrooms, and hotels, so that through him I was able to get into easy contact with an immense number of persons whom otherwise I should have known only from a distance."

Instinctively Maugham recognized how useful these gifts of Haxton's could be to him in his career. With the exception of *Of Human Bondage*, his best work was written while he was with Haxton. There was a connection between his creative output and life with Gerald. All but one volume of short stories, the best plays, and all the novels from *The Moon and Sixpence* to *The Razor's Edge* were written during his tenure.

Maugham, who confessed to liking rogues, was also drawn to Haxton's unscrupulousness. As he wrote his American friend Dillie Fleming, who was being exploited by a man named Roland Stuart: "You must expect to pay something for the amusement you get out of knowing wrong 'uns."[25] Gerald made him pay. He was alcoholic, violent, dishonest, and unfaithful. Their relationship had a dark, unpleasant side in which the roles of master and servant were interchanged and each tried to make the other suffer.

But all that was yet to come. For the moment Maugham saw in Haxton a charming adventurer. He experienced, according to Glenway Wescott, "the first completely beautiful, completely appropriate love affair he had ever had."[26] He must have had intimations of what it would lead to, however, for in 1915, just one year later, he wrote the play *Our Betters* and modeled the character of the gigolo on Haxton, calling him Tony Paxton. Tony, the Duchesse de Surennes' young lover, is a sportsman who plays bridge and the horses and chases Gaiety girls. He is, according to the duchesse, "a liar, a gambler, an idler, a spendthrift." The duchesse catches Tony with her friend Lady Grayston and says: "He's a thorough wrong 'un, and that's all there is about it. He hasn't even the decency to try and excuse himself." Lady Grayston tells the duchesse: "You seem to have a passion for rotters, and they always treat you badly." Tony makes a fool of her, which only makes her love him more. The relationship between the duchesse and Paxton was uncomfortably close to the one that was developing between Maugham and Gerald.[27]

Maugham was pulled in different directions. While he was discovering charming Gerald at the front, Syrie was pregnant in England. Maugham had told Syrie that it would be a long war and that it was no time to have a baby, but Syrie would not listen. He applied for a leave and was back in London on February 4, 1915. He wrote his friend Dillie: "I am back on a fortnight's leave, very merry and bright, but frantically busy—I wish it were all over."[28]

One wonders what he had to be bright and merry about, considering the situation. In May he learned that the war had affected him once more; his friend and producer, Charles Frohman, the man most responsible for his wealth, had been one of the 1,195 casualties aboard the *Lusitania*. Frohman had been warned not to travel in wartime, but he insisted on making his annual London trip. When his partner, Al Hayman, went to see him off on May 1, Frohman was in a jocular mood and said: "Well, Al, if you want to write me, just address the letter care of the German submarine U-4."[29] On May 7 the British liner, within sight of the Irish coast, was torpedoed by a submarine and sank in half an hour. Maugham did not waste time mourning Frohman but wrote promptly to Al Hayman: "I am very glad to know that everything is to be continued just as if poor C.F. were still alive. My play [*Our Betters*] will be ready in a few days. . . . It was C.F.'s idea to bring over American actresses for the women's parts [since the play was about wealthy American women who marry titles]. . . . I expect you know the idea was to open the Duke of York's theatre with it in the autumn. I think the chief part would suit Blanche Bates very well if she would play it."[30] *Our Betters* did not open at the Duke of York's that autumn. It opened in New York in 1917, and was not produced in London until 1923.

In July, again on leave, Maugham decided to take Syrie to Rome, where she could be delivered without anyone knowing about it. They took an apartment near the Pincio and led a quiet life. Maugham worked on *Our Betters* and played golf, but to Syrie the days seemed interminable. She livened them up by telling Maugham about her admirers. He did not know what to believe and what was invented. When she was living in Paris, she said, the Duc de Gramont had asked her to be his *maîtresse en titre*, reserving Thursdays for him, a Bourbon prince had asked her to accompany him around the world on his yacht, and Gordon Selfridge had offered to settle on her five thousand pounds a year.[31]

The time was approaching for Syrie to give birth, and her mother, Mrs. Barnardo, came to Rome to hold her hand. Maugham had never met her and was relieved that she took her daughter's situation in stride. Leaving Syrie's mother in attendance, he took a short holiday that summer in Capri, where he could swim and gossip with his homosexual friends. He was sitting in a wineshop one day when Norman Douglas came in and announced that his friend was going to shoot himself and that he could think of no reason to dissuade him. "Are you going to do anything about it?" Maugham asked. Douglas said no, ordered wine, and sat down to await the sound of the shot.[32]

Despite Gosse's prediction that the war would bring publishing to a standstill, 1915 was a lively year for books. There was a life of Robert Cecil and a profusion of war books, including *What Is Wrong with Germany*, by William Harbutt Dawson. There was *Delia Blanchflower*, by Mrs. Humphry Ward, an indictment of militancy in the suffrage movement; *The Research Magnificent*, by H. G. Wells, a novel about an idealist; and two novels by Joseph Conrad, *Within the Tides* and *Victory*. There was *A Lover's Tale*, by Maurice Hewlett, a story about Iceland; *The Little Man and Other Satires*, by John Galsworthy; *Greg and Pauline*, a love story by Compton Mackenzie; and *Fifty-One Tales*, by Lord Dunsany. And there was *Of Human Bondage*, by W. Somerset Maugham.[33]

Of Human Bondage was published by Heinemann in England on August 13 and by George H. Doran in America on August 12. Doran, a tall, courtly man with a beard, was an Irish Canadian who had started out selling newspapers in the streets of Toronto. He founded his firm in 1907, at a time when manufacturing costs were low. It was possible to publish fiction, pay a 10 percent royalty, and make a small profit on 1,500 copies. A sale of 500 copies was considered fair. Doran's first best seller was Arnold Bennett's *The Old Wives' Tale*, which sold 100,000 copies in America. This was a period when English authors were more popular in America than at home, and each year Doran went to London for three weeks, took an apartment at the Savoy, threw parties, and bought books. The content of *Of Human Bondage* seemed somewhat impious to Doran's Canadian Methodism, and its great length made the manufacturing cost appalling, but his manuscript reader, a young man named Sinclair Lewis, urged its publication with vehemence.[34]

The first printings on both sides of the Atlantic were 5,000 copies, a record for Maugham; the book cost $1.50 in America and 6 shillings in England. The English dust jacket, which showed Philip Carey in bohemian garb—black cape with a red cravat, green trousers, and wide-brimmed hat—had to be changed for the first edition. The artist had the club on the wrong foot.

Maugham's first choice of title, a quotation from Isaiah, "Beauty from Ashes," had already been used, and so he changed it to *Of Human Bondage*, one of the books in Spinoza's *Ethics*. This was the novel he had written to free himself of his obsessions, on the "misery loves company" theory that when private feelings were made public, they ceased to be his. Thirty years later, however, when he was asked in New York to read the first chapter for a recording for the blind, he broke down and could not finish. Publication had not provided that thorough a catharsis.

But it was all there: the loss of his mother, the breakup of his home, the years at the vicarage, the wretchedness of his school years, the stammer transposed into a clubfoot, the happy times in Heidelberg, the year in Paris, and medical school. "It is not an autobiography," he wrote, "but an autobiographical novel; fact and fiction are inextricably mingled; the emotions are my own but not all the incidents are related as they happened and some of them are transferred to my hero not from my own life but from that of persons with whom I was intimate."[35]

For the first and last time Maugham dropped the mask. Gone was the pose of Edwardian gentleman, of "The Jester," of epigrams to amuse society women. Here was the painful reality of the cripple, who carried through life a feeling of apartness, friendless and longing for friends, but perversely compounding his alienation by his own aloofness. Here was the true condition of life, not success or invitations to the right homes or scores of admirers, but bondage. Philip Carey is in bondage to his physical defect, to his upbringing, and to the woman who mistreats him. The novel's theme is his struggle to free himself.

Maugham adopted the form of the *Bildungsroman*, the nineteenth-century German novel of education, in which a single character is taken from childhood through a variety of encounters and experiences, as though over an obstacle course, to come out at the end a changed and better person. An example of the *Bildungsroman*, which he had read and admired at Heidelberg, was Goethe's *Wilhelm Meister*, divided into *Lehrjahre* (*The Apprentice Years*) and *Wanderjahre* (*The Years of Wandering*). Wilhelm starts out as an apprentice in the family business, but a love of the theater leads him to try the actor's life, just as Philip Carey goes to Paris to try to become a painter. Wilhelm gives up acting and becomes a surgeon, while Philip is told that he will never be a first-class painter and returns to England to enroll in medical school. Wilhelm has a series of passionate affairs, and Philip has affairs with Miss Wilkinson, a governess staying at the vicarage, Norah Nesbitt, a writer of twopenny novelettes (based in part on Violet Hunt), and Mildred Rogers. Wilhelm limits his inclinations to those who matter and arrives at a sense of dedication. He becomes aware of his social obligations and of the sense of dignity derived from being useful to his fellow man. Philip frees himself from the bondage of Mildred and decides to marry the wholesome Sally Athelny. Philip's quest for the meaning of life leads him to the conclusion that it has no more meaning than the arabesques in a Persian carpet, but having understood that, one must go on.

A second major influence was Samuel Butler's autobiographical *The Way of All Flesh*, published a year after Butler's death, in 1903. There are many similarities between Butler's protagonist, Ernest Pontifex, and Philip Carey. Both are brought up in a Victorian clerical family. Pontifex' father, appointed to a rural deanery, is a brutal hypocrite who gives his son a beating for mispronouncing a word. Pontifex rebels against his family and religion. He does not, like Philip, have a physical impediment, but struggles to free himself from the cant and pretense of his Victorian upbringing. Like Philip, he is destroyed by women, and like Philip, he suffers financial setbacks. Eventually he overcomes these obstacles and redeems himself.

Of Human Bondage placed itself in a venerable tradition, that of the autobiographical chronicle novel. There were many others, before (Arnold Bennett's *Clayhanger* and Compton Mackenzie's *Sinister Street*) and after (D. H. Lawrence's *Sons and Lovers* and James Joyce's *A Portrait of the Artist as a Young Man*). What Maugham contributed to the genre were the physical defect to explain his character's alienation and a sadomasochistic view of love. Maugham had read the works of Leopold von Sacher-Masoch, which he mentions in *A Writer's Notebook*. He described the state to which Sacher-Masoch gave his name as "a sexual desire in a man to be subjected to ill treatment, physical and mental, by the woman he loves. For example, Sacher-Masoch himself insisted on his wife going for a trip with a lover while he, disguised as a footman, suffering agonies of jealousy, performed for the couple a variety of menial services."

Philip Carey's affair with Mildred is a textbook example of this kind of behavior. Philip is drawn to Mildred, the waitress in the A.B.C. restaurant, because of her indifference. He selects someone who he senses will be cruel to him. He seeks the humiliation of being in bondage to a woman he despises: "He hated himself for loving her. She seemed to be constantly humiliating him, and for each snub that he endured he owed her a grudge." Mildred is shallow, callous, greedy, unintelligent, and utterly conventional. She goes to church one day a week because "it looks well." When Philip kisses her, she says "Mind my hat, silly." Mildred goes off with Philip's friend Griffiths. Philip offers them the money for the trip, becoming their accomplice, just as Sacher-Masoch, disguised as a footman, was the accomplice of his adulterous wife. "Though every word he spoke tortured him [as he gave them the money], he found in the torture a horrible delight." Maugham admitted to Richard Cordell that the episode was autobiographical. Seized by "a devil of self-torture," he actually gave a rival five pounds to finance a trip with the person he loved.[36] The word "person" is used because of the possibility that the model for Mildred was a young man rather than a woman. Harry Philips, who was Maugham's secretary-companion in Paris, had told Joseph Dobrinsky that Mildred was based "on a youth."

Her physical description is androgynous. She is "tall and thin, with narrow hips and the chest of a boy." With her small regular features, blue eyes, thin, pale lips and delicate skin, Mildred is pretty in a late-Victorian way, like the undernourished women of Alma-Tadema. Whether or not Maugham based Mildred on a man, the result is the same: the loved one inflicts pain on the lover.

One of the elements of sadomasochism is the reversal of roles. Philip turns the tables on Mildred, who becomes wheedling and subservient and tries to get him into bed. Philip tells her he is disgusted. Mildred burst into

> abominable invective. She accused him of every mean fault; she said he was stingy, she said he was dull, she said he was vain, selfish; she cast virulent ridicule on everything upon which he was most sensitive. . . . She kept on, with hysterical violence, shouting at him an opprobrious, filthy epithet. . . . Then she turned round and hurled at him the injury which she knew was the only one that really touched him. She threw into the word all the malice and all the venom of which she was capable. She flung it at him as though it were a blow.
> "Cripple!"

The appearance of Maugham's *Bildungsroman* in 1915 was poorly timed. There was enough misery in British homes without his contribution, and it was hardly light reading for the men in the trenches. The critics seemed to feel that Maugham had let down his public in their hour of need. He was supposed to make people laugh, not depress them with a long tale of woe. *The Athenaeum* on August 21 said the book was too long, and the hero's values "are so distorted as to have no interest beyond that which belongs to an essentially morbid person." *Punch*'s "Our Booking-Office" on August 25 found the characters of Philip and Mildred repellent. The *Saturday Review* on September 4 chided the author for overemphasizing "the drab and sordid side of things."[37]

The novel did not fare much better in America. The New York *World* described its subject as "the sentimental servitude of a poor fool." The Philadelphia *Press* dubbed the main character "futile Philip." *The Outlook* felt "the author might have made his book true without making it so frequently distasteful." *The Dial* called it "a most depressing impression of the futility of life." The Detroit *Times* said it had "no brilliancy of style." The Portland *Oregonian* said "young readers are warned off." The New Orleans *Times-Picayune* said "certainly the story cannot be said to be in any sense a wholesome one, and it would require a distinctly morbid taste for one to enjoy it thoroughly."

Of Human Bondage was rescued by one influential critic, who was also the leading American realistic novelist—Theodore Dreiser. Writing in the December 25, 1915, issue of the *New Republic* under the title "As a Realist Sees It," Dreiser called the book a work of genius. He laid it down, he said, feeling that it was "the perfect thing which we love and cannot understand, but which we are compelled to confess a work of art." Maugham, he went on, was "a great artist." Dreiser compared the novel to a Beethoven symphony, whose "bud notes and flower tones were filling the air with their elusive message, fluttering and dying." The Dreiser review was a nice Christmas present for Maugham and gave *Of Human Bondage* the lift it needed. It has not been out of print since its publication and is still widely read.

Its appeal is based on the main character's admission of weakness, something most readers can identify with. It was Maugham's one attempt to deal fully with the misery of his life, and the honesty that came across the page won him readers in the millions. One of his readers was a teenage girl living in a small town in Connecticut who would become known under her married name of Clare Boothe Luce. She was so moved that she sent Maugham one of the three fan letters she ever wrote. She poured her heart out to the unknown author, telling him of her unhappy childhood, her plan to become a writer, and her mother's lack of sympathy for her ambition. She got back a handwritten six-page letter full of compassion and encouragement. Maugham told her that an unhappy childhood could be a great blessing, for it spurred one to seek happiness in life and communicate with others. Those who had a happy childhood, he said, were seldom ambitious in later life, for they had already had the best.[38] *Of Human Bondage*, it can be seen from this example, had a large potential audience in survivors of unhappy childhoods.

Critics tended to judge Maugham's subsequent work by the standards of his one confessional novel. They beat him over the head with his own book. "Why," asked Malcolm Cowley, "did he write one book that was full of candor and human warmth? Why did he never climb back to the same level?"[39] As Maugham told Garson Kanin: "Decent people often say to me, 'Why don't you write another *Of Human Bondage?*' And I reply, 'Because I've only lived one life. It took me thirty years of living to possess the material for that one work.' "[40] He agreed, however, that it was his finest book, even though it had been slow in making its way, and was pleased to learn that it had the "doubtful honor" of being required reading in many educational institutions.[41]

While *Of Human Bondage* came out in London to bad notices, Maugham was in Rome waiting for Syrie to deliver. She had in earlier years had an operation that made normal delivery impossible, and when she began to have labor pains Maugham sent for the doctor, who suggested she be taken to the hospital and put in the hands of an obstetric surgeon. Maugham hired an ambulance in the middle of the night, the surgeon performed a Caesarean section, and a daughter was born on September 1, 1915. She was christened Liza, after the heroine of Maugham's first novel, but he was disappointed that the child was not a boy. Having a son was one of his unrealized ambitions, and when his French friend Paul Dottin had a son Maugham wrote him: "Let me congratulate you on the birth of your son. . . . We can all write books, but it is given to but few to produce a male child. I have never been able to manage more than a daughter."[42]

There is a problem of timing here. According to Maugham, it was in August 1914, while he was in Capri, that Syrie told him she was pregnant again. If that was the case, the child could not have been born in September 1915. But Maugham was always vague about dates, and it is more likely that Syrie informed him of her pregnancy later, which explains why he came back to London in February 1915. Syrie was still married to Henry Wellcome, but Maugham had no doubt whatever that the child was his. It was a delicate situation, one that he cannot have been comfortable with. A few days after the birth the doctor told Syrie that she could never have another child. She wept, but soon recovered, and three weeks later they were back in England.

Back home Maugham was eager to contribute to the war effort once more, but could not return to his ambulance unit. When no one else seemed to want him, Syrie arranged several dinners with a man in the intelligence service, whom Maugham found ordinary and middle-class. The man was the lover of one of Syrie's friends, and wanting to please his mistress, he asked Maugham to come and see him. Maugham went to a street of red brick houses, with a "For Sale" sign at the house to which he had been directed. The intelligence official—whom Maugham called "R."—suggested that with his knowledge of French and German and his profession of writer as a cover, he would make a good secret agent. He could live in a neutral country under the pretext of writing a book.[43] R. was in reality Sir John Wallinger, whose career had been served in the India police and who was in charge of the intelligence service in France and Switzerland during World War I.

On September 27 Maugham wrote Violet Hunt from his house in Chesterfield Street: "I have left the Red Cross and am now in the

Intelligence. I do not like it nearly so well, but I suppose I am a little more useful."[44] He was told that he would be sent to Switzerland to replace an agent who had suffered a nervous breakdown. He was waiting for his marching orders when he found himself in the middle of another domestic crisis. Syrie, who had given up her house in Regent's Park and was living in a hotel in Piccadilly, asked to see him. She was distraught and handed him a letter from a lawyer. "Wellcome is going to divorce me," she said. Maugham was shaken. "But you told me that by your separation agreement you were free to do what you liked," he protested. "I didn't know," Syrie said, "I thought it was all right." When he read the letter Maugham was in for another shock: he was named corespondent. He was realistic enough to know he could not defend the case, and put it into the hands of Sir George Lewis, who had a good reputation as a divorce lawyer.

What he learned was that Wellcome had hired detectives to trail Syrie and had uncovered proof of her adultery with several men, among them Gordon Selfridge. Maugham had won out over his rivals as corespondent because he was single and solvent. One evening he was having dinner at Chesterfield Street with a doctor friend when Syrie called in a panic. She had swallowed a handful of Veronal pills. He called up Mrs. Barnardo, who remained calm and composed, as though taking an overdose of barbiturates was a routine occurrence. His doctor friend treated Syrie and she was up and about in forty-eight hours. She moved to another hotel, much to the manager's relief. Maugham wondered whether she had taken the Veronal to scare him.

Soon after, Sir George Lewis asked Maugham to spend a weekend at his house in Sussex so that they could discuss the case. Syrie had told him that Wellcome had settled five thousand pounds a year on her, which explained how she could afford her beautifully furnished house with five servants, her clothes, and her parties. Sir George informed Maugham that Syrie had two hundred pounds a month from Wellcome and Selfridge made up the deficit. But since Selfridge had broken up with her she had gone heavily into debt. "She's up against it," Sir George said (if we can trust Maugham's 1962 recollection in *Looking Back* of a conversation that had taken place almost half a century earlier), "and you're to be the mug to save her. You're cruelly trapped and you'd be a fool to marry her."

"What else can I do?" Maugham asked.

"You could afford to give her twenty or thirty thousand pounds, couldn't you?" Sir George asked.

"I suppose I could," Maugham replied.

"Wellcome's solicitors have told me that if you don't marry her, he'll give her a thousand a year. She won't starve."

Maugham sighed. "D'you want to marry her?" Sir George asked irritably.

"No," he replied, "but if I don't I shall regret it all my life."

"Then there's nothing more to be said," Sir George concluded with a shrug. What Maugham did not bother to explain was that his chief concern was Liza.[45]

Shortly after his weekend in Sussex he was summoned by R., who told him that he would go first to Lucerne, to investigate an Englishman with a German wife who was living there, and then to Geneva, which would be his headquarters. "If you do well," R. told him, "you'll get no thanks, and if you get into trouble you'll get no help." Maugham left, did the job in Lucerne, and proceeded to Geneva. He took a room in the Hôtel Beau Rivage, where the other spies stayed.

By the end of 1915 Maugham had settled into the routine of espionage. Once a week he crossed Lake Geneva to the French side to file his reports and receive instructions. He was quite aware that he was violating Swiss neutrality and worried that the Swiss police would arrest him. In his spare time he went boating on the lake and wandered through the old city. He read Rousseau's Confessions, tried La Nouvelle Héloise, and found that he just barely escaped being bored. So he decided to write a play—after all, he was supposed to be a writer—which he wrote quickly, because he was afraid that if he were arrested he might not be allowed to have pen and paper, and he did not want to leave it unfinished.[46] The result was a comedy he called "The Unattainable," but the title was later changed to Caroline. Caroline learns that her long-absent husband has died in Africa. Her suitor, an eminent K.C., has been wooing her for ten years. Everything has been fine as long as she was unattainable, but now he feels obliged to propose. Caroline replies that they have been linked by "a very charming sentiment for so long that it would be a pity to expose it to the wear and tear of domestic life."

Caroline also has a young suitor, who loses interest when he learns that she is a widow and says: "A woman is more desirable when she's unattainable." The K.C. and Caroline finally decide to marry so their friends will leave them in peace. They discuss whether to keep separate establishments. He wants a bathroom with white tiles, she wants one with futuristic decoration. In the last act Caroline's doctor, to save the day, announces that her husband is not dead. The K.C.'s passion is rekindled because Caroline is once again unattainable.[47]

Caroline was a soufflé whipped up in Switzerland out of boredom, but it was also a comment on Maugham's situation. It showed that he was able to turn his own predicament into comedy. He had enjoyed his affair with Syrie as long as she was married to Wellcome. Once she became available, he had to decide whether to marry her—a situation that was less enjoyable. In bringing Caroline's husband back to life in the last act, Maugham was transposing his own wish that someone would take Syrie off his hands.

While he was writing *Caroline*, Gerald Haxton, his lover from the ambulance corps, got himself into a mess in London. On November 13, 1915, he was arrested in a Covent Garden hotel with a man named John Lindsell and charged with gross indecency, which, according to the statute, meant committing a homosexual act that was not buggery. Gerald and his partner were picked up by chance by military policemen who, while looking for deserters, had burst into their hotel room and found them *in flagrante*. On December 7 Gerald and John Lindsell were indicted in the Central Criminal Court at Old Bailey on six counts of gross indecency, under Section 11 of the Criminal Law Amendment of 1885, the same law under which Oscar Wilde had been prosecuted. Gerald and Lindsell pleaded not guilty on the advice of their expensive lawyers. Gerald's was Roland Oliver, who would later become Justice Oliver, and Lindsell's was Henry Curtis Bennett, who was later knighted. When they appeared on December 10 before the Recorder of London, Sir Forrest Fulton, they were acquitted of all offenses.[48]

Although Gerald was acquitted, the incident was a cloud that hung over him for years and was never entirely forgotten. He apparently left England shortly afterward, and when he returned in February 1919, arriving from Copenhagen, he was deported as an undesirable alien. He was never again allowed to enter England. This was the main reason that Maugham decided to live in the south of France when Gerald became his secretary. What had Gerald done to be deported four years after his arrest for gross indecency? I tried to obtain access to his file at the Home Office but found that it was in a special category of papers closed for a hundred years. Such papers are closed for three reasons: in the public interest because of security or other grounds; if certain disclosures would embarrass or distress living persons or their immediate descendants; if information has been given in confidence, to protect the informants.

1

In 1914, when he was 40 and serving in the British Ambulance Corps on the Flanders front, Maugham (1) met 22-year-old Gerald Haxton (2), an American adventurer, and fell in love with him. Gerald became his secretary-companion.

2

3

Sent to Russia as a secret agent by British spy chief Sir William Wiseman (3) in 1917, with the impossible mission of keeping the Bolsheviks out of power, Maugham was helped . . .

... by a former mistress, Sasha Kropotkin (4), who introduced him to Alexander Kerensky (5), head of the Socialist government, months before the Bolshevik revolution. "There is more of Saint-Just in him than of Bonaparte," Maugham judiciously said of Kerensky.

4

5

6

7

8

9

10

11

In the twenties and thirties, Maugham counted among his friends Carl Van Vechten and Hugh Walpole (6); Max Beerbohm (7); Barbara Back (8), whose elegance and wit he much admired; Godfrey Winn (9); G. B. Stern (10); Beverly Nichols (11); and Fred Bason (12), a cockney bookseller who tried to take advantage of him.

12

Maugham frequently traveled with Gerald Haxton (13), who, as secretary-companion, was always in his shadow.

13

Maugham sent his manuscripts to Eddie Marsh (14), a strict grammarian who corrected his errors and improved his style.

14

After his divorce, Maugham saw little of
his daughter, Liza, here skiing with her
mother in St. Moritz (15).

15

In 1936, Liza married Vincent Paravicini (16), son of the Swiss Minister in London. Tall
and darkly handsome, he was the physical opposite of her father.

16

Maugham's best-known short story, "Rain," was written in longhand in a leather-bound notebook, with few corrections (17). A triumph on the stage and screen, it offered a part that every actress hungered for.

Tallulah Bankhead (18) was shattered when Maugham vetoed her after she had been cast in the London production.

19

Among the memorable Sadie Thompsons were Joan Crawford (19), Jeanne Eagels (20), Rita Hayworth (21), and Gloria Swanson (22).

21

20

22

In the thirties, Maugham lived in his Villa Mauresque in the South of France and entertained royally. The Duke and Duchess of Windsor (23) were his frequent guests, as was G. B. Stern (24), grown older and stouter, partly on Maugham's fine French cuisine.

24

25

A number of movie stars owed their fame to Maugham. Bette Davis (26) said she divided her career between Before Maugham and After Maugham. Herbert Marshall (25) became type-cast as the urbane Maugham narrator of *The Razor's Edge*, which also starred Clifton Webb (25), Gene Tierney (25, 27), Anne Baxter (25), and Tyrone Power (25, 27). Webb played the American snob Elliott Templeton, who was based on Henry (Chips) Channon (28), a wealthy American who had spent most of his life cultivating the English aristocracy.

27

26

28

30

29

Maugham came to America in 1940 and stayed with his publisher, Nelson Doubleday, and Nelson's wife, Ellen, on their plantation in South Carolina (29). Nelson built a cottage where Maugham could live and work (30). Here his close American friends, such as the writers S. N. Behrman (31) and Glenway Wescott (32), could come to see him.

31

32

33

In 1941, Maugham went to Los Angeles to write a screenplay. Here he is at lunch in the Polo Lounge with Gerald Haxton and Liza (33). Liza later accompanied her father on an outing to Yosemite with Bert Alanson, the San Francisco stockbroker who made Maugham a millionaire, and Mrs. Alanson (34).

34

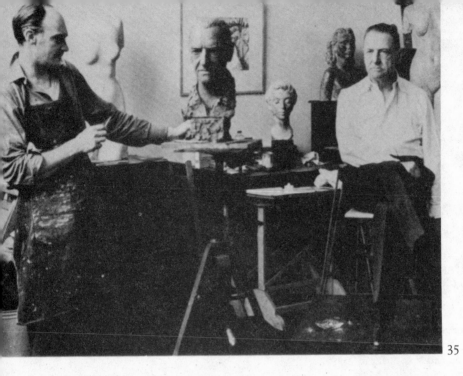

35

Maugham was accustomed to sitting for painters and sculptors. He sat for his bust by Laurence Tompkins (35), for another of the numerous portraits by Gerald Kelly (36)...

36

37

. . . and for his famous portrait by
Graham Sutherland (38), which Kelly
said made him look "like an old Chinese
madam in a brothel in Shanghai." He
was also an art collector, and on a visit to
the Rosenberg Gallery in New York
(37), he considered buying Renoir's
"Three Sisters."

38

39

Two years before Gerald Haxton's death, he and Maugham stood facing each other (39) before Carl Van Vechten's camera, in a rare moment of unguarded affection.

Mr. H. G. Pearson, the departmental records officer at the Home Office, explained that Gerald's deportation had not been connected with his morals charge. He insisted on the phrase "security or other grounds," which may have been an allusion to rumors that Gerald worked for Belgian Intelligence. Mr. Pearson had Gerald's file on his desk, and as he riffled through it he shook his head and said: "Chap's a bad lot." He added: "He was caught in a compromising situation with another man. He had money behind him and got off on a technicality. He was a dreadful fellow but we couldn't prove it. When he came back afterward, there were one or two other things floating about, and we put two and two together."

Mr. Pearson said that after Gerald was deported, applications were made over the years asking for a remission. Pressures were applied at the club level. Someone would approach the Home Secretary: "I say, you know that chap who's Willie Maugham's secretary, got into some kind of trouble years ago and had to leave England—can't something be done?" But no remission was granted.

Under the present rule, researchers will have to wait until the year 2019 before the Haxton file opens up. One final point: the hundred-year categories are determined by the Lord Chancellor. Maugham's brother Frederic became Lord Chancellor in 1938 and could have closed the Haxton file to protect Maugham. But Mr. Pearson said that was not the case, since legislation governing the hundred-year rule was passed only in 1958.[49]

Maugham came to London in January 1916 for the rehearsals of *Caroline*, which was directed by Dion Boucicault and starred his wife, Irene Vanbrugh. In the last act there was a big comic scene in which Caroline's supposedly dead husband turns up, but when he saw it, Maugham realized that the scene did not work. He asked Boucicault to give him twenty-four hours, and rewrote the last act, putting the actor who played the husband out of a job. *Caroline* opened on February 8 and was a hit: it ran for 141 performances. Here was the Maugham that critics and public wanted, the writer who would provide them with comic relief in wartime. The critics dug into their bag of adjectives for light comedy: sparkling, diverting, whimsical, light as a feather. Maugham was gratified to hear that Boucicault was playing to two thousand pounds a week, the largest sum he had known a comedy to earn in all his years in the theater.[50]

Maugham gave a supper party at 6 Chesterfield Street on opening night. Surrounded by such stars of the London stage as Irene Vanbrugh and Gladys Cooper,[51] congratulated from all sides, he could forget for a moment that the day of reckoning had come: he was due to appear in divorce court on February 14 in the case of Wellcome v. Wellcome and Maugham. On February 15 the case was reported in brief items in the London newspapers. In the *Daily Chronicle* Maugham appeared on the crime page, along with partners in a glove company who were indicted for trading with the enemy, a man who had adopted children to pass them off as his own and divert his brother's inheritance, and an Italian diplomat who was found shot in a Piccadilly hotel. He was described as "a gentleman of the name of William Somerset Maugham." Syrie Wellcome did not defend herself against her husband's suit for divorce on grounds of adultery. Evidence was introduced that she and Maugham had stayed together in a hotel in Windsor in July 1915, and counsel for Wellcome intimated that considerable evidence had also been taken in Rome, but that it was not necessary to read it, thus sparing Syrie the embarrassment of a public disclosure of her pregnancy and childbirth. Justice Bargrave Deane pronounced a decree nisi (a decree that is to take effect at a specified date unless cause is shown for nullification) and granted Wellcome total custody of his son.[52]

Maugham went back to his war job in Geneva and was joined by Syrie, who did not want to be in London just then. On March 12 he wrote his brother Frederic:

> The whole matter has been a great distress and worry to me, but I try and console myself by thinking it is only through undergoing all varieties of human experience, however distressing some of them may be, that a writer can hope in the end perhaps to produce work of permanent value. I fancy the worst of my troubles are over, but what the final result will be only time can show, and in any case the future cannot have in store any worse harassment than I have undergone in the last eight months.[53]

Maugham's schedule in Switzerland involved trips to Berne, and to the French side of the lake once a week. Left to herself, away from her friends and the London social scene, Syrie was bored, and she made scenes. When she finally decided to go back to England, Maugham was relieved. In June he went to one of his favorite French spas, Brides-les-Bains, to recover from the tensions of the divorce case and espionage work, and in July, finding that there was nothing much more he could do in Switzerland, he asked R. to release him from the assignment.[54]

Maugham had served in Switzerland for British Intelligence for about a year. It was not unusual for the intelligence departments to recruit writers and artists, and among them was Maugham's friend Compton Mackenzie, whom he had met in Capri. Mackenzie had served in military intelligence in Greece and Syria, and in 1928 he published a novel called *Extremes Meet*, based on his activities. Maugham's *Ashenden* stories, also based on his espionage experiences, came out the same year, and Mackenzie's book suffered by comparison. Piqued, Mackenzie wrote that "Maugham's work for Intelligence during the war had consisted of acting as a kind of intermediary to gather the information of agents he met in Switzerland and communicating that information to Indian Intelligence headquarters in London. My experience and Maugham's were completely different. He handled his own material in the best Maugham manner; he could not possibly have handled mine."[55]

Another writer-spy and friend was the American-born playwright Edward Knoblock, who had written such hits as *Kismet* and *Behind the Mask*, and who collaborated with Arnold Bennett on a generational play called *Milestones*. Knoblock, a naturalized Englishman, was given a commission as a Second Lieutenant and assigned to Indian Intelligence, where Maugham was working. He was then recruited by Mackenzie for his Athens operation.[56]

Then there was Gerald Kelly, who became an intelligence agent in Spain. Three of the episodes in *Ashenden* were based on Kelly's experiences. Two of these, *The Hairless Mexican* and *The Dark Woman*, have to do with a Mexican general who has been recruited by R. to kill a German agent and kills the wrong man. "Actually," Kelly said, "we trailed him [the agent], spent 100 pounds of good allied money following him. Watched him go to the station at Seville, get into a carriage bound for Madrid—and the rascal then slipped out the other side and disappeared."[57]

Maugham's work as a spy was, as Mackenzie noted, that of a go-between. He relayed instructions from his boss in London to agents in the field. He himself wrote in the preface to *Ashenden* that "the work of an agent in the Intelligence Department is on the whole extremely monotonous. A lot of it is uncommonly useless." At the same time he was able to gather enough material for a book of stories, based on actual cases and people, with many details only slightly changed. R.

asks the narrator, who calls himself Ashenden but uses the pseudonym Somerville: "Where have you been living all these years?" He replies: "At 36 Chesterfield Street, Mayfair," changing only the number of Maugham's real address from 6 to 36. The stories were so close to the truth that he destroyed fourteen unpublished ones in one of his "bonfire nights" after Winston Churchill had seen the manuscripts and informed him that they violated the Official Secrets Act.[58] It was not his practice, however, to let that many stories accumulate without offering them for magazine publication, and one can only wonder at this uncharacteristic destruction of salable material.

From the stories one can get some idea of Maugham's activities, although, as he points out, the actual cases have been rearranged, for "fact is a poor story-teller. It starts a story inconsequently and tails off, leaving loose ends hanging about, without conclusion." When Maugham was visited by the Swiss police in his hotel room in Geneva, they asked him what he was doing in Switzerland. Writing a play, he said. Why in Geneva, they asked. Because England is in turmoil, he said. He had personal problems with his fellow agents, one of whom wanted a raise and threatened to give him away to the Swiss authorities. Another agent, in Basel, was also selling information to the Germans. Maugham's job was to meet with his agents, pay their wages, pass on their information, and wait for instructions. He wrote long reports, which he was convinced no one read, until, having included a joke, he was reprimanded for his levity. He was sent to Lucerne to observe a British traitor and his German wife, and then realized that he had been used as a decoy to lure the man back to England. He was involved in an attempt to capture an Indian anti-British agitator, who committed suicide before he could be caught. There may have been other incidents set in Switzerland among the destroyed stories. Even in the humdrum role of go-between he was a part of the manipulative side of espionage, which John Le Carré later made his theme, while his relationship with an anonymous chief would be picked up by Ian Fleming in his James Bond stories.

Ashenden is equally interesting for the self-portrait it provides of Maugham in early middle age. The device of a narrator with a different name is the flimsiest of veils. In his introduction to one of the stories that was eventually made into the film *Trio* he says: "If you would like to take the character of Ashenden as a flattering portrait of the old party who stands before you, you are at perfect liberty to do so." The choice of the name Ashenden, which Maugham used again in *Cakes and Ale*, has its origin in his years at the King's School, where one of his class-mates, perhaps one whom he admired or envied, had the name, which he now adopted as his own. In 1954 the daughter-in-law of his school friend wrote to ask him about the choice of the name. "I chose the name Ashenden," he replied, "because like Gann and Driffield, it is a common surname in the neighborhood of Canterbury, where I spent many years of my youth. The first syllable had to me a peculiar conno-tation which I found suggestive."[59]

Ashenden/Maugham, the fortyish writer who spent a year in Geneva, is a tidy creature, who notices upon entering his room that his things have been examined. He is a man who sees the comic side of life, and people often tell him that he has character. He plays bridge, and has played with enough first-class players to know that he is not in the same league. His hair is thinning and he dislikes exposing an unbe-coming baldness. Abstemious by nature, he turns down a second glass of brandy. He is impatient when traveling, and worries about missing trains. He has a cool head and controls his emotions. He does not mind talking to bores, since they are his raw material "and did not bore him any more than fossils bored the geologist." He observes people and tries to discover keys to their lives from appearances. He sees an old Irish colonel and his wife rising after dinner; she waits at the door for a minute while he chats with a Swiss, and Ashenden/Maugham realizes that she had never opened a door for herself. He is by nature a very shy person and has in vain tried to cure himself of a failing that at his age seems inappropriate. He admires goodness but is not outraged by wicked-ness, and has a great tolerance for human frailty. People think him heartless because he is more often interested in them than attached to them. He likes strange people, but dislikes it when people talk to him about his books. It makes him self-conscious to be praised or blamed to his face.[60]

Maugham returned to London in the summer of 1916 prepared to marry Syrie, but her divorce was not yet final. He was fortunate to be doing war work that he could leave when he liked in order to meet the demands of his career. He was intent on arranging an American pro-duction of *Our Betters*, but he also had an idea for a novel that had long been turning in his head. He had mentioned it briefly in *Of Human Bondage*; it reflected his Paris years, when he had met the painter Roderic O'Conor, Gauguin's friend, at the Chat Blanc. In *Of Human Bondage* O'Conor turns up as Clutton during Philip Carey's time as an art student in Paris.

"D'you remember my telling you about that chap I met in Brittany?" Clutton asks. "I saw him the other day here. He's just off to Tahiti. He was broke to the world. He was a *brasseur d'affaires*, a stockbroker I suppose you call it in English; and he had a wife and family, and he was earning a large income. He chucked it all to become a painter. He just went off and settled down in Brittany and began to paint. He hadn't got any money and did the next best thing to starving."

"And what about his wife and family?" asked Philip.

"Oh, he dropped them. He left them to starve on their own account."

"It sounds a pretty low-down thing to do."

"Oh, my dear fellow, if you want to be a gentleman you must give up being an artist. . . . An artist would let his mother go to the work-house. . . ."

"But is your friend a good painter?" asked Philip.

"No, not yet, he paints just like Pissarro. He hasn't found himself, but he's got a sense of colour and a sense of decoration. But that isn't the question. It's the feeling, and that he's got. He's behaved like a perfect cad to his wife and children, he's always behaving like a perfect cad; the way he treats the people who've helped him—and sometimes he's been saved from starvation merely by the kindness of his friends— is simply beastly. He just happens to be a great artist."

This brief passage was the outline for his new novel. The artist whose conviction of his own genius makes him ruthless toward others was someone Maugham could never be. He was a gentleman who had to do the right thing. But he could write about his opposite, the artist who does exactly as he pleases, who flouts convention, who follows the gleam of a distant star. He would write a novel based on the life of Gauguin, and go to Tahiti to research this strange creature, who had died of syphilis in 1903; many of those who had known him were still alive. There was another reason for the trip: his winter in Switzerland had affected his lungs, and a tropical climate, he was told, would do him good.

He sailed for New York in August. One of his fellow passengers was Lillie Langtry, whom he had glimpsed as a child on the beach at Deauville. He introduced himself. The Jersey Lily was sixty-four, smaller than he had expected, but she still had a fine figure. She told him that one evening she had quarreled with Crown Prince Rudolf (Rudi to her) and had thrown the emerald ring he had given her into the fire. The archduke dropped to his knees and rummaged through the burning coals to find the stone. "I couldn't love him after that," she said.

Maugham stored the anecdote and later found use for it in his fiction. The Jersey Lily said that Edward VII had once told her, "I've spent enough on you to buy a battleship," and she had replied, "And you've spent enough in me to float one."[61] Maugham saw her two or three times in New York. She went to dance halls and paid men fifty cents to dance with her. The thought of this woman who had had princes at her feet paying for a dance filled him with shame.[62]

He had been in New York three or four weeks when Syrie wired that she was arriving. He met her and Liza and the nurse at the dock. When he told Syrie that he was leaving for the South Seas she made a scene. With the example of Gauguin in his mind, he told her he was going to Tahiti in pursuit of his profession, and added that he would be gone only three or four months and they would be married on his return if the divorce was final. In the meantime he had kept in touch with Gerald Haxton, at loose ends in Chicago, who was glad to accept Maugham's invitation to join him as his secretary-companion.[63]

In November 1916 they set out on the first of Maugham's exotic journeys. For years he had been promising himself to visit far-off lands but had gone no farther than Egypt, which had proved disappointing in terms of material. Now he felt that he could write no more novels set in England. He had put all his experience into *Of Human Bondage*. In the footsteps of Pierre Loti, Robert Louis Stevenson, and Zane Grey, he was off to the lands of *"paresse et caresses"* to seek new situations and new characters in unfamiliar locales. He was leaving with a novel about Gauguin in mind, but the South Seas would provide a richer harvest.[64]

He had planned to go straight to Tahiti, but George Doran, his New York publisher, told him that since he was going in that direction he should stop off in Hawaii. Doran's casual suggestion had important consequences. If Maugham had not gone to Hawaii, he would have met neither the model for his best known short story, "Rain," nor the man who made him a millionaire, Bertram Alanson. Rather than take the regular steamer from San Francisco to Honolulu, he and Gerald took a cruise ship, the S.S. *Great Northern*, thinking that the food and accommodations would be better. Among the four hundred passengers there was a chamber of commerce delegation that had been promised the key to the city of Honolulu (made of an exotic Hawaiian wood), honeymooners, and elderly persons taking the cruise on doctors' orders. Maugham and Gerald avoided their fellow passengers, kept to their cabins, played cards and rested.[65] But there was one tall and elegantly dressed man whom Maugham got to know during the trip. His name was Bertram Alanson and he was a stockbroker from San Francisco. Maugham and Alanson hit it off immediately, and after they reached Hawaii they toured the islands together. Thereafter, whenever he was in San Francisco, Maugham stayed with Alanson, an admirer of his books. The admiration was mutual, for Alanson had a talent that Maugham respected as much as his own: he knew how to make money grow.

Alanson's family were German Jews originally called Abrahamson. His father owned coffee plantations in Guatemala, and although Alanson was born in San Francisco in 1877, three years after Maugham, he spent his early years in Guatemala and attended the university there. The plantations were destroyed in the earthquakes of 1902 and 1906, and Bert came back to San Francisco in 1908 and bought a seat on the stock exchange. The youngest man on the floor, he was tall and dapper and had artistic tastes. He liked Italian opera and read Cervantes in the original. He and his brother Lionel founded Alanson Brothers and prospered. Bert Alanson was thought by his family to have little interest in women, but at the age of forty-six he married the divorced wife of one of his best friends, the beautiful Mabel Bremer, who had been a model as a girl and was known around town for her extravagant hats. Bert and Mabel had one of the finest homes in San Francisco, on Russian Hill, staffed by a butler named Lemuel and other servants. Bert had a fastidiousness that Maugham shared. He and Mabel dressed for dinner, in long gown and black tie, whether there were guests or not. Bert was a snob—he derived intense satisfaction from his friendships with the famous. Having no children, he and Mabel devoted themselves to their friends. Nothing was too good for them. When Maugham visited, there were caviar and champagne, and martinis laced with absinthe, of which Bert had a steady supply from a mysterious source. There was a grand piano in the living room so that another famous friend, Artur Rubinstein, could practice when he was in town.[66]

Maugham liked to tell the story, in various forms, that he had once given Alanson some money to invest, had forgotten about it, and years later discovered that it had multiplied. The version S. N. Behrman tells is as follows: In 1949 Alanson visited the Mauresque, Maugham's home in the south of France. Alan Searle, by then Maugham's secretary, said to him, "You've been talking so long about that fifteen thousand dollars you gave Alanson to invest for you, that he's never said a word about it since; why don't you ask him now that he's here?"

"I wouldn't think of it," Maugham said. "He's probably long ago lost it and it would embarrass him. It couldn't matter less, anyway."

At lunch on Alanson's last day Maugham said: "Do you remember that fifteen thousand dollars I gave you in Hollywood to invest? It's probably gone and it couldn't matter less. I simply ask out of curiosity."

"I remember very well," Alanson said. "It is not lost. I invested it carefully and have reinvested it ever since. It is now worth well over a million dollars."[67]

A variant was told to Robert Bruce Lockhart, an acquaintance of Maugham's who had been a British agent in Moscow during World War I. In London, in 1939, Lockhart was having lunch at Boulestin's with Maugham, Jan Masaryk, and Harold Nicolson, and Maugham told the story, which Lockhart committed to his diary: "Years ago on cruise met rich American Jew who regards Maugham as God. Maugham once able to do him service. Met him on way to Russia (on secret service) via Siberia—Yank had big holding in rubles—wanted information. Maugham afraid in official position sent telegram: 'Rachel very ill recovery impossible.' Yank sold—made 200,000 pounds. Said must give Maugham something—gave him box of cigars. Later Maugham gave him 2,000 pounds to invest (Yank is a broker)—now worth 30,000 pounds."[68]

What these versions show is Maugham's propensity to rearrange life into amusing stories. The story also enhanced his image as an Edwardian gentleman so indifferent to money matters that he forgot about large sums. The truth concerning Alanson's handling of his money was quite different. Maugham had invested about $25,000 from his American play royalties with the New York brokerage firm of Trippe & Company. He was no speculator and put the money into debentures that brought in a fixed revenue. In 1921 Trippe & Company failed, and he felt that he had been robbed of his savings. He wrote his friend Dillie Fleming that "nothing can protect us from dishonesty and there it is. I am dreadfully put out about it because I had been saving all I could so as to put myself in such a position that I would never write for money again; and here I am having to start afresh."[69]

Things were not as bad as he thought. As a Class A creditor, he got back about two-thirds of his investment. But having been burned, he decided to give his money to a broker he trusted, and he trusted Bert Alanson. For thirty-six years, from 1922 until his death in 1958, Alanson managed Maugham's portfolio, free of charge, and made him a rich man. Maugham's gratitude was sincere. He thought of Bert Alanson as his best friend. Over the years he wrote him more than six hundred letters, which form the largest single existent Maugham correspondence. His letters to "dearest Bert" are full of praise and affection: "The results of the years seem to me wonderfully satisfactory . . . I consider myself very lucky to be able to profit by your intelligent sense of finance." "This is what results in having a broker who is a wizard." "How could I have guessed that the comparatively small sums I entrusted to you could in the course of time produce such a substantial income?"

> I was delighted with what you tell me you have paid into the bank. It is a huge sum, more than ever before, and I could hardly believe it was true. I think that at present prices the investment must amount to very nearly a million dollars. Do you remember years ago you said that was the sum you proposed eventually to make for me? And it is all your doing. I do not know how I can thank you enough. What a bit of luck it was for me that I happened to find myself in the same ship as you on the way from Los Angeles to Honolulu. . . . Except for that, I should never have had this house and my pictures, nor should I have been able to get away, for useful purposes . . . All I can say is thank you, thank you, thank you.

"You have turned an investment of a very small sum into a fortune. That is exactly what you have done and you know it has changed my whole life."[70]

Maugham was exaggerating when he said the sum was small. He sent Alanson funds whenever he had a windfall, in sums of five, ten, fifteen, and on one occasion, thirty thousand dollars. Alanson invested the money in companies he knew about, such as the shipping firm Natomas. Maugham had two accounts. Alanson regularly sent him dividend checks, which grew to an imposing size. He also set up trust funds at Maugham's request for Gerald Haxton, Alan Searle (who became his secretary after Haxton's death), his nephew Robin Maugham, and his grandchildren.

The S.S. *Great Northern* docked in Honolulu on November 14, 1916. Maugham and Gerald took three weeks to see the sights, staying at the Alexander Young Hotel. Maugham had a professional interest in the Iwilei red-light district and visited a prostitute's shack but did not sample the wares. According to Wilmon Menard, the prostitute asked Maugham: "You lookin' for a virgin or a young boy?" Neither, he assured her. "Well, if you ain't in here to do nothin'," she said, "then you'll have to pay double—which is two dollars. Bed-work is fast, talk is slow."[71]

Maugham, again according to Menard, saw a line of "doughboys" from the army base, more than seventy-five feet long. They jingled silver dollars in their pockets. It was done, he supposed, to remind the woman inside that they were waiting under the stars for sexual relief. A woman's voice shouted through the wall of the shack: "Gawd dammit! Cud-oud that racket! You're drivin' me nuts!"[72]

There was a newspaper campaign at the time to close down Iwilei, and one night the police raided the area and arrested a hundred and eight prostitutes and fifteen pimps. Gerald had struck up an acquaintance with Judge Clarence W. Ashford, before whom the whores and pimps were to be brought to trial, and the judge invited Gerald and Willie to attend. They sat in the courtroom as the women were brought in and placed on a year's probation. Most of them went back to San Francisco.

Maugham and Bert Alanson took an Inter-Island Steamship Company boat to Hilo, on the big island of Hawaii, to see the Kilauea volcano in eruption. Lava cinders crunched under their feet and fissures released spirals of steam. The sulfurous smoke made Maugham cough. A man standing near him said, "Gosh, it's like hell." A priest beside him turned and said, "No, it's like the face of God." Bert Alanson said nothing, which made Maugham like him all the more.[73]

Maugham and Gerald had decided to island-hop to Tahiti, and their next destination was American Samoa, halfway between Hawaii and New Zealand. Samoa is a three hundred and fifty-mile chain of ten islands, divided into eastern and western halves. In an 1899 treaty, Germany, the United Kingdom, and the United States declared the Samoan Islands neutral territory. Eastern (American) Samoa was administered by the United States, and Western Samoa by Germany, until 1914, when the New Zealand government took it over. On December 4 Maugham and Gerald took the Sydney-bound steamer *Sonoma*, which stopped off at Pago Pago, the capital of Eastern Samoa. Wilmon Menard, who did a painstaking job of research on Maugham's trip to the South Seas, went through back issues of Honolulu newspapers to find traces of his stay and came upon this item in the *Pacific Commercial Advertiser* for Tuesday, December 5, 1916, in the "Passengers Departed" column: "By steamer for Sydney, Dec. 4: Somerset Maugham, Mr. Haxton, W. H. Collins, Miss Thompson, Mr. and Mrs. J. J. Mulqueen." Miss

Thompson was of course Sadie Thompson of "Rain," one of the dollar-a-throw hookers who had been made jobless by the crackdown on the Iwilei district.[74]

Maugham did not even bother to change her last name. She was a flashy blonde, plump and coarsely pretty, and wore a white dress, white hat, and high white boots. She was on her way to Apia, in Western Samoa, to get a job as a barmaid, and Gerald pointed her out as she stood at the rail. She had the cabin two doors down from his, and among her belongings was a gramophone with a trumpet-flower horn, which she played day and night. There was a permanent party in her cabin, and other passengers complained to the chief steward. A medical missionary and his New England wife were also on board. His district was the Gilbert Islands, which were widely separated and could be reached only by canoe. His wife managed the mission at Pago Pago during his absences. Maugham began to wonder what would happen if Miss Thompson and the missionary came into sexual conflict.

When they landed in mid-December in the steamy South Pacific port of Pago Pago he was relieved to part with Miss Thompson and her gramophone and gentlemen callers. All around the harbor rose steep green hills. It was hot, the rainy season had begun, and there was not a breath of air. The natives, many of whom were tattooed and wore a hibiscus flower behind one ear, were tall and well built, reminding Maugham of Greek statues.

It developed that the passengers bound for Western Samoa were delayed in Pago Pago because of a quarantine inspection, and Miss Thompson was again Maugham's neighbor, this time in the lodging house on Broad Street at which he and Gerald were staying. The village of Pago Pago was located at the far end of the bay, cut off from trade winds, landlocked, and in the path of tropical rains that came off Rainmaker Mountain. It was hot and damp and smelly, and Maugham caught a fungus rash that took weeks to cure. He found the natives lazy and dishonest, charity cases of the naval government. He was convinced that chambermaids had stolen a pair of gold cuff links and a silver hairbrush out of his bags. He spent listless days listening to the rain beat on the corrugated iron roof of the lodging house. Miss Thompson again proved a nuisance, for she had quickly taken a Samoan lover, and the rusty bedsprings "created a horrid disturbance."[75]

Out of Maugham's distaste came his classic story of repressed sexuality. He never spoke to Miss Thompson, and had only one conversation with the missionary couple, during which the wife spoke with horror of the natives' depravity and told Maugham that when they first got there they could not find a single good girl in any of the villages. He made this note:

> A prostitute flying from Honolulu after a raid, lands at Pago-Pago. There lands there also a missionary and his wife. Also the narrator. All are obliged to stay there owing to an outbreak of measles. The missionary finding out her profession persecutes her. He reduces her to misery, shame, and repentance. . . . He induces the governor to order her return to Honolulu. One morning he is found with his throat cut by his own hand and she is once more radiant and self-possessed. She looks at men scornfully, exclaims: "Dirty pigs!"[76]

From this note he wrote "Rain," or "Miss Thompson," as the story was first called, which opposes Sadie Thompson the life-enhancer and Rev. Davidson, the life-diminisher. Maugham still had it in for clergymen. The reverend, sullen and morose, refuses to mix with other passengers aboard ship. He is a hardhearted religious fanatic who drives a Danish trader off his island and tries to get Sadie deported. But Sadie, the life force, conquers. As Graham Greene wrote, "Mr. Somerset Maugham, I suppose, has done more than anyone to stamp the idea of the repressed prudish man of God on the popular imagination."

The enforced stay in Pago Pago gave Maugham the subject of another short story, "Red," which he said was his favorite. He met a beachcomber called Red, a young American ex-sailor who had been discharged in Pago. He ran the eating house, a little green bungalow on the edge of the jungle, while the owner was ill. No drinks were served because Pago was dry. Red was surly, refused cigarettes, and when he talked it was about women. He showed Maugham a collection of dirty postcards. From this encounter he wrote "Red," the story of a beautiful young sailor with whom a native girl falls in love. He disappears, but the girl never forgets him. Years later Red turns up again, fat, bald, and vulgar. "Red" was *The Picture of Dorian Gray* in reverse; there was no painting in the attic to halt physical deterioration.[77]

Maugham was relieved when travel restrictions were lifted and he and Gerald were able to proceed to Apia, the capital of Western Samoa, on the island of Upolu. They left Pago Pago aboard the *Manua*, a battered seventy-ton schooner, whose paint was blistered and gouged and whose decks crawled with huge cockroaches. Built for shallow waters, the *Manua* rolled badly, and stank of kerosene, which fueled the auxiliary engine. The trip made Maugham so sick that he stayed on tea and bread. The American captain, a plump Charles Laughton type, and probably the model for Captain Nichols in Maugham's 1932 novel *The Narrow Corner*, had forfeited his certificate and was reduced to the command of this disheveled tramp. He told Maugham that native women were far superior to white women, particularly in the bedroom, which was just what Maugham wanted to hear, for he had already formed the theory that native women were healthy erotic animals while white women were neurotic bitches.

Apia was prettier than Pago Pago. The white frame Catholic church stood out in a grove of coconut trees, and the harbor was dotted with cutters and native canoes. Offshore, on a coral reef, lay the rusted hulk of a German gunboat wrecked in the hurricane of 1889. Maugham and Gerald stayed in the Central Hotel, a three-story frame building operated by a former Newcastle dentist's assistant, who brewed his own beer. After a few drinks he would become patriotic and threaten to close the hotel and go off to the trenches to "do his bit." One night, according to Wilmon Menard, he picked a fight with Gerald because Gerald was American and America was neutral. When he called Gerald a "slacker," Gerald grabbed him by the collar and said: "That'll do now. I've carried more wounded and dead soldiers in a Red Cross ambulance than you've carried beer bottles down to this bar. And anytime you want to pack up and take off for the front lines, just go ahead, and I'll be only too happy to take your place behind the bar, and try to improve on the lousy bitter beer you make from old socks, assorted garbage, or horse manure."[78]

The New Zealand administrator of Apia was the first of a gallery of colonial officials Maugham would meet. "He regards the natives as willful children," he wrote, "unreasonable and only just human, who must be treated without any nonsense, but not unkindly. He boasts that he keeps the island like a new pin."[79] It was probably on this man that Maugham based the character of the administrator in "Mackintosh," a story set on Savaii, the largest island of the Western Samoa archipelago. "Mackintosh" is a thirty-page tragedy of two clashing temperaments. Walker, the administrator, is a thick-skinned, hard-driving man, who regards the natives as children, does a lot of shouting and ass-kicking, and wants to build a road clear around the island. His assistant, Mackintosh, refined and educated, grows to hate his brutal superior to such an extent that he manipulates a disgruntled native into killing him. Stricken by puritan remorse, Mackintosh then kills himself.

The fourth story to come out of Maugham's Samoan trip was "The Pool," apparently based on the English manager of the Apia bank, who had met a sixteen-year-old Samoan girl at a rock pool and had fallen in love with her. He uses this starting point to show the deterioration of the colonial in a strange place whose customs he does not understand. The Englishman marries the girl, but the marriage fails because he treats her as he would a white woman. The man sinks into drunkenness and self-loathing and kills himself. "The Pool" was essentially *A Man of Honour* with palm trees. Again, the road to disaster was paved with good intentions. If the colonial had kept the native girl as a mistress instead of marrying her, he would have been all right.

Maugham left Samoa in the first week of 1917, after making a pilgrimage to the grave of Robert Louis Stevenson, above Apia, and visiting the Fiji and Tonga islands. He had to go to New Zealand to get to Tahiti, and took a banana boat from Suva to Auckland. January 30, 1917, found him in Wellington, New Zealand, at the Midland Hotel. He wrote his friend Dillie Fleming: "The war has forced all of us to go to strange parts of the world that we never thought to visit," even though his trip had nothing to do with the war. "New Zealand is amusing," he wrote, "because it is so extraordinarily English. I was expecting to find Wellington like a city in the Western states, but it is much more like Bristol or Plymouth. . . . I confess it makes me just a little homesick."[80]

He got to Tahiti some time in February 1917, and spent from a month to six weeks there. Sharks surrounded his ship as it came into Papeete harbor, which had been shelled and partly destroyed by the German cruisers *Scharnhorst* and *Gneisenau* in 1914. Maugham saw copra schooners and pearling luggers, their lines tied to the butt ends of half-buried ancient cannons. The waterfront reminded him of a provincial town in the Touraine. He saw a brick outdoor laundry of exactly the same design as one he had seen soldiers using in Arras during his Red Cross service. He found rooms at the Hotel Tiare, which he called the Hotel de la Fleur in *The Moon and Sixpence*. It was run by a huge and shapeless part-Tahitian woman named Louvaina Chapman— renamed Tiare Johnson in the novel—who wore a pink Mother Hubbard and a straw hat. (She died in the influenza epidemic in 1918.) The Hotel Tiare (the tiare, a little star-shaped white blossom, was Tahiti's national flower) was a five-minute walk from the center of town. It had a small sitting room with a waxed parquet floor, a piano, and bentwood furniture upholstered in velvet. Madame Louvaina spent most of her time in the kitchen supervising the Chinese cook.[81]

Always purposeful, Maugham set about researching Gauguin. The painter had arrived in Tahiti in 1890 at the age of thirty-nine, but what he found there was not paradise. He was in poor health and so poor that he had to beg the local authorities for clerical work. He fought with the clergy and the gendarmerie, and made himself generally unpopular, for he was rude and blunt. In despair, he tried to kill himself with arsenic in 1898. In 1901 he left Tahiti for the Marquesas Islands, where he lived on breadfruit and water until his death in 1903. His obituary in the Papeete newspaper said: "Gauguin was a sort of anarchist. A horror of convention and contempt for all rules led him to a simplistic conception of art and life."[82] During his lifetime Gauguin said that if he could sell his canvases for two hundred francs each he would be happy. After his death they sold for hundreds of thousands of dollars.

Maugham's method of research was to send Gerald out as a retriever. Charming Gerald haunted the bars and cafés, struck up conversations, and brought back the people Maugham wanted to meet. Thanks to Gerald's winning ways, he met a number of persons who had known Gauguin, and his character, Charles Strickland, began to take shape.

He met Emile Levy, a wealthy pearl buyer, who told him that Gauguin insulted everyone, drank, ran up bills, and took morphine. Most of the locals he talked to agreed that Gauguin was a savage, but at the same time they cursed themselves for having ignored his paintings, which were fetching large sums. He met Captain "Winny" Brander, who had been aboard the schooner that Gauguin took to the Marquesas, and who had witnessed the painter's death.[83] One day Maugham drove thirty-five miles outside Papeete to visit the widow of a chief who had been awarded the Legion of Honor for his services to the French protectorate. The widow, a stout, gray-haired woman who sat on the floor smoking native cigarettes, told Maugham there were Gauguin pictures in a house not far from hers. Maugham's acquisitive juices started flowing and he asked to be taken there.

They drove a few miles down the road to a shabby frame house, its veranda swarming with dirty children. The dark, flat-nosed native who lived there invited them in, and the first thing Maugham saw was a Gauguin painted on a door. It appeared that during his illness Gauguin had been looked after by the parents of the present owner. In gratitude he had painted a picture on each of the upper glass panels of the three doors in one of the rooms. Two of the panels had been picked away by children, but the third, representing a rather crude Tahitian Eve with a rabbit and a flowering tree, was fairly well preserved. Maugham asked the man if he wanted to sell it. "But I shall have to buy a new door," he said. "How much will it cost?" Maugham asked. "A hundred francs." "All right," Maugham said, "I'll give you two hundred." Wasting no time lest the man change his mind, Maugham and Gerald unscrewed the hinges and carried away the door. Back at the chiefess', they sawed off the lower part and took the glass panel back to Papeete. When Maugham sold his art collection at Sotheby's in 1962 the Gauguin door went for $37,400.[84]

Maugham liked the town of Papeete, with its shade trees and leisurely pace. He would have his coffee at Drollet's, and stroll along the waterfront to the Parc Bougainville, in which there was a bust of the navigator. He sat on a bench and looked out across the lagoon to the barrier reef and the blue silhouette of Moorea Island. In the meantime Gerald spent his spare time spearfishing. Once, according to Wilmon Menard, Maugham joined him and watched through a glass panel in the boat's bottom as Gerald speared a squid, which discharged its inky liquid into his face and grabbed his arm and neck with its tentacles. Maugham reached down and peeled the creature off Gerald. In later years, whenever he wanted to tease Gerald in company, he would say, "Gerald, why don't you tell us about the time at Rima-tou, near Tahiti, when you wrestled a hundred foot octopus into submission."[85]

While Maugham was saving Gerald from the monsters of the deep, his play *Our Betters* opened on Broadway on March 12. This was the first time he had not been closely involved with one of his productions and was not on hand for the world premiere. *Our Betters* is the play he wrote when he was in Rome with Syrie in 1915, but no English producer would touch it, because the language was considered too shocking, and because it made fun of Americans at a time when England was counting on America to enter the war. Maugham had found an American producer, John D. Williams, when he stopped in New York on the way to Tahiti. *Our Betters* was a satire on rich and rootless American social climbers who buy their way into London society. Rumors spread before the opening that the character of the American tycoon was based on Gordon Selfridge and that there was a bold second act. The first-night critics came forewarned. At the end of the second act Lady Grayston, one of the Americans who has married a title, and the mistress of the tycoon, is seen going into the summer house of a country estate with the gigolo Tony Paxton. Arthur Fenwick, the tycoon, exclaims upon hearing the news, "The slut!" A collective gasp was heard in the audience. Lady Grayston returns with Paxton, realizes they have been found out, and turns to him and says, "You damned fool! I told you it was risky." The curtain fell to the sound of another gasp.

Most reviews, with the exception of that in *The New York Times*, which called the play "simply withering," expressed shock at the immorality and bad language. Heywood Broun in the New York *Tribune* on March 13 wrote that the overtly immoral second act "just about ruins what would otherwise be an amusing entertainment." The New York *World* on March 18 said: "Even if it were not one-half as repellent and bitter as it is, the bluntly spoken vulgarity of the end of its second act would be enough to ruin it." The New York *Dramatic Mirror* said the play was "morally sordid" and "offensive."[86] The reviews whetted the public's appetite, and *Our Betters* ran for a healthy 112 performances.

Maugham, who in mid-March was preparing to leave Tahiti, did not know what a furor he had caused. He had gathered enough notes for his novel and had arranged for his passage to San Francisco and London. He had the Gauguin-on-glass insulated and crated, and drove it down to the dock, where he found many of the Tahitians he had met on hand to wish him bon voyage.

On April 18 he and Gerald were in San Francisco. He was famous enough to deserve an item in the *Examiner*, and there was also a local angle, since his secretary was a native. They stayed at the Palace Hotel, where Gerald found waiting for him a cable from his mother in England that said: "Will my American son volunteer to serve his country? He can do no wiser thing."[87] America had entered the war twelve days earlier. Gerald decided to enlist, and he and Maugham parted company. Maugham was grateful that he had been along. He was so incurably shy that he would never have spoken to anyone unless they spoke to him first. Gerald, with his bubbling good humor, knew everyone within twenty-four hours. Maugham acknowledged that he would not have obtained his material without his gregarious associate. Gerald was sent to South Africa for training, sailing aboard a Japanese vessel, which was captured by the German raider *Sea Wolf*. The passengers and crew were brought on board the raider, and the ship was then sunk. Gerald and the other passengers were taken to Germany as prisoners of war. Gerald sat out the rest of the war in a POW camp in Güstrow, about seventy-five miles east of Hamburg.[88]

Maugham went to New York, where he had an important decision to make. Syrie was there waiting to become Mrs. Maugham. He sought the advice of his friend Ned Sheldon, who was already suffering from the slow paralysis that would cripple him. Sheldon, the old-fashioned moralist, told him that he could not abandon the woman who had given birth to his child.[89] The theme of his first play, *A Man of Honour*, was the disastrous consequence of marrying a woman one does not love out of a sense of duty. But Maugham the man was incapable of applying the lesson of Maugham the dramatist to his own situation. The Edwardian man of honor agreed with Ned Sheldon. As Basil Kent had married the pregnant Jennie Bush, he would marry Syrie.

At 3 P.M. on May 26, 1917, Maugham married Syrie—in Jersey City, in order to escape the attention of the New York press. Ned Sheldon was best man.[90] Syrie's witness was her friend Alexandra Colebrook. "My wedding lacked not only sentiment but what is more important . . . glamour," Maugham later told Garson Kanin. "I remember that immediately before the judge in New Jersey married us . . . he fined a drunk; and immediately after, he fined another."[91] This sounds like Maugham turning life into a story. Afterward there was a reception at the Hotel Brevoort, not far from Sheldon's Gramercy Park apartment, which was attended by some of Maugham's stage friends, including Ethel Barrymore. Their honeymoon was spent in a cottage on the Jersey coast.

They were hardly young lovers. Maugham was forty-three and Syrie was thirty-seven (although on the marriage certificate her age appeared as thirty-two). It was, says Glenway Wescott, "a marriage of convenience on both sides. They knew all about each other. They didn't have to apologize. Willie knew about her past and her lovers, and Syrie knew about his homosexuality. She wanted a father for her child and a man who was at the height of his fame as a playwright. He wanted a hostess, who knew the tout-Londres and would give him as much rope as he needed. The trouble was she fell in love. Willie told me himself that her physical demands were intolerable, inexcusable."[92]

Maugham was also drawn to the idea of marriage. He had ended *Of Human Bondage* with Philip marrying a wholesome, earthy young woman. In *Cakes and Ale* the narrator says that, having reached forty, "I amused my imagination with pictures of myself in the married state. There was no one I particularly wanted to marry. It was the condition that attracted me."

The reasons Maugham married were perfectly valid but did not prevent the marriage from being unhappy. He lived with Syrie for ten years and felt that they were years of misery. He soon came to detest his wife, and he bore her a grudge until the end of his life. To him Syrie was like a partner in a deal who had not lived up to the terms. Having done the right thing, he resented his own honorable behavior. He had not married for love but because of cowardice, and because he had been pressured into it. That being the case, he did not think that Syrie had the right to make demands on him. He was a forty-three-year-old writer, too old to change his ways, and he expected Syrie to accept his six-month-a-year absences in search of material, accompanied by his lover Gerald Haxton. He felt that he should be allowed to lead a double life, but Syrie did not accept the situation. She nagged, she made scenes, she said that he excluded her from his life. Maugham told her that he went on trips to get impressions, and that when she was with him he got none. He complained that when he was in London she made scenes that lasted long into the night, and that he had to get up in the morning and write amusing dialogue for the play he was working on. In 1921, when *The Circle* was produced, Syrie said: "It's funny that people say *The Circle* is your best play. I wasn't very nice to you while you were writing it."[93]

Maugham had other complaints. Syrie treated affection as a commodity, and she had no interest in things of the mind. She was the sort who says "how extraordinary" when a book is being discussed, and was as bored with his friends as he was with hers. Syrie had always been interested in interior decoration and antiques, and so, in 1923, she opened a small shop at 85 Baker Street and became known as the first of the society shopkeepers. Maugham was pleased that she had found something to occupy her but dismayed that she had "gone into trade." He would tell his guests at lunch or dinner: "I think I should warn you, ladies and gentlemen, to hold tight to your chairs. They are almost certainly for sale." Syrie's shop prospered, and she moved to more sumptuous quarters on Duke Street, at the corner of Grosvenor Square. One day, walking home from Claridge's with his journalist friend Beverley Nichols, Maugham crossed the street to avoid passing in front of Syrie's shop, saying: "Forgive me, dear Beverley, but I could not bear to look through the window and see what my wife may be doing."

"But what might she be doing, Willie?" Nichols asked.

"She is almost certainly on her knees to an American millionairess trying to sell her a chamber pot."[94]

Syrie had a great vogue in the twenties with her white-on-white rooms. Maugham said she stole the ideas from Mrs. Winkie Philipson, who, having married a coal merchant, gave vent to her creative urges with an all-white living room. Syrie had visited Mrs. Philipson's house in Sandgate and caught the all-white virus, which she adapted to the homes of the fashionable in England and America. Among her admirers were the couturier Edward Molyneux and Cecil Beaton. Beaton said that

with the strength of a typhoon, she blew all color before her. And, for the next decade, she bleached, pickled, or scraped every piece of furniture in sight. White sheepskin rugs were strewn on the eggshell surfaced floors, vast white sofas were flanked with crackled white incidental tables, white ostrich and peacock feathers were put in white vases against white walls. Her all-white drawing-room in Chelsea became a place of pilgrimage among the intelligentsia. It was unearthly. Everything was so white and hygienic that Margot Oxford, the outspoken wife of the former Prime Minister, Lord Oxford and Asquith, paused but couldn't resist voicing a word of advice: "Dear Mrs. Maugham, what you really need are a few old varnished maps on the walls." Soon, under Syrie Maugham's energetic aegis, Mayfair drawing-rooms began to look like albino stage sets. The craze wasn't to subside for a decade, whereupon Mrs. Maugham switched gears and introduced the vivid colors of a lobster salad—but she was by now an established decorator of considerable prestige, and among women, equal to Elsie De Wolfe, Sybil Colefax, Ruby Ross Wood, and Mrs. Draper.[95]

Maugham claimed that the rage for white ended when people discovered that it became grubby and had to be redecorated. He also said that Syrie sold fakes as antiques. Whether or not his accusations were true, it seems that Syrie was careless about money and not above sharp practice. There is a clue to her handling of money in a letter Maugham wrote on February 7, 1927: "I have recently paid into Mrs. Maugham's account a cheque for over 700 pounds and I cannot think that it is overdrawn."[96] A collector who had dealings with her remembers that "she was dishonest in her dealings and when she tried to open yet another decorating business in the United States she was informed that as she had been in financial difficulties once or twice she could not open again."[97] There was more carelessness in Syrie than dishonesty. She was the sort who never knows the time, leaves her purse in taxicabs, and loses theater and steamship tickets.

Syrie's freewheeling ways were described by David Herbert, the younger son of the Earl of Pembroke, who lived in Tangier and used to stay with her in her flat in Park Lane after World War II. Syrie had bought a small house in Oxfordshire for Liza and came to Morocco to buy furnishings for it. Arriving in London at the customs shed, she told Herbert: "Always choose the oldest customs official. No chance of promotion." She was bringing in thousands of dollars worth of Moroccan antiques and did not want to pay duty. She went up to an elderly man, who asked: "Anything to declare, madam?"

> "Oh, yes, a great deal, but I don't want it; our friends abroad are so kind and generous but invariably have bad taste. They are always giving me things that I can't use. Oh dear, oh dear. Now, just open that parcel, for instance. What can I do with horrible stuff like that?" She paused, looked at the customs man, and said: "Perhaps your wife could find some use for it, or some of her friends?"
>
> "Oh, madam, you're very kind, but it is illegal for us to accept anything in the way of presents."
>
> "Well, what about local charity?"
>
> "No, madam, that's impossible also."
>
> "Well, I'm not going to pay duty on something I don't want, so we'll just leave it here to rot."
>
> "Oh, madam, that would be such a waste. I shouldn't be suggesting this, but perhaps you have some favorite charity in London?"
>
> "Oh, there is Dr. Barnardo's Homes. He was my father, you know."
>
> "Well, madam, there's nothing more to be said; the question is solved."

According to David Herbert, Syrie was known as a pirate in business matters. She once sold a writing table to an American woman for a large sum and asked the decorator Alexis French to come and look at it. He examined it and said, "Syrie, to the best of my knowledge I declare that this table has no sign of worms."

"Alexis dear," she said, "as a friend, would you put that in writing; my conscience would be clear; I'd feel much happier."

"Of course," French said. When he had gone, Syrie said: "Very odd. That leg fell off yesterday and Lakey [the maid] stuck it on this morning."

When Herbert was in New York during the war Syrie called him and said: "You must help me; I'm in trouble. The Customs and Excise officers visited the shop in my absence and that silly new secretary showed them both sets of books. I'm taking the first train to San Francisco. Here are six telegrams addressed to myself at six different cities in America. I want you to send them after I've left. If they want to find me, they will have to search six cities, by which time I shall have got on a boat and left."[98]

There are two sets of books for people as well as for antique shops. The second set concerning Syrie shows her a warm, generous person with a gift for friendship and the enhancement of life. Many of their mutual friends preferred her to Maugham. Godfrey Winn, a popular newspaper columnist, remembered her as "a woman of genuine warmth, great taste and enthusiasm. Some people give, some people take. She was a giver and again a giver. It was true that there was nothing she relished more than a shrewd bargain in antiques, a coup, and equally she enjoyed charging an extravagant price for her services as a decorator, but then everything went back into the melting pot."[99]

Rebecca West said:

I didn't think Willie—whom I knew from the time I was 18—an interesting man or an interesting writer. . . . As for Syrie, she was an extremely talented and original and entertaining person with a curious driving industry that made her like a hummingbird who meant to get somewhere. I think it interesting that she should have seriously studied the craft of interior decoration before she needed to, from the man who ran the antique department at Fortnum and Mason. She knew exactly how to clean and restore old fabrics. She had a far greater command of the telling phrase in conversation than Willie, and was much more perceptive. . . . She was sympathetic and very polite, it is the only word I can use, to the people who worked for her or were on her household staff. She had extremely good taste concerning plays and acting, and was oddly well-read. And had a passion for her daughter (as well as surreptitiously acting with thoughtfulness to her unhappy son). Noel Coward said to me not long before he died that he could have used of her that phrase—"I held her in high regard." There was much more to her than there was to Willie, whose only picturesque quality was the decisiveness of his homosexuality (though he was good run of the mill stuff otherwise). . . . The vision of Syrie in "Looking Back" is pure lunacy. I remember Noel Coward saying to me that one could test the intelligence of one's friends by seeing if they had noted that Syrie was much more intelligent than Willie . . . but she loved him madly. . . . Willie had a lot of dreary friends whom Syrie would not accept joyfully, notably a very bad painter called Sir Gerald Kelly.[100]

Maugham was blind to Syrie's good qualities. All he could see was that she had trapped him into marriage and become an emotional and financial drain. He thought of her as a virago, brought up in a large family whose members were in the habit of saying terrible things to each other, and claimed he needed a drink before facing her. From the start of their marriage, however, he was an absentee husband. In New York, not long after they were married, he got a call from an old friend of the family, Sir William Wiseman. A plump, round-featured man of thirty-two, Wiseman was a baronet and a Cambridge boxing blue. Mustached and vested, he was the picture of the upper-class Englishman. A banker with the firm of Kuhn, Loeb when the war broke out, Wiseman fought in Flanders as a captain in the Duke of Cornwall's light infantry and was gassed. After that he was sent to America, ostensibly as the head of the British purchasing mission. In fact, he was head of British Intelligence operations in the United States. Wiseman got on well with Colonel Edward M. House, President Wilson's foreign policy adviser, and was credited with helping get America into the war. Soon after that Wiseman began to think of sending a mission to Russia. He wanted to counter German pacifist propaganda there. The czar had been overthrown in March, and the provisional government in power was in danger of being ousted by the Bolsheviks, who would make peace with Germany. Wiseman wanted to send a man to Petrograd with the mission of supporting the Mensheviks and keeping Russia in the war. The man he chose was Maugham.[101]

Maugham hesitated. His lungs were bothering him, and a Russian winter would not help. He did not speak Russian, and he wondered whether he was up to a mission of such magnitude. At the same time, having read Tolstoi, Turgenev, and Dostoevski, whose works he felt made the greatest Western novels seem artificial, he was fascinated by Russia. The mission appealed to his sense of adventure. He was not averse to getting away from his bride, and he very much wanted to serve his country. He may also have thought of his fellow writer Hugh Walpole, who had been in and out of Russia four times since 1914, twice as a foreign correspondent, then as a Red Cross orderly attached to the Russian Ninth Army, where he rescued wounded men under fire and was awarded the St. George's Cross, and finally in 1917, as the curtain rose on the revolution.[102] Maugham consulted a doctor, who advised against his going, but he convinced the doctor that he was taking no undue risk.

By June 20 he had decided to accept the mission, and wrote his

British theatrical agent Golding Bright: "I am going to Russia and shall be occupied there presumably till the end of the war."[103] Preparing for the journey, he consulted several prominent Russian Jews in New York, including a Rabbi Wise. He met Emmanuel V. Voska, a Czech refugee who was to join the mission with three colleagues. Voska, who wanted to free Czechoslovakia from the Austro-Hungarian Empire, was to contact Thomas Masaryk, the future president of Czechoslovakia, who controlled an organization of 70,000 men. Voska's instructions were: "Go to Petrograd. Establish there a branch of the Slav Press Bureau. Organize the Czechs and Slovaks of the empire to keep Russia in the war. You may take three other men with you. We will stand any reasonable expense. So far as we are concerned, you may have the greatest freedom of action."[104]

Wiseman's office obtained Japanese and Russian visas for Maugham; his cover was that he was going to Russia for literary purposes, to write for American publications. His code name was Somerville, the name he used in *Ashenden*. Masaryk was Marcus, Kerensky was Lane, Lenin was Davis, Trotsky was Cole, and the British government was Eyre & Company.

Maugham worried about money, and on July 7 he wrote Wiseman: "I do not know whether it is intended that I should have any salary for the work I am undertaking. I will not pretend that I actually need one, but in Switzerland I refused to accept anything and found afterwards that I was the only man working in the organization for nothing and that I was regarded not as patriotic or generous but merely as damned foolish. If the job carries a salary I think it would be more satisfactory to have it; but if not I am not unwilling to go without. I leave the matter in your hands."[105]

On July 18 he received $21,000 from Wiseman, which was to cover his expenses and enable him to finance the Mensheviks. He left for the West Coast. Syrie took his departure without a murmur. In San Francisco he saw his friend Bert Alanson, who asked him to inquire about his holdings in rubles. On July 28 he sailed for Tokyo and Vladivostok. After he had landed in Vladivostok he spent an idle day waiting for the Trans-Siberian, and dined on cabbage soup and vodka in the station restaurant. The service was bad. An English-speaking Russian sitting at his table said: "Since the revolution, the waiting in restaurants has become abominable."[106]

The four Czechs, led by Voska, also took the Trans-Siberian. Maugham pretended not to know them. In August they arrived in

Petrograd, which had been St. Petersburg until 1914, became Leningrad in 1924, and was then the capital of Russia. They set up their headquarters in the Hotel Europa. The situation was precarious. Czar Nicholas II had signed the Act of Abdication on March 16, bringing the moderate left to power. Alexander Kerensky, who represented the Labor party in the Fourth Duma, was made Minister of Justice and then Minister of War in the provisional government of Prince Lvov. While the provisional government ruled, the Bolsheviks gained control of the masses through the Soviets and agitated for immediate peace. The Germans allowed Lenin to cross by train into Russia in the hope that he would take power and remove his country from the war. At the first all-Russian Soviet Congress in June 1917 Lenin's faction was outnumbered by the Socialist Revolutionaries and the Mensheviks. His attempt to seize power by means of an armed uprising in Petrograd was put down but led to the resignation of Prince Lvov and the formation of the primarily socialist Kerensky government. Kerensky was a vacillator, who neither outlawed the Bolsheviks nor tried to conciliate them. It was in the midst of this situation that Maugham arrived, with $21,000, four Czech patriots, and the mission of keeping Russia in the war, two months before the November revolution that brought the Bolsheviks to power. It was Wiseman's hope in sending Maugham that he would "guide the storm."

A message to the British Consulate had preceded him: "Mr. W. Somerset Maugham is in Russia on a confidential mission with a view to putting certain phases of the Russian situation before the public in the United States. Please give him facilities for cabling his principals through British Consul-General, New York. Please cable if he has presented himself at the Embassy yet." This was in effect a request for a private code for Maugham, and it made the British ambassador, Sir George Buchanan, furious to have to forward his cables without knowing their contents. Before having met Maugham he already thought of him as a meddling intruder, and after Maugham presented himself at the embassy he waited for some time before being introduced to the First Secretary, H. J. Bruce. Maugham was nervous, stammered badly, and decided from the cool reception that he would get no help from the embassy.[107]

Help came from another direction. He ran into Sasha Kropotkin— the daughter of the anarchist Prince Kropotkin—whom he had known when they were living in London in exile and with whom he had had a brief affair. Sasha was painted by Gerald Kelly and described by Maugham in one of his Ashenden stories: "fine eyes, and a good, though for these days too voluptuous figure, high cheekbones and a snub nose (this was very Tartar), a wide mouth full of large square teeth, and a pale skin . . . In her dark, melancholy eyes, Ashenden saw the boundless steppes of Russia." Sasha was close to the Kerensky government and volunteered to help Maugham and act as his translator. From information provided by his Czech associates he formed a pessimistic view of the political situation. The army was mutinous, he was told, famine was staring the country in the face, and the Kerensky government was tottering. Winter was approaching and there was no fuel. The Bolsheviks were agitating, and Lenin was hiding somewhere in Petrograd.

Through Sasha Kropotkin he met Kerensky. Once a week Maugham invited him or a member of his cabinet to dine at the Medvied, the best restaurant in Petrograd, and plied his guest with caviar and vodka at the expense of the British government, with Sasha acting as hostess and interpreter. He saw quite a bit of Kerensky—at the restaurant, at Sasha's apartment, and at his office. Kerensky was a large, sallow-faced man who reminded Maugham of the theatrical producer Charles Frohman. "Both men," he said, "had the quality of exciting in others the desire to do things for him."[108] His final impression was of an exhausted man, broken by the burden of power, unable to act, and more afraid of doing the wrong thing than of not doing the right one.

Thomas Masaryk's good sense and determination made a more favorable impression. But the person who impressed him most was the Menshevik leader Boris Savinkov, who had assassinated Grand Duke Serge and the czarist chief of police, Dmitri Trepov. He endeared himself to Maugham by declaring that assassination was a job like any other. Savinkov, who was Kerensky's Minister of War, hated the Bolsheviks, and told Maugham: "Either Lenin will stand me up in front of a wall and shoot me or I shall stand him in front of a wall and shoot him."[109]

Maugham attended the Democratic Convention at the Alexandrevsky Theatre, where delegates had gathered from all parts of Russia and from all classes. The meeting was scheduled for four, began at five, and lasted until midnight. He found the speeches overlong and the orators unimpressive. These were the kind of men, he thought, who would be addressing a radical constituency in the south of London. He wondered how such mediocre men had taken control of such a vast empire.

Kerensky was the only speaker who was received with enthusiasm. Dressed in khaki, clean-shaven, with his hair cut *en brosse*, he appeared confident and spoke for an hour. But Maugham did not share his confidence. His information was that the Germans were advancing. Russian soldiers were deserting in droves, the navy was restless, and there were rumors that officers had been murdered by their men.[110]

On September 24 Wiseman sent a coded message to the Foreign Office that said:

> I am receiving interesting cables from Maugham, Petrograd:
>
> (A) He is sending agent to Stockholm for promised information, and also to Finland. He has reports of secret understanding for Sweden and Finland to join Germany on capture of Petrograd.
>
> (B) Government change their mind daily about moving to Moscow to avoid Maximalists. He hopes to get agent into Maximalist meeting.
>
> (C) KERENSKY is losing popularity, and it is doubtful if he can last.
>
> (D) Murder of officers continues freely. Cossacks are planning a revolt.
>
> (E) There will be no separate peace, but chaos and passive resistance on Russian front.
>
> (F) Maugham asks if he can work with British intelligence officer at Petrograd, thereby benefiting both and avoiding confusion. I see no objection providing he does not disclose his connection with officials at Washington. If D.M.I. agrees, I suggest he be put in touch with KNOX, but positively not under him.
>
> (G) I think Maugham ought to keep his ciphers and papers at Embassy for security. He is very discreet and would not compromise them, and may be useful as I believe he will soon have good organization there. Anyway I will cable you anything interesting he sends me.

Maugham spent his mornings taking Russian lessons, and long hours at night coding his messages. On October 16 he sent Wiseman a message repeating that Kerensky was losing favor and probably would not last. He urged full support of the Mensheviks, and outlined a program of pro-Menshevik espionage and propaganda activities, which he estimated would cost $50,000 a year.[111]

In his spare time he visited Dostoevski's grave and went to the ballet and theater. One evening he sat down to watch what, from the audience's laughter, he took to be a comedy. By the end of the first act he had a sense of *déjà vu*. Glancing at the program, he discovered that the play was *Jack Straw*, translated from the English of "Mum."[112] He also found time to write to his friends. A letter to the playwright Edward Knoblock, who was in Greece on an intelligence assignment with Compton Mackenzie, revealed him in a contemplative frame of mind: "It seems incredible that one of these days we shall all settle down again to normal existence and read the fat, peaceful *Times* every morning and eat porridge for breakfast and marmalade. But, my dear, we shall be broken relics of a dead era, on the shelf all dusty and musty. The younger generation will give us a careless glance as it passes us. We will hob-nob over our port and talk of the dear old days of 1913, and you will agree with me that these young fellows of nowadays are dreary dogs."[113]

On October 18 Kerensky summoned Maugham and gave him a message for the British Prime Minister, Lloyd George, so secret that he was not allowed to put it in writing. Kerensky wanted him to leave for London at once and deliver it in person. The point of the message was that Kerensky could not hold out, needed Allied guns and ammunition, and wanted the British ambassador replaced. Maugham left the same day for Norway, and embarked on a British destroyer in Oslo, which landed him in the north of Scotland. Arriving in London, he called the Prime Minister's secretary and was given an appointment for the following morning.

Maugham went to Downing Street and found Lloyd George most cordial. He said how pleased he was to meet him and how much he had enjoyed his plays. Afraid that his stammer would spoil his delivery, Maugham had written out Kerensky's message and handed it to the Prime Minister, who read it hastily and said: "I can't do that." "What shall I tell Kerensky?" Maugham asked. "Just that I can't do that." Maugham attempted to speak, but Lloyd George rose and said: "I'm afraid I must bring this conversation to an end. I have a Cabinet meeting I must go to."[114] Maugham went back to his hotel wondering what to do next. He supposed he would have to go back to Russia, but events overtook him. On November 7 Kerensky was overthrown, and the Bolsheviks took power and sued for peace. On November 18 Sir Eric Drummond, private secretary to the Secretary of State for the Foreign Office, wrote on Maugham's report to Lloyd George: "I fear this of only historical interest now."[115] Maugham believed that if he had started six months earlier he might have succeeded. In a kind of reverse pride, he felt he was partly to blame for the Bolshevik take-over. In fact, the failure of his mission was due to the naïve belief of the intelligence people that sending one agent with funds could have any bearing on events. Maugham witnessed the forces of history at work and his own helplessness before them.

Though his mission was a failure, it provided him with material for some of the *Ashenden* stories. As usual, they were based on fact. "Mr. Harrington's Washing," the tale of an American businessman who refuses to leave Petrograd before he retrieves his laundry, and is shot in a riot, was based on an American banker who came to Russia to close a loan to the Kerensky government. The banker was found shot in a gutter after a street skirmish, his bundle of laundry under him.[116] The story also described Maugham's state of mind as he set out on his mission: "It was the most important mission that he had ever had and he was pleased with the sense of responsibility that it gave him. He had no one to give him orders, unlimited funds (he carried in a belt next to his skin bills of exchange for a sum so enormous that he was staggered when he thought of them), and though he had been sent to do something that was beyond human possibility, he did not know this and was prepared to set about his task with confidence."

His two and a half months in Russia had made Maugham's lungs worse. He was coughing and running a fever. The lung specialist he went to told him he had a touch of tuberculosis and said cheerily, "A sanatorium is the place for you, my boy." The news of Kerensky's overthrow made another visit to Russia out of the question. One day he received a summons to go at a certain hour to 10 Downing Street. He was taken to a room where important-looking men sat on each side of a long table. Among them was William Wiseman, his intelligence chief. He was asked to read a report on his activities in Russia. Afraid of stammering, he gave it to Wiseman to read. When Wiseman was done, Maugham was asked to take on a new mission. Now that Russia was out of the war, the intelligence people wanted to send a man to Romania to counter peace initiatives there. Maugham did not want to let them down—he was surprised they still had confidence in him—but he thought he had better tell them that he had tuberculosis and had been advised to go to a sanatorium. "In that case I don't think we ought to ask you to go," one of the men said. "Go to your sanatorium and I hope you'll get well very soon."[117]

PART IV

1917-1926

Chapter Nine

So here I am, in the middle way, having had twenty
years—

. . . . .

Trying to learn to use words, and every attempt
Is a wholly new start, and a different kind of failure
Because one has only learnt to get the better of words
For the thing one no longer has to say, or the way in
which
One is no longer disposed to say it. And so each ven-
ture
Is a new beginning, a raid on the inarticulate.

T. S. Eliot, "East Coker"

BECAUSE OF the war it was impossible for Maugham to go to Davos or Saint-Moritz to treat his tuberculosis, so he settled instead for a sanatorium in the north of Scotland, some twenty miles from Aberdeen. It was in a place called Banchory, and he was admitted in November 1917. It bothered him that he could not continue his war work and that the war would probably be over by the time he was well. Syrie remained in London and did not come to see him. He was already having doubts about the marriage, wondering how long it would last, and deciding to hope for the best and leave it at that.[1]

For the first six weeks at Banchory he stayed in bed and saw no one but doctors, nurses, and the maid who brought him his meals. Finally the day came when the doctors told him he could get up in the afternoon. A nurse helped him dress, led him to the veranda, propped cushions behind him, wrapped him in rugs, and left him to enjoy the mid-winter sunshine and the view of the snow-clad fields. All along the veranda there were patients in deck chairs, some chatting with their neighbors and some reading. Once in a while someone coughed and looked anxiously at his handkerchief.

Maugham found that the time passed with a bewildering rapidity. On November 10 he wrote to congratulate Hugh Walpole, who was back from Russia and had been awarded the C.B.E., adding that "since you saw me last I am a new man, for I have broken every habit I had. I get up at eleven and go to bed at four; I drink three pints of milk a day. I do a dozen things I never thought it possible for a sane man to do and I do none of the things I ever did before. . . . Your affectionate friend . . ."[2]

"In adversity, good cheer" might have been Maugham's motto. He wrote one friend that he was playing the role of the *Dame aux Camélias*, and he cheerfully wrote his friend and fellow World War I spy, Edward Knoblock:

> I think you would like this place. There is something that would appeal to your passion for the macabre in the way the tuberculars fall in love with one another . . . you cannot imagine the effectiveness of threatening your beloved that you will have a hemorrhage (I never could spell the damned word) if she does not turn a consenting ear to your entreaties. . . . One man came here and died four days later. I had quite a success with the remark that it seemed hardly worthwhile to come to Scotland for such a short time. . . . Do write and tell me all the news. Above all (of course in confidence) tell me when the war will end. I promise it shan't go any further.[3]

Maugham quickly improved and was able to write again. He took notes on the life around him, which he would later turn into a short story called "The Sanatorium," told by Ashenden the narrator, in which a man and a woman decide to marry even though they know it will shorten their lives. The story made one of his favorite points: "There are people who say that suffering ennobles. It is not true. As a general rule, it makes men petty, querulous, and selfish."

He also worked on a farce called *Home and Beauty*. Since he was sent to bed every evening at six after an early dinner, he had plenty of time. His window was kept wide open, and he had to wear mittens to hold a pen comfortably. It was, he said, "an admirable opportunity to write a farce." On January 26, 1918, *Love in a Cottage*, a play he had written for Marie Lohr before going to Russia, opened in London. Maugham had an uncanny way of echoing the events of his life in his writing. *Love in a Cottage* was a play about money and illness, written at a time when he had married to provide financial security for the mother of his child and had been laid low by consumption. Marie Lohr played a nurse who inherits a fortune when her husband dies. There is a provision in the will that she will lose the money if she marries again, and after being pursued by fortune hunters and assorted parasites she opts for "love in a cottage" and marries a penniless doctor. Critics dismissed the play as one of the slightest of Maugham's efforts, but it ran for 127 performances, for the British public was still eager for escapist entertainment in wartime.

In the spring of 1918 the doctors told Maugham that he was well enough to leave on condition that he return in the fall. Syrie came to see him and they decided to rent a house for the summer, on a hill in the peaceful Surrey countryside, near Farnham. The house, called Charles Hill Court, had a study for Maugham and a large garden to play in for Liza, who was almost three. Maugham spent his first months *en famille* in this bucolic setting.

He was working on *The Moon and Sixpence* and on a play set in Egypt called *Caesar's Wife*. It turned out that one of his neighbors was Robert Hichens, the friend of Oscar Wilde and author of *The Green Carnation*. Still fascinated by those who had known Wilde, Maugham called on Hichens and left his card. They saw each other continually during the summer, Hichens often playing croquet with the Maughams in their garden. Since he had three saddle horses, he asked Maugham if he rode. Maugham replied that in the course of a long and varied life he had ridden all sorts of beasts in all sorts of places. Hichens gave him a gray mare and rode a fidgety roan, and they went on many delightful rides, often interrupted by tea at the Frensham Ponds Hotel. One day, thinking that he might want a change, Hichens offered him the roan. It was a hot summer day and they were trotting quietly along the high-road deep when the roan crossed its forelegs and threw Maugham. Blood gushed from his head, which had struck the road. A bump formed on his forehead. When he had recovered he insisted on re-mounting the roan, and they rode to his house, where Hichens left him in Syrie's care. Hichens had never seen a man make less of a nasty accident; it was part of Maugham's nature to pretend indifference to pain and physical discomfort.[4]

Maugham did complain, however, that Syrie did not make welcome the old friends who came to see him, but aside from that they lived together amicably. As the summer drew to an end the question arose of where they would live. He refused to live in the house in Regent's Park which Gordon Selfridge had bought for Syrie, and insisted that she move into his house at 6 Chesterfield Street, even though this meant displacing his old friend Walter Payne, who was obliged to find a home of his own. Maugham spent only two months in London before he had to be back at the sanatorium in November, and it was there that he learned the war was over. He stayed in Banchory until the spring of 1919, returning to London with a clean bill of health.[5]

With the war and tuberculosis out of the way, he was his old prolific self. In 1919 he had two plays produced and a novel published. *Caesar's Wife*, the first play to run, opened on March 27; it had been suggested by *La Princesse de Clèves*, Madame de La Fayette's 1678 classic about a woman's renunciation of illicit love. The Princesse de Clèves, married to an older man, is in love with the young Duc de Nemours, but willpower triumphs over passion. In Maugham's adaptation the young and pretty wife of the British consul general in Cairo is in love with her husband's male secretary. She nobly asks her husband to send him to another post, but the husband insists that he remain in Egypt for the good of England. Both are acting out of duty and against their feelings. Maugham, stung by criticism that he wrote only about unprincipled people, had wanted to try a play where everyone's behavior was above reproach. As the play ends, the consul's young wife realizes that she needs and loves her husband after all. Maugham may also have been inspired by his own nobility in marrying Syrie instead of going off with Gerald Haxton, who had turned up in London in February 1919 while Maugham was still in Scotland. Gerald had spent eighteen months in a German POW camp, and went to Denmark when the armistice was signed to get the smell of prison barracks out of his nostrils. He came to England to see Maugham, but was deported as an undesirable alien before they could meet.[6]

C. Aubrey Smith, the consul with the stiff upper lip in *Caesar's Wife*, played another of Maugham's empire builders, like Alexander Mackenzie in *The Explorer*, who believes that there are races born to rule and races born to serve. Fay Compton, young and inexperienced, made her reputation as the consul's wife. The London *Times* on March 28 said that "Miss Fay Compton represents her as a child of nature—perhaps rather too petulant a child. The petulance is in the part, no doubt, but the actress seems inclined to emphasize it. It is a skillful, forceful performance; also it is a little hard."[7]

Fay Compton was frightened of Maugham. She thought his dialogue was hard to learn and harder to act. When she changed lines, he insisted: "We must have the correct words. I can't pass anything." Sensing her alarm, he made an effort to gain her confidence, enlisting Syrie to help her choose her costumes.[8] In the end he admired her performance. "The gesture with which she held out her arms to her lover after she had sent him away for good and all," he wrote, "had a grace, tenderness and beauty the like of which I have never before or since seen on the stage."[9] He enlarged upon his opinion of Miss Compton in a letter to his American theatrical agent John Rumsey: "She is a beautiful creature, a slut by nature, a good actress, and has a considerable hold on the British public."[10]

Although it was rather stolid and edifying, *Caesar's Wife* ran for 247 performances. In New York it ran for 72 performances, and was made into a film by First National Pictures in 1925, under the title of *Infatuation*, with Percy Marmont and Corinne Griffith. Maugham wrote Golding Bright: "I am rejoiced that you like the play, since I have reached the age when each play may be the beginning of the end of my career as a dramatist; like everyone else my powers must fail sooner or later and I would rather take my leave of the stage decidedly than with a series of dull pieces nobody wants."[11]

In April of the same year, 1919, Heinemann brought out *The Moon and Sixpence* in a first edition of 6,000 copies (as against 5,000 for *Of Human Bondage*). Six pages of publisher's advertisements included in the edition indicated what was then being read: six novels by Eden Phillpotts, seventeen by Flora Annie Steel, and three by Israel Zangwill. Maugham had been pondering a novel based on the life of Gauguin since his first contact with the painter's work in Paris in 1905. Again, as in *Liza of Lambeth*, written when the slum novel was fashionable, his timing proved right. The post-Victorian figure of the artist as outcast was in vogue. It had been dealt with by Thomas Hardy in *The Well-Beloved*, Jack London in *Martin Eden*, Theodore Dreiser in *The Genius*, D. H. Lawrence in *Sons and Lovers*, and James Joyce in *A Portrait of the Artist as a Young Man*. For a post-World War I audience, wondering where society had led them, the time was ripe for the antisocial hero who goes his own way. It was also ripe for the exotic setting of Tahiti, far from European battlegrounds.[12]

Charles Strickland, the character based on Gauguin, deserts his family, exploits his friends, drives his mistress to suicide, and is generally ill bred. He feels impelled to paint, and it develops that he is a great painter. The moral of the story is that great art justifies despicable behavior. George Moore dealt with the same idea when he wrote: "What matters the slaughter of ten thousand virgins if they provide Delacroix with a masterpiece?"

It was a theme close to Maugham's heart. Inside the Edwardian gentleman there was a Charles Strickland trying to get out. The author's admiration for the socially alienated artist who has the courage to be ruthless is one of the problems of the book, inasmuch as the narrator, Ashenden, is supposed to disapprove of Strickland. But Maugham seems to endorse both Strickland's society-be-damned rebelliousness and his attitude of suspicion toward women. Strickland abandons his wife because women are bad for artists. They do you in with all their petty demands. Love and art are incompatible. And what is true of Strickland's wife is also true of his mistress, Blanche, for women are all alike: "Do you remember my wife?" he asks. "I saw Blanche little by little trying all her tricks. With infinite patience she prepared to snare me and bind me. She wanted to bring me down to her level: she cared nothing for me, she only wanted me to be hers. She was willing to do everything in the world for me except the one thing I wanted: to leave me alone."

Part of Maugham's misogyny in *The Moon and Sixpence* may be attributed to the fact that he wrote it in a remote country retreat, with Syrie as his sole adult companion most of the time. Such a generous ration of Syrie must have seemed less than idyllic, and he seems to have transferred some of his annoyance to the book he was writing. But women are also disparaged in his other works (which did not prevent him from having a high proportion of women readers). Indeed, he pursued the subject with the fervor of a medieval churchman equating woman with sin. He would have agreed with Saint Louis that woman was "the confusion of man, an insatiable beast, a continuous anxiety, an incessant warfare, a daily ruin, a house of tempest."

"Tell a woman you'll double her capital in six months if she'll give it you to handle," says a character in "The Round Dozen," "and she won't be able to give you the money quick enough. Greed, that's what it is. Just greed." Women are "prudish and spiteful" ("The Door of Opportunity"). They are "jealous and spiteful and lazy" ("Neil Mac-Adam"). "It is always difficult for a man to stomach the want of reticence that women betray in their private affairs," Maugham wrote in "Virtue." "They have no shame. They will talk to one another without embarrassment of the most intimate matters. Modesty is a masculine virtue." They are sexually insatiable. Fred, in *The Narrow Corner*, says of a former mistress: "I'm not particular, but really, sometimes she almost disgusted me. She was proud of it. She used to say that after a chap had loved her, other women were duller than cold roast mutton. You don't like a woman to be absolutely shameless." They are dangerous. In "P & O," a man returning from the tropics dies aboard ship, apparently as the result of a spell cast by the native wife he has left behind.

On occasion women are murderers. In "The Letter," a woman kills her lover and pretends he was trying to rape her. In "Before the Party," the wife of a judge in Borneo slashes his throat with a parang because she is furious at his drunkenness. When they are not murderers they can be the agents of death. In "Footprints in the Jungle," a plantation man takes a friend into his home, and the friend has an affair with his wife and kills the husband. As if that were not enough, Maugham's women meddle with man's freedom, undermine his power, and try to control his life. In "The Kite," a young man marries a woman who interferes with his kite-flying. He returns to his parents and she destroys his best kite.

A New York psychiatrist, Leopold Bellak, who analyzed ten of Maugham's short stories, concluded that his strongest aggressive drives were projected against women. In an article published two years before Maugham's death Bellak said he had a paranoid personality that viewed life in terms of suspicion, fear, and defensive aggression. His stories were attempts to resolve his emotional problems. Bellak recommended that Maugham (then ninety years old) be psychoanalyzed in order to develop his emotional range. Successful analysis, he predicted, could raise him from the level of superb craftsman to that of great artist.[13] (Maugham once told the playwright S. N. Behrman that he had been psychoanalyzed but that all it had done for him was to increase his sexual desires.)[14]

In The Moon and Sixpence, Maugham's view of women was given its fullest airing. They were the enemies of creative life, parasitic and manipulative, sapping the strength of men. In Charles Strickland, who says that "women are very unintelligent," he found an outlet for his gall. When Gauguin's wife read the book, however, she said that she did not find a single trait of Strickland's that had anything in common with her husband.[15] Of course, to have found Maugham's portrait a good likeness would have been to admit that she had married a scoundrel.

Nor did those who knew it recognize Maugham's Tahiti. One got no impression from the book that it had been colonized by the French, was the chief of the Society Islands, could be reached by steamship, and had a newspaper and a radio station.[16] A novelist of course is not bound to paint an accurate portrait. The book's real weakness lay elsewhere: in its failure to live up to the principle stated by the critic Richard Black-mur that "the intelligence must always act as if it were adequate to the problems it aroused." Maugham presents Strickland as a great painter and a genius but is unable to do more than tell us that this is the case. The only clue to Strickland's genius is that it is a sudden force that overwhelms him. "I tell you I've got to paint," he says. "I can't help myself. When a man falls into the water it doesn't matter how he swims, well or badly; he's got to get out or else he'll drown." The only way Maugham can show genius at work is by making Strickland boorish, as if greatness were somehow synonymous with bad manners. A more convincing book about a painter was Joyce Cary's *The Horse's Mouth*, which showed the complicated processes of a gifted painter's mind. With Gully Jimson, the reader knew that he was in the presence of a great painter. Maugham did not even come close.

Katherine Mansfield cited this flaw in the novel when she reviewed it in *The Athenaeum* on May 9, 1919: "We must be shown something of the workings of his [Strickland's] mind; we must have some comment of his upon what he feels, fuller and more exhaustive than his perpetual 'Go to hell.' It is simply essential that there should be some quality in him revealed to us that we may love, something that will stop us for ever from crying: 'If you have to be so odious before you can paint bananas—pray leave them unpainted.' "[17]

A quarter of a century later Maugham had a chance to get back at Miss Mansfield when he wrote: "She has been extravagantly praised. She was not a genius, but partly by the booming of her literary friends, partly because in the poverty of the short story in England at the time she was writing, she seemed better than she was, she was acclaimed as such. She had a small and delicate talent and sensitive feeling for visual things, but when she tried to write a story of any length, it broke to pieces in the middle because it was not supported by a structure of sufficient strength."[18]

Generally, however, *The Moon and Sixpence* was highly praised. Reviewers are often one book behind, and it received the notices that *Of Human Bondage* merited and became a best seller in the United States. The title was borrowed from a review of *Of Human Bondage* in *The Times Literary Supplement*, which said that the main character "like so many young men, was so busy yearning for the moon that he never saw the sixpence at his feet."

In the spring of 1919 the Maughams moved out of the Mayfair house at 6 Chesterfield Street, where they felt cramped. Willie and Syrie had separate bedrooms, but Syrie had also taken over his writing room, so that he had to work in a small ground-floor room overlooking the street. They found a four-story Georgian house at 2 Wyndham Place, in Marylebone, a less fashionable district than Mayfair, which had the unusual feature of a barrel-vaulted drawing room. St. Mary's Church, with its Greek columns and small rounded steeple, stood at the end of the street. The Maughams remained there until 1923. Gerald Kelly's studio was nearby, and Syrie opened her shop not far away, in Baker Street, and went to furniture auctions to pick up odds and ends that she could sell at a profit.[19]

In June, Maugham wrote Hugh Walpole to praise his novel *Second City*, which was set in wartime Russia. He particularly liked the descriptions of Petrograd, a city that both he and Walpole knew at first hand. Maugham seemed to be on the best of terms with Walpole. They were both successful writers and men-about-town who enjoyed each other's company. "Since I think you must shortly be returning to London," he wrote, "[for] is not the season in full swing and what youth of fashion can rest content with Polperro [a small fishing village in Cornwall where Walpole had a cottage] when St. James calls him?—I write to beg you to let me know when you are coming, for very soon I set out on my travels and if you do not I shall see nothing of you."[20]

Maugham's travels that summer involved a holiday in Capri, without madame, happily among his friends. He lectured his fellow writer Compton Mackenzie, who had returned to Capri after his wartime service and taken a fine villa called Casa Solitaria.

"You're very extravagant, Monty," he said. "You should try to save money."

"My dear Willie," Mackenzie said, "how on earth can I save money after somehow keeping a villa in Capri on the pay of a Captain of Marines without being able to write a book for nearly three years? I have had to pay off lots of debts and if one has paid off lots of debts one has a right to enjoy extravagance."

Maugham replied in the tone of La Fontaine's ant refusing the grasshopper's request for a loan: "I've saved one hundred and eighty-six thousand pounds."[21] Considering that he had been making money only since 1907, this was quite an achievement.

On August 30, 1919, *Home and Beauty*, the play he had written in the sanatorium with his mittens on, opened in London, with Gladys Cooper in the role of a war bride who has to choose between two husbands, one presumed dead. In the end she marries a suitor with a

Rolls Royce, and both husbands breathe sighs of relief. Maugham milked the situation for laughs, and introduced in the last act the character of an "intervener," a lady who is hired in divorce cases to help prove misconduct. Miss Montmorency, the intervener, turned out to be the incarnation of prim spinsterhood, and declined her services, saying: "One gentleman is business, but two would be debauchery." *Home and Beauty* was a hit and ran for 235 performances, adding more funds to Maugham's savings account. *The Times* called it "a little masterpiece of polite merriment" and said that Gladys Cooper, whom Maugham had met ten years earlier through Charles Hawtrey, had become an accomplished actress.[22]

A month after the opening Maugham left for China on another hunt for material. En route he stopped in New York and Chicago, where he picked up Gerald Haxton, whom he found he could not do without. The attachment was too strong; the genial, outgoing twenty-seven-year-old Gerald was the perfect counterpart to Maugham, who was a model of prim reserve. In Chicago, Maugham visited a slaughterhouse, where hogs came by on an assembly line, and was struck by the calm indifference with which a pleasant-faced young man killed them.[23] The young man illustrated one of Maugham's cherished principles: one could get used to anything, as he had gotten used to dissecting corpses in medical school and, as a spy, turning in persons he had nothing against.

He spent about four months in China, which was under a military dictatorship after the overthrow of the Ching dynasty. In December he and Gerald took a long trip in the interior, traveling by sampan fifteen hundred miles up the Yangtze River and then continuing on foot. By January 3, 1920, he was at the Astor House hotel in Shanghai boasting in a letter to Dillie Fleming that he had walked four hundred miles "on my flat feet."[24] Dillie had written that her divorce had finally come through, and Maugham, from Shanghai, replied with a little lecture on the virtue of patience in marriage, a reflection on his own situation: "You seem definitely to have made up your mind that your marriage is not a success. . . . In married life there are times when one feels things are so hateful that it is worthwhile doing anything to get out of it, but one goes on—for one reason or another—and somehow they settle down more or less, and one becomes resigned or makes allowances or what not, and time goes on and eventually things seem not so bad as they might have been."[25]

Maugham met a variety of people in China but concentrated on the British, who were there in various capacities. There was the customs official who had been in China twenty years and knew how to treat the natives; the junior partners of well known trading firms who read their London papers at the club; the man who professed socialist opinions and read Bertrand Russell but mistreated his rickshaw boys; the missionaries who hated the Chinese but had spent a lifetime trying to convert them; the smug delegates of empire; the Englishwoman who was trying to duplicate a London drawing room in a converted temple in Peking, putting a stove in the niche where the Buddha had been. These were the English abroad, whom he would put to good use in his short stories.[26]

He also took notes on the Chinese he met, such as the cabinet minister who mourned the passing of the old ways, whereas Maugham knew that the man was dishonest and cruel, and a greater contributor to his country's decline than all the factors he described. He met a Chinese professor of comparative literature, who asked him the secrets of his craft.

"I only know two," Maugham said. "One is to have common sense and the other is to stick to the point."

"Does it require no more than that to write a play?"

"You want a certain knack, but no more than to play billiards."

"They lecture on the technique of the drama in all the important universities of America."

"The Americans are an extremely practical people. I believe that Harvard is instituting a chair to instruct grandmothers how to suck eggs."

"I do not think I quite understand you."

"If you can't write a play no one can teach you and if you can it's as easy as falling off a log."[27]

By January 12 Maugham was in Hong Kong, having had a very good time and collected a good deal of material. He was returning to England via Suez, and was delighted to hear from Golding Bright that *Home and Beauty* was doing well on both sides of the Atlantic, for the cost of moving into and renovating Wyndham Place was twice as much as he had estimated.[28] The material he had collected Maugham would turn into a book of sketches, *On a Chinese Screen*, serialized in the *American Bookman*, a play set in Peking called *East of Suez*, and a novel, *The Painted Veil*, set in Hong Kong. He took special pride in his description of the Great Wall of China in *On a Chinese Screen* as an example of sinewy poetic prose. He proudly read it aloud to Harold Acton, who had been to China, but Acton thought it was trite.[29]

Maugham was planning to be back in London at the end of March, but in mid-March he received some disconcerting news. Syrie had rented their house on Wyndham Place until the end of July, cutting him off from his papers and his books and his accustomed surroundings. Syrie offered him a bed-sitting room in a house she had rented in the King's Road, Chelsea, but he refused. "I am too old to pig it," he wrote Golding Bright, "so unless I am needed for rehearsals, I shall settle down in some quiet spot on the Riviera."[30] In the end he put off his departure and left Hong Kong in April, returning to England via Mukden and Japan.

In the marriage between the Maughams each behaved in a manner certain to provoke retaliation in the other. Willie was off for months at a time, so that Syrie felt justified in renting their home. When he returned to find himself homeless, he had no qualms about going off on another long trip. In the next few years he would be gone a great deal of the time, sometimes for periods of six to nine months. He was a man divided between a wife and child, who meant social conformity, and a male lover, with whom he shared an adventurous and professionally rewarding life.

Gerald remained in Italy or France on a standby basis when Maugham was in England. Maugham liked to tell the story of coming into the smoking room of the Bath Club after one of his Far Eastern trips to be confronted by an elderly member in a high-backed chair by the fire. Before he could say "Good morning" the club member said, "Hello, Maugham, haven't seen your face recently. Been to Brighton, I suppose, for the week-end."[31]

Maugham valued the contrast between his adventures in the Orient with Gerald and his sedentary life in London, where he wrote in his study, played bridge at the Garrick, went to first nights, and worked at the part of father and husband. On a typical day, five-year-old Liza would come in to say goodbye wearing the white squirrel coat he had brought her from China, and he would play trains with her until her nurse came to fetch her. After an afternoon of bridge he would get home just in time to tell Liza a bedtime story. He thought she looked very nice in her pajamas, with her hair done up in two plaits.[32] But such moments were rare; Liza did not see much of her father. In self-justification Maugham later wrote, "I have a notion that children are all the better for not being burdened with too much parental love."[33]

On August 9, 1920, another Maugham play opened, *The Unknown*, a reworking of his Boer War novel, *The Hero*, for post-World

War I audiences. With *Of Human Bondage* and *The Moon and Six-pence* having established him once again as a novelist, Maugham felt secure enough in his reputation to attempt a serious play. *The Unknown* dealt with a wounded and decorated veteran who has lost his faith after the death of a close friend at the front. He returns to his home in provincial England, to his churchgoing parents and his pious fiancée, who breaks off the engagement because of his transformation. This was the most discursive and mirthless of Maugham's plays, but it was notable for its performances. The veteran was played by the future Sherlock Holmes of films, Basil Rathbone, and Haidee Wright played the mother of two sons killed in the war, whose incongruous gaiety shocks the village community. There were critics who said *The Unknown* was worth seeing for a single line. The characters are discussing how a benevolent God can permit war. The village vicar says that the war was due to the "loving-kindness of God, who wishes to purify the nation by suffering: to err is human, to forgive divine." And then Haidee Wright had her show-stopping line: "And who is going to forgive God?"

As *The Times* recounted it on August 10, she "spoke it with all the force of her being. . . . You can imagine the shock at that sudden outcry, the intensity of passion with which her tale of misery and brave despair came hissing through her all but clenched teeth. And at the close of that act the audience would not be satisfied until they had Miss Wright before the curtain and thundered their applause at her."[34]

A few critics admired Maugham's daring for bringing theological discussion to the stage. But Frank Swinnerton, who would become his friend, dismissed the play in *The Nation* on August 21 by saying that "the characters discuss God for three acts and reach no conclusion about Him." Desmond MacCarthy, his ambulance corps billet-mate, reviewing his first Maugham play in the *New Statesman* on August 14, did not let friendship temper his judgment that the play was a failure. He added somewhat gratuitously that Maugham's work owed more to "tenacity of purpose than to originality."[35] *The Unknown* ran for a disappointing 77 performances.

Maugham was not in London to see it close, for in October he was off again to observe his countrymen in unfamiliar settings, this time the Federated Malay States. He and Gerald traveled via New York, where his American publisher, George H. Doran, gave him the galleys of his South Sea stories, *The Trembling of a Leaf*, and Los Angeles, where an offer to write for films had come from Famous Players-Lasky.

Lasky and one of his young producers, Samuel Goldwyn, had recruited a number of famous playwrights to add luster to the film industry and had grouped them under the name Eminent Authors, Inc. Most of the eminent authors could not write for the screen, and the experiment was a flop. Among them was Maurice Maeterlinck, author of *The Blue Bird* and *Pelléas and Mélisande*, who wrote a screenplay about a small boy who discovered some fairies in the woods. Goldwyn's reaction to this fable was distinctly unfairylike. Maugham arrived in Los Angeles in December to discuss writing for the screen. His friend Edward Knoblock was already on hand, working on Douglas Fairbanks vehicles. Hollywood had not long been the center of the film industry. Sagebrush and wild pepper trees grew in vacant lots on Sunset Boulevard. Mary Pickford and Fairbanks were building Pickfair. The private swimming pool as a status symbol had not yet occurred.[36]

There was probably no writer who sold as many stories, plays, and books to the movies as Maugham, but his first experience in Hollywood left him jaundiced, and not long after, he wrote words that proved to be less than prophetic: "There are directors who desire to be artistic. It is pathetic to compare the seriousness of their aim with the absurdity of their attainment. . . . I believe that in the long run it will be found futile to adapt stories for the screen from novels or from plays, and that any advance in this form of entertainment which may eventually lead to something artistic, lies in the story written directly for projection on the white screen."[37]

The one positive result of his conferences with studio heads was that he sold them a script for $15,000. He promptly sent the money to Bert Alanson to invest. Across the hall in Maugham's hotel there was another writer, John Colton. One night Colton knocked on his door, said he couldn't sleep, and asked if he had anything to read. Maugham gave him the galleys of "Miss Thompson." The next morning Colton was all excited and said he wanted to make a play from the story. Maugham said to Knoblock: "Colton asks me whether I will let him dramatize 'Miss Thompson.' Do you think there is a play in it?" "I don't know," Knoblock said, "I don't think so. No harm in letting him try, I suppose."

Maugham agreed, and he and Knoblock went out to celebrate New Year's Eve in a tacky Los Angeles dance hall called Dreamland, which had a good black band. Prohibition was in force, and they drank whiskey out of teacups. The bottle had cost thirty dollars. Some blue-collar types at the next table said: "Say, I guess you got the real stuff. Let's have a taste, brother."

"What are you drinking?" Knoblock asked.

"Oh, this is distilled shellac. I've been a-boilin' it down for days. I'm a ship's painter. And when I'm crazy for hooch, I just lick my brushes."[38]

In Hollywood, Maugham also met Charlie Chaplin, who was already a star. His speech still had a hint of his Cockney youth, and Maugham was won over when Chaplin improvised a dialogue between two house-wives from the slums of Lambeth. Behind Chaplin's comedy Maugham sensed a profound melancholy. One night when they were walking in Los Angeles they came to a poor section of the city. Chaplin's face lit up when he saw the tenements and shabby shops. "Say," he said, "this is the real life, isn't it? All the rest is just sham."[39]

After Los Angeles, Maugham and Gerald went to San Francisco to see Bert Alanson, before embarking on February 21 on the Pacific mail vessel *Wolverine State* for Honolulu.[40] On arrival he ran into a woman he had met in his youth on Lake Como. She had introduced him to Emerson, and she always carried a volume of the essays, heavily under-lined in blue pencil (to bring out the color of her eyes, Maugham thought). Now she was Lady Rothermere, renting a house for the season. She still read Emerson. She wore a Doucet dress, with a pearl chain that he estimated was worth a quarter of a million dollars, but no shoes or stockings. "You see," she told him, pointing to her bare feet, "here we lead the simple life." Maugham felt that the unaffected charm of her appearance was somewhat marred by a large bunion.[41]

Their next port of call was Sydney, Australia, where they could catch a boat to Singapore. Maugham wrote Knoblock: "I look back on my connection with the cinema world with horror mitigated only by the fifteen thousand dollars. . . . I had a most amusing and surprising time in Australia. You know of course that Cairo is the haven of the elderly unenjoyed; well, Sydney is the Mecca of the decrepit author. The last one they saw was Robert Louis Stevenson and they still speak of him. When I arrived, with nothing more than a brass band and a steam roller to herald my coming, I was received with the most gratifying enthusi-asm."[42]

By March he was in Singapore, and he remained in the Malay States through August, with a side trip to Sarawak, on the nearby island of Borneo. The Federated Malay States, formed in 1895, were under British rule. The population of Moslem Malays, Chinese, and Indians was governed by British civil servants. The British developed Malaya's wealth, making it the world leader in rubber production, and saw to it that the ethnic groups remained at peace with one another.

The civil servants and planters formed a curious colony of their own which tried to reconstruct England in the tropics. At dinners at Government House the men wore tails or white monkey jackets. The king's birthday parade was an important occasion, involving horses imported for the officers from Australia. The Tropical Service uniform was white trousers too tight to sit down in, a white tunic with gilt buttons, black patent-leather boots, and a large helmet. There was a hunt club, although there was nothing to hunt and nothing to hunt with, for hounds could not stand the climate.

It was in many ways a better life than England. Every household had a boy, a cook, a *tukan-ayer* (water carrier), a gardener, and a driver. The women were called Mem. The men had their clubs. There was a good deal of drinking, but in the heat the highballs rapidly made their exit through one's pores. Every five years the colonists went on home leave, and if they lived in an exhausting climate, they went to the hill stations for fresh air. If they were in outstations and saw no white men for long periods, they went to Singapore. *The Times* arrived at up-country stations six weeks late. The variety of the work was interesting. There were district officers, constables, census takers, and magistrates who tried drunken Malays and thieving Chinese houseboys and who watched floggings carried out. The warder who held the cane was not allowed to bring his arm above the level of his shoulder.[43]

It was this contained world of British colonials that Maugham made his own, and soon Malaya became known as "Maugham country." Maugham was intrigued by the things that happened to the British in the tropics, by their reaction to the country and the effect that contact with nature had on them. For the first time since Lambeth he felt that he was seeing life as it really was. Behavior was unrestrained. A staid English couple transplanted to the Malay States would fall apart and become the figures in a sordid drama. Everyone he met had stories to tell—about the member of the Legislative Council who was caught *in flagrante*, about the baronet who had eloped with the sister of a Chinese millionaire, about a man who lived in an incestuous relationship with his sister. Although he seized on this gossip to create the world of his short stories, he was the first to admit that the people he wrote about were exceptions. "The vast majority of these people, government servants, planters and traders," he said, "who spent their working lives in Malaya were ordinary people ordinarily satisfied with their station in life. . . . They were good, decent, normal people."

His method was to pick up invitations and letters of recommendation as he went along, enjoying the hospitality of people cut off from their home country and glad to have a visitor.

Arriving with Gerald in some remote spot, with a letter of introduction to the Resident, he was at first embarrassed at the thought of presenting himself to a total stranger with the announcement that he was going to sleep under his roof, eat his food, and drink his whiskey. But the strangers were always welcoming and would say: "Good God, man, you have no idea how glad I am to see you. Don't think I'm doing anything for you in putting you up. The boot's on the other leg. And stay as long as you damned well like. Stay a year."[44] He stayed with them, they unburdened themselves, and he wrote it up. Such was the formula. "Would it bore you awfully if I told you about it?" they would ask, and afterward, "I'm afraid I've rather bored you with my domestic affairs." "Not at all," Maugham said, and meant it.[45]

Maugham wrote two collections of stories set mainly in Malaya, The Casuarina Tree in 1926 and Ah King in 1933. In the minds of many readers he is as closely associated with Malaya as Kipling is with India. In fact, he spent relatively little time there—six months in 1921 (of which three were spent in sanatoriums in Java because of illness) and four months in 1925.

If he had returned to Malaya, it is no exaggeration to say that he might have come to harm. More than ten years after his last trip there the anger had not subsided, as this editorial from the Singapore Straits Budget of June 7, 1938, shows:

> It is interesting to try to analyze the prejudice against Somerset Maugham which is so intense and widespread in this part of the world. The usual explanation is that Mr. Maugham picks up some local scandal at an out-station and dishes it up as a short story . . . the second cause is disgust at the way Mr. Maugham has explained the worst and least representative aspects of the European life in Malaysia—murder, cowardice, drink, seduction, adultery . . . always the same cynical emphasis on the same unpleasant things. No wonder that white men and women who are living normal lives in Malaysia wish that Mr. Maugham would look for local color elsewhere.

After those two short trips he did not return, for the publication of The Casuarina Tree had made him persona non grata. The people who befriended him—the officials who confided in him, the hostesses who asked him to dinner, the district officers who put him up—felt betrayed.

Maugham, who was such a model of Edwardian circumspection at home, had no compunctions about repeating the most intimate stories he heard about the people he met. Where material was concerned he was ruthless, exploiting his hosts and respecting no one's privacy.

In the words of Victor Purcell, a Malayan civil servant from 1921 to 1946:

> Maugham's passage in Malaya was clearly marked by a trail of angry people. The indignation aroused by his play *The Letter*, which was based on a local cause célèbre, was still being voiced in emotional terms. It was also charged against him that he abused hospitality by ferreting out the family skeletons of his hosts and putting them into books. His representation of a certain level of European life in Malaya was photographic, but as a picture of the European community in general it was not fairer than one of Britain as a nation would be in exclusive terms of racing, the News of the World, and conversation in golf clubs. The Maugham chiaroscuro always seemed to me to consist of sharp contrast exclusively, with no nuances or shading.[46]

What made things worse was that often Maugham did not take the trouble to disguise his material. In Singapore, for instance, he stayed at the Hotel Van Wyck, which became the Hotel Van Dyke in the story "Neil MacAdam." He was quite candid in later years in explaining that this story was told to him word for word while that story was based on such and such. In the fifties, when some of his stories were televised, he introduced each one, explaining its genesis. Of "Footprints in the Jungle," which is about a couple who have committed a murder that remains unsolved, he said: "It is one of those stories that I can hardly claim the authorship of, for it was told me word for word one evening in a club in one of the towns of the Federated Malay States." Of "The Vessel of Wrath," a comic account of a spinsterish missionary who reforms and marries a drunken ruffian, he said: "I traveled a good deal in the Malayan Archipelago at one time and all the people I have described in this story I met at one time or another. I only had to bring them together to invent the story."[47] Just as he had done in *Liza of Lambeth*, Maugham sometimes transcribed verbatim what he saw and heard.

An example of how faithful he could be to his material is "The Letter," perhaps his best known short story after "Rain." Published in 1926 in *The Casuarina Tree*, and made into a hit play with Gladys Cooper, and a hit movie with Bette Davis, "The Letter" is about a married Englishwoman in Malaya, Leslie Crosbie, who kills her lover and then pretends that he was trying to rape her. The facts, as related in Singapore newspaper accounts that Maugham must have studied, were these:

On April 23, 1911, Mrs. Ethel Mabel Proudlock, the wife of a headmaster in Kuala Lumpur, shot the manager of a tin mine, William Crozier Steward, on the veranda of her home. Her husband was out to dinner with one of his teachers when Steward arrived in a rickshaw. According to Mrs. Proudlock, he tried to kiss her. She asked him if he was mad. (Leslie Crosbie said she asked her lover if he was a half-wit.) Steward turned out the light, Mrs. Proudlock said, and pressed her to him. Groping for the light switch, her hand touched a revolver, left on the bookcase, and she fired. As in the story, she did not fire once, but six times. As in the story, she claimed loss of memory. As in the story, public sympathy was with the brave woman who had defended her honor against a brute.

In "The Letter" it is revealed that Leslie Crosbie shot her lover because he had a Chinese mistress. A letter she had written asking him to come and see her was in the hands of the Chinese woman, and the story ends with her lawyer buying the incriminating document and her freedom. The plot came straight from the trial testimony. The prosecutor made a strong case that Mrs. Proudlock had been on intimate terms with Steward, and established that Steward had a Chinese mistress. The only element that Maugham added was the letter. In the story, Leslie Crosbie was found guilty of justifiable homicide and was freed. But Mrs. Proudlock was found guilty of murder and was sentenced to be hanged.

Mr. Proudlock cabled the Secretary of State for Colonies, asking for clemency for his wife. A petition in her favor was circulated and obtained more than seven hundred signatures. The women of Kuala Lumpur asked Queen Mary to pardon Mrs. Proudlock as a Coronation gesture. Another petition was presented to the Sultan of Selangor, the native ruler whose jurisdiction included Kuala Lumpur; he pardoned her in July. She went back to England, without her husband, and died in an asylum. Her month in the condemned cell had broken her reason.

It was a Singapore lawyer and his wife, Mr. and Mrs. C. Dickinson, who put Maugham onto the story. He expressed his gratitude by sending them a copy of the play with the inscription: "Dear Mrs. Dickinson, Here is the play which I owe so much to you. Yours always, W. Somerset Maugham."[48]

Maugham had not been long in Singapore when he decided to make a side trip to the island of Borneo, the northern part of which was also under British rule. While he prepared for this rugged journey, the play which is thought to be his best, *The Circle*, opened on March 3, 1921, at the Haymarket Theatre. *The Circle* has worn better than Maugham's other plays, and was revived in 1944 with John Gielgud and in 1977 with Googie Withers. It is less artificial than his other comedies. The epigrams do not seem to have been added on like candied cherries on a cake. The humor arises from the characters and the situation. The play's theme, that we must make our own mistakes, is true in any generation. The romantic young wife of an insipid member of the British upper classes falls in love with an intense young rubber planter on leave from Malaya. Should she flout social convention and run away with the planter? She has before her the example of her mother-in-law, who eloped thirty years before with a lord; they are now an elderly and quarrelsome couple. Recognizing that romance does not last, the young man does not promise her happiness, but love with its pains and problems. The young woman decides that she must discover the fallacy of romance for herself, and as the curtain falls she and her planter are off for the Federated Malay States.

The Circle was the first of Maugham's plays to be booed. The gallery expressed its displeasure, whether at the actors' delivery (there were cries of "Don't mumble") or at the elopement in the final scene was not clear. It was generally well reviewed, however, ran for 181 performances, and was twice made into a movie by MGM—in 1925 as *The Circle* and in 1930 as *Strictly Unconventional*.[49] The cast included Fay Compton, Allan Aynesworth, and Ernest Thesiger, who played the pompous husband. In the midst of rehearsals Thesiger complained that he was getting no help from the director, and thought of sending the author an expensive cable to ask him what his character was supposed to be feeling in an important scene.[50]

The author could not have been reached by cable, for he and Gerald were traveling up a river in Sarawak, British North Borneo, by launch and paddle boat, and then poling, until they were in the heart of the jungle. At night they slept among the headhunters, whom they found to be polite and hospitable. At every village a feast and a dance were given in their honor, keeping them up until three in the morning. Maugham saw kingfishers and monkeys, and was warned not to bathe far from the bank, because the river was infested with crocodiles.

They were not troubled by crocodiles, but on the way back downriver, in April, they encountered the greatest danger on any river in

Borneo, a bore, an inrush of water, of tidal-wave proportions, that sweeps upstream when high tide compresses it into the narrow channels. It was three days after the new moon, the most dangerous time, and they were traveling in a paddle boat with a crew of convicts from the Simanggang jail.

Maugham saw two or three waves in the distance, but they looked harmless, until suddenly, coming closer, they seemed miraculously to have grown to an immense height. Tightening his belt so his trousers would not slip off if he had to swim, he looked up to see the bore upon them, a wall of roaring water ten feet high. The force of the wave turned the boat broadside, the crew lost control, and Maugham found himself thrown out from under the awning where he had been sitting.

The boatmen shouted to cling to the boat, and he and Gerald hung onto the gunwales and the base of the framework that supported the rattan mats of the awning. Another wave capsized the boat and they momentarily lost their hold, but regained it. Maugham, out of breath and feeling his strength going, wanted to swim to shore, which looked about forty yards away, but Gerald begged him to hang on. The boat spun like a wheel, he swallowed quantities of water, and he was about to let go when two of the Malay prisoners caught hold of a thin mattress, which they rolled into a lifebelt. He grabbed it and they struck out for shore. Suddenly Gerald cried out that he could touch bottom. Maugham swam a few more strokes and let his feet sink down into thick mud. They scrambled up the bank, grabbing the roots of dead trees, and found a little flat of tall grass where they lay down exhausted, covered with black mud from head to foot. At that point Gerald had a heart attack, and Maugham was sure he was going to die. Eventually a canoe came to get them, and took them back to a native longhouse, where they washed in a pail, unable to bring themselves to use the river.[51]

When they got back to Kuching, the capital of Sarawak, their escape from the bore was looked upon as miraculous. Maugham later wrote the Resident with whom he had been staying up-country and asked him to commute the sentences of the two convicts who had saved his life. The Resident replied that one man had been set free but that he could do nothing about the other, who, on his way back to the jail at Simanggang, had stopped off at his village and murdered his mother-in-law. Maugham and Gerald, both suffering from cuts and bruises, went back to Singapore to rest and refit, and a few days later were off again on their tour of the Malay States.[52]

Chapter Ten

There was a young lady from Guam
Who peddled her charms, charm by charm,
Inspired I suppose
By the classical prose
Of W. Somerset Maugham.

Ogden Nash

By August, Maugham's travels had exhausted him—he was forty-seven and had only two years before recovered from tuberculosis—and he and Gerald were resting in a hotel sanatorium in Java, at 6,000 feet above sea level. Bert Alanson had received his copy of *The Trembling of a Leaf*, which was dedicated to him, and wrote to thank Maugham, who replied on August 23 to remind him of the trip to Hawaii they had made together in 1916, which had led to the writing of the stories.[1]

Doran published *The Trembling of a Leaf* on September 17 in an edition of 3,000 copies, priced at $1.90. Publication followed in England on October 6, and the first edition quickly sold out. Maugham was already known as a novelist and playwright, and *The Trembling of a Leaf* established him as a short-story writer. The seven stories, the fruit of his first trip to the South Seas, were set in Hawaii, Samoa, and Tahiti.

The title came from Sainte-Beuve: *"L'extrème félicité à peine séparée par une feuille tremblante de l'extrème désespoir, n'est-ce-pas la vie?"*[2] In Maugham's characters, a trembling leaf separates despair from happiness. Edward Barnard gives up business success in Chicago and a fiancée to find happiness in Tahiti. The Scotsman in "The Pool" has every reason for happiness when he marries a beautiful native girl, but finds despair. In *The Trembling of a Leaf* Maugham filed the patent on a certain kind of story, set in the tropics and usually describing the undoing of the characters because they have failed to understand their surroundings. The collection included his most famous story, "Rain"—which had appeared that April in H. L. Mencken's the *Smart Set* after having been turned down by many other magazines—and other vintage Maugham, such as "Red," "The Pool," "Mackintosh," and "The Fall of Edward Barnard." Two minor efforts, "Honolulu" and "The Pacific," completed it.

Maugham had written the stories in a notebook with a navy-blue leather cover, the pages of which were lined on one side and unlined on the other. He wrote on the lined side and made corrections on the unlined side. Corrections were minor. Occasionally there was a line through a word. In "Rain" he made several changes of dialogue that had to do mainly with the way an American whore would express herself: "The dirty dog's asking me for a dollar and a half a day for a room you can't hardly turn round in" became "The feller's tryin' to soak me a dollar and a half a day for the meanest sized room." "That's O.K. then, said Miss Thompson. Come right in and we'll have a tiddly to settle it. You come along too, doctor" became "That's the goods, said Miss Thompson. Come right in and we'll have a shot of hooch. I've got some real good rye in that grip if you'll bring it along, Mr. Swan. You come along too, doctor."[3] When I saw the manuscript, which is now at Stanford, with its handwritten titles such as "Rain" and "Mackintosh," I was reminded of a remark Ilka Chase made about Maugham when she visited him in the south of France in the fifties: "Neither an assembly line nor a stock market nor an oil well did it, simply what came from one small skull and that one right hand."[4]

Critics agreed that here was something they had not seen before. The *Bookman* in November said the stories were "as savage and gripping as some of the paintings by Goya." The *Saturday Review* on November 5, 1921, said that "each tale is begun by inspiration and completed by artistic perfection." The most interesting review came from Rebecca West, never an admirer of Maugham's, who wrote in the *New Statesman* on November 5 that his indomitable character "enables him to make the best and most remunerative use of every grain of talent that he possesses." The Sainte-Beuve quote she considered indicative of "a certain cheap and tiresome attitude towards life, which nearly mars these technically admirable stories." She found two "more than admirable stories," "Mackintosh" and "Rain."[5]

That Maugham in these stories had demarcated a small precinct of the literary landscape was acknowledged in later years by another writer who laid claim to the same geographical area. James Michener wrote in 1952 that "one of the evil limitations put upon anyone who wants to write about the South Pacific is that he must stop reading

Maugham, Conrad, and Becke, lest he inadvertently plagiarize from those masters. . . . At the same time I must admit that before I start to do any writing about this vast area I usually take down Rain and reread those first three paragraphs to remind myself of how completely one can set a physical stage in a few absolutely correct observations. I hold those passages to be about the best beginning of a mood story extant."[6]

The use of the detached narrator was another technique admired by fellow writers. Maugham used it in two of the six stories in *The Trembling of a Leaf* and in *The Moon and Sixpence, Cakes and Ale, The Razor's Edge* (where he dropped the alter ego and called the narrator Somerset Maugham), and in many short stories. The narrator is in the story, but apart from it. He remains self-effacing and uninvolved. He is a man of the world whom nothing shocks and who tells a story much as he might in his club over drinks to a friend. He keeps the story moving, like a circus ringmaster who stands outside the ring but makes sure that acrobats somersault and lions roar on cue.

The narrator device helps Maugham achieve an offhand tone, for he begins with observations about himself and then shifts to the narrative. Almost always the narrator's remarks about himself are true of Maugham. In "The Book-Bag," for instance, he begins by describing his passion for books, saying, "I would sooner read the catalogue of the Army and Navy stores or Bradshaw's Guide than nothing at all." The narrator speaks of being imprisoned by illness for three months in a hill town in Java, as Maugham was, and running out of books, so that he had to buy the school books from which educated Javanese learned German and French. From these good-humored and largely autobiographical remarks he slips smoothly into his tale of incest. As Anthony Burgess wrote of the Maugham narrator: "Here again was something that English fiction needed—the dispassionate commentator, the *raisonneur*, the man at home in Paris and Vienna but also in Seoul and Djakarta, convivial and clubbable, as ready for a game of poker as for a discussion on the Racine alexandrine, the antithesis of the slippered bookman."[7]

Maugham's return to England was delayed by Gerald, who, after his heart attack, had developed a bad case of typhoid, and in mid-November they were still in Java. It was there that Maugham learned that his broker, Trippe & Company, had failed. (He had not yet turned over his investments to Alanson.) Trippe had misappropriated his clients' stock, and criminal proceedings against him were being considered. It was ironic that Maugham, who was so careful about money, had confided his savings to a dishonest broker. Despondent over the loss, he wrote Alanson: "Of course everyone blames me but I do not know what I could do better than invest the money in debentures. My hopes of being independent seem further off than ever and I am going to London now to start serious work. Fortunately the success of The Circle will help. It is playing to $20,000 a week and if this keeps up I should make a tidy sum."[8]

Maugham stopped in San Francisco on his way back to England early in 1922, and after conferring with Alanson about his financial situation, asked him to handle his investments. In January he sailed from New York. A shipboard photograph, showing him with a fedora on his head and a pipe in his mouth, appeared in a New York newspaper over the caption: "Versatile English novelist and playwright sailing aboard the Aquitania after concluding a year's tour of the Orient with a brief visit to America."

Another passenger on the *Aquitania* was Dwight Taylor, the twenty-year-old son of the actress Laurette Taylor, off on his first trip to Europe, with a letter of introduction to Maugham among his most prized possessions. He had not expected to meet him so soon. Spotting him at the purser's desk, he went up to him and thrust the letter at him, like a man presenting a subpoena. Maugham opened the envelope, read the contents, and fixed him with large, melancholy brown eyes. All hopes for a peaceful voyage had vanished.

"Dwight," Maugham said, "I am a man of very rigid habits. In the morning I remain in my cabin going over letters and business correspondence with my secretary. At precisely twelve o'clock I appear at the Dutch door in the smoking room, where I have one Martini cocktail. I then walk around the deck until a quarter to one, at which time I descend to the dining salon for my lunch. After lunch I retire to my cabin again and remain incommunicado for the remainder of the day."

Dwight nodded, looking dazed and disappointed.

"I would be happy if you would care to join me for my noonday cocktail and the walk around the deck," Maugham said.

"Thank you," Dwight said, "and after all, we've still got evenings." From somewhere deep in his throat Maugham emitted a curious sound somewhere between a sigh and a groan.

The next day at noon Maugham appeared with Haxton, whose hair stood up on his head like the bristles on a brush and who struck Dwight as messy. He did not know that Haxton was recovering from typhoid, and it seemed odd to him that a man of Maugham's refinement would allow his secretary to go around looking like a scarecrow. Dwight accompanied Maugham around the deck. Two women stopped and asked for his autograph. He placed their books on the ship's rail and scrawled something in French.

"What did you write?" Dwight asked.

"An obscene curse on autograph hunters," Maugham said. "But it is in an obscure Parisian patois which they are unlikely ever to understand."

That night Dwight sat in on a poker game in the lounge. "I hear you were playing cards last night," Maugham said when they next took their turn on deck. "How much did you lose?"

"About sixty-five dollars."

"I wouldn't play with strangers if I were you," Maugham said. "I daresay they're all good chaps—but they're much older than you are, and I imagine on a much less stringent budget."

"Oh, I know just about how much I can afford to lose, and when I've reached my limit I'm going to stop."

"How much is your limit?"

"A hundred dollars."

"All the same, I'd save it for other things. You have no idea what Europe has to offer."

"Cheap women?"

Maugham looked away as he framed his answer. "Expensive ones," he said.

That evening Dwight joined the poker game again, and this time Haxton appeared. "How about dealing me in?" he asked cheerfully.

"Too late, Mr. Haxton," a man in a checked cap who was holding the cards said. "The cards have been cut and the game has begun."

"What do you mean, it's begun," Haxton said. "The deck is still in your hands and there are only six in the game."

"No room," the man said.

"Why there's plenty of room," Haxton said, grabbing a chair from another table and swinging it around. "Move over, Dwight."

Dwight was losing. When Haxton's turn came to deal, Dwight found himself holding three aces. He took two cards and drew the fourth ace. He won a big pot. Haxton loaned him some chips so he could keep betting. After a few more hands the man with the checked cap said, "That's all for tonight" and stopped the game.

The next day Dwight took his turn on deck with Maugham. "I hear you were playing cards again last night," Maugham said. "How much did you win?"

"Oh—I got back what I lost and a little bit over."

"That's good," Maugham said. "Don't forget you owe Mr. Haxton for some chips."[9]

Gerald Haxton was such a skillful gambler that he could cheat at a table with professional shipboard poker players and not get caught. Maugham had asked him to retrieve Dwight Taylor's losses, and he had obliged by dealing the young man winning hands. But most often, Maugham despaired of Haxton's compulsive gambling, which, in addition to his other passions—drink and sex—cut heavily into his travel expenses.

Maugham had been away almost a year and was glad to be back in London, enjoying the comforts of home. His short stories had been a great success and he was once again lionized. On February 2 Hugh Walpole asked him to lunch to meet Sinclair Lewis, who had made his name with *Main Street* and had been in London since January, living in a service flat in St. James and working on *Babbitt*. Maugham had read and admired *Main Street*, the first book that helped him understand Americans. Lewis wrote his wife on February 3, 1922: "A happy lunch with Hugh, Somerset Maugham, and St. John Ervine. Much talk of books, of writers. Maugham seems to fancy me; invites me to dinner for both the tenth and 22nd of this month."[10]

Maugham sent Lewis a reminder: "My dear Lewis, I am expecting you to dinner (dressing jacket or do they call it a dinner jacket—I mean of course a Tuxedo!) next Friday at 8. Also on Feb. 24th: not the 22nd as we arranged the other day."[11] To the Friday dinner he also invited Walpole and the drama critic St. John Ervine, to whom he wrote "This will not hamper your right to stick my next play LIKE HELL."[12] The dinner went well, even though Lewis in London went out of his way to play the boorish American. At one party he had kissed all the female guests. On another occasion he had thrown his arms around two elderly British men of letters and insisted on teaching them an American square dance.

Maugham was to get a glimpse of this side of Lewis at his dinner on February 24, to which he had invited Edward Knoblock, Osbert Sitwell, Eddie Marsh, Charles McEvoy, and the painter Christopher Nevinson. After dinner Lewis snatched Eddie Marsh's monocle, stuck it in his eye, and began parading up and down, with Marsh following like a dog on a string. Then he parodied highbrow conversation with his version of an Oxford accent, and imitated McEvoy's cracked voice, which was sometimes bass and sometimes treble. Everyone was embarrassed. McEvoy, poised for a counterattack, interrupted the parody and asked Lewis if he was American. "Yes," Lewis said, "that is what makes me so sick with you condescending Englishmen." "I don't care if you are sick," McEvoy replied calmly. "In fact I should be rather pleased. But you are just the man to tell me why old Americans are so much nicer than young ones." The monocle fell from Lewis' eye and he was meek for the rest of the evening.[13]

Maugham's admiration for Lewis' work remained intact, although as a rule he was not very perceptive about American writers. He admired Hemingway, whom he called "to my mind the most versatile and powerful contemporary writer of fiction in the English-speaking countries," but he did not like either John Steinbeck or F. Scott Fitzgerald. "Oh yes," he said to S. N. Behrman about Steinbeck, "he is a leading American novelist now, but how long will that vogue last for these limited characters?"[14] As for Fitzgerald, when Behrman sent him Arthur Mizener's biography, *The Far Side of Paradise*, in 1951, Maugham wrote back: "The thing that shocks me about the whole story is how mean all his ideas were. He never seemed to realize how ignoble his ambition was to shine at parties. Of course his conceit was absurd, he was never more than a writer with a very small talent, and unless I am greatly mistaken, even his best work didn't amount to much."[15] "I find it true of most Americans," he said, "that they write a good first book and then they fizzle out."[16]

In April, Maugham went to Florence to see Reggie Turner and Norman Douglas. Hugh Walpole was there on his first visit to Italy and went on to Sicily in May. Maugham went back to London to finish his play set in China, *East of Suez*, which went into rehearsal during the summer. It was directed by Basil Dean, who had started with a repertory company in Liverpool and then taken over London's most prestigious theater, His Majesty's, following the death of Herbert Beerbohm Tree. The play opened with a spectacular street scene near the Great Gate of Peking, requiring forty Chinese extras. Eugene Goossens, who wrote the incidental music, had found among the Chinese workingmen in Soho an amateur orchestra. An interpreter had to be hired to relay instructions. Maugham sat in on rehearsals but did not offer advice unless he was asked for it. When Dean asked him if he could cut lines, he said: "Why not? The stage is a workshop." But he seemed to Dean to lack genuine enthusiasm for the theater and to resent having to attend rehearsals. In the first act, Daisy, the Eurasian heroine, pays a call on her English fiancé at his office in Peking and tea is served. The stage manager looked up and asked: "China tea, I suppose, Mr. Dean? And what sort of sandwiches would you like?" "Oh, I don't know," Dean said, "cucumber, I should think." Maugham stirred himself to life and spluttered: "It's the last thing they'd have."[17]

East of Suez opened on September 2, with Meggie Albanesi and Basil Rathbone, and ran for 209 performances. As a spectacle it succeeded; the opening scene, with its coolies and water carriers and rickshaws and a Mongolian camel caravan, was effective. Maugham wrote: "I cannot think that anyone who saw the play will have forgotten the thrilling strangeness of the mob of Chinese, monks and neighbors, who crowded in when the wounded man was brought in after the attempted assassination in the fourth scene. With their frightened gestures and their low, excited chatter they produced an effect of great dramatic tension."[18] But as a play, it failed. Maugham had simply transported the conventions of the Edwardian theater to an Oriental setting. Daisy, a half-Chinese woman with a past, is engaged to marry one Englishman but is in love with another. Maugham added to the convention of the woman with a past the convention that marriage with a half-caste is doomed. This was what his West End audience devoutly wanted to believe. After embroidering on this theme for seven scenes he ended the play by having the English lover kill himself, and the English husband realizes that he has made a mistake to marry a Chinese. Critics were disappointed that he had written such a trite melodrama after *The Circle*. The *Spectator* on September 9 warned: "Another piece of work like this and his reputation as a serious playwright will be gone." A positive review came from St. John Ervine, who, contrary to Maugham's invitation, did not "stick it LIKE HELL" but called it a story well told and skillfully presented.[19]

Maugham was eager to be off again. He found London pleasant to come back to but boring to live in, like an artificial comedy on which one waited for the curtain to fall.[20] Having finished his book of Chinese sketches, he was impatient for more travel. He wanted more material for short stories to follow up on the success of *The Trembling of a Leaf*. He was, he said, "in a period of my life when almost everyone I met, almost everything that happened to me and every incident I witnessed or was told of, shaped itself into a short story."[21]

He left London in September and was in New York on the twenty-first for the opening of *East of Suez*. This time he would be gone nine months—in Burma, Siam, and Indochina. About a month after he had left, on the evening of October 19, 1922, Mrs. New Gladys Cooper (not to be confused with the actress Gladys Cooper), one of London's leading accompanists, cycling down Park Lane on her way to a concert, was knocked over by a car and died of a fractured skull. The driver of the car was Syrie Maugham. An inquest was held on October 22. Mrs. Cooper's brother-in-law testified that she had good sight and good hearing and had long ridden a bicycle in London. A bus driver testified that Syrie's car had passed him and then he had heard a crash. Syrie said she had not seen the bicycle but had heard a clatter and felt an impact. She had never dreamed such a thing could happen and was completely shaken up. The ruling of the inquest was "accidental death."[22]

It was also in October that Maugham's book of travel sketches, *On a Chinese Screen*, was published. This was not a book but the material for a book, which Maugham had decided to publish as notes, with slight alterations. There were fifty-eight sketches, some less than a page in length, which *The Times Literary Supplement* called "a very pretty piece of Maughamware."[23]

When Maugham traveled he did not like to take the same route twice, so this time he and Gerald went first to Ceylon and took a boat from Colombo to Rangoon. On board they met a man who said he had spent five years in Kengtung, a Burmese market village near the Tibetan border, to which came natives of half a dozen countries and members of half a hundred tribes. It was twenty-three days from the railhead and could be reached only by mule through the jungle. The man said he would rather live there than anywhere in the world. Maugham asked what it had to offer. "Contentment," the man said. Intrigued, he decided to see for himself.

He began the journey in Rangoon, from which he took the train to Mandalay, in the heart of Kipling country, and then continued by car as far as he could to the village of Taunggyi. Here the British Resident found him mules and ponies, a Gurkha boy, and an interpreter named Kyuzaw. Maugham's plan was to go to Kengtung, then south to Siam, hoping to reach Bangkok by Christmas. He set out from Taunggyi some time in November, at the end of the rainy season, riding at the head of his caravan like a minor Oriental potentate, armed with the Resident's warning to avoid headhunting tribes, snakes, and tigers.

There were about six hundred miles to cover, and a day's march could range only from twelve to fifteen miles without exhausting the mules. Along the way they stayed at monasteries and government rest houses, which were usually built on piles and furnished with teak tables and chairs, 1918 copies of *Strand* magazine, and a summary of the Burma game rules. It took them ten days to reach the Salween, one of the major rivers that rises in the Tibetan steppes and empties into the Indian Ocean. They crossed on a raft and came to a tiny village, where Maugham met an Italian priest in a shabby cassock and a battered pith helmet who had been in the jungle for twelve years and had not seen a white man in eighteen months. Maugham admired this sort of man, one who had renounced the world and its pleasures and seemed none the worse for it. Indeed, the priest was filled with enthusiasm for his work, even though he had made few converts, for most of the population were Buddhists who held strong beliefs of their own. The priest had not had a cup of coffee in two years, so Maugham had his Gurkha make some. "Nectar!" the priest exclaimed after tasting it. "People should do without things more often—it is only then that you really enjoy them."

It took them twenty-six days to reach Kengtung. There they stayed a week, visiting the market, where vendors used lead casts in the form of the Buddha for weights. Maugham soon saw what his shipboard acquaintance had meant, for he too was drawn to a simple life, far from the bustle of the West, where one could read and think. From Kengtung they crossed the border into Siam. They were out of the jungle, and the country was open and pleasant, scattered with neat little villages, each surrounded with a fence, with fruit trees and areca palms growing in the compounds. Where the country was flat, rice was cultivated, but where it undulated, teak forests grew. Eventually they reached a large village on a road. "I saw waiting for me," Maugham wrote, "shaded by palm trees and diapered by the sun, red, substantial, reliable but unassuming—a Ford car. My journey was over."[24]

The car meant a return to civilization. Maugham was an affluent middle-aged man accustomed to the formal elegance and servant-assisted comfort of London life, but there was a side of his nature that hankered for the dangers and difficulties of jungle trips. He crossed some very rough country but never complained about the hardship, just as he had not complained that summer in Surrey when a fall from a horse had gashed his forehead. He was always happy, however, to leave the jungle behind him.

He and Gerald drove to Bangkok, a city of green-roofed temples, klongs (canals), and street touts, one of whom handed them a card that said: "Oh, gentleman, sir, Miss Pretty Girl welcome you Sultan Turkish bath, gentle, polite, massage, put you in dreamland with perfume soap. Latest gramophone music. Oh, such service. You come now! Miss Pretty Girl want you, massage you from tippy-toe to head-top, nice, clean, to enter Gates of Heaven."[25]

One of the first things Maugham did in Bangkok was not to go to see Miss Pretty Girl but to mail a letter he had written in Taunggyi to congratulate Sinclair Lewis on *Babbitt*:

> My dear Sinclair, you will think me very uncivil not to have written you about your book before, but it reached me the day I was leaving England and I carried it off from Syrie right away. It was very good of you to send it to us. I have read it with great enjoyment and have now sent it back to her. I think in many ways it is a much better book than *Main Street*. It seems to me a more complete and rounded work of art; of course I read it with interest and amusement but, as you will not be surprised to know, also with horror. I cannot imagine that such a ruthless depiction of a certain type and a certain class has ever been attempted; and the objectivity, so cold and merciless, with which you have written gives one a very curious sensation; except that people never recognize themselves I should say that you must be on the high road to being one of the most disliked men in America. I read *Babbitt* with sweating palms at the thought of how shy all those people would make me if I met them in real life. I thought I knew from *Main Street* what the man was like in his high stiff collar and ready-made suit of clothes whom I saw in the smoking compartment of a Pullman, but now I know that this was only an optimistic sketch of him. After reading *Babbitt* he stands before me in all his fleshiness.
>
> I hope the book will have as great a success as *Main Street*; I am curious to know with what you will follow it up, for it seems to me that you have in *Babbitt* exhausted a vein, and I shall look forward to his successor. You are a very lucky young fellow. I am writing to you from Taunggyi, a place you have doubtless never heard of, in the Shan States, from which I am starting on a march to the borders of China and then down into Siam. I expect to be about sixty days on the way. My respects to Madame.[26]

In Bangkok, Maugham was laid low by malaria, which was not the result of the rigors of his jungle trip but of a misplaced sense of politeness. Driving through Siam, he had been invited by the king's uncle to spend the night in his palace. After a splendid meal he was shown to the principal guest bedroom. An immense red-and-gold-lacquered four-poster dominated the room, and he did not have the nerve to ask one of the numerous servants for a mosquito net. Maugham ran a fever of 105, and heard the German woman who managed the Bangkok hotel where he was staying say: "I can't have him die here, you know. You must take him to the hospital." "All right," the doctor said, "but we'll wait a day or two yet." He was so weak he could not move, but slowly he improved.[27]

While Maugham had been exploring the jungle of upper Burma his most successful play opened in New York, but it was one that he had not written. The dramatization of "Rain" had been the result of John Colton's insomnia that night in Los Angeles when he had asked Maugham for something to read. Colton had written the play with Clemence Randolph, and it opened on Broadway on November 7, 1922, with Jeanne Eagels (whose real name was Aguila, the Spanish for "eagle") playing Sadie Thompson in a costume she had picked up on Sixth Avenue for six dollars.

The play spelled things out more than the story. The Reverend Davidson's fall from grace, for instance, is shown in this stage direction: "Sadie goes back to bed and Davidson stands watching her door. . . . Suddenly his head drops, his hands clasp convulsively, and a bitter struggle between Davidson, the man of God, and Davidson, human creature, takes place. . . . With studied deliberation, he grasps the handle of Sadie's door, opens it and steps inside." The story ended with Sadie shouting: "You men! You filthy dirty pigs! You're all the same, all of you. Pigs! Pigs!"

But the play required a more explicit ending, with Sadie being told that Davidson has cut his throat, at which she says: "Then I can forgive him. I thought the joke was on me—all on me. I see it wasn't." Mrs. Davidson then appears and says: "I understand, Miss Thompson, I'm sorry for him and I'm sorry for you." "I'm sorry for everyone in the world," Sadie says, and begins to sob as the curtain falls. Seven hundred and fifty gallons of water poured down on the stage at each performance. The showers worked so well that spectators were heard during the intermission complaining about the terrible autumn weather.[28]

The opening-night audience in New York was so involved with the story that they booed the Reverend Davidson when he tried to have Sadie deported. On November 7 The New York Times called Rain "a drama of altogether extraordinary grip and significance." Robert Benchley in Life on November 30 said the play provided "a powerful thrill."[29] The public agreed, and Rain was soon the hottest ticket on Broadway, sold out for eighteen months. It ran for 648 performances.

By 1935 there had been sixty Sadies in stock companies, and Sadie Thompson became a part that every actress wanted to play.

Rain was sold to the movies in 1923 for $150,000, a high price in those days, and was made three times, which may be a record for the filming of a literary property. (Maugham, who was not the play's author, got 25 percent of the sale price.) *Sadie Thompson*, a silent version, in 1928, starred Gloria Swanson and Lionel Barrymore. The first talking version, *Rain*, with Joan Crawford and Walter Huston, was made on Catalina Island in 1932, with a Maxwell Anderson script and Lewis Milestone directing. Joan Crawford wore bangles and open-work stockings, and Walter Huston, as the minister went around looking dazed and repeating the Lord's Prayer. *Miss Sadie Thompson*, the third version, in 1953, starred Rita Hayworth and José Ferrer. It was also made into a musical called *Sadie Thompson* in 1944, with music by Vernon Duke, starring June Havoc. It closed after less than two months.

Recovered from malaria, Maugham proceeded on his swing through Southeast Asia. From Bangkok he went to Pnompenh and visited the ruins of Angkor Wat, and thence to Saigon, where he admired the Third Republic opera house and the electric fans in the Hotel Continental. He visited Hué, and spent some time on a sampan. Peripatetic as he was, he managed to keep in touch with his various agents and publishers concerning his many projects. J. B. Pinker had died the year before, in 1922, and so Maugham had acquired an American agent, Charles Hanson Towne, an engaging man-about-town. Towne had one of the most varied careers in the world of letters. Born in Louisville, Kentucky, in 1887, he was, at one time or another, editor of The Smart Set, poet, novelist, newspaper columnist, author of amiable books such as *Loafing in Long Island*, and an agent determined to specialize in only the best fiction. In later life, this genial man who knew everyone and belonged to all the right clubs became an actor and was a hit as the Anglican clergyman in *Life with Father*. From Hué Maugham wrote Towne that he wanted better terms from Doran, his American publisher. He held a strong hand, for he was being courted by Harper, who "are prepared to meet me in any way whatever."[30] He wanted a guarantee from Doran of two and a half times the English sales on each of his books.

From Hué, Maugham went to Haiphong, where the local newspaper printed the names of foreign visitors, and he was approached by a man who had seen his name in the paper and with whom he had been at St.

Thomas's. The man had "gone native"; he lived with an Oriental woman and smoked opium, and asked Maugham if he had tried it. Once, in Singapore, Maugham said. What happened? the man asked. "Nothing very thrilling, to tell you the truth," Maugham said. "I thought I was going to have the most exquisite emotions. I expected visions, like De Quincey's, you know. The only thing I felt was a kind of physical well-being . . . But next morning—Oh God! My head reeled. I was as sick as a dog. I was sick all day, I vomited my soul out, and as I vomited I said to myself miserably: And there are people who call this fun."[31]

He then proceeded to Hong Kong and Shanghai, and sailed to Vancouver aboard the *Canadian Empress* on April 13, 1923, spending the ten nights that the trip took playing poker with an inscrutable mien.[32] He took the night boat to Seattle and the train to San Francisco, where Bert Alanson had booked rooms at the St. Francis. On April 30 he was in Hollywood; he was paid part of his share of *Rain* and sent Alanson $4,500 to invest. (The royalties on *Rain* eventually came to more than a million dollars.)

On May 23, having traveled to New York by train, and fortified by liquor that Alanson had provided, Maugham and Gerald sailed aboard the *Aquitania*. He sent Bert a check for $10,000 and asked him to invest half in the name of Gerald, who had played some part in having *Rain* made into a play. "He has been very faithful and devoted to me for many years," Maugham wrote Alanson. "Of course he has not been able to save anything and I should like this to be the nucleus of some provision for him in case I die. If you see fit will you invest it for him in the Portland company and pay the dividends to him at my address. . . . For the rest of the money I should be very happy if you put it also in the same concern; but of course I am only too glad to leave the disposal of it in your capable hands. I should be a richer man now if I had done that from the beginning."[33]

Maugham was back in London by June 1923, an event of sufficient significance to have been recorded in a newspaper interview. "You run across people in these out of the way places who give you a lot of material," he said in the interview. He was looking for people who were "not rubbed down by civilization." "People tell you things they would not tell in an acquaintance of 20 years," he said.[34]

Maugham had broken away from the clubby confines of literary London, where he made infrequent appearances. In his absence the establishment of letters kept feeding upon itself. Hugh Walpole scattered messages of congratulation like confetti. H. G. Wells discoursed on the contemporary novel at *The Times* Book Club.[35] Certain reviewers carried on their trade of puffery in exchange for a dinner or some other favor. Arnold Bennett played tennis at Lord Beaverbrook's, was mentioned in the *Evening Standard* as a first-nighter, lunched at the Reform Club with H. G. Wells, dined with John Galsworthy in Hampstead, gave a party for Ravel, and crossed France aboard his yacht, the *Marie Marguerite*, sailing along the canals.[36] New blood was injected to keep the club from becoming anemic. In June of 1923 those three relentless self-promoters, the Sitwells, staged a happening. From behind a curtain Edith declaimed her verses through a megaphone:

> *The stars in their apiaries*
> *Sylphs in their aviaries.*

Someone in the audience asked if she meant ovaries. There were hoots and catcalls, and Noel Coward walked out, starting a thirty-year feud.[37] The twenties were the decade of modernism and determined frivolity. It was the decade of Noel Coward, Jack Buchanan, the Astaires, and Gertrude Lawrence. Maugham watched the cavalcade and knew he was no longer young. In 1923, at the age of forty-nine, he wrote for *Vanity Fair* an essay on middle age. He knew he had reached that stage, he said, when, after having lunch with a friend and her seventeen-year-old niece, they got into a taxi to go to a matinee and the girl took the tip-up seat. He realized that she looked upon him with the respect due to age. He preferred to list the advantages of his station, one of which was that he no longer had to pretend to like and to know things that he did not. Poses had become unnecessary. What made middle age tolerable was reconciliation with oneself, even though "yesterday he was a young man and today he drinks lithia water."[38]

As usual when he returned after a long absence, there was trouble at home. Syrie's reputation as an interior decorator was growing. She had been commissioned by *House and Garden* to write articles such as "Framing Kakemono Pictures" and "Lighting the Piano." She now felt that the house in Wyndham Place was not up to her standards, and she convinced Maugham to sell it and buy a larger, more imposing house. A block away, at 43 Bryanston Square, she found a five-story house with a slate mansard roof, to which they moved in August.[39] After initial grumbling Maugham was delighted with the house, which was spacious, and he blessed the *Rain* that had bought it. Arnold Bennett, after going to dinner there, pronounced it "simply magnif . . . the fellow's study is larger than my drawing-room . . . I think."[40]

At the end of August, Maugham learned that Gerald Haxton's mother, who had been bedridden for years and in constant pain, had died. "It was a dreadful life she led," he wrote Alanson, "and although I personally had much affection for her I am thankful that she is dead at last."[41] Gerald was in great distress, but there was little Maugham could do to comfort him, since he was in England and Gerald was on the Continent. He was as attached as ever to Gerald, who seemed to personify freedom and adventure.

On September 12, 1923, *Our Betters*, the satire on American women who marry titles, which Maugham had written in 1915, opened at the Globe Theatre. The Lord Chamberlain required small changes at the end of the second act, where the word "slut" was used. To offset conjecture that the character of the American tycoon was based on Gordon Selfridge, the program noted that "owing to various rumors which were circulated when the play was produced in America, the author wishes to state that the characters in it are entirely imaginary." *Our Betters* turned out to be Maugham's biggest London success. It ran for 548 performances. Margaret Bannerman got good notices as Lady Grayston, but Constance Collier as the Duchesse de Surennes was criticized for her mannerisms. She said "muh" for "me," as in "Bertie, you could never forsake muh."

Maugham was amused by critics who did not know how long ago he had written the play and pointed out the ways in which it showed progress over earlier plays. One such critic was Desmond MacCarthy, who wrote in the *New Statesman*: "I do not know if Mr. Somerset Maugham, who has traveled a good deal lately, has visited Mr. Coué at Nancy, but certainly every day and in every way his work gets better and better." *Our Betters* was filmed by RKO in 1933, with Constance Bennett and Gilbert Roland.[42]

In the meantime Maugham had written a farce called *The Camel's Back*, which was opening in New York that November, and he went there in October with Gerald for rehearsals. Alanson sent him a flask adorned with a camel's back to celebrate the occasion. They stayed in an apartment that Knoblock had found in his building at 222 West Fifty-ninth Street. One evening Maugham and Chaplin, who was in New York making a movie, went to the theater together. As they came in, the audience rose to applaud Chaplin, and though they left through a side door to avoid the mob, they still had to fight their way through thousands of people. Chaplin was delighted, and Maugham could not help thinking that it must be an intoxicating experience to receive so much acclaim.[43]

Maugham was not exactly obscure, however, and there were those who sought him out as eagerly as the fans did Chaplin. Among them was Ray Long, the fiction editor of *Cosmopolitan*, who offered him a contract for eight stories at $2,500 a story. Maugham accepted, remembering the time when he had lived for two years on that sum.[44]

While working on the production of *The Camel's Back* Maugham moved in theatrical circles, and met the noted drama critic George Jean Nathan, who had once called him "merely an inferior Hubert Henry Davies." Nathan asked him whether *The Camel's Back* was any good. Maugham replied that it was the sort of play that was good if the audience liked it and bad if they didn't. In fact, the play was in trouble, and Maugham had to rewrite the third act, although he blamed the star, Violet Kemble Cooper, for botching her big scene. He could not tell anymore whether the jokes worked, for he knew them too well. At tryouts in Worcester, Springfield, and Washington the audience was unresponsive. Gerald did his best to reassure Maugham, telling him that the play went over their heads because it was so sophisticated.[45]

On November 7 they were at the Shoreham Hotel in Washington for the first night of the tryout. Maugham wanted to play bridge, and Gerald recruited a nineteen-year-old college student named Karl Pfeiffer, who was said to be a good player, to make up a foursome. It was the start of a long friendship, which ended bitterly when Pfeiffer wrote an unflattering book about Maugham in 1959.

Pfeiffer was delighted to meet Maugham but found him rather standoffish. Perhaps it was simply that Maugham did not like to make conversation when he played bridge, one of the things in life he took most seriously. Pfeiffer asked him about book titles.

"A good title is the title of a book that's successful," Maugham said.

"That isn't much help to a writer when he has to choose a title," Pfeiffer replied.

"No, it isn't," Maugham said.

"I think *The Moon and Sixpence* is a very good title," Pfeiffer said.

"Do you?" Maugham asked. "Do you know what it means? People tell me it's a good title, but they don't know what it means."

Pfeiffer did not know what it meant and asked for an explanation.

"It means reaching for the moon and missing the sixpence at one's feet," Maugham said.

At one point Maugham made a remark that struck Pfeiffer as odd. Maugham had won a hand, and one of his opponents commented that he must be unlucky in love. Maugham asked what he meant. The man explained that he had in mind the old adage "Lucky at cards, unlucky in love." "Oh, I thought you meant my wife was unfaithful to me," Maugham said.[46] It was a peculiar thing to say, since the man knew nothing about his wife.

The Camel's Back opened in New York on November 13, and closed after 15 performances. It was thin gruel. Critics called it infantile and profoundly boring. In London, where it opened in January 1924, *The Camel's Back* did slightly better, running for 76 performances.[47]

Maugham returned to London in January to find that there was much talk and apprehension at the prospect of the Labor party's coming to power. He thought they should be given a chance—that they would not make more of a mess of things than any of the other parties had done. Politics was not an interest of his, and he seldom expressed an opinion except to say that politicians were all alike.

He was working on a novel set in China, *The Painted Veil*, his first novel in several years. It was hard work, and on some days he looked with misgiving at the blank pages that had to be filled. He promised himself a holiday in Spain when he was done.[48] *Our Betters* was running to capacity and money was coming in from all sides. On March 2, at dinner at Arnold Bennett's at 75 Cadogan Square, he boasted that he expected to clear forty thousand pounds from *Rain*. This did not make him any the less thrifty. The following day he wrote Bumpus of Oxford Street, his bookseller, "I did not know that the collected works of Hazlitt were so expensive and do not think I care to have them at the price you mention."[49]

In April a Maugham book appeared that was one inch high and written in his own hand. Called *Princess September and the Nightingale*, it was unveiled at the British Empire Exhibit at Wembley as one of the thousand volumes in the library of the Queen's Doll's House, a million-dollar tribute to those two complementary sides of the English character, thoroughness and whimsy. Designed by the noted architect Sir Edwin Lutyens, on the scale of one inch to the foot, it had taken four years to build. It was a record of English craftsmanship, the ultimate period piece, and a present to the king and queen, who came from a long line of home-loving monarchs.

The doll's house was a stately home of 1923, an updated version of a house by Christopher Wren, complete in every detail, except for dolls, which would have cluttered it. The wine cellar was stocked with tiny magnums of champagne, two dozen bottles of Romanée-Conti 1904, and an 1820 Madeira. There were portraits of King George V and Queen Mary by Sir William Orpen. There was a gramophone that played "God Save the King," a strong room with replicas of the crown jewels, plumbing that worked, an elevator, two pianos, tiny clocks, and in the cellar, a tin with boot polish and brushes. The boot polish tin was the size of a farthing. There were three cars in the garage, in perfect running order, a Lanchester, a Sunbeam, and a Rolls. The library had a painted ceiling, pile carpets, walnut paneling, recessed bookcases, leather armchairs, and a writing table with a leather top. The books, one inch high and bound in yellow calf, with Queen Mary's bookplate on the inner cover, included two hundred works by authors of the period, who had been asked to contribute an original composition or a passage from a published work, writing it by hand in a volume the size of a postage stamp. Wells, Shaw, and Masefield were conspicuous by their absence, but Barrie, Bennett, Chesterton, Gosse, Housman, and Maugham, among others, helped to give a diminutive idea of the state of English literature in the 1920s. Barrie wrote his autobiography, and Lady Jekyll wrote *The Doll's House Cookery Book*.[50] Maugham contributed, in fifty-three leaves of compressed manuscript, a fable that had previously been published in the December 1922 issue of *Pearson's Magazine*: A nightingale came to sing for Princess September each day. Her envious sister persuaded her to put the bird in a golden cage. "I cannot sing unless I'm free, and if I cannot sing I die," the nightingale said. The princess freed the bird, which returned to sing at its convenience. It was a parable of Maugham's life as a writer. He could not sing unless he was allowed to come and go as he liked, while his wife tried to keep him caged. She was not very successful, for Maugham was planning another long trip, this time to Mexico and Central America.

Chapter Eleven

*He was a man who could never get the two sides of
his nature together.*

Gerald Heard to Clare Boothe Luce.

BY 1924 Maugham felt that he had exhausted the material in Southeast
Asia. He spoke Spanish and planned to write a novel set in Mexico. He
asked Bert Alanson, who had grown up in Guatemala, for introductions, and said, "I cannot tell you how much I am looking forward to
breaking into a new hunting ground." Having finished *The Painted
Veil*, and glad to get it off his chest, he sailed with Gerald Haxton for
New York on the *Majestic* on September 17, 1924. One of their fellow
passengers was Basil Dean, the director of *East of Suez*, who had an
aversion to Haxton but played shuffleboard with Maugham on the
voyage.[1] Maugham spent ten days in New York, staying at the Gotham,
the prices of which, he said, "are enough to make one's hair stand on
end."[2]

In New York, Maugham made a new friend, Carl Van Vechten, a
man who had pushed his slender talent through many doors. Critic,
essayist, novelist, photographer, and jazz enthusiast, he was a famous
figure on the New York scene in the twenties and thirties. Born and
educated in Cedar Rapids, Iowa, he established himself in New York
with a whirlwind of activity. He was America's first ballet critic, he wrote
two books about cats, dozens of prefaces and introductions, two hundred magazine articles, and seven novels. He was a phenomenon of
dispersal. He was also held responsible for the Harlem renaissance of
the twenties through his support of black musicians. His apartment at
150 West Fifty-fifth Street, a few doors down from the Gotham, where
Maugham was staying, was known as the midtown branch of the
N.A.A.C.P. At his parties one was likely to meet Bessie Smith rubbing
shoulders with H. L. Mencken, or Paul Robeson singing spirituals as
Dreiser and Tallulah Bankhead listened.[3]

Thanks largely to Van Vechten, Maugham's ten days in New York were one continuous party, which left him exhausted. He managed to see ten plays, including the success of the year, *What Price Glory*. He lunched and dined out every day, and enjoyed most his lunch at the Coffee House with his new agent Charlie Towne. By October 7 he and Gerald were in New Orleans, heading south, and he was reading Van Vechten's novel *The Tattooed Countess*, the story of an Iowa girl who marries money and comes home after a long series of European affairs to face small-town disapproval. "It is a delightful book," he wrote, "and it distresses me to think that not one in a hundred of your readers will ever see how witty and brilliant and entrancing it is."[4]

They got to Mexico City in the second half of October. At about the same time D. H. Lawrence and his wife Frieda arrived. Lawrence had left England after the suppression of *The Rainbow*, unsold copies of which had been destroyed six weeks after publication, in 1915. He had lived in Capri for a while, but felt that it was a stewpot of semiliterary cats, and had migrated first to Sicily and then to Mexico.

Lawrence and Maugham were fated to dislike each other. They had nothing in common except a love of travel. To Lawrence, Maugham was a commercial, superficial writer, a member of the London establishment from which he had been banned. To Maugham, Lawrence was a pathological case. On October 25 Maugham sent a wire to Lawrence's hotel, the Monte Carlo, asking if they might meet before he left for Cuernavaca, a pretty town about sixty miles south of Mexico City. They met briefly, and afterward Lawrence wrote his friend Witter Bynner that Maugham was "disagreeable, with no fun left in him, and terrified for fear he won't be able to do his next great book, with a vivid Mexican background, before Christmas. A narrow-gutted 'artist' with a stutter."[5]

When Maugham and Gerald got back from Cuernavaca they and the Lawrences were invited to lunch by Zelia Nuttall, an American writer and archeologist who lived in the suburb of Coyoacán and whom Lawrence used as the model for Mrs. Norris in *The Plumed Serpent*. Maugham had Gerald call Lawrence and say, "I hear we are going out to a friend's to lunch together who lives rather far out; let's share a taxi." Lawrence was miffed that Maugham had not bothered to call himself and said, "No, I won't share a car."[6] He did not realize that Maugham never made phone calls because of his stammer.

The lunch, according to Frieda, was "drowned in acidity." Mrs. Nuttall, for some reason, held a grudge against Haxton. Maugham sat next to Frieda, who asked him how he liked Mexico. "Do you want me to admire men in big hats?" he answered crossly. "I don't care what you admire," Frieda said. She felt sorry for Maugham, who struck her as an unhappy man who got little joy out of living. "He seemed to me to have fallen between two stools as so many writers do. He wanted to have his cake and eat it. He could not accept the narrow social world and yet he didn't believe in a wider human one."[7]

Maugham and Lawrence had an opportunity to meet again, in Florence in 1926, when Reggie Turner acted as the go-between. Turner must have written Lawrence to suggest that he meet a brother artist, for Lawrence replied on May 1: "I met Maugham in Mexico City too, and was annoyed with him. And for sure he didn't love me like a brother. So don't expect us to be two roses on one stem. But perhaps he's nice. I don't pretend to know him. And if he'd like to see me, I'd like to see him."[8]

Lawrence was bitter about always having to scrounge for money, while writers like Maugham and H. G. Wells, whose work he considered inferior to his own, were financially secure. On January 6, 1930, he wrote Aldous Huxley: "I hear Maugham and Wells and Co. were rolling their incomes around Nice for Christmas, rich as pigs."[9]

Lawrence's one published opinion of Maugham's work was a review of *Ashenden* in the London *Vogue* on July 20, 1928. He gave it the back of his hand. "Mr. Ashenden," he wrote, ". . . is almost passionately concerned with proving that all men and all women are either dirty dogs or imbeciles. . . . These stories, being 'serious,' are faked. Mr. Maugham is a splendid observer. He can bring before us persons and places most excellently. But as soon as the excellently observed characters have to move, it is a fake." In fairness to Maugham it should be noted that Lawrence's opinion may have been tempered by personal dislike, and that in any case the *Ashenden* stories were outside his range of sympathy and interest.

Fifteen years later Maugham gave his view of Lawrence, which was equally unfavorable:

> I have never thought Lawrence's short stories very good. I find them formless and verbose. . . . To my mind his view was the view of a sick man of abnormal irritability, whose nature was warped by poverty and cankered with a rankling envy. He may have had a streak of genius; I don't know; I have a notion that he was a better poet than prose writer. He had a wonderful felicity for stringing words together, and

you can go through his works and find sentence after sentence of ravishing beauty, but the general effect, to me at least, is lush and airless.[10]

At the end of his life, in 1962, Maugham was asked by an English professor from Baltimore what he thought of Lawrence. "I only met Lawrence once," he replied, "and we certainly had no discussion. He didn't like me."[11]

Maugham did not like or understand Mexico, and he abandoned the idea of a novel set there. He needed the contrast between the transplanted British colonial and an exotic foreign setting. If only Mexico had been a British Colony. "Mexico City is not thrilling and I do not think we shall stay here long," he wrote Knoblock. "My chief object, of course, was to find material for stories, and so far I can see there is not the smallest likelihood of it . . . it is exasperating to have come so far and feel that one is wasting one's time."[12] Mexico City did, however, offer a few pleasures, among them the boys Gerald brought back for his employer. One of them was a thin, large-eyed child who said he was fourteen. He undressed in Maugham's hotel bedroom, knelt to say his prayers, and crossed himself before getting into bed.[13]

From Mexico City they went to Vera Cruz, staying at the Hotel Diligencias, overlooking the plaza, and took a Ward Company ship to Yucatán. They proceeded to Havana, where they stayed about a month, then went on to Jamaica, where Maugham spent a few quiet weeks working on the dramatization of his story "The Letter." Anthony Prinsep, the manager of the Globe Theatre, where *Our Betters* had been produced, was much taken with its star, Margaret Bannerman, and sent Maugham frantic cables about casting her in *The Letter*. Maugham wrote his American play agent John Rumsey: "I suppose he is rich enough to let his affections stand before his business interests. I think a law should be passed to prevent managers from falling in love with their leading ladies." There were also casting problems for the American production of *The Letter*, and Maugham advised Rumsey that "if you ask me to choose between Estelle Winwood and Peggy O'Neill I am in a quandary. I like neither pork nor beans and would rather eat neither of them."[14]

He spent the first month of 1925 in Guatemala, where he found enough material for a couple of uninspired short stories and approved of the dry martinis in the bar of the Palace Hotel. In February he was back in New York, writing Knoblock: "I am reaching the end of my exotic materials. I have of course notes for a good many more stories . . . but I have not the capacity to assimilate much more."[15]

Maugham was in New York in time for the publication of *The Painted Veil*. The novel was serialized in *Hearst's International* magazine from November 1924 to March 1925, and in *Nash's Magazine* in London from December 1924 to July 1925. In London the serialization attracted a libel suit and a protest. A couple with the same names as the main characters, Walter and Kitty Lane, threatened to sue, but they settled out of court when Maugham offered them two hundred fifty pounds and changed "Lane" to "Fane." Then the Hong Kong government objected to the use of the colony as the setting for the novel, and he changed the locale to the mythical colony of Tching-Yen. In an author's note he complained that with writers

> choosing the names of their characters at haphazard, from Bradshaw's Guide, the telephone directory, or, as is the practice of the author of this novel, from the obituary column of "The Times," it is inevitable that they should sometimes hit upon the name of a living person who may suppose that a reference to him is intended; and if for purposes of verisimilitude they give one of their characters a post or office which exists in an actual place, the holder of that post or office is liable to assume that a reflection is cast upon him. It is hard to believe that any writer would be such a fool as deliberately to libel a total stranger.[16]

Heinemann had on his hands some 8,000 copies of the novel, printed, bound, and ready for distribution. Review copies had already been sent out; they were recalled, although about 70 escaped. The physical alterations the book had to undergo to incorporate the author's changes were a major problem. As many as 27 leaves had to be literally cut out of every copy by hand and replaced with 27 reprinted ones, each new leaf being glued in place. The novel that at last was published on April 23 bulged like an overfull stamp album.

Maugham was pleased, for the publicity helped the sales of *The Painted Veil*, which in England went through five printings totaling 23,000 copies. "I got something like 500 pounds of free advertisement," he wrote Alanson, "and the book went with a bang. George Doran writes to me from New York that it jumped straight into the best-seller list and he hopes very soon to reach the hundred thousand."[17]

The roots of *The Painted Veil* went back to Maugham's reading of Dante on his first trip to Florence, and particularly to the lines:

Siena mi fe; disfecemi Maremma:
Sulsi colui, che, innanella pria
Disposando m'avea con la sua gemma.

(Siena made me, Maremma unmade me: this he knows who after betrothal espoused me with his ring.)

His Italian teacher had explained that the lines referred to a gentlewoman of Siena whose husband, suspecting her of adultery, exposed her to the noxious vapors of his castle in the Maremma. She did not die, so he had her thrown out of a window.

Maugham adapted the situation to a British colonial setting. Kitty Fane, who dislikes her bacteriologist husband, who is stationed in Hong Kong, has an affair with the dashing Charlie Townsend (a character partly based on his agent Charlie Towne). Her husband Walter finds out and insists that Kitty go with him to a Chinese town that is in the midst of a cholera epidemic, where death is taking lives "like a gardener digging up potatoes." Unlike the husband in Dante's tale, however, it is Walter who catches the disease to which he exposes his wife. With her husband dead, Kitty feels freed and thinks she is also free of her attraction to Townsend, but upon returning to Hong Kong she lets him sleep with her again before heading back to England.

This steamy tale concerning the high contagion of passion and cholera had mixed reviews. *Bookman*, in May 1925, called it "one of the great short novels of our time," while the *Spectator*, also in May, found it trite, pretentious, and insincere.[18] Lytton Strachey, reading it in bed with the flu, graded it "class II, division I."[19]

Maugham had now been writing for more than a quarter of a century and had built up a substantial body of work. In 1925 he was mentioned in a work by Cornelius Weygandt, a professor at the University of Pennsylvania. Weygandt rated him as a "lesser late Victorian," along with such forgotten writers as Sabine Baring-Gould, Arthur T. Quiller-Couch, Eden Phillpotts, and Olive Schreiner. "His writing is always a little uncertain, a little like the writing of a man not born to English," Weygandt wrote. "He is prone to inversions and unrhythmical as a rule." And yet Weygandt did not know that French had been his first language and thought that Maugham had been born in Kent. "There is no ease, no urbanity, no mellowness in the man," he went on. "He is very like a certain type of medical student of the late

19th century, a man liberated by science from tradition of many sorts, but not as yet humanized by experience of suffering into that sort of doctor who is above everything the friend of man. Maugham is a keen student of humanity but hardly an artist at all."[20]

Always juggling half a dozen projects, Maugham had to leave New York on March 14, 1925, for the London rehearsals of *Rain*. Basil Dean, having paid a high price for the English rights, was directing it at the Garrick Theatre. Every actress in London wanted to play Sadie, but Dean was partial to Tallulah Bankhead, who had just scored a personal triumph in Gerald du Maurier's *The Dancers*. With her honeyed accent and golden hair, Tallulah had become the idol of the upwardly mobile London working girl, who saw her as the embodiment of the modern woman. Tallulah was bold and irreverent. She was a free spirit who said such outrageous things as "I'll come and make love to you at five o'clock. If I'm late start without me."

When Dean approached her she agreed to take a salary cut because she wanted the part so badly. She wrote him: "I agree to play the part of Sadie Thompson at a salary of forty pounds per week. I note that the management is to commence the production of the play not later than 30th June 1925. I agree that if Mr. Somerset Maugham should definitely disapprove of my engagement, I will cancel it and your company will not be under any liability to me in respect of it." Tallulah left for New York to see Jeanne Eagels' performance, so determined to shine that, in her cabin on the boat back to London, she played the jazz records Sadie played in *Rain*. She wanted Sadie to be her first all-out hussy.[21]

Maugham sat in the dark auditorium through the first rehearsal and watched Tallulah give what she thought was a brilliant imitation of Jeanne Eagels, sure to electrify the author. Not a word escaped his lips. He remained equally inscrutable at the second rehearsal. Tallulah was alarmed. Maugham told Dean that she was not right for the part. Dean called her into his office and broke the news. The author, he said, did not want her, and he was in no position to defy so majestic a force. Dean felt that it had nothing to do with her performance but was a spiteful expression of personal dislike.[22] Tallulah left in tears. She was contemplating suicide when Noel Coward asked her to star in *Fallen Angels*, in which she was a huge success. Maugham wrote Alanson that "I had the bother of getting rid of [Miss Bankhead]. It was more bother than you would imagine since she used every scrap of influence she had to sway me and when finally I put my foot down I was the object of the obloquy of all her friends."[23] To smooth things over he sent her a check for a hundred pounds and a note saying that when he was upset he always found that a week or two abroad helped. Would she please accept the enclosed? Tallulah sent back the check and wrote Maugham that she did not plan to make a career out of disappointment. She had been dismissed after two days' rehearsal, she said, whereas actors were usually given four weeks to learn a part. She had not had a word of advice from the author. She hoped that he was no more offended at getting his check back than she had been upon receiving it, and suggested that he turn it over to his favorite charity, which she had no intention of becoming. Maugham took her to lunch and told her that her performance in *Fallen Angels* was brilliant.[24]

Rain opened on May 12 with Olga Lindo, who had no sex appeal but was paid an opening-night tribute. Among the first-nighters were Galsworthy, Wells, and Bennett. The fire department, fearing that the onstage downpour would short-circuit the lighting system, insisted on having buckets of sand everywhere, but the 1,500 gallons of water came down without a hitch. "We got such a reception as I have never heard before in a London theatre," Maugham wrote Alanson. But the play ran for only 150 performances, and Basil Dean was convinced that it was Maugham's fault for vetoing Tallulah.[25] That June there was a heat wave in London, which hurt the box office. Maugham asked the authors of *Rain*, John Colton and Clemence Randolph, to join him in waiving their royalties should the weekly gross fall to a figure at which the production would have to close. He felt that every effort should be made to get a London run of at least six months.[26]

Tallulah Bankhead was not his only casting problem. He had to decide whether Margaret Bannerman was right for *The Letter*. He went to see her in a play called *The Grand Duchess*, found her dreadful, and told the management that he did not want her. "You can imagine the scenes this occasioned," he wrote Alanson. "After ten days of hysterics the unfortunate young woman retired to Aix-en-Provence with a nervous breakdown and there has been the devil to pay."[27] Maugham seems to have derived a nasty pleasure from the power he had over actresses. He appears to have enjoyed turning them down for parts, as if through them he were punishing all women.

One woman whose part he could not veto was his wife. Relations between them were increasingly strained, but for some reason he made no attempt to suggest a break. Instead it was Syrie who asked one day, out of the blue: "If you divorced me you wouldn't try to take my child away from me, would you?" Maugham took this to mean that she had a lover, a fact of which he had already been apprised. Syrie was afraid that he would sue for divorce, as her first husband, Henry Wellcome, had done, obtain proof of her infidelity, and take custody of Liza, as Wellcome had taken custody of their son.[28] But Maugham had no such intentions.

In 1925, having prospered as a decorator, Syrie bought some land in the pine forest at Le Touquet, a fashionable beach resort in Normandy, where she built a house called Maison Eliza. Le Touquet had a casino and a golf course, it was close to England, and it was a good place to entertain her growing American clientele, among whom she numbered Astors and Mellons who were sold on the all-white look. In keeping with the style that had brought her fame, Maison Eliza had a long white salon with skeepskin rugs, white-leather sofas, and a screen of slated mirror that reflected bowls of white peonies.

When Maison Eliza was finished, Syrie decided to give a weekend housewarming, which she also intended as the scene for a reconciliation with her husband. She invited Gerald, to show that she accepted him, along with Noel Coward and his handsome American friend Jack Wilson, Barbara Back, the wife of a well-known London surgeon, Frankie Leveson, a society dance instructor who had taught the Prince of Wales the fox-trot, and Beverley Nichols. Maugham had befriended Nichols, an aspiring writer and journalist, when he wrote a book about himself, at the age of twenty-five, appropriately called *Twenty-Five*. Maugham had reviewed the book glowingly in the *Sunday Times* as a birthday present for Beverley, who was hailed as representing the spirit of the twenties. If so, the twenties were vain, shallow, and ambitious. Beverley was pretty—he looked like a faun escaped from the woods. Beverley was amusing. While at Balliol College he had convulsed the Oxford Union with the facetious remark that "women should have the courage of their complexions." Beverley was ingratiating with the famous. He made friends with Nellie Melba, and had as a scarfpin an *M* set in small diamonds. Beverley was facile, and could write a two-thousand-word interview based on a two-minute meeting. Beverley was flamboyant, like young Byron minus the talent. Beverley was homosexual, and Maugham wrote him letters that began "My precious" and "My sweet." Beverley wrote books of cozy interviews with the famous and always managed a tone of engaging banality. In *Are They the Same at Home?* there was this exchange with Maugham:

BN: "Haven't you had the most shattering rows with people?"

WSM: "I don't think so. I don't like rows. I think you do."

BN: "I don't. And, anyway, I feel sure you must sometimes have ended great friendships in a blaze of fury."

WSM: "Not fury. It's usually been because I was bored."[29]

The account of the weekend at Le Touquet that follows is based on Beverley Nichols' *A Case of Human Bondage* and describes how Syrie was the loser in "one of the strangest triangles, perhaps, that life, fiction's master, can ever have devised." Nichols' account bears listening to, for he was present, and it is consistent with what Syrie was later to tell her friends.

On the first evening, the guests were assembled in the drawing room listening to Noel Coward play "Parisian Pierrot." Gerald told Syrie a story about his recent trip to Siam—he said he had seduced a twelve-year-old girl in exchange for a can of condensed milk. Nichols was sure that he had told the story to hurt Syrie. He felt that Gerald had about him "the aura of corruption." That evening they all went to the casino, only a few minutes away from the house. From the table where he sat with a tall pile of chips in front of him Gerald shouted to Nichols, "Come over here, you pretty boy, and bring me luck." Nichols declined the invitation and went back to the house. At three in the morning he heard some noise in Gerald's room, opened his door, and found him naked on the floor, covered with thousand-franc notes and vomiting. As Nichols stood in the doorway Maugham came up behind him, furious, and asked, almost hissing the words, "What are you doing in Gerald's room?" Nichols said he had heard him groaning. "Did he ask you to come to his room?" Maugham asked. The implication annoyed Nichols, who replied that Gerald was in no condition to ask anyone anything. Maugham shook Nichols' shoulders and said, "Get out."

The strain between Syrie and her husband was evident. Greeting her guests on the following day, she made her entrance, opening her arms and saying "Darlings" with a forced brightness, and approached Maugham to be kissed. He turned away. Trying to make the best of it, Syrie said, "I always think that Gerald makes the best sidecars in the world."

That evening Nichols came down early for dinner, and found Syrie, Maugham, and Gerald in the music room. Their positions, he thought, illustrated the nature of their relationship. Maugham and Gerald sat together on a sofa, laughing as they turned the pages of a book, while Syrie, in a long white dress, stood at the open window staring into the garden. The book was a copy of Bartlett's *Familiar Quotations* that belonged to Nichols.

"What's so amusing in my *Familiar Quotations*?" Nichols asked.

"Yours?" Gerald said. He turned the title page. "So you pinched it, did you?" The book had been inscribed to Nellie Melba by an admirer, with the date and the quotation, "The living voice it is which sways the soul."

"No," Nichols said. "She gave it to me."

"That's what you say."

"Yes, that's what I say. Anyway, what's so amusing about it?"

"It's all this hooey about . . . Love," Gerald said. He then read, in a jeering voice, some of the three hundred references to love and lovers, constantly glancing at the figure in the long white dress. His reading was interrupted by laughter outside, and Noel Coward joined them. Gerald snapped the book shut and turned his attention to the cocktail tray.

On Sunday morning at breakfast, guests were sitting around reading the Paris edition of the New York *Herald*. Maugham sat at the table in a Chinese dressing gown, waiting for Syrie, who took breakfast in bed in her ground-floor bedroom, to summon him. Beverley Nichols had a habit of touching the pears and apples in the fruit bowl on the dining room table. "Weren't you taught when you were young not to stroke the fruit?" Maugham asked irritably. A maid arrived and said, "Madame has finished her breakfast." Maugham went in, and they started arguing, and you could hear him saying, "Don't shout, please . . . don't make me a scene." This was one of the phrases he kept from the French: *"Ne me fais pas de scènes."*

Maugham was furious because that morning he had found a laundry bill on his dressing table. There was no laundress; Syrie had her guests' laundry sent into town and presented each one with a bill. Maugham took it as an insult. When Syrie had dressed she came into the drawing room and noticed that an armchair had been moved.

"Who moved the arm-chair?" she asked.

Gerald said that he had.

"Then would you mind putting it back?"

Gerald started to rise.

"Sit down, Gerald," Maugham said. "We moved the chair because it makes the room look more comfortable."

"It doesn't," Syrie said. "It makes the room look vulgar and suburban. Put the chair back, Gerald. Now, if you please."

Maugham, his voice trembling with rage, said: "I'd imagine you'd want the place to look vulgar and suburban—since you run it as a boarding-house. Already your lodgers are made to pay their laundry bills. Soon, I suppose, we'll get our weekly bills for our food and rent."

Syrie turned and walked out of the room.

Nichols decided that the tension between them was spoiling the weekend and said he had to leave on Sunday afternoon. He was astonished when Syrie said she would leave with him. She too had had enough. She would leave her houseguests and her daughter behind. She said she did not mind leaving Liza with Maugham. "You see," she said, "Willie is really terribly proud of being a father at all." They took the 5.30 boat to Dover, and in the dining car, on the train to London, Syrie delivered a soliloquy on her predicament, which according to Nichols went something like this:

> "It is not only the sex angle, Beverley darling. As far as the sex is concerned . . . if one's marriage has been broken up, what does it matter whether it's been destroyed by a woman or by a man? . . . No, what does distress me, what really does make the whole thing intolerable, is the fact that Gerald is a liar and a forger and a cheat. . . . Nobody would deny that Gerald is extremely attractive. . . . Of course, he drinks like a fish and lies like a trooper and if one has any sense one doesn't leave one's bag out of one's sight for a moment if he's in the same room, but he is attractive. Not only physically . . . though of course that does come into it, and we all know that if he thought it would be of the faintest advantage he'd jump into bed with a hyena. . . . Of course it repels me and I don't pretend to understand it and I hate Liza having to grow up in this sort of atmosphere, though I suppose the poor darling will have to learn the facts of life sooner or later. But I might have managed to rise above it if Gerald had been a different sort of person. . . . What one can't cope with is this appalling sort of mental domination. I used to give darling Willie ideas for stories . . . he even used to read them aloud to me because he said it helped his stutter. But if I give him an idea nowadays it's strangled at birth. By Gerald. If I buy a picture, it's damned, by Gerald. If I decorate a room, Gerald finds some way of making it look cheap and vulgar. If I make any friends, Gerald poisons Willie's mind against them. He's dedicated his whole life to getting me out . . . out . . . out."[30]

There was more to the failure of Maugham's marriage than Gerald. From the start it had been a marriage of convenience between two ill-assorted persons, whom the years did not bring closer. Syrie now was forty-five and Maugham was fifty-one and the sexual side of the marriage had long been over. Maugham had been away much of the time, first in Russia on an intelligence mission, then in Scotland with tuberculosis, and finally on six- and nine-month trips to collect material. In his absence Syrie had made a life of her own. It is not surprising that she took a lover. She was no Penelope, unraveling at night the yarn she wove during the day while her husband roved. Gerald was a factor, for Maugham both loved him and needed him as an information gatherer. But Syrie was broad-minded; she could have lived inside the triangle, particularly since Gerald was not allowed to come to England. The truth was that there was no marriage, there was only the thin façade of a marriage, and even that was something Maugham found hard to keep up.

His own account of his stay at Le Touquet, which he wrote in a letter to Edward Knoblock, one of the few friends to whom he confided his personal problems, was not quite so dramatic as Beverley Nichols' and made no reference to Syrie's sudden departure:

> I am afraid Syrie and my affairs have been a great trouble to you. I went over to Le Touquet and spent a week there. Syrie was as nice as nice could be and is evidently bent on turning over a new leaf. She did not ask me if I had seen you. I hope during my absence she will cease her complaining about me to all her friends (which must be tedious for them) . . . you will do me a service by reminding her that she has only to say the word and I am willing to let myself be divorced. I cannot change and she must either live with me as I am, or take her courage in both hands and make the break. But of this more than enough.[31]

Maugham was willing to let himself be divorced but not to initiate divorce proceedings. Like his heroine Constance Middleton in *The Constant Wife*, which he would write the following year, he wanted to get away from his spouse with "a divine young man" but not to sever the marriage tie. He needed the respectability of marriage. If a break came, it had to come from Syrie, so that he could claim that he had tried to keep the marriage together.

By July 9, 1925, Maugham was recovering from his week at Le Touquet at the spa of Brides-les-Bains. He and Gerald were taking the cure. One of the secrets of Maugham's longevity was that he took very good care of himself. Having suffered from tuberculosis and malaria, he was in the category of the physically frail who live to be ninety because they are more attentive to their well-being than strong persons. Every year, and sometimes more often, he took the cure at Vichy, or Badgastein, or Brides-les-Bains. From the age of sixty-four until his death he made three visits to Dr. Niehans' Swiss clinic for rejuvenation treatments. Like the proverbial one-owner car with low mileage that has been kept in a garage, waxed weekly, oiled and greased monthly, and tuned up annually, he did not wear out. Maugham wrote Alanson:

> You would be amused if you saw us here, for we are leading a life of unimaginable strenuousness and virtue. We get up at half past seven and go down to the well, like Jacob, but finding no Rebecca, to drink a glass of hot medicated water. Then a medicated bath, and after that a cup of coffee and a bun for breakfast, eighteen holes of golf follow, another drink of water and then a frugal luncheon. A short rest, tennis till six, more water, and a still more frugal dinner. A little bridge and bed. I don't know whether this is going to make us strong and young, slender and beautiful as we anticipate, but it is certainly preparing our entrance into the kingdom of heaven.[32]

Maugham was delighted with Bert's news that the dividends from the shipping company Natomas now came to a considerable annual sum. He wanted the money sent to his Paris banker, Bernhard Scholle, for "in this way I hope to avoid the English income tax."[33] He promised to send Bert a copy of the withdrawn edition of *The Painted Veil*. "There are not more than 25 in existence," he said, "and in the course of the next few years they should be worth their weight in gold."[34] Alanson was now married to the beautiful Mabel Bremer, a model from Warren, Pennsylvania, and Maugham felt they were well suited to each other. He had sent Bert a piece of old Dutch brass as a wedding present, warning him that cleaning it would destroy the patina.[35]

Maugham was planning a second trip to the Malay States in the fall to pick a fresh crop of stories. Prior to that, however, he spent a fortnight in Capri in August, saw Brooks again, and considered buying a house there. He asked Brooks to look around for one and to write his friend Walter Payne about the down payment. He was so thrilled at leaving for the East again, he told Brooks, that he could think of nothing else.[36]

Before leaving for Malaya, however, he indulged in one of his periodic outbursts against his American publisher. Despite the fact that *The Painted Veil* was on the best-seller list, he was dissatisfied. Doran had promised to issue a booklet about his work before its publication and had not done so. He complained to Towne that Doran had sent *The Painted Veil* out "like a parcel of tea, and let it sell on its own merits."

> I do not think the sale of *The Painted Veil* has been unsatisfactory, but I am fairly sure that with a little pushing and some judicious work they would have been much larger than they have been. I do not wish Doran to look upon me as a goose which lays regularly a golden egg . . . My suggestion is therefore that we go to Doran and unless he is prepared to guarantee success for my next books (which will consist of a volume or two of short stories, a travel book, and, last, a novel), to make arrangements elsewhere. There is only one way I know by which a publisher can guarantee success, and that is by giving so large an advance that it is necessary for him to do everything he can for the book in order to get his money back.[37]

Doran was in fact about to issue the missing booklet. Called *W. Somerset Maugham, Novelist, Essayist, Dramatist,* and including five articles by admirers, it was calculated to soothe his ego. When Towne advised him that the booklet was forthcoming and that Doran intended to do his best by him, Maugham's anger subsided. He wrote Towne: "As you may know, my inclinations are very much to stick to whatever publishers I have. I have been with Heinemann in London for twenty years and have resisted very substantial offers to leave them. So long as Doran will do his best by me I am very willing to do my best by him. . . . I am not so anxious to make a large sum of money out of a book as to have it as widely read as possible. I seek distinction rather than lucre."[38] He could afford to affirm this lofty sentiment because he already had the lucre.

Maugham left for Singapore on October 6, 1925, after the September 24 opening of a play based on *The Moon and Sixpence,* by Edith Ellis, with Henry Ainley playing Charles Strickland. E. A. Baughan wrote in the *Daily News* on September 25: "Somerset Maugham and his adaptor are responsible for what may be called the essential truth of this strange picture of a man at war with his environment and with civilization itself. It is that the longing and yearning for absolute freedom, for the achievement of which Strickland is merciless to himself and to all who stand in his way, is true to the secret life of most men in differing degrees. But they have not the courage or the incentive of big enough ideas to fight for that freedom." Maugham was gratified to learn that the first four performances had earned eight hundred pounds, and felt that the play would be a success. In fact, it closed after 75 performances. In 1942 *The Moon and Sixpence* was filmed by United Artists, with George Sanders and Herbert Marshall, who from then on was typecast as the Maugham narrator on screen.[39]

Maugham spent four months in Malaya collecting stories from those he met. He wrote Charlie Towne that he wanted to visit the various places in the Malay Archipelago in which the scene of his new novel was laid, "and since that will cost me a good ten thousand dollars you can imagine that I should not go unless I thought it very well worth while."[40] In mid-February 1926 he took a French ship from Saigon to Marseilles, a thirty-day trip, during which he spent most of the time in bed with a recurrence of malaria. Shortly before landing he was feeling better, and as he walked to the smoking room he saw the sunny coast of Corsica from a window. Seeing Europe again made him realize how tired he was of wandering and how much he now wanted to remain quietly at home.[41] But this was not to be: in Marseilles there was a letter from Syrie's secretary informing him that she had rented their house on Bryanston Square, and the tenants would not be moving out for a fortnight. This was the second time that Syrie had made him homeless upon his return from a long trip. Fed up, he decided to stay in France and look for a house of his own.[42]

He set up headquarters at the Réserve de Beaulieu, a hotel on the Riviera, and spent the rest of March and April house-hunting with Gerald. The Riviera at that time was becoming a fashionable place to live: in 1921 the Cole Porters had rented the Château de la Garoupe, a large house on the Cap d'Antibes, and among their guests were Sara and Gerald Murphy, who had a lot of writer and artist friends, such as Scott Fitzgerald, Stravinsky, Léger, and Picasso. "At the time," Gerald Murphy wrote, "no one ever went near the Riviera in the summer. The English and the Germans—there were no longer any Russians— who came down for the short spring season, closed their villas as soon as it began to get warm. None of them ever went into the water."[43]

Agents showed Maugham house after house, but none pleased him. At last, in despair, they took him to see a white elephant on Cap Ferrat that had been vacant for years because no buyer wanted to pay for the cost of making it habitable. It had belonged to Leopold II, King of Belgium from 1865 to 1909, and a real estate wizard. He bought the Congo, which made Belgium a major colonial power, and he bought Cap Ferrat, a narrow peninsula jutting into the Mediterranean between Nice and Monte Carlo, which was said to have the most pleasant climate on the Riviera. Leopold built himself a palace in a large park and three houses for his three mistresses, the size of the house corresponding to the rank of the mistress. Since he was pious as well as dissolute, the rotund and bearded Leopold wanted a priest close at hand. His greatest pleasure was fornication, and his greatest fear was dying without absolution. He built a house in 1906 for his confessor, Monseigneur Charmeton, close enough to his own so that the priest could be at the king's side in five minutes. Monseigneur Charmeton, who had spent most of his life in Algeria, asked for a house that was Moorish in style.

This was the house that Maugham was shown. It had keyhole windows, domes and minarets, colonnades and columns, and a large garden overrun with weeds. Maugham saw that the Moorish decorations were lath and plaster, which could be scraped off, leaving a plain square house. It was on the west side of Cap Ferrat, with a fine view of the bay of Villefranche, and had eight acres of terraced land. Nice was nine miles away, Monte Carlo eight miles away. He made an offer to the agents, Knight, Frank & Rutley, which was not accepted, and months of haggling began.[44]

While in Beaulieu he learned that during his absence Charlie Towne had signed a new contract for him with Doran. He was not pleased. "You seem to have paid no attention whatever to my letter," he wrote Towne. "I asked you as clearly as I possibly could *not* to make any agreement with Doran if he refused my demand of a guarantee of two and a half times the English sale without consulting me first. It is quite true that I did not want to change publishers . . . [but] you seem now to have bound me hand and foot for the rest of my career as a novelist." According to the new contract, Doran would pay Maugham an advance of five thousand dollars on a novel. "It is to be presumed that with such a reputation as I have any novel I write will earn that sum in royalties without any effort on the part of the publishers," he said. ". . . I should prefer no further contracts to be signed on my behalf without their being previously submitted to me." The incident led Maugham to fire Towne soon afterward. "I hope that this step of mine will cause no break in the friendly, cordial relations we have always had," he wrote him. "Though I consider you too arbitrary to be an agent I continue to think you a charming and amicable companion."[45]

Maugham's problems with Doran became academic, for that year his firm was absorbed by Doubleday. Frank Nelson Doubleday (the Doubledays were French Huguenots whose original name was Dubaldy) had founded his firm in 1897 with S. S. McClure, who retired in 1902. Walter Hines Page, later ambassador to England, was a partner, but he too left the firm. In the twenties Doubleday became the wonder of the publishing world. He published Frank Norris, Theodore Dreiser, and Rudyard Kipling, whom his two sons, Felix and Nelson, called "Uncle Rud." Kipling often visited Doubleday at his farm on Long Island. Young Nelson had liked Kipling's story "How the Whale Got His Throat" and suggested to Uncle Rud that he write more stories like that. If Kipling agreed, he told his father, he should get a share of the royalties. Doubleday promised him a penny a copy. The *Just So Stories* sold half a million copies. It was Kipling who dubbed Doubleday "Effendi," after his initials, which he said meant "master" in Turkish.

It was young Nelson who negotiated the merger with Doran—for his father was ill—and it was he who insisted that Doran stay on. "It should be a union for life," he said. "Very well," Doran said, "I will remain until I am carried out feet first in a wooden box." But Doran could not get along with Effendi and remained less than two years. Effendi, Doran said, believed "in the Doubleday Bible. It was the record to the minutest fraction of a percentage of the profits or the losses in each and every department of his business. It was his vade-mecum. It contained his matins, his vespers, and his collects. Long since I had learned that in the Doubleday economics of publishing, the auditor-in-chief and not the editor-in-chief was the final arbiter of the publishing policy." Thus Maugham became a Doubleday author and a close friend to Nelson, who took over the firm in 1929. Doran, who had started in publishing as a two-dollar-a-week office boy, went back to Canada, where he died in 1956.[46]

While he was in Beaulieu, Maugham learned that Syrie was giving a large Easter party at Le Touquet to which he had not been invited. This was good news, indicating that she might agree to a divorce, and he wrote Knoblock: "I cannot imagine what has made her reverse her very definite desire to have nothing of the sort with which I left her last autumn." He returned to England in early May, "not knowing whether it is to be war or peace."[47]

It was neither war nor peace, it was more of an armed truce. When Maugham told his wife that he had made an offer on a house on the Riviera, she received the news with icy silence, although she soon became reconciled to the idea. Maugham wrote Alanson:

> I have made a very agreeable arrangement with my wife. She is to have the house in London and I my house on the Riviera and we are going to stay with one another as guests when it suits our mutual pleasure and convenience. I think this is the best thing for both of us and it will give me the opportunity which I need to work in pleasant surroundings and without interruption. I am at present in negotiation for a house . . . but I do not know whether the owner and myself will come to an agreement . . . I suppose we shall haggle for three months and then we shall do what we both had in mind in the first place and that is split the difference. But it's a lovely house.[48]

In May 1926 there was a general strike in England. It started with over a million miners leaving their jobs. When they were joined by a million and half skilled workers, England was paralyzed. There was no gas to cook one's food, there were no trains or tubes or buses or taxis. Drivers of private cars could not use the roads without union permits. The red flag over London was the chief topic of conversation, and Londoners were reminded of the worst days of the war. Winston Churchill, then Chancellor of the Exchequer, edited the official government newspaper, the *British Gazette*, and resolutely opposed the strikers. Prime Minister Stanley Baldwin, the son of a Worcestershire ironmaster, who had become leader of the Conservative party, broke the strike by moving the army and navy into position and enrolling thousands of volunteers as special constables. One of the volunteers was Henry (Chips) Channon, a wealthy Chicago homosexual turned London social figure, who became a friend of Maugham's. Channon wrote in his diary: "Terror grips my heart at the prospect of the unpleasant baton charges."[49] Maugham, ever patriotic, was another volunteer. He had a friend at Scotland Yard, Sir Ronald Howe, who recruited him to work there. Arnold Bennett noted in his diary for May 12: "Willie Maugham was working at Scotland Yard till 8.30 of a night—I don't know what at. Special constables abound."[50]

With the strike over by mid-May and the British congratulating themselves that there had been an almost complete lack of violence, life went back to normal, and Maugham was able to concentrate on his work. He had finished his second volume of Far East stories and was putting the finishing touches to a new play, *The Constant Wife*.

In June, *Caroline*, the play about the woman whose suitors court her because her husband is away and they think she is unattainable, was revived with Irene Vanbrugh, who had played the title role ten years earlier. Neither the actress nor the play showed much sign of age. *Caroline* ran for 152 performances, and the critic for *The Nation and Athenaeum* said on June 26 that Maugham's phrasing had "the genuine Congrevian ring."[51]

July found him back in Brides-les-Bains taking the cure. "All goes well and I am losing weight rapidly," he wrote Barbara Back, his closest woman friend. ". . . I have arranged to meet Syrie earlyish in August for the festival at Salzburg and after that I shall come back to London and work. . . . I shall be curious to hear if you have seen anything of Syrie since I left. I had a letter from her after the production of *Caroline*, but since then nothing. . . . Gerald sends his love and so do I."[52]

Barbara Back was the exception to the rule that Maugham did not like women. There were others, but Barbara occupied a special place in his life. Née Nash, she was the wife of the London surgeon Ivor Back, who had been at Cambridge with Gerald Kelly and Aleister Crowley. Back, who had taken his medical training at St. George's Hospital, where he remained as a surgeon until the end of his life, was a brilliant and handsome man, with as many friends as interests. A prominent figure in London society, he was painted by Sir William Orpen, in his hospital coat, with his rubber-gloved hands on his knees.[53] He always introduced himself to literary folk by asking, "Didn't I meet you at Willie's?"

Barbara was blonde, beautiful, and elegant. At the time when Maugham met her she was an up-and-coming London hostess, whose Tuesday lunches in her house on Charles Street invariably featured kedgeree (rice and smoked haddock) and treacle pudding, cooked by the estimable Mrs. Pert. Her parties were known for the size of the homosexual contingent. Maugham appreciated a good hostess, and when Syrie was out of the picture Barbara sometimes entertained for him on opening nights. He also appreciated good guests, and Barbara was asked often to the Mauresque. She was decorative, she dressed well, her conversation was bright, and she was good at games. Maugham liked to have her as a partner at golf and bridge. He inscribed a copy of *The Narrow Corner* "For Barbara, because she never calls on his diamonds to the Queen, from her appreciative partner the author."[54]

More important, she was his London informant. After he took up residence in the south of France he came to London only two or three months out of the year. Barbara kept him up on the Mayfair gossip, telling him in long chatty letters who was sleeping with whom and what marriage was on the point of breaking up. Her correspondence over a period of thirty-five years was for Maugham like a subscription to a private *Tatler* column. Barbara also had a knack for handling Maugham with a mixture of flattery and irreverence. As Beverley Nichols wrote: "The Master's friendship with Barbara Back was probably the happiest he enjoyed with any woman throughout the course of his long life. It was gay, spontaneous and completely untroubled by emotional undertones."[55]

In September 1926 *The Casuarina Tree*, a collection of seven stories set in Malaya and Borneo, was published. In it were to be found some of Maugham's best work: "The Outstation," "The Yellow Streak," and "The Letter." Cyril Connolly awarded *The Casuarina Tree*, along with two other Maugham collections, *Ah King* and *Ashenden*, a place among his hundred key books of the modern movement (1880–1950), because "he tells us—and it has not been said before—exactly what the British in the Far East were like."[56]

In "The Outstation" the only two white men, the Resident and his assistant, are at odds because the difference in their social backgrounds is magnified in the jungle. The Resident dresses for dinner and reads the Monday *Times* on Monday, even though it is six weeks late, breaking its wrapper with his tea. The assistant is careless in dress and manners, openly disdainful of his superior, and tactless with the natives. In England they would never have met. They are thrown closely together in a strange place, whose atmosphere Maugham conveys with touches of local color—the house on piles, the Dayak soldiers, the *atap* awnings, the *praus* (local boats), and the gin *pahits*. When his assistant is killed by a native he has mistreated, the Resident resumes his stuffy routine. Edwin Muir, poet, novelist, and one of the best fiction critics of the twenties, wrote in *The Nation and Athenaeum* on October 9 that "The Outstation" was "one of the best stories written in our time."[57]

"The Yellow Streak" was based on Maugham's near-drowning in Sarawak. The description of the bore was almost word for word as it appears in *A Writer's Notebook*. From this incident Maugham devised a subtle study in cowardice. Izzart the half-caste saves himself when his boat is overturned, leaving his companion behind. The companion, Campion, reaches shore and thinks that he got away before Izzart. But Izzart reveals his cowardice to Campion. Campion promises not to say anything more about it but adds: "There's only one thing I'd like to ask you: I've made a good many friends here, and there are one or two things I'm a little sensitive about; when you tell the story of our upset, I should be grateful if you didn't make out that I have behaved badly. I wouldn't like the fellows here to think that I'd lost my nerve."

"... I don't know why you think I should do that."

Campion chuckled good-naturedly, and his blue eyes were gay with amusement.

"The yellow streak," he replied, and then, with a grin that showed his broken and discolored teeth: "Have a cheroot, dear boy."

The story succeeds because Maugham shows that the problem is not that Izzart behaved like a coward in a crisis but that his nature will make him blame his companion in order to throw off suspicions that exist mainly in his own mind. The moral of the story is that we do ourselves in and drag others down with us. L. P. Hartley, the author of that fine novel *The Go-Between*, wrote in the *Saturday Review* on September 18 that *The Casuarina Tree* was distinguished by "great narrative power, an unfailing eye for dramatic effect . . . and a ruthless insight into and insistence upon the ignobler motives." It was an almost perfect work, he said, although Maugham's subject matter was limited by his cynicism.[58]

The title, Maugham said, came from a Malayan superstition that anyone who took a piece of the Casuarina tree in a boat would have his journey impeded by contrary winds or perilous storms. "Looking at them [the stories] in cold print," he wrote the anthologist Grant Overton, "I have an impression that they are rather tight and I believe that I could attempt with advantage a greater looseness of construction and style. Have you not noticed that the tightrope walker skips now and then in order to rest his audience from a feat too exactly done?"[59]

His new comedy, *The Constant Wife*, was opening in Cleveland with Ethel Barrymore on November 1, and he was planning to leave for America in October. Just before his departure the agents for the property on Cap Ferrat accepted his last offer, $48,500, and after six months of haggling he found himself the proud possessor of a house on eight acres of land between Nice and Monte Carlo. He entrusted the remodeling to a Nice architect, Henri Delmotte, hoping that he could move in by the spring of 1927.[60] In the meantime Syrie had found a house in King's Road, Chelsea, with a sort of annex around the corner at 72 Glebe Place. She wanted Maugham to sell the house on Bryanston Square and give her the money to buy the King's Road house and the annex. He agreed, with the stipulation that he would be allowed to keep his bedroom furniture, his books, his theatrical paintings, and the various objets d'art he had collected on his trips. These he sent to Cap Ferrat.[61]

By October 11, 1926, Maugham and Gerald were in New York at the Gotham. They got in touch with Van Vechten, who took them, along with John Colton, on a field trip to a Harlem whorehouse. It was the fashion then to go slumming, moving from club to club and party to party, and getting drunk, a fashion that persisted until 1929, when everyone sobered up.[62]

When *The Constant Wife* opened in Cleveland, Ethel Barrymore had one of her worst nights of stage fright. She did not know her part. Pages containing her lines were scattered about the stage so that she could consult them, and the director hid in the fireplace to prompt her. Maugham suffered agonies. The Cleveland papers made Miss Barrymore's lapses a case of civic pride. Cleveland deserved to have an actress who knew her lines. Contrite, Miss Barrymore went up to Maugham afterward and said, "Oh, Willie, I've ruined your play. It will run a year." It ran two years, a year in New York and a year on the road.

> I think I can honestly say that the one single performance that satisfied me most was that of Ethel Barrymore in *The Constant Wife* [Maugham said]. There was one line which I shall never forget. It wasn't even a line. It was a single word, the word "when." I had written it because it was the natural, obvious word for the heroine of my play to say, and it had never occurred to me that there was anything more in it than the inquiry it made. But Ethel Barrymore put such a wealth of meaning, humor, innuendo, and malice—none of which I had seen—into that little word that the audience rocked with laughter until I thought they'd never stop. It just shows you what a great actress can do when the author gives her half a chance. If I hadn't fallen madly in love with Ethel during the rehearsals, I should have fallen in love with her then.

Her brother John attended a performance of *The Constant Wife* and noticed that no one in the audience coughed. He asked Ethel about this.

"But I don't let them cough," she said. "You don't? And how is that done?" "I just turn on something inside myself, and they don't dare cough."[63]

The Constant Wife was a comedy of marital maneuvers in which Constance Middleton (Miss Barrymore), upon learning that her husband is having an affair with her best friend, takes her revenge not by having an affair of her own but by making herself financially and emotionally independent. In the last act she decides to leave on a holiday to Italy with an old flame, and her husband says he does not want her back. She is almost out the door when he exclaims: "You are the most maddening, wilful, capricious, wrong-headed, delightful and enchanting woman man was ever cursed with having for a wife. Yes, damn you, come back!" The curtain falls.[64]

At least one spectator wondered whether the constant wife had remained constant and wrote Maugham to find out. Mrs. Ruth Buddington said that after she had seen a revival in 1935 in Cape Cod, "unexpectedly, the old discussion of the interpretation of the conclusion came up again as to whether she really went off with Bernard or disciplined her husband by making him think she was planning that infidelity. Although I suspect that you must have been approached a weary number of times on the subject I am venturing to write you to ask whether the authentic solution makes the title ironic or literal . . . We should all welcome your reply to settle our dispute and should appreciate your trouble on our account. I enclose an envelope for your convenience."[65] Maugham replied, using his own envelope: "I think Constance went off with Bernard and did not think much of it when she did. But I may be wrong. The author does not always know."[66]

After the New York opening of *The Constant Wife* Maugham went back to London to help Syrie move out of 43 Bryanston Square. On November 24 he wrote a lady admirer that he could not send her a portrait of himself because he had sold his house and all his things were in storage.[67] In the new house on King's Road he had been allotted a study on the top floor which was also the gentleman's cloakroom, so that when there was a party he had to put away all his writing things. Syrie suggested that he should rent a small flat to work in, but that did not appeal to him. He put up with the inconvenience while waiting for his house on the Riviera to be made habitable.[68]

On February 24, 1927, his dramatization of "The Letter" opened. He wanted Gladys Cooper, who had turned down *The Constant Wife* because of another commitment, to do it, and offered her options on his next three plays as an incentive. It was her first venture as actress-manager of the Playhouse, and *The Letter* ran for 338 performances. Miss Cooper found Maugham easy to work with. He came to rehearsals with a blue pencil, ready to make the necessary cuts. "I've had so many of my lines cut," he told her, "that I'm going to collect them and make a play out of them."[69]

The Letter was Maugham's first and only thriller. The curtain rose on a darkened stage. A series of shots fired in quick succession rang out, accompanied by the smell of cordite, and a figure was seen staggering across the stage to the veranda. "He tried to rape me and I shot him," Leslie Crosbie tells her husband. Why did she fire all six shots? She can't remember. The dead man's Chinese mistress wants $10,000 for the letter incriminating Leslie. Her lawyer arranges its purchase and she is acquitted. Her husband insists on seeing the letter and asks, "What does it mean?" "It means that Geoff Hammond was my lover," Leslie says. The husband breaks down and goes offstage. "He's going to forgive you," the lawyer says, "he can't do without you." Leslie replies that although she does not love her husband she will never let him know it. "That will be your retribution," the lawyer says. "No," Leslie replies, "my retribution is greater. With all my heart I still love the man I killed."

"*The Letter* is superb theatre throughout," said the *Sunday Times* on February 27. "The evening was sensationally successful, and the audience delighted almost to hysterics." Gladys Cooper's acting "could not have been bettered by any living English actress." Another critic, however, said that she played "like a Victorian duenna at a croquet party." The play did well in New York with Katharine Cornell, and was twice made into a movie—in 1929 with the temperamental Jeanne Eagels, who was famous for walking off the set, and Herbert Marshall as the lover, and in 1940 with Bette Davis and Herbert Marshall, this time cast as the husband.[70]

Maugham by now was beginning to come to the attention of foreign critics. His books and plays had been widely translated, and the French recognized him as one of their own, a disciple of Maupassant and Flaubert. He was hailed as a great novelist and dubbed "the Kipling of the Pacific" and "the British Maupassant." He was compared to Joseph Conrad, Robert Louis Stevenson, and Edgar Allan Poe. *The Trembling of a Leaf* was said to be far superior to the romantic exoticism of Pierre Loti. In February one of his French fans, Paul Dottin, a professor at the University of Toulouse, sent him a questionnaire for a critical study he was writing. Flattered, Maugham replied at some length. "I wrote steadily from the time I was 15," he said. "I became a medical student because I could not announce to my guardian that I wished to be a writer . . . I never write anything till I have thought of it so long that it begins to annoy me and then to write is to get rid of it. I write with a pen. I write as quickly as I can, never delaying to get things right, but just eager to set them down somehow and then go over the mss. again, twice, three times, often four." *Of Human Bondage*, he said, was "to a large extent an autobiography."[71]

The Constant Wife opened in London on April 6, 1927, produced by Basil Dean, with Fay Compton in the lead. The first night was a disaster. In those days a rope barrier separated the stalls (seats in the front part of the orchestra) from the pit and was moved forward or back according to the demand for stalls. The advance booking for a new Maugham play was so heavy that the front rows of the pit were sold as stalls, but instructions to move back the rope barrier were forgotten. When ticket-holders for the additional rows of stalls arrived they found their seats taken by those who had been in the pit queue since eight o'clock that morning. The "pitites" refused to budge, and quarrels broke out. The manager, Horace Watson, went onstage to explain the mix-up and appealed to the usurpers to leave their seats, promising them tickets in the stalls on some other night. They would not move, so he asked for volunteers from the stalls to give up their seats. The aisles were full of standees. Maugham and Syrie sat in a stage box looking dismayed. The cast was so upset that its timing was off, and performances lacked the finish that a Maugham play requires. Fay Compton stepped out afterward to make the usual first-night speech and said that the author was not in the house. (Maugham and his wife, who were giving an afterplay party, had gone home.) Her speech was received with unmannerly interruptions. Mistaking a cry of "Shut up" from the gallery as intended for her, she turned to the rows of stalls and thanked "the civil members of the audience." Loud booing then broke out in the gallery. Only with the playing of the national anthem was calm restored.[72]

The opening-night party, which was also Syrie's housewarming party for the house in King's Road, was a greater success than the play, according to Arnold Bennett, who wrote: "As soon as she saw me Marie Tempest kissed me on both cheeks, and Tallulah Bankhead wanted to emulate her, but I calmed her. Only Maugham and his wife were a bit gloomy. He always is. I hear the play is rotten. Crowds and crowds at the party."[73] Maugham admitted that Syrie was an admirable hostess—amiable, lively, and charming. But he had had enough of her and was planning a final break.[74]

The Constant Wife was panned in London with terms such as "banal," "tedious," "devoid of wit," "straw figure," "trite," and "dismal." It reminded one reviewer of Congreve's line: "Raillery, raillery, Madame; we have no animosity. We touch off a little wit now and then, but no animosity." Maugham felt that the London production and cast were to blame, and noted that everywhere else, even in the English provinces, it was highly praised.[75]

He was still in London in June when Arnold Bennett came to dinner on the twelfth. "Syrie was not down," Bennett wrote in his diary, "but W.S.M. awaited us. The new house is now practically finished and looks very strange and agreeable. I saw Liza Maugham (aged 13) for the first time, after having heard of her for years and years. This evening was very agreeable. Just us four, and some nice talking."[76] Actually, Liza would have been twelve that September. From the time she was seven or eight she had realized that her parents did not get along. Her father was often absent, and it was natural for her to take the side of her mother, who adored her. When her father was home, there was constant quarreling and her mother was unhappy. She could not detect all of the undercurrents of the situation but felt relieved when the marriage ended.[77]

In June the London season was over, and Syrie left for Le Touquet while Willie went to Cap Ferrat. They parted on amicable terms. Though his house was full of workmen, he was able to move in.

PART V

1927-1940

Chapter Twelve

A Great Artist needs all the comfort he can get.
Arnold Bennett to Virginia Woolf

THE RIVIERA in the late twenties was a haven for successful English and American writers, and almost an English-speaking enclave. Beaulieu had an avenue Edith Cavell, Nice had a Scotch Tea Shop, and Monte Carlo had tea shops with such names as Bide-a-Wee, where customers could read the *Illustrated London News.* James Barrie and Michael Arlen were in Cannes, Frank Harris was in Nice, H. G. Wells was in Grasse, E. Phillips Oppenheim was in Cagnes, Edith Wharton was in Hyères, and now W. S. Maugham was in Cap Ferrat. He lived in his house, which he called the Mauresque, after its North African origins and his own Moorish trademark, for the rest of his life, with a five-year interruption during World War II. Far Eastern trips were over for the time being, although he still traveled constantly, being restless by nature and unable to stay put for more than three or four months at a time, so that the Mauresque was part home and part operational headquarters.

After the aspiring writer, the successful playwright, and the world traveler, Maugham was now the established man of letters. He had published eleven novels, three collections of short stories, and twenty plays. He was ready at last to face the world on his own terms.

The Villa Mauresque was his fortress. He could raise or lower its drawbridge as he liked. Everyone else who lived there, including Gerald, was an employee. Finally, after thirty years of compromise, he had everything exactly as he wanted it. In this new manorial phase Maugham regressed to Edwardian formality. He was hospitable, but guests had to abide by house rules. Life was conducted according to the rhythm of his personality, and whoever was too tone-deaf to hear it was swiftly banished.

Maugham in residence was the antibohemian, the writer as man of means who had by his pen alone been able to afford a style of life available only to tycoons and princes of the blood. The Maugham legend began with the Mauresque. Here was the aging writer in his setting, the neighbor of millionaires and duchesses, surrounded by paintings, servants, and cypresses, retiring at designated hours to his study, host to the Windsors, Churchill, and Beaverbrook. The Mauresque became a landmark, like Berenson's I Tatti near Florence, or Beerbohm's Villino Chiaro in Rapallo. Invitations were prized: to have been bidden to Maugham's table on one's European tour ranked on a par with a private papal audience. The list of the famous who stayed there would take several pages, and it was Maugham's secret satisfaction that they all came to him.

The stylized Fatima's hand etched in red in the white plaster gatepost told each visitor that he had arrived. The drive curved up between rocks and clumps of agapanthi. The lawn on each side of the driveway had to be dug up at the end of every spring and replanted every fall, because the summer sun scorched it. Gardeners on steep slopes pruned orange and avocado trees. Maugham was the first to grow avocados on the Riviera (where it was illegal to import agricultural produce), smuggling California cuttings into France in his golf bag. They bore no fruit for seven years, but he was patient. Eventually he picked between three hundred and four hundred pears a year.

At the end of the drive one reached a square white house with long green shutters, which opened onto a broad terrace overlooking the Mediterranean. There was no doorbell, for the crunch of tires over gravel was sufficient to alert the servants. On the lintel above the entrance was carved another red hand. The pool, dug out of a rock in a hillside overlooking the house, was framed by four lead-cast pinecones. At one end was a Bernini faun through whose mouth water gushed.

The villa was built around an interior arched courtyard, a fine place to dine on a summer night. It had seven bedrooms, two of them on the ground floor, and four bathrooms. Maugham's bedroom was the corner room on the first floor, with a view of the sea and a marble chimneypiece. His narrow eighteenth-century Sicilian bed had flowers painted on the head- and footboard. On the mantelpiece were photographs of his mother. The bed was set at an angle at which he could get the best light for reading, and behind it stood a Spanish baroque sculpture. "I was prepared to die in the painted bedstead in my bedroom," he wrote. "I sometimes crossed my hands and closed my eyes to imagine how I should look when at last I lay there dead."[1] A bookcase built into the wall contained his favorite books, including the complete works of Hazlitt and Samuel Butler. The guests' shuttered bedroom windows opened unto row after row of orange, lemon, and tangerine trees. Goldfinches sang and the mimosa bloomed the year round. There was rarely a frost, and rain fell, on the average, only sixty-seven days a year. The single drawback was that there were so many mosquitoes that nets were essential at night.

The entrance hall had a black slate floor and led past Kuan Yin, the Chinese goddess of mercy, to a marble staircase. Siamese bronze heads decorated the landings. The dining room, small and high-ceilinged, could seat eight. The large drawing room had a fireplace of Arles stone, over which a gilded wood eagle spread its wings. A round table was piled high with books, and there were more books on shelves, the highest of which Maugham could reach only by standing on a chair. Spanish furniture, including an altarpiece that served as a humidor, and gilded wooden chandeliers gave the room a baroque flavor. It was here that Maugham greeted his guests, coming forward with arms outstretched in welcome, then dropping them to his sides to avoid contact. French windows at either end of the drawing room led to a front patio and a garden with a paved surface surrounded by shade trees. Beyond a high hedge clipped into an arch was a lily pond. At night you could hear frogs croak.

Maugham's writing room, reached by a small green staircase, was like an oblong box that had been placed on the flat roof of the two-story house. Long French windows ran the length of one wall, and another wall was solid with books. His desk, facing the books, was an eight-foot-long Spanish table. Light came through the Gauguin window he had bought in Tahiti, which was placed in a raised recess where there was a small fireplace and a sofa covered in blue batik.

A second house was converted into apartments for the staff. There were thirteen servants: a cook, two maids, a butler, a footman, a chauffeur, and seven gardeners. "Sometimes it fills me with uneasiness," Maugham said, "that no less than thirteen persons should spend their lives administering to the comfort of one old party."[2] He also had four dachshunds, named after characters in Wagner operas. His favorite was Elsa, the heroine of *Lohengrin*.

It was all very grand and designed to impress. Maugham had silver plates; they were economical, he said, because he broke so many china plates he had to buy two services a year. In the garage were two cars, a

Voisin and a La Salle. Objects collected during his travels were everywhere. There were stuffed birds from Borneo and African masks in the guest bathrooms. When S. J. Perelman visited with his son Adam, the young man asked: "What do they do in this place? It looks like some kind of a damn movie joint."[3] And, indeed, if life at the Mauresque was a movie, Maugham was both director and producer. Everyone who came there was in *his* movie, or rather, his drawing room comedy, decorous and meticulously stage-managed, with punctual entrances and exits, clever dialogue, and servants as smooth and silent as the butlers on West End stages.

His first visitor was Syrie. Maugham asked her to lunch in July 1927 when he heard that she was in Antibes. He gave her a guided tour, and she was properly appreciative. When she left he had his car drive her back to Antibes; it returned with a note saying that she wanted a divorce. Maugham wrote back asking whether she would agree to a French divorce. He wanted to avoid the publicity of proceedings in England. Syrie agreed, and the lawyers went to work.[4] They dissuaded her from citing Gerald as corespondent. She filed a divorce petition in a French court in the autumn of 1928, and the decree was granted in Nice on May 11, 1929, on grounds of incompatibility. Maugham gave her the house in King's Road, fully furnished, a Rolls Royce, and 2,400 pounds a year for her and 600 for Liza.[5]

He saw Syrie only four or five times after that, and then just to deal with business matters or at Liza's weddings, but he developed a greater aversion to her than he had felt when they were married. It was not only that he resented having to pay alimony, it was that a side of him would have preferred to remain married, as long as they kept separate homes. It was Syrie who had insisted on the divorce. Maugham wanted the cover of a marriage, no matter how synthetic, so that he could live with Gerald respectably. He was horrified at the idea that he might become known, in Quentin Crisp's phrase, as one of the "stately homos of England." The divorce exposed him as such, for Syrie told whoever would listen that her marriage had been broken up by a homosexual liaison, and that she refused to tolerate any longer the *ménage à trois* with Gerald. Liza was forbidden to visit her father at the Mauresque because of Gerald's pernicious influence, and Maugham never forgave Syrie for spreading the tale of his homosexuality. She prospered as a decorator, opened a shop in New York, and went on giving the best parties in London. Sometimes she would say that she was still in love with Willie.[6]

By August 1, Maugham was writing letters on Mauresque station-ery that featured the Moorish symbol. "Getting this house in order seems to take all the money I can lay my hands on," he wrote Alanson. ". . . The swimming pool is a great success. We go in four or five times a day and lie about in the heavenly sunshine. . . . Of course, I am not nearly ready yet. These workmen here are very slow. . . . The only thing is to arm oneself with patience."[7]

There were four categories of persons who had easy access to the Mauresque: the titled, the wealthy, the famous, and attractive young men. One of Maugham's first guests, Hugh Lygon, was in the fourth category. The son of Lord Beauchamp, then leader of the Liberal party in the House of Lords, Lygon was at Eton and Oxford with Anthony Powell, who described him as "a Giotto angel living in a narcissistic dream." That August he was invited to the Mauresque. Anthony Powell, who had gone abroad after graduating from Oxford, was sitting in a café in Nice one day when Lygon came in with a girl. He went over to Powell and said: "I'm staying at Willie Maugham's villa. I've been stuck for the afternoon with this terribly boring Rumanian. May I sit down and talk to you for a minute or two? She'll be all right on her own for a bit." Powell felt not the slightest interest in hearing about the Maugham household and party. Maugham seemed to him an irretriev-ably third-rate author, and he could well believe that staying with him was a bore.[8] With time, Powell reconsidered. Maugham had his failings as a writer, he felt, but "Rain" and "The Outstation" were good short stories, while the goings-on at the Mauresque were always worth an anecdote.[9]

Hugh Lygon was in the vanguard of regiments of guests. There were often five or six staying at the same time. There were regulars who came each year, sedate ones, such as Kenneth Clark and his wife in March, more lively ones, such as Cyril Connolly and Noel Coward in the summer. But sedate or lively, they were not allowed to interfere with the master's inflexible schedule. He had his breakfast tray— porridge and cream and tea and milk—brought with the papers at 8 A.M. Then he took his bath, in which he would repeat lines of dialogue to see how they sounded. He shaved in his bath, thanks to a fixture called the Gentleman's Helper, which fitted across the tub, with a mir-ror and space for a razor and a shaving brush.

After breakfast he conferred about the day's menus with his cook, Annette Chiaramello, an Italian woman whom he had promoted from kitchen maid. Annette came to him with the menu book and stood behind his chair, and Maugham put on his spectacles and the consultation began. *"Alors, pour commencer, une vichyssoise. Et ensuite, des escalopes de veau au madère. Et pour terminer, une crème brûlée."* *"Bien, monsieur,"* Annette would say. *"Merci, monsieur."* *"Merci, Annette."* Among Annette's specialties were *brie en gelée*, with the crust removed, and avocado ice cream, a Riviera exclusive, laced with Barbados rum. Maugham enjoyed asking his guests if they could guess what it was. Annette would leave to do the shopping with Jean Larregle, the chauffeur. Maugham was resigned to the practice of the cook's getting kickbacks from the stores where she shopped. "In France," he wrote, "your cook has a tacit right to charge you five per cent more for everything she buys in the market than she has paid for it, and if she does no more than double that you must consider yourself the happy employer of an honest woman."[10]

There came a time when Annette protested that she was overworked. "I cannot bring myself to be very sorry for you," Maugham said, "because you work for three months and then we go away for three months and all the time you are paid full wages." "But, monsieur," said Annette, "for the months while you are away I lose my commissions on everything I buy."[11]

Maugham then went to his study to write until 12.45. He said he worked mornings, because "my brain's dead by one o'clock." He felt that if Darwin could work no more than three hours a day and still develop the theory of evolution, that was enough desk time for him. He wrote with a specially designed fountain pen, with a thick collar for a better grasp, on San Remo pads purchased from *The Times* bookshop, each page of which held about two hundred and fifty words of his handwriting. He thought of himself as the last professional writer to write everything with his own hand. "I wish some learned professor of English would think it worth his while to write a brief treatise on the possible difference this may make in the production of literature now that every author uses a machine on which to express himself." He cannot have known that Mark Twain used a typewriter and that Tolstoi's niece took dictation on a typewriter. He sat with his back to the view because the seascape was distracting. He preferred to look at the bookshelves;[12] the view of his collected works spurred him on.

At 12.45 cocktails were served. Maugham never had more than one—a very cold dry martini. He would sometimes scowl at a guest who ordered seconds and say, "Mr. So-and so seems to want another martini," his voice shivering with irritation. Lunch was informal.

Maugham generally wore white ducks, espadrilles, and a blazer with a folded scarf. He had good English silver from Phillips in Bond Street, and silver *sous-plats* with large ducal crests. He would apologize for the lightness of the lunch and then serve an egg dish, followed by a joint which he liked to carve, salad, fruit, and cheese. When there was chicken, he liked to say that he had not been able to afford white meat until he was thirty.

In good weather lunch was served on the patio. The service was brisk, and if you were caught up in the conversation, the servants removed your plate before you had finished. On the other hand, Maugham wanted the food to be appreciated. He told a young man at lunch one day, "You may think you're eating gruel, but it is in fact zabaglione—and very expensive to make." He had a sweet tooth and would say while eating one of Annette's desserts, "I like Gide, I like Claudel, but I prefer caramel." Coffee was taken in the garden. If there were guests of note, he liked to do autopsies on them after they had left. When Jean Cocteau, his Riviera neighbor, came to lunch and held the floor, Maugham said, "He talks for the benefit of the servants."[13] (But he would have approved of Cocteau's definition of fiction: "Literature is a force of memory that we have not yet understood.") At 2.30 Maugham took a nap, and then went for a walk or did his correspondence with Gerald. He also liked to play golf and tennis. In golf, said George Doran, "he disdains the beaten path of the fairway, adventuring to the right and to the left and to the slightly discovered bramble or gorse. As he emerges his sentences are scarcely printable, but on the putting-green his accuracy restores his score to approximate par."[14]

Dinner at eight was a more formal affair. Maugham wore a velvet jacket, a black tie, and initialed velvet slippers from Peal, a gift from Churchill. The meal was served by a butler and a footman, who wore white jackets with silver buttons bought in Italy. There was always champagne, and more courses on the menu than for lunch. Guests were expected to leave early unless a game of bridge had been arranged.

One of the few who turned down an invitation to the Mauresque was Max Beerbohm, who objected to being summoned by telegram, which led to the following response from Maugham in February 1928, written in a parody of Beerbohm's style:

> Cher Monsieur de Max,
> I should have considered it MOST PRESUMPTUOUS to write to stay with me

(i) a master of English style

(ii) a distinguished hermit

(iii) the only caricaturist in the world who has never been able to do a caricature of me

by means of a vulgar telegram.

Anyone of those persons, should I ever have found in myself the temerity to communicate with him on such a matter, I should have thought worthy of a special envoy. I should have sent a Chevalier de la Rose in white satin who would have caroled my invitation in a pure contralto. How much less then would I have made use of a piece of wire attached to a post when these three are one, and that one, by Heaven (have not newspapers drummed it into my envious ears for five and forty years?) none other than

THE INCOMPARABLE MAX

And did you really think that modest wire could be meant for you? Truly the modesty of the great is admirable. I will not conceal from you that a little while ago I asked Reggie [Turner] whether he thought you would like to come here and his reply was as follows:

Yes, I think he'd like it very much. I don't think he'll come. He never goes anywhere. Perhaps you'd better not ask him. He might like to be asked, of course. He's in very bad health. I'm quite sure he won't come. On the whole I wouldn't ask him if I were you. I'm quite sure he won't come. Perhaps you'd better ask him. I don't see why he shouldn't come. I don't think you'd better ask him. It'll bother him to be asked. There's no reason why you shouldn't ask him. Yes, ask him. But perhaps you'd better not.

So what can I do? What indeed can I not do? But this I will say, I have a very good cook and a very nice garden, and if you and Madame *were* passing this way—there now, I was just going to say you would be very welcome; and in your letter you say that nothing will induce you to accept any invitation from me. I will not expose myself to the mortification of another refusal.[15]

As he had pointed out to Annette, Maugham spent about six months a year at the Mauresque. The rest of the time he traveled—to England for one or two months, or to America when one of his plays opened, or to one of his favorite spas for a cure, or to Spain, which held a special place in his heart. He was back in London in the spring of 1928 to attend the cycle of the *Ring* at Covent Garden and for the publication of *Ashenden*. He kept a small flat at 18 Half Moon Street, which connected Piccadilly and Curzon Street. The Ritz and the

Berkeley were close by. It was in that part of London where whores and duchesses shared the pavement.

England was a welcome contrast to the south of France. When one of his Riviera friends said, "I hate the food in England," Maugham replied, "What rubbish. All you have to do is eat breakfast three times a day." It was to England that he went to keep up Edwardian appearances, to buy Floris soap in Jermyn Street, to have his suits made by Leslie & Robert, and to have his thinning hair cut at C. F. Trumpers by George, who went to Buckingham Palace once a week to cut the hair of another George.[16]

Ashenden, the book of spy stories based on his World War I experiences in Switzerland and Russia, came out in England on March 29 and in America on March 30 (it was Maugham's first Doubleday, Doran book), in first printings of 10,000 copies each. He wrote Paul Dottin that it was "on the whole a very truthful account of my experiences during the war when I was in the Secret Service. I venture to think that at all counts in England it is the first time anyone has written of this business who knew anything about it."[17] He had delayed publication for ten years while he waited for clearance of classified material from his mysterious bosses in British Intelligence.

The book's merit lay in getting away from cloak-and-dagger romances with Mata Hari seductresses and heroic spies. Ashenden's work was unheroic and unromantic. He was a cog in a chain of manipulation, who did not fully understand the reasons for what he was asked to do. Although Ashenden never fired a shot, he was asked to do appalling things, such as issue an order to sabotage munitions factories in Austria, in which the death of civilians was certain. When the Nazis came to power, Goebbels cited *Ashenden* as an example of the unscrupulousness of the British Secret Service. Maugham was the first to say that espionage was not only a dirty job but a boring one. He anticipated the work of Eric Ambler, Graham Greene, and John Le Carré, who wrote that "the Ashenden stories were certainly an influence in my work. I suppose that Maugham was the first person to write about espionage in a mood of disenchantment and almost prosaic reality."[18] As *The Times Literary Supplement* put it on April 12, 1928: "Never before or since has it been so categorically demonstrated that counter-intelligence work consists often of morally indefensible jobs not to be undertaken by the squeamish or the conscience-stricken."

It was on the occasion of Maugham's spring visit to London in 1928 that he met Alan Searle, who would succeed Gerald Haxton as his secretary. Searle was then twenty-four, a small, unobtrusive, sweet young man with soft features and dark curly hair. His family origins are unknown, but he was thought by some of his friends to have West Indian blood.[19] Born in the London slum of Bermondsey, the son of a tailor, he dropped his aitches like one of the characters in *Liza of Lambeth*. He had already been taken up by older homosexuals, including Lytton Strachey, who called him "my Bronzino boy." Maugham met him at a stag dinner given by an antique dealer named Robert Tritton. A weak, affable little man, addicted to voluntary social work, where he met Alan, Tritton later married the tobacco heiress Elsie Baron.[20] Invited at the last minute, Alan was, as a favor, seated next to the guest of honor. When he told Maugham that he worked for the Discharged Prisoners Aid Society, visiting convicts in prison and helping them after their release, Maugham asked, "Do you want to do that all your life?" No, Alan replied, he wanted to travel. "Look here," said Maugham, who was taken with the shy, submissive, doll-like youth, "I'm leaving for the Continent next week. If you want to travel, come with me." Alan told his mother about the offer. She knew the kind of men who took innocent youths on trips to Europe, she said, but Alan did not listen. He and Maugham got along well together and continued to see each other whenever Maugham was in London.[21]

Another young man whom Maugham met and liked while in London that spring was Godfrey Winn, a sandy-haired and freckled young writer with an engaging smile. They met at a bridge evening, and Winn thought that Maugham was charming. Maugham told Winn that he had run into George Moore in Paddington Station and had politely asked the author of *Esther Waters* what fresh piece of literary creation he was engaged upon. Moore, who was seventy-six, replied, "Maugham, the only thing that I am interested in at the moment is whether I shall ever again be able to pee through my penis."

Upon hearing that Winn had written one novel called *Dreams Fade* and was at work on another, Maugham asked him to spend August at the Mauresque. He liked young men who were good at games, and Winn, aside from being a first-rate bridge player, was one of the best tennis players in England, having won the South of England Junior Championship at the age of thirteen. Winn had started life as a child actor, playing in Noel Coward's *The Marquise*. He later became one of Fleet Street's most popular columnists, after climbing the rungs of women's magazines with such articles as "The Daughter I Would Like to Have," "The Girl I Hope to Marry," "Should Wives Have a Career," and "Why I Like Working with Women."

With his chatty column about beautiful people in the *Daily Mirror*, he was a sort of English Leonard Lyons. He displayed the magic personalities against the cozy backdrop of his cottage in Esher, his dog Mr. Sponge, and wonderful old Mum, forever pruning roses in the garden. When Lord Beaverbrook found out that he was getting five hundred fan letters a week, he hired him for the *Daily Express*, and told him to "go out and speak for the inarticulate and the submerged." Asked why Winn was paid more than the rest of his staff, Beaverbrook said, "Because he shakes hands with people's hearts." When he died in 1971 of a heart attack in the middle of a game of tennis, his will was probated at 361,000 pounds.

At the time of their meeting in the spring of 1928, Maugham told the impecunious and aspiring young writer, upon inviting him to the Mauresque: "I hear that your tennis is even better than your bridge, and you'll find that we are all eager to improve our game, and ready for some expert coaching. I write every morning, and no doubt you'll want to do the same. In the evening there's usually a game of bridge. If the stakes are too high for you, I will insure any losses." Maugham gave him a check to cover the first-class fare on the Blue Train, and Winn arrived at the Mauresque with the feeling that he was entering a rare and privileged world.

On the first day Winn showed up at lunch in a gray flannel suit. "This is the South of France in August," Maugham said, "not Finals Day at Wimbledon." "Take Godfrey into Nice this afternoon," he instructed Gerald, "and get him some linen slacks, shirts, and espadrilles at the Bon Marché, like yours." Winn looked at Gerald, who was handing round drinks dressed in pink beach clothes, and thought: I don't want to resemble you in any way, ever.[22]

Gerald was then thirty-six, but the signs of dissipation were already on his face. To be the secretary of a famous writer was a mixed blessing. When they went to parties, he knew that he was invited only because he was with Maugham. Snubbed and ignored, he drank too much and made a spectacle of himself. He wavered between gratitude for the easy life he had and rage at being the prisoner of a much older man. His moods changed from manic gaiety, when he would insist on staying up all night and visiting the dives of Nice and Monte Carlo, to angry outbursts when he insulted his employer. Gerald's escape valves were drinking and gambling, and when Maugham put his foot down over

Gerald's losses at the casino, Gerald borrowed a thousand dollars from Bert Alanson. On August 6, 1928, he wrote Alanson: "Thank you again for your kindness in so quickly responding to my signals of distress. I had a most awful winter in the various casinos along the coast, never getting a win at all. Fortunately this summer has smiled upon me and I have made nearly ten thousand dollars. I have decided that that is enough and will gamble no more till winter. Would you please let me know how much I owe the bank in interest? I have already had two cheques for $500 sent to you by Bernhard Scholle to return the principal."[23]

Gerald Kelly's wife Jane recalls that when Gerald was in the chips, he spent extravagantly. He once blew a thousand pounds on a party. Another guest at the Mauresque in those years, Arthur Marshall, recalls that Gerald "charmed the birds from the trees. No matter how badly he behaved, Willie was always enraptured by him. I remember once we were waiting to play tennis and Gerald hadn't turned up, and he was seen coming through the trees towards the court, and Willie said—very rare for him to be sentimental—'Oh look, good, here comes Master Hackey.' It was said with love, you know, and deep affection."[24]

Winn, determined to earn his keep, gave Maugham tennis lessons on his new court. One morning Maugham had him summoned and asked how he was coming on his novel. "I'm afraid I'm stuck," Winn said.

"Stuck," Maugham repeated with disdain.

"Yes, my inspiration seems temporarily to have given out."

"Is that why you've been spending your mornings up at the pool, while I have been in my study?"

Winn replied lamely that he was overhwlemed by the beauty of the Riviera.

"I did not pay your fare to come down here in order that you should spend your days lazing beside the pool," Maugham said. "You are too young to need a holiday, what you need is discipline. I wanted you to learn from my example. I hoped that it would not be necessary to have to speak to you so plainly. Your first novel was fresh and showed such promise that I was anxious to meet its author. I was not disappointed. But I am now. . . . There is no such thing as inspiration. At least if there is I have not discovered it. There is, instead, dedication and complete absorption in your craft. I am a self-made writer. I started with a poor prose style, and had to fine it down as best I could. You must appreciate right from the start that writing is a profession like Medicine or the Law . . . I keep the same regular hours today as I did when I was a medical student. I suppose you could say that today, the public are my examiners."

Maugham told Winn to spend his mornings at his writing desk, just as he did, and never to write fewer than a thousand words. He invited Winn to visit his study, in the hope that it would encourage him to work. "You see the third row from the bottom, Godfrey?" he asked pointing to the bookshelves. "It is exactly on the level of my eyes. When I look up because I am momentarily at a loss for the right word, I remind myself, however weary I am, that the whole of that shelf is filled with copies of my own books. . . . One day, no doubt, you will have a full bookshelf too."[25]

Work habits were forgotten for the moment that August when Michael Arlen, who was on the Riviera after having conquered London with *The Green Hat*, the first novel with a nymphomaniac as heroine, challenged Maugham to a tennis match. Arlen was an Anglo-Armenian whose real name was Dikran Kuyumjian. Despite Arlen's polished manner, Rebecca West could not resist remarking that he was "every other inch a gentleman," and Noel Coward cattily observed that despite the yellow Rolls Royce and the Riviera elegance, "the odor of recent shabbiness lingered in his nostrils."

Winn coached Maugham for the great match, which was to take place on the Mauresque court. Maugham sharpened his game, responding well to suggestions. The day came and all Cap Ferrat turned up. There were no tie breakers in those days, and the score went to 10 all. The two writers, evenly matched, were wilting in the August sun when Winn took over the umpiring. Maugham won, 13–11, and Winn was back in the master's good graces.

One day before lunch Winn was astonished to see Gerald appear unshaven and unwashed. He had clearly been out all night on a binge and was now making a point of showing Maugham the results, to embarrass him in front of his guests. Gerald opened his mouth to speak, but Maugham interrupted him, saying angrily: "Gerald . . . don't talk now. Don't say anything. Just make the cocktails, do you hear? Mix the cocktails. That's all you're fit to do, and then go and clean yourself up." Soon after, at lunch alone with Winn, something broke through Maugham's reserve and he said: "You do not know what it is like, Godfrey, and I hope you never will, to be married to someone who is married to drink."[26]

317

When Maugham moved to the Riviera, Alexander Woollcott, critic and author, and the model for Moss Hart and George S. Kaufman's *The Man Who Came to Dinner*, had rented a villa at Antibes that summer with Harpo Marx. "A stream of incredible people came and went at our luncheons," he wrote. "Bernard Shaw and Elsa Maxwell, Cornelia Otis Skinner, Mary Garden and Grace Moore, Somerset Maugham and Irene Castle, Lady Mendl and Daisy Fellowes, Ruth Gordon and Frank Harris."[27] One day Woollcott, Harpo, and Ruth Gordon were invited to the Mauresque. Maugham welcomed Woollcott warmly but ignored the two others. Harpo felt rejected. He picked up *Variety* from a terrace table and read it while the others drank tea. When he had finished he tossed it on the terrace floor. Maugham rose, picked it up, and said in a tone meant to indicate that he knew what it was to deal with barbarians, "I'll just put this away."[28]

In October 1928 Maugham left for New York on the *Mauretania* for the rehearsals of his new play, *The Sacred Flame*. He had decided to stop writing plays but still had four "lying pigeon-holed in my fancy all ready to be written."[29] He wrote them in the order in which he expected them to be increasingly unsuccessful, not wanting to damage his reputation with the public until he was through with it. The first of the four was *The Sacred Flame*, a somber story about a paralyzed pilot whose wife is pregnant by his brother, and whose mother puts him out of his misery. It was one of the first plays about euthanasia, but in New York, where it opened on November 19, it bored the audience rather than shocked them, and closed after 24 performances. It was Maugham's worst flop in five years. It did better in London, opening in February 1929 with Gladys Cooper as the unfaithful wife. Its success was due in part to the Bishop of London, who called it the most immoral play in town. The bishop and other religious figures attacked the play, which condoned killing an invalid, as destructive of the entire fabric of English national life.[30] Gladys Cooper played the part for eight months, when she had to retire to produce her own offspring. "That is what I call a conscientious actress," Maugham wrote the producer, Messmore Kendall, "a woman who having to represent a character who is in the family way goes and gets into that condition herself. *True Art*."[31]

While in London in February, Maugham had supper with Godfrey Winn on the balcony of Ciro's while, below them, couples danced the tango. Winn had just sent Maugham a copy of his new novel, *Squirrel's Cage*, and asked whether he had read it. "Indeed, I have read it," Maugham said. "Every word, though I am not a masochist by nature."

He advised Winn to turn to journalism, and asked him to come to the Mauresque in April.[32]

Maugham was back among his avocado trees in April after having had his tonsils removed, which proved to be a painful business for a man of fifty-five. For two weeks he could not swallow anything without agony. Arnold Bennett came to tea. The two writers, both hugely successful, liked to impress each other with their affluence, and Bennett was duly awed by the house, the garden, and the white-clad servants.[33]

Maugham heard from his favorite niece, Kate Mary (Kitty) Maugham, his brother Frederic's daughter, whose first novel he had helped place with Heinemann, that she was now at work on another novel; she complained that her love life interfered with her writing. Maugham, who was hard at work on *Cakes and Ale*, and who liked to think of himself as someone who could produce a given number of words a day in any circumstances, replied on April 2: "If you can only write when you are not in love will you ever be able to finish a book? I was almost continuously in love from the time I was 15 to the time I was 50 and it did not prevent me from turning out novels and plays year in year out."[34]

Kitty also informed her uncle that Syrie was spreading ugly rumors about him. Concerned, he wrote Barbara Back, who sometimes saw Syrie on the London social scene, about the rumors, and added: "When you see her, tell her that no one attaches the smallest importance to anything said by that abandoned liar [Syrie]."[35] He told Barbara Back that everything with Syrie was "absolutely finished" and that all he now had to do was "hand over twelve thousand pounds and resign myself to paying six hundred pounds a quarter free of income tax until Syrie marries again. I have learned from the papers that Mr. Johnnie McMullen [a homosexual playboy] is spending the summer with her at her house in London and have a strong hope that at the end of the season when debutantes settle these matters she will make an honest woman of him."[36] Maugham was thus paying a large cash settlement to Syrie in addition to 2,400 pounds a year alimony plus 600 pounds a year for Liza's support. The divorce became final that May, but Syrie never did marry again.

Godfrey Winn arrived once more, in April of 1929, and Maugham felt that he had improved over the previous year. "He is much better behaved and more willing to put himself out to be of service to others," he wrote Barbara Back. "He may be as big a snob as ever he was but he has certainly learned to hide the fact."[37]

In May, Gerald was the life of the party at a Riviera festivity, but it almost killed him. He got so drunk that he dove into an empty swimming pool, breaking his neck. Maugham, however, told a less embarrassing version: Gerald had dived onto a rock, he said, cut his head open, broken one of his vertebrae, and dislocated his spine.[38] It was worse than anything that had happened to him driving ambulances on the Flanders front in World War I. If he had been a decent and respectable person, Maugham said, he would certainly have been killed. As it was, he was encased in plaster and suffering a great deal of pain. He recovered quickly, however, and Maugham wrote Charlie Towne: "The only thing is that perhaps he cannot turn his head in the street to look back at someone who has caught his fancy as spryly as was his wont."[39]

While Gerald was self-destructing, Ellingham Brooks died in Capri on May 31, 1929, of cancer of the liver. Maugham's first lover, the companion of his happy year in Heidelberg, the esthete who had opened the gates of literature for him, was to his last day a Capri eccentric, still supported by his rich American wife Romaine. In his sixties, he lived on the Matromania Road with his dogs and his books and his wheezy old piano, in two shabby rooms littered with unpublished manuscripts.[40] The translations and poetry he had spent a lifetime working on had come to nothing. In terms of the lofty aspirations of his youth, he was a failure. "I once got five guineas for a sonnet," he would boast. He became ill and went to Naples for an operation, but it was too late, and he returned to Capri to die. "Somewhere beneath the ash of his laziness there burned the authentic fire," wrote E. F. Benson, who with Maugham had shared Brooks's villa.[41]

This was a kinder appraisal than he received from Maugham, who wrote unflattering accounts of Brooks in three books and a short story. In *Of Human Bondage*, published at the time they were sharing a villa, the character of Hayward the esthete was based on Brooks. Like Brooks, Hayward moved in intellectual circles in Cambridge, read Browning, and dabbled in art. "When he got only a 'pass' degree his friends were astonished; but he shrugged his shoulders and delicately insinuated that he was not the dupe of the examiners." Like Brooks, Hayward read for the bar in London and was ploughed in the final. In *The Summing Up* Maugham wrote that "having gradually wasted his small fortune, he preferred to live on the generosity of others rather than work, and often he found it difficult to make both ends meet. His self-complacency never deserted him . . . I do not think he ever had an inkling that he was an outrageous sham. His whole life was a lie." In *A Writer's Notebook* he wrote that Brooks "has no will, no self-restraint, no courage against any of the accidents of fortune. If he cannot smoke he is wretched; if his food or his wine is bad he is upset; a wet day shatters him. If he doesn't feel well, he is silent, cast-down, and melancholy. The slightest cross, even a difference of opinion, will make him angry and sullen." Finally, Maugham based a story called "The Lotus-Eater" on Brooks: a man leaves a bank job to settle in Capri and has enough money to last until he is sixty, when he intends to end his life. When the time comes he cannot do it, and he lives out his remaining years in poverty and humiliation.

Compton Mackenzie, who knew Brooks in Capri, felt that Maugham had treated him very badly and that there was no excuse for what he wrote about him.[42] No excuse, perhaps, but an explanation: Maugham, who resented and tried to conceal his homosexuality, could not forgive Brooks for having introduced him to the love that (in those days) dared not speak its name. There was also a grasshopper-ant antagonism between the two. Brooks had wasted his gifts. He had talked a good book and accomplished nothing. To hard work he had preferred a life of warm, indolent days in Capri. Maugham had been duped into admiring a poseur. By contrast, he had tended his own gifts and made them bloom. He felt toward Brooks the professional's disdain for the dilettante, perhaps touched with envy: "For twenty years he amused himself with thinking what he would write when he really got down to it, and for another twenty with what he would have written if the fates had been kinder," he wrote in *The Summing Up*.

Maugham threw himself into the Riviera life that summer. He played the golf course at Mont Agel and went to dinner parties in Antibes, Monte Carlo, and Juan-les-Pins. In July, Gerald organized a picnic for sixteen on the Iles de Lérins, off Cannes. The women wore beach clothes and the men tennis shirts and white ducks, but Arnold Bennett, refusing to permit himself such *sans-gêne*, dressed in a checked suit, striped shirt, and starched collar. A storm broke, which prevented their return to the mainland until 2 A.M., when they went to a night club and danced until 4.15. They got back to the Mauresque at six o'clock, with Bennett looking as dapper and well-groomed as when they had set out at noon the previous day. Bennett remembered it as "the longest and finest picnic I ever took part in."[43]

In September the stock market crashed in New York. Thanks to

Alanson's foresight, Maugham was not badly burned, but according to Noel Coward, "poor old Syrie has lost practically all she had."[44] Coward was then coming into his own, and Alexander Woollcott declared him "Destiny's Tot." He had equaled Maugham's record of four plays running at once in the West End. Maugham admired him and said so in an introduction to *Bitter Sweet*, published that year: "The future of the English drama is in the hands of Mr. Noel Coward." Coward was invited often to the Mauresque. One summer day he was in the patio with Maugham, Gerald, Beverley Nichols and Godfrey Winn waiting for Edna St. Vincent Millay, who was coming to lunch. The butler showed her in, wide-eyed and beaming as she looked out at the blue Mediterranean and said, "Oh, Mr. Maugham, but this is fairyland."[45]

Noel Coward managed to remain friends with both Maugham and Syrie. When he bought his country house in Kent, Goldenhurst Farm, Syrie decorated it with white roughcast walls, long sofas, and two pianos back to back. In 1934 he dedicated his first serious drama, *Point Valaine*, to Maugham. It was a flop.[46]

In November 1929 Maugham went to Greece and Egypt to celebrate his finishing *Cakes and Ale*. From Cairo he kept up his gossipy correspondence with Barbara Back, telling her he did not believe the rumor that Michael Arlen, while in London, had had "a little flutter." His reasoning was that if Arlen had gone to London for that, he would not have had his evenings free, "and be forced to ring up here and there to find someone to give him a dinner. I do not believe human nature has altered so distinctly since I was of an age to be interested in these matters but my recollection is that the object of my temporary affections was not prepared to requite them without a dinner and the pleasure of my company for some part of the evening."[47] Arlen had become a friend, for he was successful and he was a snob. *The Green Hat*, written in two months, had created a sensation, and Arlen had been catapulted to fame on the strength of one book, whereas it had taken Maugham years to win his reputation. But Maugham was too successful himself to envy the overnight success of another writer. Morever, the man who pretends to be a gentleman, adopting all the values of a class to which he does not belong, and gets away with it by sheer force of conviction, was a character Maugham knew well. He shows up in a number of Maugham stories, such as "The Lion's Skin," and here he was in the flesh.

In December, on his way home to the Mauresque from Egypt,

Maugham wrote a young Cockney admirer named Fred Bason, whom he had never met. He always answered his fan mail, and in the case of good-looking young men sometimes made an effort to pursue the relationship. "If you have a snapshot of yourself," Maugham wrote Bason, "you might send me that too so that I may know to what sort of boy I am writing."[48]

The rise and fall of Maugham's friendship with Bason is an example of what could happen when a famous, aging author came to know a younger reader. Bason was a pale, thin sparrow of a youth, born in 1904 in the London slum of Walworth, the son of a harness maker. He attended a London City Council elementary school, dropping out at the age of fourteen to help his parents make ends meet. From collecting and selling cigarette cards he had progressed to barrow boy, carrying books in wheelbarrows to outdoor stalls, and eventually set up the Greyhound Bookshop in Walworth. Bason had a passion for books. By the time he was sixteen he had read all the novels Maugham had published. Having won five pounds betting on a fight, he wondered whether to spend it on a girl for the night or a first edition of *Of Human Bondage.* "I think the bondage of that book a better investment than a bird in bed," he decided.

Bason had first written Maugham around 1928, after reading his play *The Unknown* and finding it "all on the meaning of life and the destiny of man. It's not a play, it's an argument." Maugham replied with a warm and friendly letter, and the correspondence continued, with Maugham occasionally ordering a book from Bason.

Maugham was anxious to meet Bason, for he was thinking of writing another novel set in a London slum, and Bason, a lifelong resident of Walworth, could serve as guide. It was with a view to cultivating his acquaintance that Maugham, in May 1930, went to Walworth to have tea with the Basons. Fred lived with his mum and dad at 152 Westmoreland Road. Maugham autographed Fred's copies of eight of his books, and Fred snapped his photograph in the backyard, next to the garbage can. As he was leaving, Fred's father came in. He was a true Cockney, whose favorite reading was the racing edition of the *Star.* He had never heard of Maugham. But he was won over when Maugham offered him his first cigar in ten years, and Mr. Bason paid him the highest Walworth compliment, calling him "a toff."[49]

Fred did not expect to see Maugham again, but in September 1931 Maugham wrote saying that he wanted to attend the variety theater in Walworth. Fred took him to the South London Palace, near the Elephant and Castle. As they walked to the music hall Fred, who was single, said something about the gamble of matrimony. "Gamble," Maugham said. "Yes. You get better odds on dogs!" Bason was impressed by Maugham's elegance. His long-filtered cigarettes were made to order for him in a shop in Vigo Street, and his cigarette case, with its ruby-and-diamond clasp, was the gift of a maharajah. And yet when it came to buying seats Maugham chose the cheaper circle over the stalls, saying that from the circle he could see the audience without looking round at them. Fred said that for a tanner in the gallery they could have looked down at the whole bloomin' lot, but Maugham replied that he was no good at heights.

The red light went on, the number board changed to two, and the show started. The first act was a team of acrobats called the Three Elysses. When Maugham wondered how they got their name, Fred volunteered to go backstage and find out. Maugham said it was useless knowledge. Fred then questioned whether any knowledge was useless. Maugham said it was useless to know that at the moment it was 4 A.M. in Peking. Supposing you took it into your head to ring up the Emperor of China, Fred said, he would be bloomin' displeased to be awakened so early in the morning, even by you. Maugham said that in Monte Carlo he had seen a woman dive a hundred feet into eight feet of water. "It made me sick to watch her do this," he told Fred, "yet she did it twice a day for weeks and thought nothing of it." (Four years later he wrote a short story based on the Monte Carlo high dive, called "Gigolo and Gigolette.")

Following the acrobats came the comedy team of Varney and Butt. Maugham laughed when the man said, "How far did you sink to get those fine clothes?" and the woman replied, "Only as far as Selfridge's basement." Then there was a male dancer whom he applauded heartily, and after the intermission came the second part of the program, "Stars of the London Theatre Queues." These were the performers who worked on the sidewalks outside theaters for coins. Maugham was particularly interested in a man who tore newspapers into amazing designs. When they left the theater it was raining hard, and Fred found a taxi for Maugham, who said he was going to the Garrick Club, but did not invite Fred to come along. He did, however, invite Fred to the Mauresque. The next day Fred ran into an actor he knew, Miles Mander, and told him about the invitation. "I will not forget how emphatically Miles Mander told me not to go there," he said. "He also told me some facts of life I didn't know. As God is my judge I did NOT know. No one in the world had told me and some things are quite impossible to guess. Well, there ain't no reason to go further in this little matter— but whenever the matter of a visit to Mister Maugham's home cropped up, I told him I was too busy. . . . I had no wish at all to offend him. . . . There is a Cockney saying that one doesn't pee on one's own doorstep."⁵⁰

Apparently Maugham's homosexuality was widely known in the London theater world. One wonders, however, whether Bason's virtue was ever in serious danger. He was small and unattractive, and Maugham seems to have sought him out for material rather than pleasure. In all likelihood, if he had really been invited to the Mauresque, he could have gone without having to defend himself against an unwanted approach.

Later in 1931 Maugham said he wanted to find out what the election was like in Walworth, a Labour stronghold. Fred made all the arrangements, but Maugham stood him up to go to Selfridge's election-night party. "He let me down," Fred said. That year Bason produced the first bibliography of Maugham's work. He was not a trained bibliographer, and the book is full of errors and omissions. Maugham agreed to write a preface, however, in which he said: "When I look at it, well printed and smartly bound, I seem to look at my own tombstone."

Maugham was generous with Fred. One time he gave him signed copies of his books and told him to sell them and go on a holiday. Fred sold them and went to Madeira. Another time, when he said it was impossible to spend a week in Paris on five pounds, Fred said he could do it. "If you can go to Paris and stay there for a week on my fiver," Maugham told him, "I will reward you with another fiver for your enterprise." Fred did, and had "the time of my young life." He did what he could to pay Maugham back. "My mother was making a cardigan for Maugham as a Christmas gift," he wrote. "It was a lovely jumper. He had given her the best box of chocs she ever chewed. We cockneys try to repay. But not in the way he *really* wants. That never never."⁵¹ Fred sometimes helped Maugham with research. "I know you are an expert on Cockney dialogue," Maugham wrote him, "please send me a post-card to say whether 'ain't' is used now or if the spread of education has made 'isn't' universal."⁵² Fred had tried his hand at writing a play and wanted Maugham to look at it, but on this point Maugham was adamant: "No, I do not think I want to read your new play," he wrote Bason. "I read one of yours earlier in the year. Remember that there are a great many people who want my opinion on their unpublished works and in the last fortnight I have had to cope with no less than five different authors."[53]

In March 1933 Bason wrote Maugham that he had received an inquiry from a collector in California who wanted to buy some Maugham manuscripts. Maugham did not want to sell them piecemeal, he wanted to sell them all for a lump sum of $50,000, with which he planned to establish a prize for young writers. In addition, he did not want anyone to know that he was selling them. Maugham decided to let Fred Bason act as his agent, promising him a thousand pounds if he made the sale. This was an error in judgment, surprising in a man who prided himself on his knowledge of the world and its ways. Bason, a brash, shabby, semiliterate urchin from the wilds of Walworth, proved an unsuitable choice.

Fred was ecstatic at the chance. Golly, he thought, I need that thousand pounds more than anyone else in the world. Pull up your socks, Freddie! This is the chance to buy a house. Go to it![54] He bought some high-grade stationery and wrote dozens of letters to wealthy bibliophiles. A response came from the American rare-book dealer B. Ruder, with whom he worked out the following plan: Ruder would feature Maugham's manuscripts in his catalogue at a price of 10,000 pounds (the pound was worth $5.00). The listing would say: "The original autograph manuscripts of the works of W. Somerset Maugham offered for sale by consent of the author, the entire proceeds to be devoted to the founding of an annual literary prize, with the author and the purchaser as co-founders." Maugham would write a preface telling about the proposed prize. The listing, Fred hoped, would attract a buyer.

All he attracted was Maugham's fury. "I will have nothing to do with any such scheme," he wrote. "I have told one or two people privately for what reasons I wish to sell my manuscripts but to advertise the fact would seem to be excessively vulgar. . . . I am afraid I think that you have put me in an embarrassing situation and I hereby withdraw from you any authority to deal with my manuscripts in the future."[55]

Their friendship further deteriorated when Maugham found out that Bason had kept the money from the sale of some mint copies of his early play *A Man of Honour*, which he had unearthed and given to Bason on consignment. There was also the matter of signed books. Maugham had been glad to autograph an occasional novel to add to its value when Bason sold it. But now in every mail there arrived books that Bason wanted him to sign and dedicate, and it came to his attention that Bason was selling them at high prices to American dealers. "This is a racket which brings discredit on me," he wrote Bason. "I think you have done very well out of me so far. I notice that you have turned everything I have written for you into cash, for which I cannot blame you, but I think you must rest satisfied with what financial benefit you have got out of me hitherto and expect no more."[56] Bason lost his Cockney temper and wrote an angry letter, to which Maugham replied: "One of the reasons I ceased coming to see your mother, whom I like very much, is that I found it quite intolerable to be put down to write in a large number of books and I much resented the way in which you tried to dictate to me what I had to say. . . . I very much resent the rudeness of your letters the moment things do not go absolutely as you would wish them to go."[57]

At that point Maugham decided to have nothing further to do with Bason. When he was evacuated on a coal barge from the south of France at the outbreak of World War II, Fred sent him a box of six cakes of the most expensive soap he could find, Imperial Leather, but received no acknowledgment. When Fred was injured in the London blitz and developed palsy and a stammer, he wrote Maugham for advice and did receive a friendly note that said: "Dear Fred, the man who helped me [with his stammer] is Dr. Leahy, 47 Clarges Street, Piccadilly; but I expect he is now in the army. I am sorry you are so afflicted and hope the matter is only temporary. Yours, WM."[58]

In September 1946, hearing that Maugham was back in London, Bason wrote him at the Dorchester:

> If this is deemed impudent then skip it. I hear you are in town. I would love to see you, sir, for old times sakes. I don't want your autograph! I don't want anything signed! I do not want anything whatever, save just to see how time has used you, to exchange greetings and chat ten minutes. For it's years of much excitement and some little distress on both our lives in our ways—and both our homes much blitzed and much lost—that's never regained. I am now FIT AND WELL. Nearly my old self again save a little less hair and considerably less cheek! . . . May we meet? You are still the Boss to me and I won't beg—I just say I will be happy to meet you if you can spare the time someday. . . . Always grateful—and never never forget. Made many mistakes when very young—cannot atone or repay. But remember always.[59]

Maugham did not reply, but some years later Fred ran into him by accident while waiting for a friend in the lobby of an expensive hotel.

He was sitting in an armchair. Bason went up to him and said: "Good afternoon, Mr. Maugham. It's a long time since we met. I'm Freddie Bason, your first bibliographer. You remember me? How are you, sir?" Maugham looked him up and down. Then, in a carefully measured voice, he replied, "None the better for your asking."[60]

Maugham's lack of charity was his least attractive trait. It's true that he had helped Bason considerably, writing a preface for him, signing books to increase their value, sending presents to his family, giving him advice on writing, and offering him the chance to earn a large sum by selling Maugham's manuscripts. It's equally true that Bason exploited Maugham and tried to make as much money out of him as he could. But Maugham also had reasons for cultivating Bason. There was the possibility of sexual favors, and there was the London slum novel, for which Bason provided material. Writers, and perhaps Maugham more than a good many others, always get their pound of flesh. The relationship was based on mutual exploitation. But Maugham had a trait that Bason lacked—unwavering vindictiveness. Those who disappointed him were summarily dismissed.

The year 1930 probably marked the peak of Maugham's career. He published *Cakes and Ale* and *The Gentleman in the Parlour*, an account of his travels through Burma, Siam, and Indochina in 1923. His last comedy, *The Breadwinner*, was produced. In addition, his books and plays were being translated all over Europe. In France his Riviera friend and neighbor Horace de Carbuccia adapted *The Letter* and *The Circle*. Carbuccia was a Corsican politician and publisher with Fascist convictions, which did not seem to trouble Maugham. Wealth and a fine house on the Riviera covered a multitude of sins. Carbuccia was the editor of the anti-Semitic, right-wing sheet *Gringoire*, and during World War II he collaborated with the Germans. Maugham was interviewed by *Gringoire* in July 1929, apparently indifferent to its political bent.

Maugham told Carbuccia that he wanted the proceeds from his French adaptations to go to Gerald. In January 1930 Carbuccia wrote him that it would not be a good idea to produce *The Circle* and *The Letter* in Paris at the same time. "There is a very violent campaign in Paris right now against foreign authors," he said. "Jealous colleagues would protest, despite their respect and admiration for you, if you occupied two stages at the same time. Let us wait for the storm to pass."[61] *The Letter* went on at the Athenée and ran for 200 performances. At this time Maugham was also considering a screenwriting offer from Basil Dean, the producer of *Rain* and *East of Suez*, and he wrote Dean on January 26: "It would be grand if the pictures ceased to be an outrage to the intelligence of an educated person."[62]

In February *The Gentleman in the Parlour* was published. The title was taken from Hazlitt's *On Going a Journey*, and expressed what was perhaps Maugham's main reason for traveling—it was a way of becoming anonymous and approaching total freedom: "Oh! it is great to shake off the trammels of the world and of public opinion—to lose our importunate, tormenting, everlasting personal identity in the elements of nature, and become the creature of the moment, clear of all ties—to hold to the universe only by a dish of sweet-breads, and to owe nothing but the score of the evening—and no longer seeking for applause and meeting with contempt, to be known by no other title than The Gentleman in the Parlour." The book, a series of rambling impressions loosely connected by his trip, ended with a remark attributed to a Jewish commercial traveler, which Maugham seemed ready to adopt as his own: "I'll give you my opinion of the human race in a nutshell, brother; their heart's in the right place, but their head's a thoroughly inefficient organ."

On February 10 Maugham's dramatic agent and friend, Golding Bright, came to the Mauresque with his wife, who wrote under the name George Egerton, and was enough impressed by the Mauresque to write a good description of it in a letter to a friend:

> Built round a patio with orange trees in tubs, lower bachelor bedrooms . . . long windows open on the terrace bordered by orange and lemon trees—beds of auriculas and other flowers and view of the sea. The terraces, three, go up to an enormous marble swimming and diving pool. It is deep and very wide, marble slab and big old-bronze gong, from the East, near the seats, to strike for cocktails . . . a queer, gossipy, cliquey community all emulating one another's gardens and expenses . . . WSM has a femme de chambre for ladies, otherwise a chef, butler, and footman. Perfect unfussed service—no woman's house has such . . . everything of any kind is somewhat precious. The raffinement de luxe.[63]

In London that May, Maugham submitted to the usual chores. Newspapers wanted interviews. An artist named Alfred Wolmark asked to paint his portrait. He agreed to sit and went to Wolmark's studio, and they talked for more than an hour while Wolmark waited for a natural expression. Finally Maugham blurted out: "When are you going to make a start? I have been sitting here for more than an hour and you have done nothing." "I have been waiting all this time for you to relax your expression of bitterness to the world," Wolmark said, "and now that we understand each other we will get to work."[64]

One of the feature writers who came to the flat on Half Moon Street to interview Maugham was Derek Patmore, another of those young men in a hurry, like Beverley Nichols and Godfrey Winn. Patmore, who was writing a series in the *Sunday Referee*, got on well with Maugham and asked him to lunch with the society beauty Hazel Lavery in his maisonette in St. James's Square. The lunch went well, with Maugham reminiscing about his plays, but after he had left, Hazel Lavery turned to Patmore and said: "You know, much as I admire Willie Maugham, he always rather frightens me. Perhaps it's because he was a doctor once. For when I'm with him, I always feel that I've been placed like a butterfly on an operating table."[65] She was not alone in her opinion. Many persons were put off by Maugham's cold and clinical eye.

Three years later, when Patmore was visiting H. G. Wells in Grasse, the conversation turned to love. Wells surprised Patmore by saying: "The trouble with artists and writers is that we all demand the *surrender* of the loved one. There is no difference between myself and my mistress and Willie Maugham and his American friend Gerald Haxton." The reason Wells's remark took Patmore by surprise was that Maugham's homosexuality was never publicly discussed. "His private life was complex and secretive," Patmore said. ". . . Unlike other famous writers, he was extremely faithful in his attachments, and never descended to abandoned living. Although his intimate friends knew that he, like Marcel Proust, another great psychologist, was a secret homosexual, it was never referred to in public."[66]

In contrast to Maugham, Wells had a disorderly personal life. While remaining married to his wife, Jane, he conducted a series of affairs, including one that lasted ten years with Rebecca West, who gave birth to his son. Wells was a victim of what might be called the paradox of the polygamist. The search for passion in successive infidelities led him to devalue and discard the women he possessed.

He had settled on the Riviera before Maugham, around 1923, after breaking up with Rebecca West. He moved to Grasse with a French mistress named Odette Keun, and built a house called Lou Pidou, a Provençal contraction of *Le Petit Dieu* (The Little God). An inscription over the fireplace said: "Two lovers built this house." Now in his sixties, Wells was no longer the prophetic writer at the height of his powers whom Maugham had met at Reggie Turner's in 1908. His best work, such classics of science fiction as *The Time Machine* and *The War of the Worlds*, was far behind him. His reputation slipped as he turned out potboilers such as *The Way the World Is Going* and *The Common Sense of World Peace*, and he was written off as a relic of the past.

But on the Riviera he still enjoyed star status and played the *bon vivant* to the smart set. Once, confiding to Maugham about one of his cooled passions, he said: "You know, women often mistake possessiveness for passion, and when they are left, it is not so much that their heart is broken as that their claim to property is repudiated." Wells and Maugham were both friendly with Elizabeth Russell, a cousin of Katherine Mansfield, who described Elizabeth as "a little bundle of artificialities." Raised in Australia, she had married the German Count von Arnim and gone to live on his estate in Pomerania. E. M. Forster and Hugh Walpole were employed as tutors to her children. She wrote fan letters to Wells and had an affair with him before becoming his neighbor in the south of France (she had a house in Mougins). Maugham asked them both to lunch. Wells, the child of domestic servants, said he had been to see the house where he had spent his boyhood and where his mother had been a lady's maid. He had lived there "below stairs." "And this time, H.G.," Elizabeth asked, "did you go in by the front door?" Wells flushed and grinned and did not reply.[67]

Eventually the two lovers who had built Lou Pidou parted, and Odette Keun got the house. But Wells kept coming to the Riviera, often staying with Maugham. In gratitude, he sent him his complete works, bound in red. On a subsequent visit he looked at his books on the shelf, ran his finger along them, and forlornly remarked: "They're as dead as mutton, you know. They all dealt with matters of topical interest and now that the matters aren't topical any more they're unreadable."[68]

Back at the Mauresque at the end of May 1930, Maugham caught up with his correspondence, writing his letters by hand, for Gerald was in Paris being treated for his broken neck. He had dinner with Prince and Princess Ghika, but the evening was disastrous because he lost fifty pounds at bridge, which he thought was too much to pay for dinner.[69] He answered fan letters, as he always did, considering it bad policy to ignore his readers. "I was very glad to get your charming letter," he wrote Benjamin Moore-Fine. "One has to accept with a show of pleasure and interest the compliments of so many people whose opinion does not matter a two-penny damn, that it is a novelty and a delightful one to be able for once to express sincere gratification at praise for one's book. I am glad you liked *The Gentleman in the Parlour* and glad you liked it for the reasons you did."[70] He wrote the novelist and critic Frank Swinnerton, who had said in a review in the *Observer* that a certain novel was skillful but not very good, asking: "Would you kindly inform a hard-working and struggling novelist why the fact that a novel is extraordinarily, fascinatingly skillful prevents it from being very good? And would you say that *Madame Bovary* and *Vanity Fair* . . . were very good or very skillful?"[71]

Now that he was fifty-six, Maugham was bored without Gerald, who represented youth and vitality. He wrote Barbara Back on June 25: "Here everybody is so old and decrepit that there are no scandals any more. Nobody seems to fall in love with anybody else and the Riviera is the last home of propriety."[72]

Chapter Thirteen

I'll tell you the sort of book I want to write: a sort of intimate life, with a lot of those little details that make people feel warm inside, you know, and then woven in with this a really exhaustive criticism of his literary work, not ponderous, of course, but sympathetic, searching and . . . subtle.

Alroy Kear in *Cakes and Ale*

IN 1930 Sinclair Lewis won the Nobel prize for literature. Maugham, his friend and admirer, did not send him a letter of congratulation, while E. M. Forster, who knew him hardly at all, did. In England, King George V celebrated the twentieth anniversary of his accession. The *Graf Zee* zeppelin cruised over London. John Masefield succeeded Robert Bridges as poet laureate. Mixed bathing was allowed for the first time in Hyde Park's Serpentine. Prime Minister Ramsay MacDonald laid the foundation stone for the largest municipal library in England, in Manchester. The price of the *Daily Telegraph* was reduced from two pence to one penny. Some of the notable novels that year were D. H. Lawrence's *The Virgin and the Gypsy* (his last book, for he died in 1930, at the age of forty-five), *Angel Pavement*, by J. B. Priestley, *Soldiers' Pay*, by William Faulkner, *The 42d Parallel*, by John Dos Passos, *Imperial Palace*, by Arnold Bennett, and *Cakes and Ale*, by W. S. Maugham.[1]

Two years earlier, in January 1928, Thomas Hardy had died at the age of eighty-eight, closing an era. There was a curious separation of the corpse in two parts to satisfy both his personal wishes and those of the nation. His heart was buried beside his first wife in the churchyard at Stinsford, near his home. The rest of him, reduced to ashes, was buried in Westminster Abbey. His pallbearers, the cream of the political, academic, and literary worlds, were Prime Minister Stanley Baldwin, Ramsay MacDonald (who would become Prime Minister for the second time in 1929), James Barrie, John Galsworthy, Rudyard Kipling, Edmund Gosse, A. E. Housman, George Bernard Shaw, A. B. Ramsay, Master of Magdalene College, Cambridge, and Dr. E. M. Walker, Pro-Provost of Queen's College, Oxford.[2]

It was the great pomp of Hardy's funeral that gave Maugham the idea for *Cakes and Ale*.[3] For years the character of Rosie had lingered in his mind, and he now thought of a way to dispose of her and made the following note: "I am asked to write my reminiscences of a famous novelist, a friend of my boyhood, living at W. [Whitstable] with a common wife very unfaithful to him. There he writes his great books. Later he marries his secretary, who guards him and makes him into a figure. My wonder whether even in old age he is not slightly restive at being made into a monument." It struck Maugham that a writer, simply by enduring, became a legendary figure. He wondered at the difficulties of maintaining the dignified exterior that his admirers demanded. As the novel expanded he introduced the unfaithful wife—based on Sue Jones, the actress he had loved—and Alroy Kear, a self-promoting writer who bore more than a passing resemblance to Hugh Walpole.

Maugham denied the likeness to Walpole at the time but recanted in an introduction to the Modern Library edition, published in 1950, in which he said:

> Hugh Walpole then was the most prominent member of that body of writers who attempted by seizing every opportunity to keep in the public eye, by getting on familiar terms with critics so that their books may be favorably reviewed, by currying favor wherever it can serve them, to attain a success which their merit scarcely deserves. They attempt by push and pull to make up for their lack of talent. It was true that I had Hugh Walpole in mind when I devised the character to whom I gave the name of Alroy Kear . . . I had no wish to hurt Hugh Walpole's feelings. He was a genial creature and he had friends who, though they were apt to laugh at him, were genuinely attached to him. He was easy to like, but difficult to respect.[4]

Small things set off the mechanism of Maugham's spite. It may have been the Rede Lecture at Cambridge that Walpole gave in 1925, "The English Novel, Some Notes on Its Evolution." Listing novelists of quality, Walpole had mentioned E. M. Forster, D. H. Lawrence, Virginia Woolf, Frank Swinnerton, Sheila Kaye-Smith, Francis Brett Young,

Aldous Huxley, David Garnett, Romer Wilson, and Margaret Kennedy. Maugham was pointedly omitted.[5]

When Maugham finished *Cakes and Ale* he sent it off to Alexander Frere at Heinemann, a man respected by his authors, who included Graham Greene, Thomas Wolfe, and Sinclair Lewis (to whom he was affectionately known as "you lousy little limey"). Frere had been at Heinemann since 1923 and was joint managing director with C. S. Evans. He became chairman in 1944 when Evans was killed by a flying bomb. "In all the years I was associated with Willie," Frere said, "I never had a cross word with him about anything connected with his work. It was quite remarkable. It doesn't usually happen that way with authors. He would deliver the manuscript to us and he would correct the proofs, meticulously and professionally, and that was that."[6] Did Frere edit Maugham? "Oh my God, no. He wouldn't have tolerated it and, really, it never occurred to anyone to try. It would have been like going out to the bull ring and telling Belmonte how to do a veronica."[7] Frere sent Maugham's manuscripts straight to the printer and forwarded proofs, which he got back within ten days. "We didn't alter a comma. He used to say: When I finish the proofs I don't want anything more to do with it. He never commented on the jackets. Our arrangement was: I'm going to write a book and I'm not going to give it to you until it's fit for publication."[8]

Frere sent a set of proofs of *Cakes and Ale* to the Book Society, which had been founded in 1928 in emulation of the highly successful Book-of-the-Month Club in America.[9] As chairman of the selection committee, Hugh Walpole was one of the first to see *Cakes and Ale*.[10] One evening in September 1930 he went to the theater, "then home and, half-undressed sitting on my bed, picked up idly Maugham's *Cakes and Ale*. Read on with increasing horror. Unmistakeable portrait of myself. Never slept."[11] Walpole, who had always been friendly with Maugham, praising his work and success, was shocked by what he felt to be the book's malice. Alroy Kear, the novelist and lecturer who is bent on making himself the Grand Old Man of English letters, was clearly he. Walpole called Frere in the middle of the night and said, "You've got to stop the publication of this book." "Well, sir," Frere said, "I can't see any resemblance to you in any of the characters." The next day Frere met Walpole at lunch at the Reform Club with H. G. Wells, Arnold Bennett, and J. B. Priestley, another Book Society author. After lunch he urged Priestley to persuade Walpole that the character was not he.[12] Priestley spoke to Walpole and said that Maugham absolutely denied that it was. "But how can he," Walpole asked, "when there are in one conversation the very accents of my voice?" For days Walpole could think of nothing else. Why had Maugham written a book that would serve no purpose other than amusing his enemies? "It is the stab in the back that hurts me so," he wrote in his diary. "He has used so many little friendly things and twisted them round. Anyway, it's a caddish book."[13]

When *Cakes and Ale* came out Walpole wrote a letter of protest, and Maugham replied, from 18 Half Moon Street:

I really am very unlucky. As you may have seen I have been attacked in the papers because they think my old man is intended as a portrait of Hardy. It is absurd. The only grounds are that both died old, received the order and were married twice. You know that for my story I needed this and that there is nothing of Hardy in my character. Now I have your letter. I cannot say I was surprised to receive it because I had heard from Charlie Evans that Priestley and Clemence Dane had talked to him about it. He told them that it had never occurred to him that there was any resemblance between the Alroy Kear of my novel and you; and when he spoke to me about it I was able very honestly to assure him that nothing had been further from my thoughts than to describe you. I can only repeat this. I do not see any likeness. My man is an athlete and a sportsman, who tries to be as little like a man of letters as he can. Can you really recognize yourself in this? Surely no one is the more complete man of letters than you are and really you cannot think of yourself as a furious golfer and a fervid fox-hunter. Nor is the appearance described anywhere like yours. Nor so far as I have ever seen do you frequent smart society. Frankau or E. F. Benson might just as well think themselves aimed at and Stephen Mackenna much more. The only thing that you can go on is the fact that you also are a lecturer. I admit that if I had thought twice of it I would have omitted this. But after all you are not the only English man of letters who lectures, but only the best known; and it is hard to expect a writer, describing such a character as I have, to leave out such a telling detail. The loud laugh is nothing. All big men with the sort of heartiness I have described have a loud laugh. The conversation you mention in California has entirely slipped my memory and I cannot place it or the book. I certainly was not conscious of repeating it. Really I should not have been such a fool. I certainly never intended Alroy Kear to be a portrait of you. He is made up of a dozen people and the greater part of him is myself. There is more of me in him than of any writer I know. I suggest that if there is anything in him that you recognize it is because to a greater or lesser extent we are all the same. Certain characteristics we all have and I gave them to Alroy Kear because I found them in myself. They do not seem to me less absurd because I have them. I do not think for an instant that there will be any reference to this business in the papers, but if there is I promise you that I will immediately write, protest and vehemently deny that there has ever been in my mind any thought of portraying you. Yours always, W. S. Maugham.[14]

Walpole wrote a brief reply, signed "Alroy Maugham Walpole," thinking that was the end of the matter. But when *Cakes and Ale* was favorably reviewed in *The Times Literary Supplement,* he said: "People really do like malice and cruelty in their literature these days." Walpole decided that Maugham was "a cynic and an uneasy unhappy man. . . . It is his nature to be deeply sentimental and to be revolted by his sentimentality, so that he turns on anyone he thinks sentimental."[15]

Even after having been pilloried by Maugham, Walpole continued behaving toward him in a friendly manner and sending him his books. He made several halfhearted attempts to get back at Maugham in his novels, but the spite and gall that went into the baking of those cakes and the brewing of that ale were not in him. In *Captain Nicholas: A Modern Comedy* (1934) there is a fictional novelist named Somerset Ball, who is ridiculed by younger writers exasperated by his falseness. But Captain Nicholas says that Ball's novels are redeemed by a "real sense of terror. . . . He knows what it is to be frightened—unlike all your splendid young Siegfrieds who go cynically up the mountain although they know the fire's false. Ball knows the fire's real. He was burnt once." In *John Cornelius: His Life and Adventures* (1937) Walpole describes a cynical, pessimistic writer whom he calls Archie Bertrand: "He has a fine narrative gift, humor, drama and a philosophy that is neither as original nor as true as he thinks it is. He is more delightful to read than any of his contemporaries, but he does not give joy in retrospect. Joy and loving compassion are elements of his life altogether omitted from his work."[16]

Walpole also, when he got the chance, made unkind remarks about Maugham in his reviews. In an article written for the *New Statesman* on June 14, 1941, shortly before his death, he praised Virginia Woolf's novel *Jacob's Room,* and wrote: "It was this book, I suppose, that made me unjust to Maugham's *Of Human Bondage,* read by me at this time. How melodramatic and cheap did it seem and still does seem beside *Jacob's Room*."

A more immediate reprisal came, not from Hugh Walpole but from a woman writer of travel books who was a friend of the second Mrs. Hardy. Her name was Evelyn May Wiehe, née Clowes, but she usually wrote under the pen name of Elinor Mordaunt. In 1931 she published *Gin and Bitters* under the name A. Riposte. The book was an obvious attack on Maugham, who was called Leverson Hurle, "a small dark man, proud of his smallness; rather sallow, showing, even then, yellow pouches under his dark eyes: eyes as sad and disillusioned as those of a sick monkey." It was said that he "secreted bile as snakes secrete poison in their fangs: the bile of sheer venom."

Hurle goes to the Malay Peninsula with his secretary, who writes people in the district that they are coming to stay, will need a cool, airy room with a nice view, a room to write in, and a car to meet them. The planters joked to one another: "Got a royal command yet?"

> Only after Mr. Leverson Hurle, his secretary and valet, were back in England, and a volume of short stories dealing with life in the Malay States, and a play fabricated from one of these same stories, became public property did his many hosts and hostesses—these people who had turned out of their own rooms, on the cool side of their houses, spent both themselves and their money to do him honor—come to the conclusion that never—never—again, whatever his credentials might be, would they entertain any traveling author.
>
> . . . .
>
> Toward the end, in his decadence, he lost all sense of decency. In particular he took to lambasting his fellow writers, alive and dead . . . in this, indeed, he followed out the old name for medical students, "corpse snatchers." . . . One living writer in particular, a man of about his own age, or maybe a little younger, he held up to ridicule—a writer whose books, in general, ended as weakly as his own began, apart from one single effort.[17]

"Maugham Mauled," wrote *Time* magazine when *Gin and Bitters* came out in New York in April 1931. "Consecrated Butchery," said the New York *Herald Tribune*. The *New Republic* said on May 27 that *Gin and Bitters* had "only spindly legs of its own, and even as parody it falls pretty flat, the author's knowledge of Mr. Maugham apparently being confined to gossip and the internal evidence of his writings. The sum total is neither malicious enough to be amusing, nor penetrating enough to be of much interest."

On May 7, *The New York Times* ran a story under the headline: " 'Gin and Bitters' Held Up: English Edition Called Off After Friends of Maugham Protest." On May 14 *The Times* ran a letter from Elinor Mordaunt denying that her book had been held up. Martin Secker was publishing it in England in the fall under the title *Full Circle*.[18]

Walpole was alarmed that Mrs. Mordaunt was "making a fuss. Shall I ever be free of the *Cakes and Ale* controversy? I may certainly with my hand on my heart, wish that W.M. had never been born."[19] Not wanting him to think that he had anything to do with the book, Walpole wrote Maugham:

> I've just read *Gin and Bitters* and I do most earnestly beg you to injunct its publication in England. It is a *foul* book (I have no idea who wrote it save that it is a woman). . . . It will undoubtedly make a sensation and although you may not care what anyone says it is a disgrace that people who don't know you should have that impression of you. . . . I am sure you can obtain an injunction—I'm willing to give evidence on your behalf to any extent and I'm sure many others would. The book is *foul* and you ought to stop it. I'm not writing this from hysteria or any motive but one of real and true affection for yourself. I do beg you to stop the thing as I'm sure you can. Yours affectionately . . .[20]

"It never struck me for a moment," Maugham replied, "that you could have wasted your time in writing a parody on a book of mine and whatever attack on me *Gin and Bitters* may contain I am prepared to bear with FORTITUDE. I do not mind very much what anybody says about me. I am used to the slings and arrows of outrageous fortune."[21] In fact, however, he minded a great deal, and wrote Frank Swinnerton: "I am assured on very high legal authority that the book constitutes a gross libel. I am likewise assured that I can do nothing till it is published. If it is I must obviously seek what redress the law allows."[22]

Full Circle came out in England in September. *The Times Literary Supplement* said on September 17 that the author was "abundantly clever even when she is administering slightly malicious raps here and there in the English literary world. She has humor and insight and an easy and entertaining way of writing."

Maugham's own riposte came in October, when he sued for libel.

"The writ was received some days ago," the publisher told the London *Times*, "and the matter is now in the hands of our solicitors. They will advise us whether any copies of the book are to be issued while the action is being considered."[23] Martin Secker withdrew the book, although he did not think Maugham would take the matter to court. As Frederic, Maugham's barrister brother, told Secker, "Willie would never have gone into the witness-box with that stammer of his."[24] This was not certain, for Maugham had on two previous occasions been involved in law suits that could have landed him in the witness box— the Colles copyright suit and the Syrie Wellcome divorce suit—but in both those cases he had had no choice, whereas this time he did.

In later years Maugham denied an account by Karl Pfeiffer that he had tried to suppress *Gin and Bitters*. He wrote the author Myrick Land, who was working on a book called *The Fine Art of Literary Mayhem*, on September 6, 1961: "Mr. Pfeiffer's inaccuracy is well matched by his vulgarity. I never met the author of *Gin and Bitters* and I would never have dreamt of trying to suppress it. Walpole's reputation was never great and *Cakes and Ale* certainly never inhibited the last eleven years of his life. Mr. Pfeiffer apparently cannot put pen to paper without writing nonesense."[25]

"There is no kick in the milk of human kindness," Maugham liked to say. *Cakes and Ale* was his most malicious but also his funniest book. The *arriviste* writer has never been better done:

> Than Roy no one could show a more genuine cordiality to a fellow novelist whose name was on everybody's lips, but no one could more genially turn a cold shoulder on him when idleness, failure, or someone else's success had cast a shade on his notoriety. . . .
>
> . . . I could think of no one among my contemporaries who had achieved so considerable a position on so little talent. This, like the wise man's daily dose of Bemax [a breakfast food with laxative properties], might have gone into a heaped-up tablespoon. . . .
>
> . . . When someone has written a stinging criticism and Roy, especially since his reputation became so great, has had to put up with some very virulent abuse, he does not, like most of us, shrug his shoulders, fling a mental insult at the ruffian who does not like our work, and then forget about it; he writes a long letter to his critic, telling him that he is very sorry he thought his book bad, but his review was so interesting in itself, and if he might venture to say so, showed so much critical sense and so much feeling for words, that he felt bound to write to him. . . .

. . . It sounds a little brutal to say that when he had got all he could out of people he dropped them; but it would take so long to put the matter more delicately, and would need so subtle an adjustment of hints, half-tones, and allusions, playful or tender, that such being at bottom the fact, I think it as well to leave it at that. . . .

. . . He was never impatient with the persons who call up the celebrated on the telephone at inconvenient moments to ask them for the information of newspaper readers whether they believe in God or what they eat for breakfast. . . .

. . . He was an example of what an author can do, and to what heights he can rise, by industry, common-sense, honesty, and the efficient combination of means and ends.[26]

This was character assassination raised to an art form. Perhaps Maugham saw in Walpole a side of himself that he had done his best to suppress. Perhaps when he wrote Walpole that there was much of himself in Alroy Kear he was telling the truth. For Maugham too was a careerist, not above flattering social contacts and critics. He went about it with greater subtlety and less determination, and it was not for him a full-time occupation. In the kindest light, his attack on Walpole, particularly after twenty years of professed friendship, might be explained as an attempt to exorcise certain tendencies that he found latent in himself.

Nor was Edward Driffield, the Thomas Hardy character, spared: "If, as I think, longevity is genius, few in our time had enjoyed it in a more conspicuous degree than Edward Driffield." Willie Ashenden, the narrator of *Cakes and Ale*, knew Driffield when Willie was a boy growing up in Blackstable. Alroy Kear, who is writing a biography of Driffield, asks Ashenden to remember some of his remarks, which enables Maugham to get in a crack at Henry James: "I overheard him saying that Henry James had turned his back on one of the great events of the world's history, the rise of the United States, in order to report tittle-tattle at tea parties in English country houses." "I don't think I can use that," Alroy Kear said. "I'd have the Henry James gang down on me like a thousand of bricks."[27]

Maugham in any case had the Hardy gang down on him "like a thousand of bricks." "Trampling on Thomas Hardy's Grave," "Hitting Below the Shroud," and "Grave Profaned by Literary Ghoul" were some of the responses in the press. James Douglas in the *Daily Express* wrote:

Any scribbler may heap contumely on his memory and torture his relatives with vilification and aspersions concerning his private life. . . . Mr. Maugham denies that Driffield is Hardy, just as Dickens denied that Harold Skimpole was Leigh Hunt. He gives Driffield the O.M. But Meredith was also an O.M. and Mr. Maugham argues that Driffield might be identified with Meredith as plausibly as Hardy. But Driffield's novel is banned by the libraries, like *Jude the Obscure,* and there is no record of their banning any novel by Meredith. This rules out Meredith. Driffield's first wife is represented as being notoriously unfaithful. If Driffield was a portrait of Hardy, some people may think there is an unfortunate aspersion on the character of the first Mrs. Hardy. Mr. Maugham swears that he never thought of Hardy at all when he was writing the book. But the career of Driffield is peppered with resemblances to the career of Hardy.[28]

Maugham enjoyed the notoriety, which helped boom sales. He started the rumor that Alroy Kear was really based on the poet John Drinkwater, another literary apple-polisher, who described his own style as "the best words in the best order." Maugham wrote his French admirer Paul Dottin: "They are telling the story in England that Hugh Walpole, piqued and mortified by the attribution of the character to him, went on a walking tour in Cumberland and happened to meet John Drinkwater who had come for precisely the same reason."[29]

For months the London literary community talked of nothing else. Lytton Strachey, a leading figure in the Bloomsbury group, wrote his sister Dorothy Bussy in November 1930: "This book is causing some excitement here as it contains a most envenomed portrait of Hugh Walpole, who is out of his mind with agitation and horror. It is a very amusing book, apart from that—based obviously on Hardy's history (more or less)—only marred, to my mind, by some curious lack of distinction."[30] Another Bloomsbury writer, David Garnett, author of *Lady into Fox,* remembers getting a great deal of pleasure out of *Cakes and Ale,* "the plot of which must have been told Maugham by Desmond MacCarthy, who met Hardy when he was a schoolboy staying with some stuffy people in a country house. . . . I always found Maugham difficult to read because of his prose style: like a choppy sea . . . He must have been a beastly man."[31]

Beastly or not, *Cakes and Ale* was his best written novel. His style in the past had often been hackneyed. In his effort to achieve a casual tone, "like the conversation of a well-bred man," he used colloquialisms that bordered on clichés. He did not use them, like Evelyn Waugh, to reveal character through dialogue, but in the narrator's voice. His characters "got along like a house afire," or "didn't care a row of pins for each other," or exchanged "sardonic grins" and "disparaging glances." A person was "as clever as a bagfull of monkeys," the beauty of the heroine "took your breath away," a friend was "a damned good sort," a villain was "an unmitigated scoundrel," a bore "talked your head off," and the hero's heart "beat nineteen to the dozen." To describe an island, he wrote about "the unimaginable beauty of the island."

There was nothing slipshod in this use of clichés; it was, on the contrary, a deliberate attempt to achieve an easily accessible, conversational style. In this he was influenced by Hazlitt, who had written in his essay "On Familiar Style": "To write a genuine familiar or truly English style, is to write as anyone would speak in common conversation, who had a thorough command and choice of words, or who could discourse with ease, force, and perspicuity, setting aside all pedantic or oratorical flourishes." In the eyes of critics, however, the familiar style often worked against him, for they concluded that he was either writing down to the reader or could do no better. He had to defend himself against charges that his prose was cliché-ridden and sometimes ungrammatical. A young man visiting the Mauresque once chided him on the use of double negatives, as in "It was not impossible for him to go to Paris that year." Maugham defended himself: "If I say 'I am not unprepared to lend you fifty pounds,' it's not the same thing as saying 'I can lend you fifty pounds.' It implies a greater obstacle. You do feel the difference, don't you?"

He could also write extremely well. Here, for example, is the description of a famous woman pianist in the short story "The Alien Corn":

She got up and went to the piano. She took off the rings with which her fingers were laden. She played Bach. I do not know the names of the pieces, but I recognized the stiff ceremonial of the frenchified little German courts and the sober, thrifty comfort of the burghers, and the dancing on the village green, the green trees that looked like Christmas trees, and the sunlight on the wide German country, and a tender cosiness; and in my nostrils there was a warm scent of the soil and I was conscious of a sturdy strength that seemed to have its roots deep in mother earth, and of an elemental power that was timeless and had no home in space.

On the whole, however, as Alexander Frere acknowledged, "he wasn't a very good stylist, but he had an inestimable gift of story-telling. . . . My test is, read a story like 'The Alien Corn,' read this story and then sit down and try to do it yourself. When people say he writes like a man with a club foot, I say try to do what he does."[32]

"We do not write as we want," Maugham said, "but as we can." His output was prodigious and had its ups and downs. *Cakes and Ale* was one of the ups. He went on writing for another thirty years but never matched it in style or structure. It was a pity that the scandal surrounding the models for the main characters drew the attention of the literary community away from the book's real merit. It was, Maugham said, his favorite. "I am willing enough to agree with common opinion that *Of Human Bondage* is my best work," he wrote. "It is the kind of book that an author can only write once. After all, he has only one life. But the book I like best is *Cakes and Ale*. It was an amusing book to write." By amusing Maugham meant that it was in contrast to the message novels of H. G. Wells, for whom fiction was "the vehicle of understanding, the instrument of self-examination, the parade of morals, and the exchange of manners." It was also amusing because it was a book about writers: the three main male characters, Edward Driffield, Alroy Kear, and Willie Ashenden, are novelists, and Ashenden, who knew whereof he spoke, tells Kear, "It's very hard to be a gentleman and a writer." Finally, it was amusing because it gave Maugham the chance he had been waiting for for years to put his affair with Sue Jones between hard covers. Maugham the misogynist and Maugham the homosexual created one of the most memorable female characters in twentieth-century English fiction.

Cakes and Ale did not get its effects from an exotic setting, or the confession of an unhappy youth, or the ruthlessness of genius. It was not an attempt to cash in on a fashionable topic. It was Maugham at his best, dealing with themes and people that he had spent a lifetime absorbing through his pores, rather than with the shock of the unfamiliar that gave their special character to his Far East stories. It was as an expatriate that he wrote his best book about England, and that too was fitting, for it contributed to the tone of urbane detachment. In showing the narrator as a boy in Whitstable, a young man in medical school, and an established author, Maugham passed gracefully through historical periods. He went over some of the material already used in *Of Human Bondage*, but if *Bondage* was a *pièce noire, Cakes and Ale* was a *pièce rose*. This time the stress is on the moments of happiness in childhood, such as a cycling lesson from Driffield as Rosie yells, "Go it, go it, two to one on the favourite." "I was laughing so hard," the narrator says, "that I positively forgot all about my social status." This is a Maugham we have not seen before.

Cakes and Ale was admired by other writers—by Alexander Woollcott and Mark Van Doren in America, by Cyril Connolly and J. B. Priestley in England. Arnold Bennett found it "first rate." Frank Swinnerton said that after *Cakes and Ale*, "Maugham's reputation as a novelist had no immediate parallel. Within a few months of its publication all active novel-writers were considerably his juniors."[33] Until 1910 the great literary figures in England were Shaw, Galsworthy, Wells, Bennett, and Conrad. The period from 1910 to 1930 was dubbed "the age of Lawrence," and Maugham was usually excluded from "best writer" lists, but with *Cakes and Ale* came the long-awaited conse-cration. The Annual Register, which had often ignored him in the past, said in its section on the year's literature that "the accomplishment of *Cakes and Ale* and his earlier *Of Human Bondage* gives him a distinction in the literature of this century that is shared by very few indeed." In 1933 the *Daily Mail* hailed him as a literary giant, the heir to Galsworthy and George Moore.[34]

To say that *Cakes and Ale* was the peak of Maugham's career invites the question of a subsequent decline. His popularity continued to grow, like a firm that dispenses franchises and sprouts branches worldwide. The small artisan in his shop had become a multinational corporation. But *Gin and Bitters* and the outcries in defense of Hardy foreshadowed a gathering critical distrust of Maugham. The negative aspects of his work were a lack of compassion for his characters, a dislike of women, and a cynical point of view. In 1929 a young graduate student at the University of South Carolina, Elizabeth Douglas, wrote Maugham that she was preparing a thesis on his work for her Master of Arts degree and asked whether he would answer her questions. Why did he depict the most depraved and abominable individuals? Why were his women so unscrupulous and cruel? What were his future writing plans? He replied with a nine-page letter in which he set out his creed:

> I do not consciously preach anything. I do not think that to preach is the business of the novelist or the dramatist. I put it to you that those who do soon grow tiresome, for the doctrines they preach grow old-fashioned: can anything date more lamentably than Ibsen? [This was an uncharitable remark for Maugham to make, for his deepest influence

in the theater had been Ibsen. It was also untrue, for Ibsen's plays today show more signs of life than Maugham's.]

[The writer] sees character through his own personality and so must betray himself in every line he writes. To my mind in the end his work is interesting if his personality is interesting. . . . I think I have described people as I have found them. . . . You say the characters I create are abominable: they are not to me; I am not shocked by many things that shock other people. What fills you with horror only makes me shrug my shoulders or smile. I do not see people all of a piece . . . I see them capable of every meanness and of every heroism: that indeed is why I find them so interesting, sympathetic, and amusing. . . . Remember that I had a very useful training in a large London hospital. It taught me lessons I have never forgotten, and for which I can never be sufficiently grateful. There I saw human nature in the raw. . . .

You say that my women are unpleasant. That is a reproach I have often heard. I suppose it's justified. On the other hand let me say this: I have great difficulty in recalling in fiction or the drama the figure of what is generally meant by a good and noble woman who is alive and human; it must be a very difficult thing to create. Do not talk to me about the Shakespearean heroines; Beatrice and Rosalind are the only ones who are not fools or prigs. And then there is this: I belong to a generation in which women were in a stage of transition. . . . The average woman of my generation . . . had neither the merits of her mother nor of her daughter. She was a serf set free who did not understand the circumstances of freedom. She was badly educated. She was no longer domestic; she had not yet become companionable. . . .

My aim in the rest of my work is to round off and complete my production so that my writings and my life together shall form a finished, symmetrical and as it were coherent structure. This letter is written so hastily . . . Perhaps when you have read it you will oblige me by tearing it up.[35]

Maugham saw life and work as complementary, somehow elevating each other, the quality of his work connected to the quality of his life. The nature of this connection in an artist resists explanation. A strict separation between life and work seems artificial, for they mix and overlap. Is there, in the end, a true distinction between the man who lives and the writer who creates? Indeed, Maugham thought so only in the sense that the hours he spent in his study were privileged. When he was writing he entered an orderly world of his own making, where he was in complete control of his material and in which there was a beginning, a middle, and an end; he was freed from the contingencies of everyday life. Everything was relevant. If a gun was shown in the first act, as Chekhov said, it had to be fired in the third act. He took incidents and characters from his life and rearranged them on the page. But he also tried to impose on his life the kind of order and high polish that he achieved in his work. Is it possible that his passion for respectability, his need to present himself to the world as a fashionable gentleman of means, made him lose touch with an intensity of emotion that could have raised the level of his art? What one misses in Maugham is surrender to the muse; he is always holding back.

Yeats wrote in "The Choice":

> The intellect of man is forced to choose
> Perfection of the life, or of the work,
> And if it takes the second must refuse
> A heavenly mansion, raging in the dark.

For Maugham, as for most of us, the relation between work and life was never a choice between two forms of perfection. It was more a matter of certain pretenses in his life intruding on the creative process and delineating the limitations of his work.

In the fall of 1930 Maugham's attention was distracted from the flap over *Cakes and Ale* by the rehearsals of his new play, *The Breadwinner*. It was his last comedy and the second of the last four plays he wanted to get out of his system before retiring from the stage. *The Breadwinner*, which opened on September 30 and ran for 158 performances, was Ibsen's *The Doll's House* in reverse. A London stockbroker walks out on his parasitic children and pretentious wife and starts a new life. This was a variation on the theme of bondage dear to Maugham's heart, but played for laughs. Like Charles Strickland, the stockbroker abandons his family, but instead of leaving for Tahiti, he stomps on the symbol of his respectability, his top hat. Maugham, now divorced, was in the last stage of his treatment of marriage—open revolt from the marriage contract. Ronald Squire was the broker, Marie Lohr his wife, and the two children were played by Jack Hawkins and Peggy Ashcroft, who packs her father's tailcoat when he decides to leave, in case he finds employment as a waiter. Critics were shocked by one of her lines in Scene 2: "Don't you know that since the war the amateurs have entirely driven the professional out of business? No girl can make a decent living now by prostitution." The London *Times* said that "Peggy

Ashcroft is made to say things of fantastic callousness." One critic wrote that she blushed when she spoke the line. Another claimed that his review, headlined "Terrible Lines in New Play," had brought the Lord Chamberlain to the second performance, by which time the offending passage had been cut. Maugham had not lost his power to shock, and to gain publicity by it.

The Breadwinner was on in London at the same time as Noel Coward's *Private Lives*, and Desmond MacCarthy, comparing the two, said that Maugham was "not so deft at catching life-rhythm in dialogue and his wit is deliberate rather than quick . . . on the other hand he has a far firmer grip of what he is writing about, and the implications of his subject." Maugham's works could hardly be described as the harvest of an indulgent eye, MacCarthy said. He approved of selfishness, saw it masquerading everywhere, and preferred it naked and unashamed. But he thought that some women, such as the wife in *The Breadwinner*, carried it too far; they took without giving and had no notion of fair play.[36] *The Breadwinner* did less well in America, where Brooks Atkinson called it "a feeble shuffle in the old bag of tricks."[37]

By December 1930 Maugham was back among his orange trees, with a houseful of guests, including Bob Tritton, who had introduced him to Alan Searle, and Rowland Leigh, a writer of lyrics. The house was so crowded he was afraid he would have to put up some of the guests on mattresses in the halls. Gerald was almost recovered from his broken neck, sleeping without drugs, but carrying his head a bit askew, which made him look strange, particularly since he was not yet able to brush his hair.

Maugham had recently bought a new car, which he claimed made him feel like a dowager duchess,[38] and he was fitting in nicely with the social set of the Riviera, which H. G. Wells called "a luminous eczema on the fringe of the sea." There was a group of regulars who played bridge and invited one another to dinner, where they discussed their gardens and the servant problem. There was Charlie Monroe, a handsome American who had made a fortune in utilities and bought the Château St. Jean in Cap Ferrat, an ostentatious pile with gold faucets and a regiment of servants. Charlie was renowned for his rudeness, but with Maugham he was a lamb, inviting him over for tea and calling him "sir." There was Lady Kenmare, an Australian beauty, much married and much widowed, who was known as Lady Killmore because of the mysterious demises of her husbands. She owned one of the loveliest villas on Cap Ferrat, La Fiorentina, and gave Maugham a pair of her prize poodles. There was Prince Pierre de Polignac, the father of Prince Rainier, and Daisy Fellowes, one of the first women to have her nose bobbed, who spent most of the summer aboard her yacht, the *Sister Anne*. There was Lloyd Osbourne, Robert Louis Stevenson's stepson, and Violet Trefusis, the daughter of a mistress of Edward VII. She was the great love of Vita Sackville-West and the model for the Russian princess in Virginia Woolf's *Orlando*. There were the actresses who had married well: Denise Orme, once a reigning beauty of the musical-comedy stage, who became Lady Churston, Mrs. Wessel, and Duchess of Leinster; Charlotte Ives, who had been in several plays in America, and who married a Dutch Huguenot named Boissevain and settled in Antibes; and Maxine Elliott, who had a theater named after her in New York, bought a villa called l'Horizon, and kept a black-and-white monkey named Kiki, who sometimes bit the guests. They were the models for one of Maugham's Riviera stories, "Three Fat Women of Antibes."[39]

On New Year's Day, 1931, Cecil Roberts, a minor English novelist who "knew everyone," came to lunch at the Mauresque. Barbara Back was there—slim, beautiful, intense, famed for her earthy wit and common sense. She had a teasing, humorous way of drawing Maugham out, although Roberts found it didn't help Maugham's disposition, which seemed grim and abrupt. There was something saurian in Maugham's manner, and Roberts, aware of his reputation for unkindly caricaturing his guests, was on his guard.[40]

In March, Maugham was shocked to learn that Arnold Bennett had died after catching typhoid in France. They had met when they were struggling writers in Paris, in 1905, and had become friends, although each continued to harbor reservations about the other. But they had things in common, including a stammer, and genuine admiration for each other's work smoothed over personality differences. Maugham thought *The Old Wives' Tale* was a masterpiece, and Bennett considered *Of Human Bondage* one of the half dozen major English novels of the century. Once they became successful they also shared a taste for high living. Maugham had the Mauresque and Bennett had his yacht, his country estate, and his town house in Cadogan Street, which had belonged to the Marquess of Dufferin. Maugham believed, however, that although he was at ease with affluence, Bennett had never completely shrugged off his factory-town origins. Bennett had once said to him: "If you've ever been really poor you remain poor at heart all your life." Maugham had last seen him in November in London at a party given by the producer Messmore Kendall. They had sat on the floor with Michael Arlen and shared a bottle of 1911 Lanson champagne. Maugham remembered him beating his knee with his clenched fist to force the words from his writhing lips until he finally said: "I am a nice man." Maugham agreed.[41]

That spring Maugham had been rewriting a stage adaptation of his novel *The Painted Veil*, by Bartlett Cormack. His first instinct had been to throw it overboard, but Gerald, who was supportive when it came to Maugham's writing, had convinced him that it was worth trying. In June he sent it to Gladys Cooper, actress-manager of the Playhouse, and wrote: "I have done a lot of work on it and I think I have made it shipshape. I think it has color and movement, and certainly a very fine part. You will notice that the actress who plays Kitty has not much time to sit about in her dressing room and play patience."[42] Miss Cooper bought the play and asked Maugham to come to London for rehearsals, but he begged off because he was expecting more guests and was within fifty pages of finishing his new novel, *The Narrow Corner*." "I hear you are a trifle sore about the terms on which you have got the play," he said. "All I am getting is a straight 7½%, and as the story and the characters are mine, I have entirely rewritten the dialogue so that I don't think there are thirty lines by the American author, and I invented the last scene altogether, scrapping his idea completely, I don't think I am being exorbitant."[43]

In the home stretch of his novel, Maugham cut down on the social life. He went to Violet Trefusis' for the weekend, but it rained the whole time and he was disappointed that "it was one of those parties where no one did anything but talk, no bridge, no backgammon, no patience, nothing."[44] Always alert to gossip, he heard that Ian Campbell and his wife (Lord Beaverbrook's daughter) had broken up and that their Riviera property was being sold by Beaverbrook to pay their debts. Maugham had decided that it was "absurd to waste my time and tire myself to death in going to parties that seldom amuse me."[45] But Gerald, who had recovered from his broken neck and was his merry old self, went to all the parties. Nelson Doubleday arrived in July, just divorced, and a lunch was arranged so that he could meet Dorothy Caruso, the tenor's widow. Mrs. Caruso was much taken with the large and outgoing Nelson and wanted to marry him, but nothing came of it.[46]

There were many long faces on the Riviera that summer, for the crash two years before had eroded the most rocklike fortunes. Charlotte

Boissevain was so hard up she had to rent her house. Syrie Maugham, due to arrive, was too broke to come. Maugham wrote his niece Kitty, now married to a broker named Robert Bruce, that "everyone is burnt owing to the American crash. Syrie has lost everything. Lucky for me the agreements were signed months ago or she would have opened her mouth as wide as a brothel door."[47]

One of the Mellons told Maugham that the world was on the brink of disaster. "If the worst happens," Maugham replied, "we shall keep a cow and pigs and live on the produce of the estate."[48] He had nothing to worry about: Bert Alanson had saved his capital, and his stocks continued to pay a dividend in the midst of the Depression. "Money from the clouds is the very best money of all," he wrote Bert, "because it is so very good to spend."[49] He was rich enough to hire a masseur for a month; he came to the Mauresque every day and pounded the flabby physiques of Maugham's pale English guests. These included Godfrey Winn, the critic Raymond Mortimer, and Eddie Sackville-West.

Maugham heard that Alec Waugh was in Villefranche and wrote to ask him to lunch. Alec, who had made a stir as a very young man with *The Loom of Youth*, a novel based on his public school experiences, was flattered. Maugham was, along with Compton Mackenzie, George Moore, and John Galsworthy, one of the four modern writers he most admired. When *The Painted Veil* came out he was staying at the Savile Club, and he hid the club's copy behind the Encyclopaedia Britannica so that he could have it to himself. In England, where he came less and less often, Maugham had become an object of legend. No English writer, it was said, had ever made so much money. His house was purported to be the most lavish on the Riviera and the scene of bac-chanales arranged by Haxton. Now Waugh would see for himself.

What he found was a dignified, temperate gentleman of fifty-seven, who played golf and tennis and was at his desk each morning. Waugh, knowing that Maugham did not like to discuss his books, was deter-mined not to mention them, but at lunch, *à trois* with Gerald, he could not resist asking if he considered *Of Human Bondage* his best book. "I haven't read it since I corrected the last proofs," Maugham said. "I wouldn't know." Waugh asked him if he had met his brother Evelyn, whose *Vile Bodies* had been a great success in 1930. "Yes and no," Maugham said. "I met him when I was with Godfrey Winn. Godfrey introduced him to me, but not me to him; paying me the compliment of assuming that he would know who I was. Apparently your brother didn't." Alec had the good sense not to say that his brother knew perfectly well whom he was meeting.

Waugh had been warned that Maugham made his guests feel ill at ease. One of the reasons was the stammer, which made Waugh nervous, because he never knew whether or not Maugham was going to finish a sentence—when he did, Waugh felt like applauding. He got on well with Maugham, however. He felt that Maugham was the one person who would always understand whatever problem he had, but he resisted the temptation to be overconfidential, for he knew that Maugham would simply have said: "If that's your trouble, then you must learn to live with it."[50]

Waugh passed the test and was asked again. One evening he came to dinner with his brother Evelyn, Patrick Kinross, a Scottish peer who wrote books on the Middle East, and a young novelist who would make his mark with a book revealing the goings-on among the staff of an English boy's school. Kinross and the Waughs went home after dinner, but the novelist stayed the night. When he returned the next morning to the hotel in Villefranche where they were all staying he was very pleased with himself: Maugham had told him how well he used his fingers. Alec Waugh thought of Charles Strickland, who despised the people he was enjoying. Evelyn Waugh in his diaries referred to the novelist as "a catamite of Somerset Maugham's," but the reference was deleted in the published version. Later that year Alec Waugh saw Maugham and the young novelist at a cocktail party. As the young man was getting a drink he touched Willie's hand," Alec said, "and I saw a look of pure lust cross Willie's face."[51]

Maugham left for London in September 1931 for the opening on the nineteenth of The Painted Veil, which the critics sniffed at. He had warm praise for Gladys Cooper. "I have never seen you act so naturally," he told her, "with so much variety, ease and command of your medium. You have the whole technique of acting at your finger's end. There is no one in Europe who can hold a candle to you."[52] Maugham had given up his flat in Half Moon Street and taken rooms at 14 Harcourt House, on Cavendish Square, near Oxford Circus. He wrote the critic and playwright St. John Ervine:

I am reaching the end of my career as a dramatist; it is a young man's job (I think) and in a very little while now I propose to make my final experiment in this direction . . . Of course I am very glad that your great success as a dramatist has enabled you to give up the dreary work of criticizing one play after another, but from my own standpoint I have always regretted that you should have withdrawn from a field in which you alone had a solid knowledge of the conditions and at the same time common sense and worldly wisdom. My God, how ignorant these fellows are who are writing upon the current drama.[53]

Also in September, his new collection of short stories was published, *Six Stories in the First Person Singular*. They were set in England and on the Continent. Maugham meant to show that his countrymen could misbehave at home just as well as in the tropics. In "Virtue" a middle-aged woman leaves her husband for a younger man because she thinks it is the honest thing to do. Her husband then kills himself, and the lover deserts her. Maugham had made the point before that a virtue taken to an extreme leads to disaster. If she had had an affair with the younger man, things would have been all right. "It's her damned virtue that caused the whole trouble," the narrator says. "I prefer a loose woman to a selfish one and a wanton to a fool." The woman, Janet Bishop, tall and fair and good to look at, a gossipy woman who loves to become involved in her friends' mishaps and has long talks with the narrator, seems based on Barbara Back.

As was his custom, Maugham the narrator dispensed casual information about himself: "I am a man who likes to cross a t and dot an i." And later, "There are few things better than a good Havana. When I was young and very poor and smoked a cigar only when somebody gave me one, I determined that if ever I had money I would smoke a cigar every day after luncheon and after dinner."

One of the stories, "The Round Dozen," was a gift from Alan Searle, who in his work as a prison visitor had met the main character, a notorious bigamist. Another, "The Alien Corn," a story Maugham particularly liked, was based on a young man he knew "who had made a hash of his life." The son of wealthy English Jews, he determines to become a concert pianist. Told by a great pianist that he will never be first-rate, he kills himself. "I've told you the story as it happened," Maugham said when it was dramatized for television. It was one of his conceits to claim that his stories came to him like something in a kit, which he had only to assemble. He also liked to say that writing was therapy. In "The Human Element," the story of an upper-class English girl who is having an affair with her chauffeur, the narrator says: "That's the great pull a writer has over other people. When something has made him terribly unhappy, and he's tortured and miserable, he can

353

put it all into a story and it's astonishing what a comfort and relief it is."

"Jane," later made into a play by S. N. Behrman, was another of Maugham's tales about middle-aged women who marry younger men. Cyril Connolly saw "Jane" as the story of a homosexual young man with a mother fixation.[54] "The Creative Impulse" poked fun at a pretentious woman writer who "had given the world half a dozen volumes of verse, published under Latin titles, such as Felicitas, Pax Maris and Aes Triplex." Maugham's books were now printed in first editions of 10,000 copies, and sold well, but he had lost ground with the critics in a decade when social realism such as George Orwell's was much admired. While granting his stories technical perfection, the critics found his vision of life hollow and artificial. "What, one wonders," asked Forum in November, "has happened to the man who wrote Of Human Bondage? Why should he have traded his heritage for so slick a mess of pottage?"[55] In fact, Maugham was remarkably consistent. It was critical fashion that had changed.

Before returning to the Riviera, Maugham went to a dinner party given by Osbert and Sacheverell Sitwell, at which T. S. Eliot was present. Maugham considered Eliot the best modern poet and had read Four Quartets many times, each time with increasing enjoyment. What Eliot thought of Maugham's work is not recorded, but the dinner was a flop. As sometimes happens when eminent authors are brought together on a social occasion, neither was willing to make the first move. They kept their distance, like lords expecting homage. It was not in Maugham's nature to go up to Eliot and tell him how much he had liked The Waste Land. As for Eliot, he was notoriously shy, and as the time dragged, Maugham looked surreptitiously at his watch, longing for the moment when he could leave without being rude. He was sorry the evening had not been a success, for he had heard that Eliot could be delightful company with one or two intimate friends. The two men scarcely spoke, and never met again.[56]

Things were dead that winter on the Riviera. Hotels were nearly empty and the casinos were going broke. Maugham caught up with his mail, which invariably included requests for advice from aspiring writers. On December 24, 1931, he wrote Harold Cater at Syracuse University:

> I think any sort of experience is valuable to a writer and evidently to be a reporter on a newspaper must give a varied insight into life. It is a

specialized business and to exercize it too long may very well unfit a man for anything else. I think it is absurd to try to write like anybody else, but I do think it very useful to study carefully the great English masters such as Dryden, Swift, and Addison . . . I do not see why anyone should expect to become a good writer without working very hard any more than he can become a good physician or a good architect.[57]

In January 1932 he went to Berlin with Gerald for a jaunt. By April he was back at the Mauresque, working in the morning, swimming and playing golf and tennis in the afternoon, and going to bridge parties in the evening. The stakes were high. His bridge partner Hazel Ghika had lost 100,000 francs in a year, and Maugham begged her in vain to play for stakes she could afford. The chief topic of conversation was that the croupiers at the Cannes casino had been fired after being caught cheating.[58]

Gerald continued to haunt the casinos and cultivate his "bad boy" image. Now that the adventurous Far Eastern days were over, he was bored. Middle age was approaching and he had nothing to show for his life except fifteen years spent in Maugham's shadow. He hated himself for accepting the easy, luxurious routine that Maugham offered. To punish Maugham for keeping him in gilded detention, he drank himself into a stupor, gambled away borrowed money, and made himself generally objectionable. Arthur Marshall, the Cambridge don who was one of the regular summer visitors, remembers seeing Gerald pour himself a predinner glassful of gin, which he swallowed like water. Maugham was late coming down to greet his guests, who included several women, and when he arrived, explaining that he had lingered in a hot tub, Gerald asked, "And did you masturbate?"[59]

Some of Maugham's friends and relatives, however, found Gerald attractive. His niece, Kitty's sister, Diana Marr-Johnson, thought of him as "a fawn-like creature, magnetic and vital." Once she went with him to the casino, and he thrust a bundle of bank notes into her hands and told her to bet. Instead she put the money in her purse, returning it to him when he came back from the roulette tables, having lost his last penny. Her husband Kenneth, however, felt that Gerald radiated an unpleasant sexual self-consciousness. He sensed something inherently evil about Gerald—here was someone who would do terrible things for his own amusement. Gerald's presence in a room made him uneasy, and he called him "the black bishop."[60]

In October, after the usual guest- and gossip-filled Riviera summer,

Maugham went to London for the opening of his next-to-last play, *For Services Rendered*. Once again he changed his London address, taking rooms in Ormonde House in St. James Street, off Piccadilly and close to his clubs. He mentioned to an interviewer that he was giving up the stage and was surprised to find that the matter "aroused nearly as much interest as if a well-known prize-fighter had announced his intention of retiring from the ring. For a week, from dawn till dewy eve, I received in my parlour a succession of gentlemen of the Press from all parts of the world. . . . I was rung up from the offices of great newspapers that till then have never communicated with me but to ask me what I ate for breakfast or what was my opinion of the Modern Girl and invited, sometimes for nothing and sometimes for fifteen, twenty, or even thirty guineas, my bitter tale to tell."[61]

For Services Rendered, which opened on November 1, was Maugham's most somber attempt at social criticism. It was an antiwar play, an indictment of a whole nation, a bitter comment on what he chose to call "this muddle of a post-war world." There were no epigrams or happy endings to make West End audiences go home smiling. Like the stockbroker in *The Breadwinner*, Maugham the writer of elegant comedies had stomped on his top hat. As in his Boer War novel, *The Hero*, he showed the influence of war on a family in a quiet town in Kent, but it seemed hardly possible that so much misery could have been visited upon a single family: the son has been blinded, an ex-naval officer commits suicide, and one of the daughters is a tormented spinster driven to madness by her blind brother's demands.

The patriots and promise-makers, the apostles of a better world, were shown up as rogues and hypocrites. "I know that we were the dupes of the incompetent fools who ruled the nations," says the war-blinded son. "I know that we were sacrificed to their vanity, their greed and their stupidity. . . . They muddle on, muddle on, and one of these days, they'll muddle us all into another war. When that happens, I'll tell you what I'm going to do. I'm going out into the streets and cry: Look at me; don't be a lot of damned fools; it's all bunk what they're saying to you, about honor and patriotism and glory, bunk, bunk, bunk."

This was not exactly music to the ears of English audiences, but there was worse to come. The play ended with the right-thinking father smugly announcing: "I don't think we've got very much to complain of. . . . This old England of ours isn't done for yet, and I for one believe in it and all it stands for." The mad daughter is left alone onstage and begins to sing "God Save the King" in a cracked, crazed voice, as an ignoble and dissonant song. Once again Maugham had shocked, but this time to no commercial advantage, for the play closed after 78 performances.[62] One of the spectators was the novelist Cecil Roberts, who had lunched at the Mauresque in 1931. He was so enraged by the play's sentiments that he denounced it on the editorial page of the *Daily Express*, calling it an overt slander on the army, with undertones of pacifism. It was this sort of thinking, Roberts later wrote, that had led to the notorious encouragement of Hitler by the young men of the Oxford Union who passed resolutions saying they would not fight for king and country. Had he not given up responding to attacks on his work, Maugham might have said that his war record was the best evidence that he was no pacifist.[63]

But the critics saw the play differently. Maugham's World War I friend Desmond MacCarthy said flatly in the *New Statesman and Nation* on November 12 that *For Services Rendered* was Maugham's best play. High praise also came from John Pollock in the *Saturday Review* on November 12. Pollock called Maugham "the first of living dramatists, the best short-story writer since Kipling, and the only contemporary English novelist with a first-rate European reputation." Just as the critics were about to give up on him, he produced a work that sent them back to their typewriters for reevaluation. On November 14 he gave a cocktail party in the Pinafore Room at the Savoy for the cast, which included Flora Robson, who had a triumph as the crazed daughter, Cedric Hardwicke, convincingly portraying blindness, C. V. France (one of his favorite actors), as the complacent father, and a young actor named Ralph Richardson, playing the naval officer whose financial worries drive him to suicide.

Maugham was so productive that his works were often released in tandem. His second novel set in the East, *The Narrow Corner*, was published the same month that *For Services Rendered* opened. He could solace himself from mixed reviews of his play with good reviews of his novel, and vice versa, although he claimed he never read reviews: "I have never read a review of anything I have written except when by chance I happened to find one in the newspaper I was reading. The advantage of this is that when I am told that an old friend of mine has violently attacked me in some paper I can greet him, when I run across him, with my usual cordiality."[64]

The Narrow Corner, set in the Dutch East Indies island of Banda Neira (Twin Islands), which Maugham called Kanda Meira, was a philosophical novel disguised as a thriller. The title came from the

Roman emperor and stoic Marcus Aurelius: "Short therefore is man's life, and narrow is the corner wherein he dwells." Maugham's stoic was Dr. Saunders, struck from the register for unethical practice and settled in the East, where he smokes opium and observes life with detached benevolence, expounding the author's view that "life is short, nature is hostile, and man is ridiculous; but oddly enough most misfortunes have their compensations, and with a certain humour and a good deal of horse-sense one can make a fairly good job of what is after all a matter of very small consequence."

Dr. Saunders is on a boat with Captain Nichols, a character borrowed from *The Moon and Sixpence*, who is looking after a young fugitive named Fred Blake, wanted for murder in Australia. They arrive on the island and meet an old scholar named Frith, whose lovely granddaughter Louise is engaged to a Danish planter called Erik Christessen. Louise falls for Fred Blake and spends the night with him. Finding out, Christessen kills himself. Nichols leaves with Fred Blake and disposes of him at sea after Fred has won a large sum of money from him at cards. A number of Maugham's familiar themes are woven through the narrative. Like Mrs. Craddock, Louise Frith feels liberated when her fiancé commits suicide: "At the back of my mind I know it has given me freedom," she says. Christessen, the good man, cannot survive in the world as it is, while Louise cannot live up to his vision of a pure woman. Goodness is a frail plant that feeds on illusion, while evil, in the person of the scoundrel Captain Nichols, is a sturdy and adaptable weed. Nichols, although a murderer and a thief, has a redeeming quality—professionalism. "He seemed to take pleasure in the mastery of the little boat he managed with such confident skill; it was in his hands like a horse in a horseman's when he knows every trick and habit it has."

Another view of life is given by Frith, the elderly clover-and-nutmeg planter, who studies Indian philosophy. In the first treatment of a theme he would pursue more fully in *The Razor's Edge*, Maugham considered Buddhist nonattachment as a viable solution to life. "Of course," says Frith, "Brahma is the only religion that a reasonable man can accept without misgiving." When Swan, another old man on the island, tears up a translation he has been working on for a year, Frith reacts with Buddhist resignation: "Never mind, old man, you've only torn up a few dozen sheets of paper; they were merely an illusion and it would be foolish to give them a second thought; the reality remains, for the reality is indestructible." Through his characters Maugham the unbeliever was in search of a rule of life, and was interested enough in Buddhist thought eventually to travel to India for a firsthand look. The book ends with Dr. Saunders offering the Buddhist-like remark, "If the richest dreams the imagination offered came true, in the end it remained nothing but illusion."[65]

The Narrow Corner sold well (in the United States, according to Doubleday trade figures, it sold 67,073 copies, and Maugham was now getting a 20 percent royalty on his American sales), but the critics were not kind. Anne Armstrong in the *Saturday Review* on November 26 complained that his "women are all of a piece—100 per cent uninteresting angels (off stage) or passionate and consuming vamps in the spotlight. . . . He does not . . . attempt to draw credible women." The *New Statesman and Nation* on November 12 said that his "natural sentimentality has so long frozen into cynicism that he forgets how much can be done by a little warmth. His characters, except the villains, move stiffly through lack of it."[66] Like so many of his novels and stories, *The Narrow Corner* was made into a movie (in 1933), in Laguna Beach rather than in the Dutch East Indies. Ralph Bellamy, with a Danish accent, was the planter, and Douglas Fairbanks, Jr., played the fugitive from Australian justice. He got seasick during a scene in a ship, which was being rocked on a cradle in the studio to simulate a rough passage.

While in London that fall Maugham was asked to tea at the home of E. M. Forster in the village of West Hackhurst. Maugham had a grudging admiration for his work. Forster had also invited William Plomer, who had published a first novel, and the poet Herbert Read. The tea party ended disastrously when Read, addressing Maugham, referred to "contemptible people who write for money, like you."[67]

In December, Maugham went to Paris to attend the trial of Guy Albert Davin, who had been sentenced to life for murdering his rich American friend Richard Wall.[68] The crime had homosexual overtones, but Maugham was more interested in the character of the murderer and the French penal system. From the trial and a subsequent visit to French Guiana he fashioned his 1939 novel, *Christmas Holiday*.[69] He now kept a flat in Paris, in the quiet sixteenth *arrondissement*, at 65 rue La Fontaine. Gerald spent a good deal of time there whenever he could get away from Maugham, and had an amusing set of friends, mainly homosexual.

By March of 1933 Maugham was back at the Mauresque working on his last play, *Sheppey*, whose hero was a working-class Londoner. It

359

was at this time that he asked Fred Bason to do a bit of research for him. "I want to know whether people habitually speak of board school or if they speak of it as a county council school or what? Also I should like to know what salary a young man would get as a teacher in one of those schools, a young man say of 23 or 24."[70]

Nelson Doubleday arrived at the Mauresque that spring with a new wife, Ellen, a wealthy New Jersey woman. "They tell me she is as big as a house," Maugham wrote Barbara Back, "but it escaped my eagle eye. I merely thought she had a rather poor figure."[71] The crash continued to affect the expatriate colony, and Maugham said that Americans were leaving Cannes at the rate of a hundred a day. There were still visitors aplenty from England, however, and he had lunch with Sydney and Beatrice Webb, influential leaders of the Fabian Society, who had recruited H. G. Wells, and with Wells's former mistress, Odette Keun, who told him that she loved H. G. more than ever.

That May, Maugham went to London for a fortnight to see his daughter Liza, who was nearly eighteen and "who now if you please is a young woman going to balls every night,"[72] and to attend to business. More than ever, since moving to Cap Ferrat, he was an absentee father. His aversion to Syrie made him reluctant to go through the necessary arrangements to spend time with his daughter, and Liza recalled that between 1927 and 1936, when she married, she saw her father once a year for lunch at Claridge's. "Rather stiff and awkward affairs," she remembered. "I really don't know him. I don't know him at all."[73] That July, Liza would have her coming-out party in Syrie's King's Road house, a grand event that was reported in the society pages. She entered the standardized world of the debutante and went to dances that were marriage markets. Liza was short and trim, bright-eyed, with bobbed hair, and there was something that was definitely Maugham's in the tilt of her chin.

While in London, Maugham asked his brother Frederic, who had become a noted barrister, to read a short story of his and a passage in the book it was based on and give him legal advice on whether the story was libelous. Robin Maugham, Frederic's son, has said that his father and Willie detested each other, but in fact their relationship was much more complicated. Willie disliked the patronizing hauteur of his older brother, and Frederic disapproved of Willie's Riviera life and—although the subject was never broached—of his homosexuality. Each admired the other's achievements, however, and would not permit third-party criticism. Maugham always remained on cordial terms with Frederic, inviting him to the Mauresque and occasionally seeking his legal advice. There was also a keen but sublimated sense of rivalry between them.

On May 26 Maugham had lunch at the Jardin des Gourmets with Robert Bruce Lockhart, a squat, broad-shouldered, broken-nosed Scotsman who had been British agent to the first Bolshevik government in Russia in 1918. When he and Maugham reminisced about their respective experiences in Petrograd, Maugham repeated what continued to be one of his most cherished illusions—that if he had arrived in Russia sooner to bolster the Mensheviks, the Bolshevik revolution of November 1917 would have failed. In his diary Lockhart described Maugham as having "a very Mongolian face, a very precise manner, rather short fingers with broad, flat ends. Rather conceited. Hates the English climate."[74]

Having returned to the Mauresque in June for the summer season, Maugham as usual entertained freely. He was delighted to see his guests arrive and just as delighted to see them leave. "I cannot make up my mind," he wrote Barbara Back, "whether it is better to have a guest who has charming manners and plays bridge and tennis like nothing on earth and is stupid, or one that plays them very well and is vulgar, bumptious and rude, but clever and amusing."[75] He had become an authority on guests and was tempted to write an essay on them:

> There are the guests who never shut a door after them and never turn out the light when they leave their room. There are the guests who throw themselves on their bed in muddy boots to have a nap after lunch, so that the counterpane has to be cleaned on their departure. There are the guests who smoke in bed and burn holes in your sheets. There are the guests who are on a regimen and have to have special food cooked for them, and there are the guests who wait till their glass is filled with a vintage claret and then say: I won't have any, thank you. There are the guests who never put back a book in the place from which they took it, and there are the guests who take away a volume from a set and never return it. There are the guests who borrow money from you when they are leaving and do not pay it back.

(One of the borrowers was Rowley Leigh, who finally settled the debt. "I should not have liked him to go to the jug for three months or so," Maugham said. "I believe French prisons are lousy.")

> There are the guests who can never be alone for a minute and there are the guests who are seized with a desire to talk the moment that

they see you glancing at a paper. There are the guests who, wherever they are, want to be doing something from the time they get up in the morning till the time they go to bed at night. There are the guests who treat you as though they were Gauleiters in a conquered province. There are the guests who bring three weeks laundry with them to have washed at your expense and there are the guests who send their clothes to the cleaners and leave you to pay the bill. There are the guests who telephone London, Paris, Rome, Madrid and New York, and never think of inquiring how much it costs. There are the guests who take all they can get and offer nothing in return.

Guests took large quantities of his writing paper, embossed with the Moorish sign, and on occasion pinched one of his first editions, which he subsequently kept in a locked cabinet.

The role of the crusty, difficult host, alert to the foibles of his guests, was one that Maugham did not always assume. He could be surprisingly gracious with persons he had never met before. That June, Alexander Frere came to visit and mentioned that a promising young novelist on his list, John Lodwick, was in the vicinity. Maugham asked Frere to bring him to lunch. When Frere relayed the invitation, Lodwick made a fuss, said he didn't know whether he should go, Maugham made him uneasy, and the whole idea was a mistake. "Are you or aren't you coming?" Frere asked. Lodwick sullenly replied that he was. At the appointed time on the appointed day there was no sign of him. "The boy is probably having trouble getting here because taxis are so expensive," Maugham said. Lodwick turned up an hour late, so drunk he could scarcely stand, his face darkened by a two-week growth of beard. Maugham, who would normally have been infuriated by tardiness, drunkenness, and hirsuteness, stuck out his hand, smiled broadly, and said "John Lodwick, I've always wanted to meet you, I'm so glad you could come and have lunch."[76] He understood vulnerability. In 1959, Lodwick was killed in a car accident in Barcelona.

Having defeated Michael Arlen at tennis, Maugham now tried him on the golf course in the pinewoods near Cap Ferrat. Arlen's pregnant wife Atalanta was having a difficult time, with constant vomiting. Maugham told them their doctor was no good and tried to persuade them to go to another.[77] It was in his nature to take the problems of his friends in hand, but he was vexed if they did not heed his advice.

In July, Maugham and Gerald went to Vichy, the former for his rheumatism and the latter for his liver. Since recovering from his broken neck, Gerald was a reformed character. Maugham found him cheerful, easy to get on with, reasonable, and in every way delightful. After Vichy they went to Paris for the Davis Cup matches.[78]

As in the previous year, Maugham had a play and a book coming out in London in September. The play was the last of the four he had written in order of their lack of appeal to the public. Called *Sheppey*, it was a reworking of his 1899 short story "A Bad Example," in which a city clerk, moved by the misery he sees while sitting on a coroner's jury, decides to live a perfect Christian life and is declared insane. In this case, Sheppey the barber is the working-class Christ figure, who wins 8,500 pounds in the Irish sweepstakes, intends to give it to the poor, to the consternation of his wife and children, and dies of a heart attack before the doctors can certify his lunacy. The theme that goodness is intolerable was recurrent in Maugham's work. Society would turn on any man who tried to apply the Gospel in twentieth-century England. He also touched on the arrogance of do-gooders:

> SHEPPEY: Sometimes I think the kingdom of 'eaven's in me own 'eart.
> FLORRIE [his daughter]: You're barmy.
> SHEPPEY: Because I want to live like Jesus?
> FLORRIE: Well, who ever heard of anyone wanting to live like Jesus at this time of day? I think it's just blasphemous.[79]

John Gielgud directed *Sheppey* despite his reservations. He thought the first act was Pineroesque, the second act was Shavian, and the third act was fantasy. Maugham turned up at the end of the second week's rehearsals, but Gielgud did not find him helpful. This was his last play, and his indifference to the stage was evident. Gielgud could not tell what he thought about the production as a whole, but apparently he liked it, for at a lunch at Claridge's after the opening on September 14 he drew Gielgud into the cloakroom and pressed his dedicated copy of the script into his hands.[80]

Sheppey puzzled the critics. They searched in vain for the Maugham they knew. He had moved far away from the comedies that had made him famous, from the Mrs. Dots and Lady Fredericks. When, in the last scene, a woman who announces that she is death comes to take Sheppey away, one critic observed that not even Shakespeare could write a convincing part for a ghost. The *Illustrated London News* said on September 23: "This bitter, discontented play . . . will leave the average playgoer wondering what lesson it is desired to teach, or what particular vice it seeks to flagellate." One critic who understood *Sheppey* was Charles Morgan in *The Times*, who wrote on September 15: "Mr.

Maugham has not written a play about a saint, he has written a play about the world's reluctance to part with its money, and has written it with fluency, judgement and wit—with everything, indeed, except that supreme devotion that might have exchanged success for a master-piece."

James Agate, the dean of London drama critics, wrote in his diary on September 16 that he was

> terribly bored by Maugham's new play. . . . Bored not only because it was common but because it all seemed so hopelessly beside the point. Maugham was out to prove that "a man who tried to live like Jesus Christ today would be certified as mad and put into a lunatic asylum." That statement seems to me to be so foolish as to be almost meaningless. . . . What Maugham ought to have meant is that that man would be regarded as insane whose life had differed from the normal life of today as that of Jesus differed from the normal life of 1800 years ago. . . . I had a terrible tussle with my Sunday Times article about this play and was at it from 11 in the morning till 10 at night. . . . On these occasions I write in nodules, in the way a rabbit stools. . . . I gather I am the only critic who disapproves of Maugham's play.

The following day Agate discussed *Sheppey* with Sir Cedric Hardwicke. He said that an author who is indignant because Christ's command-ments are not kept could be convincing only if the whole body of his work had been an argument for Christ. Did Agate mean that *Sheppey* was a subject for Shaw rather than Maugham, Hardwicke asked. "Of course," Agate replied.[81]

Sheppey closed after 83 performances, convincing Maugham that he had lost touch with the theater-going public and was right to put an end to his thirty-year career as dramatist. The only difference not writing plays made to his life, he said, was that when he went to a first night he was relegated to the twelfth row with leading ladies of a generation ago and relatives of members of the cast. When the Australian drama critic Leslie Rees went to see him that September and asked why *Sheppey* was his last play, Maugham said: "The main thing I've always asked from life is freedom. Outer and inner freedom, both in my way of living and my way of writing. If you have a small pretty idea for a play you must pad it out to fill the requisite two and a half hours. If you want to deal with a really big theme you're perpetually hedged with time limits, cast limits, you have to restrict yourself everywhere."[82] There was a lack of sincerity in blaming the restrictions of the form rather than his own limitations, but the remark about freedom was deeply felt.

A better reason for Maugham's giving up playwriting was that the theater had come a long way since he first started writing for it, when one could not get a play accepted unless there was a titled person in the cast. In America, the Edwardian comedy of manners had been laid to rest by Clifford Odets, Thornton Wilder, and Robert Sherwood. In France, Giraudoux and Anouilh wrote subtle philosophical plays that did well in London. Maugham had the good sense not to try to keep up with the new generation of playwrights. His oeuvre for the stage was substantial enough. He bridged the quarter century between Oscar Wilde and Noel Coward. Several of his plays are regularly revived. *The Circle* had a successful London run in 1977, and Ingrid Bergman played in *The Constant Wife* in 1975. As Congreve said of Dryden, "What he has done in any one species, or distinct kind, would have been sufficient to have acquired him a great name."

The man most upset by Maugham's decision to give up playwriting was his dramatic agent of more than thirty years, Golding Bright, even though he had not liked Maugham's last two plays, which, he said, made audiences uncomfortable. Bright's wife defended Maugham, saying that since he could make 10,000 pounds for the serial rights to a novel, and a dollar a word for a short story, why should he continue with the risky business of writing plays?[83]

In September 1933 another volume of short stories set in the Malay States came out, called *Ah King*. One of the six stories, "Footprints in the Jungle," concerning a couple who live together in perfect respectability after having done away with the woman's husband, was, Maugham declared, "told me word for word one evening in a club in one of the towns of the Federated Malay States. I was shown two of the people concerned in it and believe me, when I looked at them, knowing their story, I could hardly believe my eyes." Another, "The Vessel of Wrath," later made into a movie with Charles Laughton, was "Rain" backward. In "Rain" a minister is corrupted by a prostitute. In "The Vessel of Wrath" a drunken bum marries the local clergyman's sister and is turned into a missionary.

"The Back of Beyond" and "Neil Macadam" were fairly routine stories, one about a lover who gets cold feet and the other about one of Maugham's pretty androgynous boys (Neil Macadam's "most striking feature was his skin . . . It would have been a beautiful skin, even for a woman") who is being pursued by a nymphomaniac.

The focus, as in Maugham's other Far East stories, was on the terrible things that happened to the British in the colonies. Proper middle-class men and women went to pieces and committed murder and incest. In "The Book-Bag," which was turned down by Maugham's editor at *Cosmopolitan*, Ray Long, because of its scandalous nature, he managed to tell a story of incest between a brother and sister without once mentioning the word.

The way this conjuring trick was performed was as follows: the narrator, a writer traveling in Malaya, visits a planter named Featherstone.

"Do you play bridge?" asked Featherstone.

"I do."

"I thought most writers didn't."

"They don't," I said, "it's generally considered among authors a sign of deficient intelligence to play cards."

From this casual beginning the story unfolds, with Maugham planting oblique references to incest. In his book bag, which he always takes on trips, the narrator has a new biography of Byron, which he lends to his host. The two men discuss the allegedly incestuous relations between Byron and his sister, Augusta Leigh, preparing the reader's mind for the revelation to come.

Featherstone tells the narrator about a young woman he loved, who lived on a plantation with her brother. The brother returns to England and brings back a wife. The sister kills herself. The wife insists on leaving for England. "It's too horrible," she tells Featherstone. "Did you know what she meant?" the narrator asked. "He gave me a long, haggard look. 'There was only one thing she could mean. It was unspeakable. Yes, I knew all right. It explained everything. Poor Olive. Poor sweet.'"

The outstanding story in *Ah King* is "The Door of Opportunity." A young couple, the Albans, are stationed in an isolated district. They are not the usual colonials. He plays Stravinsky on the piano and is learning Chinese, and she hangs Gauguin reproductions on the walls. He is a bit superior and diffident and does not fit in with his colleagues, "the men who had come out to the colony as lads from second-rate schools, and life had taught them nothing. At fifty they had the outlook of hobbledehoys. Most of them drank a great deal too much. They read nothing worth reading. Their ambition was to be like everybody else. Their highest praise was to say that a man was a good sort. If you were interested in the things of the spirit you were a prig. They were eaten up with envy of one another and devoured by petty jealousy."

Despite their limitations, these men do their jobs according to the rules. But when a riot breaks out in his district among the Chinese coolies, Alban refuses to act, because he has only eight policemen and is badly outnumbered. He does the sensible thing, and he is sure he is right. But he has betrayed the assumptions of Empire. "If the officers of this government had hesitated to take unjustifiable risks," the governor tells him, "it would never have become a province of the British Empire." Alban's career is broken, and he loses the respect of his wife, who leaves him. Maugham shows that fate is the inevitable result of character. Alban's demise comes not from cowardice but from intellectual arrogance. His decision is sensible, but it is wrong from the standpoint of the community and its values. His wife rallies to the herd. "I would rather be the wife of a second-rate planter," she tells him, "so long as he had the common human virtues of a man than the wife of a fake like you."[84]

By now Willie was "Old Master Maugham" (*Time* magazine, November 13). Edwin Muir called him one of the "most skillful novelists writing today," and William Plomer said his short stories were "among the best now being written." A dissident voice was Hugh Walpole's; he was still smarting from *Cakes and Ale*. In an article called "Tendencies of the Modern Novel," which came out in October in the *Fortnightly Review*, he refused Maugham one of the "vacant chairs" in English letters because he had never matched the dignity of *Of Human Bondage*.[85]

In October 1933 Maugham left for Spain to research another book of impressions. He covered much of the same ground as on his first trip in 1898, going to Granada, Seville, and Córdoba, and attending a bullfight. This time he paid more attention to paintings. He found the Murillos "very good furniture for sacred buildings," and decided that Velázquez was "the greatest court painter that ever lived."[86]

While in Granada he learned that he would have to appear before the income tax authorities in England. Syrie had sworn that she and Maugham had continued living together during the first four years he was at the Villa Mauresque, and had not filed tax returns for those years. Maugham was being asked to pay two thousand pounds in back taxes. This was to him just one more example of her irresponsibility in financial matters. He thought it was all "a bit thick" and dreaded the unpleasant confrontation that would take place if they both had to appear before the tax inspector.[87]

Chapter Fourteen

A man wounded and aloof, who has sought consolation in excelling in his profession.

V. S. Pritchett

ON JANUARY 25, 1934, Maugham celebrated his sixtieth birthday at the Mauresque in the company of Gladys (G. B.) Stern, a writer of light novels, who was his closest woman friend after Barbara Back. It was a stiff and rather formal occasion. The staff arrived in deputation to present him with a basket of azaleas and the butler made a lugubrious speech in French to the effect that Monsieur Mawam could not be expected to live much longer. That evening they had dinner in Monte Carlo. Contrary to habit, Maugham went into the casino's Salle Privée and sat down at a chemin de fer table. He played until he had won forty pounds and then left. Gladys Stern asked him what he planned to do with his winnings. He had seen a pair of carved dolphins in the window of a Nice antique dealer, he said, which would look perfect in his inner courtyard. In a triumphant voice he added, "At last I can afford them."[1]

Gladys Stern, like Barbara Back, had succeeded in piercing Maugham's defenses, sailing past the legendary Place of Awful Politeness, which kept most people at bay. Maugham, who prized physical attractiveness in men and women, made an exception in her case, for she was bursting fat. She understood that, above all, he liked to be entertained. In medieval times he would have kept a jester. Like Barbara Back, she sang for her supper, keeping the conversation light and amusing and writing gossipy letters. She was famous for her ability to draw people out. Maugham adopted with her a bantering tone, of which he was rarely capable with women, and called her "sweetheart" and "dear heart" and "blessed among women." He congratulated her on her good reviews. "Gratters, old man," he wrote her on one occasion. "Isn't that what the girls at your school said to you when you'd done well in a hockey match?" Gladys (or "Peter," as she was known to her friends), was thrilled at being treated as an equal, for she was a terrible snob when it came to writers.

She and Maugham also shared a passion for Jane Austen and a cynical attitude concerning romantic love. Peter liked to quote the French proverb: *Il y a toujours un qui baise et l'autre qui tend la joue* (There is always one who kisses and one who offers the cheek). Peter was one of his few friends who could get away with criticizing Maugham. When his book of essays *The Vagrant Mood* was published, she told him that she had found them all fascinating but one.

"The one on Kant, I expect," he said.

"No, I liked Kant. On Burke."

"You surprise me, Gladys," he said. When he called her Gladys, she knew there was trouble ahead. "That essay was acknowledged by everybody who knows anything about it as by far the best in the book." Gladys had a sharp reply on the tip of her tongue but held it.[2]

At sixty Maugham was settling into the fourth and final stage of his writer's life. The sentimental realist had drawn on his unhappy childhood and the obsessions related to his mother's death to write a great autobiographical novel. The man of the world and the theater, Gerald Kelly's Jester, had made West End audiences laugh for a quarter of a century. The traveler to the Orient had gone to little known corners of the globe for his material and had shown that good stories are more the result of legwork than inspiration. Maugham disagreed with Chekhov, who had written: "People don't go to the North Pole and fall off icebergs. They go to the office, quarrel with their wives, and eat cabbage soup." In Maugham's experience, people did go to the North Pole, and to the South Seas, where different things happened to them than would happen at the office. Now, in the final stage, Maugham was developing into that legendary ancient, the Grand Old Man of Letters. Most of his important work was behind him, reissued in collected editions, of which there were several that year. He was about to experience the phenomenon he had ridiculed in *Cakes and Ale*, that the less an aging author writes, the more famous he becomes.

Letters arrived from all over the world, many of them asking for advice or money. One letter was from a woman in a distant British colony who wanted to know what she should do about her husband, who had been unfaithful for seventeen years. Maugham had to devise form letters to cope with the huge volume of mail, such as: "Thank you for your charming letter and all the nice things you say. It was extremely kind of you to write to me; I was touched and much pleased." Had he been so inclined, he could have established himself as the oracle of Cap Ferrat. But he could never be sure that his glory was deserved. When a gushing woman asked what it was like to be famous, he replied: "It's like having a string of pearls given you. It's nice, but after a while, if you think of it at all, it's only to wonder if they're real or cultured."[3]

In terms of success, they were real. He was the Midas of writers, who wrote not novels and stories but properties. In 1934 Bette Davis made the film Of Human Bondage with Leslie Howard. She had appeared in twenty-one forgettable films such as Fog Over Frisco. "I had been wandering aimlessly until Of Human Bondage came along and brought me out of the fog," she wrote. "We have such reverence for the chance this picture gave my fast-disappearing career that everything in our family dates BB (Before Bondage) and AB (After Bondage)."[4]

Maugham, at the top of a profession he liked, continued to derive intense satisfaction from his work, once telling his friend Glenway Wescott that "there is a particular drawback in the career of writing. When you have finished the day's work, and you have to take your leisure and wait for your creative gift to be restored the next morning, anything you can do in the remaining hours of the day seems a little pale and flat."[5] He enjoyed shutting himself up in a room every morning. He said he was like the elderly Frenchman who spent every evening with his mistress. When a friend asked him why he didn't marry her, he said, "Where would I spend my evenings?" "If I didn't write," Maugham said, "how should I spend my mornings?"[6]

Thanks to his annual cures and the moderation of his appetites, he was in good health and looked younger than his age. Rebecca West said that "with his ordered black hair, his neat white mask, his compact and unobtrusively graceful figure, and his detached manner, he might be one of those prize Siamese cats who treat their owners with distant condescension, refusing to be softened because their owners paid a fortune for the pleasure of acquiring them."[7]

He was inscrutable as a cat, except with Gerald, with whom there could be no poses. The passion between them was spent but had been replaced by a mutual need. Gerald exercised over Maugham the tyranny of the weak. He had to be watched over and kept from excess, like a delinquent son. Maugham, who was so quick to dispense with people over trivial offenses, put up with a great deal of irresponsibility and destructiveness from Gerald. He was determined to remain loyal to the man with whom he had shared the happiest years of his life, the man for whom he had left his wife and moved to France and to whom he was still deeply attached, for only with Gerald was he capable of intimacy.

Toward the rest of the world he presented a system of impregnable defenses. It was as though the vulnerability of his youth had hardened over the years into enamel. He was proud of not displaying emotion, and he believed that he let out his inner conflicts by transferring them to the written page. The only flaw in the enamel was his stammer, by which he revealed his fear of communicating or his inability to do so. But even this he had been able to turn to his advantage. In 1926 the *Daily Express* had come out with a series on famous men who overcame their handicaps. There was Major J. B. Cohen, who had lost both legs at Ypres, Cecil Rhodes, who had gone to South Africa to cure his lung trouble, and Maugham, who had won fame despite his stammer. He had not overcome the stammer but had turned it into a weapon that made everyone else feel ill at ease.

Maugham's behavior fits quite neatly into the list of negativistic syndromes developed by the psychoanalyst Harry Stack Sullivan in his *Conceptions of Modern Psychiatry*. In the syndrome of the stammerer, Sullivan observed, "people make use of vocal behavior—or misbehavior—not for communication but for defiance and domination. They have discovered a magic of articulate sounds that really works. By demonstrating their inability to produce a word . . . they immobilize the other person and arrest the flow of process in the world. This is a power operation of no mean proportions. It represents a grave disorder of development at the time . . . when the consensual validation of verbal behavior was beginning."

The traits already evident in Maugham as a child had firmed: the lines on his face and the downward-turning mouth corresponded to emotional lines. The world was a hostile place, loveless and desolate, which no amount of material wealth could alter and against which he had to protect himself. As a schoolboy he "found that he had a knack of saying bitter things, which caught people on the raw; he said them because they amused him, hardly realizing how much they hurt, and was much offended when he found out that his victims regarded him with active dislike."[8] This knack remained, although it now coexisted with the Edwardian gentleman's code of manners, and kindness toward dumb animals, and not interrupting people when they tell you what you already know. Maugham was at the same time exquisitely courteous and gratuitously cruel. Being a gentleman, he would say, "When I wrote a book called *The Moon and Sixpence*," and not "When I wrote *The Moon and Sixpence*," the latter implying that it was common knowledge. But when he was told about a woman whose hair had turned gray overnight after her daughter died, he said, "It's more likely she couldn't make her regular visit to the beauty parlor."[9] He was both generous and mean-minded. Through Alexander Frere and others he gave money anonymously to such hard-up writers as Richard Aldington and G. B. Stern. But when an editor sent him a book asking for a comment, he wrote back that he was sick and tired of young writers' climbing on the backs of their betters. He was extremely judgmental and extremely thin-skinned. No one escaped his barbs, and friends and acquaintances were constantly being excommunicated for small or imagined offenses. At the same time, the slightest criticism of his work could upset his writing schedule for a week. A misquote in an interview could send him into a trembling rage.

Maugham had enough self-awareness to know that his shyness was a mixture of diffidence and conceit, that his cynicism was inverted sentimentality, and that he lacked a certain quality of feeling. "I have long known that there is something in me that antagonizes some persons," he told Richard Cordell. "I think it is very natural, no one can like everyone; and their ill will interests me rather than discomposes me. I am only curious to know what is in me that is antipathetic to them."[10]

This was disingenous, for he knew how off-putting he could be, how his whole manner was designed to keep the rest of the world at bay. Despite the constant stream of visitors to the Mauresque, he shrank from human contact. "I do not much like being touched," he said, "and I have always to make a slight effort over myself not to draw away when someone links an arm in mine." As he admitted, he was incapable of receiving love. "Though I have been in love a good many times," he wrote, "I have never experienced the bliss of requited love. . . . I have most loved people who cared little or nothing for me and when people have loved me I have been embarrassed." In describing M. Corbin, the French ambassador in *Ashenden*, Maugham might have been describing himself: "He was a cold, distant, severe man, who gave you the impression that any friendly advances you might make to him would fill him with embarrassment."

Sixty was an age for assessment. As the list of his published works grew longer with each new book, Maugham asked himself where he stood in the English literature of his time. He felt that he was not taken seriously by critics, and it pained him. He saw himself as isolated, excluded from the lists of best novelists and the "Whither literature?" symposiums. In 1925, when Virginia Woolf attacked Bennett, Wells, and Galsworthy, and listed the significant writers as E. M. Forster, Lytton Strachey, D. H. Lawrence, and T. S. Eliot, she did not even mention Maugham, so easy was he to overlook.

There was a "Maugham problem," one that he was all too conscious of. He tried to dismiss it with the explanation that he was a teller of tales: "Though I am not less concerned than another with the disorder of the world, the injustice of social conditions, the confusion of politics, I have not thought the novel was the best medium for uttering my views on these subjects; unlike many of my more distinguished contemporaries I have felt no inclinations to preach or prophesy."[11]

There was more to it than a failure to preach. There was the feeling that Maugham was a writer in the shade. As a playwright he was in the shade of Pinero and Shaw. As a novelist he was in the shade of Henry James and Conrad. As a short-story writer he was in the shade of those writers who had pioneered the exotic setting, Kipling and Robert Louis Stevenson. In terms of style, he had not improved on his models, Maupassant and Chekhov. Maugham had to face the fact that he would never rank among the giants, which contributed to the discontent of his last thirty years.[12] He was the best known English writer in the world, but in his heart he knew that he was second-best. The disproportion between his fame and his worth gnawed at him. His bitterness was so evident that Malcolm Cowley wrote in a review of his collected short stories in the New Republic that August:

> W. Somerset Maugham is utterly tired of being told that he is a competent story-teller. He feels that the word is used superciliously. It gets under his skin like a chigger, itches and keeps him from sleeping, fills him with blind resentment against all critics who apply it to his work. Nor does his resentment stop with them. He hates the lucky writers they praise, he hates the magazines that print their book reviews, he even hates people who read these magazines. I am not in the least exaggerating: every time one of Maugham's characters is seen with a copy of the London Mercury or the New Statesman and Nation, you can be quite sure that he will end by revealing himself as an unspeakable bounder. Years ago, when he wrote Of Human Bondage, Maugham was praised by the highbrow critics of whom he now complains. He is like a boy who used to win prizes in school, and feels he is doing just as good work as ever, and wonders resentfully why he is given only a passing grade.[13]

"I have no illusions about my literary position," Maugham wrote. "There are but two important critics in my own country who have troubled to take me seriously, and when clever young men write essays about contemporary fiction they never think of considering me. I do not resent it." Indeed, he resented it fiercely. The two critics, whom he cultivated with invitations to the Mauresque, were Desmond MacCarthy and Cyril Connolly, who said of his work that "if all else perish, there will remain a story-teller's world from Singapore to the Marquesas that is exclusively and forever Maugham, a world of verandah and prahu which we enter, as we do that of Conan Doyle's Baker Street, with a sense of happy and eternal homecoming."

In his breast-beating Maugham forgot or ignored the fact that he had admirers among his peers. Over the years his books were reviewed by important writers who found much to praise. As early as 1905 Virginia Woolf liked his *Land of the Blessed Virgin*, and thirty-two years later she praised *The Summing Up*. The success of *Of Human Bondage* was made by Theodore Dreiser's tribute. Maxwell Anderson praised *The Moon and Sixpence*, and Rebecca West found several of his stories "admirable." L. P. Hartley and William Plomer called him a great short-story writer. Victor Sawdon Pritchett said he was "the most readable and accomplished English short-story writer of the serious kind alive." Graham Greene said he was "a writer of great dedication," and Elizabeth Bowen said he was a "first-rate professional writer." Stephen Vincent Benét called *Of Human Bondage* a masterpiece. Evelyn Waugh said he was "the only living studio-master under whom one can study with profit." His fan club included Alec Waugh, Anthony Burgess, Frank Swinnerton, Glenway Wescott, Jerome Weidman, S. J. Perelman, S. N. Behrman, James Michener, Christopher Isherwood, and Raymond Chandler. The great Latin American writer Gabriel García Márquez said Maugham was one of his favorite writers. One unexpected fan—considering the difference in their views of life—was George Orwell, who wrote in an autobiographical note: "The writers I care most about and never grow tired of are Shakespeare, Swift, Fielding, Dickens, Charles Reade, Samuel Butler, Zola, Flaubert, and among modern writers James Joyce, T. S. Eliot, and D. H. Lawrence. But I believe the modern writer who has influenced me most is Somerset Maugham, whom I admire immensely for his power of telling a story straightforwardly and without frills."[14]

Perhaps one of the reasons Maugham fell into critical disfavor was that he kept writing for such a long time. In *How Writing Is Written*, Gertrude Stein said: "Everybody is contemporary with his period. A very bad painter once said to a very great painter, 'Do what you like, you cannot get rid of the fact that we are contemporaries.' That is what goes on in writing. The whole crowd of you are contemporaries with each other, and the whole business of writing is the question of living in the contemporariness."

But a writer with a career as long as the average human life crosses over generations and trends. This is made clear in Maugham's case when we see who his contemporaries were on the publication of some of his books.

When he published *Liza of Lambeth* in 1897 his contemporaries were George Moore, Thomas Hardy, Rudyard Kipling, Joseph Conrad, and H. G. Wells.

When he published *Of Human Bondage* in 1915 his contemporaries were Arnold Bennett, James Joyce, D. H. Lawrence, and Theodore Dreiser.

When he published *Cakes and Ale* in 1930 his contemporaries were Graham Greene, Evelyn Waugh, F. Scott Fitzgerald, Ernest Hemingway, William Faulkner, and Sinclair Lewis.

When he published *The Razor's Edge* in 1943 his contemporaries were Norman Mailer and Irwin Shaw.

When he published *Purely for My Pleasure*, his last book, in 1962 his contemporaries were J. D. Salinger and John Updike.

Maugham was never the spokesman for an age or a generation or a decade. His work was not contemporary in that sense. He did not write the great Edwardian novel, or the great between-the-wars novel, or the great World War I or World War II novel, although he lived and wrote through all those periods. What he did was create an oeuvre, a body of work, all of it bearing the imprint of his particular sensibility. He was convinced that building an oeuvre was the mark of the great writer. "Copiousness is not a defect in a writer," he said, "it is a merit. All the great authors have had it. Of course not all their production is of value; only the mediocre can sustain a constant level. It is because the great authors wrote a great deal that now and then they produced great works."

By "contemporariness" Gertrude Stein meant what would last, what would remain of value to subsequent generations of readers. This is the watershed of literature, dividing period pieces from classics. Many books are judged great in their own time and then are forgotten. They please the reader because they are shaped by the same forces that mold his nonreading hours, they recreate a sense of the present with which he can identify, but the work's value dies as soon as the present becomes the past. The book that endures because succeeding generations find it meaningful is on its way to becoming a classic. Much of Maugham's work has endured, many of his books are still in print, and his plays are often revived. *Of Human Bondage* can be regarded as a modern classic, in that each generation finds in it an echo of its own miseries.

If Maugham had been willing to balance the ledger he would have found cause for cheer, but it was his nature to believe his bad notices, as he had written to Ada Leverson back in 1908. He had not changed, although he now kept up the pretense that he did not care what was said about him. In February 1934 it came to his attention that Alexander Woollcott had made fun of a sentence of his in his Town Crier broadcast. He asked Woollcott for a copy of the script. "I hope you will not hesitate for fear of hurting my feelings," he wrote, "since in matters of this sort I have no sensitiveness. I take great pains with my writing but I am conscious that as one grows older it is very easy to fall into mannerisms." Woollcott wrote back that he had merely chided Maugham for using one word instead of another. "I was afraid you had discovered me using a pet phrase or a mannered construction with indecent frequency and I was haste [sic] to correct myself in time," Maugham said.[15]

In March he went south to finish his research on his second Spanish book, *Don Fernando*, and was caught in the middle of a street riot. "I got all the material I wanted for a book," he wrote Bert Alanson, "and now they can have all the revolutions they want."[16]

In May he went on his annual spring trip to London, again to see his daughter, who had been named the most beautiful debutante of the year, and his Mayfair friends. He was fought over by the two reigning London hostesses of the thirties, Sybil Colefax and Emerald Cunard. Sybil Colefax, the wife of a prominent English jurist, was two years older than Maugham. It was said that she had launched herself in literary London by inviting Shaw and H. G. Wells, telling each that the other wanted to meet him. She lived at Argyll House in Chelsea, not far from Syrie Maugham, with whom she competed as a hostess and decorator. For thirty years her home was the gathering place for political, artistic, and literary people. Her generosity was proverbial, as was her sharing of friends with friends. Virginia Woolf called her "a shiny cupboard, carved with acanthus leaves, to hold whiskey." Her handwriting, someone said, was like a collection of primitive fishhooks. When one of her guests complained about not being able to read the invitation, she said, "After all, you are here." Maugham went there regularly when he was in London.

Emerald Cunard, the same age as her archrival, was born Maud Burke in San Francisco. She came to England, and wanting to meet George Moore, changed the place cards at a dinner party they were both invited to so that she could sit next to him. She eventually became his mistress and longtime friend. In 1895 she married Sir Bache Cunard, the grandson of the founder of the shipping line, who was twenty years her senior. His chief interest was fox hunting in Northamptonshire, where he had a large property called Neville Holt, but the only game his wife was interested in hunting were artists and writers.

Sir Bache finally agreed, at Maud's constant urging, to invite George Moore to Neville Holt for a weekend, but was shocked when he scoffed at religion, saying, "You can't change God into a biscuit." In 1911 they separated. Sir Bache kept Neville Holt and the Fernie hounds and Maud got a house on Grosvenor Square. She had an eye for the rising young man, and entertained on a grand scale. (In 1926, after the death of her husband, who did not mention her in his will, she changed her name to Emerald.) The great love of her life was the short and lecherous Thomas Beecham, then conductor at Covent Garden, who had been involved as corespondent in several divorce cases. She did not like homosexuals, whom she called "popinjays," but never suspected that Maugham was one.[17]

While in London that spring Maugham received from the *Bookman* a request to contribute to a symposium in which writers were asked the following: "1. Can you, as an individual, declare the state of things today, even in our own country, as in their totality humanly bearable? 2. If not, can you as an artist disregard that state of things? 3. If you cannot, how would you define, plainly in a brief sentence or so, the relevance of your art to these existing conditions?"

This was the kind of thing Maugham thought was nonsense, and he wrote back: "I am not going to answer your questions. Why should a professional writer, who makes his living by his pen, cry stinking fish?"[18] He was on principle antisymposium. The only such request he could not turn down was from his Capri friend Compton Mackenzie, who was editing the *Gramophone Monthly Review* and wrote three dozen distinguished contemporaries to ask them about their favorite songs and composers. Maugham replied:

> What a devilish fellow you are to ask a harmless and respectable gentleman like myself to answer such questions, but here they are:
>   Favorite Song—The Prize Song.
>   Favorite Composer—Wagner.
>   Favorite Music—The Fire Music.
>   Favorite Singer—Lotte Lehmann.
> Curses on Your Head![19]

It was an unusual year for Maugham in that he had stopped writing plays and did not have a new book out. The Maugham industry kept going on its own momentum, however. A collection of thirty short stories, called *East and West* in the United States and *Altogether* in England, came out, as did reprints of five novels, *Liza of Lambeth, The Painted Veil, Ashenden, Cakes and Ale,* and *The Narrow Corner,* bound uniformly in rose-colored cloth and representing the first titles in an ambitious "Collected Edition of the Works of W. Somerset Maugham." The author contributed a new preface to each volume. His play agents in America sold the film rights to *The Sacred Flame* and *East of Suez,* but the latter was never made. As John Rumsey of the American Play Company explained it: "Several million churchmen are attacking 'indecent' films, [and] motion picture companies are going to the other extreme in their search for material. You will say, of course, that *East of Suez* could not be considered indecent, but when I tell you that fine pictures like *Of Human Bondage* and another fine English motion picture called *The Constant Nymph* have both been put on the indecent list by churchmen you will realize how far these fanatical reformers have gone."[20]

In June, back at the Mauresque, Maugham invited Barbara Back to join him later in the summer at the Austrian spa of Badgastein, "which we are told is pleasant and amusing and very good for harassed nerves."[21] An example of his attention to detail is a letter he wrote her husband Ivor concerning the trip:

> Will you see that she does not bring a trunk too large to go into the car and will you see that it locks because it will have to go back to Cap Ferrat by Grande Vitesse. Will you see that she brings her golf clubs. Will you see that she brings the same sort of clothes as she would if she were going to stay at Scarborough. It may be chilly and it may be

very hot. . . . Will you also see that she brings shoes that she can walk in. Not too pointed and the heels not too high. Will you see that she brings a small valise for the journey back by car from Bad Gastein. Will you also give her something she can take if she gets a blister on her heel, a dislocated knee and gall-stones. If I can think of anything more in the next few days I will let you know.[22]

Hearing that his seventeen-year-old nephew Robin had arrived in Vienna that June, Maugham offered to send him some money if he ran short. "If you get into any hole, trouble or jamb [sic], I recommend you to communicate with me rather than with the above-mentioned sainted parents," he wrote. "Having led a vicious but not unpleasant life for a vast number of years, I am conscious that there are difficulties which even the best brought-up young man cannot always avoid and being as you know a hardened cynic I have a great tolerance for the follies of the human race."[23]

Robin was the only son of Maugham's barrister brother Frederic, who also had three daughters, Diana and Kate Mary (both published novelists), and Honor Earl, a portrait painter. Robin had just left Eton, where he had been as miserable as his uncle at the King's School. Small and slight of build, he had been bullied and teased, and nicknamed "the walking dictionary" because he used long words. He had responded to the sexual advances of older boys in the hope that they would treat him kindly. Reading *Of Human Bondage*, he identified with Philip Carey. He was musical, sang in the choir, took piano lessons, and wanted to go to Vienna to become a pianist, as Philip had gone to Heidelberg. It would be an escape from his stern, punctilious father, whose every word was a rebuke, and an example of whose tone was: "I have told you time and again that it is the sign of a second-rate mind to sprinkle your every sentence with stock phrases such as 'well actually,' or 'as a matter of fact.' Now please tell us what you want to say directly, without meaningless verbiage."[24]

Robin wanted to follow in his uncle's rather than his father's footsteps. His uncle was a man of the world, who lived the good life in the south of France. Robin wanted to be a writer and started a literary magazine at Eton called *Sixpenny*. He sent his stories to Maugham, who replied: "Your first story has a slight sentimentality which is surprising in anyone who bears your name, but I liked the second story very much. I think it is very cleverly written. You will remember, I trust, that you are seventeen and that to write is a very difficult business

379

so do not think that you can achieve anything without an immense amount of work. It is a very good thing to see oneself in print. I think it shows one what one's work looks like in a way that is impossible to get even from a typescript."[25]

Maugham saw in Robin the son he never had. He befriended him, gave him advice, took an interest in his work, and settled a trust fund on him. Maugham played the role of benevolent uncle so well that young Robin preferred him to his father. When he was in London he invited Robin to lunch at the Garrick, and in the summer Robin had an open invitation to the Mauresque.

In his autobiography, *Escape from the Shadows* (the shadows being his famous father and famous uncle), Robin tells a story that deserves to be repeated only so that it may be refuted. According to Robin's account, Gerald Haxton was there to show him around when he arrived in Vienna in June 1934. Gerald went back to the Mauresque and started writing Robin letters that began "Beloved one" and "Sweetheart." Robin thought Gerald was being facetious and replied in a similar vein. Gerald then sent Robin a ticket to Venice so that they could meet. He took Robin to his double room at the Danieli and tried to make love to him. Robin pushed him away, explaining that his letters had been written in jest, but apparently spent the night in Gerald's room, for he was there the next morning when the phone rang. He says he heard the following conversation:

"Good morning, my dear Gerald."

"Good morning, Willie."

"And was the young man satisfactory in bed?"

"I'll telephone you later."

Robin says he felt shocked and disgusted, and wondered whether Maugham had planned that Gerald should seduce him because he loathed Maugham's father, or because it amused him to think of his own lover having his nephew, or because he hoped that once Robin had been seduced by Gerald he would accept his own advances.

This story is improbable for a number of reasons. When Maugham wrote Robin in June to offer money, he made it clear that Gerald was with him at the Mauresque. There was no way Gerald could have met Robin in Vienna. There was no way Gerald could have tried to seduce Robin in Venice, for he remained with Maugham at the Mauresque until they joined Barbara Back in Austria in July. By that time the Austrian chancellor, Engelbert Dollfuss, had been assassinated, and a Nazi putsch was expected. Robin's mother was worried about him and urged him to come home. When she did not hear from him, she asked Maugham to put him on a plane to London, and Maugham went to fetch him by the lake at Klopeinersee, where he was staying.

Moreover, it would have been out of character for Maugham to plot Robin's seduction. Maugham wanted authority over Robin, which would have been compromised by physical intimacy. There is no hint of any such intimacy in the more than one hundred letters he wrote his nephew. In addition, one wonders how Robin could have heard Maugham's end of the telephone conversation. Finally, it was out of character for Gerald, whom we have seen mocking the entries on love in Beverley Nichols' copy of Bartlett's *Quotations*, to write love letters.

According to Robin, Maugham took him to dinner in Badgastein before sending him home that July. They had blinis and blue trout, and Maugham told him: "I would like, if I may, to give you a word of advice. You are quite an attractive boy. Don't waste your assets. Your charm won't last for long."[26]

In August, Willie and Gerald went to Salzburg, taking excursions on the various lakes. "Gerald wishes you could see the leather shorts he has bought himself," he wrote Barbara Back. "He can't help yodeling when he puts them on."[27]

Maugham was back at the Mauresque on August 12, receiving visitors, among them Carl Van Vechten, who took his photograph. He received copies a month later and wrote "Dear Carlo" that he was as pleased "as if I had written the Encyclopaedia Britannica with one hand."[28] Still trying to set up his literary prize with funds from the sale of his manuscripts, he offered a New York dealer, Henry Schuman, exclusive rights for six months to dispose of them. He had fifty items, including *Of Human Bondage* and its never-published early version. He was hoping to get $50,000 for the lot. "It does not seem to me an extravagant price for fifty items," he wrote Schuman on October 8, 1934, "and I should have thought a dealer buying them could by selling them separately make a handsome profit for himself. But the best sum I have been offered so far for the whole lot is seven thousand and five hundred pounds and so it seems to me it would probably be better for me to attempt to dispose of the items separately. I have had three thousand five hundred pounds offered me for the two versions of *Of Human Bondage*."[29] Nothing came of his dealings with Schuman.

Gossipy letters arrived from Barbara Back telling of the sexual involvements of Beverley Nichols and his lover, Cyril Butcher, a hard-drinking clerk turned actor. Maugham was offended by her holier-than-thou tone. "Everybody's sexual affairs are his own business," he wrote. "It is idiotic to set oneself up on a pedestal and turn up one's nose. My own belief is that there is hardly anyone whose sexual life, if it were broadcast, would not fill the world at large with surprise and horror."[30]

In December, Maugham went to England to see his friends, and had lunch with his fellow agent to Russia, Robert Bruce Lockhart. "Maugham is a peculiar man," Lockhart wrote in his diary. "Has terrific inferiority complex, hates people yet is a snob and cannot refuse a luncheon where he is to meet a countess. Life ruined by wife who is coarse and irritating. Once he was having tea in his own house with a friend, when his wife came in. Her voice downstairs irritated him so much that he hid behind the sofa and stayed there until his wife left again."[31] Although divorced for five years, Maugham continued to tell spiteful stories about Syrie.

He was back at the Mauresque for Christmas, where he gave an enjoyable party for H. G. Wells and his new mistress, Moura Budberg. Wells had first met this Slavic femme fatale in Petrograd in 1914, when she served as his interpreter. In 1917 she had an affair with Lockhart, and was arrested and imprisoned on suspicion of plotting to overthrow Lenin. She became Gorki's mistress and joined him in Berlin in 1922, but when Gorki returned to Russia she went to London and took up with Wells. She remained with Wells until his death in 1946, but would not marry him. "We live in open sin," Wells told a friend, "but for two grandparents with lives of their own there is neither marrying nor giving in marriage."[32] Maugham once asked Moura, a tempestuous and beautiful woman with high cheekbones and expressive eyes, what she saw in the paunchy, played-out writer. "He smells of honey," she said.[33]

Gerald, who had gone to bed exhausted after the party, was taking care of a Great Dane he had brought back from Austria. "A Great Dane is a dog, dear," Maugham wrote Barbara Back. "It is quite huge, but very sweet and extremely decorative. . . . Oh, by the way, Gerald and I are quarreling madly over your soap. He will use it on his hands though I tell him it should only be used on the face. No difference in my complexion."[34] Only with Barbara Back and a few others did Maugham drop his guard and allow himself to make mild homosexual jokes such as the one about the Great Dane.

While in London in December he had run into an old acquaintance who would make an important contribution to the editing of his manuscripts. This was Eddie Marsh, as curious a relic of the Edwardian age as Augustus Hare had been of the Victorian era. Born in 1872, Marsh was Maugham's contemporary. He had gone to Cambridge and then joined the civil service, where his urbanity and discretion led him to become private secretary to Churchill, Asquith, and Chamberlain. He had, Harold Nicolson said, a gift for allaying the irritability of cabinet ministers. But this was only one facet of the man. He was primarily known as a patron of the arts, and a London taste-maker who knew everyone and held opinions on everything.

A fixture at fashionable dinner parties, Marsh had a high, reedy voice and bristling eyebrows, and wore a monocle on a black silk ribbon and shirts with starched fronts. The little crash of his monocle falling onto his shirtfront was like a call signal announcing his presence. His humor was on the precious side. At a picnic in the south of France where cold meats were served, one of the ladies complained about the light in her eyes and he said, "My dear, it must be the *glare* from the veal." Renowned as a raconteur, he was said to rehearse the stories with which he hoped to captivate dinner parties. One of these was that he was strolling with the Duke of Devonshire and they passed a silversmith's. The duke pointed to six silver rings in a velvet case in the window and asked what they were. "Napkin rings," Marsh said. "What are napkin rings?" the duke asked. Marsh explained that they were for holding rolled napkins so that they could be used again. "Good God," the duke said.

Marsh was equally renowned for his generosity. Among the writers whom he helped financially were James Joyce, Dylan Thomas, and D. H. Lawrence. He was not as rich as he was thought to be, but the origin of his money was curious. His great-grandfather, Spencer Perceval, Prime Minister in 1812, was shot dead as he was entering the House of Commons by a disgruntled citizen called Bellingham. Commons voted 50,000 pounds in trust for the surviving children. The eldest boy was Marsh's grandfather, and about a century later Eddie Marsh found himself the heir to one-sixth of the trust. He called it his "Perceval murder money" and used it to help artists. His helpfulness was such that it became the object of jokes. The story was told that a young woman approached him at a ball and said, "Mr. Marsh, I want you to do something for me." "Yes," Eddie said. "Mr. Marsh, I want you to marry me." "When?" Eddie asked. His other notorious trait was an infinite capacity for appreciation. His friends played a game of trying to discover a book or a play or a painting that he disliked. "Eddie's a miserable fellow," Arnold Bennett complained, "he likes everything."

Eddie Marsh had one of those unambitious natures that prefers helping others to doing original work, but he made a genuine contribution

383

to literature. In editing five volumes of Georgian poetry, including the work of his close friend Rupert Brooke, he was largely responsible for defining the poetic spirit of the postwar years. Max Beerbohm called him "one of the ornaments of his time," but he was more than that. He was a literary figure who toiled in the shadow of others.[35]

Maugham had first met him when Churchill was at the War Office, before World War I. He saw him at Edmund Gosse's and asked him to dinner as an extra man. On this occasion, in December 1934, Maugham was chatting with him at a party when Marsh mentioned that he was correcting the proofs of Churchill's *History of the English-Speaking Peoples*. Churchill had told him that his notes were an education in writing. Maugham asked how he could undertake anything so tiresome. It was boring enough to correct one's own proofs; to correct someone else's must be deadly. To Maugham's surprise, Marsh said there were few things he enjoyed more. Maugham had finished his book of Spanish impressions, *Don Fernando*, and was tempted to ask Marsh to look at the proofs. But he thought of Marsh as a highbrow who mixed with highbrows, and he was humiliatingly conscious that they did not consider him a member of their set. It was Marsh who offered to go over Maugham's proofs. "He spoke," Maugham recalled, "as though I were positively doing him a favor." Marsh felt that way too, for he jotted in his diary on that day: "There's glory for me!"

Thus began a collaboration that lasted eighteen years. From 1935, with *Don Fernando*, to 1953 and *The Vagrant Mood*, Maugham received from Eddie Marsh hundreds of pages of critical notes on fourteen of his books. Maugham suggested that they should come to some sort of business arrangement, for why should Eddie work long hours and get nothing for it? Marsh would not hear of it and persisted in saying that what he did was pure pleasure. "If in the last 20 years I have learned to write better English," Maugham said, "the credit is largely owing to Eddie." When he read the first batch of notes, Maugham was startled: "Here was [sic] not the few casual corrections I had expected, but an imposing series of remarks on punctuation, grammar, style, and fact . . . for instance, in *Tom Jones*, Fielding made Partridge see Garrick play *Hamlet* in London on a day in 1745, when in point of fact Garrick was in Dublin and did not return to London till six months later. Eddie would never have passed such an error, nor in the same great novel would he have allowed a respectable woman to have two children seven years apart when she had been married only five years."

Maugham was astonished to see that Marsh, so lenient in society, was a despot when it came to grammar. In fact, Marsh called what he did "diabolization," the art of finding fault and being as carping as possible for the eventual benefit of the work. "His comments are by turn scornful, pained, acid and vituperative," Maugham complained. "No obscurity escapes his stricture, no redundance his satire, and no clumsiness his obloquy. I think few authors could suffer this ordeal and remain persuaded that they wrote tolerably well."

Occasionally he fought back. When he wrote "lunch" and Marsh changed it to "luncheon" he protested that it was natural to say, "Will you come and have lunch with me?" "But it isn't natural to me," Eddie responded. "I won't come and have lunch with you. I will, however, if I am disengaged, be pleased to come and have luncheon with you."

Maugham knew that in Eddie Marsh he had found a rare creature totally devoid of envy or personal spite, whose sole concern was language. Marsh kept a brown envelope he called his "vanity bag," in which there was this letter from Maugham:

> I sometimes read in the papers (A) that I write well and (B) that I am modest. They little know, the people who say this, that it is not I but you who write well; and as for modesty, those pages of corrections of yours are iron heels on great Nazi boots that grind my face into the dust; each time I say to myself—Now this time I'm sure he won't see much to find fault with, and then the proofs come back . . . all my conceit has got to be hurriedly packed away again. So it is not only the correctness of my language that I owe to you, but also the beauty of my character.

The curious image of bootheels grinding his face was in keeping with the vocabulary of bondage that Maugham instinctively adopted, but the feeling of gratitude, although oddly expressed, was genuine.[36]

Maugham spent the first months of 1935 in Cap Ferrat waiting for May, when he would go to London for the publication of *Don Fernando*. In February, Robin, now at Trinity College, Cambridge, wrote to tell him that his first attempt at writing a play had flopped. Maugham, at his most avuncular, told his nephew: "You are so monstrously conceited that I am afraid you will find failure very difficult to bear . . . to bear failure with courage is the best proof of character that anyone can give. . . . You will find that people forget the failures of others very quickly. . . . My last piece of advice is not to let anyone see your mortification, but whatever you fancy people are saying about you to go on with your ordinary life as though nothing unpleasant had happened to you."[37] Having had his share of failure, Maugham knew that the only way to deal with it was to step carefully over the wreckage and move on.

His variations on Spanish themes came out to glowing reviews. Never had his style won higher praise, which must have pleased Eddie Marsh as much as the author. *The Times Literary Supplement* on June 27, 1935, called it "a beautifully written book." The critic for the *Forum* in September said it was "almost flawlessly written." Graham Greene said in the *Spectator* on June 21 that *Don Fernando* was "Mr. Maugham's best book." "I have never read a book with more excitement or amusement," Greene said.[38] "Mr. Maugham [is] at the peak of his achievement as an artist." Maugham knew that he owed a debt to Eddie Marsh, for after receiving his first comments, he had written: "I scampered hurriedly through your notes, and then I went straight down to the Bath Club to look you out in *Who's Who*. I heave a great sigh of relief. Thank heaven you'll last my time, for what I should do without you I can't imagine."[39] But Marsh did not last his time. He died in 1953, and Maugham was to continue writing, unedited, for ten years after his death.

All praise aside, *Don Fernando* was one of the least structured of Maugham's books. He threw together material he had gathered for an unwritten picaresque novel set in the time of Philip III, material based on his travels and his reading of more than two hundred books on the period in Spanish. *Don Fernando* rambles and digresses, moving from the story of the founder of the Jesuits, Saint Ignatius of Loyola, to discourses on El Greco and Cervantes, to a celebration of the values of Spain's Golden Age. As Charles Poore pointed out in *The New York Times* on July 21, reading it was "like reading all the material someone has gathered for a historical novel, and everything else that had entered his mind as he went along."[40]

In London, Maugham saw old friends and made new ones. At lunch on May 4 at Emerald Cunard's he met Henry (Chips) Channon, another curious figure of the period, whom he would see from time to time over the years. Channon, the son of a Chicago businessman, devoted his life to repudiating the land of his birth and making himself accepted by London society. "I have put my whole life's work into my anglicization," he wrote in the diaries published after his death. "The more I know of American civilization, the more I despise it. It is a menace to the peace and future of the world. If it triumphs, the old civilizations, which love beauty and peace and the arts and rank and privilege, will pass from the picture. And all we will have left will be Fords and cinemas. Ugh!"

As a young man Channon went to Paris in 1917 with the American Red Cross. He claimed that he had once sat at dinner between Proust and Cocteau, and that Cocteau had told him that his eyes were set by Cartier. If they were bright then, they sparkled even more when he came to England and made friends with lords and ladies.

Chips was short, bustling, reddish of hair, and anxious to please. Unselfconscious about having enough money to pursue social success, he wrote: "I belong definitely in the order of those who have—and through no effort of my own, which is such a joy." He was taken up by the American-born Emerald Cunard and by Juliet Duff, a pillar of the English aristocracy. Channon was able to measure the chasm between old world and new when Lady Juliet took Doris Duke to visit Wilton Castle, the ancestral home of the Herbert family, which Holbein had designed. She showed Miss Duke the great double-cube room with the portrait of the Herbert family by Van Dyck. They reached the great hall. "This tapestry was a gift of Henry VIII to the Herberts," she said. "I'm not interested in textiles," Doris Duke replied.

Chips Channon judged everyone according to the lofty standards of the *parvenu*. The only essential question was whether one qualified as an English gentleman. Thus he found Hugh Walpole "noisy, common and uninteresting, and quite devoid of the rarities—the *voluptés* almost— that make an English gentleman, such as Thomas-made boots and Eton-made inflections."

Since he did not belong to the nobility by birth, the next best thing was to marry into it, even though his sexual interests did not lie in that direction, and in 1933 he married Lady Honor Guinness, the eldest daughter of the second Earl of Iveagh. They set up house at 5 Belgrave Square, next door to Prince George, Duke of Kent. Monsieur Boudin of Jansen designed the dining room—at a cost of more than 60,000 pounds—in imitation of the dining room of Schloss Nymphenburg's Amalienburg. Chips gave lavish parties, lacing the cocktails with Benzedrine to make sure everyone had a good time. "I am the Lord of Hosts," he wrote, "the only person with a large establishment who entertains on the grand scale and enjoys it." In politics he was pro-Chamberlain and anti-Churchill, with strong sympathies for the Germans and an undisguised streak of anti-Semitism.

At the lunch at Emerald Cunard's, Chips studied the guests. There were "a lot of boring old antiques," and there was Sir Harry Stonor, who had been in attendance on British monarchs for half a century, as Quarterly Waiter in Ordinary to Queen Victoria, and Gentleman Usher and Groom in Waiting to King Edward VII and George V. Stonor had it over Maugham in Chips's eyes. "Though he [Maugham] is a brilliant writer," he wrote, "he is not, of course, a gentleman. . . . There was a trace of subservience in Maugham's manner to the supercilious Stonor and a touch of contempt in Sir Harry's condescension to Maugham."[41] What Chips did not know was that Maugham was also studying him and filing him away for future use in one of his novels.

On May 13 Robert Bruce Lockhart gave a lunch party for Maugham and invited Harold Nicolson and Moura Budberg. Lockhart cultivated Maugham and seems genuinely to have enjoyed his company, but in his diary he was critical of the man and his work. "Conrad was very good on women," he wrote. "Maugham as pederast, always cruel and unfair to women. Discussed literature with Michael Arlen, who is a Conrad fan, puts him miles above Maugham."[42]

On May 28 Maugham attended a celebration for Marie Tempest's stage jubilee. She was over seventy and had been on the stage for fifty years. In face and figure she looked middle-aged. She led a highly disciplined life and was happy with her middle-aged husband Graham Browne, who directed her in many productions. She was still appearing in "Marie Tempest" parts, as she had in 1908, when she starred in Maugham's second successful comedy, *Mrs. Dot.* The jubilee, sponsored by Lord Camrose's *Daily Telegraph*, included a lunch at the Savoy, at which speeches were made. Maugham was one of the speakers. "Others will have written of Marie Tempest's wonderful talent, of her charm and irresistible gaiety," he said. "I have written this because it may have escaped the notice of many who had admired her brilliant performances that they are due not only to her natural gifts, which are eminent, but to patience, assiduity, industry, and discipline. Without these it is impossible to excel in any of the arts. But this is something that not all who pursue them know."[43]

After the lunch there was a Grand Matinee on the stage of the Drury Lane Theatre, at which she performed excerpts from her best roles. The king and queen attended, as did every important English actor and dramatist.

In July, Maugham was off for his annual cure, this time at Badgastein. Robin had asked if he might come to stay at the Mauresque. Maugham replied on July 13: "You know of course that you are always welcome if you want to stay here—with a boy friend, for I could not cope with you alone—but only if your respected parents permit. For if they look upon this house as likely to corrupt your morals and weaken your character, it is not for me to say stuff and nonsense."[44] This was hardly the tone of a man who had tried to arrange the seduction of his nephew, and Robin found other ways to spend the summer.

In his efforts once more to sell his manuscripts Maugham had enlisted the aid of Marie (Missy) Meloney, editor of the New York *Herald Tribune* Sunday Magazine, who did the rounds of New York dealers. Maugham explained that he wanted to found a prize to be used for travel by British writers, who he felt were too provincial. "If only one out of five benefited from a year's travel it would be worth much to English literature," he said, "and so, I like to think, to the welfare of the world. . . . I cannot found this prize for less than 10,000 pounds—that is the sum I am asking for my MSS—and I do not think it is excessive. . . . I have had this scheme in my heart for many years . . . it would be a great pleasure if I could carry it out in my lifetime."[45] But again there were no takers.

Through most of 1935 Maugham was working on a kind of autobiography, for which he had as yet no title. He was also planning his first working trip outside Europe since moving into the Mauresque in 1927. As part of the research for the novel *Christmas Holiday*, based on the French murderer whose trial he had attended, he was going to French Guiana to meet the young man, who had been sent to one of the penal colonies there.

Arriving in New York with Gerald in November aboard the liner *Europa*, after an absence of eight years, Maugham was pursued by the press. He said that he had given up plays because "a novelist can have a lot of fun boring people." He said he had seen twenty-eight of his thirty plays but did not want to see the films made from his work because "they change your story, and I am not crazy to have seen something I have written done by a film director in another way." In December the New York *American* wrote: "To be invited to swim in Willie Maugham's pool is tantamount to being invited to loll in the reigning dowager's box in the Horseshoe Circle."[46]

He and Gerald made their way to French Guiana via Haiti. In December, Haxton sent Carl Van Vechten a postcard from Haiti showing a naked black woman, with the message: "Am still on the wagon. . . . I'm following your good example."[47] In French Guiana they visited the penal colony of St. Laurent du Maroni. Maugham was sixty-one, but the promise of finding new material offset the discomfort of the trip.

The French had been deporting criminals to Guiana since 1794, and the eighteenth-century method of execution, the guillotine, was still in use. The executions, orders for which had to be confirmed by the Minister of the Interior in Paris, fascinated Maugham. The condemned man did not know his time had come until the warden appeared in his cell with the words "Have courage." The executioner Maugham saw at work had been recruited from among the convicts and was paid a hundred francs per head. He was given the silent treatment by the other convicts, and had two mastiffs to guard him, for the previous executioner had been found knifed to death—an incident upon which Maugham based a short story. The guillotine was in a small room inside the prison. A banana stem, the same size as a man's neck, was used for practice to make sure it worked smoothly. The whole operation took thirty seconds. When the head had fallen, the executioner held it up by the ears to show the witnesses and said, "*Au nom du peuple français justice est faite.*" Blood spurted over the executioner, who was given a new set of clothes after each job. Maugham was told the story of the doctor who asked a man about to be guillotined to blink three times after his head was cut off. The doctor swore that the man had blinked twice.

As always when he traveled, he had come armed with letters of introduction. He was welcomed cordially by the prison director, a short, stout man in a white uniform, with the cross of the Legion of Honor on his tunic. His salary was 60,000 francs a year and he had obtained his job through political influence. He had a large white frame house facing the sea, with a chandelier in every room. He was looking forward to retirement, when he would build himself a house on the Riviera. Maugham and Gerald were put up in a bungalow that belonged to the governor in Cayenne, and took their meals at the local hotel.[48]

The convicts, in pink-and-white pajamas, round straw hats, and shoes with wooden soles, had the run of the town, and walked to their various jobs as clerks or servants. They suffered from fever and hookworm and the knowledge that they would never see their homes again. The *relégués*, or habitual criminals, sent to St. Laurent for the protection of society, were given better treatment than the murderers. They caught butterflies and beetles and made ornaments from buffalo horn, which they sold in order to buy the great St. Laurent luxury, rum.

Maugham estimated that three-quarters of the convicts were there for murder. Among these were the two men assigned to clean his bungalow. "I may tell you that I took the precaution to bar the windows and lock the doors of my bedroom when I went to bed," he told Barbara Back.[49] Curious about motive, he found that it was usually money. "In one way or another," he said, "money was at the bottom of every murder I inquired into but one. The exception was a young lad, a shepherd, who had raped a little girl and when she cried out, afraid people would hear, he had strangled her. He is only eighteen now."[50] When he asked a convict why he had slit his wife's throat, the man replied, "*Manque d'entente*" ("We didn't get along"). He could not help thinking that if the generality of men killed their wives on that account no penal settlement would be large enough to hold them.[51]

Pleased with his material, Maugham left St. Laurent du Maroni in January 1936 with the final impression of "a brutishness that must reduce all but a very few to apathy and despair."[52] He and Gerald returned to New York by way of the Panama Canal. "You can 'ave the Panama Canal, and the zone too, if you want it," Gerald wrote Barbara Back.[53]

They took the *Twentieth Century* to New York, arriving on March 22, and stayed at the Hangar Club, 30 East Sixty-third Street. A collection of very short stories he had written for *Cosmopolitan* magazine at intervals between 1923 and 1929 had come out in February under the title *Cosmopolitans*. The critics felt that the stories were second-best. "It would be impossible for Mr. Maugham to write a dull story, or an incompetent one," wrote Florence Haxton Britten in the New York *Herald Tribune* on February 22. "But in this collection of twenty-nine little anecdotes of the wide, wide world and the seven seas he comes as close to going over the edge about twenty-nine times as Charlie Chaplin on roller skates does in 'Modern Times.' His recoveries—like Charlie's —are occasionally superb." Graham Greene in the *Spectator* on April 17 said that the stories had "no echo of the general life," and Peter Quennell, in the *New Statesman and Nation* on April 4, said that "the stories flick by like houses and gardens seen from a railway carriage: no sooner have they aroused our interest than they vanish for good."[54] The London *Times* titled its review "The Mixture as Before," a term the British use when they ask a pharmacist to refill a prescription. It was on the basis of *Cosmopolitans*, however, that Christopher Morley nominated Maugham as the most readable writer of his time.[55]

In New York he heard from Robin, who was in Berlin and had

important news: he was in love. His uncle congratulated him on having that "pleasant experience" and advised him, in his best tutorial tone, to go to the Kaiser Friedrich Museum and not to miss "the archaic Greek statue on the ground floor, and above all don't miss the early XVIII century stuff all the way at the top. . . . I seem to remember a bishop or two in windswept draperies that struck me as quite wonderful." Again he invited Robin to stay at the Mauresque whenever he liked but to bring a boyfriend, as "you will find Gerald and me alone very dull."[56]

In May 1936 Maugham went to London, where his twenty-one-year-old daughter was about to be married to Vincent Paravicini, the son of the Swiss minister to England. On July 24 he gave Liza away at St. Margaret's, a fashionable church in Westminster. Vincent Paravicini was said to be one of the best-looking men in London—tall, but not too tall, dark, but not swarthy. He was the physical opposite of Maugham, who thought him "a most beautiful young man."[57] Syrie did not particularly like Vincent but decided that he was acceptable. Liza was short and blonde and pert, with bright eyes and a lively face. The London newspapers dubbed them the best-looking bride and groom of the month. The columnist William Hickey said of the wedding: "Is it a Cochran first night? No, it's an issue of *Vogue* come to life."

Liza wore a Schiaparelli headdress and a white brocade gown embroidered in silver lilies, with a long double train and a tulle veil. Her bridesmaids were Tessa Kindersley, Sylvia Regis de Oliveira (the daughter of the Brazilian ambassador), Virginia Gilliat, and Lady Anne Bridgeman, who wore a black patch over one eye, having been kicked by a horse. The pages were dressed in Swiss Guards' uniforms. Among the guests were a royal princess, a burnoused sheik, and a large contingent of the diplomatic corps. Lady Mendl, a decorator and friend of Syrie's, was there, as were Serge Lifar, Osbert Sitwell, Marie Tempest, Jessica Mitford, and assorted lords and dukes. At the reception at the Swiss Legation the guests consumed a wedding cake designed by Oliver Messel, the noted stage designer. The wedding presents stood the test of elegance and included pale-blue sheets embroidered with white swans, given by Lady Jowitt.[58] As her gift, Syrie decorated the young couple's London flat at 15 Wilton Street.

Maugham's presents were a house near Henley-on-Thames and a large block of the shares that Bert Alanson was holding for him. Pleased by the match, he arranged for the newlyweds to spend their honeymoon at the Mauresque. The only drawback of the ceremony for him was that he had to see Syrie again. He sat next to her in St. Margaret's but uttered not a single word. He refused to be photographed with her, scooting away when a camera was trained upon them. He continued to bear her considerable ill will, feeling that she was a futile woman, who had botched Liza's education. As he later told Garson Kanin: "Liza has never shown the slightest inclination toward looking after herself or supporting herself in any way. . . . This unfortunate condition is entirely the fault of her . . . mother, a foolish woman who has never been interested in anything really except . . . social position. She is, and always has been, a snob. She brought Liza up to believe that nothing in life is more important than the right sort of marriage. I blame her not only for what she caused me to miss in my life, but for what I know she is going to cause Liza to miss in hers."[59] This was a case of the pot calling the kettle black, for Maugham was himself a snob, and he had shown no inclination to fill the gaps in Liza's education.

While Liza and Vincent honeymooned, Willie and Gerald went to Budapest. They sat in cafés on the Danube, drank apricot cordial, and listened to tzigane music.[60] Moving back into the Mauresque, Maugham invited his brother Frederic and his wife and Lady Juliet Duff to come for a short stay. Considered one of the most brilliant lawyers of his generation, Frederic had risen to High Court Judge and Lord Justice of Appeal. His career was as successful as his younger brother's—which did not make him any more amiable. It was his first stay at the Mauresque, and he was tight-lipped and censorious. He disapproved of his younger brother's life-style, thought the Mauresque too theatrical to be in good taste, and made ironic comments about the French cuisine. Maugham was amused after his departure to hear Juliet Duff say of him: "He has such wonderfully high spirits, hasn't he? He's simply bubbling over with fun all the time."[61]

It was at some point during the summer of 1936 that the painter Marie Laurencin, whose favorite subject was young girls, told Maugham that she wanted to paint him. She was a Riviera neighbor, and Maugham owned four of her works, which he had hung in the dining room. When she came to lunch she inspected her pictures. "What a pretty little thing," she murmured about the first. Before the second she said one word: "Exquisite." In front of the third she gasped, turned to Maugham, and said, "There can be no doubt about it, it's a masterpiece." At the last picture she turned to the man who had asked her to lunch and said, "It's delicious."

Maugham reminded her that he was not the customary Laurencin subject, a young thing with a milk-and-rose complexion and gazelle

393

eyes, but an elderly gentleman with wrinkles and pouches. But to Laurencin it did not matter. As he sat for the portrait in her studio she told him the story of her life and loves. Her great love had been a famous French politician who was so busy that he could see her only at eight in the morning, on the way to the office. "Wasn't that an inauspicious hour to make love?" Maugham asked. "Not for Philippe," she replied.

At the end of the fourth day she put down her brush and said: "*Vous savez, on se plaint toujours que mes portraits ne sont pas ressemblants. Je ne peux pas vous dire à quel point je m'en fouts.*" ("You know, people always complain that my portraits are not good likenesses. I can't tell you how little I care.") She then asked Maugham for the exact English translation of the French slang expression "*Je m'en fouts.*" "If you really want to know," Maugham said, "it means 'I don't give a fuck.'" She took the canvas off the easel and handed it to Maugham as a gift. It was not a good likeness. She had made Maugham look like a fawn-eyed romantic rather than a hardworking writer in his sixties.[62]

Robin finally came in September for his first stay at the Mauresque. At twenty he was studying law at Cambridge and had become a socialist, but he still wanted to be a writer. He was much impressed by the splendor of the villa, by the efficient servants who kept his glass filled with champagne, and by the famous guests who arrived daily, such as Michael Arlen, Noel Coward, and Harold Nicolson, who was upset by Jean the chauffeur's demon driving. Nicolson felt that Jean was taking his revenge for all the times he had to go to fetch guests.

Robin told his uncle that he was in love with a girl in London named Gillian. "You don't really love that girl," Maugham said. "You just want to go to bed with her. You're a vigorous young man. You need a romp. And after dinner tonight Gerald has decided to drive you into Nice and to take you round to a brothel or two. You'll soon find out what you want." Robin found a girl who was a stenographer in Paris and worked in a brothel twice a week to pay for her holiday in Nice. This, in his eyes, made her not quite a prostitute.

To keep Gerald out of casinos and bars Maugham had acquired a 45-ton fishing boat with two masts and a Diesel auxiliary, which was named the *Sara*, but which he called "the yacht." It could sleep four and had a crew of three. The day after the trip to the brothel they all went on a cruise to Villefranche. Robin felt a strong physical attraction for the sixteen-year-old cabin boy, golden brown in his bathing trunks, and had to lie on his stomach to hide his excitement. That evening he went to the Nice casino with Gerald, who got drunker and more abusive the more he lost at chemin de fer. He called a French player "frog-face" and a lady "you silly old bitch," and finally the manager asked them to leave. Gerald took Robin aboard the *Sara*, where a seventeen-year-old boy named Laurent was waiting. "This is my little friend Laurent," Gerald said. "Have a good time with him. He's a sweet boy. You've nothing to fear." Robin made love to Laurent, who got up early the next morning to go to his job in a carpenter's shop. Robin told Gerald that he had fallen for Laurent, and Gerald advised him to enjoy himself while he could, for he still had plenty of time to become a respectable Lord of Appeals like his father. Robin met Laurent again the next night on the boat, and this time Laurent professed amour, but in the morning he had to leave, even though it was Sunday, so Robin went back to the Mauresque. That afternoon, as he was opening the door of his bedroom on his way to the pool, he saw the door of his uncle's room down the hall open and Laurent emerge. Robin felt sick. He went to the pool, where he found Gerald. Taking one look at Robin's face, Gerald guessed what had happened and said, "Well, ducky, you must remember you're not the only queer around the place."

That evening Maugham was at his card table spreading out seven cards face down for a game of solitaire, and he beckoned to Robin. "Gerald tells me you've got a lech on Laurent," he said.

"I'm in love with him," Robin said.

"Balls!" Maugham said. "You've just got a simple lech on him, that's all. You want his body and you enjoy having him. . . . Do you think for one single instant that he's in love with you?"

"Last night Laurent told me that he loved me."

"And you believed him. You poor idiot! Don't you realize that he says that to every one of his clients? The boy may well be attracted to you, but that's because you're lucky enough to have an extremely well-formed body. However, that's not the reason he lets you fuck him all night. He lets you have him because each time he goes with you, I pay him his standard tariff—which, in fact, is almost the equivalent of three pounds. The boy's nothing more than an accomplished little prostitute. The fact that he has persuaded you to believe that he's in love with you has annoyed me quite considerably. I refuse to allow you to make a complete fool of yourself while you're staying under my roof." Shaking with anger, Maugham told his nephew that he would never see Laurent again.[63]

Maugham was apparently attempting to prove to his nephew the futility of romantic love. As a young man he had suffered from unrequited love, and the experience had hardened him. He had come to believe that love should be kept distinct from sex, a healthy appetite that had to be satisfied; and for that purpose attractive boys were obtainable. But to go around moon-eyed over a boy prostitute was a form of folly that Maugham, having been through similar experiences himself, was not about to indulge in others. He decided to teach his impressionable nephew a lesson that he might not be able to learn elsewhere, on the necessity of keeping physical urges in a separate compartment from the yearning of the heart.

Maugham was a member in good standing of the PEN Club, which was giving a dinner to celebrate the seventieth birthday of its president, H. G. Wells, at the Savoy Hotel on October 13, 1936, but he was not a very active member. In 1934 he was asked to join the executive committee but wrote the secretary, Hermon Ould, "I am afraid I cannot be of the smallest use to you. I am abroad almost all the year and I loathe attending meetings." He was elected anyway, "in spite of the fact that you are unlikely to attend the meetings," and in 1935 he was named to the council, "the members of which are required to do nothing except maintain an attitude of good will towards the PEN."

In 1936 he was also asked to attend the PEN congress in Buenos Aires as one of the three English delegates, along with Aldous Huxley and H. G. Wells, but he refused to go. He also refused to get involved in PEN campaigns to help refugee writers and in PEN's stand against European fascism.[64] But the dinner for his old friend H. G. Wells was a PEN event he wanted to attend, and he advanced his departure for England in order to be there. He came with Barbara Back and sat at the high table. George Bernard Shaw, who was eighty, proposed the toast, to which Wells replied. They had been friends since 1895, when they were both drama critics trying to make their way in the world of journalism. Now they were considered the two great English sages of their time. Shaw gave the kind of performance that could be expected of him, lacing his praise of Wells with a few well chosen barbs about his more recent whither-the-world books. He spoke with admirable elocution in his Irish brogue, while Wells read his speech in a high-pitched voice, with his nose in the text.[65] It was a pessimistic speech, in which Wells warned that the world would be worse before it was better. Reviewing his long career, which he knew was coming to an end, Wells said that he felt like "a little boy at a lovely party, who has been given quite a lot of jolly toys and who has spread his play about the floor. Then comes his Nurse. 'Now Master Bertie,' she says, 'it's getting late. Time you began to put away your toys.' . . . I hate the thought of leaving. . . . Few of my games are nearly finished and some I feel have hardly begun."[66] To Maugham, who was only eight years Wells's junior, these intimations of mortality must have sounded inauspicious.

On October 28 he went to a party at Sybil Colefax's. Her husband, Sir Arthur, had died in February, and she was selling Argyll House, the scene of so many enjoyable social occasions, to Lord Crewe. This, the last party in Argyll House, was attended by the Churchills, the Duff Coopers, Artur Rubinstein (who was often recruited to play Chopin at Sybil's functions), Desmond MacCarthy, and Harold Nicolson. The burning topic was the king and Wallis Simpson, who was a close friend of the hostess. Would there be a morganatic marriage? Would the king give up the woman he loved? And what about poor Mr. Simpson?[67]

That same month Maugham contributed an essay on the detective story to Cyril Connolly's literary magazine, *Horizon*, and had an experience that he had not had for a quarter of a century: his work was rejected. The writer J. MacLaren-Ross remembers the incident; he was present on the day in October when Connolly tapped some proofs on his knee with a pencil and said, "Maugham."

"I beg your pardon," MacLaren-Ross said.

"Somerset Maugham. His article on the detective story for *Horizon*."

"When's it coming out?" MacLaren-Ross asked.

"D'you know anything about detective stories?" Connolly asked.

"As it happens, quite a lot."

"Then tell me what you think of this."

"You want me to read the article?"

"A quick glance through should be enough," Connolly said, folding his hands across his briefcase.

"Well," Connolly asked as MacLaren-Ross handed back the proofs, "d'you think it's a good article?"

"Of course. Don't you?"

Connolly folded the galleys and thrust them into his briefcase. "No," he said. "I don't think it's a good article."

"You don't?"

Connolly shook his head and smiled. "In fact, I've decided not to print it."

"Not print it," MacLaren-Ross gasped, "but it's by Maugham!"

"I have the greatest respect for Maugham as a novelist," Connolly said, "and I don't say this is a *bad* article. It's good enough to be accepted by *Horizon* but not quite good enough for me to publish."[68]

MacLaren-Ross got the point. Two of his own stories had been accepted by *Horizon*, but if Connolly could reject a long commissioned article by an author of Maugham's stature, he realized that his stories stood little chance of appearing, and indeed they did not. He did not dare ask Connolly whether Maugham had been paid. The rejection did not trouble Maugham, who included a revised form of the article, "The Decline and Fall of the Detective Story," in his book of essays *The Vagrant Mood*.

In November, Maugham went to the coal-mining district in Derbyshire to spend a long weekend with the Sitwells in their seventeenth-century mansion, Renishaw Hall. The Sitwells were less a family than a literary cartel with a gift for self-propagation. Edith, a kind and generous person surrounded by hangers-on, gave tea parties in her tiny flat at St. Petersburg Place, and was famous for her hats and bons mots, while Osbert and Sacheverell were known as wits and dandies. "Both brothers," said the drama critic James Agate, "are artists who enjoy pretending to be asses." [69]

Renishaw, a crenelated mass of gray stone, was the family seat. It gave Maugham a peculiar satisfaction to go there and think that the Sitwells were surrounded by possessions that had been in their family since the reign of Charles II. From his room he could see a formal garden with yew hedges, a lake, and then the park stretching out to the horizon line. Chimneys in the distance indicated the origins of the Sitwell fortune. There were coal mines under the property and huge fires in every room. The passages were icy but the company was good.[70] One of the guests was the dancer Robert Helpmann, who was told that everyone would wear costumes in Maugham's honor. He dressed up as Queen Alexandra, and made his entrance to find that none of the others had worn costumes. Maugham shook hands with him without comment. Osbert was a charming and gracious host. Renishaw stood for permanence and decorum, which was what Maugham liked best about England.

After his weekend with the Sitwells, Maugham visited Canon F. J. Shirley, the new headmaster of the King's School, which was facing bankruptcy. Seeking the help of rich old boys, Shirley had asked Hugh Walpole, "What about Maugham?" "Hopeless," Walpole replied, "he hates the school." Shirley nonetheless wrote Maugham, asking him to let bygones be bygones. He said the school was facing extinction and suggested that Maugham write a play that could be performed as a benefit. When he did not get a reply, he thought, "This proves that the fellow is really just the damned shit everyone says he is." But Maugham was traveling, and it took time for Shirley's letter to catch up with him. "That sort of thing is not at all in my line," Maugham replied. "I have retired from the theater and I am too old a dog to learn new tricks." He added, however, that he would come to call when he was in London. This he now did, touring the place in which he had spent the most miserable years of his childhood. Won over by Shirley's tact and attentiveness, he promised to help. On November 6, back at his London flat at 5 Portland Place, near Cavendish Square, he sent Shirley a dozen eighteenth-century mezzotints to brighten up the masters' common room.[71]

This was the first of many gifts. In 1937 he (who had been so helpless at games) sent a check for 200 pounds toward laying down three tennis courts. He later gave 3,000 pounds to build a boathouse for the "Eights" and 10,000 pounds to establish a scholarship for working-class boys. His motive, he wrote Shirley, was

> to diminish the class-consciousness of the ordinary schoolboy by throwing him into contact at a formative period of his life with boys of another class, and thus to some extent to diminish the exclusiveness and snobbery which have resulted in the universal dislike for the English, which no traveler can fail to notice. The Duke of Wellington is supposed to have said that the Battle of Waterloo was won on the playing fields of Eton. I think a future historian may with more truth say that India was lost in the public schools of England.[72]

Shirley could find no takers among working-class families, and the money was spent to build a physics laboratory. Maugham also gave 5,000 pounds to build a library room on top of the physics lab, and left his 1,300-book library to the school. "I am glad you can make use of the books," he wrote Shirley. "Otherwise on my death they would have to be sold for what they could fetch to local booksellers. My descendants are ignorant of foreign languages and uninterested in things of the mind."[73] He also gave the school the manuscripts of his first and last novels, *Liza of Lambeth* and *Catalina*. He later wrote Shirley: "I

399

don't know if you saw in the newspapers that the manuscript of a novel of mine was sold at Sotheby's the other day for two thousand six hundred pounds. It looks as though on a pinch the School could raise a sum on the manuscripts I presented."

It was Maugham's peculiar turn of mind to return bearing gifts to the place where he had been unhappy. He made up for his unpopularity as a student by becoming a generous old boy. It was his way of triumphing over the dismal experience of his days at King's. With the passage of time he came to feel a real fondness for the place, in which part of his best known book was set. Perhaps on another level he was competing with Hugh Walpole, who had presented to the school his portrait by Augustus John, paid for the returfing of the Mint Yard, donated his collection of manuscripts, and had a prize, a society, and a dormitory named after him.[74] But most likely his generosity had a great deal to do with the personality of John Shirley, who made Maugham feel valued, appointing him a governor of the school. Maugham, who could not abide clergymen or committees, sat alongside the dean and chapter of Canterbury on the governing body of the school, and tried to make his annual stays in London coincide with its meetings.

On December 11 the political crisis pitting King Edward VIII against the government of Stanley Baldwin was solved. The king insisted on his right to marry Wallis Simpson. The government opposed the marriage and interpreted the king's refusal to obey its wishes as a threat to constitutional procedure. The king abdicated and gave a moving radio speech. He was given an annual income of 60,000 pounds and the title of Duke of Windsor; he left for France, where he and Mrs. Simpson were married. Maugham was in the lounge at Claridge's with Graham Greene, Eddie Marsh, and Osbert Sitwell when the king made his abdication speech. Borrowing a portable radio from one of the porters,[75] they sat huddled around the little box listening to history being made. "I have found it impossible," Edward said, "to carry the heavy burden of responsibility and to discharge my duties as king as I would wish to do without the help and support of the woman I love."

Before returning to the Riviera for Christmas, Maugham saw Robert Bruce Lockhart again. Lockhart committed to his diary some preposterous gossip that he had picked up: "Maugham has had relations with women. (After all, he married and had a daughter.) One was————.[76] She has a hold on him still. One reason is that because of his homosexual nervosity he could not perform alone. The liaison was à trois. The third was Godfrey Winn! Maugham . . . is a man who has tried everything: drugs etc. but has an iron self-discipline and is now master of himself."[77]

Maugham was now sending each of his books in proof to be read by Eddie Marsh, and in January 1937 he received the corrected proofs of his new novel, *Theatre*. Pleased with the result, he wrote Marsh on January 27: "You are wonderful, you are so invaluable that I cannot see any help for it, I am afraid you are condemned now to look through my proofs till the end of the chapter. The only mitigation I can offer is that two days ago I celebrated my 63d birthday, so you can console yourself that the chapter will not be an unreasonable time in coming to an end. I think you must know grammar better than anyone in England." That same month Marsh retired from government work, which gave him more time to pursue his avocation.

Theatre came out in March in America and England, where the first printing was 20,000 copies. Like *Liza of Lambeth*, the novel was based on direct observation; it was the story of the private and professional life of a famous actress. Maugham had worked in the theater for thirty years, with the finest actresses of his day—Ethel Irving, Marie Tempest, Gladys Cooper, Irene Vanbrugh, Fay Compton, Billie Burke, and Ethel Barrymore, among others. He knew the material so well that *Theatre* read almost like reportage.

He returned to such favorite themes as the bondage of the senses and the penalties of a creative life. Julia Lambert, like Mrs. Craddock, marries a handsome and masculine man, Michael Gosselyn, her manager. She is passionately in love, but he is unresponsive. When he returns from war she finds that she has become indifferent. This is her liberation: "It seemed a revenge that she had enjoyed for the unhappiness he had caused her; she was free of the bondage in which her senses had held her to him and she exulted. Now she could deal with him on equal terms."

Julia lets herself be seduced by a young accountant in her husband's office. He is very shy, but once he gets her alone he becomes increasingly bold. The bedroom scene is done in the before-and-after nineteenth-century mode: "He was on his knees, and she was in his arms" (before); "she sent him away a little before Miss Phillips was due" (later). At the end of the book she frees herself from her dependence on her young lover, for her true dependence is on her profession. Creative work is salvation, Maugham says, and it absolves hypocrisy, shallowness, and sexual license. In describing how Julia approaches a character he was also describing how he shaped character in his fiction:

She was not aware that she deliberately observed people, but when she came to study a new part vague recollections surged up in her from she knew not where, and she found that she knew things about the character that she had had no inkling of. It helped her to think of someone she knew or even someone she had seen in the street or at a party: she combined with this recollection her own personality, and thus built up a character founded on fact but enriched with her experience, her knowledge of technique and her amazing magnetism.[78]

Reality for Julia was on the stage, as reality for Maugham was in his study.

Theatre was written at a time when Maugham was reading and admiring Colette, and the romance between the aging actress and a young lover whom she cannot hold was an English version of *Chéri*. Maugham found Colette's ease of expression so formidable that he could not believe she took any trouble over it. She was a neighbor, living in Monte Carlo, and Maugham arranged to meet her and was surprised when she told him that she often spent a whole morning on a single page.[79]

Many of the actresses Maugham had worked with, and some with whom he had not, were convinced that they were the model for Julia Lambert. The passage in which Julia steals scenes by waving a red scarf was attributed to Marie Tempest. Mrs. Patrick Campbell, who had never acted in a Maugham play, asked James Agate what actress had been the model for Julia. No one in particular, Agate said, since Julia was a second-rate actress, with no reverence for her art. "No actress could be great in Willie's presence," Mrs. Campbell said. "He lives in hell and likes it."

Theatre was received as the latest product from a firm with high standards of manufacture. Bernard De Voto said in the *Saturday Review of Literature* on March 6 that it was "as fine a specimen of the well-made novel as this generation has known." *Time* said on March 15 that it was "well up to Maugham's high professional standard." Elizabeth Bowen in the *New Statesman and Nation* on March 27 called his style "neutral, functional, and fully efficient." She thought of the novel as "an astringent tragi-comedy" in which Maugham "anatomises emotion without emotion" and "handles without pity a world where he finds no pity." His "disabused clearness and hardness" may diminish his subject, but he is "a first-rate professional writer." A demurral came in *Books of the Month* in April from Maurice L. Richardson, who found

Theatre Maugham's worst book in terms of improbable characterization and action, but who added that his storytelling was so expert "that he could get away with a triangle drama between a charwoman, a crocodile, and a pillar-box."[80] James Agate, the dean of London drama critics, did not review *Theatre*, because it was not a play, but the book violated his ideal of the theater and made him very angry. He believed that a great actress, no matter what her private life was like, had to think nobly of her art. But Julia Lambert, he thought, came across as a common bitch with no reverence for genius, a quality without which no actress had ever been great.[81]

If Maugham had not given up playwriting, *Theatre* might have been written for the stage. It was, several critics pointed out, constructed like a play, and was eventually dramatized by Helen Jerome and Guy Bolton. A French version by Marc-Gilbert Sauvajon, called *Adorable Julia*, was a huge success in Paris.

In the first months of that year—1937—there was a crisis in the Maugham household. Gerald Haxton, who was now forty-five, had to face the fact that the best years of his life had been spent in the master's shadow. He typed the master's letters, ran the master's household, and accompanied the master on his travels, making the arrangements. On trips Maugham depended on him for material, which made Gerald more of an equal, but as Maugham aged, the trips were less frequent, while at the Mauresque he was little more than head steward. Gerald looked at himself, his hair graying, his face puffy and dissipated, and saw a glorified servant. The love he had once felt for Maugham soured into resentment of a life devoted to doing the great man's chores.

Drink had been in the past one way of dealing with what he felt to be a humiliating servitude, but now it was also his way of getting back at Maugham, who hated any form of excess. Drunkenness meant loss of control and sloppiness, which Maugham, whose two greatest virtues were self-control and orderliness, could not abide. The Mauresque was a fortress against the forces of disorder, but inside the fortress there was a double agent. Gerald would come stumbling in after a night out, his eyes bleary, his breath reeking of liquor, his clothes rumpled, his speech slurred, and his presence was an insult to the tidy elegance that the Mauresque and its owner represented.

Alcoholism was ruining Gerald's health, and in February 1937 he became so seriously ill that he thought he was going to die. He was frightened enough to go on the wagon, much to Maugham's relief.

Maugham told him that if he started drinking again he would kill himself. If he did start drinking again, Maugham said, it meant that he would rather drink and die than not drink and live, and if that was the case, they would be better off going their separate ways. Maugham would pension him off, sell the Mauresque, and go back to England to live. He had hired Gerald to take care of him, and instead his days were spent taking care of Gerald. The situation was becoming intolerable. As he wrote Barbara Back, "I cannot spend the remaining years of my life acting as a nurse and keeper to an old drunk."[82]

By March, Gerald had recovered and was spending much of his time racing a small sailboat. Maugham was growing tired of the Riviera—he felt that he had no friends there any longer and no one to talk to—and he wanted to get away.[83] An opportunity arose when *The Constant Wife* was revived that spring, starring Ruth Chatterton. Maugham accepted an invitation to join the play in tryout in Manchester and Brighton prior to opening at the Globe in May. In London in April he went to a party given by Alice Astor von Hofmannstahl and ran into the actress Ruth Gordon, whom he had met on the Riviera. "Miss Gordon," he said, "my play *The Constant Wife* is being revived in Brighton. Your friend Miss Ruth Chatterton is starring in it. Will you meet me in Brighton tomorrow night and see if you can do something about her performance?"

She went. She saw. Maugham asked, "Well?"

"Well," Ruth Gordon said, "I think Ruth Chatterton is fine. But I think your play has gotten old-fashioned and you should do something about *it*."[84] Maugham, who admired frankness, always liked Ruth Gordon after that. The revival ran for 36 performances in London.

In May, Robin came of age and celebrated with a birthday party to which he invited fifty Cambridge undergraduates and Osbert Sitwell. Maugham, in Canterbury on one of his pilgrimages to the King's School, wrote him: "My good Robin, I am assured A. that tomorrow is your birthday and B. that being a born fool you have C. mucked up your beautiful car, therefore, in celebration of A. and because you cannot be accounted responsible for B. which is obviously the fault of your progenitors, I am sending you a cheque which may in part repair the results of C."[85]

In mid-May, Maugham left for Paris to gather more material for his new novel, *Christmas Holiday*. His chauffeur, whose driving Harold Nicolson so feared, had an accident, and the car had to be towed to

Rouen.[86] From the Victoria Palace Hotel, Maugham wrote Bert Alanson that he had asked Nelson Doubleday to send Bert his $5,000 advance on *Theatre*. He had opened a second account with Bert, in which he wanted to collect $50,000 to found his prize, and the $5,000 should go toward that. Later that year he sent Bert another $8,500 for the number-two account, which represented his English earnings on *Theatre*.[87]

On June 10 he sent Robin another birthday present, a cigarette case. His research was finished, and he was off to Scandinavia with his lady novelist friend G. B. Stern and Gerald. The tour was a washout. Maugham did not like Sweden or the Swedes, whose faces he found dull and mean. Fortunately he had the canvas-and-leather book bag he always took on trips, which looked like a postman's sack. He did like Denmark, however, and wrote Barbara Back that "you might do worse than fly over to Copenhagen for a few days when you want to take a little fling with a new lover."[88] In Copenhagen, their rooms were not ready when they arrived at the hotel, and the others went sight-seeing. But Maugham, refusing to forgo his habit of an afternoon siesta, lay down on a couch in the lobby and napped from two to four. He wrote Bert Alanson that Sweden was "very dull, the country monotonous and the people uninteresting . . . but Copenhagen was gay and cheerful and one has divine things to eat there." Since he was getting older and older, and not, like the prairie flower, wilder and wilder, he was thinking of spending his money rather than let it accumulate "for the benefit of my daughter."[89]

Briefly back at the Mauresque in July, Maugham reached an agreement with Gerald. There would be no more drinking, and he would sell the Mauresque and take a flat in London, spending at least five months a year there. He would try to have Gerald's persona non grata status lifted so that he too might return to England. He was not sure that Gerald could keep his resolutions but was willing to give him a chance. He was tired of the Riviera. He put the Mauresque on the market at a price of 25,000 pounds, unfurnished.[90]

At the end of July, Maugham was off again, to Salzburg, Munich, and Badgastein, where there was a Toscanini concert, and then to Venice to see the Tintorettos. He congratulated Robin on having graduated from Cambridge and told him that he now faced the world. In Munich he ran into the novelist Cecil Roberts, who had been his guest at the Mauresque. Hitler had taken all the modern paintings by Jews out of the German galleries and exhibited them in Munich as Jewish art. "I must say, from what I see here," Maugham told Roberts, "that awful man seems justified."[91]

Back among his orange trees in August, Maugham felt discouraged and out of date as a writer. "Today, with the world in the mess it's in," he wrote Richard Cordell, who had just finished a flattering book about him, "novelists feel compelled to deal with the conditions that obtain. That is natural enough. Critics take little interest in the entertainment value of a piece of fiction and they are angry with the readers who demand just what they, the critics, have no use for. There is nothing to do about it."[92] His spirits lifted when he heard that Alexander Woollcott was including *Cakes and Ale* in an anthology. "Last time I was in America, I listened with joy to your Sunday evening performances," he wrote Woollcott. "It must be very wonderful for you to have that enormous audience in the palm of your hand."[93] Woollcott did three broadcasts a week for Cream of Wheat, as the Town Crier. There was an introductory *ding ding dong* and a "Hear ye, hear ye," and then Woollcott came on to discuss the latest play or chat with an author. A great success in the thirties, he was known as the first stylist of the airwaves.

Maugham saw less and less of Gerald, who spent his time playing bridge in a club "frequented by cads, crooks, and Jews."[94] Although he was not much use, he was at least keeping sober and staying out of mischief. Prospective buyers came to look at the Mauresque. "I really think there is a chance of disposing of it," he wrote Barbara Back. He had put the books and expenditures in the hands of an agent, which saved him a hundred pounds a month.

Maugham thanked Frank Swinnerton, who was now a reviewer for the *Observer*, for sending him copies of his autobiography and his novel *Harvest Comedy*. He praised the autobiography's vitality and Swinnerton's ability to put before the reader the look of people.[95] Maugham had become friendly with Swinnerton after admiring his novel *Nocturne*, in which there is a scene on a yacht with a man in a state of sexual excitement. He wrote Swinnerton that it was "full of cock!" and that what gave *Nocturne* its peculiar flavor was that "it has a cockstand in it and there are very few novelists who can put *that* on to a printed page."[96] He included an excerpt from *Nocturne* in a one-volume anthology called *The Traveller's Library*, published in 1933 and comprising selections from fifty modern English writers.

Compiling anthologies was a sideline that Maugham took very seriously. He felt that he was performing a service to literature by bringing his favorite writers to what he hoped would be a wider audience. Aside from *The Traveller's Library*, his anthologies were: *Tellers of Tales* (the hundred greatest stories of all times), in 1939; *Introduction to Modern English and American Literature* (a selection of stories, poetry, and nonfiction), in 1943; and *Choice of Kipling's Best*, in 1953. He also prepared abridged editions of what he considered the ten greatest novels, which were: *Tom Jones, David Copperfield, Madame Bovary, Le Père Goriot, Wuthering Heights, The Brothers Karamazov, The Red and the Black, Pride and Prejudice, Moby Dick,* and *War and Peace.*

Swinnerton's autobiography included a perceptive portrait of Maugham. He had, wrote Swinnerton, a mind without fat, which did not flinch from the unpleasant but turned it to sportive account. He had a faculty which some would never be able to relish, the power to be interested without becoming attached. The core of his nature was wounded sensitiveness, determination, clear-sightedness, a resistance to pity, and an indifference to empressment which some might regard as flippancy. Maugham was saving Swinnerton's novel to read on his first trip to the East in more than ten years—he was leaving for India in December. Swinnerton was the proud father of a daughter, and Maugham hoped that "she will grow up to be good, good-natured, and good-looking."

In October, Maugham became a grandfather. Liza gave birth to a son, and he went to England to have a look at the baby. "Liza thinks herself very clever to have produced a son and she wants to call him Nicholas Somerset," he wrote his favorite niece, Kate Mary Bruce. "I have seen the infant and he is very red and wrinkled and angry-looking. I didn't get the impression that he thought very much of the world."[97] Maugham wondered how best to play his new part and was hesitating between (1) a long white beard and a beaming benevolence and (2) a frail cadaverousness set off by a skull cap and an acidulous manner.[98]

On October 11 Robert Bruce Lockhart gave a lunch for him, to which he invited Moura Budberg and Harold Nicolson. Maugham talked about his forthcoming trip to India to research another novel. He was annoyed with Nicolson for asking him to let himself be interviewed by a young female French journalist and for making a facetious remark about Robin.[99]

He was still in London in November when Richard Cordell's book *W. Somerset Maugham* came out. This was a generally flattering treatment, which included an introductory biographical chapter and a summary of everything Maugham had written. Cordell concluded that Maugham had achieved notable success in every genre he had attempted. On November 27 *The Times Literary Supplement* said that Cordell "shows little insight into the reasons why Mr. Maugham, notwithstanding that his inventive and emotional range both as a storyteller and a playwright is a narrow one, has so much to teach the aspiring writer of fiction."[100]

In December, Maugham gave a farewell party for himself at Claridge's and returned to the Mauresque for a few days before his departure for India. He obtained letters of introduction to various maharajahs from one of his Riviera neighbors, the Aga Khan. Maugham had been resisting India for twenty years because it was Kipling country and he felt that all the good stories had been written, he did not care for Indian art, and he had a prejudice against the English colony.[101] But he had in mind a novel about a young man who adopts the Hindu philosophy of renunciation, and he thought he had better go to see the country for himself. He would be sixty-four in a few weeks, but age did not deter him from a tiring trip. After all, with Kipling and a few others, he had pioneered the territorial expansion of the English novel. "I have never been able to write anything," he said, "unless I had a solid and ample store of information for my wits to work upon."[102]

Maugham's plan was to discover India without the English and spend the three months he had allotted mainly in the southern states under native rule. He and Gerald sailed in December for Bombay, and played bridge with an Egyptian ranked player who relieved him of substantial sums of money, but Maugham felt it was worth it to play with someone of that caliber. Arriving in Bombay in January 1938, he found that his reputation had preceded him. In an interview for a Bombay newspaper he said things he would never have said in the London press. From the lofty vantage point of the retired playwright, he declared that the English stage had degenerated (the implication being that this was so because he was no longer writing for it), and that there was not a single great English actor or actress still playing. He was besieged in his hotel by streams of earnest Indian students who wanted to have long and profound talks about the meaning of life. They seemed to want answers that he could not provide, for he had come to find answers to his own questions. What a vast country, he thought, and how hopeless to try to understand anything in three months.[103]

After about ten days in Bombay, Maugham went south, passing through the Portuguese and Catholic enclave of Goa, where he met a Catholic priest whose Brahmin ancestors had been converted by one of the companions of Saint Francis Xavier. Maugham wondered whether, even with four hundred years of Catholicism behind him, the man was not still at heart a Brahmin. He did not think man's essential nature could be changed, and certainly not by religious conversion. The priest told him that even among Christians the caste system was still observed. "We're Christians," he said, "but first of all we're Hindus."[104]

By January 25 he was in Madura, near the southernmost tip of India, where he visited the large seventeenth-century temple built to honor the goddess Siva. In the temple he felt he had found the real India, which knew nothing of the West. Men stripped to the waist, their chests smeared with the white ash of burned cow dung, lay face down in the ritual attitude of prostration. At the foot of each sculptured column a religious mendicant was seated with a bowl for offerings. Groups of priests followed by pupils prayed at shrines. Maugham sensed in the temple "something secret and terrible."[105] He wrote to Frank Swinnerton that his visit to Madura was "something which I shall always treasure." He had finished Swinnerton's novel *Harvest Comedy*, and said that its main character, William Harvest, was "one of the greatest lambs I remember in fiction. I am glad you have rehabilitated the name of William; I always thought it a silly name and a great misfortune to own it."[106] It seems odd that such a respectable name as William, the name of four English kings, including the one who conquered England, would incur Maugham's displeasure. Either he was being facetious, or his dislike of his first name was a part of his general dislike of himself, for his name was the most immediate way by which others knew him. Another indication of his dislike for his first name was the way he signed his work: W. Somerset Maugham.

From Madura, Maugham went north to Madras. He had been told that a few hours by car from Madras, in a place called Tiruvannamalai, at the foot of the sacred mountain of Arunachala, there lived a great Indian sage and holy man, Ramana Maharshi. He was called Bhagavan, which means "Lord," and in his ashram there was a stone hall where he received his disciples. The Bhagavan was a strict vegetarian; he sat for long hours in samadhi, a state of deep meditation attained by those who have proved capable of spiritual illumination. The Bhagavan had reached the egoless state, the point at which his ego was, he said, "like the skeleton of a burnt rope—though it has form, it is of no use to tie anything with."[107]

Maugham set out by car on a dirt road rutted by the heavy wheels of oxcarts, with a basket of fruit to offer the Bhagavan. As he waited to be presented he fainted, and was taken into a hut and laid on a pallet bed. The Bhagavan, a plump, dark-skinned man with close-cropped white hair and beard, came to see him. He walked with a slight limp, leaning on a stick, and wore nothing but a white loincloth. He reminded Maugham not so much of a scholar as of a sweet-natured old peasant. Followed by two or three disciples, he sat down close to Maugham and stared at the wall over his shoulder, his body absolutely still except for a foot that tapped on the floor. He sat like that for a quarter of an hour, in meditation. Then he asked Maugham whether he had any questions. Maugham said he was feeling too weak to ask questions. The Bhagavan smiled and said, "Silence is also conversation." He resumed his meditation for another quarter of an hour, then got up, bowed, smiled a farewell, and limped out, followed by his disciples. Maugham instantly felt better, and wondered whether it was the result of the meditation. He went into the hall, where the Bhagavan sat on a low dais on a tiger skin, near which a brazier burned incense. The faithful sat on the floor, some reading, others meditating. Two strangers came in, prostrated themselves before the Bhagavan and offered a basket of fruit. He accepted it with a slight inclination of the head, motioned for a disciple to take it away, and became abstracted in meditation. After a short time Maugham tiptoed out.[108]

Among the disciples there was an American ex-sailor from Long Beach named Guy Hague, who had found peace and spiritual serenity in the ashram and who may have been one of the models for Larry Darrell in *The Razor's Edge*, as the Bhagavan was the model for the sage in the same novel.[109] The word spread that Maugham's fainting spell had been a special grace of the Bhagavan—he had been rapt into the infinite. It may simply have been the altitude. Doctors, however, had told Maugham that the fainting was due to an irritability of the solar plexus, which pressed his diaphragm against his heart.[110] When the Bhagavan died in 1950, millions in India mourned him. It was said that when his pulse stopped, a bright ball of light rose from his head and moved slowly across the sky.[111]

From Madras, Maugham went north to Hyderabad, where he had an introduction to the Minister of Finance, Sir Akbar Hydari. When Sir Akbar learned that he had not come to India to shoot tigers but to meet scholars and religious teachers, he went out of his way to find some. He introduced Maugham to a holy man, a tall, courtly fellow wrapped in a scarlet cloak. Maugham's heart sank when the holy man repeated like a parrot the same things other holy men had said. The truth might be one and indivisible, but it soon grew stale. Maugham asked how he could acquire the power of meditation. The holy man told him to sit on the floor cross-legged in a dark room and stare at the flame of a candle for a quarter of an hour a day. He tried it for as long as he could, and when he could stare no longer he looked at his watch; three minutes had passed.[112]

Traveling by car from Hyderabad to Bidar, Maugham saw a large crowd, at least three hundred persons gathered around a pipal tree. He was told that this was the shrine of a healer, a former well-to-do contractor who had felt the call to serve God. The healer wore a dirty white turban, a shirt with no collar, and silver earrings. He asked Maugham to give him his blessing, which Maugham did, feeling foolish. He also met a saffron-robed swami who practiced asceticism, and Maugham asked him whether he minded being deprived of the pleasures of ordinary men. "Why should I?" the swami asked. "I had them in a previous life." In a Moslem cemetery he saw fakirs put skewers through their eyes and cheeks, and another gouge his eye out with a short dagger and walk around with his eyeball hanging down his cheek, and still another pass a skewer through his tongue. Maugham, who was not a believer, was mystified by their imperviousness to pain.

From Hyderabad he went north to Nagpur, where he had an introduction to the Prince and Princess of Berar, who asked him to lunch. "I suppose you've been to Bombay?" the prince asked. "Yes," Maugham replied. "I landed there." "And were you put up for the Yacht Club?" "Yes." "And are you going to Calcutta?" "Yes." "I suppose you'll be put up for the Bengal Club?" "I hope so." "Do you know the difference between them?" "No." "In the Bengal Club at Calcutta they don't allow dogs or Indians, but in the Yacht Club at Bombay they do allow dogs."[113]

The racism and provincialism of the British in India exasperated Maugham. When he had tea with the wife of a minor official, he told her that he had spent most of his time in the states administered by Indians. "You know," she said, "we don't have anything more to do with Indians than we can help. One has to keep them at arm's length." Maugham reflected that in England she would have been a manicurist or a stenographer.

By February 26 he was in Calcutta, and wrote Karl Pfeiffer, the young bridge player he had kept up with, who was now a college professor:

> I can only regret that I did not come years and years ago. . . . I have met all sorts of fantastic people—Indians, yogis, mystics, philosophers, magicians, I know not what—and seen some unbelievable things. I can only stay three months and it is nothing . . . it is like seeing the Himalayas at night only in one flash of lightning. . . . I can only leave to the future to decide what use I can make of all that I have seen and done here and what will come when all these vivid impressions have settled down and the subconscious gets a chance to work upon them.[114]

From Calcutta he and Gerald drove westward through the jungle to Banares. Gerald was glad to be traveling again; after years of boring social life at the Mauresque, this was like old times, like their trips to Malaya in the twenties. India was great hunting country, and he carried a rifle in case they saw any game. They caught sight of a peacock among the trees, its beautiful tail outspread, its walk so elegant that Maugham was reminded of Nijinsky on the stage at Covent Garden more than twenty years before. Rarely had he seen a more thrilling sight than that peacock threading its solitary way through the jungle. Gerald told the driver to stop. "I'm going to have a shot at it," he said. Maugham was appalled, but said nothing, not wanting to start a quarrel. Gerald fired and Maugham hoped he would miss, but he didn't. The driver jumped out of the car and brought back the dead bird. Maugham thought it was a cruel sight, but it did not spoil his appetite when they ate the breast that night for dinner, for it was a welcome change from the usual scraggly chicken.[115]

In Banares he took a boat ride down the Ganges at sunset and marveled at the minarets of the city's two mosques against the pale sky. In the morning the river was crowded with bathers, who splashed sacred water on themselves with brass bowls. Continuing northwest, they reached Agra, where Maugham saw the Taj Mahal. Overcome by its beauty, he realized that "it took my breath away" was no idle phrase, for he actually felt shortness of breath.

By March 15, 1938, he was at the Maiden's Hotel in New Delhi, where he learned that Prime Minister Neville Chamberlain had named his brother Frederic Lord Chancellor, the highest office in the British Empire that a lawyer could attain. The appointment astonished the political and legal worlds. Frederic was seventy-one years old and had never met Chamberlain. He had no idea how he had been chosen. But he told the Prime Minister that he was like the Roman soldier to whom Caesar had given a high command, who had said: "Why should I doubt whether I am fit for the job if *he* thinks I can tackle it?" The Lord Chancellor was a member of the cabinet, Speaker of the House of Lords, and Custodian of the Great Seal; he appointed magistrates and was generally responsible for the administration of the courts and of the law. With the office came a life peerage. When Frederic was presented to Queen Elizabeth, she informed him that although she had not read any of his brother's books, she had looked at all of them.

Willie was proud of his brother. "It is very wonderful, if you come to think of it," he wrote Bert Alanson, "that an obscure young man, without money or influence to help him, should by sheer merit in his profession achieve a position which in nine cases out of ten is looked upon as the greatest reward for political services that a lawyer can hope for."[116]

In New Delhi, Maugham let the English viceroy, Lord Linlithgow, know that he was passing through. He was hoping that he and Gerald would be officially received at the palace, which created an awkward situation. Linlithgow's son, John Hope, a young man who was on holiday in India prior to taking his bar exams, remembers his father discussing the problem of the famous author whose secretary had been persona non grata in Great Britain and the Commonwealth since 1919.[117] Linlithgow decided to ask Maugham to lunch without Haxton, an invitation that was turned down. Maugham felt that Linlithgow had snubbed him by ignoring Gerald, and he never forgot a snub.

At the end of March the two travelers were back in Bombay, at the Taj Mahal Hotel, waiting for the ship that would take them to Naples on March 31. Maugham left India with a poor impression of the English presence there, to which the incident in New Delhi no doubt contributed. "Oh, the doddering old fools who are running this country," he said, "it is a wonder India has not been lost long ago."[118]

Chapter Fifteen

This tartness, this capacity for suffering which was obviously very deep in him, this lack of self-pity, this sort of harsh self-irony: I think that is really what one reads him for.

C. P. Snow

WHILE MAUGHAM was in India *The Summing Up* came out, in January 1938 in England, and in March in America, where it sold more than 100,000 copies. One group of critics made flattering comparisons with other writers, while another group explained why the book fell short. Stephen Vincent Benét likened it to Kipling's *Something of Myself* (in the *Saturday Review of Literature* on April 16), while the *Observer* compared the author to Pascal and the *Manchester Guardian* likened him to Swift. David Garnett in the *New Statesman and Nation* on January 8 said the book was too long and diffuse. Graham Greene in the *Spectator* on January 14 said Maugham was limited by his agnosticism, for if you "rob human beings of their heavenly and their infernal importance you rob them of their individuality." V. S. Pritchett in the *Fortnightly Review* in March said Maugham's indifference had led him to be merely a commentator on character who had confined himself to debunking the conventional view.[1] Maugham's friends felt the book was a tour de force of circumspection. "Never have I read an autobiography," said G. B. Stern, "that contains so little auto as his Summing Up."[2]

Maugham, however, had specified on the book's first page that it was not an autobiography or a memoir but an attempt to sort out his thoughts on the subjects that had interested him in the course of his life. If at times it read more like a philosophical treatise or a manual on the craft of writing than the story of his life, that was intended. It was, as the title indicated, a sum of beliefs and opinions. Maugham could be accused of many things, but not of misleading his readers. Episodes in

414

his life were described, out of chronology, to illustrate some point. He avoided posturing and self-congratulation, but rancor showed in his comments on "the Maugham problem." If critics did not take him seriously, he said, if "the world of letters should have attached no great importance to my work," it was because "as a writer of fiction, I go back, through innumerable generations, to the teller of tales round the fire in the cavern that sheltered neolithic man." It was the lament of a man who felt misunderstood. "In my twenties," he said, "the critics said I was brutal, in my thirties they said I was flippant, in my forties they said I was cynical, in my fifties they said I was competent, and now in my sixties they say I am superficial." There were, he concluded, no great critics in his time.

The book ended with a discussion of the meaning of life for someone like himself, who acted as if God did not exist. Pleasure was not the answer, for "it is one of the faults of my nature that I have suffered more from the pains, than I have enjoyed the pleasures of my life." There were values that gave life significance, values that gave man the illusion that he was escaping from human bondage, oases in the vast desert of existence, and these values were Truth, Beauty, and Goodness. But Maugham destroyed the scaffolding he was standing on by saying that we cannot know what truth and beauty are, for man lives by make-believe, and standards of beauty change with time.

That left goodness, or loving-kindness, "the only value in this world of appearances to have any claim to be an end in itself," the only quality that made reverence rise naturally in Maugham's heart. And where had he found such goodness? The only example he gave was the mother who died when he was eight. With her he had known disinterested love, unclouded by demands and dominance. And so Maugham was back where he had started, still unable to budge from the scene in his childhood when he learns that his mother is gone. "Her death," he wrote, "was a wound that fifty years have not entirely healed." What was there left but to resign oneself to one's nature and to find solace in one's profession? *The Summing Up* ends with these words from Fray Luis de Leon: "The beauty of life is nothing but this, that each should act in conformity with his nature and his business."[3]

The Summing Up had been gone over by that unforgiving grammarian, Eddie Marsh, whose comments Maugham preserved, giving some indication of the process of "diabolization." Here are a few examples taken at random, showing (a) what Maugham wrote and (b) what Marsh preferred.

p. 45—(a) I would sooner a writer were vulgar than refined; for life is vulgar, and it is life he seeks.

(b) I can't help boggling at the last sentence of 1st para. To say that an author should be vulgar in his search of vulgar life lays you open to Dr. Johnson's "who drives fat oxen must himself be fat . . ."

p. 50—(a) . . . sometimes the stars shine more brightly from the gutter than from the hilltop.

(b) The sense is clear, and the sentence may stand, but I can't help observing that stars don't shine *from* the gutter or the hilltop.

p. 182—(a) In France and Germany to write is an honorable profession.

(b) Here is this substantial infinitive again. I do think it's awkward.

p. 239—(a) Others may despise us because we do not lend a hand with a bucket of water; we can do no more, we do not know how to handle a bucket.

(b) "do no more." The point is not that you "can do no more," it is that you can't even do *that*, i.e. lend a hand with a bucket.

p. 314—(a) . . . there are few things that cause greater wretchedness than to love with all your heart someone whom you know is unworthy of love.

(b) Either "who you know is" or "whom you know to be" (otherwise you are landed with "whom is").

p. 317—(a) It is not action that aims at happiness; it is a happy chance if it produces it.

(b) Here are three "it's," all different in meaning. You could get rid of two by saying "it is a happy chance if happiness results."

And on and on for page after page, correcting a man who had been at his trade for forty years. "I know what I want to say and I say it," Maugham grumbled, "and then Eddie comes along and tells me I haven't."[4] In gratitude, he sent Marsh some eighteenth-century emerald cuff links he had brought back from India. "I like to think they may have adorned the sleeve of one of the Mogul's page-boys," he said.[5]

Docking at Naples in April 1938, Maugham returned to the Mauresque via Florence, where he saw his old friend Reggie Turner for the last time. Reggie was sixty-nine, and he had been operated on the year before for a cancerous growth on the tongue. He was despondent, both about his health and about the political situation, with the Fascists ruling Italy under Mussolini. Maugham took him to Montegufoni, the

Tuscan castle Sir George Sitwell had bought in 1909, where Edith Sitwell was visiting her father. Reggie was glad to get out of Florence, which was festooning for an appearance by the Duce, accompanied by his new ally, Hitler. Reggie's world was crumbling, and perhaps mercifully, he died that December. He had lived too long as the survivor of a coterie, a sort of walking and talking footnote to the nineties.[6]

Maugham too was preoccupied with the political situation. In March 1938 German troops had occupied Austria and forced the Anschluss. Austria, renamed Ostmark, was governed by the Austrian Nazi Arthur Seyss-Inquart. Maugham was concerned because he had a substantial sum of money in German marks, which he could not get out because of currency restrictions. He thought of going to Germany and buying a work of art with his frozen marks. "I do not think there is any danger of war," he wrote Bert Alanson, "but the Austrians have a little lost their heads just now and are behaving in such a manner that it is better for foreigners to keep out of the country."[7] There would be, for the time being, no more summer opera in Salzburg or walks through the pine forest in Badgastein.

The plight of the Jews was also on his mind, for he received a PEN Club request for money to help Austrian refugees, and replied: "I have not waited until I received your letter to do what I could for the Austrian Jews of my acquaintance who had had to leave their country and so I must ask you to be content with a cheque for ten guineas and to look upon it more as a mark of my sympathy than as a reasonable contribution to so worthy a fund."[8]

Robin, the ardent socialist, had misgivings about his father's peerage, but Maugham wrote him in May to defend the value of titles:

> If you can get your ennobled father to accept a full peerage, I think you would be all sorts of a damned fool to make any objection. For my own part I do not believe it can hurt a barrister to be a peer. . . . Remember also that while your father is one of the most distinguished men in the country, he is distinguished by reason of his office; to be the son of a deceased Lord Chancellor is to be very small fry, to be a peer is always to be something . . . a peerage makes it a trifle easier to make one's way in the face of the obstacles offered by all the other people whose aim is similar, and it is a very nice consolation prize if one falls and fails. What you say about the middle class origins of the family is all stuff and nonsense. How do you suppose the Percys and the Grosvenors started? The Percys who were Smiths?[9]

As the summer approached, Maugham slipped into his familiar Riviera schedule, working in the morning on his new novel, *Christmas Holiday*, swimming or catching up with his correspondence in the afternoon, and enjoying his "blessed peace." Gerald the furious yachtsman spent most of his day at sea.[10]

As always, there were requests for advice from aspiring writers. A typical answer to a Mr. Wilensky warned:

> The chances of one's writing anything of permanent value before one is thirty are small. And if one is a literary man who has to earn his living the probabilities are that one will waste very good themes which one realises afterwards one could have made much more of with greater knowledge and experience. My advice to you therefore is to adopt any occupation which will give you a living and keep writing for your spare time. In that spare time you will be able to write a novel in a year or two and from its result you can judge whether it is worth your while to go on. The life of a writer is extremely specialized and by following some other avocation it is likely that he will gain experience which will be of great value to him afterwards. So far as I personally am concerned I can only wish that I had remained a doctor for three or four years instead of writing books which have long been dead as mutton.[11]

Plans to sell the Mauresque had been suspended and, as always, there was a flock of guests: Robin, Barbara Back, Vincent and Liza, Sybil Colefax, G. B. Stern, the Paris businessman Jacques Raindre, the critic Raymond Mortimer and his friend Paul Hyslop. Harold Nicolson arrived in August with a compliment for his host. His wife, Vita Sackville-West, was staying with Virginia Woolf, who said that she much admired *The Summing Up*. She liked the clarity of the style, the honesty with which he had tried to get at the truth, and the analysis of his own methods of writing. This was praise indeed, coming from one of the highbrows who Maugham claimed ignored him.

What a perfect holiday, Nicolson thought as he settled in at the Mauresque: the heat was intense, the garden lovely, the chair long and cool, the lime juice at hand, the swimming pool nearby, the sunsets splendid, and the people pretty. He also felt the disquieting sensation that all this could not last, that it was part of an era that was drawing to a close.[12]

There was exciting news on the Riviera that summer—the Duke and Duchess of Windsor had rented a villa at Cap d'Antibes from Sir Pomeroy Burton. She kept house and he dug in the garden, and they were careful about whom they saw. After their marriage in June 1937 King George VI had written his brother that the cabinet had made a formal submission that while the duke could use the title Royal Highness, it could not be extended to the duchess. The duke was deeply hurt; in his eyes it was a slur against his wife, and therefore upon himself.

Maugham invited the Windsors to dinner—no easy matter. He had to let the duke know who would be there, the guests had to be screened, protocol had to be observed. Negotiations between Maugham's butler and the duke's butler went on for days. The dinner was scheduled for August 5, and Maugham briefed his houseguests: the duke got cross, he warned, if the duchess was not treated with respect. Harold Nicolson wondered what to call her, since she was not supposed to use the title Royal Highness.

When they arrived, Maugham and Liza went into the hall to greet them while the others stood sheepishly in the drawing room. In they came, and there was a lot of bowing and curtsying and listening intently to what the duke said. The duchess had a sort of metallic briskness. She wore her hair smoothed off her brow and falling down the back of her neck in ringlets, which gave her, Harold Nicolson thought, a placid, less strained look. Her voice now mingled the accent of Virginia with that of a duchess in a Pinero play. The duke, who had as a young man attended the Royal Naval College, walked with a swinging naval gait, plucking at his bow tie, and seemed in high spirits. Cocktails were served, and everyone stood around the fireplace. "I am sorry we were a little late," the duke said, "but Her Royal Highness couldn't drag herself away." To Nicolson the three words fell into the circle of guests like stones in a pool. "Her (gasp) Royal (shudder) Highness (and not one eye dared to meet another)."

They went in to dinner. Nicolson sat next to the duchess and across from the duke. They called each other "darling" a great deal. The duke spoke casually of "when I was king." Nicolson called him "Your Royal Highness" and her "Duchess." He found the duke glamorous and charming and sensitive about his wife. They still hoped to return to England, and when he asked the duchess why she didn't buy a house, she said, "One never knows what may happen. I don't want to spend all my life in exile."[13]

After dinner Maugham walked in the garden with the duke, who told him: "Every day I feel more privileged and grateful that the duchess consented to marry me."[14] These were sentiments difficult for

Maugham to grasp, and he said of the duke: "I don't know about his intelligence, but he's *bien élevé.*"[15]

The Windsors came to the Mauresque on other occasions, and Raymond Mortimer remembers having lunch with them. "We drank pink champagne," he said. "I called her Ma'am. I found her physically attractive—*un morceau de roi.* He looked so wretched and sad. He wanted to talk to me alone because I was a journalist, he wanted to know what was going on in England."[16] Another time Maugham invited the Duchess of Sermoneta, once the reigning beauty of Rome, to lunch with the Windsors and Wallis' close friends, Mr. and Mrs. Rogers. The Duchess of Sermoneta admired Maugham for not taking part in "National Rat Week"—dropping Edward when he abdicated—which Maugham could hardly have done, not having known him when he was king. The Duchess of Windsor was dressed all in purple, with a purple hat, and after lunch they played bridge until teatime. She powdered her nose at intervals, using a gold vanity case encrusted with large diamonds, rubies, and emeralds, protected by a chamois leather sheath in which she replaced it carefully each time. The vanity case was the only remarkable thing about her, the Duchess of Sermoneta thought. She found it hard to believe that the British Empire could have been given up for the love of this woman.[17]

It may have been from the Duke of Windsor that Maugham heard of Paul Niehans, a Swiss doctor who claimed to have invented cellular therapy. Niehans had a clinic in Clarens, near Vevey, where he treated famous patients for a variety of ailments with injections of cells scraped from unborn lambs. According to Niehans, cellular therapy cured cancer, heart disease, diabetes, cirrhosis of the liver, insomnia, depression, and impotence. It also halted old age, promising rejuvenation in a syringe. There are two schools of rejuvenation, the lift school and the pump school, and Maugham was drawn to the latter, even though he was a doctor and a skeptic.

Niehans did not explain how his treatment worked. A promising surgeon and an authority on endocrine glands, he had stumbled on cellular therapy in the course of his experiments and was so startled by the results that he devoted the rest of his life to disseminating its benefits. The idea was that cells from animal fetuses would revitalize human organs, somewhat in the manner of Achilles eating the bone marrow of a lion for strength. Underactive organs were treated with cells of the same organ, and overactive organs with the cells of antagonistic organs. Menopausal disturbances, for instance, were treated with ovary cells.

The medical community was dubious about cellular therapy, but satisfied customers included over the years the Aga Khan, the Duke of Windsor, Konrad Adenauer, Pope Pius XII, Thomas Mann, King Ibn-Saud, Bernard Baruch, Georges Braque, Charles Lindbergh, Gloria Swanson, and Merle Oberon. "I reject nine out of ten patients," Niehans said. "I choose persons who represent a certain value to society by their individual prominence." He saw himself as a savior of great men.

At the age of sixty-four Maugham somehow persuaded himself that cellular therapy could do wonders and left in September for the Niehans clinic, La Prairie. Gerald did not want to come, for he was taking his boat on a cruise around Sicily,[18] so Maugham invited Alan Searle, the young Bermondsey boy he had met in 1928, who was now thirty-four, to join him. He had taken a liking to Alan and usually saw him when he was in London. With Gerald destroying himself with drink and increasingly useless as a secretary, Maugham was considering Alan as a replacement. Alan suffered from psoriasis that covered his whole body—he could not expose his skin to the Riviera sun when he came to the Mauresque—a condition that Niehans might cure.[19]

On September 7 Maugham arrived at La Prairie, a large chalet with flower boxes in the windows. He and Alan were given the red-carpet treatment and taken to visit the clinic's private slaughterhouse, stocked with pregnant ewes. The merit of the Frische Zellen, or fresh-cell, treatment depended on injecting the cells immediately after they had been scraped from the fetus. The cells were ground up and made soluble in a saline solution known as "the miracle serum," which was injected into the patient's buttocks. Ideally, no more than an hour elapsed between slaughter and injection.

Patients usually stayed at La Prairie from a week to ten days. They were given the Abderhalden test, a urine enzyme reaction test invented by the Swiss physiologist Emil Abderhalden, which was supposed to reveal physical malfunction. After three or four days a doctor, or Niehans himself in the case of prominent patients, arrived with syringes like those veterinarians use on horses, filled with a pinkish solution. No more than one organ's cells were placed in one syringe. All the injections, as many as ten, were given at one time, after which the patients needed three or four days to recover. Patients were segregated to keep their identities secret, and took their meals in their rooms. They were told to stay off tobacco and alcohol for three months, which was apparently why Churchill never took the treatment.[20]

As a famous patient, Maugham was attended by Niehans, a tall, distinguished man through whose veins flowed the blood of the royal Hohenzollerns. His mother was the illegitimate offspring of the King of Prussia, Frederick III, and one of his mistresses, the Countess Fürstenberg. This bastard daughter of a king married a Bern surgeon named Niehans.[21] When Niehans examined Maugham, he complimented him on the youthfulness of his body, the healthy tone of his skin, and the excellent condition of his sexual organs. "You have lovely soft testicles," he said with his best bedside manner. After examining Alan he said, "I'll give you a new skin." They took the shots on the fourth day. Niehans came in with a trayful of syringes the size of rolling pins, which he administered. "I woke up in a tent every morning," Alan said, "feeling randy as could be. Here I was with all this bull and lamb and whatnot in me . . . and I didn't know what to do with it." The shots had the same effect on Maugham, who found himself, according to Alan, "with very distinct urges . . . usually in the bath."[22]

Once he had received the injections Maugham was impatient to leave the clinic. Time hung heavy on his hands. The newspapers filled him with gloom, although everyone at the clinic was convinced there would be no war. He was glad to be leaving for England. He would spend a day in Geneva and then go on to Paris and London.[23]

He did not keep to his schedule, for on the way to Paris he was injured when his car went off the road. He wrote Bert Alanson that he had been "nearly killed," but it cannot have been quite so serious, for he did not require hospitalization. Recovering at the France et Choiseul Hotel in Paris, he was grateful that Alan was with him. Except for Alan, who had been an angel, he said, he would have had to go into a nursing home, for he could not even change his position in bed without help. He was in pain, but fortunately the doctor who was looking after him gave him shots of morphine.[24] This was Alan's first opportunity to demonstrate how devoted he could be in a crisis.

Maugham was well enough to be in London in October in time for a grand dinner given by G. B. Stern in the upstairs room at Quaglino's for her sixty-four closest friends, mainly from the world of letters. Peter drew twenty seating plans, and resisted the impulse to have a bores' table. She submitted the seating to Maugham, who said, "Peter, forgive me for saying so, but you've put all your plums at one table." These included Maugham, J. B. Priestley, H. G. Wells, Max Beerbohm, and Rose Macaulay. "Give me a difficult table if you like," Maugham said, "and I'll look after it for you." A reporter approached Miss Stern at the party and asked what its purpose was. She thought of Alice ("If a fish came to me, and told me he was going on a journey, I should say, with what porpoise?"). "Couldn't you say," she replied, "that I wanted to see my friends?"[25]

One Sunday in October, Maugham visited the poet and novelist Siegfried Sassoon and his wife at their house in Wiltshire, Heytesbury, which was set back from the road by a hundred yards of lawn. Among the guests was the American playwright S. N. Behrman, upon whom Maugham made a powerful first impression. "His features were strong and clearly cut," Behrman recalled. "He was smallish but one felt great strength, enormous self-control. The expression on his face was hard to define, elusive in spite of the clarity. It conveyed a kind of punitive resignation, as if he expected very little from life, but that he meant to make up for that little by distributing petty revenges."[26]

In November, Maugham went to one of Sybil Colefax's dinner parties. Among the other guests were Virginia Woolf, still beautiful in her mid-fifties and brimming over with wit and gossip, Max Beerbohm, with red-tinged, pouched blue eyes, looking like a porcelain figurine from another era, and a young novelist named Christopher Isherwood, whose book, *Goodbye to Berlin*, had been much admired. Maugham's dark, watchful, bridge-player's eyes intimidated Isherwood; his stammer made Isherwood feel that it was he who had a speech defect. But behind the wrinkled mask of his face Isherwood was aware of a shy warmth to which he was eager to respond. If Maugham had let him, he would have liked to adopt him as his "Uncle Willie."

Isherwood had had too much to drink, and he interrupted a story Maugham was telling to say, "Mr. Maugham, on the boat to China, last winter, we had an experience which was exactly like one of your stories." He started telling the story, but his slurred voice lost the thread, and he left the room, thinking himself in disgrace. As he let himself out of the house a parlormaid came forward with a pen and asked him to sign Lady Colefax's guestbook. Scrawling his signature with a shaking hand, he put so much pressure on the pen that it snapped in half. After he had left, Maugham, far from being annoyed at his behavior, turned to Virginia Woolf and said, "That young man holds the future of the English novel in his hands."[27] Aside from admiring Isherwood's work, he felt a sort of compassion for the young writer who had behaved clumsily because he was intimidated. He and Isherwood became friends when they met in California during the war, and Maugham referred to him as "that delightful strange man whom you could never really know."[28]

Maugham also saw Frank Swinnerton, who told him he was concerned about the Americanization of the language. Maugham was making visits to Bermondsey with Alan, with the thought of writing another slum novel, a sequel to *Liza of Lambeth*. His conversation with Swinnerton still in mind, he asked a Bermondsey man whether, if he wanted to tell someone to " 'op it," he would say "beat it." The man looked at Maugham for a moment as he thought the question through and then said, "Do you mean, if I wanted to say fuck off?"[29]

In September, Prime Minister Neville Chamberlain had gone to Germany and signed the Munich Pact, which gave the Sudetenland to Hitler and abandoned England's ally, Czechoslovakia. Chamberlain returned to London (the Lord Chancellor drove to the airport to welcome him) and proclaimed "peace in our time." The policy of appeasement seemed to be a success. Even Maugham thought so, for he wrote Alanson in October, "Well, we've escaped war for many years."[30]

England was nonetheless preparing for war, and many young men joined the armed forces in 1938, among them Robin, who thought of forming a commando unit called "Maugham's Own." As a law student, he went to Lincoln's Inn to join the Inns of Court Regiment, but he stood in the wrong line and was recruited by the tanks section. Maugham was amused to hear that the Lancers, a cavalry regiment that had been mechanized, had changed its motto from "Love and depart" to "Screw and bolt."[31]

One of the strongest supporters of Chamberlain and appeasement was Maugham's brother, the Lord Chancellor. On December 14, 1938, at the Constitutional Club, he made an inflammatory speech that combined a passionate defense of Chamberlain's policy with an attack on its chief critic, Winston Churchill. The Lord Chancellor, who as a cabinet member had access to classified information, warned that the Germans were able to drop 3,000 tons of bombs in a single day and that they could do irreparable damage to London and other great cities. The men who did not consider these alarming facts, he said, "ought to be either shot or hanged." This obvious reference to Churchill did not wait long for a reply, for in the evening paper several days later there was a headline that read: "Churchill's Attack on Cabinet Ministers." "It may be doubted whether the highest legal luminary in the land, the head of our whole system of judicature," Churchill said, "is well advised to use language which savours of lynch law and mob law abhorrent equally to the British character and Constitution."[32]

The appeasement policy also began to worry Maugham, who tried to warn his brother that France was a shaky ally. Through his influential Riviera friend, Horace de Carbuccia, he was well versed in French political scandal, and he went to the House of Lords to see the Lord Chancellor. When Frederic appeared he removed his long-bottomed wig, placed it on a wig stand, and hung up his robe. Willie told him that he had proof that a member of the French cabinet was in the pay of the Germans. He had seen a photograph of a check paid to the cabinet member's wife. Frederic was skeptical and said it was probably a forgery. When Willie tried to explain that France was riddled with corruption, Frederic said: "My dear Willie . . . You will appreciate that the most secret Intelligence documents are sent to me as a member of the cabinet. You are not even a politician; you are a novelist out of touch with reality. I therefore have every reason to disbelieve almost everything you've said. . . . And in any case—you can take it from me—there will be no war."[33]

Maugham's concern with the state of Europe came out inferentially in *Christmas Holiday*, which was published in England in February 1939 and in the United States in October. On the surface this was the story of a young and naïve upper-middle-class Englishman, Charley Mason, who goes to Paris for a five-day vacation at Christmas. He meets a young woman who is working in a brothel and whose husband has been sent to the Guiana penal colony for murder. The story of the murder and life in the penal colony, based on Maugham's research, is told in detail. The young Englishman finds all the assumptions of his background questioned. He is thrown from a life of cozy complacency into a life of risk and crime. When he returns to Porchester Close, W.2, "only one thing had happened to him, it was rather curious when you came to think of it, and he didn't just then quite know what to do about it: the bottom had fallen out of his world."[34]

In a larger sense *Christmas Holiday* was Maugham's comment on the approaching end of the between-the-wars era. He sensed that the established order in Europe, and with it his own *douceur de vivre* in Cap Ferrat, were about to collapse. The bottom was falling out of Europe. Charley represented the liberal middle class that had ruled Europe and was now being outflanked by extremists. In the character of Simon, Charley's friend, Maugham drew the portrait of a revolutionary, an outsider who tries to detach himself from human needs and becomes a political fanatic. In the character of Robert Berger, the murderer, Maugham suggested that his real motive was a perversion of the creative instinct, an urge for self-fulfillment. Men such as this, failed artists, capable of anything, were responsible for the social upheavals in Europe and for the war that would break out in a matter of months.

Christmas Holiday could be read as a political allegory, as Glenway Wescott noted in *Images of Truth*. Maugham, he said, "explains more of the human basis for fascism and nazism and communism than anyone else has done: the self-fascinated, intoxicated, insensible character of all that new leadership in Europe; the womanish passivity of the unhappy masses dependent on it and devoted to it; the Anglo-Saxon bewilderment in the matter, which still generally prevails; and the seeds of historic evil yet to come."[35]

None of the reviewers at the time saw the larger meaning of the book, which they read as a straight melodrama laced with a satire on English middle-class smugness, in lines such as "Oh well, we English have a wonderful capacity for making our wild oats into a nourishing diet." In the *London Mercury* in March, Graham Greene said *Christmas Holiday* was cliché-ridden and displayed an "odd ignorance of human feeling," while Frank Swinnerton in the *Observer* on February 5 said it was "very nearly a masterpiece," with the "beautiful simplicity of Manon Lescaut," and Evelyn Waugh in the *Spectator* on February 17 praised its "accuracy, economy and control."[36]

By the time *Christmas Holiday* appeared in England, Maugham was in the United States in search of an osteopath to straighten out a kink in his back caused by his car accident the previous September. He saw the Broadway shows and expressed admiration for Robert E. Sherwood's *Abe Lincoln in Illinois*.[37] He went to San Francisco to see Bert Alanson, and then to Washington via Chicago. He wrote Robin from the Palmer House in Chicago to congratulate him on passing the first part of his bar exam and to warn him about drinking too much. "You were quite obviously drinking a great deal too much and the immediate effect was to make you very nervous and then depressed; I have had too much to do with soaks not to look with dismay upon the prospects of anyone I know becoming one."[38]

In Washington, Maugham had a touch of flu but was kept busy with interviews and photographs "in every position except standing on my head." He was pleased with himself, for he had won a dollar at bridge from a member of Roosevelt's cabinet. Editors were anxious to entertain him, and he was being paid five hundred dollars to speak for two minutes on the radio. "Gerald has been trying to reckon that at eight hours a day for a year," he wrote Alanson. "The amount of commissions I am pressed to accept here and there is quite fantastic. So you see, your little friend is on the crest."[39] One commission he accepted was an article on tolerance for the *Reader's Digest*.

In mid-March he was a guest on Rudy Vallee's radio show. *Variety* reported "five minutes of philosophical cross-fire emerging from a question put to Maugham about embryonic writers. The air actually dripped with deep thinking, Vallee matching observation for observation until it became difficult to differentiate between the literati and the obligato."[40]

Planning to return to France on the Italian line, Maugham found the offices picketed by hundreds of women carrying placards that said "Get Out of Spain." He canceled his booking and took the *Queen Mary* to Cherbourg. From Paris he wrote Barbara Back that "the Americans, as you probably know, are growing all the time more and more anti-German. I think there is little doubt that if war breaks out they will come in very soon. Here people seem to think it is imminent."[41]

But for the moment it was life as usual when he returned to the Riviera. Alan Searle came to visit, and Maugham saw a good deal of the Windsors, who had wanted to go to Morocco but were advised that they had better not. The mystery writer E. Phillips Oppenheim came to lunch and told how he had been robbed of $100,000 by his agent in America, who was none other than Eric Pinker, the son of J. B. Pinker, the canny Scotsman who had been Maugham's agent.[42] Eric, who had founded the American branch of the agency after his father's death in 1922, was a sporty type who liked to gamble. Oppenheim complained to Thomas E. Dewey, New York's crusading Attorney General, and Eric Pinker was convicted of fraud and served a term in Sing Sing. The agency went into liquidation. Pinker was paroled on the understanding that he would not handle other people's money again, and went to work for Dunhill's selling cigars in a frock coat.[43]

In spite of Maugham's efforts to maintain life as usual, the outside world butted in. One day he received a notice that the French Navy wanted to confer with him. Several days later two cars came up his driveway and half a dozen officers in impressive uniforms got out. One, gold-braided, with a rosette in his buttonhole, was an admiral, who said they wanted a strip of his land for a gun emplacement. If war broke out, he explained, it would be a source of satisfaction to Maugham to have a big gun to fire at Italian ships. The admiral said that Maugham was a well-known friend of France—surely he would not hinder a plan that was of urgent necessity to the security of the state. They made Maugham feel that he alone was responsible for the safety of France's southern flank.

Intimidated by men in uniform, he was stripping them in his mind and imagining them in their underwear to make them seem more human. He said he was only too glad to comply. The admiral congratulated him on his public spirit, which the English were so famous for. A gunnery expert explained that they wanted only so many meters by so many meters. The gun would be so well camouflaged that he would not even see it. How much did he want for the use of the property? Nothing, Maugham said.

"We are quite prepared to pay a reasonable price," one of the officers said.

"I'm sure you are," Maugham said, "but I have lived many years in this country and have received many favors from the French people. I couldn't think of asking you to pay for a little strip of land that you need for the defense of your country."[44]

The admiral said he greatly appreciated Maugham's generosity, and two days later Maugham received a stiff official letter telling him that on mature consideration they had decided not to place a gun on his property. Gun emplacements were built elsewhere—on high ground above the Mauresque and along the sunny coast—barbed wire was strung, and machine-gun nests were dug. The bridges were guarded and there were soldiers everywhere. If the Italians attacked, the Riviera would become a battlefield. On the other side of the border Mussolini decreed that Italians who were not in Italy for mobilization would have their property confiscated. There were 250,000 Italians between Marseilles and Ventimiglia. Maugham lost his footman and three of his gardeners.

Still hoping that peace could be kept, he went to Montecatini with Gerald in May to take the cure while he could still travel to Italy. He took the mud baths and went to bed at half past ten. He wrote G. B. Stern that he was "getting rid of rheumatism, malaria, envy, malice and all uncharitableness."[45] Gerald was taking the cure for the liver. He was pleased that *Christmas Holiday* had sold 20,000 copies in England and hoped to reach 30,000. *Redbook* had paid $16,000 for the serialization rights. "Here in Italy," Maugham wrote Alanson, "everyone seems convinced that there will be no war, so unless the Germans do something idiotic I think we are safe."[46]

Returning to the Mauresque in June, Maugham went through the paces of a normal summer, with all the usual guests, and golf and tennis, and cruises aboard the *Sara*. Everyone had a reason why there would be no war. Hore-Belisha, the British Secretary of State for War, was on the Continent, someone said, and if there was going to be a war, he would obviously be in England. Maugham said he hoped Hitler realized that. One of his guests, the French financier Jacques Raindre, argued that German businessmen wanted peace. War would ruin them. Hitler was bluffing. Raindre had just bought a large block of shares in a Polish oil company and convinced Maugham to go in with him.[47]

Vincent and Liza were there. Vincent went to Monte Carlo to play in the tennis tournament, and reported that everyone was leaving and there were no seats on the Blue Train. The mayor of St. Jean called to say that mobilization orders were about to be posted. War clouds drifted over the Mauresque. Maugham told his guests there was no danger, until the Senegalese troops from the colonial infantry base at Fréjus began appearing on the roads. Vincent said he had seen them guarding the railway bridge at Cap Ferrat, and Maugham decided it was time for Vincent and Liza to go back to England. When he went to the garage, Jean, the chauffeur, informed him that he had just been called up and swore the French Army would be in Rome in two weeks. Ernest, the Swiss butler, went to Nice to see his consul, who told him Switzerland was mobilizing. François, the head gardener, was too old to be called up, but soon the other servants were gone. A young English writer and his wife came for lunch. They were carefree and gay and would not believe Maugham when he told them that war might break out at any minute. He convinced them to leave at once for Paris.[48]

Maugham wondered what to do. The Mauresque without servants was uninhabitable, and yet he did not want to leave his home unless he had to. He worried that French troops would occupy it and fire revolvers at his pictures. One day Gerald came back from Villefranche and said the Chasseurs Alpins had left at dawn for the frontier, and the harbor master had told him that all private yachts had to leave the harbor within twenty-four hours. It was then that Maugham decided to take the *Sara* down the coast with Gerald. If war was declared, they would sail at once for England. In Nice they stocked up on sardines, canned soup, corned beef, tongue, sliced ham, macaroni, and rice.[49]

They sailed out of Villefranche harbor and down the coast to Saint-Maxime, where they stopped to see Maugham's friend Horace de Carbuccia, the editor of the pro-Fascist sheet *Gringoire*. Carbuccia, a fat, bald Corsican, bragged that he had paid three million francs to get elected to the French parliament. His magazine had become increasingly pro-German and -Italian and anti-Semitic. It was rumored that he was subsidized by Mussolini. *Gringoire* specialized in personal attacks and invective, which had in one instance driven a cabinet minister to suicide. At the time Carbuccia had said to Maugham: "It's not playing the game to commit suicide. It's taking an unfair advantage in a political controversy." Now, as they sipped pink champagne before dinner, Carbuccia said he was furious that France and England were going to war over Poland. "Why should we care about Poland?" he asked. "The Poles have always been worthless people." Maugham defended the Franco-British alliance. It was the end of their friendship. In 1942 Carbuccia wrote a malicious article in *Gringoire* called "Farewell to My British Friend." He said that Maugham's story "The Treasure," about a man who sleeps with his maid, was in reality about Maugham and his footman at the Mauresque. He also claimed that Maugham smoked opium and that "the tips of his fingers were slightly damaged by the dross of the opium which he had smoked with moderation since his return from China."[50] After the war, on January 13, 1950, Carbuccia was sentenced as a collaborator to five years' hard labor.

Leaving Saint-Maxime, Maugham looked in the *Mediterranean Pilot* for a good place to berth, and chose Bandol, a pretty but unfashionable resort town near Toulon. In Bandol he and Gerald and the crew of three were virtual prisoners aboard the yacht. The movements of individuals were restricted and they could not go even as far as Toulon without a permit. A blackout was ordered and they had to paint over the *Sara*'s portholes. The cabin boy jumped ship and the second mate left for Italy. Summer visitors had fled, most hotels were closed, and the Bandol casino had been turned into a hospital. Maugham settled down to a quiet life. It was the first time since his student days that he had done his own shopping. An honest-looking shopkeeper sold him a Camembert guaranteed to be *coulant*, but it was hard as a rock; things were never what they seemed. In the morning he drank his *café au lait* and read the *Petit Marseillais* and the *Petit Var*. At ten he got the English papers, and at noon there was a radio broadcast from Marseilles. After lunch and a nap he strolled through town and watched games of boule. At five there was *Le Soleil* from Marseilles. At dusk they shut down and air-raid wardens patrolled the docks and called out if chinks of light showed.[51]

On September 1 Gerald came on board the *Sara* and told Maugham that the Germans had invaded Poland. "Good," Maugham said. "No, bad," Gerald said. "It means war." "I know," Maugham said. On September 3 England and France declared war. Chamberlain appointed Churchill First Lord of the Admiralty, and Maugham's brother Frederic, the outspoken supporter of appeasement, resigned as Lord Chancellor, having served in that office about a year and a half. He had been involved in the passage of several important pieces of legislation, but perhaps his most notable achievement was reviving the medieval custom of the Lord Chancellor's breakfast, which took place at 12.45 in the Royal Gallery of the House of Lords. As part of this preposterous ritual, guests wore chain armor, knee breeches, buckled shoes, and gold swords. An almoner announced, "Be it ye will of ye justices and barristers that ye be forthwith seated," and a boar's head was brought in.[52]

Maugham had been planning a second trip to India that winter, which was now out of the question. With a war on, he wanted to be of use, and wrote the Ministry of Information to offer his services. By September 25 he was back at the Mauresque. There was an antiaircraft battery on Cap Ferrat, and soldiers were bivouacking on the Nice golf course. Maugham was despondent at not contributing to the war effort. "I realize that with the whole country eager to get some occupation connected with the war," he wrote Robin, "they can find as many people as they want younger and perhaps more competent than I; so I much fear that I shall be left to twiddle my thumbs indefinitely."[53] Gerald wrote Robin: "Willie and I are back here but feeling very aged and on the shelf—nobody seems to want our services. He is very low and gloomy about it. I am trying to take it easily but only succeeding at times. If you young people insist on running this war I can only hope that you will end it quickly and make a peace that will last out my few remaining years."[54]

When Frederic Maugham resigned as Lord Chancellor, his reward for loyal service was a hereditary peerage. He became Lord Maugham, first Viscount of Hartfield, and Robin upon his death would inherit the title. Maugham was so pleased by this development that he decided to settle a trust of $25,000 on his nephew. He was hoping that Robin, with his title, his law degree, and a little capital, would launch a successful political career. He asked Alanson to draw up a trust, which Robin would receive after his uncle's death. "I want to do something to make his future position somewhat easier," he wrote Alanson. "You see, his father has three daughters and with only a fourth share Robin cannot hope to inherit a large fortune."[55]

Maugham remained unwillingly at the Mauresque, but in October a job was found for him. The Ministry of Information asked him to write a book on the French war effort, intended to boost British morale. Pleased to be actively involved, although the role of journalist was far from his favorite, he wrote Alanson on October 21 that he was off to the front and that "everyone seems very confident about the results of the war, and it looks as though it really couldn't last the three years the British are preparing for."[56]

He was given a six-week Potemkin tour that convinced him that the French were resolute and single-minded and would fight to the finish. This was during the inactive opening months of the war, when French troops remained huddled behind the Maginot Line and not a shot against the Germans had yet been fired. He was escorted to the front and given an interview with the Minister for Armaments. In Nancy he visited the headquarters of General de Lattre, who had beautiful manners and looked very elegant in his well-cut uniform. He visited a *casemate* on the Maginot Line, whose commandant reminded him of a wellfed Dutch burgher. "If necessary I could stand a siege of six months," he said, "but I should hope they would come and rescue us before then." He found the French soldiers highly motivated, the morale good, and the rapport between officers and men based on camaraderie. In short, he adopted the propaganda line the ministry wanted, ignoring all evidence to the contrary.[57]

While in Nancy he ran into Godfrey Winn, who, with his column for Beaverbrook, speaking for the inarticulate and the submerged, had become the best known journalist in England. Winn was also writing a series on the French war effort. According to Maugham's account, Winn came up to him and said, "There's something I particularly wanted to ask you, and I thought I might never have another opportunity."

"What is it?" Maugham asked.

"I want to know why you've dropped me."

"I don't know that I've done that."

"Yes, you have. It's obvious. I never see you now. When I've written to you to ask if I could come and see you, you've made excuses to put me off. When I've asked you to lunch, you've refused. You never ask me to come and stay with you on the Riviera. What have I done to offend you?"

Maugham protested that there was nothing, that they led different lives now, that it was force of circumstance, the course of events. Winn kept insisting, until at last Maugham said, "Well, if you insist on having the truth, you can have it, but I'd rather not tell you."

"I want it," Winn said.

"I'm horrified at the stuff you write. I think it's muck. I think it's ignoble."

"D'you mean to say that's why you've dropped me? Can't you distinguish between the writer and what he writes?"

"No, I can't be on terms of familiarity with somebody whose writing I despise. . . . The tragic thing is that you write straight from the heart; that's why it goes to the heart of your readers. In your case certainly the man and the writer are one and the same.

"After all," Maugham went on, "what can it matter to you what one solitary person thinks of you? You've an enormous success and you earn a huge income. A lot of people worship you, and you've got masses of friends without me. . . . Why should you bother about me? One out of so many?"

"You wouldn't understand," Winn said, and walked away.[58]

Maugham was the writer he had admired and emulated, and his friendship was all the more precious because Winn had not been able to live up to him. He went on to earn a reputation as a war correspondent. He was the only reporter to sail on the disastrous P.Q. convoy from Iceland to Archangel in 1942, in which 23 of 36 ships were lost. After the war he renewed his friendship with Maugham.

On November 18 Maugham wrote Alanson that he had spent "a thrilling week with the French army at the front."[59] He had been in the coal mines of Lens, in Flanders, not far from the battlefields from which he had evacuated the wounded in the early days of World War I. He visited the miners' small red-brick houses, and went down into the shafts, creeping through holes until he came to places where they were actually mining coal. The mine manager told him that the work looked much harder than it really was. He got black with coal dust, and though he washed and washed, he could not get it out of his eyelashes and eyebrows. He later used the material from his visit to the mines in *The Razor's Edge*.

Maugham also visited armaments factories, and found the French very confident, turning out tanks and planes. "I have never seen them more united and more serious. They have taken the war as though it was a crusade." He visited areas from which the inhabitants of Alsace-Lorraine had been evacuated, and wound up with a tour of a battleship in Toulon. He was home before Christmas and began to write. "When I was at the Front," he said, "I would have said that the whole nation is under arms, but after visiting the armaments works I was almost inclined to say that the whole country is one huge factory. . . . I do not believe that we in England yet realize how intense the French effort is and with what determination the whole country has applied its energies to the prosecution of the struggle."[60]

The fruit of Maugham's reportage, a book called *France at War*, was published in England in March 1940. Three months later France fell, and publication was discontinued. The *Saturday Review of Literature* on June 1 called it the worst kind of propaganda, which "reminds one of nothing so much as a goody-goody book written by a pious lady for Sunday school scholars."[61] Maugham made a quick recovery from *France at War*, and in October 1940 *Redbook* published his "Inside Story of the Collapse of France."

Having done his bit for the propaganda effort, he turned to other matters. William Lyon Phelps had sent him his autobiography, in which he quoted John Galsworthy as saying that he couldn't think why Maugham had written *Cakes and Ale*. "A silly remark," Maugham wrote Phelps in January 1940. "I wrote it because I had had the character of my heroine with me for twenty years and at last hit upon a plan which gave me the opportunity of using it. . . . Galsworthy was a very nice man, but so anxious to be the perfect gentleman (which indeed he very nearly was) that it made him a trifle obtuse."[62]

There was also the matter of Robin's trust. Robin was now a trooper in the army expecting to get his commission soon, and Maugham was delighted to get a photograph of him in uniform. "You look about fifteen," he said, "and if you really look like that I don't think your mother should let you out at night, with blackouts and what all, by yourself." He told Robin that the trust documents would soon be signed, and after that "you can look forward to my demise with fortitude. . . . I am giving Bert power to change securities as he thinks fit, in the confident hope that he will gradually increase the capital, so that the longer I live the more you are likely to receive."[63] Robin wrote Alanson a thank-you note replete with yoicks, hallelujahs, and tralalas. In April, Maugham sent Alanson a check for $25,000, and in May he signed the trust documents.[64]

By that time Maugham was in London, haunting the Ministry of Information, hoping for an assignment, and feeling like a performing dog in a circus whose tricks the public would probably like but who somehow couldn't be quite fitted into the program.[65] Sounding out friends who might be able to help, he had dinner on April 2 with Kenneth Clark, director of the film division of the Ministry of Information, Harold Nicolson, and Leslie Howard. They discussed British writers who remained in America in spite of the war, such as Aldous Huxley, W. H. Auden, Christopher Isherwood, and Gerald Heard. Why should these four eminent men have flown, Nicolson wondered, and wrote in the *Spectator* on April 19: "How can we proclaim over there that we are fighting for the liberated mind, when four of our most liberated intellectuals refuse to identify themselves with those who fight and with those who oppose the battle?"[66] The *Spectator* later printed the following epigram, addressed "To Certain Intellectuals Safe in America":

> *This Europe stinks, you cried, swift to desert*
> *Your stricken country in her sore distress.*
> *You may not care, but still I will assert,*
> *Since you have left us, here the stink is less.*

For many America seemed the safest place to be, and Liza, pregnant with her second child, was persuaded by her mother to go there in the summer. Liza's husband, Vincent Paravicini, had become a naturalized British subject and had enlisted in the army. Liza at first stayed on Long Island with the Doubledays.[67]

In June, Maugham was sent back to France to write some more optimistic articles. This time there were no guided tours to the front, for the front had collapsed. The Maginot Line *casemate* he had visited six months before had fallen in less than a day. He stayed on at the Mauresque, restless and anxious, and worried that if the Italians occupied the Riviera they would intern British subjects. He also heard that Goebbels had mentioned *Ashenden* on the radio as an example of British cynicism, and that he was on a blacklist and would be arrested and sent to Berlin to be tried as a spy.[68]

By June 4 English forces had been evacuated from Dunkirk, and not long after that Maugham heard Premier Paul Reynaud announce in faltering accents on the radio that France accepted defeat and that Marshal Pétain would sign the armistice. François, the gardener, wept. Maugham wept. He had ordered 20,000 tulip bulbs to be ready for planting in December, and now he would have to leave. He went to see the British vice consul in Nice, John Taylor, who told him that all British subjects had to be evacuated. In the absence of available ships,

Taylor requisitioned two empty English coal barges, the *Saltersgate* and the *Ashcrest*, which came into Cannes harbor. The barges were ordered to take back to England about 1,300 British subjects stranded on the Riviera.

Maugham decided to join the exodus, leaving Haxton behind to close up the Mauresque and sell the *Sara*. He took a last look at his paintings and chose from his bookcase three books: Plato's *Trial and Death of Socrates*, Thackeray's *Henry Esmond*, and Charlotte Brontë's *Villette*. He locked the door to his writing room and went to his bedroom to pack. He could take only one suitcase on board, and with a pang left behind a new tailcoat, thinking he would never need full dress again. He said goodbye to Gerald, wondering whether he would ever see him again. He drove to Cannes, where an unlikely group of refugees was assembled on the dock, made up in part of prominent Riviera hostesses of venerable age, accustomed to traveling first class, and their servants.

They waited for hours on the dock in the summer heat. Maugham was sixty-six, and he had not been so uncomfortable in a long time. One woman died of the heat while waiting. Finally, with 537 others, including the crew, he boarded the *Saltersgate*, whose iron decks were thick with coal dust. Maugham slept in the hold and queued up for the daily stew with dowagers wearing pearl necklaces and diamond rings, and washed in water that a hundred before him had used. Social distinctions were buried in coal dust. He watched Mrs. Norman Craig, a popular Monte Carlo resident who often had her meals at the Hotel de Paris, eating her soup on the steps of the galley. He heard a woman ask a crew member where the games deck was. "It's all over the ship, madam," he replied. He admired an Australian who had made a pail out of an empty jam jar, and a spoon out of the top of a biscuit tin.

There was talk of Italian submarines, and the skipper, Captain Stubbs, joined a French convoy in Marseilles that was headed for Oran. Maugham decided that if they were hit he would not try to save himself. He asked a doctor for advice. "Don't struggle," the doctor said. "Open your mouth, and the water pouring into your throat will bring on unconsciousness in less than a minute." From Oran they headed for Gibraltar, arriving on June 25. They spent three days there, and were let ashore in batches of fifty to shop. Finally, on July 8, after twenty days "without even taking our clothes off," Maugham wrote, "we reached the blessed shores of England." No one but Gerald knew where he was, and *The New York Times* had listed him as missing.[69]

But he was a survivor, and in more ways than one. In June his new collection of short stories, *The Mixture as Before*, was published. The title was taken from the London *Times* review of his last volume of stories, *Cosmopolitans*, which had been intended to brand him as a formula writer. Maugham wrote in a foreword that "after pursuing the art of fiction for over forty years I have a notion that I know a good deal more about it than most people," so why not the mixture as before, since the mixture was effective? He also announced that "I have now written between 80 and 90 stories, I shall not write any more." When another volume called *Creatures of Circumstance* appeared seven years later he explained that he had written "I shall not write many more," but that a typesetter had dropped the *m*.

The publication of *The Mixture as Before* was the occasion for an important review by V. S. Pritchett in the *New Statesman and Nation*. Taking a long look at Maugham's oeuvre, Pritchett said that his indifference over the years to political and social positions had been vindicated by events. "The last forty years of the English novel," Pritchett wrote, "have seen an enormous and optimistic social preoccupation. . . . The present war has, on the short view, dashed all that and Maugham the skeptic, who would have nothing to do with it all either in politics or belief, survives among the wreckage of public Utopias and private sensibilities."

Pritchett also noted Maugham's debt to Kipling, for "Maugham is Kipling, turned inside out, discovering alcohol, beachcombing and middle-class sex, where Kipling portrayed the Roman overlord and evoked the secret, savage hierarchy of the jungle. . . . People go to pieces in the Maugham jungle and, living happily as wreckage, disconcert the conventional; they do not, as in Kipling, discover the masonic ritualism of the animals. Of the two writers it is hard to say who is the more romantic, the more masochistic, the more knowing."

These ten new stories, however, were not set in Kipling country, but on the Riviera, in England, and in the penal colony that Maugham had visited. "Gigolo and Gigolette" was based on the circus act Maugham had described to Fred Bason. "Three Fat Women of Antibes" was based on some of his Riviera neighbors. "The Voice of the Turtle," in which a young writer is invited to the Mauresque to meet a famous prima donna, was based on an incident involving Godfrey Winn. The story about the crown prince and the ring flung in the fire was one that Lillie Langtry had told him. "The Treasure," the story of the perfect parlormaid who enjoys a night of love with her employer and then reverts to type, was the one that Horace de Carbuccia said concerned a valet rather than a maid. "The Lotus Eater," set in Capri with a good deal of local color (drinking the light Capri wine and eating Bel Paese and figs for dessert), was based on Ellingham Brooks, the man who had given up London life for Capri but ran out of money.

The collection contained three of Maugham's best stories. In "The Facts of Life" a young man goes to Paris, and against his father's warnings, lends money to a stranger, gambles, and picks up a woman. There are no disastrous consequences, and he comes out 6,000 francs ahead. This was the happy side of *Christmas Holiday*, showing that a naïve youth could benefit from a trip to the corrupt Continent. It was Maugham at his most lighthearted, exposing the fallacy of the moralist position. "I'm glad to be able to tell you that it has a moral," he said, "and that is: it's better to be born lucky than to be born rich."

"The Lion's Skin" concerns the son of a waiter posing as an English gentleman, who, in a moment of crisis, loses his life because he behaves the way he thinks an English gentleman should. The mask he wears proves fatal. Of "Lord Mountdrago" Maugham said: "I had it in mind for years before I wrote it, and I put it off because I thought it was a terribly difficult story to make convincing. At last I said to myself, come on, let's have a shot at it." The lord in question is a foreign minister and suffers from nightmares about a Labour MP whom he has ridiculed so thoroughly that he has practically ruined the MP's career. Lord Mountdrago seeks medical help, and the doctor is Maugham's familiar *raisonneur*: "Nothing could shock him any longer. He knew by now that men were liars, he knew how extravagant was their vanity; he knew far worse than that about them; but he knew that it was not for him to judge or to condemn." The doctor suggests that the only way to find relief from the nightmares is to make an apology. But this Lord Mountdrago cannot do, and he kills himself. On the same day the Labour MP dies. The story might have been written by Edgar Allan Poe. It was one of Maugham's few departures from the naturalistic terrain he was comfortable on, but it is entirely convincing and has a haunting quality not often found in his work.

Exhausted by his ordeal but glad to have escaped from France, Maugham settled into a suite at the Dorchester Hotel, which he liked because it was in the heart of Mayfair. He submitted to interviews and wrote an account of his trip. One day he ran into Syrie in the lobby. As Edith Sitwell told the story in a letter to a friend: "I hear that Willie (I do not know if this is true) found himself being reconciled—(One of those air-raid shelter reconciliations)—with his ex-wife, at a hotel in London the other day. That great woman, who was about to leave for America, said, in an effort to enlist his sympathy: 'Oh, Willie, I know I shall be torpedoed!' 'Then,' said Willie, true to type as ever, 'I have only one piece of advice to offer you. Keep your mouth open, and you will drown the sooner.' Mrs. M. began to cry."[70]

Syrie was leaving for New York in response to a wire from the Doubledays informing her that Liza was gravely ill. In the midst of her pregnancy she had caught the measles, chicken pox, and pneumonia, and the Doubledays did not want to shoulder the responsibility alone.

Maugham found London marvelously unchanged. "Life here goes on in a manner that is almost normal," he wrote Alanson. "There is no shortage of anything . . . we all have an implicit belief in Winston Churchill. If he had been Premier six months sooner, I really think the war would have been over by now."[71] In August the air raids began, but although there were shelters, no one could be persuaded to use them. People collected in the hotel lounge and gossiped and had tea or cocktails. "I am staggered by the difference between what I see here and what I saw in France," he wrote Richard Cordell. "There they were terrified of the Germans, here they don't care a damn for them. Slow to rouse, these people, but by God when they are roused!"[72]

One day when he was walking in Hyde Park he saw a stalled car that a young woman was pushing while her escort sat in the driver's seat pumping the accelerator. He watched her struggle and push the car until it started, and the scene was to him symbolic of British resolve. Londoners went about their business to the sound of bombs, and Maugham continued to dress for dinner, not seeing why, just because there was an air raid, a gentleman should not dress like a gentleman. He invited a friend to dinner at the Dorchester, and the friend, walking home, saw a bomb drop in Piccadilly fifty yards away. He threw himself on the ground and later told Maugham, "Lucky it hadn't been raining. I would have ruined my clothes." Toward the end of August the herbarium at the Natural History Museum was destroyed. Acres of vitrines were shattered, and the carcasses of prehistoric animals were reduced to dust. Londoners responded with air-raid humor. An elderly lady told Maugham, "I find the raids much less boring than my sons-in-law."[73]

He went to a dinner party at Sybil Colefax's new house at 19 Lord North Street, one of those charming old houses with paneled walls and pretty chimneypieces. After dinner a string quartet played a Haydn sonata as sirens sounded, antiaircraft guns fired, and bombs echoed down the Thames. The musicians continued playing as though nothing had happened.[74]

In September the battle of London began in earnest. The planes arrived each night at dusk. The first intensive raids on central London were on September 7. The East End, poor and Cockney, bore the brunt of the raids because it was near the docks.

"Why doesn't Hitler bomb the West End," the Cockneys grumbled. It seemed like class prejudice on the Führer's part.

On September 10, because of a navigational error, German bombs damaged the north side of Buckingham Palace, and Queen Elizabeth said, "I'm so glad I've been bombed. It makes me feel I can look the East End in the face." It was now the turn of fashionable London. Bond Street, the Albany where Bryon had once lived, the Burlington Arcade, Mayfair—all were bombed. There were gaps where William and Mary houses had once stood, and whole streets were paved with broken glass. Burglar alarms rang away in shops. West End hotels provided bunks in cellars for regular patrons who came in to dine and dance and stayed the night. At the Dorchester, Maugham dined to the accompaniment of a band trying to drown out the sound of the anti-aircraft guns in Hyde Park.[75] He could hear the bombs, which sounded like the tearing of a giant linen sheet, and the wailing of the sirens, and the sound of the all-clear. The Dorchester's air-raid shelter was in the Turkish bath, and one stepped over hotel-mates to find an empty mattress. All the talk was so consumed with bombs and shelters that the gossip about a noted woman-about-town was that she had the deepest shelter in London.

At the height of the September bombing season Maugham went to lunch at Sybil Colefax's with H. G. Wells, Vincent Sheean, Diana Cooper, and Moura Budberg. Maugham produced a prose poem by François Mauriac with a great many invocations to God, about which H.G. teased him. The conversation was studded with "that sort of thing," and "don't you know." Mrs. Colefax was nervous. "I don't like this one bit," she said. "What if a bomb should land here now? It's much too good a bag for the Germans. Why don't we go to the shelter? It's better than just sitting here."

"I refuse to go to the shelter," H. G. Wells said, "until I have had my cheese. I'm enjoying a very good lunch. Why should I be disturbed by some wretched little barbarian adolescents in a machine? This thing has no surprises for me. I foresaw it long ago. Sybil, I want my cheese." Fleming, the elderly maid, came into the dining room and put up the wooden frames that covered the windows, which had already been broken three or four times. They finished the lunch with the lights on.[76]

Maugham kept waiting for an assignment. He tried the Intelligence Department at the War Office, his old boss, but the head of it, Ian Hay, did not want him.[77] His age was against him, but he was hoping that he could still be of use. Although he lived out of England and felt that he could never completely identify with his countrymen, the war brought out a latent patriotic side. It was a clear-cut situation in which everyone had to do his duty. He had done his bit in World War I; missions in Switzerland and Russia had laid him low with tuberculosis. In periods such as this Maugham's worldly wisdom and tolerance of human failings were in abeyance. The author of the antiwar play *For Services Rendered* stood fully behind the war effort. A good example of his changed attitude concerns a consumptive young writer named George Bullock, to whom he was giving financial assistance. Bullock, a homosexual who lived with a writer named Raymond Marriott, suffered from a shriveling of the lungs and was often bedridden. He and Marriott had written Maugham a fan letter and then met him in 1937. Between 1937 and 1940 Maugham had sent Bullock a total of six hundred pounds to cover his medical expenses. But on his return to London in 1940 Maugham learned that Marriott and Bullock were conscientious objectors, or "conchies." Marriott had gone before a tribunal and had been sent to a community in Worcestershire to work the land. Bullock, then twenty-eight, who would have been refused for active service on medical grounds, also took a pacifist stand, but was so ill that he was admitted to Brompton Hospital.

Maugham went to see him and told him that Marriott had a bad influence on him and that he would give him no more help. Marriott wrote Maugham to protest, and Maugham replied: "I am sorry George should have told you I thought you despicable. I am sure I did not say so to him. I think your influence on him has been unfortunate and it is true that I do not approve of your attitude. It is true also that I do not think any good can come out of our meeting at present, for our views on most subjects are obviously irreconcilable. We must agree to differ and leave it at that."[78]

> Willie got it into his head that I had influenced George to be a pacifist [Marriott recalled]. I asked him for money to go to the country with George, and he said he thought I was fleeing and he wanted to

stick up for his principles. When he heard that we were conchies his help stopped, he said you have had so much, you mustn't expect any more, that enormously wealthy man said that. I was also friendly with Hugh Walpole, and I had thought that of the two of them Walpole would be down on me and tell me I had to fight for king and country, but it was the other way round, Walpole the establishment Englishman wrote me that he understood but Maugham the man of the world was finished with me.[79]

In September the Ministry of Information asked Maugham if he would like to go to the United States to present the British case. He was famous there and would have no trouble getting invitations to speak. He had always refused to speak because of his stammer, but while in London he went to see the same specialist who had helped King George VI, Dr. Leahy, of 47 Clarges Street, Piccadilly. Dr. Leahy taught him the trick of snapping his fingers hard when he stammered, to get himself unstuck. When this failed he would lose patience and smash his right fist into his left palm.[80] With his impediment somewhat under control, Maugham was ready to leave for America. He may have thought that helping to nudge America into the war was similar to his World War I mission, when he had tried to keep the Mensheviks in power so that Russia could stay in the war. He may also have thought of his daughter, of his many friends there, and of the reception he would be given.

One of the last persons he saw before leaving England was Virginia Woolf, at a dinner party in Westminster. She was enchanting, and they all stayed late. The air-raid sirens had sounded and Maugham offered to take her home, but she insisted on leaving alone. There were no taxis, and Maugham, concerned for her safety, followed her at a distance. She reached Whitehall and all was well, but just past the Admiralty two planes flew over and the barrage began. Maugham shouted at her to take cover, but she could not hear him in the din. She made no attempt to move but stood in the middle of the road and threw her arms in the air. She appeared to be worshiping the flashing sky. It was strange to see her there, lit up now and then by the flares of the guns. Then the planes passed by and she moved on.[81] It was the last time Maugham saw her, for the following year she killed herself. But the incident was consistent with his role in life as an observing writer, standing always slightly apart from the event as he watched the antics of humanity.

PART VI

1940-1953

Chapter Sixteen

I think there is in the heroic courage with which man confronts the irrationality of the world a beauty greater than the beauty of art.

Maugham, *A Writer's Notebook*

ON OCTOBER 2, 1940, Maugham left for New York, an example of lend-lease in reverse. He flew from Bristol to Lisbon, where he spent a week. He did little sight-seeing, having been allowed to take only ten pounds out of England. He took the Clipper from Lisbon to New York, which stopped in the Azores and Bermuda. He was an elderly gentleman making his first transatlantic flight after having been forced out of his home by European turmoil. When the plane ran into a storm, which frightened him, he resorted to sleeping pills. The war had affected him as little else in his life had, and his escape from France was still on his mind. If brutality and treachery paid, he thought, what the hell was the use of art and literature?[1]

Liza and Ellen and Nelson Doubleday were on hand to greet him at La Guardia Airport when he landed on October 11. Immigration laws to the contrary, he was allowed to go through customs with only three dollars in his pocket. He was not likely to become a public charge. His first remark was a request for an old-fashioned. The Doubledays took him into the airport bar, and he dramatically exhibited a vial of poison, which he broke into little pieces, saying, "I won't be needing this now, Nelson."[2]

The Doubledays invited him to spend a fortnight at Barberry's, their home in Oyster Bay, to recuperate and decide what to do next. His first order of business was to ask Alanson to send him some money, for the British government had frozen his London bank account. His next problem was where to live. After his speaking tour was over he wanted a quiet place where he could finish the novel he was working on, *The Razor's Edge*. Nelson Doubleday offered to build him a house on his plantation, Bonny Hall, in South Carolina, and a separate cottage to write in. He would approve the plans, and the Doubledays would provide him with a maid, a cook, and a yardman.[3] The plantation was in Yemassee, on the Combahee River, which was pronounced "Coomby." This amused Maugham, for Americans were always accusing the British of pronouncing their place-names differently from the way they were spelled.[4]

By the end of October, Maugham was in New York, staying at the Ritz-Carlton. He had heard from Gerald, who was in Lisbon, trying to find passage to America. Gerald had closed the Mauresque, leaving the best pictures with Maugham's neighbor Lady Kenmare. He had little hope of seeing his home again. The Italians had occupied the Riviera as far as Nice, and he supposed that his property would be expropriated.[5]

In November he started giving speeches on behalf of the British war effort. He felt that England had an image problem. When a young theatrical producer named Peter Daubeny came to see him, Maugham described himself as a goodwill ambassador.

> We are hated for our reserve and our shyness [he told Daubeny], which they put down to coldness and bad manners. I am about the only resident Englishman here who has scrupulously and successfully avoided giving offense. But it is amazing how stupid and tactless some of our prominent citizens have been. Before we adjourn for dinner let me give you two words of advice for your trip here—never criticize an American to his face, unless it's to rave about something, and never call an American by his surname if he's already calling you by your Christian name—which he will do automatically.[6]

Maugham was lionized. Warner Brothers gave a cocktail party for him and introduced him to two hundred and fifty people, none of whom he had ever met before and to all of whom he had to try to say something pleasant. Photographers trailed him around the room and, whenever he was taken to meet a celebrity, raised their cameras and told him to engage in natural conversation. When his stock of natural conversation gave out he started reciting the Lord's Prayer. One of his fans called him at the hotel to read him a poem. Maugham told him he was going out. The fan asked if he could come the following day. Maugham said he would be out of town, but nothing would deter the fan. In desperation, Maugham said, "But I don't want to hear your poem, sir." There was a pause, and then the fan said: "Oh, go to hell."[7]

Persistent fans were not his only problem. Syrie was in New York, giving interviews in which she said she was the originator of the all-white room and that she had decorated for Wallis Simpson before she became the Duchess of Windsor. She wanted to do something for the war effort, she said, and would give lessons on interior decoration and send her fee to Refugees in England, Inc.[8] But since she had come as a visitor, she could not get a working permit. She went to Canada and reentered the country as a resident alien, with Nelson Doubleday posting bond for her. The Doubledays put her up at the River Club, and soon the bills started coming in. She was entertaining constantly and putting it on the tab, and even drawing cash from the club. Finally Ellen Doubleday told her that she could stay there two more months and no longer. "Of course," Syrie said, "it would not look very well if this should get out in the papers." "I had never in my life come so close to feeling that I was being blackmailed," Ellen Doubleday recalled.[9]

"Syrie has been making a terrible nuisance of herself and leading Liza a hell of a life," Maugham wrote Barbara Back in December. "She has been making dreadful scenes and threatening to commit suicide: in fact the whole bag of tricks. . . . Liza has only stood firm on one thing and that is a refusal to live with her."[10] Liza was unhappy, pining for her husband in England, slowly recovering from her illness, and worried that it would affect her pregnancy. The Doubledays had put her up with relatives near their estate, and she felt alone and homesick. The relatives had a daughter who resented Liza for getting too much attention and who would come to her room, bang on the door, and say: "Don't you know you are going to die? Of course you are. I heard the doctor say so."[11]

Maugham was now living alone for the first time since he had moved into the Mauresque in 1927, but he had many friends in New York, including the playwright S. N. Behrman. They had hit it off at their first meeting at Siegfried Sassoon's country house in 1938, for they had several things in common. Sam Behrman, the son of a rabbi in Worcester, Massachusetts, had, like Maugham, trod the uphill road to success, writing seventeen plays before the first one was produced on Broadway. Also like Maugham, he was short and believed that he was physically ugly. On a squat body perched a large head with a high forehead and nearsighted eyes that blinked through thick-lensed glasses. A cigarette constantly dangled from his lips, which he consumed by sucking it into his mouth with spasmodic lip movements, never touching it with his hands. He never looked freshly shaven because his beard successfully resisted all razors. His walk was like the waddle of a penguin. And yet Sam Behrman was more attractive than a matinee idol, for there emanated from him an extraordinary warmth and charm. Everyone who met him felt the better for it afterward. He was witty, he was wry, he enhanced the moments spent in his company.

He and Maugham developed a kind of bantering cronyism that Maugham had with few other men. Maugham would kid Sam about his looks, saying that he was glad his beauty had stood the test of time. He wrote Sam: "I don't know why I go on liking you, but somehow I do. Do you think I ought to consult a psychoanalyst?" Sam responded to Maugham's fondness with an unconditional admiration for his work, and said that his feeling for Maugham was one of "unashamed love." But the love had a veil of teasing and humor. Maugham said that Sam was anti-Semitic, in response to which Sam sent him a set of phylacteries (small boxes containing strips of parchment inscribed with the Hebrew Scriptures), telling him that his standing with the Lord was not secure and that the phylacteries would fortify it. They carried on running jokes, such as Maugham playing the Jew to Sam's *goy* and offering to lend him money at usurious rates. Another was that Sam had written *Cakes and Ale* and Maugham would hear from his lawyers if he had not already done so.[12]

Sam Behrman saw a good deal of Maugham, for he had committed himself to dramatizing the short story "Jane," the tale of a middle-aged lady from the provinces who becomes the wonder of smart London society because she always tells the truth, and marries a man half her age, only to leave him for an older man. They discussed casting; Sam had offered the play to Katharine Cornell, who had turned it down. Maugham said that when he was writing plays, actors were simply informed when rehearsals began, but that in America it was easier to get the president of U.S. Steel for a part than an actor. Sam said he had reservations about dramatizing a story that took place in the untroubled thirties, now that England was at war.

"It's only meant to be a light entertainment, you know," Maugham said. "Is this a time for light entertainment?" Sam countered. Maugham mentioned Jane Austen. "Look at her novels," he said, "they were written at one of the gravest moments in English history, when we might have been invaded at any moment. Jane Austen is blithely indifferent to all that—never mentions it." Sam was not convinced, and determined to make "Jane" more topical.[13]

Among Maugham's other New York friends there were Carl Van

Vechten, who was now devoting himself mainly to photography, and the ebullient real estate heir Jerry Zipkin, not to mention the swiftly growing British contingent, which included Cecil Roberts, Harley Granville-Barker, and Emerald Cunard, accompanied by Sir Thomas Beecham, who had adjoining tenth-floor suites at the Ritz-Carlton, the hotel where Maugham was staying. Emerald Cunard lost no time improvising a New York salon, of which Maugham, Beecham, Virgil Thomson and Frederic Prokosch were the pillars. One afternoon Maugham was there while Beecham rehearsed a lecture on Mozart, and he and several others delivered a running commentary while Sir Thomas illustrated his points at the piano. This civilized gathering of exiles was in odd contrast to the state of the world at that moment.[14]

Maugham was asked out for more meals than he could manage. Richard L. Simon of Simon & Schuster gave a small dinner party for him to which he invited a young writer and Maugham fan named Jerome Weidman. Simon wanted to surprise Weidman and did not tell him Maugham was coming. "The Simons lived in a delightfully renovated brownstone on West 11th Street," Weidman recalled, "the part that abandons its gridiron correctness when it passes, or used to pass, Loew's Sheridan and heads for the Hudson." Simon was mixing drinks. Suddenly Mrs. Simon clapped her hand to her forehead and said, "Oh, my God, we have no cigars." "Cigars?" Simon asked. "For God's sake, Dickie, he's an Englishman. They always smoke cigars after dinner." "Jerry," Dick said, "would you mind running up to the corner and getting a cigar?" "How many?" Weidman asked. Having established that none of the other guests smoked cigars, Simon said, "Get one." "Any special kind?" Weidman asked. "A twenty-five-center should be okay," Simon said. Weidman went trotting off to the corner cigar store, examined the contents of the cigar counter, and saw the kind he used to be sent out to buy for his boss when he was a kid working in the garment centre, Garcia y Vega. He bought one and went back to the Simon house, where he found a neat little man standing on the stoop. They stood together in silence until the door opened and Simon introduced Maugham to the others.

Weidman thought Maugham looked as thoughtful and precise as a mathematician. At dinner, when the butler passed the roast around for seconds, Maugham said, "Tell me, will there be any dessert?" Mrs. Simon looked as if she thought Maugham had mistaken her home for a diner. "Why yes, I think so," she said. "Yes, of course there will be

449

dessert." "Then I won't have any more of the meat," Maugham said. "You see, I make it a rule never to eat more than two dishes, or two servings of one dish, at any meal. If there were no dessert in the offing, I should be delighted to have another serving of this delicious roast. Since I am very fond of dessert, however, I prefer to have that." Weidman admired Maugham's sound common sense. He struck him as a man over whose eyes no wool was going to be pulled.

When they went into the living room for coffee, Simon went to the bar, picked up the cellophane-wrapped Garcia y Vega, and said, "Cigar, Mr. Maugham?" Maugham took the cigar, looked at it as though it were a stool specimen, and said, "Thank you, no." "He handed it back to Dick," Weidman recalled, "and drew from his breast pocket one of those silver cases that look like miniature sets of pipe organs, and pulled out a cigar more to his liking."[15]

In December, Maugham left for Chicago to give some more speeches. Gerald, who had taken the American Export Line vessel S.S. *Excambion* from Lisbon on November 24, landed in New York and joined Maugham in Chicago. He told Maugham that he was on the wagon, and that he had left the Mauresque in the care of a French boyfriend of his named Louis Legrand. Annette, the cook, and Nina, the maid, were still there. He had locked the wine cellar and stored the paintings. Legrand was trying to sell Gerald's sailboat, the *Tenace*. Gerald missed the Riviera and his friends and complained that Chicago was the filthiest city in the world.[16]

Maugham was pleased with the turnouts he was getting for his speeches but worried that audiences in the isolationist Midwest would be less receptive to his message that America should contribute to the war effort. He also felt uncomfortable in the unaccustomed role of pleader, although the biggest handicap, his stammer, was under control. One of his speeches that has survived was an appeal on behalf of the R.A.F.

> If we ask you on this occasion to contribute what you can to the Benevolent Fund of the R.A.F., it is because we know from old experience that your generosity is boundless. . . . The members of the R.A.F. have fought on without respite. . . . Many of them have been so wounded that life henceforth must be a constant struggle with adversity. Will you not do something to make it a little easier for them? Many of them have been killed. They were young men, hardly more than boys; they have left young widows and young children. Will you not do something

and help them? It is for you and me they fought and died; and not only for you and me and all of us—for truth and charity, honor and loving kindness.[17]

Maugham whiled away the time between speeches visiting Chicago, where he would later set sections of *The Razor's Edge*. He went to see the Seurats in the Art Institute. He sought out Ruth Gordon, whom he had met on the Riviera and who was then playing in Chicago and staying at his hotel, the Ambassador. One morning her phone rang: "Miss Gordon, this is Somerset Maugham. I'm stopping at this hotel and should like to see something of you."

"Would you like to come to the theater tonight?" she asked. "It's a celebration of my having been on the stage twenty-five years. Alexander Woollcott is doing a radio broadcast after the second act." At the party afterward Maugham signed everyone's napkins and programs.

A week later the Lunts opened in Chicago. Lynn Fontanne called Ruth Gordon and said, "Darling, Mr. Somerset Maugham is staying in our hotel."

"I know," Miss Gordon said.

"Darling, tonight is New Year's Eve and Alfred and I think it would be a good idea to have supper up here in our apartment and invite Mr. Maugham, will you come, dear?"

"I'd love to, but I have Jones [her son] and my secretary and . . ."

"Bring them and you ring up Mr. Maugham."

"Me?"

"Yes, darling. Ring him up and invite him."

"But Lynnie, let's be practical. We stand a much better chance of getting him if you or Alfred ring up."

"Well, perhaps you're right, darling."

A few hours later Lynn Fontanne was on the line again. "Darling, I've been trying to ask Mr. Maugham, but I've taken a fright! I can't get up the courage. I've met him, of course, but it was so long ago he may not remember me. *You* do it."

"But Lynn, it's after three o'clock. Anybody as celebrated as Mr. Maugham must be *booked* for tonight."

"Don't give up so easily, darling! Alfred and I *both* say *you* should ask him."

Ruth Gordon wrote Maugham a note and sent for a bellboy. She waited, but no reply came, so she called to invite him, but he was going to the opera.

"Oh, dear," she said, "they will be so disappointed. And so will I. It's been a sort of horrible mix-up. Lynn was to phone you earlier, but she got scared you wouldn't remember her."

"I'm old," Maugham said, "but I'm not in my dotage."

"No, Lynn wanted to ask you but she was too frightened. But happy new year and it's been lovely talking to you."

"Miss Gordon, I've changed my mind. Please tell Mr. and Mrs. Lunt I shall be delighted to take supper with them."

Maugham saw the new year in with the Lunts and Ruth Gordon. He was in good spirits. Lynn Fontanne said he was the sexiest man she knew except for Alfred. At 2 A.M. he went up to Miss Gordon's son Jones, then eleven, and said, "I think all of us under sixteen and over sixty should now retire." The next morning he sent her a note dated January 1, 1941: "Dear Miss Gordon, you are as sweet as you are good and kind. Happy New Year."[18]

In January he went to San Francisco, where there was a warm reunion with Bert Alanson. Maugham launched a fund drive to raise $400,000 to buy ambulances for Britain. A number of ambulances, each one driven by a professional football player, were going on a national tour to collect money. "Make no mistake about this," Maugham said. "This war isn't going to decide only who shall command the seas, who shall own this or that part of the earth's surface, who shall control the raw materials of South America. It is going to decide whether honesty is the best policy, whether truth is better than falsehood, whether it is better to keep a promise you have truly made or break it when it no longer suits your convenience, whether what we called goodness is to be banished from the earth, and whether the only meaning of right is might."[19]

His next stop was Los Angeles, where he had been summoned by David Selznick to discuss writing a film about England at war. Taken up by the aristocracy of celluloid, he was asked to a dinner given by Fanny Brice, at which he was seated next to Dorothy Parker, who was dressed in demure black silk. "We were waited on by Russian noblemen or Japanese samurai," Maugham said, "I forget which." Maugham told Miss Parker that he had all her books bound in red leather. Discussing the state of English literature, he patronizingly said, "We have a novelist, E. M. Forster, though I don't expect he's familiar to you." Miss Parker assured him that she had not only heard of him, she would go on her hands and knees to get to him.[20]

"Why don't you write a poem for me?" Maugham asked.

"I will if you like," Miss Parker said. "Give me a pencil and a piece of paper."

She wrote:

> Higgledy Piggledy, my white hen;
> She lays eggs for gentlemen.

"Yes, I've always liked those lines," Maugham said.

Miss Parker gave a thin smile and added:

> You cannot persuade her with gun or lariat
> To come across for the proletariat.[21]

Maugham said that, thanks to her, Higgledy Piggledy had joined the august company of Jove's eagle, Boccaccio's falcon, Shelley's skylark, and Poe's raven.

He also saw some old friends now working in Hollywood: Edmund Gwenn, who had starred as Gann, the gamekeeper, in Maugham's 1910 drama *Grace* and was now a bald, spry seventy, and John Van Druten, whom he privately thought of as the dramatist who had had the greatest success with the least talent. At a party attended by Joan Crawford and Hedy Lamarr, Maugham was impressed at being among so many extravagantly lovely women. It was, he said, like being offered an enormous dish of peaches and saying, "Oh, I'll have an apple," for the men stood apart in a group. "Do go and talk to the girls," the host said. Maugham approved when one of the men replied, "We're having a good time, we don't want to get cluttered up with a lot of women."[22] At a studio party he met George Jessel, who was then a producer for Zanuck and 20th Century-Fox, and who scampered around the room shouting, "Somerset Maugham, a Schlemiehl he ain't." And yet Maugham did not feel that he had been a success in Hollywood, for he was not invited to dinner by Mrs. Jack Warner, the acknowledged arbiter of social importance. "I just never made the grade," he said.[23]

Maugham's friendship with young Jerome Weidman had grown to the point where Weidman's publisher, Simon & Schuster, sent him Weidman's first two novels, *I Can Get It for You Wholesale* and *What's in It for Me?* Maugham wrote Weidman from the Beverly Hills Hotel: "When people send me their books my practice is to say what I like about them and keep silent about what I like less; but you are so clever and you have it in you to write so many more good books that I feel justified in going a little further. Of course these two books are written and published but I am thinking of the future. . . . In fiction the motivation must be very much stronger than it actually is in life to convince the reader. . . . Of course I do not speak as Sir Oracle, I am only offering you a small technical hint."[24]

Weidman replied:

> I don't think there is any way I can really tell you how much your letter meant to me, but I feel I must make the attempt or I will explode. If you are a bricklayer, let us say, and a tailor or a cab driver says, "That's a pretty good wall you made there," your reaction will be one of pleasure, naturally. But when another bricklayer, a bricklayer (I wish I had chosen a happier word) whom you regard as the best in the whole business, says the same thing to you, there is very little you can say . . . to tell him how much you have been pleased and excited and moved by his comment.[25]

Maugham left Los Angeles in early March, with the film projects still up in the air, to give more speeches in Chicago. His schedule was beginning to tire him. "Now I am going back to Chicago to deliver four blasted lectures in 11 days," he wrote a friend, "and then to New York to speak again there and in Philadelphia. A dog's life."[26] He was pleased with his speeches, however, particularly the one on the family in England in wartime, which he said brought tears to the eyes of the most hardened midwestern businessman.[27] Between speeches, he made a side trip to Lafayette, Indiana, to visit his first biographer, Richard Cordell, and he discussed English prose style with twenty-four of Cordell's students at Purdue University.

In Chicago, Maugham learned that Liza had given birth to a healthy, blonde, blue-eyed daughter, whom she named Camilla, and he wrote Kate Bruce: "Liza, after keeping everyone waiting for an unconscionable time, women are so silly about natural history, has given birth to a female child."[28] This flippant remark about a pregnancy that had almost killed his daughter was out of character for a writer who had been obsessed with the dangers of childbirth in his early novels, but Maugham was a different man in his sixties, not always consistent with the preoccupations of his youth.

He returned to New York in April, while Gerald went to Detroit to take delivery of a new Oldsmobile. Looking in on his daughter and granddaughter, Maugham found Liza looking prettier than ever. She had decided not to return to England with a young son and infant daughter, and Maugham hoped that her husband would not be angered by her decision. Continuing on his rounds, he spoke at Yale, and came down with the flu.[29]

In April there appeared *Up at the Villa*, a novel that Maugham had apparently written several years earlier. It was the story of a wealthy English widow in Florence who befriends a young Austrian refugee and sleeps with him out of kindness. When she refuses to see him again he shoots himself. She seeks the help of a disreputable Englishman, who helps her dispose of the body and then blackmails her into marrying him. Maugham did not think much of his latest and wrote Eddie Marsh that it was intended "to pass an idle hour." It was serialized in three issues of *Redbook*, from February to April 1941, under the title *The Villa on the Hill*. Warner Brothers bought it for $30,000 and put Christopher Isherwood to work on it, but no script could be written to satisfy the censor. In any case, Isherwood admitted that he had written "a bad script from a bad story."

Hastily written, stilted, and implausible, *Up at the Villa* was scorched by the critics. *Newsweek* on April 7 said that it could have been dictated while Maugham was talking in his sleep. Nigel Dennis in the *New Republic* on May 19 called it his worst novel. Morton Zabel, a professor at the University of Chicago, used the novel as a launching pad for the most furious attack on Maugham in years, "A Cool Hand," in *The Nation* on May 3.

> This novel [Zabel wrote], as unmitigated a specimen of fictional drivel as has appeared under respectable authorship within living memory, might be flatly dismissed as the latest triumph of servant girls' literature were it not for the phenomenal value that still attaches to Maugham's name among modern authors. The standard argument of his case is familiar. He is the Complete Cool Hand Technical Expert among writers; he has never been taken in by literary gangdom, aesthetic pretensions, or anything else in the life around him. . . . We are also used to hearing Maugham called "the greatest living English novelist," the implication always being conveyed that were he so disposed he could, at any time he feels like it, produce another *Cakes and Ale* or *Of Human Bondage*. One is moved to ask: then why hasn't he done so? . . . If any doubt remains on this score, *Up at the Villa* should dismiss it. The screaming falseness of its dialogue should alone be enough to turn the stomachs of even moderately sensitive readers. . . . And incidentally, if the title of "the greatest living novelist" is to be thrown around any

further, it is time it landed in the right quarter. The greatest living English novelist is E. M. Forster.

It might have been pointed out to Mr. Zabel that Forster had not written a novel since 1924, having suffered a sort of creative paralysis after the success of *A Passage to India*, while Maugham was still a working novelist, not content to be judged by his best work of twenty years earlier. But the chief interest of *Up at the Villa* was biographical, for Rowley Flint, the English scoundrel and blackmailer, was clearly based on Gerald Haxton:

> He had not a single feature that you could call good; he had white teeth, but they were not very even; he had a fresh colour, but not a very clear skin; he had a good head of hair, but it was of a vague brown between dark and fair; his eyes were fairly large, but they were of that pallid blue that is generally described as grey. He had an air of dissipation and people who didn't like him said he looked shifty. It was freely admitted, even by his greatest friends, that he couldn't be trusted. . . . He was in short a young man with a shocking reputation which he thoroughly deserved.

He did, however, have sex appeal. The Princess San Ferdinando, an American lady married to a Roman prince, said, "Of course he's a bad lot, but if I were thirty years younger and he asked me to run away with him I wouldn't hesitate for a moment even though he'd chuck me in a week and I'd be wretched for the rest of my life."[30]

Gerald did double duty in *Up at the Villa*, for the character of the Englishwoman's dead husband was also based on him. The woman, Mary Panton, describes her husband as "a dreadful gambler and when he was drunk he'd lose hundreds of pounds." He had been killed in a car accident, which may have been wishful thinking on Maugham's part. "He'd come home and make love to me with his breath stinking of whiskey," Mary says, "all hunched up, his face distorted, and I knew it wasn't love that made him passionate but drink, just drink. I or another woman, it made no difference, and his kisses made me sick and his desire horrified me and mortified me. And when he'd satisfied his lust he'd sink into the snoring sleep of drunkenness."[31] One wonders to what extent Maugham was writing from experience.

Up at the Villa could be read as a *roman à clef* about Maugham and Haxton. There was a theory that the hold Gerald had over Maugham was blackmail. The novel could be seen as an account of Haxton's blackmail. Rowley Flint helps Mary Panton dispose of the dead Austrian and then she has to marry him. Perhaps Haxton had helped Maugham out of some homosexual scandal and held it over him. This was the way Glenway Wescott, who became a close friend of Maugham's during the war years, explained the book. "When I read it," he said, "I saw that there it all was, it made my flesh creep. Willie hated it so. He said to me, 'It's the only thing I've ever done for money, and you pretend to be such an appreciator of my work, and you praise that story, you don't know hack-work when you see it. I'm ashamed ever to have done it.' "[32]

While Maugham kept up his propaganda work on the lecture circuit the Doubledays were building his house, which would be finished at the end of the year. In the meantime he was working on a novel commissioned by the British Ministry of Information, intended to show America the effect of the war on a typical British family, and called *The Hour Before the Dawn*. Hollywood was interested, and he thought of spending the summer there. In May he sat for Laurence Tompkins, considered one of the best portrait sculptors in America. He thought Tompkins made him look like a Roman senator. In June he settled into a roomy house at 732 South Beverly Glenn Boulevard, with an acre of garden. It cost $700 a month, and he was told that it was a bargain, because the swimming pool was rectangular. He had a studio in the garden where he could work undisturbed.

Gerald took flying lessons, hoping to qualify as a pilot in the event that America entered the war. His landings were bumpy, but he took his first solo flight in August. Gerald wrote his friends in France about life in Hollywood, including all the gossip: one of the Dolly sisters had committed suicide; he had met Loretta Young and Rosalind Russell. He sent money, parcels, and autographed pictures of movie stars to Louis Legrand, who was house-sitting in the Mauresque.[33]

Liza planned to come from New York with her two children, but she had misgivings about joining her father, because she disliked Gerald and did not want to be a witness to his alcoholic misconduct. Her father wrote to reassure her: "I know it's because of Gerald and I can assure you that he is not drinking." But Gerald was drinking in secret, and several times during their visit Liza saw him go through fits of delirium tremens.[34] In spite of that it was a pleasant family summer, with Maugham practicing the art of being a grandfather. The only drawback was that he did not like working with movie people. "I loathe the people I am working for," he wrote Kate Bruce. "I will never again have anything to do with pictures."[35] He also hated the book he was working on. His credo as a writer had always been to shun "messages." He felt that he had no gift for writing tales of stalwart patriotism. He was also sick of writing propaganda, and he had come to hate giving lectures, with all the preliminary tiresomeness of having to shake the hands of innumerable persons and say a few polite words to each.[36] He complained that although people were cordial and hospitable, he could find no one to talk to. Living in Los Angeles, he said, was like being on a diet of candy.[37]

Things improved when he learned that Aldous Huxley, Christopher Isherwood, and Gerald Heard were in the area. All three were engaged in the study of Vedanta, a Hindu system of belief dealing with the ultimate nature of reality. Vedanta postulated a universal moral order that accounted for cycles of growth and destruction in nature. The purpose of philosophy, it said, was the extinction of suffering caused by ignorance. Vedanta advised meditation and a vegetarian diet. The three British writers had become disciples of Swami Prabhavananda, one of the first Indian gurus to migrate to the green shores of California. He had a mission in Hollywood, and his new disciples spread the word.

Gerald Heard was the initiator of their geographical and spiritual migration. A prominent figure in the British intellectual world of the thirties, he knew most of the leading scientists and philosophers and gave scientific talks on the B.B.C. He was reputed to read two thousand books a year and had an extraordinary flow of information about everything. He was, it was said, an example of the Wellsian supermind. Heard had begun expounding Vedantist principles in the thirties. In *The Social Substance of Religion* (1931) he wrote that the chaos of the modern world could be cured only by religion. In *The Third Morality* (1937) he advocated vegetarianism and yoga. Heard became a close friend of Aldous Huxley, to whom he fed ideas. Huxley's *Eyeless in Gaza* ended with the Vedantist belief that there was a unity in all things in the universe, and his *Ends and Means* (1937) called for Eastern nonattachment. In 1937 Heard came to California to follow the teachings of Swami Prabhavananda and a year later Huxley followed, taking a house on North Linden Drive in Beverly Hills.[38]

Heard had founded a meditation community called Trabuco College and thought of himself as a full-fledged yogi. He meditated with Huxley, urging him to eat natural foods, and refused to drive a car, which made get-togethers somewhat problematic. Huxley combined his interest in Vedanta with screenwriting. He worked on the scripts for *Madame Curie* and *Pride and Prejudice*. Heard was working on a book called *Pain, Sex, and Time*. Edmund Wilson, hearing about their conversion, wrote that "Mr. Huxley and his ally, Mr. Heard, will be lucky if they do not wake up some morning to find themselves transformed into yogis and installed in one of those Wizard-of-Oz temples that puff out their bubble-like domes among the snack bars and the lion ranches."[39]

When Christopher Isherwood arrived, in the spring of 1939, to clarify his pacifist ideas with Heard and Huxley, they introduced him to Prabhavananda. Isherwood, who had hitherto been an atheist, became a believer, a disciple, and eventually an editor of Prabhavananda's magazine, *Vedanta and the West*.[40] The three writers played an important part in disseminating Hindu philosophy in California, although Arthur Koestler belittled their efforts as "Yogi-journalese of the Gerald Heard type."[41] They remained in America throughout the war. Isherwood, like Huxley, became a screenwriter, but they continued to write novels with Vedantist themes: Huxley wrote *Time Must Have a Stop* (1944) and Isherwood wrote *A Meeting by the River* (1967).

In June, Maugham wrote Eddie Marsh: "Aldous Huxley, Gerald Heard are here, both a godsend to me, and Christopher Isherwood has retired from the world and is living in a Quaker camp. Gerald, terribly emaciated, with a long beard and a very red nose, is spreading the word with diligence, striking success, and a certain incoherence."[42] Maugham met Huxley on various social occasions, including a dinner at the Ronald Colemans', where Maria Huxley found Maugham tired but much mellowed and more gentle. Huxley seemed pleased to see him, for he too needed someone to talk to.[43] Maugham thought of Huxley as the most *learned* novelist who had ever lived, now living in a colony not noted for its learning.

It was a treat for Maugham finally to be with people who spoke his language, and a relief from the large Hollywood parties where everyone seemed to be a stranger. On one such occasion he met John Barrymore. "What a ham," he wrote Gladys Stern. "He now wears his hair dark red with a white *mèche* sweeping up from the forehead, but he still has a perfect nose."[44] More than that, the three British writers provided source material at a time when he was working on *The Razor's Edge*, which dealt with a young American's quest for meaning through Hindu philosophy. Maugham did not become a convert, but had a keen professional interest in their views, and borrowed traits from Heard and Isherwood for his character Larry Darrell.

During that summer Liza enjoyed Hollywood and the handsome leading men who took her out. Maugham preferred her escorts to be ushered into the living room to wait for her, and was annoyed one evening when the butler announced Errol Flynn and brought him to the room in which Maugham was sitting. Maugham mixed a drink and tried to make conversation. There was good news about the war in the evening paper, and Maugham said, "Have you heard the news?" "You mean about Mickey Rooney?" Flynn asked.[45]

At a cocktail party an actress who had what seemed to be a pronounced thyroid condition approached Liza and said, "Please do thank your daddy for Mildred; it was like having an acting textbook to guide me." The lady with the bulging eyes was Bette Davis, whose performance as Maugham's heroine in Of Human Bondage had made movie history and established her as a star.[46] Maugham asked Miss Davis to lunch on August 3, and told Gerald that he found her very ugly. He was relieved to have finished The Hour Before the Dawn. He sold it to Redbook for $25,000, and Paramount bought the movie rights for $65,000. Christopher Isherwood worked on the script. Maugham was hoping to clear $50,000 after taxes. "Not bad for two months' work," he wrote Alanson.[47]

In September, Karl Pfeiffer, who taught in Chapel Hill, North Carolina, came to visit. He and Maugham had first met in Washington in 1923 when Pfeiffer had been recruited to make up a foursome at bridge. Maugham had lost track of him after that, but Pfeiffer wrote in 1937 to inform him that he was now a professor of literature at a university, and Maugham invited him to the Mauresque, saying that Pfeiffer's letter "was all a letter should be, gay and personal and interesting, indicating a personality which I should like to know better."[48] Pfeiffer had come to the Riviera that summer and stood outside the Mauresque but was too shy to go in. "You cannot think me such an ogre that I devour alive young professors of literature who adventure into my den," Maugham admonished. "Next time you come my way let there be no nonsense." But the war intervened, and this was the first time Pfeiffer had seen Maugham since their original meeting.[49]

Pfeiffer's true ambition was to write, and he published articles such as "Are You a Fertile Male?" for the Reader's Digest and other journals. From the moment he saw Maugham again he began taking notes on what the great man said, wore, ate, and looked like, with a view to writing a book about him someday. He would slip out of the room to jot down Maugham's remarks or make notes before going to bed after spending the evening with him. He noted Maugham's less attractive traits, such as his disregard for the feelings of others, a privilege of the elderly. To a woman chattering at bridge Maugham said, "If we're going to play cards, you'll have to keep your mouth shut." And to a bridge partner who protested against his smoking a cigar he said, "I'm sorry you don't like it, but I intend to smoke it anyway."

Maugham, despite his recent windfalls, complained to Pfeiffer that he had to live on $1,500 a month. Pfeiffer said he could live on that without inconvenience. "Of course you could," Maugham said. "You're a college professor and everybody knows you haven't a cent. But I am supposed to have money, and I have obligations." He was giving Liza $300 a month and paying Gerald a salary. He could not afford a chauffeur and was not a good driver. One afternoon, wary of a sharp turn in his driveway, Maugham asked Pfeiffer to put his new Oldsmobile in the garage. They changed seats, and Pfeiffer managed to dent a fender. "I could have done as well myself," Maugham huffed. As soon as a Hollywood gossip columnist reported that Maugham was taking driving lessons, he stopped taking them.[50]

Pfeiffer brought him a copy of Richard Cordell's book, which had come out in 1937. Maugham, who claimed he never read anything about himself, made several remarks that proved to Pfeiffer that he had read it. Gerald mailed the book back to Pfeiffer after he had left. "I beseech you to throw it in the waste basket," he wrote, "as he seems to have got almost every fact wrong, including the name of Willie's grandfather. DON'T USE IT for any sort of reference."[51] This was an unfair comment on one of the best factual accounts of Maugham's life then available.

Maugham was back in New York in October, waiting to move into his house on the Doubleday plantation, which was supposed to be ready in December. At the end of October he and Gerald spent a weekend with Henry and Clare Boothe Luce in Port Chester, New York. He saw H. G. Wells, also on the American lecture circuit, and found him looking "old, tired, and shriveled." His lectures were a failure, and he was hurt and disappointed.

Maugham was increasing his income with magazine work, for which he was much in demand. There was hardly a magazine one could open without finding something by him: short stories in *The New Yorker*, political articles, such as "We Have Been Betrayed" in the *Saturday Evening Post*, prophecies, such as "What Tomorrow Holds" in *Redbook*, personal reminiscences, such as "Paintings I Have Liked" in *Life*, advice to writers, such as "Write About What You Know" in *Good Housekeeping*, and miscellanea, such as "Reading Under Bombing" in *Living Age*.

He was so busy with commissions that he decided to get an agent, for he had not had one since Charles Hanson Towne, whom he had dismissed in the twenties. He engaged a dapper, cigar-smoking, fast-talking fellow named Jacques Chambrun, who had offices at 745 Fifth Avenue. Chambrun had taste, charm, and intelligence, and was enormously enterprising. His only flaw was that he did not like to separate himself from the money that came in for his authors. When Maugham told Ken McCormick, who had become editor in chief of Doubleday, about his new agent, McCormick said, "Let me give you some case histories," and told him seven or eight horror stories about Chambrun. He was so bad about paying that the Curtis Publishing Company, which published the *Saturday Evening Post*, had a policy of sending their fees directly to the writers. Maugham listened and went to Chambrun and said, "Why do you want to represent me when these stories about you are circulating?"

"I've changed," said Chambrun. "Those stories concern the first years I was here, when I didn't know how business was done." Maugham went back to McCormick and said, "I think I will keep him." "There was something in Willie that dearly loved a scoundrel," McCormick recalled. "He ended up hiring a lawyer at 2½ per cent to watch over Chambrun's 10 per cent."[52]

Once he had Maugham, Chambrun used him to attract other writers. A writer named George P. Morrill was impressed when Chambrun told him that he "had the honor of representing Somerset Maugham, among others." Morrill bombarded Chambrun with fiction but appeared to sell nothing. When he saw some of his stories in magazines, he went to Chambrun's office, and, going through his file, saw that he had earned more than $2,000. Morrill confronted Chambrun, who feigned surprise and wrote him out a check for $2,214. The check bounced, and Morrill retained an eminent literary lawyer, Philip Witternberg, who took the case without a fee, because, he said, "this man is a menace to the literary profession."[53]

And yet Chambrun continued to operate, and Maugham kept him until 1948, despite ample proof of his irregularities. Maugham had, for example, promised an article to Marie Meloney, the editor of *This Week* magazine, who had a few years before tried to find buyers for his manuscripts. "I hope Chambrun does not haggle," he wrote her in November. "Being naturally long-winded I frequently give editors more material than they are paying for, but I do that for my own satisfaction because I want to make a piece as good as I can and I never expect extra remuneration for it."[54] The article, "They Also Serve," appeared in *This Week* in 1942. Chambrun sold it for $1,000 and gave Maugham $625, which meant that on this particular transaction, he pocketed a commission of 37.5 percent. He was robbing Maugham, the flagship of his agency.[55]

In December, Maugham moved to South Carolina, but his house was still not quite ready. The plumber was a drunk and the electrician was running for Congress, and neither the central heating nor the lights were working. The furniture had not arrived from Macy's, and there was no landscaping.[56] But Maugham liked the house that Nelson had built, which had three bedrooms, each with its own bath. It was white clapboard, with a fireplace wall paneled in Carolina pine. The bookshelves were filled with ready-made sets of "great classics." In addition, there were two cottages, one for his study and one for the servants, all black. There was Nora, the cook, Mary, the maid, and Sunday, the yardman, who wore dark glasses indoors because he thought it looked elegant. Sunday had a nephew called Religious, who did odd jobs around the place. The plantation overseer told Maugham, "They're good niggers, they're humble." The address was Parker's Ferry, Yemassee, South Carolina, but on his stationery Maugham crossed out the word "Ferry." An arrangement was made to deduct part of the cost of the house from his royalties.

He moved in before Christmas, and hung reproductions of the paintings he owned on the walls. This would be his home for the next four years, and he adopted the same schedule as at the Mauresque, working in the morning and taking a nap after lunch. He wrote Eddie Marsh that he was in "a very solitary spot, two miles from the nearest house, thirteen miles in fine weather from the nearest village and twenty miles in bad—when the dirt road is deep in mud, over fifty miles from a town. But I have a spacious view of a thousand acres of marsh, and a river flowing to the right of me, behind a row of splendid pines. . . . The only real inconvenience is the long distance one has to go for provisions."[57] He was twenty-four miles from Beaufort, the nearest town, and fifty-five miles from Charleston.

The furniture from Macy's was adequate, but he took great care over finding exactly the kind of writing chairs he wanted, asking a friend: "If you can find me two Windsor chairs I should be glad to have them. They need not be old ones and they need not match as they are to go in different rooms. I want to use them as writing chairs and I should like them to be of any wood except maple. Do you know what a Windsor chair is? Something like this." Maugham proceeded to draw one, pointing out that it was all wood and not upholstered. "I do not think they should cost much if you can find them at an auction," he said.[58]

The Doubledays spent their holidays in South Carolina and were good hosts, often inviting Maugham to "the big house," where Nelson, hearty and gregarious as ever, threw back copious mint juleps, which he called "phlegm-cutters." Maugham would sometimes join them for dinner parties at neighboring plantations. On one of these occasions the host, mistaking him for Michael Arlen, asked, "Well, sir, have you found any pretty girls in green hats to write about?" Maugham stared hard at the man through his monocle and said he was too busy to write about girls in green hats. On another occasion he was taken to meet a member of the local gentry, a Miss Manigault. "She doesn't like foreigners," Maugham was told. "It's rather a pity she asked us," he said. "Oh no, you're English. It's New Yorkers she doesn't like."[59]

Nelson had good news about the publishing business. He was selling as many books as he could print, he said. In 1940 he had sold 30 million. If he could only get his hands on more paper he could sell twice as many. He was placing inexpensive books in the five-and-ten-cent stores to form a new reading public. He wanted Maugham to prepare an anthology of English and American literature of the past fifty years that could give an ignorant person, anxious to learn, a bird's-eye view of the period. Maugham agreed, thinking it would be a useful book. He was also working on *The Razor's Edge*. Now that America had entered the war, his propaganda duties were over.

During this time in America Maugham suffered from alternating fever and chills, the result of a malarial condition he had picked up in Siam. A number of doctors had previously treated him without success, but in January 1942 the malaria got so bad that he decided to go to New York to see a Viennese doctor named Max Wolf. Gerald was also sick and went with him. Wolf, a disciple of Niehans, practiced cellular therapy and made something from goats called Bogomolets serum. He worked out of a five-story home-office on the upper East Side and had a blue-chip clientele. He claimed that the Mountbattens telephoned him from England for medical advice. Wolf examined Maugham and said he had found a huge gelatinous tumor in the pylorus that was blocking the stomach. The tumor was benign, Wolf said, but it was bigger than a baby's head. Wolf treated the tumor with enzymes and gave Maugham 125 grains of quinine, twenty-five times the normal dose, in one injection. According to Wolf, Maugham told him: "I'll take it. I can't live this way. If you don't cure me I'll take my own life. I have not been able to work for the past two years anyhow."[60] In fact, he had been working steadily. Miraculously, the tumor and the malaria vanished, and Maugham sang Wolf's praises. Haxton's condition was not so easily cured. He spent three weeks in the hospital and then went to Florida to convalesce at the Angler's Hotel in Key Largo, where he went fishing for sailfish.

On January 25 the Doubledays gave a party in Oyster Bay for Maugham's sixty-eighth birthday. When he returned to Yemassee they loaned him a horse so that he could go riding three or four times a week "with an engaging young negro to show me where to go and see that I come to no harm."[61] He sent his friends in England parcels of coffee and sugar and copies of his articles. He still felt strongly that the British had a long way to go to make themselves liked by Americans. "You know of course that they hate us," he wrote G. B. Stern. "Oh yes, they hate us all right and the worst of it is about half of it is our own damned silly fault. It makes me so angry. Of the other half, well, we can do nothing about George III and his Hessians now, and we can do nothing about our Nineteenth Century Imperialism, nor can we do anything about the inferiority complex of Americans."[62]

With Gerald in Florida, Maugham was alone, but in February, Glenway Wescott came to spend a few weeks. The son of Wisconsin farmers, Wescott had placed himself in the front line of young American novelists with his second novel, *The Grandmothers—A Family Portrait*. There followed a long sojourn in Paris, where he was taken up by the *beau monde*. The fruit of his Paris years was a short psychological novel, *The Pilgrim Hawk*, a minor classic. Returning to America, he wrote a World War II novel, *Apartment in Athens*. Wescott had met Maugham briefly at the Mauresque in 1928. "You're another one of those young Americans who think they know everything because they've read Proust from cover to cover," Maugham told him. The meeting was not memorable, for when they met again, at lunch at Emerald Cunard's in 1941, Maugham said, "How curious that we have never met."[63] But in 1942 they became friends. Maugham liked this civilized, subtle young American who had somehow assimilated the best values of both the new world and the old, and they formed an attenuated master-disciple relationship.

Maugham found Wescott an agreeable houseguest, since he worked all day long and they met only for meals. He lectured Wescott about the sort of books he should write. He liked *Apartment in Athens,* which had a strong plot and plenty of action, but felt that *The Pilgrim Hawk* was thin stuff. "But isn't that what a novelist is supposed to do," Wescott responded, "get the biggest bubble from the smallest piece of soap?" Wescott was partly supported by a brother who had married a wealthy woman, and Maugham advised him that the spur of economic hardship would make him more productive. He railed against E. M. Forster, who had taken the easy way out by becoming a don, while he, Maugham, continued to write every morning. Maugham hated Forster because such young writers as Wescott and Christopher Isherwood seemed to admire Forster more than they admired him. They studied his style and thought he had more depth than Maugham, although they agreed that Maugham had the magic of narrative at his fingertips. One morning Wescott heard Maugham talking to himself in the bathroom. He explained that before he began to write he tried out the dialogue to see if it sounded right.[64]

Wescott asked Maugham whether he would go back to France after the war. Maugham said he did not think so, for "the French have eaten so much shit that they will stink of it." He was also fed up with Gerald, and went into long harangues on what he had done for Gerald and what Gerald had done to him, and why did he have to go through any more of this? He told Wescott that he had found a replacement for Gerald—a sweet, submissive, devoted young man named Alan Searle, who was everything Gerald was not and whom he had come to love and who loved him. Alan was working in a YMCA camp in North York, but Maugham hoped that he could join him after the war.

Although Maugham freely discussed his sex life with a close friend, Wescott found him essentially prim. "Willie hated to be touched except by arrangement," he said. "If you touched him by surprise, he was like an oyster quivering when you pour lemon juice over it." Maugham told Wescott that his happiest sexual encounters had been with anonymous boys in far-off lands. The amorous high point of his life, he said, had been a night on a sampan in Indochina. Wescott gained the impression that Maugham was sexually naïve when he showed him a book he had written called *Calendar of Saints for Unbelievers,* with illustrations by

Pavel Tchelitchew of the signs of the zodiac. Maugham studied the sign of Gemini, which showed two male figures entwined to suggest the 69 position. "What a shame that can't be done," Maugham said. Wescott started to tell him but decided against it.[65]

On several occasions Maugham had mysterious visitors to his South Carolina house, some of them in uniform. When Wescott asked about these visits, Maugham explained that he had not been sent to America merely to make speeches but also to work for British Intelligence and report on his fellow countrymen. If they kept bad company, or expressed pro-German sentiments, or spent large sums of money of mysterious provenance, Maugham reported them. "Do you realize," he told Wescott, "that there isn't a week that passes that I don't get one of my poor wretched countrymen sent back to England?"

Maugham was proud of saying that he did not judge the conduct of his fellowman. What shocked others only made him shrug his shoulders and smile, for he saw man capable of every meanness and every heroism. But he cast aside his tolerant attitude in wartime to play the political commissar. He felt so strongly about the way the British should behave in America that he agreed to snoop on his countrymen. "The manners of some of our fellow countrymen are frightful," he wrote his nephew Robin. "You would think they were deliberately going out of their way to offend Americans."[66]

The head of the British secret service in America at that time was Sir William Stevenson, known as Intrepid, who in a letter to the author indicated in a roundabout way that Maugham was under his orders:

> With regard to Somerset Maugham, he is typical of a problem we had in working with material from BSC files. Quite a large number of volunteers in warfare against Nazism were loath to be known as part of any intelligence agency, arguing that their services were given in a period of desperate emergency. Few had much taste for the business and became involved because they saw no alternatives. Their wishes had to be respected. . . . Intrepid had a variety of friends and contacts working for him; and those that we identified in *A Man Called Intrepid* were those who subsequently made it plain that they were not opposed to being acknowledged publicly. I don't think Somerset Maugham ever made this feeling known.[67]

Glenway Wescott left Parker's Ferry in March, and Gerald returned from Florida, still looking unwell but on the mend. He told Maugham that he did not intend to spend the rest of the war on a plantation and was going to look for a job in Washington, where he had friends. While he remained in South Carolina, Maugham kept up an active correspondence with Liza, who was working in the British Library of Information in New York. Her son Nicholas was wondering whether to become a Red Indian or a gangster when he grew up, and her husband, Vincent Paravicini, had been sent with the British Army to Australia.[68]

As for Robin, he was a lieutenant in the 4th County of London Yeomanry. In August 1940 he had been sent to the Middle East as part of the 22d Armoured Brigade. As the commander of a Crusader tank, with a crew of three, he took part in the great desert war that started in September along the coasts of Egypt and Libya. The British fought first against the Italians, whom they defeated. But in February 1941 the Afrika Corps under Rommel entered the battle, and in March the British were driven out of Libya, except for the Tobruk enclave. General Auchinleck took command, and Robin's brigade became a part of the newly formed Eighth Army. By March 1942 Robin had seen a year and a half of action, interrupted by riotous leaves in Cairo. He wrote his mother that he had had four tanks shot to pieces under him and that he and his crew had destroyed three Italian and four German tanks. He wrote the Alansons, with whom he had stayed on a trip to America, that he was having a very exciting time in various tank battles. The desert was fascinating, he said, like a mirror in which one's every mood was reflected. It could be cold and sinister or bright and friendly.[69]

If any doubt remained about Maugham's unchallenged position at that time as Grand Old Man of English Letters, the *Harvard Advocate* party of April 1942 might well be cited to dispel it. Needing some sort of *action d'éclat* to promote their financially anemic literary magazine, the editors of the *Advocate* invited Maugham to a party in his honor. He replied with a telegram that said "Certainly not." But the *Advocate* editors went ahead anyway and sent out invitations. "This piece of news," wrote Norman Mailer, recalling the incident, in which he took part, "ran around the ring of Cambridge like a particle in a cyclotron. Nothing in four years at Harvard, not Dunkirk, Pearl Harbor or the blitz, not even beating Yale and Princeton in the same season for the first time in years, could have lit up Harvard more. Not to be invited to that party was equal to signifying that one had mismanaged one's life." Four hundred of Harvard's best and brightest turned up for the party. The *Advocate* people passed the word that their absent guest of honor was in the building: Maugham was climbing the stairs, Maugham was through the door, Maugham was in the other room. After a proper interval the word was passed that Maugham was at the door, Maugham was going down the stairs, Maugham had left. The guests walked distractedly from room to room. What was the point? Maugham was gone.[70]

Maugham at the time was still in Yemassee, but it was getting hot and he planned to leave for New York on April 30. He had written an article about America's opinion of the English in the *Saturday Evening Post*, "Why Do You Dislike Us?," which appeared in April and caused a furor. Within two weeks he received three hundred replies, most of them aspersive. One of his readers wrote: "Do you think we shall ever forget the Battle of the Boyne?" He was looking forward to New York, where he could research *The Razor's Edge* in a good library.[71]

From New York, Maugham wrote Robin to keep him up to date. Gerald had found a job in Washington with the O.S.S., and he was without a secretary. His house in South Carolina was solitary and romantic, and in the spring the woods were like the setting of a Maeterlinck play. He was concerned that with gas rationing and the tire shortage he would be confined to the plantation. His two black maids looked after him and laughed at everything he said. He was also concerned about Rommel's spring offensive against the Eighth Army. "I hope you have got through this present fighting unscathed," he wrote, "and are successfully smashing German and Italian tanks as you have done in the previous battles."[72]

In fact, Robin had been wounded in the first days of the offensive. The tank battles had started on May 26, and Robin was in the battle of Knightsbridge, a mound of stones near a disused desert well, where the British lost 230 out of 300 tanks. On May 28 he was standing by his scout car watching the enemy positions through binoculars when a flat piece of shrapnel hit him in the chest. As he waited to be evacuated he fell asleep and was hit again, this time in the head. He was taken to a hospital near Suez and released with a piece of shrapnel still lodged in his brain. Invalided back to England with a 50 percent-disability pension, he had blackouts and fits of vomiting and headaches and was given further treatment.

His uncle believed that he was never the same after his wound. He had behaved gallantly in battle. His commanding officer, Brigadier Carr, in a letter home to his wife, had said of him: "He is one of the bravest men I will ever see. I should think he has saved about forty mens' lives in the 4th Co. of London Yeomanry by rescuing them from destroyed tanks, for each of whom he has risked his own life." Mrs. Carr, relaying the letter to Robin's mother, said the brigadier had never praised so highly any other officer under his command.[73] "Who would have thought," Maugham said, "that that flighty boy had it in him to do what he has done?"[74]

In June *The Hour Before the Dawn* was published. Maugham had first written it as a film script, purely for propaganda purposes, and then was prevailed upon to promote the film by making it into a novel. He liked it so little that he prevented its publication in England and probably destroyed the manuscript, for it was never found. It did nothing to add to his reputation. The plot is easily summed up: a well-to-do country-bred English family copes with the war. The menfolk are called up, and evacuees descend on the women. The son is a conscientious objector. In a denouement that is meant to be suspenseful, the refugee Dora Friedberg turns out to be a spy. *Newsweek* on June 22 said it sounded "pre-war, brittle, and trivial." *Harper's* in August said: "The mind rebels at accepting from Mr. Maugham so over-simplified a version of There'll Always Be an England."[75] The third-rate movie made from this fourth-rate novel came out in 1944 and starred Franchot Tone and Veronica Lake. In it the author made his screen debut, saying a few introductory words.

Maugham decided to spend the summer of 1942 in Edgartown, on Martha's Vineyard. It was cool, he liked ocean bathing, and he could work undisturbed at the Colonial Inn, which had been highly recommended. When he arrived in July the Edgartown Yacht Club called the local newspaper, the *Vineyard Gazette*, and asked whether he was important enough to be sent a guest card. Among the people he met, his favorite was the writer Max Eastman, whom he found a handsome and engaging companion. At a clambake he met Katharine Cornell, who had played *The Constant Wife* in America. "I'm afraid he was so reticent and observing that I became rather frightened of him," she said.[76]

One day he was walking along a dirt road wondering what to say about the poems he had collected for the Doubleday anthology of modern English and American literature. He came upon a broken-down cottage. At the door stood a tree tall enough to reach the roof, covered with pink cup-shaped flowers, so thick they hid the leaves. The tree's loveliness made him catch his breath. A stumpy, dark-haired, Portuguese woman came out, and he asked her the name of the tree. "I don't know," she said. "I never thought to ask. It's pretty, isn't it?" It occurred to Maugham that the pleasure the tree had given him was of the same kind that he derived from poetry. He felt it intensely but could no more communicate it than he could communicate what he felt about the quintet in the *Meistersinger* or Titian's "Man with a Glove."[77]

He liked Edgartown and stayed there into September. Jerome Weidman had kept in touch with Maugham and wrote that he had seen Gerald lunching at the Ritz in New York. "I could not catch his eye," he said, "because Miss Fannie Hurst, wearing on her head an edifice that looked like the illegitimate offspring of a monk's cowl mated with a stale wedding cake, kept crossing the room at three-minute intervals, blocking the view and rendering communication impossible."[78] Gerald, who had a clerical job with the O.S.S., hinted to his friends that he was involved in top-secret intelligence work. One of his stories was that he had been put in a cell with a captured Nazi of high rank to pry information out of him. Jerry Zipkin, Maugham's real estate friend, ran into him in Washington, acting mysterious. "I'm going to quietly say goodbye now," Gerald said, "and you won't know where I'll be."[79]

In November, Maugham went to a screening of Noel Coward's *In Which We Serve.* He was in the elevator on his way up to the projection room when a portly gentleman got in with him and immediately knelt before him. Not to be outdone, Maugham knelt too. It was Alexander Woollcott, the Town Crier. Woollcott, a man who liked to express his enthusiasm, was moved to tears by the Coward film, because "it is of courage all compact and courage is the only thing that makes me cry— courage and, oddly enough, miracles."[80]

On November 9 Maugham went to New Haven to give a Francis Bergen Memorial Lecture on democracy at Strathcona Hall. At the suggestion of his friend William Lyon Phelps he chose the grim topic of political obligation. He intended to end his speech with a peroration on the price of liberty, enlarging on how costly it was but how necessary it was to pay the cost. He was congratulating himself on having come to the end of the speech without stammering when he had a blackout and forgot what the price of liberty was—which was out of character for someone who usually remembered what things cost. He rumbled and fussed with his notes, but the final paragraph of his speech would not come, and to this day the students of Yale are in the dark about Maugham's accounting of the price of liberty.

In December he returned to his temporary home in South Carolina, where he found people complaining about the coffee and sugar rationing. He was glad that rationing had brought the war into every American home, but he too complained that he was restricted to three gallons of gasoline a week. The Doubledays had bought cows and chickens and grew their own vegetables, and there were bass in the river by his house, so his kitchen was not severely deprived. He had begun to train his cook, Nora, to prepare French cuisine, making her repeat the same dishes over and over. She agreed to cook French food but refused to cook such Yankee dishes as baked beans. When the Doubledays were there, he had dinner at the "big house" several times a week. Jerry Zipkin, who visited him, said:

> Ellen Doubleday ran the worst household in America. The roast never went around, if you were sitting on her left you starved. Nelson roared at her, and she would come in tears to see Willie and ask him how to run a house. Nelson was big on duck-shooting and was up at five, heading for the marsh. Willie was in his study on the stroke of nine and put his pen down exactly at five minutes to one, even in mid-sentence. He saw the servants in the kitchen eating a fish stew and said "That's the kind of food I want," while Ellen Doubleday served roast beef and mashed potatoes.[81]

Disturbing news arrived from France. "I hear that the Wops have looted the English and American houses on the Riviera," Maugham wrote a friend. There was also a rumor that the Germans were going to demolish Riviera houses and build fortifications, and Maugham was afraid there was not much hope for the Villa Mauresque.[82]

In the early months of 1943 Maugham had a recurrence of the stomach trouble that caused him sometimes to lose consciousness. Max Wolf and his enzyme treatment had failed to cure him and he feared he had cancer, but specialists assured him that the malady was purely nervous. "It appears that I have some complaint of the solar plexus which caused spasms," he wrote his brother Frederic, "and by pressing the diaphragm against the heart made me lose consciousness, and there was always the chance that the pressure would not relax soon enough to let me recover from it."[83]

He was well enough to receive guests, however, and invited Dorothy Parker to spend a few weeks at Yemassee. She was intimidated, saying that "whenever I meet one of these Britishers, I feel as if I have a papoose on my back." But she went, staying for three weeks, and saying that it was the longest three weeks of her life. She had hoped to find interesting people, but there were only Willie and various young men indifferent to ladies. All Maugham wanted to do was play bridge, and she finally said of him, "That old lady is a crashing bore." She had never liked homosexuals, and perhaps she felt a trace of envy because Maugham was rich and prolific and she was not. Yet she did not cut short her stay and must have made a good impression, for Maugham wrote—for a fee of $250—the introduction to her collected works, which were published in 1944.[84]

In 1943 the war news was increasingly encouraging and Maugham suddenly thought he saw the end in sight. He feared the Allies would be soft on the Germans and wrote Marie Meloney: "I am very much afraid that as soon as the war is over you Americans and we British will start that old story of those poor Germans, which to my mind did so much harm after the last war. I feel that, if only in fairness to the small nations who have suffered, retaliation is necessary, and since you Americans and we British are bad haters, I think we should allow the said small nations to do their damnedest. But I do not expect you for a moment to approve of this."[85]

His brother Frederic, now Lord Maugham, had written a book in defense of Chamberlain's policies, a copy of which Maugham received in April. Willie congratulated him but added: "I don't think you can expect your readers to absolve Chamberlain from great blame for having allowed . . . the humiliation that Munich surely was. . . . I expect your book will make quite a stir."[86]

In April, Gerald's assignment in Washington came to an end. Nelson Doubleday, who liked to connect the jobless man with the manless job, hired him to run a commissary in his plant in Garden City, Long Island, which sold fruits and vegetables to employees at wholesale prices. Maugham joined him in New York in May and marveled at the virtuous, hardworking life he was leading, getting up at 6.30 to feed the multitudes. "He appears to be giving his employers great satisfaction," he wrote Robin.[87]

Although he was sixty-nine years old, Maugham was still capable of romantic attachments. It was in the spring of 1943, when he was staying at the Ritz-Carlton in New York, that he received a letter from a seventeen-year-old senior at Lawrenceville saying that *Of Human Bondage* was one of the books that had shaped his life. He replied that he was touched that young people could still be moved by the book and invited the young man, David Posner, to come to see him. Posner, who became a prize-winning poet, was a handsome and precocious youth

473

with smooth olive skin and dark curly hair. He went to see Maugham and they made love. It was not a question of the "old party," as Maugham described himself, seducing an innocent teenager. If there was a seduction, it was on the part of Posner. "I was starry-eyed," he said, "I was hoping it would happen. I thought that the way to intimacy and to an understanding of his work was through his body. And I was hardly the only pebble on the beach."[88]

Posner continued going to bed with Maugham on the average of once a week, even though what he felt was affection rather than desire. "He wasn't particularly virile," he said, "but he was full of lust. He was rather businesslike about sex, but it's equally true that there were occasions when we would spend a long time just fondling. I treated him with tenderness and affection. You couldn't go anywhere without people stopping and staring. But when we were alone he could be the world's most enchanting conversationalist."[89]

Posner found Maugham a deeply suspicious man who believed that he could not achieve intimacy without being taken advantage of. "I've never been good-looking, and I know that no man could ever fall in love with me," Maugham said. "It's always for something they can get out of me." If you assume the worst, Posner thought, that is what you get. If you expect ulterior motives, you cannot form a satisfactory relationship. Maugham's assumption was a self-fulfilling prophecy. Posner made a point of never asking for money, but Maugham was generous with his protégés and eventually paid Posner's way through Harvard.

"He profoundly disliked women sexually," Posner said. "He didn't like his boy friends to have girl friends and he was very disturbed once when he saw me with a girl. He was hostile to me for a long time. 'What a queer thing you are,' he would say. He didn't like going to bed with a man unless the taint of women was off them."[90]

Maugham remained in New York through June, suffering from the heat. "To be half-way comfortable one has to sit in one's shirt-sleeves and to go out to dinner in evening clothes is intolerable," he wrote his brother.[91] He had been asked to go to Brazil for more propaganda work, but he decided instead to spend his second summer in Edgartown and finish The Razor's Edge. This time the Colonial Inn gave him a sitting room at no extra charge.[92] He worked, swam, played bridge, and kept up his correspondence. He heard from Robin's mother that Robin was highly excitable, still suffering from his head wound, and from Gerald that he had rented a cottage in Garden City to avoid commuting from New York.

On August 18, 1943, he sent the last pages of *The Razor's Edge* to the typist. Since the main character was American, he asked Karl Pfeiffer to read the manuscript. "If you find any obscurities or clumsiness of language," he wrote, "I should be deeply grateful if you would point them out. Although I do not aim at making my characters talk as Americans do, I do not want them to say anything that is too startlingly British, so if you come across anything of that sort I should like you to note it. . . . You know me well enough to know that it is impossible to hurt my feelings in a matter of this sort; I may not take my critics' advice, I didn't take Desmond MacCarthy's on the end of *The Narrow Corner*, but I am not affronted by it."[93] By this time Pfeiffer was in the army, stationed in Hawaii, and never got the typescript. Maugham showed it instead to Ken McCormick of Doubleday, whom he found intelligent and sympathetic.

Finishing *The Razor's Edge* left Maugham so exhausted that he promised himself it was the last long novel he would ever write. To recuperate he went to stay with friends in Woods Hole, who manufactured the paper on which U.S. bank notes were printed. He heard a corny joke that amused him about a woman who had triplets. A friend visited her in the hospital and said how wonderful it was. "Yes," answered the mother, "the doctor tells me it only happens once in 167,000 times." "Goodness," said the friend, "how did you ever find time to do your housework?"[94]

Wherever he went, Maugham remained sensitive to anti-British feeling, which he always managed to find. In August, back at the Colonial Inn, he wrote a friend that "they are prepared over here to admit that the British can take it, they admire their courage, their stubbornness, and their high spirits under disaster; but that does not prevent them from being annoyed with the British because they feel that *they* chiefly are responsible for their being dragged into the war, nor exasperated with their slowness, the mistakes they have made and the complacency of which they accuse them."[95]

Maugham was pleased with the way things were working out for Gerald, who liked his job running the commissary at Doubleday, and was resigned to having lost him as a secretary. As the head of his department, Gerald had forty-seven employees under him and was able to feel his own master for the first time. He had always resented his subordinate position and wanted to boss things, Maugham knew, and now he could. The Germans had seized his boat, the *Sara*, and Gerald had nothing to go back to on the Riviera. Maugham hoped he would settle comfortably in America.[96]

But at the end of October, Gerald quit the Doubleday commissary when he was offered a permanent job with the O.S.S. in Washington. Maugham encouraged anything that would keep him busy. His salary was a modest $300 a month, and in view of the cost of living in Washington, Maugham decided to start giving him the income from a $35,000 trust fund he had set up for him through Alanson.[97] He wrote Karl Pfeiffer:

> Gerald has a good job in Washington under Henry Field and is delighted with it. He has got hold of a tiny apartment, is keen on his work and happier than he has been for many years. I am hoping he will stick to it not only for the duration, but for long after. One of the troubles with him was that he thought himself too good for the work he had to do with me, and so did it grudgingly and badly, and he had too much time on his hands without resources in himself to occupy his leisure. He hated to be in what he thought a subservient position and though now only very small fry in a minor office attached to the State Department, he has a satisfying feeling of self-importance. . . . It is a wonderful relief to me to be free of that responsibility and of the constant worry and anxiety that he was to me. It has disembarrassed me of strain and stress.[98]

But Maugham was not without worry; he was concerned about rumors circulating in London that Liza was going to divorce Vincent Paravicini, who was now a lieutenant colonel in an armored-car unit serving in New Guinea. "She has promised not to do anything till after the war," he wrote Barbara Back, "and when they meet again I don't see why everything shouldn't turn out all right. Obviously it is hard when two young things are separated for three years, one mustn't expect too much from human nature."[99]

Their meeting was not long in coming, for Vincent turned up in November in New York. His unit was being transferred from the Pacific front to Italy. He was suffering from malaria and dysentery, which gave him a pasty look, but Maugham found him still handsome. He went to Washington and various other places to lecture on tank warfare. "All the girls in New York went mad about him," Maugham wrote Barbara Back, "and Liza came to the conclusion that there must be a great deal more to him than she had been inclined of late to think. So far as I could grasp, notwithstanding the long separation, things went very well and there is no question of a divorce."[100] Maugham believed that passion was temporary and that they could settle down sensibly like most married couples to make the best of it.

His thoughts were now often on his family, whom he tended to view as characters in his fiction who should act according to the plot devices he provided. Robin had expressed interest in becoming a writer, but Maugham was of another opinion. "Your future more probably lies in politics than in journalism or literature," he wrote. "It is always best to bend one's efforts in the direction in which one's gifts lie."[101]

In December, David Posner, who was now a freshman at Harvard, visited Maugham in Yemassee, lying to his family about where he was going. While Maugham worked in the morning Posner walked in the marsh, where there was a sand dune from which he could watch birds. The Doubledays were in residence, but Nelson was not interested in bird-watching. "It's just the same sort of thing you see on Long Island," he said. One afternoon Posner and Maugham were strolling when Maugham said, "Walk very slowly." An orange-brown snake at least four feet long lay in the path. Posner ran to the main house, where he found Raymond Ditmars' book on snakes and identified it as a copperhead. He came back with an axe and chopped at the snake as one of the servants yelled, "Kill it, massa, kill it." Posner was surprised that Maugham had not known what the snake was. He thought of him as an authority on everything.[102]

Posner had used sex to get close to Maugham but now found the physical part of their relationship trying. Maugham was old enough to be his grandfather, and Posner had to simulate a desire he did not feel. Maugham gave him books to read (the first was Thomas Mann's *Buddenbrooks*), which they later discussed, and he gave him advice on writing. A great writer reaches his maturity when he discovers his limitations, he said. Familiarity shrank Posner's admiration—he was no longer starry-eyed. He was shocked when he saw Maugham use *Roget's Thesaurus*. Great writers, he felt, did not need the crutch of a thesaurus. "It was his way of rephrasing clichés," he said. "He didn't want to say 'lean and hungry' so he looked up two words for 'lean and hungry.'" He decided that Maugham was not the master he had once worshiped, for Maugham could be read without any mental effort at all. "Maugham was no more capable of thinking of a person's life as a metaphor than a fly," he said.[103]

The new year, 1944, dawned with Maugham despondent, thinking with foreboding of his seventieth birthday on January 25. His stomach was bothering him, and with Gerald out of the picture, he had no one to answer his mail and do his typing. He felt alone. Liza had promised to come and stay, but her children came down with the mumps and she could not leave them. Karl Pfeiffer, sizing up the situation, offered to replace Gerald as soon as he got out of the army. Maugham replied that for the moment he could not afford the luxury of a secretary. His government allowed him to keep only a fraction of his earnings (he did not mention that the British government had no control over his American income or the trusts he had set up through Alanson), and he had to support Liza and her children. In addition, he said, he would be joined at the end of the war by his old and dear friend, Alan Searle, who was willing to take Gerald's place, and who would give him a happiness he had not known in the last ten years with Gerald. "I want someone kind, unselfish and considerate who will look after me till my death," he said, "and that I think my little Alan will be only too glad to do. He has neither Gerald's vitality and [sic] energy but he is sober, modest, affectionate and of a great sweetness of nature. He will have nothing much to do when the end of the war liberates him and asks nothing better than to step at once into a permanent job."[104]

On January 25, for the first time in many years he was alone on his birthday. He worked in the morning and went for a walk in the woods in the afternoon among the gum trees and the pines and the live oaks shrouded with Spanish moss. He made himself a cup of tea and read until dinner time. Then he played solitaire and went to bed. Apart from a few words to the maids, he had spoken to no one all day.[105]

It was a day for recapitulation. He had reached the proverbial three-score and ten, man's allotted span, and whatever years he had before him were in the nature of a reprieve. When he was thirty, his brother had told him, "Now you are a boy no longer." At forty he thought he had reached the end of youth, at fifty that it was time to accept middle age, and at sixty that he should put his affairs in order. "Now I am just an old man," he told himself.[106]

Old age had a kind of aloofness. He found himself living more in the past, studying the scenes that lingered in the chambers of his memory, gazing backward through the mist of years—perhaps to the smell of fresh thyme in the fields above the Mauresque, and Gerald's laughter echoing through the pines, and the very old and cheerful Sufi who had blessed him in Hyderabad, and gin *pahits* in the sultry Malayan evenings, and the stammering Arnold Bennett asking him to share a mistress, and first love in Heidelberg, and the apple-cheeked boys in their starched collars in the Mint Yard of the King's School, and an orphaned ten-year-old seeing the shores of England for the first time, and the Punch and Judy show in the Champs Elysées, and the empty bed in his mother's room.

And now he was in a temporary home in South Carolina wondering what the future held. What plans could he make? He was an exile, an Englishman who had chosen to live in France because he never felt quite at home in England. Ever since he had been thrust into the arms of strangers after his mother's death he had known that he belonged nowhere. His land of origin was the body of his work. As a writer he had done what he had set out to do. *Of Human Bondage* was still widely read. The present generation had found it significant. But eventually it would be forgotten. One or two of his comedies might retain a kind of pale life. A few of his best stories would find their way into anthologies. It was a fragile monument to a life's work, but it was better than nothing. There were men with greater gifts, but he did not envy them. And if he was forgotten a month after his death, he would never know.

At least he had lasted. So many were dead in the fullness of their years, like Henry James and Arnold Bennett, or cut down in mid-journey, like D. H. Lawrence or another Lawrence, Lawrence of Arabia, killed in 1935 while riding his motorcycle at high speed, hoping for the accident that would end his life while still in full possession of his powers, to spare him the indignity of old age. This was senseless, Maugham thought, for the pattern of a full life included old age. Old age undertook tasks that youth was too impatient for. The elder Cato had started to learn Greek at the age of eighty.

And yet old men were on sufferance. They were not quite human anymore. If they had made a stir in the world, the young sought them out so that they could prattle about it afterward with friends their own age. The famous old man was like a mountain climbed not for the fun of the ascent, but so the exploit could be recounted. What remained was his own company. Now that solitude was forced upon him, he found that it contented him. He was neither lonely nor bored. He was sound of limb and wind and still had twenty-six of his own teeth. He might have a few years left.[107]

"I have survived my seventieth birthday and be damned to it," he wrote Carl Van Vechten. "I look forward with equanimity to such years as I may still have to pass on this earth, but honestly I have had above enough of it, and am quite prepared to call it a day any day."[108]

479

Such pessimism was temporary, and news from his publisher put him in a better frame of mind. *The Razor's Edge* was coming out on April 20 in a first edition of 375,000 copies, of which the Literary Guild was taking 170,000. This was phenomenal, even for Maugham, who may have thought back to his first book, *Liza of Lambeth*, published in a first edition of 2,000 copies. His sales had always been higher in America than in England. *The Summing Up* had sold more than 100,000 copies, and a recent novel, *Christmas Holiday*, had sold 44,751. But *The Razor's Edge* was the brightest star in his galaxy.

It was an ambitious novel for a man of seventy, his first with Americans as the main characters. It charted the spiritual odyssey of a young American who is converted to the Eastern gospel of nonattachment. It was in a sense a prophetic novel, announcing the coming disaffection of thousands of young Americans with the bitch goddess Success and their quest for an alternative in the teachings of the East. It was the first novel in Western literature whose main character was an American dropout and guru-tripper. How unexpected that a seventy-year-old English writer should have divined the allure of Eastern nonattachment for a later American generation. Larry Darrell, indifferent to the business world and the girl he is supposed to marry, was the precursor of every young American of the sixties and seventies who ever spent time in an ashram. Just as he had, in *Christmas Holiday*, written an allegory of Europe's collapse, Maugham now dealt with the conflict between materialism and the spiritual quest, which would one day become an issue for thousands of young Americans.

The title came from the *Katha-Upanishad*: "The sharp edge of a razor is difficult to pass over; thus the wise say the path to Salvation is hard." Maugham felt comfortable with the theme of the returning veteran whose life can never be the same, having already used it in *The Hero*. Larry Darrell, a World War I aviator who has seen his best friend killed, drops out of the Chicago business world to devote his life to self-improvement. He spends five years in India, and then moves to Paris. The process of his conversion is carefully charted, and the gospel of his new faith, based partly on Maugham's 1938 trip to India and partly on his own reading and his exposure to the ideas of Vedanta West in Hollywood, was explained in a discussion with the narrator.

Larry becomes detached to the point of apathy from worldly things, including sex. Isabel Bradley, his fiancée, marries the successful Chicago businessman Gray Maturin, who is based on Nelson Doubleday. He is a large, hearty fellow who owns a plantation where the woods are like the woods in a Maeterlinck play. He speaks in clichés. He does not go to bed, he hits the hay, and when it rains it rains to beat the band.

In counterpoint to Larry, Maugham brings on the snob Elliott Templeton, whose *raison d'être* is knowing the right people and being invited to the right parties. But Elliott represents another form of escapism from brutalizing American values. Like Larry, he has fled America and lives in France. He is one of those Americans who dislike their own country and are enchanted by the decorum and titles of the old world. "My poor country is becoming hopelessly middle-class," he says. "You wouldn't believe it, my dear fellow, but last time I was in America a taxi driver addressed me as a brother." Templeton was based partly on Henry (Chips) Channon, whom Maugham had met at Emerald Cunard's in 1935 and had not seen since. Like Chips, Elliott Templeton lived abroad. Like Chips, Templeton had served in the ambulance corps in World War I and had converted from Protestant to Catholic. Since his meeting with Maugham, Chips had succeeded brilliantly in scaling the bastions of English society. In 1936 he became a member of Parliament, which he called "this smelly, tawny, male paradise." Later he served as private secretary to the Undersecretary of State for Foreign Affairs, R. A. Butler. Eventually he was awarded the seal of his Anglicization, a knighthood. When that day came, his Parisian friend Princess Marthe Bibesco sent him a telegram: "Goodbye Mr. Chips."[109]

Templeton may also have been based partly on Jerry Zipkin, the young friend of Maugham's who was part of the international set, went from party to party, and knew everyone. Maugham, who had observed the goings-on among the social butterflies on the Riviera for more than ten years, had a field day with Elliott Templeton. Tragedy struck when he was not invited to a masked ball given by Princess Novemali, who was based on one of Maugham's Riviera neighbors, Princess Ottoboni (eight goods turned into nine evils). Princess Ottoboni was an American who had married a homosexual Roman prince, and they were known as *Pédéraste et Médisance*. As Maugham said of Princess Novemali, "She could not help saying beastly things about even her intimate friends, but she did this because she was a stupid woman and knew no other way to make herself interesting."[110]

The narrator, who is given the author's own name for the first time, manages to get an invitation to the ball for Templeton, who is dying. In an oddly touching scene he insists that, as a man of the world, he must dictate a reply: "Mr. Elliott Templeton regrets that he cannot accept

Princess Novemali's kind invitation owing to a previous engagement with his Blessed Lord." Templeton was a scene-stealer, and many critics preferred him to the elusive Larry Darrell, who was like "a reflection in the water."

But the book was about Larry's quest, and ends with his return to the United States to take a job in a garage or become a taxi driver. He had no desire for fame and was without ambition. "He is too modest to set himself up as an example to others," Maugham concluded, "but it may be he thinks that a few uncertain souls, drawn to him like moths to a candle, will be brought in time to share his own glowing belief that ultimate satisfaction can only be found in the life of the spirit, and that by himself following with selflessness and renunciation the path of perfection he will serve as well as if he wrote books or addressed multitudes."[111] Indeed, Larry would in time have thousands of disciples, from Timothy Leary to Carlos Castañeda. Maugham added that he himself was incapable of finding complete satisfaction in the life of the spirit. It was not a solution for everyone.

In the quality of the writing, the depth of the characters, and the enduring validity of its theme, *The Razor's Edge* was one of Maugham's important novels, to be ranked alongside *Of Human Bondage* and *Cakes and Ale*. For once the narrator was not a detached observer but the novelist inside the novel, on the same level as the other characters, which gave the book a warmth that some of Maugham's other books lack. For once reviewers could not use that overemployed word "cynical."

Commonweal said on April 28 that it was "unbelievably cheap and trifling," while *Time* said on April 24 that it ranked as one of his three major novels. Some critics felt that the snob's progress was better charted than the pilgrim's. *Library Journal* on April 15 said it was far from required reading in days when time and paper were precious. Diana Trilling in *The Nation* on May 6 said: "He reveals the flirtatious nature of his occasional excursions into mysticism as he suggests the reason for the failure of his whole literary career. Mysticism, that is, is bound to be inviting to the person who is afraid of the deep emotions; yet it can never fully win him, any more than humanity can fully win him. All the characters in Maugham's latest novel inevitably inhabit the non-dimensional universe which is all that is left when the deep emotions have been disavowed."[112] Cyril Connolly, referring to the unfavorable reviews, asked: "Are we becoming incapable of recognizing excellence when we see it?"[113]

Christopher Isherwood, a convert like Larry to the teaching of the East, considered *The Razor's Edge* a successful religious novel:

> If I ever write a religious novel, I shall begin by trying to prove that my saint-to-be really *is* Mr. Jones. Somerset Maugham, for example, does this quite successfully in *The Razor's Edge*. Larry, when we first meet him, is an entirely reassuring character, lively, natural, normal, a typical American boy. . . . How am I going to show, in terms of dramatic fiction, that decisive moment at which my hero becomes aware of his vocation and decides to do something about it? Maugham is rather vague at this point: he merely suggests that Larry's change of heart is caused by his experiences in the First World War.[114]

The Welsh writer John Cowper Powys misread the book, taking it to mean that Maugham had "got religion. He's got it in his way, and his rough-and-tumble Saint Larry or whatever his name was, wasn't the kind that wd. suit Aldous Huxley or Graham Greene or Rex Warner, but nevertheless for an ex-man-of-the-world and ex-virtuoso in Brandy this Piccolo Santo will serve. . . . Yes, I think this admirable craftsman and most honest cod has seriously 'got religion,' & thus naturally doesn't like what he liked (either in men or books) in his primrose days."[115]

Maugham had not "got religion." Nonattachment was not for him. The book's staggering success brought him back to the material world. It sold 507,000 copies in a month.[116] Once again his timing had been right. Religious novels, such as *The Song of Bernadette* and *The Keys of the Kingdom*, were wildly popular during the war years.

It was at the moment of his greatest triumph that the blow came. While working in Washington, Gerald had an attack of pleurisy, which he ignored. He finally became so ill that in May he was admitted to Doctors Hospital in New York, where it was discovered that he did not have pleurisy but tuberculosis. One lung was gone and the other was affected. The doctors also diagnosed Addison's disease, a rare but fatal form of tuberculosis that destroys the adrenal glands and gradually turns the skin brown.

Maugham's first reaction was shock, followed by surprise that Gerald's lungs were affected rather than his liver. He was hopeful that Gerald could be cured, for tuberculosis was no longer fatal. In fact it was an illness he himself had survived. But when Maugham saw him he was stunned. Gerald, once the life of the party, looked wasted. His weight had dropped to a hundred and twelve pounds, and a painful cough tore him to pieces. Doctors collapsed his lung, and he was so weak he had to be given blood transfusions.[117]

Maugham came to see him every day and brought him books. Gerald wanted to do needlepoint to pass the time, and Maugham borrowed a rare book of Matisse cutouts from Monroe Wheeler, Glenway Wescott's friend, who was a curator at the Museum of Modern Art, so Gerald could use Matisse's forms as patterns. "He bullied Monroe into giving him the book," Wescott recalled, "and it never came back, and Monroe was furious. Willie was fussing around Gerald as if he were his son, after all that Gerald had poured out in the way of venom and resentment. I suppose it was the memory of the most beautiful love affair he had ever had."[118]

There began a vigil that would last six months. For the moment Maugham remained in New York so that he could be at Gerald's side. He saw quite a bit of Chips Channon, who was in town. Channon had brought over a remark of Emerald Cunard's which Maugham found charming: "This is a very middle-class war; one simply doesn't know anyone who's killed."[119] Channon recorded in his diary: "I saw much of Somerset Maugham, who never before was a friend. He has put me in a book, *The Razor's Edge*, and when I dined with him, I asked him why he had done it, and he explained, with some embarrassment, that he had split me into three characters, and then written a book about all three. So I am Elliott Templeton, Larry, himself the hero of the book, and another: however I am flattered, and the book is a masterpiece." Maugham, in finding a tactful way to avoid offending Channon, had admitted that Elliott Templeton was based on him.[120]

Liza and her children were returning to England, and Maugham was glad they were going. He felt she had been in America too long and hoped she would settle down with Vincent to a contented life, but he knew things would be difficult.

> There have been faults on both sides [he wrote his sister-in-law Helen Mary Maugham]. Vincent, I hear, has been drinking and gambling heavily, but I am sure Liza can check all that, she has at least learned the value of money here and has acquired a lot more sense than she had. The difficulty from her side appears to be that she finds Vincent putty in her hands and she has an idea that she wants to be putty in someone else's hands. I am not sure that she would enjoy that as much as she imagines. Fortunately there is no strong silent man in the picture. . . .

Her stay here will have enabled her to amass quite a nice sum of money, and I have promised her four hundred a year for the present.[121]

Maugham was distressed to learn that Robin had undergone another brain operation. Since he was alone, he invited Robin to join him in South Carolina later that year. "The house is comfortable and the food good," he said. "You would lead a virtuous life and save money. Think about it."[122]

In the meantime Gerald was no better. The collapsed-lung operation was a failure. With the benefit of his own medical training, Maugham followed the daily bulletins closely. Gerald was in such pain that he was given morphine daily. Twice at the end of June it seemed that he would not last out the day. He was so emaciated and looked so dreadful that it was agonizing for Maugham to see him.[123]

In early July 1944, as a last resort, Maugham took Gerald to Saranac Lake, a noted place for tuberculars in the Adirondacks. He hoped the air would improve him. He went with him because he could not bear the thought of his dying alone. He had received a first payment of $50,000 on the film rights to *The Razor's Edge*, of which he sent Alanson $30,000 to invest. He complained that his earnings would place him in the 85 percent tax bracket, but added: "It's funny, at seventy, money doesn't seem important any more, at least saving it doesn't."[124]

In Saranac, Maugham stayed at the Altavista Lodge, which discouraged tubercular convalescents and in fact noted on its stationery: "Tuberculous patients not received." He found Saranac "a hell of a place, nothing but nursing homes and hospitals and a very indifferent hotel." Gerald, who stayed at one of the hospitals, improved slightly; he was in less pain and soon began to breathe a little better. Maugham went to see him twice each day and was making plans to take him to Arizona in the winter.[125]

Gerald's decline was a terrible blow. He had been with Maugham through all the best years of his life, those in which they had traveled up and down the world together and had such fun, and with him all of Maugham's happiest recollections would die. Gerald had made out a will, leaving his money to Robin and his personal effects to Maugham.[126] He had a small sum in England which he left to his French friend Louis Legrand, also a tubercular.

The Saranac doctors said Gerald needed an exploratory operation and recommended the Leahy Institute in Boston. Gerald was moved to the New England Baptist Hospital in August, and Maugham went to Edgartown for a rest. He enjoyed the bathing and the bridge but was anxious about the verdict from the Leahy Institute. The doctors there came to the conclusion that Gerald did not have Addison's disease but tuberculosis of the duodenum.[127] As he was carted from hospital to hospital, no two specialists agreed on the nature of his illness.

Gerald was bearing up with courage and uncharacteristic patience. On August 15 he wrote Barbara Back:

> Babs my sweet, I am in Boston at the moment and it is 101 in the shade, not very good for my T.B. but that is getting along fairly well. My trouble is that after every meal or even half a glass of warm milk I blow up as though I was going to have quintuplets. I am here to see specialists and so far beyond deciding that the trouble is *not* tubercular [evidently the doctors were not telling him the truth] they've found nothing but ounces of morphia to relieve the very bad pain. It's the pain which tires me so much that writing is difficult and even getting washed is a burden.[128]

Gerald was so unhappy in the grim Baptist Hospital that Maugham took him back to New York. He had to be carried to the train in a stretcher. Maugham was beginning to lose hope. "The only thing that keeps me from despairing," he wrote his old friend the playwright Eddie Knoblock, "is that I know how great a power of resilience he has and I still think that if he can go through this winter he may pick up. All the best years of my life were connected with him. I always counted on his surviving me by the years he is younger than I am. They say as one grows older one feels less; I wish it were true."[129]

Now, when Maugham came to see him at Doctors Hospital, Gerald lay on his back, not even reading, just staring into space. If he spoke, it was sometimes to denounce him violently, as Mildred had denounced Philip Carey in *Of Human Bondage*. Appalling obscenities poured forth from his feverish lips. He raved like a lunatic, screaming and railing against the man who had been his companion for nearly thirty years and who was now doing his utmost to help him get well. He predicted that Maugham would die before he did and made wild forecasts of the fun he would have once Maugham was out of the way. Nurses tried to lead Maugham away, but he would not move, he sat quietly listening to the stream of filth coming from the cadaverous figure on the hospital bed.[130]

Gerald's hostility, expressed over the years through drinking and making a spectacle of himself, was finally in the open. For years he had been dependent on Maugham. Now, after a brief attempt at emancipation, illness had made him dependent again, at the mercy of Maugham's concern, as he had formerly been at the mercy of his commands. While Gerald had lived with Maugham he had been able to maintain a more or less stable balance. Maugham had looked after him when he broke his neck and had the DT's, and had put up with his outbursts. It was only after he left Maugham that he contracted the illness that was now killing him. For a man as physically active as Gerald to be bedridden and useless may have given him the feeling that he was being punished for his entire life, and for all the pain he had inflicted on others.

The best lung specialist in New York examined Gerald and said the only chance of saving his life was an exploratory operation. But he was much too weak, and the doctors began a program to make him strong enough so that he would survive the operation. "I have been in bed six months now," Gerald wrote Barbara Back in early October, "and it looks like another eighteen more. I had what is now called an acute case but used to be called galloping, so it will be at least six months before they can start a thoracoplasty. Ask Ivor [her doctor husband, Ivor Back] what that is—and then it'll take a year to get over that. It is very tiresome to be in bed instead of in Washington."[131]

Maugham had completely given up hope. Even if Gerald recovered, he would be a semi-invalid for the rest of his life. He sometimes wished that he would go to sleep one night and never awake. At the end of October the doctors decided to operate. They found a large ulcer in Gerald's stomach and could not determine whether it was tubercular or malignant. They did not think he could survive having it cut out, and closed it off. Gerald seemed to be getting on fairly well after the operation, but a week later he had an attack of edema (an excessive accumulation of fluid) in the lung, which proved fatal.[132] He became unconscious, and died in Doctors Hospital on November 7, 1944. He was fifty-two years old.

"I warned him, all the doctors he went to warned him that he was killing himself," Maugham wrote Barbara Back. "He did not want to die, but he would not do what they told him; it looked as though he was rushing to death."[133]

Gerald's death was the last scene in a drama that had been played out over more than a quarter of a century. It sometimes seemed that his relationship with Maugham was based on the amount of hurt they could inflict on each other. Even in their happier moments they were opposites. Maugham was thrifty, and Gerald was a spendthrift. Maugham was cautious, and Gerald was reckless. Maugham was moderate, and Gerald was excessive. Maugham was a survivor, and Gerald was a casualty. As the dynamics of such relationships went, Maugham played a restraining and cautionary role, which provoked Gerald to indulge his excesses all the more.

In his life with Gerald, Maugham had lived out the principal theme of his work, love as bondage. Like Mildred in *Of Human Bondage*, Gerald was an unworthy object of passion—dishonest, mocking, and unfaithful. For twenty-eight years, for reasons that perplexed his friends, Maugham had accepted the situation. Now Gerald's death freed him, just as death had freed Mrs. Craddock, Basil Kent, and others of his characters. Early in their relationship Maugham had placed under Gerald's pillow this poem by Yeats: [134]

> *I turn round*
> *Like a dumb beast in a show,*
> *Neither know what I am*
> *Nor where I go,*
> *My language beaten*
> *Into one name;*
> *I am in love*
> *And that is my shame.*
> *What hurts the soul*
> *My soul adores,*
> *No better than a beast*
> *Upon all fours.*

On November 9 there was a funeral service at the fashionable Episcopal Church of St. James at 865 Madison Avenue. The Doubledays attended, as did Glenway Wescott and Monroe Wheeler and several others of Maugham's friends. Maugham was sitting next to Glenway Wescott, and in the middle of the service he broke down and sobbed. Wescott watched him, bent over with his head in his hands, with mixed feelings. And all these years, he thought, you've been bragging about how tough you are, and you've never displayed emotion, and you've been trying to extend your life into the life hereafter through your work, and here in this church, where the very words "life hereafter" are being uttered, here you sit blubbering, you can't even keep your composure and you're making a fool of yourself in public. What good was an upper-class Anglo-Saxon manner if it left you weak as a kitten in the common plight, the hour of every man?[135]

After the service one of Maugham's New York friends, the Countess Palffy, an American woman who had married European nobility, came up to Maugham and said, "I can't abide your weeping over that man." It your weeping over that man." It was God's blessing, she said, that had saved Gerald from a miserable downhill life. Maugham walked away from her, and never saw her again. Gerald was buried in Ferncliff Cemetery, Hartsdale, New York.[136]

Shortly after Gerald's death Cecil Roberts, the English novelist, who was in New York doing propaganda work, called Maugham and offered to come to see him. "I don't want to see you," Maugham said. "I don't want to see anyone. I want to die!" Roberts went anyway, and Maugham opened the door looking haggard. They had lunch in the hotel and Maugham perked up. Appreciative of Roberts' concern, he took his hands in his and thanked him: "You are a good friend, Cecil."[137]

In December he went back to Parker's Ferry, where Robin joined him at the end of the month, but Maugham was still dwelling on Haxton's death. "With the pills they've given me," he said, "I sometimes manage to sleep or doze for as much as six hours a night. But I think of him every minute that I'm awake."[138]

Robin was worried about his uncle, who refused to leave Parker's Ferry or see anyone. If something reminded him of Gerald, he would break down and sob. Robin was not in much better shape himself. He had developed a stammer like his uncle's as the result of his head wound and suffered fits of amnesia and depression.[139] He told Maugham that he could never become a lawyer because of the amnesia, and that his essential nature lay in writing. Maugham advised him to marry a rich woman and go into politics, so that he could end up as governor-general of a remote island.[140]

Robin's presence soon had a tonic effect. Maugham found him good-humored and amusing. Everyone was charmed by him. But in his charm, Maugham felt, there was the disturbing element of always wanting to shine and be the center of attention.[141] Toward the end of January 1945 Robin went to New York to visit friends. Maugham sent him to Max Wolf, the Viennese doctor who had treated him with enzymes. Robin returned to Parker's Ferry so ill that he had to be put to bed. Max Wolf, Maugham reported to Robin's father, Lord Maugham, said he was suffering not from his wounds but from neurasthenia. "Of course neurasthenia is just as much of a disease as scarlet fever," Maugham pointed out. "Dr. Wolf thinks (strange as it may seem to you) that it is due to an inferiority complex occasioned by the fact that he is the son of his father and the nephew of his uncle."[142] Robin craved a position attained by his own efforts, the doctor said, and advised hard work and no drinking. By May, when he went home to England, Robin had gained weight and seemed calmer. He was planning to write the story of his life in the tank corps.

With Robin gone, Maugham resumed his quiet life, working in the morning on a historical novel set in Renaissance Italy, reading or walking in the afternoon, and sometimes playing cards in the evening at the Doubledays'. The news from the Riviera was that the American Seventh Army under General Patch had landed on the beaches on August 15, 1944. Maugham was pleased to hear that the Americans had taken over the Mauresque as a rest house for officers on leave and were demining the property. He had been concerned about the possibility of a mine blowing up while he walked in the garden. The Mauresque had been occupied by both Italians and Germans, and shelled by the British fleet, but Maugham did not know the extent of the damage. One of his maids had been arrested as a Gestapo agent. Maugham could not bring himself to believe that she was anything of the kind, but there was nothing he could do to help her. She was sentenced in October 1945 to a three-year prison term. His apartment at 65 rue La Fontaine in Paris was being looked after by his businessman friend Jacques Raindre. Gerald's friend Louis Legrand was living in it.[143]

In June, Maugham was asked to go to Hollywood to work on the script of *The Razor's Edge*, which he had sold to the movies for $250,000. Darryl Zanuck, the head of 20th Century-Fox, had bought it, and wanted George Cukor to direct. But Cukor did not like the script and told him he would do the picture only if Maugham worked on it. This was just the sort of challenge he needed to stop his brooding over Gerald, and he spent most of June and July as Cukor's houseguest.

Maugham had sent Zanuck a telegram saying that he would work on the screenplay for nothing. Zanuck kept the telegram, never having received a similar offer, but did not like the idea of anyone working for the studio gratis and asked Cukor, "Would he like some nice cuff links?" "He's got some nice cuff links," Cukor said. "Would he like a gold cigarette case?" "He's got a gold cigarette case." "Would he like a

After the war, Maugham returned to the Villa Mauresque, where he is shown (1) in white ducks and espadrilles, in 1951, a youthful 77.

VILLA MAURESQUE

The wall surrounding the property bore his trademark, the Moorish symbol (2). He sometimes stood on his doorstep to welcome guests (3) . . .

4

. . . or led them upstairs, past the imposing Picasso (4), to their rooms, or waited for them in the drawing room (5), furnished in Spanish baroque.

5

7

After Haxton's death, Alan Searle became Maugham's secretary, sharing his meals (6). Sometimes Maugham sat in gloomy silence, but he always had a morsel for his dog (7).

8

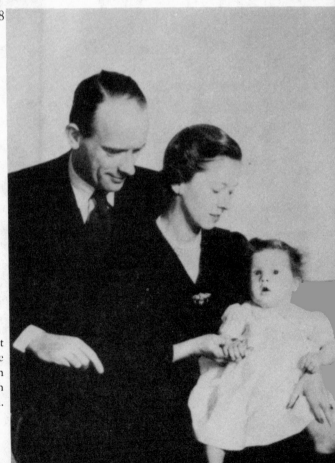

Liza, divorced from Vincent Paravicini, married John Hope (later Lord Glendevon) in 1948. They are shown (8) in 1958 with their son Julian.

Katharine Cornell and Allan Jeayes (9)
were in the American dramatization of
Maugham's second-most-famous story,
"The Letter." The ladies with the pistols,
Jeanne Eagels (10) and Bette Davis (11),
starred in the film versions of the same story.

9

10

11

12

At the Mauresque, Maugham received his famous friends, such as Jean Cocteau (12) and Noel Coward (13).

13

15

14

The Aga Khan (14), who invited Maugham onto his houseboat on the
Nile, and Ian Fleming (15), who asked him for a blurb for his first James
Bond thriller, were among Maugham's Riviera friends.

Maugham enjoyed playing bridge with Elsa Maxwell (16).

16

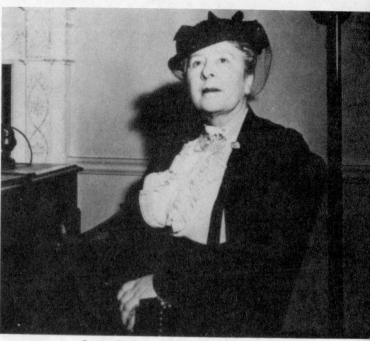

17

18

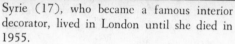

Syrie (17), who became a famous interior decorator, lived in London until she died in 1955.

Jerry Zipkin (19), a man who loved parties, was a frequent correspondent with Maugham.

Robin, Maugham's nephew (18), was a frequent visitor to Mauresque, and the recipient of a handsome trust fund Maugham settled on him.

19

20

Maugham tried to keep young by visiting the rejuvenation clinic of Dr. Paul Niehans (20), shown here supervising the extraction of a lamb fetus, from which his miracle serum was made.

Maugham placed his trust in few men, one of them being his editor at Heinemann's, Alexander Frere (21).

21

22

W. Somerset Maugham (22), upon receiving honors from the Queen in 1954.

His brother, Lord Frederic Maugham, and daughter Liza attended a reception for Maugham's 80th birthday (23) in 1954.

23

"NURSE, HE'S JUST SAID DADA"

24

Maugham with Liza and his two Paravicini grandchildren (24) in 1962. He later tried to disinherit Liza and adopt Alan Searle, with whom he often played cards (25). News of the adoption proceedings was greeted in the London press with jocular cartoons (26).

25

His paintings, including Picasso's "Death of a Harlequin," were sold
at Sotheby's (27).

Maugham visited the King's School (28), where he had been miserable as a boy.

In his last years, Maugham still had friends of his generation: Bernard Berenson in Florence (30), his Riviera neighbors Winston Churchill (31) and Lord Beaverbrook (32), Bert Alanson (33) in San Francisco, and Max Beerbohm (34) in Rapallo.

29   30

31

33

But he outlived them all (29), and was left alone.

34

35

One of the last photographs of W. Somerset Maugham (35),
taken at Mauresque.

Maugham died on December 15, 1965, in the South of France, at the age of 91, and his
ashes were buried on December 22 at the King's School (36), beneath the spires of Canterbury Cathedral.

36

car?" "He's got a car." "Well, what the hell would he like?" "I think he'd like a picture."[144]

Zanuck asked Maugham to come and see him and told him he would be happy if he bought himself a painting at the expense of 20th Century-Fox. "You can't buy a picture for nothing," Maugham said. "What would 20th Century-Fox be prepared to pay?" "Anything up to $15,000," Zanuck said. Maugham was thrilled. He had never in his life spent so much for a picture, and he ended up buying his first Impressionist painting, a scene of the harbor in Rouen by Pissarro.[145]

As it happened, not a word that Maugham wrote was used in the film. Zanuck turned over his version to the screenwriter Lamar Trotti, who rewrote it twelve times before the studio was satisfied. But the life was pleasant. He went to parties, and met Greta Garbo. A masseur came in twice a week to pound him into shape. Zanuck asked him to write a sequel to *The Razor's Edge*, and Maugham replied: "The only example in history of a sequel being as good as the original is *Don Quixote*, and I should be crazy to attempt one to *The Razor's Edge*. For one thing, it would need a far greater knowledge of American life than I can possibly pretend to possess."

The movie starred Tyrone Power, whose first role it was after three years as a Marine Corps pilot. He went to a Hindu swami for insight into the character of Larry Darrell. The swami told him that Larry had been transformed by "an inner light."[146] Clifton Webb played Elliott Templeton with a bitchy parvenu snobbishness and Herbert Marshall was properly suave as Somerset Maugham. Perhaps the most interesting bit of casting was that of Anne Baxter as Sophie, the debutante turned tramp. It happened one afternoon that Darryl Zanuck, at his home in Palm Springs with his crony Gregory Ratoff, was pacing around the pool in his bikini, swinging his polo mallet and cursing the problem of casting Sophie. "Darryl, darling, what about Anne Baxter?" Ratoff suggested. "Nah," Zanuck snarled, "she's a cold potato." Ratoff, a friend of Anne Baxter's, who wanted her to get the part, said with an evil leer: "Please, darling. I have had it. It's marvelous." "You're kidding," Zanuck said. "That's right, Darryl. Marvelous!" On the basis of Ratoff's recommendation, Anne Baxter got the part.[147]

His work done, Maugham went to San Francisco to visit the Alansons, who took him on excursions to Lake Tahoe and Yosemite National Park. By October 1945 he was in New York, staying at the Plaza, where he had two rooms on the sixteenth floor. He liked the Plaza. The barman made good martinis, the hansom cabs outside had an archaic turn-of-the-century look that agreed with the building, and he could exchange *cher maîtres* with Salvador Dali in the restaurant. He wrote G. B. Stern: "Everyone who comes in says: what a beautiful view of the park you have and I say: yes, it's a beautiful view of the park. Then they say: it must be simply lovely at night, and I say: yes, it's simply lovely at night. Then they say: you know, I'm never tired of this view and then I say: will you have a cocktail and they say: yes, and turn their back on the view with a sigh of relief."[148]

Now that the war was over, Maugham wondered what to do. An incendiary bomb had destroyed part of his garden, and every window in the villa was broken. He thought of selling the Mauresque and finding a smaller house in England. Wherever he decided to live, of one thing he was sure, he wanted Alan Searle as his secretary, and he was pulling strings so that Alan could join him in America. Travel out of England at that time was still severely restricted. As a way of thanking America for its wartime hospitality, Maugham had offered the manuscript of *Of Human Bondage* to the Library of Congress. The manuscript was in England, and bringing it to America gave Alan a valid reason to travel. Maugham asked Lord Halifax, the British ambassador to the United States, to endorse this plan. He also asked his British publisher, Alexander Frere, who was doing war work in the Ministry of Labour, to ask the minister, Ernest Bevin, to give Alan the necessary exit permit.[149]

While waiting for Alan's arrival Maugham saw New York friends and English transients. Peter Daubeny, the young theatrical producer to whom Maugham had lectured on Anglo-American problems in 1940, came through New York with plans to revive some of his plays. Daubeny had been in the Coldstream Guards, and a mortar shell had taken off his left arm at Salerno. Maugham found him charming and appealing and wished he could see more of him. S. N. Behrman took him to lunch at "21" with Harold Ross, the editor of *The New Yorker*. They were joined by Leonora Corbett, the young actress who had made a hit in Noel Coward's *Blithe Spirit*. She told Maugham that *The Razor's Edge* should be made into a play. "I'd love to play the heroine," she said. Maugham had described the heroine as having oversized legs. He looked her up and down and said, "Well, my dear, you have the legs for it, haven't you?" Miss Corbett cooled noticeably toward Maugham after that remark. When he had gone, Behrman mentioned it to Ross, who said, "It's his nature, I guess."[150]

Maugham went back to Parker's Ferry after Thanksgiving. Americans were jittery about the atom bomb (the first of which had been dropped on Hiroshima that August), he wrote Robin, but Maugham himself took the new weapon in his stride. "One destructive weapon after another has been invented during the world's history, and filled people with terror," he wrote, "and yet the world has gone on and things, bad as they were, were never quite as bad as was feared."[151]

He had finished the novel set in Renaissance Italy and was embarking on another, set in seventeenth-century Spain, the Spain of Philip III and Don Quixote. For several years he had been carrying on a correspondence with a Spanish psychiatrist living in New York, Dr. Félix Martí-Ibáñez, whom he now wrote to ask: "What exactly were the qualifications in the Golden Age of Spain which entitled a man to be called Don?"

Martí-Ibáñez was one of those unconditional admirers whom Maugham seemed to pick up like disciples. He had come to the United States after fighting on the anti-Franco side in the Spanish civil war. During the South Ebro campaign he was hit in the arm and scalp by a dumdum bullet and took refuge in a bombed house in the village of Torre del Español. In the house he found a tattered volume of Maugham's short stories, and marveled at the prose, which he found "taut and dry as Toledan leather, and endowed with that 'difficult simplicity' so dear to Cervantes." Settling in New York, he sent Maugham two articles he had written on Don Fernando in 1941. Martí-Ibáñez also wrote short stories, which he sent to Maugham for criticism. Of one of his stories Maugham wrote him: "Of course you are a scientist, a psychologist and a moralist. These are very good things, but the writer of fiction must take care that his special interests do not cause harm to his fiction. In effect your story is a piece of propaganda in condemnation of the atom bomb."[152]

Maugham asked Martí-Ibáñez to edit his Spanish novel, Catalina, for historical accuracy, and Martí-Ibáñez replied that he would be delighted to, enclosing an article he had written connecting chess with the Oedipus complex. He held the capture of the king to be analogous to the child's subconscious wish for the death of his father. Maugham was not impressed. "I should have thought the desire to win and therefore show one's superiority was a sufficient explanation of the chess-player's enthusiasm," he wrote, "without bringing in the Oedipus complex . . . the motive of playing is that sense of power one feels when things go favorably."[153]

In December, Karl Pfeiffer sent Maugham some saffron so that he could have one of his favorite dishes, *arroz a la Valenciana*, but his cook produced a soft, dark, inedible mess. Maugham was annoyed with Pfeiffer, who kept wanting to write articles about him. His latest idea was to publish a selection of Maugham's fan letters. This Maugham found unacceptable, and he wrote Pfeiffer: "I have kept none of my fan letters. As soon as I have answered them I throw them in the waste-paper basket. But even if I had kept any of them I wouldn't send them to you. Most of them were written out of kindness and some because the writers were in trouble and thought I could help them. I should look upon it as a shameful action to pillory them in the pages of a magazine."[154]

Maugham was still waiting for Alan, who had his papers to leave England but whose ship had been delayed by Atlantic storms. Alan sailed from Newcastle with the manuscript of *Of Human Bondage* on December 2, 1945, landed in Hoboken on Christmas day, and went straight to Parker's Ferry.[155] Maugham was stunned by the change in Alan's looks. He was now a portly and chipmunk-cheeked forty-one. Alan liked to say that as a young man he had been quite a dish, but now he was quite a tureen. When he told Maugham that Lytton Strachey had called him his Bronzino boy, Maugham replied: "Lytton Strachey be damned. You may have looked like a Bronzino once upon a time but now you look like a rather depraved Frans Hals."[156] Looks did not matter, however, for what Maugham needed was someone to take care of him, and this Alan did with diligence for the last twenty years of Maugham's life. He was, in Glenway Wescott's phrase, "the nanny of his second childhood." He answered the mail, made travel arrangements, acted as a buffer between Maugham and the outside world, and finished his sentences for him when he got stuck. In addition, he provided sexual relief whenever Maugham required it. Alan told close friends, "He was the most marvelous lover I ever had."[157]

In many ways it was a duplication of the ill-defined relationship between Maugham and Gerald Haxton, part employee and part lover, a relationship based on affection but not between equals. Alan had been understudying the part for years. He had accompanied Maugham to the Niehans clinic in 1938 and submitted to the painful series of shots, just to be agreeable, and when Maugham had had a car accident on the drive to Paris it was Alan who took care of him and kept him out of the hospital. Maugham knew that Alan was as devoted as an anchorite. There was, however, about as much resemblance between Gerald and Alan as between a wolf and a poodle. Gerald was thin and mercurial,

Alan was plump and shy. He reminded Maugham's friends of the beadle in *Oliver Twist*. Alan was sweet where Gerald had been abrasive, peaceful where Gerald had been quarrelsome, domesticated where Gerald had been wild. There was no fire in Alan, no capacity for storms. Gerald could have made something of himself, and resented Maugham for giving him an easy life. Alan had no education or ambition; he had been rescued by Maugham from a dull career in social work and was grateful. As a Riviera friend of Maugham's who knew them both put it: "Gerald was vintage, Alan was *vin ordinaire*." David Posner, whom Maugham was then putting through Harvard, felt after meeting Alan that he was sweet and kind on the surface but unctuous and moneygrubbing inside.[158] Edith Sitwell called Alan "a saint" on account of his years of prison visiting, but there was a side of Alan that she did not want to know about, which had to do with what she called "piggy things."[159]

Alan felt inadequate around Maugham's friends, and so he chose to be relentlessly ingratiating. Since he could not compete on the level of intellect or achievement, he would make up for it by fawning. Everyone was marvelous, and a pet, and grand. He scattered his heart around like birdseed. In addition, Alan was a hypochondriac, forever complaining about this or that ailment. "When you asked him how he was, he never said I'm fine," Jerry Zipkin said. This too was an appeal for sympathy in a world in which he felt he did not come up to the mark.

When Maugham was annoyed with Alan, he compared him unfavorably with Gerald. "Willie didn't respect Alan," Jerry Zipkin said. "Alan was namby-pamby." One time they came to New York from London, and Daphne du Maurier asked Alan to bring some of her jewelry, but his luggage was searched at customs and he had to pay duty on it. Maugham was furious and said that such a thing would never have happened to Gerald.[160]

One of Alan's ways of coping with his situation was to pretend to be what he was not. When S. N. Behrman first met him before the war at Siegfried Sassoon's, someone pointed out that he was wearing an Eton tie, to which he was not entitled.[161] He told people that he had been private secretary to William Temple, who became Archbishop of Canterbury. But according to Mrs. Dorothy Howell-Thomas, who *was* the archbishop's secretary: "Alan Searle was never secretary to Archbishop William Temple, and indeed was no more than a wartime acquaintance. From I think about 1940, when Dr. Temple was Archbishop of York, and lived at Bishopthorpe, Mrs. Temple became interested in a YMCA

Forces 'hut' for soldiers at Strensall Camp, York. This included a canteen and leisure facilities for the troops. . . . Alan Searle was one of the organizers employed by the YMCA to run the place. . . . Mrs. Temple used to invite the organizers to come and rest and relax at Bishopthorpe. It was therefore as an occasional guest that Alan Searle knew the Archbishop."[162]

Alan's principal virtue in Maugham's eyes was his doglike devotion. Having had to cope over the years with Gerald's sarcasm and wild behavior, he found it restful to have this housebroken, tail-wagging, petlike little man attending to his needs. He was useful, pleased with everything, and easy to get on with. "Alan is a great comfort to me," Maugham wrote Alanson. "He is falling into the work very easily and is taking a lot of tiresome chores off my shoulders. He is so happy to be here that it is heart-warming."[163]

One of Alan's duties was to relieve moments of tension, as on the day when Clare Boothe Luce came to lunch. Maugham was proud of his cook, whom he had turned into a *cordon bleu*, and a special effort was made for Mrs. Luce. When the first course arrived she looked at it, poked at it, and passed it up. The second course she treated in the same manner. Maugham's frown made Alan nervous and he prayed that she would do better by the third course, but she didn't. "I see," said Maugham in a quiet but dangerous tone, "that you don't like my food." "Oh no," Mrs. Luce protested, "it's just that I don't eat at midday." "If you don't eat, why do you come to lunch?" Maugham asked. Alan did what he could to change the subject.[164]

Maugham was planning to return to the Mauresque with Alan as soon as he could. In the meantime he heard from England that Vincent and Liza, whose marriage had not stood the strain of wartime separation, were getting divorced. "I suppose Liza will marry again very soon," Maugham wrote Robin, "and I can only hope she will make a job of it next time. I shall continue to think it very hard on the children."[165] As a precaution, Maugham asked Bert Alanson to set up a trust fund for them.

In January 1946 Karl Pfeiffer, a civilian once more, asked again if he could write an article on Maugham—this time about Maugham and food. Maugham felt that Pfeiffer was another Fred Bason, who wanted to get what he could out of him. On a previous occasion he had come to Parker's Ferry with a photographer who had followed Maugham about all day. "I do not at all like this sort of writing about me," he wrote Pfeiffer, "and such a piece as you suggest would make me rather absurd. After all, my cooking is no better nor more remarkable than that of anyone who is prepared to take a little trouble. I was very patient when you brought a boring photographer down here, but with that you exhausted my patience; if you want to write such an article as you suggest you are naturally at perfect liberty to do so but you will get no help from me."[166]

Maugham was working on his Spanish novel and wrote his niece and fellow novelist Kate Mary Bruce that "it is on entirely new lines for me, or rather on a line that I haven't attempted for 50 years. I don't know how it will pan out; if it is no good I hope I shall have the sense to suppress it; yes, I think I'd have the sense to do that; what I must look out for is that I have the sense to see that it's no good if it isn't."[167]

In the meantime his Renaissance novel, *Then and Now*, due to appear in May, was being promoted by Doubleday. An ad in *Publishers Weekly* on April 20 said:

> Top fiction title on Doubleday's spring list, *Then and Now*, tells the witty and amorous story of Niccolò Machiavelli, guileful diplomat and self-confessed great lover, who is outwitted in both diplomacy and love by Caesar Borgia. Maugham's sure touch brings these characters to life in a spritely, ironic chronicle of Renaissance Italy. The enormous success of *The Razor's Edge* assures an eager market for the new Maugham novel which, although a departure from his earlier books, bears the unmistakable hallmark of his deep understanding and talent. One of our largest advertising campaigns will assure the best-selling of this rich, human comedy.
>
> * Initial printing 825,000 copies.
> * A Literary Guild selection.

In his seventies Maugham had become the most popular English-language novelist alive.

In March, Maugham agreed to write the introduction for Charles H. Goren's *Standard Book of Bidding*. His terms were that Goren would be his guest at dinner and bridge. Goren's *Better Bridge for Better Players* was Maugham's bible. Playing with the grand master was the chance of a lifetime. Writing the introduction, he said, made him feel "as proud as a lieutenant bidden by his admiral to lead the flagship into battle."[168]

When they played together, Goren made a mistake that led Maugham to remember him as the fellow who had trumped his ace. Goren had a singleton heart, and Maugham bid one heart and three hearts. The final bid was four spades by the other two players. Goren was put in the position of trumping Maugham's ace of hearts. He should have let Maugham win his two heart tricks with ace and king and then trumped his third heart lead and collected the next trick by leading to Maugham's ace of diamonds. Maugham never forgot that hand. "By expert standards," Goren said of him, "he was not to be feared as a player, yet he had the ability and the wisdom to bring something quite special to the game."[169]

On April 20 Maugham went to Washington to present the manuscript of *Of Human Bondage* to the Library of Congress, which was giving him, he wrote his brother Frederic, "a great beano." The State Department asked him to make a record of his part of the address to use as propaganda. He was filmed by a newsreel camera team. "You don't seem at all self-conscious," the director told him, and he replied, "If I were self-conscious after facing cameras for forty years or more, really I would be a fool."[170]

The manuscript, written in sixteen medium-sized notebooks, was accepted in the Coolidge Auditorium by the Librarian of Congress, Luther H. Evans, who said:

> Something of this sense of historic episode is conveyed by an examination of tray no. 6314 in the Public Catalog of the Library of Congress; for it contains, under Maugham, William Somerset—1874—an entry for the first American edition of a novel entitled *Of Human Bondage*, and it bears in its upper left-hand corner a smudged notation in pencil: copy 1 worn out—to be replaced. I suggest to you, sir, that this citation is the accolade which a modern democracy confers upon a modern masterpiece—for when the American public takes a book to its heart it shows its love not merely by reading it, but by consuming it utterly.

Of Human Bondage had not made the best-seller lists when it was published in 1915, Evans pointed out. The best sellers that year were Booth Tarkington's *The Turmoil*, Winston Churchill's *A Far Country*, and Eleanor H. Porter's *Pollyanna Grows Up*. *Of Human Bondage* went through three printings. Four years later it had another printing. "It refused to lie down," Evans said. "By 1923, it ran through three more printings. In 1946 it was still selling 30,000 copies a year. It became a classic. It falls to my lot to serve as agent for its naturalization, but in the name of a people who will cherish it, I gratefully accept this testament of experience and pledge it a place of honor and our stout devotion."[171]

Maugham repeated before those assembled that he was no more than a storyteller. "The novelist need not eat a whole sheep to know what mutton tastes like," he said. "It is enough if he eats a chop . . . but when he goes on from this to give you his views on sheep raising, the wool industry, and the political situation in Australia, I think it is well to accept his ideas with reserve."[172] Howard Mumford Jones, professor of English at Harvard, then said that *Of Human Bondage* was a classic that had taken its place alongside *Vanity Fair*, *Tom Jones*, and *Wuthering Heights*.

On the occasion of Maugham's gift, *The Times Literary Supplement* wrote: "There are English authors today who are more indubitably world figures, intellectual forces in public life; but among the novelists and playwrights pure and simple of his generation none has attained a more active eminence or achieved a more lasting success."[173]

Then and Now came out in May, just as Maugham and Alan were preparing to leave for Marseilles aboard a French ship. It was a return to the sixteenth-century Italy in which Maugham had set his second novel, *The Making of a Saint*, published in 1898. Maugham had later admitted that it was a young writer's mistake. Nearly half a century later he returned to the historical novel, committing an aging writer's mistake, for *Then and Now* was as dull and wooden as its predecessor. It dealt with Machiavelli's stratagems to bed down a married woman who has taken his fancy. He fails, but his page and nephew succeeds. It was a Boccaccio anecdote of the *trompeur trompé* variety, strung out to 278 pages. The power politics, the duplicity, the machinations, the rivalry between Borgia and Machiavelli, all had the musty smell of library research. Maugham was at his best working from direct observation and personal experience. When he tried to recreate the past, he failed. Reviewers saw *Then and Now* as a minor work. Orville Prescott in the *Yale Review* called it "stale and obvious." Diana Trilling in *The Nation* on June 29 said it alternated between "a textbook dryness of historical outline and an embarrassing primitive effort to liven things up."[174] Maugham had told Kate Bruce that he hoped he would have the sense to see if it was no good, but the sense failed him.

Edmund Wilson, who had never thought much of Maugham, used *Then and Now* to launch a general attack on his work in *The New Yorker* on June 8.

499

It has happened to me from time to time to run into some person of taste who tells me that I ought to take Somerset Maugham seriously, yet I have never been able to convince myself that he was anything but second-rate. His swelling reputation in America, which culminated the other day in his solemn presentation to the Library of Congress of the manuscript of *Of Human Bondage*, seems to me a conspicuous sign of the general decline of our standards. . . . My experience has always been with Maugham that he disappoints my literary appetite and so discourages me from going on.

As for *Then and Now*, Wilson found it on the level of "one of the less brilliant contributions to a prep-school magazine. . . . The language is such a tissue of clichés that one's wonder is finally aroused at the writer's ability to assemble so many and at his unfailing inability to put anything in an individual way.

"The defenders of Somerset Maugham," Wilson went on, "will tell me that he is 'old and tired' now, and that historical novels are not his forte—that it is quite unfair to judge him by *Then and Now*, which is one of the least of his books." But to Wilson the quality of his work was "never that either of a literary artist or of a first-rate critic of morals." He then dressed Maugham down for using his eminence to disparage his betters, as he had done in his *Introduction to Modern English and American Literature*. Of Henry James, Maugham said: "he never succeeded in coming to grips with life"; of James Joyce: "like many of his countrymen, he never discovered that enough is as good as a feast, and his prolixity is exhausting"; of Yeats: "though he could at times be very good company, he was a pompous, vain man; to hear him read his own verses was as excruciating a torture as anyone could be exposed to."

"There is something going on," Wilson wrote, "on the higher ground, that halfway compels his respect, but he does not quite understand what it is, and in any case he can never get up there."

Wilson's article brought numerous protests from Maugham admirers, who said he was unfair and should read the short stories. Wilson did so and later wrote a postscriptum:

They *are* readable—quite entertaining. The style is much tighter and neater than it is in *Then and Now*—Mr. Maugham writes best when his language is plainest . . . [but] these stories are magazine commodities —all on about the same level as Sherlock Holmes; but Sherlock Holmes has more literary dignity precisely because it is less pretentious. Mr. Maugham makes play with more serious themes, but his work is full of bogus motivations that are needed to turn the monthly trick. He is for our day, I suppose, what Bulwer-Lytton was for Dickens': a half-trashy novelist, who writes badly, but is patronized by half-serious readers, who do not care much about writing.[175]

Later, discussing his Maugham article with a colleague of Richard Cordell's at Purdue who was his neighbor for the summer, Wilson said: "You know, I think I settled that fellow's hash. And do you know, I've never read *Of Human Bondage, Cakes and Ale,* or *The Razor's Edge.*"

Wilson's was the single most damning critique of Maugham's work in his more than fifty years as a professional writer. In his determination to cut Maugham down to size he was more like a prosecutor trying to win a case than a critic trying to evaluate a reputation. Even the most severe critics of Maugham's work would have to admit that his best short stories were more than magazine commodities and that they dealt seriously with serious themes and said something about the human condition.

But Wilson raised "the Maugham problem," as had other critics before him. For all his success and after consideration of his best work, was Maugham a writer of the first rank? He himself was not sure that he possessed the necessary equipment to scale the heights. He said that he had small power of imagination, that he was a Constable and not a Michelangelo, who had painted easel pictures, not frescoes. "I know just where I stand," he wrote. "In the very first row of the second-raters."[176] Consumed with self-doubt, he may have secretly agreed with Wilson, for years later, when the eminent critic was investigated for nonpayment of taxes, Maugham told S. N. Behrman that he deplored the standards of a civilization that hounded literary men, and said of Wilson, "the most brilliant man you have, you know."[177]

Chapter Seventeen

I have tried to remember that life is there, not to be written about but to be lived. I have tried to have every experience that was possible to me within the limitations that Nature imposed upon me, and I have looked upon the practice of literature, not as my sole aim, though my chief one, but as an activity that must be combined in due proportion with the other activities proper to a human being. I have sought freedom, material and spiritual, and now, on the threshold of old age, I am not disinclined to think that I have at last achieved it.

Maugham, autobiographical statement for *Portraits and Self-Portraits*, by George Schreiber

MAUGHAM AND ALAN took the French ship *Colombie* to Marseilles on May 29 and immediately went to Cap Ferrat to start repairs on the Mauresque. They stayed in the Hotel Voile d'Or, run by an Englishman, Captain Powell, who had been there for thirty years and said that he had never on arising failed to have been moved by the view. Maugham was pleased by the rates, 600 francs a day for three rooms, including breakfast. In the morning he bathed in the harbor of the Villa Singer, built by one of the sewing machine heirs for Isadora Duncan. He had brought enough cigarettes from America to allow himself five a day until October, when he planned to go to London.[1]

It was a shock seeing the Mauresque, which bore the scars of German and Italian occupation, British shelling, and French looting. The windows had been blown out, the roof was damaged, and the outside walls looked as though they had a bad case of smallpox. A number of the garden's finest trees had been killed by shellfire, and there was a great deal of replanting to do. Maugham began making plans for repairs in the hope that he could move in by the end of July. His former cook, Annette, once again took over the kitchen, and the gardener's wife did the housework. The Germans had drunk up his wine cellar. His cars had been stolen and there were no taxis. "Wherever we go, we go on our flat feet," he wrote Robin.[2]

Maugham was also concerned about his apartment in Paris. It was occupied by Louis Legrand, known as Lulu, a boy from a mining family whom Gerald Haxton had picked up and more or less kept over the years. Gerald introduced Lulu to some of Maugham's homosexual friends, including Harold Nicolson, who once wrote Lulu to thank him for a "soirée délicieuse."[3] Robin, when he was in Paris, also stayed at the rue La Fontaine with Lulu. During the war Gerald had sent Lulu food parcels and 3,000 francs a month, and on his deathbed he made Maugham promise to look after him. But Maugham had heard some disconcerting news about Lulu and the apartment, and when David Posner told him that he was going to Paris on a holiday, Maugham asked Posner to find out what was going on. Posner arrived at the rue La Fontaine and was greeted sullenly by Legrand, a tall, thin young man with chalk-white skin. He stayed there for a month and noticed that Lulu received a large number of male visitors. It dawned on him that Legrand was a male prostitute and was using Maugham's Paris flat for his rendezvous. Posner reported the situation to Maugham, who sold the flat but made Legrand a cash gift to honor Gerald's deathbed request.[4]

In July, Maugham was gratified to hear that *Then and Now* had sold 750,000 copies in America. "No one could be more surprised than I," he wrote Eddie Marsh, "for it would be very natural if at my age my powers such as they are failed."[5] Even dour Lord Maugham, of whom Willie complained that he never said anything about his work, was impressed. In early August 1946 Alexander Frere was having tea with Lord Maugham in the dining room of the House of Lords when Evelyn Waugh, sitting at the same table, boasted that he was the best-selling English author in the United States. Upon overhearing Waugh, Lord Maugham rose and stood over the table and said, "Young man, I don't know who you are or how many copies you've sold in the United States, but I have a brother whose latest book has just sold a million copies."[6]

Even more unexpected than his brother's approval was the disapproval of his plays expressed by the Russian magazine *Culture and Life*, which announced in September that *The Circle* and *Penelope* should be banned in Moscow. Maugham was accused of "bourgeois reactionary ideology and morality" and of attempting to poison Soviet minds.[7]

This was proof of a sort that the plays still had life. Proof of another sort was the revival of *Our Betters* in London that October, directed by Peter Daubeny. Maugham went to the opening at the Playhouse on October 3. James Agate, dean of London theater critics, was there, sitting next to Eddie Marsh, and during an intermission he went to Maugham's box and told him the play stood up perfectly. But privately he wondered whether Maugham's tale about title-hunting Americans was not dated. The famous line that closes the second act, "You damned fool, I told you it was too risky," had fallen flat. Agate, who had attended the opening of *Our Betters* in 1923, recalled that "at the first performance the audience was shocked at the goings-on in the Grayston household—the young people of today think that goings-on are what summer houses are for. Cecil Beaton's scenery, as usual, reminded me of Pinero's French governess—'overgowned and overhatted.' "[8]

Also in October, S. N. Behrman arrived in London for the rehearsals of *Jane*, the play based on Maugham's short story about the middle-aged lady who always tells the truth. He had turned the story's first-person narrator into a character based on Maugham, a cynical, well-traveled English writer named Willie Tower, who has a house in the south of France and writes stories in which people are swallowed up by a destiny they can't escape. In case the similarity to Maugham was not transparent enough, Behrman added in a stage direction: "The actor who plays William Tower will do well to study the portrait and read the works of W. Somerset Maugham. It will be particularly helpful to him to read *The Summing Up* by this writer."

Behrman based his portrait on Maugham's confidences to him about his private life. Willie Tower's wife, who pickles furniture, is flighty and superficial. "I have made very serious mistakes in my life," Tower says. "Many of them come from my abnormal inability to cause other people pain. The truth is, my marriage with Millicent was no good the moment it occurred—even before." There were several allusions to Maugham's own sexuality, as in this exchange:

MRS. TOWER: To think that my daughter—yes, and your daughter too, Willie—though you won't acknowledge it.

TOWER: I have never denied my share in Ann's paternity. Is there something I don't know?

The daughter, Ann, refers to "my fascinating, remote father," to whom she says: "You know, you do have a knack for diminishing people! You're supposed to be heartless, cynical." Tower replies: "Now, Ann dear, don't take on your mother's patter. Develop your own. It'll be equally shallow, but at least it won't be borrowed."

Maugham and Behrman went together to the first reading of the play. Ronald Squire, playing Willie Tower, was as cutting as Maugham often was. At one point the juvenile, an avant-garde writer, referred to Tower as "a glorified hack." Behrman took a sidelong glance at Maugham, whose impassive face revealed nothing. Behrman had found it troublesome to turn a story twenty-five pages long into a three-act play, and after the second act Maugham told the producer, Binkie Beaumont, "It's too long, it goes on forever."[9]

That evening, October 17, Maugham took Behrman to a dinner party at Juliet Duff's, assuring him on the way over in the taxi, "You can't go higher in the British aristocracy." At the dinner a titled lady said of Churchill, "Let's face it—Winston has *not* had a classical education." Behrman whispered to Maugham, "What would Jane say to that?" "That's for you to discover," Maugham replied. Perhaps he was thinking of what Jane had said of William Tower's books: "They have everything in them but joie de vivre—they have wit, they have wisdom, they have pity even, but no joy in just living. Have you noticed that?" After dinner Maugham reminisced about Kipling. "To the end he had the mind of a 5th-form boy at a second-rate school," he said. "He dined with me on the day after Gene Tunney beat Jack Dempsey. 'Gene is a white man,' he said. I made a bet with myself that his next two words would be 'pukka sahib.' They were."

In general, Maugham found the situation in England gloomy. Rationing was still in force, people looked drab, and a friend told him he was sleeping in his father's tablecloths. Every Englishman's explanation of the peacetime restrictions was: "Well, you see, we won the war." "The wretched people groan but bear," Maugham wrote Alanson.[10] He was glad to get back to Cap Ferrat in December. The Mauresque was finally in order. His paintings, hidden by Enid Kenmare during the occupation, were back on the walls. The number of his servants was cut from thirteen to five, and the number of his trees and the size of his garden were reduced. But the statue of Kuan Yin, the Chinese goddess of mercy, still decorated the marble entrance hall, and on his narrow Sicilian bed rested the cushion embroidered by Marie Laurencin.

Maugham resumed his interrupted life. Once more guests began to appear. One of the first was Peter Daubeny, the director of the *Our Betters* revival. Alan took him to his room and warned him facetiously that the mirror in his bathroom was two-way. Maugham took him for a walk on the Corniche. Daubeny told him that he was about to be married. A car with a baby carriage strapped to the roof roared by. "That's what you'll be doing a year from now," Maugham said, slipping his hand into Daubeny's. There was something faintly suggestive in his tone of voice, and Daubeny pulled his hand away. Sensing that he had been tactless, he gave Maugham an uneasy smile, which was met with a look of freezing scorn. The walk continued in silence.

For the rest of his stay Daubeny felt hostility in the air. Maugham had been rejected, and his manner alternated chilling sarcasm and pedantic harshness. Here was a man, Daubeny felt, who bore a deep grudge against life. Almost as a psychological reflex, he robbed any relationship of grace and the excitement of discovery. At meals Maugham disparaged everything that Daubeny had done in the theater, and implied that he could do no better.

During Daubeny's stay a young man came to lunch. "Why did you come to the South of France?" Maugham asked.

"I felt I wanted to come when you wrote that marvelous play about the South of France," the young man said.

"But I have never written a play about the South of France," Maugham said.

"Didn't you write about it in *Lady Frederick*?" Daubeny asked, coming to the rescue.

Maugham took two angry munches of boeuf à la mode and said, "If you have come to the South of France because I mentioned it in a play, I feel very sorry for you."

After lunch the young man said goodbye, and as the front door closed behind him Maugham threw his head back, emitted a sort of hiss, and said, "That little Welsh tyke will never come here again."

When Daubeny developed a sore throat Alan warned him: "For God's sake, don't tell Willie, he can't stand anyone being ill. If you can't hide it, keep out of his way as much as you can." Daubeny left the Mauresque convinced that Maugham was interested in only one aspect of life: human frailty.[11]

The querulous side of Maugham's nature had become more pronounced. It was partly age and partly Alan, who, instead of opposing him, as Gerald had done, was always conciliatory. Gerald had maintained a position of strength with his "go to hell" attitude. Alan, far less sure of himself, always fearful that Maugham would throw him out in a fit of temper, gave in to Maugham's moods.

When S. N. Behrman came to visit in December 1946, he learned that an old New York friend was staying in Monte Carlo. "It would be very pleasant for me if I could invite him to lunch," he told Maugham. "It might be pleasant for you," Maugham said, "what would it be for me?" Behrman, the most gracious of men, was stung by Maugham's rudeness and went up to his room to pack. Alan, ever the soothing arbitrator, came in and said: "You mustn't go. You mustn't. He feels terrible already. He won't sleep tonight. I beg you—don't go."

"I won't stay here another night," Behrman said.

"Please," Alan said. "He says these things. When I think of the people who come here! I think he wants to talk to you and perhaps that's why he said it—so as not to be disturbed. He can't help it. He just says them. He particularly wants you this time. He begged me to bring you. It will be terrible for him if you go. For me too! Please."

Behrman unpacked, and the rest of his stay was pleasant. Maugham went out of his way to be entertaining. They went to a village fête and he danced with one young girl after another. After the fête he said: "You know, I suppose, that everybody there, including the mayor with whom we sat, they're all Communists. This village is solid Communist."

A young man from Doubleday who was there said: "I don't understand, Willie—you're saying they're all Communists. They're Catholic, aren't they? And what you say about their sleeping with everybody—it just doesn't make sense."

"It does to them," Maugham said. "They're Communist because they're poor and want to be rich; they're promiscuous because they are highly sexed; they're Catholics because they don't want to go to hell."[12]

Bert and Mabel Alanson came for Christmas, bringing items that Maugham had asked for: shaving sticks, candles, a dozen cocktail glasses without stems, green blotting paper, two pots of Keiller's marmalade, and six plain white servants' jackets. Maugham had been hoping to take them on excursions in the foothills of the Alps, but it rained the whole time they were there. He told Alanson that he wanted to draw up a trust in favor of Alan. He would pay three thousand dollars a year into the trust, and Alan would receive the interest after his death.[13]

In February 1947 Alexander and Pat Frere arrived. They were glad to get away from England, with its cold and rationing, and spent the afternoons basking in the Mediterranean sun. In Monte Carlo, Maugham saw Peter Quennell, who spoke to him with admiration about his daughter Liza. Maugham was worried about Liza. Her divorce from Vincent Paravicini was coming through, and he was anxious to know that everything had gone as she wished. He knew from his own experience how painful divorce proceedings could be.[14]

In March he heard from George Bullock, the young tubercular writer against whom he had turned because he was a pacifist. Bullock had published a biography of Marie Corelli, the best-selling turn-of-the-century novelist, but was now so sick that he had to go to a sanatorium. Maugham sent a promise of money, accompanied by a lecture:

> You know I had TB once and spent the best part of two years in a sanatorium and completely recovered. . . . I have the top of one lung all scarred over and for the last twenty-five years I have got along perfectly well. . . . You can occupy your time to great profit. You can learn to write English. Your one and only book caused a stir because you had the good luck or the good sense to hit upon a new and curious subject, but you must know that it was very badly written. . . . Contrariness has given you the opportunity to equip yourself for the difficult art of writing . . . one has to work like the devil to become a decent writer, but if it is one's nature to write, that work is the greatest of all delights. . . . You may think it of some slight interest that when I was in my sanatorium I wrote a couple of plays and while still ill *The Moon and Sixpence.*[15]

Maugham then wrote Frere to send a check for fifty pounds to Bullock, "an obscure and rather indifferent writer and journalist who has been dying of tuberculosis ever since the war and would have died long ago if I hadn't from time to time come to his help. He seems to cling to life, miserable as it is for him."[16]

Helping young writers was much on Maugham's mind. For years he had wanted to establish a prize that would allow British writers to spend time abroad. He had tried to sell his manuscripts to finance the prize, but the offers were too low. Now, with the royalties and film money from *The Razor's Edge,* he could finally afford it. In April he announced the establishment of a 500-pound annual Somerset Maugham prize, to be administered by the Society of Authors. The judges were C. V. Wedgwood, C. Day Lewis, and V. S. Pritchett. The prize was financed by a $49,000 trust fund and was to go to a British-born writer under thirty-five who had published one book. As Maugham wrote one of the winners, the poet Elizabeth Jennings: "My whole idea in founding this award is that authors, by spending a sojourn abroad, should broaden their minds and acquire a more catholic standpoint. If the result of this were to enable one recipient of the award in ten years to add something to the riches of English literature, I should feel fully rewarded."[17] Subsequent winners included Kingsley Amis, John Le Carré, Doris Lessing, John Wain, V. S. Naipaul, Thom Gunn, and Ted Hughes. The prize is still in existence.

One immediate reaction to the prize in a time of strict currency restrictions came from Evelyn Waugh, who wrote in a letter to the *The Times*: "Does Mr. Maugham realize what a huge temptation he is putting before elderly writers? To have 500 pounds of one's own—let alone Mr. Maugham's—to spend abroad is beyond our dreams. We may not even spend the royalties of our translations in the countries where they are earned. What will we not do to qualify for Mr. Maugham's munificence? What forging of birth certificates, dyeing of whiskers, and lifting of faces? To what parodies of experimental styles will we not push our experienced pens?"[18]

While he cheerfully donated a large sum to finance his prize, Maugham grumbled about current expenses. The restoration of his house had cost too much, he felt. He had applied to the French government for war damages, but did not expect to be paid "until some time in the twenty-first century."[19] Still, life was not too difficult, as he wrote his American biographer Richard Cordell, "except that the bread is bad and that there are a number of things unobtainable. . . . But France is obviously in a critical condition, and a flare-up may break out any day. . . . But if you were in Nice or Cannes or Monte Carlo and walked about among the crowd, you could see no sign that everything wasn't for the best in the best of all possible worlds."[20]

More of his time than ever was taken up by requests for advice from aspiring writers who wanted to know the magic formula for success. To Dan Farson, a young American serving with the U.S. Army in Germany, he wrote: "If you want to become a writer it is very necessary to expose yourself to all the vicissitudes of life, and it isn't enough to wait for experience to come to you, you must go out after it. Even if you bark your shins now and then, that again will be grist for your mill. . . . The more highly cultured you can make yourself, the richer your work will be. Few people know how much industry and how much patience are needed to achieve anything worth doing. I speak exactly like Polonius."[21]

His last book of short stories, *Creatures of Circumstance*, came out in July. In a preface he seemed to be replying to Edmund Wilson's remark that his stories were "magazine commodities." Defending the fact that most of the fifteen stories in the book had been written for magazines, he pointed out that Balzac, Flaubert, Maupassant, Chekhov, Henry James, and Kipling had all published their work in magazines. "To damn a story because it is a magazine story is absurd," he said.[22]

At the same time he repeated his credo, for anyone too deaf or too stubborn not to have heard it already: "I have never pretended to be anything but a storyteller. It has amused me to tell stories and I have told a great many. It is a misfortune for me that the telling of a story just for the sake of the story is not an activity that is in favor with the intelligentsia. I endeavor to bear my misfortune with fortitude."

Two of the stories, "The Kite" and "The Episode," were based on Alan's experience as a prison visitor at Wormwood Scrubs, an institution for first offenders. In the course of telling them, Maugham provided a thumbnail description of Alan, who was given the name Ned Preston. He got on well with the warders, the governor, and the prisoners, for "he was entirely lacking in class consciousness, so prisoners, whatever their station in life, felt at ease with him. He neither preached nor moralised. He had never done a criminal, or even a mean thing in his life." It was his business to cheer the prisoners up, and "his breezy manner, his natural kindliness, often worked wonders." He read them the sports page, gave them news from home, and helped them find jobs when they got out. "He took his duties seriously and made the prisoners' troubles his own."

The two Ned Preston stories were among the best in the book, for they were based on recent experience rather than culled from notes taken forty or fifty years earlier. In "The Episode" a Brixton mailman goes to jail for stealing money from letters to take out his girl friend, whose family stands slightly higher than himself on the social ladder. Alan Searle was amazed at the accuracy with which Maugham described people he had never met. In "The Kite" a young man makes the transition from son to husband and back again after his wife destroys the object of his passion, a kite.

The other stories were drawn from many periods of his life. "Sanatorium," one of the best, went back to his confinement in Scotland after World War I. "The Colonel's Lady," which has become something of a classic, was the story of a colonel's mousy wife who confesses to a grand passion in a book of poems. "I made a note of it something like

50 years ago," Maugham said, "and then forgot it till just after the war when I was going through some old notebooks and came across it." "The Unconquered" was his only story with a World War II setting. A French girl is raped and becomes pregnant by a German soldier who comes to love her and wants to marry her, but her hatred of the Germans makes her drown the child on the day it is born. "A Point of Honor" was a Spanish tale of vengeance. Maugham said he had written it many years before in Spain and that Spaniards had told him it represented the Spanish point of view on honor as few foreigners had ever seen it. "A Woman of Fifty" was set in Italy and told of a son who murders his father when the son's English wife comes between them. "In a way, it's a terrible story," Maugham said, "one of those stories that the Elizabethan dramatists have made a play out of. Most stories owe a lot to the invention of the author, but in this case the author hadn't to do much more than write it down. The story comes straight from my life."[23] The moral of "A Point of Honor" and "A Woman of Fifty," which Maugham never tired of repeating, was that a code of honor destroys those who uphold it.

Critics had a ho-hum reaction to the collection. "Old Hand, Old Stuff," said *Time* magazine on July 28. *The New Yorker* on August 2 said: "There aren't many uncontrived situations in *Creatures of Circumstance* and there are even fewer unforeseeable developments, but Mr. Maugham has so deftly hand-polished his patent-leather entertainment that the age of the material hardly shows at all." V. S. Pritchett in the *New Statesman and Nation* on August 2 said that Maugham did not have Wells's imagination or Chekhov's or Maupassant's "taste for familiar landscape," but that he remained "the most readable and accomplished English short-story writer of the serious kind alive." That was in the nature of a eulogy, for Maugham wrote no more short stories.

In August, Liza came to the Mauresque with her children. Maugham's New York-born granddaughter Camilla's favorite phrase was "Grandpa, can you give me a dime?" Alan, meeting Liza for the first time, made a great show of friendship and said, "Oh, I'm so glad you're here, I've been longing for this moment."[24] Privately he was unhappy about the daughter's visit, for he felt that he was Maugham's real family. He complained to Bert Alanson that Liza and the children were a disturbing element, and that he did not like them at all, but had resigned himself to their presence.[25] Maugham was worried about food shortages and asked Alanson to send him a monthly parcel of rice. He had been buying rice smuggled in from Italy, but border guards had clamped down on the smugglers. He was afraid he was in for a hard winter.[26]

Another visitor that August was the writer S. J. Perelman. Ken Mc-Cormick at Doubleday had sent Maugham some of Perelman's books, which Maugham had liked. Perelman had just finished a round-the-world trip, ending up in the south of France. One morning he went to the Hotel Negresco barbershop in Nice to get his hair cut. He was waiting for his turn when he noticed something familiar about the man in the barber's chair, and he said to the reflection in the mirror, "Would that by any chance be Mr. Somerset Maugham?" And the reflection replied, "And would that by any chance be Mr. S. J. Perelman?"

Maugham then launched into a very formal speech of welcome. Perelman, he said, had seen the splendors of the East, traveling the silk road, and had finally arrived on the Riviera. The barber interrupted Maugham's oration to say, "Excuse me, Mr. Maugham, shall I snip out the little hairs in your ears?"

"Please, Maurice," Maugham said, continuing his rotund words of welcome.

"What about these little hairs in the nose?" the barber asked.

"Maurice, how many years have you been cutting my hair?" Maugham asked.

"Twenty years, Mr. Maugham."

"Then why do you have to ask? You always interrupt at exactly the wrong moment."

Thereafter Maugham and Perelman established a friendship. To Perelman, Maugham was a marvelous technician, with a kind of diligence that he felt was necessary to good writing. Some of his short stories, he thought, were classics, and *Cakes and Ale* was a model of that difficult genre, the comic novel. "If I were forced by some awful fate to be a teacher," Perelman said, "I would make my students read *The Summing Up* and *On a Chinese Screen*, where there is a section on dinner parties at treaty ports that is so brilliant you can pick it up and admire it like a piece of jewelry."

Back in England for a few months, Maugham went to stay with Lady Juliet Duff in November in her small but lovely house at Bulbridge, Wilton. Lady Juliet was an avid gardener and took Maugham on a guided tour of her flower beds. Since he had a garden of his own, he liked to think that he was knowledgeable about flowers. Approaching a thicket of roses, he said, "Oh, what wonderful Queen Hortense roses."

"Don't be a silly old bugger," Lady Juliet croaked, "they're Queen Olga of Wurtenburg."[27] Chips Channon arrived by train and found Maugham "in high spirits and agreeably anecdotal. He twitted me about my sex life, or apparent lack of it, and quoted Emerald [Cunard] as saying that I had once been a great voluptuary, but that now I was 'too preoccupied and too cerebral.' He then told Juliet Duff, who passed it on, that I was one of the most colorful characters of the day. That from Willie!" Later that month Maugham went to a grand dinner that Channon gave in his Belgrave Square mansion in connection with the royal wedding of Princess Elizabeth and Philip Mountbatten. The queens of Spain and Rumania attended, as well as various other queens. As Maugham left he whispered to Channon, "This is the apogee of your career."[28]

Once again he was embroiled in disagreements with publishers and agents. He was furious with Heinemann for selling the American rights to his propaganda book *France at War* and keeping 50 percent of the royalty. "I take it very ill," he wrote Frere, "that you should have made this attempt by a misrepresentation of the facts to obtain a profit to which I cannot see that you have any right. . . . Since your negligence over *Cakes and Ale* [Frere had shown the galleys to Hugh Walpole as a possible choice for the Book Society] and what I can only regard as your sharp practices over the American rights of *France at War* have persuaded me that I can no longer have the confidence in you which I have hitherto had that you will deal with me to my best advantage, I have put my affairs in the hands of A. P. Watt."[29]

Maugham had for years done without a London agent, trusting Heinemann to give him the best prevailing terms. He was also annoyed with Doubleday for giving him a royalty of only 5 percent on the deluxe edition of his collected stories, *East and West*, and asked Watt to do something about it. He still had Jacques Chambrun acting for him in New York, but was growing disenchanted with him. In 1947, for instance, Chambrun reported American earnings for Maugham of $284,865.19, of which the biggest items were $150,000 for the film rights to *Then and Now* and $75,000 for the film rights to *Ashenden*. Chambrun withheld $51,482.99 in commissions, close to 20 percent, and $85,459.55 for American taxes. Maugham asked Douglas Black, the new president of Doubleday, to call Chambrun and complain about the way he was handling his accounts. He was further annoyed because he was due to receive a percentage of the profits on the film of *The Razor's Edge*, which he felt he had been done out of by 20th Century-

Fox. The gross by November 29, 1947, was $6,032,781.71, one of the highest in movie history, but the studio still managed to show a deficit of $266,944.57. Maugham had Chambrun hire a C.P.A. in Hollywood to investigate the accounts.[30]

Returning to the Riviera in December, Maugham discussed with Sydney Box, the producer, the possibility of filming some of his short stories. The original idea was to take five stories and call the film "Quintet." Ruby Miller, an actress friend of Maugham's, got wind of the project and asked him to give her a letter to Box. "I shall be glad if you will see Miss Ruby Miller, the bearer of this letter," Maugham wrote, "on the chance of there being in one of the stories in 'Quintet' a part that would suit her." In a separate letter to Box he added: "A friend of my youth, Miss Ruby Miller, whom I have not seen for nearly thirty-five years, has written to ask me to give a letter of introduction to you. I could not refuse to do this, but I write to tell you confidentially that I know nothing whatever of the lady's capacities."[31]

Maugham's granddaughter Camilla came to stay over the Christmas holiday, accompanied by a French governess. His grandson Nicholas was in school in Switzerland, and in view of their expensive upbringings, he was pleased that the trust he had founded for them was growing. "You should see me in the role of grandfather," Maugham wrote Alanson. "We read French half an hour every evening." In the same year Alan had received his first dividend check from his $3,000-a-year trust, $168.75, from the Anglo-California National Bank, and was duly impressed. "This is what results in having a broker who is a wizard," Maugham said.[32]

In January 1948 Douglas Black wrote Maugham to tell him that Nelson Doubleday was so ill that he no longer had anything to do with the business. He was failing fast. His gait was uncertain. On the rare occasions when he came to the office it was almost as if he were not present. Most of the employees were unaware of the situation, but Black made a point of informing the officers and directors of the company. It was a strain, he said, but by no means an unbearable one.[33]

There was nothing Maugham could do to help the publisher, whose guest he had been during the war years, but upon hearing that George Bullock was worse, he arranged to give him $400, even though he was bedeviled by currency restrictions. His London bank informed him that he was allowed to spend 20 pounds a week out of his current account. He was worried that the Secretary of the Treasury in Washington planned to freeze the current accounts of foreigners, for he had

$250,000 in a savings account in the Guaranty Trust. He asked Watt to pay Bullock the money out of his earnings. It was the last sum of money he sent Bullock, who stayed alive another ten years, looked after by his faithful companion Raymond Marriott. He died in St. Charles hospital, with half a lung left, in 1958, at the age of forty-six.[34]

It seemed that the less Maugham wrote, the more illustrious he became. His fame had a momentum of its own, unrelated to productivity. Maugham the writer had expanded into Maugham the conglomerate. His correspondence, as Alan often complained, was enormous. Alan had to write an average of 400 letters a week. There were begging letters, and letters from would-be translators, and letters about movie deals, and squabbles over foreign rights, and requests of every sort. There were letters from admirers, which he was always glad to answer. He wrote William Archer, a fan in Santa Monica: "It's extremely pleasant to realize that someone you don't know finds so much to like in what you write and the way you write it. . . . No, you can't get autographed copies of my books from booksellers, but if at any time you would like to send me your books I will gladly sign them for you. Bless you."[35] There were letters enclosing stories, about which he was candid. "I am very sorry but I can say nothing about your story," he wrote Frederick Stanley Smith. "It does not seem to me very ingenious and is written in a very amateurish way."[36] There were requests for blurbs, which he invariably refused. Roger Senhouse, one of Lytton Strachey's last lovers and in 1948 a partner in the publishing firm of Secker & Warburg, asked for a comment for one of the books on his list. Maugham replied:

> The answer is no. I have such requests from England, France and America on an average of once a fortnight throughout the year. If I accepted them I should make myself as ridiculous as Hugh Walpole did. I have made it a rule not to let myself be used in this way, and I have been obliged to refuse intimate friends. I think it is very hard that when an acquaintance sends you a book, and you write civilly about it, you are immediately asked to let your remarks be used for publicity. It must be obvious, that in writing to an author about a book one strives to please him, and one's expressions do not necessarily correspond with one's private opinions.[37]

Equally time-consuming was the constant stream of visitors. The Mauresque was a landmark that had to be seen, like the Nice cathedral, and it was part of Alan's job to keep away intruders. At the same time

Maugham continued to entertain almost daily, seeking out whoever was of interest on the Riviera. In the spring the painter Graham Sutherland, who had bought a house in Menton in 1947, came to lunch. Sutherland was a landscapist in the English tradition, and Maugham's head reminded him of the *objets trouvés* he was fond of painting at the time. He told a friend that if he were a portrait painter, Maugham's was the kind of face he could do something with. The remark got back to Maugham, who asked him to try. At first Sutherland refused, thinking the task too complicated, but eventually he agreed on condition that the painting be considered an experiment, with no obligation on either side. He did not begin, however, until 1949.[38]

In April, Maugham left for Spain to spend some of his Spanish royalties and gather material for an essay on the seventeenth-century painter Zurbarán. He went to Barcelona to see his publisher, José Janes, and stayed in out-of-the-way *paradors* in Oropesa and Ubida. He complained that in Madrid he spent his time being interviewed and photographed, signing books, and going to lunches that began at two and ended at four. His fame was international, for he had been translated everywhere. Fifteen of his books had even been translated into Icelandic. He was invited to see the Duchess of Sueca's eleven Goyas, one of which, a portrait of her husband's ancestor, he thought finer than any Goya in the Prado. He met the Duchess of Montpensier, a jolly old girl who amused him because she looked like her ancestor, Louis XIV. The Duke of Alba asked him to lunch and showed him his collection of paintings. The Infante Don Alfonso invited him to his palace at San Lucas.[39] Maugham was happy hobnobbing with grandees. Alan was happy too, for different reasons. His heart was broken three times a day by handsome Spaniards, he wrote Bert Alanson. Exciting adventures of an amorous nature had occurred, of which he thought Alanson would approve. He reminded Alanson of the time before the war when he had stayed with him in San Francisco, and would pop into Alanson's bedroom to pay his morning call, which gave him such pleasure. With a few of Maugham's friends, including Alanson, Alan was quite open about his amorous adventures.[40]

Returning to his estate in late May, Maugham learned that Liza was engaged to be married to Lord John Hope, the son of Lord Linlithgow, who as Viceroy of India in 1938 had refused to receive Gerald Haxton. Lord Linlithgow was also one of the largest landowners in Scotland. Hope was thirty-six, the younger of twins, an engaging and highly eli-

gible bachelor who had done all the right things. He had gone to Eton
and Oxford and served in the Scots Guards at Narvik, Salerno, and
Anzio. After the war he had entered politics and been elected to the
House of Commons in 1945 for North Midlothian. (His title was a
courtesy title, given to him because his father was a marquess. He still
ranked as a commoner and could therefore run for election to the
Commons.)

Maugham still harbored a grudge against Lord Linlithgow but tried
to keep an open mind about his son-in-law to be and said he was
pleased by the engagement. From the letters that Hope and Liza sent
him he gathered that they were furiously in love. Everyone told him
that Hope was clever and nice and keen on politics. He thought they
had every chance of leading a happy and interesting life.[41]

In the meantime Hope was being introduced in London to various
members of the Maugham family, including Liza's mother, Syrie. When
the couple came into her flat, they found her leaning out the window
waiting to see them arrive by taxi. "I do hope you're pleased about Liza
and me," John said. "How do I know?" Syrie replied. "I don't know
you yet." Lord Maugham gave Hope lunch and warned him about his
future father-in-law. "Remember," he said, "that my brother subscribes
to Belloc's lines: 'I do not like the human race. I cannot bear its silly
face.' "[42]

But Maugham in his letters to Hope was friendly, and proposed to
settle twenty thousand pounds upon his daughter. In addition, he
pointed out that, thanks to his assistance, Liza and her children were
self-supporting. It was therefore with more curiosity than trepidation
that Hope went to the Mauresque in June to meet Maugham, who came
to fetch him at the railroad station in Beaulieu. Hope found him absolutely charming. Maugham was delighted to have as a son-in-law someone who could keep him informed on the political scene. He told Hope
that he wanted to give the wedding reception at Claridge's and handed
him a list of the people he wished to be asked to the party. The headwaiter should be told, he specified, that he wanted a tip of 12½ percent
added to the bill for the waiters. Alan did his best to be ingratiating and
wrote Liza: "I liked John so much. Did he like me?" John did like Alan
at first but came to mistrust him on a subsequent visit to the Mauresque.
Gasoline was still rationed in France, and Alan gave John some of
Maugham's coupons, telling him that they had more than enough.
Maugham was furious when he discovered that Hope was using his

coupons, and when Hope explained that Alan had offered them to him Maugham confronted Alan, who denied it, placing Hope in an embarrassing position.[43]

In July the Mauresque was full of guests. There was Irwin Edman, a philosophy professor at Columbia, Ken McCormick and his wife, and Cyril Connolly and his wife. Alanson continued to send parcels to help feed these many mouths, but Maugham asked him please not to send any more Ritz crackers, for they arrived in fragments and were good only to feed the chickens.

Liza's wedding was approaching, and Liza and John both sent letters to tell him the date, but each gave a different date. "Could we get one thing clear?" Maugham replied. "Are you getting married on the same day?" On July 20 he flew to London, to give Liza away on the twenty-first. He could not get into the cutaway he had worn at her first wedding in 1936 and had to rent one at Moss Bros., commonly known as Moss Bross. During the ceremony he and Syrie sat at opposite ends of the room. At the reception at Claridge's he had to give a toast to the groom and his father, but his stammer gave him trouble getting past "Linlithgow."[44]

In August, Maugham made his exit as a novelist with the publication of *Catalina*. It was a preordained success, with a first printing of 50,000 copies in England. In America it was, along with Thomas Mann's *Doctor Faustus*, a double selection of the Book-of-the-Month Club. It was serialized by *Harper's* magazine, which had in 1930 complained to his agent J. B. Pinker that "Maugham still needs a good deal of advertisement to put him across." Now he was an automatic best seller.

In the slackness of the writing, the descent into cliché, and the contrived plot devices *Catalina* betrayed Maugham's declining powers. Set in Spain during the Inquisition, it told of a crippled girl to whom the Blessed Virgin appears in a vision. She will be healed by one of three brothers, the one who has best served God. One brother is a bishop, another is a soldier, and the third is a baker. It comes as no surprise that the humble *panadero* succeeds in healing the girl. After that the story unravels and Catalina marries and becomes an actress.[45]

Catalina was a feeble book with which to end a fifty-year career as a novelist. The *New Statesman and Nation* on September 11 said that Maugham was a survivor of "early Edwardian de-bunking, a functionalist among writers, sworn enemy of just such incrustations as overlay the faltering design of Catalina. . . . Every one of the lay-figures . . . might have been borrowed from the prop department of M.G.M. or Universal." The *Atlantic Monthly* in November found the writing "outrageous in its use of cliché" and the plot "contrived with the patness of slick magazine fiction."[46]

The most interesting review appeared in *The Times Literary Supplement* of August 21, 1948, unsigned but written by Anthony Powell, who took the occasion of Maugham's last novel to survey the body of his work. He found Maugham to have an essentially materialistic viewpoint. If a woman was beautiful, she would make a better marriage than if she were ugly. Passion was no more than sexual attraction. Marriage was an arrangement whereby a man offered a woman board and lodging for life so that he could sleep with her. Such a vision was crude, Powell wrote, and did not allow for halftones. It excluded large areas of life: "The complicated gradations of community of interest and instinctive attraction seem to play an almost negligible part in the lives of his characters, as does the desire to have children for their own sake." Powell concluded that "although we can be deeply grateful for the brilliance of the companionship that he has provided in an increasingly prosy world, it may be wise to reserve judgment on the subject of his more didactic moods."

Exhausted by the Riviera social scene, Maugham went to Vichy in September for a cure. One of his neighbors, Marion Bateman, née Knapp, the rich widow of an English baron, wrote him how much she had liked *Catalina*. "I had a lot of fun writing it," Maugham replied, "and all the time I was doing so I enjoyed besides the reflection that it was the last novel I ever should write."[47] He also received congratulations from the Duke of Alba, who praised his faithful rendition of seventeenth-century Spain but pointed out that he had made a mistake in the color of the cross worn by Don Manuel, the soldier, on the mantle of his order.[48]

Now that he was writing no more fiction Maugham kept busy with the "from my studio window" sort of book. In September *Great Novelists and Their Novels* was brought out by a Philadelphia Bible publisher, John C. Winston Company. This consisted of Maugham's choice of the world's ten greatest novels, in versions that he had abridged, on the theory that "even the greatest novels are imperfect and carry with them into posterity no small amount of excess baggage," along with essays on the ten novelists. The one thing the ten had in common, Maugham said in a rather self-serving introduction, was that they told good stories in a direct way, without literary tricks such as stream of consciousness and flashbacks. Whether Melville and Dostoevski, to name two of the ten, could be accused of directness or plain prose was something Maugham's readers may have pondered.

He also went into the novelists' personalities in some detail, for he believed that "to know something about Flaubert explains a great deal that would otherwise be disturbing in *Madame Bovary*, and to know the little there is to know about Emily Brontë gives a greater poignancy to her strange and wonderful book." He poked around in their private lives for clues to their art with a thoroughness that he would later do his utmost to keep from being applied to his own. He studied Dickens' strange relations with his wife's sisters, Melville's fascination with male beauty, the tyranny of the Brontë sisters' parson father, Balzac's shabby treatment of his mother, and Fielding's lechery.[49]

Maugham had agreed to write introductions for the abridged novels on the understanding that they were chiefly for schools and colleges. He was horrified when Winston used his name in an ad campaign and more horrified when they started selling the books in England. Looking into the matter, he found that the contract drawn up by Chambrun, which he had signed after a cursory glance, had given away world rights.

Furious with Chambrun, Maugham wrote him a sharply worded letter, to which there came a contrite reply: "I hope I can make amends for the dissatisfaction I have caused you and that you will not have occasion to write me in similar terms again. The whole Winston matter has given me very great concern indeed. . . . I told them once more that they must expect legal action if they infringed our clear understanding with regard to England."[50]

Maugham wrote the president of Winston that owing to his agent's negligence he had signed an agreement giving them world rights to the book. He did not wish to repudiate the agreement but asked them to alter it as a matter of courtesy. An executive of the Winston Company wrote Chambrun that "possibly this is one of those cases where we can say we have seen everything when an author resents the fact that his books are selling."[51] Maugham placed the matter in the hands of lawyers, and obtained the changes he wanted.

Quartet, the first film made from his short stories, opened in November. The script by R. C. Sherriff adapted "The Facts of Life," "The Alien Corn," "The Kite," and "The Colonel's Lady." Maugham was appalled by the changes required by censorship. In "The Colonel's Lady" he had to tack on a lame explanation that the good woman had not had a lover after all. He agreed, however, to make personal appearances to introduce each story, and said in his opening remarks: "In one way or another I have used in my writings pretty well everything that has happened to me in the course of my life. . . . To tell you the truth, fact and fiction are so intermingled in my work that now, looking back, I can hardly distinguish one from the other."

"I hear people talking on all sides with great pleasure about *Quartet*," he wrote the producer in November, "and I very much hope that the financial returns are satisfactory. I should hate to think that you were out of pocket on anything connected with me."[52]

In December, Maugham left for New York with Alan aboard the *Queen Mary*. There were several reasons for the trip. First, Nelson Doubleday was dying and had asked to see him. Maugham, who considered Nelson Doubleday largely responsible for building up his reputation in America, wanted to make the effort. Also, he had years ago promised the Alansons that he would celebrate his seventy-fifth birthday with them in San Francisco, and that three-quarters-of-a-century mark was coming up on January 25, 1949. Finally, he wanted to confer with his psychiatrist friend, Félix Martí-Ibáñez, who was translating *Catalina* into Spanish.

When Martí-Ibáñez came to lunch at the Plaza he asked for Maugham on the house telephone and was told he would be out until three. Disconsolate, he went into the Oak Room and had lunch alone. Walking out, he spotted Maugham pacing in the lobby. "I always knew Spaniards had no idea of punctuality," he said, "but you beat all records. I've been waiting for you nearly an hour and I'm faint with hunger." Martí-Ibáñez mumbled something about the message on the house phone. "Of course," Maugham said, "I left that message so that no one would disturb me while we were lunching." Back to the Oak Room they went, astounding the waiters when Martí-Ibáñez ate a second lunch.[53]

Maugham spent grim weekends with the Doubledays in Oyster Bay. Nelson was given only weeks to live, and there was death in his face and the fear of death in his eyes. His illness had provoked a crisis in the company. Douglas Black was trying to have him declared incompetent and gave him papers to sign turning the business over to trustees. Nelson signed, but then tried to regain control of the company. There was a great deal of bitterness in the Doubleday family and in the higher echelons of the company. Maugham went to Black, and, as he put it, "I was in some small measure able to help in the settlement of the grave disagreement that had arisen between Nelson and Ellen on one side and Doug Black and Dorothy Doubleday on the other, so that his last days were relieved of anxiety and the action has of course been stopped."[54] Ken McCormick, then editor in chief, said that "Maugham apparently prevailed on Black to put off the action of incompetence since Nelson was dying anyway. He may have said: You and I know he can't live long. Why fight this battle which will depress him and tie him up in legal actions?"[55]

Nelson Doubleday died in January, at the age of sixty. Maugham usually disliked tall men, but Doubleday was an exception. He would never forget his hospitality during the war, and his remarks read at the funeral spoke of his "great power of affection and need for affection. It was touching to see the thoughtful tact with which the great big man sought for ways in which he could give pleasure to his friends, the little attentions of which he was so lavish. . . . For thirty years Nelson Doubleday gave me his constant and affectionate friendship. The recollection of it is a treasure that can never be taken away from me."[56] Douglas Black took control of the firm, and Maugham thought he was the only person who could have.[57]

Arriving in San Francisco in time for his birthday, Maugham was fêted like a foreign chief of state. Cameramen were in attendance, he said, from the moment he got up until he retired, exhausted, to bed. There was a lunch at the stock exchange club, and a birthday dinner for twelve, with candles on a cake outlining the numerals 7 and 5. Interviewed, Maugham expounded on the benefits of old age. He now had time to read Gibbon and Dante. In the past he had read for research, now he could read for enjoyment. For the benefit of photographers he riffled through a sheaf of congratulatory telegrams from all over the world. Alan in the meantime had contracted jaundice and missed the festivities.

Returning to New York in February 1949, Maugham saw his old friend Glenway Wescott, who was living with Monroe Wheeler in an apartment at 410 Park Avenue, where they conducted the closest thing then existing in Manhattan to a literary salon. The apartment, painted chocolate brown, was hung with Tchelitchews and Bérards and Cocteaus, and a new painter everyone was raving about called Magritte. Wheeler, a curator at the Museum of Modern Art, could draw on the museum collection to decorate his walls.

Maugham was the guest of honor at the Wescott-Wheeler salon. Wescott brought other guests up to meet him one at a time, and Alan stood by, ready to translate in case the stammer erupted, as it still did. One of the guests that February was a fine-looking redheaded young man named Patrick O'Higgins, who was just out of the Irish guards and still held himself with a military bearing. Maugham, who liked redheads, told Alan, "Get that boy, he has nice manners." Alan invited O'Higgins to dinner at the Plaza. Then Marlene Dietrich arrived and upstaged Maugham, who went home.

At the Plaza, O'Higgins noted, Maugham had a first-floor suite—but not on the park—called the Cecil Beaton Suite. He was in a huff because someone—he suspected a *Life* photographer—had unscrewed the plaque from the door. It was in his nature to exaggerate the most trivial annoyances. Maugham, O'Higgins found, was a money snob. He was impressed by Jock Whitney's Manhasset estate, where Mrs. Whitney was building quarters for her pet crocodile. But he also wanted value for his money. Every young man, he let it be known, had to pay for his dinner, and O'Higgins was no exception. Alan later told O'Higgins that Maugham had once taken to the Pavillon a young man who ordered foie gras and champagne. "It seems to me you're very extravagant," Maugham said. "Are you that hungry?" "Sure I'm hungry," the young man said, "but I'm also going to get fucked for it."[58]

Maugham was due to leave New York on February 11, and spent his last days there in a flurry of activity. Alan was unwell, so Maugham went shopping for food and other items still unobtainable in France. With Monroe Wheeler as his guide, he did the rounds of art galleries, spending nearly $80,000 of his American royalties. From Durand-Ruel he bought a Rouault "Crucifixion" for $10,000 and Renoir's *"Bateaux à Argenteuil"* for $50,000. From Wildenstein he bought Monet's "View of Holland" for $14,000. From Paul Rosenberg he bought Utrillo's *"Une Rue au Conquet"* for $4,500. All these paintings were bought in the name of his daughter, Lady John Hope, to whom the receipts were sent. Maugham planned to leave them to her, and in this way he avoided death duties.

Liza and John happened to be in New York, visiting America, and he surprised them with the news of his acquisitions, which would one day be theirs. He gave a cocktail party for them in the White and Gold Suite of the Plaza. John Hope's father, who was chairman of the Midland Bank, had previously suggested that Maugham form a company in the Channel Islands to avoid paying inheritance tax. But Maugham was worried that he would lose control of his fortune, and decided to keep the bulk of it with Alanson in San Francisco.[59] Maugham left on the *Queen Mary*, which sailed at midnight. Friends came to his cabin, M-60, to see him off. On one side of the cabin leather trunks were piled up. Among the friends was Félix Martí-Ibáñez, to whom Maugham said in farewell; "The best thing that Spain ever produced was her men."[60]

Home again, Maugham began to sit for Graham Sutherland on February 17. "He is the best painter in England," he wrote Alanson, "and he took it into his head that he wanted to paint me, so he and his wife have been staying here, very nice, easy guests. My publisher [Alexander Frere] and his wife are here too, so we are having quite a gay and jolly party."

This was Sutherland's first important portrait, and it launched him on a career as the portraitist of famous people. He liked to paint men and women who had directed great enterprises and whose faces showed the strain of tremendous pressures. Such faces reminded him of scenes in nature, such as a tree struggling to remain standing or a branch beaten down by animal hooves—they were studies in survival. Among his subsequent sitters were Helena Rubinstein, Konrad Adenauer, Winston Churchill, and Lord Beaverbrook.

Sutherland stalked his sitters, waiting for them to reveal themselves and compose their own portraits. He tried to combine their physical and psychological truths by catching characteristic expressions and attitudes. "I have to be as absorbent as blotting-paper and as watchful as a cat," he said. What he found was not always popular with the sitter, and it was often said that his portraits were cruel.

Maugham sat ten times, for an hour a day. Sutherland began by filling sketchbooks with small drawings, sometimes of a single feature, sometimes of the head, sometimes of the seated figure. The drawings of Maugham's face accentuated its folds, pouches, and wrinkles. From these sketches he made two or three large preparatory drawings. Then he began to paint the definitive portrait, in the studio, away from the sitter. He asked for additional sittings to make more detailed studies—of the right ear, of Maugham stammering, and of the left foot—squared up for transfer to the canvas.[61]

The portrait, four and a half feet high and two feet wide, was finished in June. It showed Maugham sitting on a bamboo stool with his arms and legs crossed, against an apricot background. The stool, and a few palm fronds at the top of the painting, evoked his travels to the Orient. He wore a brown velvet smoking jacket, a red scarf, gray-blue slacks, and tan loafers. His chin was raised with the defensiveness of someone about to be struck, and the downward-turning mouth conveyed resignation to a lifetime of pain and disappointment. The hooded eyes were the lenses of the inscrutable observer, the aloof and sardonic recorder of human frailty.

To compare it with Gerald Kelly's lighthearted portrait of Maugham in his thirties as "The Jester" was to witness a slow process of astringency. The cost of fame could be measured in the change in Maugham's appearance from a handsome, debonair fellow to a sort of wrinkled crustacean with a hard, shell-like, protective exterior.

Gerald Kelly's reaction to the Sutherland portrait was predictable. "Mr. Graham Sutherland is, they tell me, a very important artist," he said, "and his remarkable study of Willie is certainly revealing. To think that I have known Willie since 1902 and have only just recognized that disguised as an old Chinese Madam, he kept a brothel in Shanghai."[62]

Maugham liked the painting, or said he did, and bought it for $35,000. He did not, however, want it in the Mauresque, and gave it to Liza, who presented it to the Tate Gallery in 1951. Alan wrote Bert Alanson that it had actually been given to the Tate by Maugham in Liza's name, and that she was not pleased that it had gone to the nation. In his thrift and wisdom, however, Maugham kept the copyright, and received a percentage of the proceeds on the tens of thousands of postcards of the painting sold by the Tate.

A Writer's Notebook, a collection of notes taken over more than half a century, between 1892 and 1944, was to be published in 1949, and *Cosmopolitan* bought the serial rights for $10,000. For years Maugham had been building up a case against Jacques Chambrun, and now he found the occasion for a final break. In June he wrote Chambrun:

> I am astounded to learn that the extracts from my *Notebooks* are being published in *Cosmopolitan* in three numbers. I have given you permission to have them published in one number simultaneously with the production of the book. I cannot allow my instructions to be disregarded by you. With this letter I withdraw your authority to act as my agent. . . . You will cease to use my name as one of your clients, as you have done in the past when you have been touting for work, nor will you in any case represent yourself as my agent from now on. . . . Your whole conduct of the negotiations concerning the film rights of *The Razor's Edge* were inept owing to your complete ignorance of the business, and your negligence with regard to the contract with Winston was quite inexcusable.[63]

The letter put Chambrun in a panic. Maugham was the cornerstone of his agency. He cabled in answer: "Your letter this morning greatest blow I have had in view of our long association I ask you please to withdraw decision until you receive my letter explaining Cosmopolitan circumstances which through absolutely no fault of mine resulted in advance publication."[64]

Chambrun's plea for forgiveness, sent the same day, said:

> In the years I have represented you in America, the returns to me in commissions were very handsome and very gratifying, but far more gratifying and important was the prestige it gave my agency. It is true that I took advantage of it in letters to writers; if I had not done so, I should have been neglecting the strongest card I had to play. The loss of the opportunity to do so would give my business the most serious blow it has ever sustained. I know you have always been convinced that the chance to turn a penny is for me a consideration overriding every other, but I must ask you to believe that I appeal to you not to let your decision stand not only for the above commercial reason but for reasons of sentiment and pride also.[65]

Maugham's mind was made up. Not only did he drop Chambrun but he had his accounts audited, and found that he had been holding back more than $30,000 in royalties, mainly from the Brazilian publisher Editora Globo, in Porto Alegre. He threatened to prosecute unless Chambrun paid up, and agreed to take the money in installments. By 1963 Chambrun had sent him $30,092.72. Whenever he could, Chambrun continued to act for Maugham, who had to threaten legal action and send cables such as the following: "As you well know you are no longer my agent and you have no right to enter into negotiations of any sort on my behalf stop I strongly resent your interference."[66]

In June, Maugham spent three weeks in Vichy with Alan, preparing for the onslaught of guests in August. Alan had a hacking cough he could not get rid of, and doctors discovered a slight scar on the lung. On the Riviera, Maugham heard, his friends were taking baths in Vichy water, for there was a water shortage.

Back at the Mauresque at the end of June, Maugham was faced with one of the drawbacks of fame, unwanted callers. Two young men from Cambridge arrived, saying they had been sent by the son-in-law of his niece Kate Bruce. He was not home, and they waited by the gate until dinner time, when they presented themselves with their luggage, apparently expecting to be asked to stay. Alan put them off, and Maugham wrote his niece that he was extremely annoyed. "I am not a monkey in the zoo for people to come and stare at," he said, "and I very much resent being treated as such. . . . I shall be obliged if you see to it that he [the son-in-law] does not repeat a proceeding which is highly offensive to me."[67]

Maugham was all the more irritated because of the rush of invited guests. The Schermans, who owned the Book-of-the-Month Club, came, and Sam Behrman, and Jerry Zipkin, one of Maugham's favorite bridge partners, on his first trip to the Riviera. Zipkin, Maugham wrote Bert Alanson, "went completely mad. We had the greatest difficulty in preventing him from buying up the entire contents of every shop he went into. As it was, he went back laden with antiques, shirts, and pull-overs, most of which he could have got in New York at half the price. But as he owns not apartment houses on Park Avenue, but blocks of apartments, I don't suppose it mattered."[68] Before he left, Zipkin asked Annette, the cook, what she wanted for a present. Annette had her heart set on a girdle. The staff measured her with a tape, gingerly circling her ample derrière and taking notes. Zipkin went to Bloomingdale's with her measurements. "There was a choice of black or white or blue and I took black because Mediterraneans are so dirty," he recalled.[69] When the servants at the Mauresque started rating the guests, Zipkin rated number one, because he always closed doors behind him and left generous tips.

Liza and John Hope arrived. Liza was expecting, and her husband, Maugham wrote Alanson, "acts as though no one had ever had a baby before. Just chock-a-block with responsibility. They both appear to think that I ought to come down handsomely to celebrate the event, but I propose to turn a deaf ear to the demands I foresee. I wonder how it is that it never occurs to people that you may prefer to spend your money on yourself rather than on them?"[70] Maugham liked to pretend to Alanson that everyone, including the members of his family, was after his money, but in fact Liza and John demanded nothing.

The Riviera social scene glittered once again, thanks to the presence of such celebrities as the Windsors and Coco Chanel. Alan made a hit with jokes told with a Cockney accent, such as: "I don't know which way to turn, as the vicar's wife said on her return from the choirboy's outing." Maugham wrote Sam Behrman in August to make sure that the $1,782.64 which Chambrun had sent him as Swedish royalties on Behrman's adaptation of "Jane" was the correct amount. He also wanted to know who Gilbert Seldes was. Seldes had written to ask whether he was interested in having his short stories turned into television dramas under an omnibus title such as "The World of Somerset Maugham."[71] Behrman replied that "Gilbert Seldes is the author of many books and a kind of marathon authority on all the arts. One of his books was called, I believe, *The Seven Lively Arts*. He has omitted no single art. . . . I met him on the Cape . . . and we fell to talking about you, and he told me that he had had an orgasm (it is my way of putting it and not his) simply from the position of the commas in some piece of writing of yours. The sexual problems of a man who can get such a kick out of a comma must be comparatively simple, don't you think?"[72]

Had Maugham been a careful reader of his reviews, he would have known who Seldes was. For Seldes in the twenties had been drama critic for *The Dial*, in which he regularly savaged Maugham's plays. Of *The Constant Wife* he said that it was "one of the most negligible plays in years, one in which all the epigrams are machine-turned and the wit heavy-handed." He called *Our Betters* an unimportant and complacent comedy. *The Circle*, generally considered Maugham's best play, he found vulgar and stupid, with dialogue totally lacking in mental fineness. Over the years, however, Seldes' opinion of Maugham's work seems to have improved.[73]

In August, Maugham was once again a target in the Cold War, which had spread to cultural life. For the second time he was attacked by a Soviet publication. This time it was the *Literary Gazette*, which called him "an unsuccessful British spy who has now placed himself at the disposal of Wall Street bosses to aid in the spiritual disarmament of the masses." It must have amused Maugham, who had always shunned political bias in his writing, to be thus condemned as "an ideological esthete in the service of the dollar."[74]

In October 1949 *A Writer's Notebook* was published. It was made up of extracts from fifteen large volumes of notes he had kept since the age of eighteen. After compiling the extracts, he destroyed the notebooks, and with them much material of value to future biographers. Some reviewers were disappointed because the book was not revealing, but it had not been intended as autobiography. The notebooks were warehouses in which the professional writer kept his inventory. He recorded material that might serve, such as comments on people, travel notes, random thoughts, snatches of dialogue, character sketches, and story outlines. In the nineties he favored epigrams; at the turn of the century there were touches of fashionable cynicism, such as: "Bed. No woman is worth more than a fiver, unless you're in love with her. Then she is worth all she costs you."

In the selection process itself, however, there shone through Maugham's determination not to bare himself too much. He betrayed the sentimental reverse of his tough side in remarks such as: "The love that lasts longest is the love that is never returned." But the greatest fascination of the book lay in wondering what he had left out. Sometimes years passed without a line.[75]

A few critics saw through the reticence. The New York *Herald Tribune*'s Walter Prichard Eaton on October 23 called it Maugham's "De Senectute. It is cool, a little hedonistic, and will seem to many self-satisfied. It will also seem to others not a little sad. The man who studied men to make stories of them seems at the end alone, with his books."

Above all, *A Writer's Notebook* was a book to be enjoyed by other writers. It was reviewed by three important British writers, each of whom, through the filter of his own sensibility, breached Maugham's defenses. Charles Morgan in the *Spectator* of October 7 said that "if he has an affectation or mannerism it is of ruthlessness. This is partly honesty and courage, but partly fear. Fear of what? Of sentimentality? Of being duped? Of self-deception? Honorable fears, but still fears, and fears are conditions of the imagination which criticism too seldom attempts to understand. They run like a shudder across these pages. They are among the winds that drive Mr. Maugham's powerful ship." Morgan went no further in defining Maugham's fears, although he may have been alluding to his fear of revealing his homosexuality.

V. S. Pritchett, in the *New Statesman and Nation* on October 8 said that the notes did not add "a new sensation to our lives, or open us to a new experience. They suggest, rather, the price Maugham has paid for it." And in an unsigned review in *The Times Literary Supplement* on October 14, 1949, Anthony Powell noted Maugham's exceptional degree of social conformity. When Maugham wrote that "the world is an entirely different place to the man of five foot seven from what it is to the man of six foot two," Powell asked "whether self-assurance is not as attainable at five foot seven as it may be out of reach at six foot two." When Maugham wrote that "a woman not very young, not very pretty, not very intelligent, suffered hellish tortures and accepted death, for a country not her own, rather than betray her friends," Powell asked "what on earth good looks and intelligence have to do with gallantry and self-sacrifice." More than social conformity, however, these were comments on Maugham's own condition. He saw himself as ugly, and truly believed that physical appearance was destiny. Anthony Powell, a handsome young man, judging from his photographs, probably never had to surmount a strong sense of physical self-disgust.

Maugham did not see these reviews, for he was in Spain spending his accumulated pesetas with Alan, whose heart was broken by a bull-fighter, a dancer, and a gypsy. Their holiday was cut short when they both suffered some form of food poisoning. They left for London, where Maugham took to his bed at the Dorchester. Upon learning that his old friend Gerald Kelly had been named president of the Royal Academy, he sent congratulations: "I write this in the hope that my letter will be the first to reach you addressed P.R.A. I need not tell you how thrilled and excited I was to hear the good news. Do you remember Paris in 1904? We did not imagine then that either of us would come to the point we have. . . . Finally, I hope you will be as urbane and as tolerant of other people's stupidity in your new position as your irascible temper will permit. After all you have to make up for your predecessor's mistakes if you want to maintain the dignity of your institution."[76] (The predecessor was Sir Alfred Munnings.)

Maugham wrote Sam Behrman that since he had dropped Jacques Chambrun, agents hounded him to offer their services. "So far I have only written evasive replies," he said. "The fact is that now, I am not, like you, a miserable hack with my nose to the grindstone, in the hope of keeping body and soul together, but on the contrary a gentleman of leisure, of which the result is that I have nothing that any agent can profitably deal with. I am not writing anything that is of any commercial value. Most of my plays and stories have already been sold to the movies, and those that haven't are, owing to their obscenity, offensive to the susceptibilities of the chaste American public."

Behrman had a play on Broadway starring the Lunts, and Maugham asked him what he was going to do with all the money he made. Alan, who typed his letters, spelled "Lunts" with a lower-case *l*, and Maugham added in his own hand: "I don't know why Alan doesn't give the Lunts a capital letter. Lunts, c. . . ., no, no, no, Lunts, Lunts."[77]

Although he wrote Behrman that he was now a gentleman of leisure, he was busy writing a preface for a twenty-five-cent edition of *Of Human Bondage* and another for the Modern Library edition of *Cakes and Ale*. He was rewriting the scripts for a second movie based on his short stories and he was reading four short stories for Columbia records. "For an old party who has retired from the literary world," he wrote Alanson, "I seem to be kept pretty busy."[78]

From Spain, Maugham had gone to London to see his daughter and son-in-law. In December he left for Paris, and was pleased to see that Scotland Yard sent a C.I.D. man to escort him on board the boat train at Dover. He and Alan made quite a sensation, as the other passengers took them for undesirable aliens being deported from England. In Paris, Maugham could not resist opening his Christmas presents, a scarf from Liza, which he was glad to have because it was bitterly cold, and the *Oxford Dictionary of Quotations* from John, which he enjoyed reading in bed between parties. At one dinner party at the Tour d'Argent, however, he was taken ill with gastric flu, and he decided to cut short his stay and return to the Mauresque.

Before leaving Paris he bought himself two Christmas presents—a small Renoir nude and a large Sisley landscape. The dealer told him that the model for the nude had been Renoir's cook, who used to sit for him for an hour or so in the morning. Then he would say to her, "Now put your clothes on and get your washing-up done and start on the lunch."[79] As was his custom, Maugham bought the paintings in his daughter's name, and wrote her: "Dearest Liza . . . it may interest you to know that you now own a very fine Sisley and a Renoir of a nude lady, rather buxom and light tomato color, not very big but very beautiful. We brought her down with us in the car and she already hangs in my bedroom. The Sisley is a large picture and will come by train. . . . My love to you all. Daddy."[80]

The new year, 1950, began with an onslaught of guests. Cecil Roberts, who had comforted Maugham after Gerald Haxton's death, came to lunch on January 9. They discussed Augustus Hare, the late-Victorian travel writer. He was a finicky snob, spinsterish and petty, Maugham said, but his travel books were unique. He walked everywhere, which was astonishing for such a hot-bottle-and-mittens type. Maugham lived very quietly now, Roberts observed, and did not let anything interfere with his afternoon nap. Half an hour after lunch he vanished, and if they were tactful, so did his guests.[81]

Lord Maugham came to spend a week over his brother's seventy-sixth birthday. He was eighty-four, and age had not improved his humor. He disapproved of the festivities arranged by his younger brother's friends and neighbors to celebrate his birthday. Baron von Seidlitz gave the birthday dinner at the Hotel de Paris in Monte Carlo. The menu was poached salmon hollandaise, chicken Souvaroff, asparagus, and a pistachio dessert, washed down with Krug 1938 and Hospices de Beaune 1929. Lord Maugham had an attack of gout, which did nothing to make him more agreeable. He insisted on calling Willie "my boy." Over the years the two brothers had perfected their techniques for getting on one another's nerves. Alan complained that he had a terrible time keeping the peace between them. Maugham thought that his brother looked frail and that both his movements and his mental processes had slowed down. "Oh dear," he wrote Robin, "I do hope I don't go like that. I should hate to see people being tolerant to me because I was so old and rather foolish and allowances must be made for me because of my past."[82]

His brother's visit made him peevish, and Maugham complained about the currency restrictions and the coming election in England. He thought Labour would get in again and the workers would increase their demands and go on strike after strike. He complained about the unending flow of guests. Adding up the meals he had served during a three-week period, not counting breakfasts, he found that the total came to a staggering 1,060. He complained to Bennett Cerf of Random House about the shiny paper the proofs for the Modern Library edition of Cakes and Ale were printed on, which rebelled against the use of ink. "Is this to discourage authors from making corrections?" he asked. "If so, I have failed you."[83]

His son-in-law, John Hope, was canvassing in Scotland for his seat in the House of Commons, which he retained with a majority of more than five thousand. Maugham was pleased, but he was anxious about Liza, who was due to deliver in March. "You will get John to send me a wire, won't you," he wrote her in February, "when everything is satisfactorily over, and I'm sure it will be satisfactory. This is the sort of occasion when your native toughness stands you in good stead."

The Freres arrived in February, and Maugham told Alexander Frere that he was thinking of writing Liza a letter asking her to confirm that the pictures he had bought in her name would remain in his possession while he was alive. He had just acquired from the Paul Rosenberg gallery in New York a fine Matisse for $10,000, called "*Intérieur au Parquet Gravé, Femme Assise dans un Fauteuil Jaune.*" The receipt, as usual, was sent to Lady John Hope. Frere improvised the wording of the letter.[84]

On March 6 Liza gave birth to a son. He was christened Julian John Somerset in the crypt of the House of Commons, with Anthony Eden as godfather and Mrs. Paul Mellon as godmother. Maugham wrote John Hope to say that he was delighted that Liza and the baby were getting on so well.[85] Hope had been ill with the flu but got up from his sickbed to register his vote in the House of Commons, which Maugham thought of as the height of party loyalty.

Desmond MacCarthy came to stay, but he was so frighteningly ill and frail that Maugham felt it was best to let him just sit about in the garden. MacCarthy died two years later, at the age of seventy-five. He had known Maugham since World War I, and as he grew to eminence as a critic, continued to admire his work. His Bloomsbury friends had hoped that he would be a great novelist, but he did not live up to their expectations.

March 30 Maugham left for Morocco, armed with a letter of introduction to the French governor-general, Marshal Juin. Alan was quivering with excitement at the thought of the trip, but Maugham felt that when you have seen one Arab country you have seen them all. One morning at his hotel in Fez the young French waiter who brought him breakfast asked him to write a letter for him. Maugham asked what it was about. "It's like this," the waiter said. "I think it is about time I got married, and I want you to write a proposal of marriage to a girl in my village in France."

"I can't possibly do that," Maugham said. "After all, I have never seen the girl. I shouldn't know what to say to her."

"But I thought you were a novelist," the waiter said.

Maugham admitted that he was and took pen and paper in hand. "My well beloved," he began.

"Oh no, you can't say that," the waiter said, "I don't know her well enough for that."

"How do you want me to start?" Maugham asked.

"Well, her name is Erminie. Can't you start 'Dear Erminie'?"

"Of course I can," Maugham said, "but it sounds rather standoffish."

Maugham began to write and found the first three or four lines difficult, but after a while the "divine afflatus" seized him, and he grew more and more lyrical and passionate, until by the time he had finished he was saying to himself: "Well, if she doesn't accept him after a letter like that, she isn't worth having."

He showed the letter to the waiter, who did not look pleased.

"What's wrong with it," Maugham asked, "don't you like it?"

"Yes, it is all right as far as it goes. Of course, I am in love with her, and all that, but I wish you could put in something to the effect that it would be convenient if I knew how much money her father is going to give her when we marry."[86]

Maugham was glad to get back to his own surroundings and to servants who did not ask him to be a scribe. With advancing age his reaction to guests was unpredictable. With some, like Chips Channon, he was the soul of bonhomie, while with others he was a terror. When Channon came to stay for a week in April, Alan Searle, bright-eyed and devoted, met him at the Beaulieu railway station, and they drove to the villa, where Maugham, looking like a mandarin and flanked by footmen, greeted him at the door. Channon approved of everything, the villa, the sweet-smelling garden, and the orderly pace of life. He found Maugham youthful in bearing and interested in everything. At dinner Maugham and Alan appeared in elaborate dressing gowns, and he felt drab in his dinner jacket. The dinner conversation was of a licentious nature, with "many reminiscences of every kind from Willie, who has had a long amorous career, and now at 75 is still lusty. He has been everywhere, met everybody, tasted everything. His interest in the world and in Society and food and drink is acute, though he occasionally has flashes of amnesia."[87]

Other guests did not have such pleasant memories of their stays, for Maugham had developed tactics to get rid of those he felt had offended him. One of these was the writer Patrick Leigh-Fermor, who had attended the King's School. Nervous and on his best behavior on his first visit to the Mauresque, Leigh-Fermor did the worst possible thing. He said that at the King's School all the heralds stammered, and went into a long imitation. Maugham saw it as a personal attack. At the end of the meal he held out his hand and said, "Well, I'll say goodbye to you now because I won't be seeing you in the morning."[88]

Another guest who suffered a similar fate was Patrick O'Higgins, the young redheaded guardsman who had met Maugham in New York and came to spend a week at the Mauresque that June. O'Higgins was impressed. There was nothing but the best—Floris soap from Jermyn Street in the bathrooms and English silver from Phillips at meals. Maugham padded about in velvet slippers from Peal. Dinners were formal, with Maugham facing Alan in the middle of the table, à la française.

Maugham retired early, and Alan sometimes took the car to Ville-franche to pick up sailors. He told them not to make any noise, gave them champagne, and took them for a midnight swim around the pool, and sometimes a bit further. It was natural for Alan, who was thirty-five years Maugham's junior, to look for "a bit of fun" now and then. His escapades with sailors were an escape valve and did not threaten his relationship with Maugham. Alan was known up and down the Riviera for his proclivities, but since he was a heavy tipper, no one minded.

One evening O'Higgins borrowed one of the servants' bicycles and went to Madame Fontaine's, a brothel in Villefranche. Emerging in the wee hours somewhat the worse for wear, he found the bicycle gone. He walked back to the Mauresque, arriving there with the dawn. The gate was open and the pebbles in the driveway crunched under his feet. The servants were asleep and the front door was locked. O'Higgins pounded on the bronze knocker, sat on the steps, and waited for results. The door creaked slowly open and behind it O'Higgins saw what looked like a gila monster in a bathrobe. It was Maugham, his gnarled neck disappearing into the folds of the robe. His mouth was working, but he had trouble getting the words out. Finally he said, "You look very festive, Patrick. I suggest you go to bed." At lunch that day he said to Alan, "The Graham Sutherlands are coming and I'll need Patrick's room." O'Higgins packed and left.[89]

Although he was no longer writing fiction, Maugham faithfully kept to his work schedule, climbing the steps to his studio every morning and shutting himself in for three hours. He was writing an essay on Kant, a philosopher he had long admired, prodded by his friend Irwin Edman, to whom he wrote:

> Kant seems to have taken a perverse pleasure in writing badly. But when I had once got over that I was entranced. Why had no one told me about it before? . . . Of course it was a trifle disconcerting to find that many of the ideas I had thought out for myself on art and taste and so forth had been neatly set down by Kant a hundred and fifty years ago. . . . I am filled with the propagandist's urge to go out and tell everybody they must read it. You will laugh at me but when I have put my ideas on these matters before my friends they have come down on me like a ton of bricks and now I find that Kant formed pretty much the same opinions way back in the 18th century.[90]

Maugham finished the essay in August and sent it to Edman, saying: "If you said to me what you have written is just a lot of stuff and nonsense, I should be neither hurt nor mortified. . . . You will see at a glance that I am nothing of a philosopher." Edman replied: "The paper is philosophically accurate and sound. What gives it a particular freshness are the pertinent observations few philosophers would make." He said he could find no boners.[91]

Maugham was coming to the United States in September, and Edman prevailed upon him to read his paper at Columbia. As it turned out, this was Maugham's last visit to America, and it was a particularly busy one. He was giving a speech at the Morgan Library, presenting the manuscript of "The Artistic Temperament of Stephen Carey" to the Library of Congress, being inducted into the Institute of Arts and Letters, and attending the premiere of *Trio*, the second film to be made from his short stories.

Before starting out on this wearing trip Maugham went to Vichy to gather strength. He wrote his Riviera friend and neighbor Romaine Brooks: "You can't think how many ugly people there are here and what mean faces they have. I haven't seen anyone, male or female, on whom one's eyes can rest with pleasure."[92] The ugliness he saw in others may have been a reflection of his feelings about himself.

Maugham and Alan sailed for New York on the *Queen Mary* on September 22, arriving on the twenty-seventh. Maugham was looking forward to a series of treatments from Dr. Wolf, whom he trusted to keep him primed. He wondered whether to stay at the Sherry Netherland, where Serge Obolensky would do his best for him, or at the Plaza, where he had always been treated very well, and decided to remain faithful to the Plaza, where he was given a ninth-floor suite.[93]

He met and played bridge with Bennett Cerf, who had brought out the Modern Library edition of *Cakes and Ale*. Maugham accused him of "fooling around" at the bridge table. Cerf tried to make the most of this new friendship and sent Maugham a novel by Neil Paterson, *The China Run*, saying, "We are going to publish the American edition of *The China Run* and we would dearly like to carry on the jacket some comment from you." This was against Maugham's practice and he replied, "Dear Mr. Bennett Cerf, that was a very unfortunate thought you had."[94]

On October 5 there was a private showing of *Trio* at the Museum of Modern Art, followed by a celebrity-studded buffet supper at the Plaza. *Trio* was made up of "The Verger," "Mr. Know-All," and "Sanatorium." In an interview Maugham said that "Sanatorium" was based on his own experience in Scotland, "when I injudiciously contracted TB." His interviews had by now achieved a standard form: I'm just an old party, I'm living on borrowed time, I'm not writing any more novels, old age has its advantages, there is so much one can do without.

On October 11 he presented the manuscript of "The Artistic Temperament of Stephen Carey" to the Library of Congress, on condition that it never be published.

> I haven't looked at it since I corrected the typescript, and that was more than fifty years ago. When I had taken my medical degree I went to Spain with the intention of becoming a professional writer. I was twenty then. No one dissuaded me from taking this hazardous step because there was no one to care what I did with myself. When I look back I can only wonder at my foolhardiness and my self-confidence. I settled down in Seville and began to write. I finished the book still in Seville six months later. I had had a small success before with a novel and a volume of short stories and it was something of a mortification to me when, on going back to London with this new novel, which I called "The Artistic Temperament of Stephen Carey," it was refused by all the publishers it was sent to. I had not the experience of life to write the sort of novel I wanted to write and I made the great mistake which many very young writers fall into, of writing about what I didn't know instead of about what I did. I tell you this in order to make it quite clear that it is not a work of any importance. . . . I should be ashamed to see it printed and Dr. Evans has promised me that it never shall be. It is merely an insignificant curiosity like those fragments of pottery which you see in archeological museums and which have been dug up in the burial places of extinct races. . . . Fortunately these two shabby little volumes don't take up much space. It was fifteen years later that I began to write *Of Human Bondage* and when I did I never even thought of looking at this earlier book to see if there was anything in it that I could make use of. For what there is in *Of Human Bondage* of autobiography I trusted to my memory.

If, Maugham said, a learned professor were ever to study the manuscript, "and if, after doing this he came to the conclusion that if I had had any sense I should have burned it right away, my disembodied ghost will be very much inclined to agree with him."[95]

After the Library of Congress there was the Institute of Arts and Letters dinner at the Knickerbocker Club on October 17. Irwin Edman introduced Maugham, recalling a visit to the Mauresque:

> I remember in the evening after dinner, lounging in the sunlight after a swim, and having discussions on the true, the good, and the beautiful.

537

The Mediterranean sunlight fortified me in the conviction that Mr. Maugham was a philosopher and that we were both virtually Greek philosophers. . . . A man of letters is a philosopher, he has his ultimate comment on life, but his commentary is a picture, his judgment has the fascination of a well-told tale. Mr. Maugham is a celebrated story-teller. His stories are exercises in humane wisdom, or philosophy at its best.[96]

In the midst of his being heaped with honors, sad news reached Maugham. His sister-in-law Helen Mary Maugham, of whom he had been fond, had died. His brother, Lord Maugham, was grief-stricken. After thirty-four years of marriage he felt lost and wondered how to get through the time still before him with courage.

The Morgan Library dinner was coming up, at which he would be introduced by Glenway Wescott, who went to see him at the Plaza. He found Maugham feeling rejuvenated after his treatments by Max Wolf. Maugham showed him, under his silk bathrobe, that he still had, as Wescott put it, "quite a respectable phallus."[97]

On October 23 he gave the manuscript of his short-story collection *Ah King* to the Morgan Library and spoke on the writer's vocation. Some did it for money, he said, some because it was a pleasant life, and some for fame. But few made money, it was not always a pleasant life, and fame was fickle.

Finally, there are people who write because they damn well can't help it. And that is the only really good reason for anyone writing at all. And that, I suppose, was the case with me. But unfortunately the urge to write does not guarantee that you will write anything worth reading. That is quite another matter. And it has always seemed to me one of the strangest things in the world that this gift should descend on certain people. Heredity doesn't account for it. Environment doesn't account for it . . . Balzac's grandfather was a farmhand, his father was a dull and not too respectable attorney. Why should Balzac have had this power granted to him to create that world of characters? And Jane Austen. The daughter of a rather dull and perfectly respectable father, a clergyman, and a rather silly mother. How did she come to write *Pride and Prejudice*? The whole thing is a mystery.[98]

Irwin Edman had invited a number of Columbia luminaries for a stag dinner at the Coffee House to precede Maugham's Kant reading on November 2. Among the guests were Lionel Trilling and Corliss

Lamont. Edman provided Maugham with capsule profiles: Trilling "wrote a novel, a little too intellectualized, called *The Middle of the Journey*. One reviewer in England—I think it was V. S. Pritchett—said 'this is the best novel by a non-genius since E. M. Forster.' I have not been able to make up my mind whether that was a compliment or not." Corliss Lamont "is not first-rate as a thinker but his intellectual heart is in the right place, or perhaps I should say in the left place, because he is well-known as a supporter of left-wing causes, which makes him somewhat a problem child to his mother, Mrs. Thomas W. Lamont."[99]

The lecture was set for 8.30 at Columbia's Casa Italiana. It was Maugham's debut as a lecturer in philosophy. There was no microphone, it was unseasonably warm, the windows were open and he had trouble making himself heard above the street sounds. But Edman thought Maugham's talk, "Beauty and the Professor," had gone well, and reported that a student had asked him, "Why can't philosophy always be taught in so polished and wise a way?"[100]

On the day after his talk at Columbia, Maugham was invited by Douglas Black to a bridge party with the president of that University, Dwight D. Eisenhower, and several other persons, including Alexander Frere of Heinemann. By the end of the evening Maugham had lost twelve dollars to Eisenhower. He was a sore loser, and in the taxi with Frere on his way back to the Plaza he said, "That is probably a very great general, but he's a bloody bad bridge player and a very stupid man."[101] His irritation wore off, however, and he wrote Alanson that Eisenhower was "very nice, absolutely simple, no frills or pose or anything, and we had a very agreeable game."[102]

Sated with honors, Maugham was leaving for England on November 10, and his last days in New York were hectic. He attended a party at the Stork Club, at which he drank Ovaltine. *Life* magazine spent a "typical" day with him, during which he shopped for seeds at Max Schling's, ordered large quantities of food from Gristede's, and bought a painting. He took advantage of his last trip to America to add to his daughter's art collection. She was the purchaser of record of Renoir's "*Trois Jeunes Filles*" for $29,000, of Toulouse-Lautrec's "*Le Raboteur*" for $10,000, and of Bonnard's "Woman and Child" for $2,000. Maugham spent his evenings playing bridge. His last afternoon in the United States was spent in the company of Irwin Edman and S. N. Behrman.[103]

Spending a few days in England on his way home, Maugham caught up on his family. Robin had bought a yacht and was planning to sail down the French canals to Villefranche and thence to the Greek islands. His brother he found unexpectedly cheerful, wearing his widower's weeds lightly and planning to go on a trip to South Africa by himself. He spent a few days in early December at Juliet Duff's in Wilton. Chips Channon was there and thought that Maugham was "growing gentler and more mellow and is, in fact, sweetness itself. Before every meal he boyishly and with fiendish efficiency mixed the Martinis, 'Maugham Specials.'"[104]

He returned to the Mauresque to face domestic problems and the worst winter on the Riviera since the war. He had to fire a lazy and dishonest butler named Clément. He was also fighting the French tax people in order to avoid double taxation, and arranging for the shipment of his theatrical paintings to England, for he had donated them to the National Theatre, as yet unbuilt. He had by then collected enough Impressionists to cover the walls left bare. He was furious that as a result of the publicity in *Life*, French authorities were charging him two thousand dollars' duty on the Renoir he had bought in New York.[105]

The new year came in, and with his seventy-seventh birthday approaching, Maugham went through one of his despondent periods. He thought once more of selling his house and giving up the Riviera. He had no friends and no yacht. There were no amusements. He was asked to large parties, such as Princess Ottoboni's Christmas bash (he had apparently been forgiven for caricaturing her in *The Razor's Edge*), but did not enjoy them. "It is dead and dull," he wrote Kate Bruce. "I have good servants, good food, a beautiful house and a nice garden. But that does not prevent me from being bored." He would be sorry to leave the Mauresque after having had everything exactly as he wanted it for so many years, but he was too old to play golf or tennis, and many of his friends were dead. Although Alan was against it, he was thinking of moving to London and wondered whether he would be comfortable there. He would need a house and servants, and because of taxes, he would have to dip into capital. "I would not much mind where it was," he said, "Chelsea or Regent's Park. I think if I gave them decent food my friends would come almost anywhere to lunch with me. Does all this seem crazy to you?"[106] The mood passed and the Mauresque seemed habitable once again.

In March 1951 Gerald Kelly invited Maugham to speak at the Royal Academy dinner. This was a formidable occasion, broadcast live to the nation on B.B.C. The other speakers were Clement Atlee, then Prime

Minister, Winston Churchill, Lord Samuel, and Admiral Lord Cork and Orrery. Maugham, who was seated between Churchill and Lord Samuel, the head of the Liberal party in the House of Lords, stole the show with a speech about the lady from Cheltenham. This was a tweedy lady he pretended to have met, who had come up from the country for a morning's shopping and lunch and was going to see the summer exhibition at the academy before catching the 4.57 home. From chatting with her, Maugham said, "I knew exactly who she was. She was the lady we have all heard about but very few of us have met. She was the lady who doesn't pretend to know anything about art, but knows what she likes." The lady quoted Keats: "A thing of beauty is a joy forever." Maugham disagreed, for he believed that beauty responded to fashion.

"The first President of the Royal Academy," he said, "recommended Ludovico Caracci as a model for style in painting and compared him with Titian to Titian's disadvantage. Would any of us do that now? . . . It would be foolish to suppose that our opinions are any more definitive than those of our forefathers, and we may be pretty sure that our descendants will look upon them with the same perplexity as we look upon Sir Joshua's high praise of Pellegrino Tibaldi and Hazlitt's passionate admiration for Guido Reni."[107]

This homily went over well after the high-flown oratory that had preceded it. The stuffed shirts came up to Maugham afterward and said they had never heard such a speech at an academy banquet.[108]

It was fitting that Maugham should speak at the Royal Academy, for he had long been a lover and collector of art, first of theatrical paintings and now of Impressionists. He would see a painting he couldn't afford and would keep thinking about it until he said "Damn the expense" and bought it. Whenever he was in New York or Paris he haunted the galleries. He bought Pissarro's "Winter Landscape," Matisse's "The Lady with a Parasol," and two Renoirs. He also bought Fernand Léger's "Les Toits de Paris," an arrangement of squares, oblongs, and spheres in black, white, gray, and red. He thought it was decorative but wondered what was in Léger's mind when he painted it. One day he found Annette, the cook, who, like her employer, had grown increasingly bad-tempered with advancing years, standing in front of the Léger with a look of rapture on her face. When he asked what had so affected her, she said, "Mais ça me plaît, ça me dit quelque chose" ("But I like it, it says something to me").

His Toulouse-Lautrec was a strong and uncharacteristic painting of a naked man polishing a stone floor. The dealer told him that if the nude had been a woman he could have gotten three times the price. Maugham enjoyed asking his guests if they could guess who had painted it and confounding them by saying it was Toulouse-Lautrec. In New York he bought two Picassos, a large portrait of a standing woman, and the blue period "Death of a Harlequin," which showed the harlequin lying on a bed with folded hands, being mourned by two other figures, and may have reminded him of Gerald Haxton, who could fit into the doomed-clown category.

He took great pride in his collection and was gratified to hear one of his wealthy Riviera neighbors say, *"Aujourd'hui un particulier ne pourrait pas avoir une collection comme celle-ci"* ("Today an individual would not be able to amass such a collection"). It was through his passion for collecting that he met his Riviera neighbor Henri Matisse. In his eighties and bedridden, Matisse continued to paint in a big old-fashioned double brass bed with knobs at the four corners, the kind of bed the French call *conjugal*. "I am not a sick man," he told Maugham, "I am a wounded man—*un grand mutilé*." He painted on the ceiling above his bed with a brush attached to a long wand.

The chapel he had designed in Vence was being built, and he asked Maugham to take a look and see how the work was coming. When Maugham reported back, Matisse said, "Look what I did this morning." He had made line drawings of a model's head on sheets of paper measuring nine inches by twelve, which he had pinned in rows on the wall facing the bed. Maugham counted about forty drawings, and thought it was an amazing feat for a feeble and bedridden man to be doing work of such distinction. "You must look at them again and again," Matisse said, "you must look at them and look at them, it's only then that you'll see their power, the depth of thought in them, and their philosophy." Maugham looked but saw only forty lovely drawings, and thought to himself that artists are apt to see more in their work than is apparent to the eye of the beholder.

He bought Matisse's "The Yellow Chair" because he marveled at the apparent effortlessness of the brushwork. A happy inspiration must have allowed him to finish it in a single morning, Maugham thought. When he said as much to Matisse, he grunted and sent his middle-aged housekeeper after some snapshots of the painting at different stages. He showed Maugham that he had scraped the canvas down three times before getting the effect he wanted. Its colors were so brilliant that it eclipsed the paintings next to it, and Maugham had to hang it on a wall by itself. He said to Matisse, *"Vous savez, j'achète des tableaux pour fleurir ma maison"* ("You know, I buy paintings to flower my home"). Matisse muttered angrily, *"Ça, c'est de la décoration. Ça n'a aucune importance"* ("That's just decoration. It is totally without importance").[109] As they left, Maugham turned to Alan and said, "He is a grouchy old brute."

Maugham heard that his friend Barbara Back was in difficulty, for her husband had died, leaving no life insurance. Gone were the Rolls Royce, the house in Regent's Park, and the wonderful cook. She wrote a beauty column for the *Daily Mirror* and taught debutantes at the Constance Spry classes how to curtsy to royalty.[110] Maugham had always been a loyal friend. When she wrote a book of stories about life in Mayfair, he had encouraged her, telling her that they were amusing, "but you must be on your guard against monotony, you cannot always write about people going to bed with one another." Now he advised her to sell her inscribed copies of his books. "You should get quite a good sum for *Of Human Bondage*," he wrote. "The last copy that was sold in the U.S. brought $400—which is more than 100 pounds. And my stock will never be higher than it is now. It is bound to slump soon."[111] He continued inviting her to the Mauresque, sending her round-trip tickets via his travel agent.

The year ended for Maugham with a New Year's Eve dinner at the Sporting Club in Monte Carlo, where he found himself seated next to exiled royalty. The lady in question looked at the menu and said she could not eat a thing, as she was on a strict diet. Maugham suggested that she have a grilled sole, but she said no, she would just nibble on some green vegetables. Then she started on the caviar, and went on with soup, partridge, paté de foie gras, and ice cream. Maugham could not keep up and stopped after the partridge.[112]

The first important news that arrived in the new year, 1952, was that Liza was pregnant again. Maugham felt that she had done enough to increase the population and fired off a petulant letter. "Your news came as a great surprise to me," he said, "and I gather from what you say that you are pleased; so everyone connected with you has every reason to be pleased too. But though it is no business of mine, I venture to suggest it would be imprudent of you to make a yearly habit of having a baby. I think four children should sufficiently satisfy your maternal instincts."[113]

Perhaps Maugham was remembering his own childhood. He was born the youngest of four, but his mother had gone on to bear a fifth and had died as the result. A fifth child was linked in Maugham's mind with the death of his mother, and he may have superstitiously believed that his daughter would suffer the same fate, which would explain his warning about having another child.

Maugham's mood did not improve when Alan had to go into a Nice clinic that month for an abdominal operation, just when he was expecting his brother and the Freres.[114] He had hired Alan to nurse him through his declining years, but he often had to do the nursing, for Alan was seldom without some physical complaint. Alan was terrified, thinking he had cancer, but Maugham found him a good surgeon, and he was looked after by nuns. When Maugham came to get him in late February, he was astounded to see Alan kiss the mother superior on both cheeks. "I don't suppose she had been kissed for 50 years," he wrote Barbara Back. "Alan now has a fine long scar on his abdomen and he is ready to show it to anyone on the slightest provocation."[115]

Compounding Alan's poor health was his tendency to worry about what would happen to him after Maugham died. He was too old to make a fresh start. Concern for his future gave him insomnia. Maugham had in fact provided for Alan, "first because I have got him used to a very different kind of life and secondly because if I live another five years he will be over fifty and it would be hard for him to get another job."[116]

By March, Alan was back at work, typing sixty letters in two days, but now it was Maugham's turn to be ill. He went to Switzerland to consult specialists, who told him he was suffering from nervous exhaustion and sent him to the mountains to rest. Back at the Mauresque in late March, he received a succession of guests: Kenneth Clark and his wife, who were the kind of guests he liked, self-supporting; and Evelyn Waugh and Diana Cooper—she was a famous beauty and one of the great ladies of her time. They were traveling in the smallest car Maugham had ever seen and carried an immense amount of luggage. One evening, after Maugham had gone to bed early, Waugh came into Diana Cooper's bedroom to read aloud from his work in progress. Alan, who enjoyed snooping on the guests, with whom he never felt completely at ease, told Maugham that Waugh had spent the night in her room. "Willie didn't like that," she recalled, "and he was cool to me during the rest of my stay."[117] Alan was not above passing on untrue and malicious gossip to his employer.

Maugham was annoyed that he had not heard from his daughter since January. "I thought you had entirely forgotten my existence," he wrote her when a letter finally arrived. He hoped that her pregnancy was progressing without complication, adding: "After all, you should be getting used to this particular condition by now."[118]

But even at his advanced age professional problems pursued him. He had to defend himself against a plagiarism suit by Konrad Bercovici, who claimed that Maugham's story "The Verger," filmed in *Trio*, was stolen from a story of his, "It Pays to Be Ignorant." Maugham wrote Alanson that he had heard the story from his friend Ivor Back and that it was a well known bit of Jewish folklore. "My conscience is clear," he said, "and I shall fight the claim to the end."[119] He was also worried about taxes. Compton Mackenzie had sold the copyright to twenty of his books for ten thousand pounds and claimed it was a capital gain, but the British tax authorities ruled that the transaction should be taxed as income. Maugham was worried that some of his stories, sold to the Rank organization and taxed as a capital gain, would now fall under the Mackenzie ruling. "I am not very enthusiastic," he wrote Watt, "at paying over to the income tax authorities something like thirty thousand pounds if it can be avoided."[120]

There was good news to make up for the bad. Eisenhower, now the Commander in Chief of SHAPE, had ordered a complete set of his works, because all the copies in the SHAPE library were worn out; broadcasting rights had been sold for *The Moon and Sixpence*; "The Luncheon" was included in a *New Method English for the Arab World*.[121] Now that he published less, Maugham was like the managing director of a large company, overseeing the worldwide distribution of his product. More good news, of a personal nature, was that Liza had given birth to a second son, Jonathan Charles, on April 23.

In June, Glenway Wescott came to stay. It was the last time he would see his old friend. He remembers him at the pool, naked except for a broad-brimmed straw hat, saying, "I must take my dive." He complained of a pain in the groin, but otherwise looked fit. "His face was lined," Wescott recalled, "but his body had the most lovely skin in the world. He was shapely but tiny and with his little pot-belly he looked like the king of the frogs in the fairy tale. With his satiny worn skin he looked as if he was bound in the best quality English calf, you know, the kind of glove leather that doesn't last very long."[122]

Another guest was Ian Fleming, who, after a long romance, had married a friend of Maugham's, Anne Rothermere. Fleming, who held Maugham in some awe, had not yet published his first James Bond book. He was grateful that Maugham did not unleash upon him any of the irony and contempt with which he sometimes deflated guests he did not like.

In the last week of June, Maugham went to Oxford to receive an honorary Doctor of Letters degree, along with Sir Charles Kingsley Webster, history professor at the London School of Economics, and Gisela Richter, curator of Greek and Roman art at the Metropolitan Museum in New York. At the same ceremony R. A. Butler and Dean Acheson were given the degree of Doctor of Civil Law, and two American students were honored for winning Oxford's most coveted awards: Donald Hall won the Newdigate prize for poetry, and George Steiner won the Chancellor's English Essay prize. It was a moment of triumph for Maugham, who had always regretted not going to a university. The public orator, Mr. T. F. Higham, a fellow of Trinity College, gave an address in his honor in Latin, saying that he had used the advice of Horace's *Ars Poetica* in his plays:

> *Say nothing now but what you now should say;*
> *The rest cut out—or use another day.*

In July the pain in the groin he had been complaining about turned out to be from an acute intestinal infection. He ran such a high fever that Alan said you could have fried an egg on his forehead. He was so debilitated that he lay in bed and cried. Alan flew him to Lausanne, where doctors diagnosed a hernia but said he was too weak for an operation.[123] He spent all of August in Lausanne, and played bridge with the Queen of Spain. "Alan has been wonderful," he wrote Alanson, "and looks after me as no trained nurse could or would have done."[124] Alan complained that none of Maugham's family did a thing, although they would have been the first to blame him had anything gone wrong. Daniel Longwood, a Doubleday editor, sent him *The Old Man and the Sea*, which Maugham considered "vintage Hemingway. The story is both thrilling and touching and you end it with a very vivid impression of the brave old fisherman. Monologue and duologue are admirably reproduced with realism and also with poetic sense. The reader gets a wonderful impression of the horror and beauty of the tropic sea."[125]

Maugham's surgeon, Pierre Decker, was considered the best in Switzerland. He said he had never operated on a hernia in anyone over sixty, but after giving him a thorough examination, he told Maugham: "*Vous n'avez rien de la vieillesse sauf l'age*" ("You have nothing of old age except the years"). The operation took place in September; six hours after it Maugham was walking across his hospital room. The doctors were astonished at his rapid recovery. He passed the time reading his get-well mail—a hundred telegrams and four hundred letters. His hospital room was filled with flowers, among others carnations from the Queen of Spain and roses from the Aga Khan.[126]

Maugham left the clinic in late September and went to London, in time for the publication of a book of essays, *The Vagrant Mood*. This was Maugham at his most relaxed and convivial, looking back on a long, full life, pleasantly anecdotal, and allowing the reader to share the scope of his interests. The essay on Augustus Hare was a memorable evocation of a period that seemed as remote as the seventeenth century but one that the author had lived through—the end of Victorian England. The essays on Kant and Zurbarán were based on long months of research, while "Some Novelists I Have Known" gave bittersweet profiles of Arnold Bennett, Henry James, and Edith Wharton. The London *Times* on October 29 said that Maugham's principal moods were the disillusioned moralist of Graham Sutherland's portrait and the top-hatted exquisite of Gerald Kelly's early painting, and that it was the latter who had written these essays. *The Vagrant Mood* sold 40,000 copies in England, a record for a book of essays.

One of the essays, "The Decline and Fall of the Detective Story," a revised version of the article Cyril Connolly had turned down, was in part the outcome of a correspondence between Maugham and Raymond Chandler. A fan of Maugham's, Chandler had written his British publisher Hamish Hamilton in 1950 that the only inscribed copy of a book he had ever desired was one of *Ashenden*. Hamilton sent him a signed copy, and Chandler wrote to thank Maugham, saying, "The nearness of your name to mine on the title page of a book is as near as I am likely to get to distinction, and a good deal nearer than I deserve." He valued *Ashenden*, Chandler said, because "there are no other great spy stories—none at all. I have been searching and I know. It's a strange thing. The form does not appear so very difficult. Evidently it's impossible. There are a few tales of adventure with a spying element or something of the sort, but they always overplay their hand. Too much bravura, the tenor sings too loud. They are as much like Ashenden as the opera Carmen is like the deadly little tale that Mérimée wrote."[127]

Chandler sent Maugham some articles on the detective story, and formed an opinion of him, which he confided to Hamish Hamilton: "I have a feeling that fundamentally he is a pretty sad man, pretty lonely. His description of his seventieth birthday [in *A Writer's Notebook*] is

547

pretty grim. I should guess that his declared attitude of not caring much emotionally about people is a defense mechanism, that he lacks the kind of surface warmth that attracts people, and at the same time is such a wise man that he knows however superficial and accidental most friendships are, life is a pretty gloomy affair without them . . . he's a lonely old eagle." Maugham's own essay concluded: "I do not see who can succeed Raymond Chandler."[128]

Maugham learned that the $25,000 he had placed in trust for Robin had under Bert Alanson's judicious handling grown to $75,000. He wrote Alanson:

> There seems to be no reason why I should provide him with an income so much larger than he expects. He has been a grave disappointment both to his father and to me. He is now getting on for forty and is as frivolous and scatterbrained as he was as a boy. He has never grown up. He mixes with very disreputable people and throws his money about in the most reckless fashion. He has tried all sorts of ways of making a living, writing, farming, and hasn't made a success of any of them. Now he is writing scripts for a second-rate movie company, but how long that will last heaven only knows. He drinks a great deal too much. I don't suppose he will ever marry now. . . . What I suggest in view of all this is that the sum settled should be a straight $50,000, which is double the amount he expects, and that the balance should go into the trust for Liza and the children.[129]

In November, S. N. Behrman forwarded to Maugham a letter he had received from Mark Goulden, the publisher of W. H. Allen: "Some little while back, I discussed with Edmund Wilson the possibilities of a full-length biography of William Somerset Maugham, which might be ready by the time Maugham retired from active writing. Mr. Wilson suggested that you might be willing to undertake the task . . . it just occurred to me that a joint effort by yourself (on the man) and Wilson (on the writer) might result in a worthwhile book." Behrman made this handwritten addition: "I am planning a tremendous chapter: The Most Important Thing About W. Somerset Maugham—it will be about your cook."[130] "There is no race in the world as stupid as publishers," Maugham replied to Behrman. "Here is a man who has been slating me for years and they pick him to collaborate on a book about me."[131]

Later that November, Maugham visited Canon F. J. Shirley, the headmaster of the King's School. He confided to Shirley, who had become a friend over the years, that he was unhappy because he was almost eighty and had received no honors from the British government. With all the intensity of which he was capable, he wanted the O.M. (Order of Merit). "I think I ought to have the O.M.," he told Shirley. "I don't want anything else—I would refuse anything like a knighthood. But they gave Hardy the O.M., and I think I am the greatest writer of English, and they ought to give it to me."[132] The O.M. was one of the few honors whose recipients were personally selected by the monarch. But it was one of the traditions of the British Crown, dedicated as it was to producing an heir, to be horrified by homosexuality. As King George V had said, "I thought men like that shot themselves." The announcement of the list for the O.M. came from Buckingham Palace, and the number of living members was limited to twenty-four, chosen from a wide range of fields. There were not many writers. Maugham never got the O.M., although lesser writers than he won the award. Galsworthy got it, and J. B. Priestley got it in October 1977, at the age of eighty-three. E. M. Forster won it in 1969, even though he was a homosexual, but that was two years after homosexuality had been decriminalized in England.

Maugham had a secret to tell Shirley: he wanted his ashes buried somewhere within the precincts of the school. Shirley suggested that they look for a spot, and they ambled off, rather like the Walrus and the Carpenter, Shirley thought, past the infirmary ruins. Arriving near Forrens Gate, Maugham stopped and asked, "How much did you say that boathouse would cost?" This was an urgently needed boathouse for the Eights so that the school could develop a rowing team. "Four thousand pounds," Shirley said. "Ah, that is a lot of money," Maugham said. "I couldn't afford four thousand, but I think I could find three thousand." "Right," Shirley said, "it shall be done for three thousand." It was as if Maugham were offering the gift as the price for his burial plot. They resumed their stroll, entering the early Norman memorial chapel. Shirley thought this would be the perfect place, an oasis of peace in the midst of the school's bustle, but Maugham looked at the gray walls and said, "Hmm, a bit grim, isn't it?" The next step was to obtain the consent of the Canterbury Cathedral authorities, which took longer than expected, perhaps because of Maugham's proclaimed agnosticism. The delay dejected him, and he wrote Shirley that "it didn't matter a damn where one was buried; and so, if it is convenient and the Chapter agree let me be buried where you say, and if not my ashes can be put in the Cemetery at St. Jean among the bones of the inhabitants of the village." Consent was not long in coming, however, and the matter of Maugham's burial place was settled.[133]

After a year overshadowed by illness Maugham wanted a change of scene and decided to take Alan on a tour of Greece and Turkey in the spring. Alan needed a holiday. He had a skin infection and had to take eight agonizing injections all at once, and was blistered from head to foot in order for a serum to be obtained. In addition, his sinuses had been washed out twice. Living with Maugham was a great nervous strain because he was insulted almost daily by the people he had to keep at bay. He behaved like a disagreeable old spinster, and people gave him hell, and even though he enjoyed the reflected glory, it left him exhausted. Then there was the family, whose visits he dreaded and resented. They were coming at Easter, and had not come the year before, he said, only because they had something better to do.[134]

Just before their departure Maugham received the first of Ian Fleming's James Bond books, *Casino Royale*, and wrote Fleming on April 15: "I started it last night in bed and at half-past one, when I was about halfway through, I said to myself: I really must get to sleep; though what I really wanted to do was to read on till the end. I finished it an hour ago. It goes with a swing from the first page to the last and is really thrilling all through. I particularly enjoyed the battle at the casino between your hero and M. Chiffre. You really managed to get the tension to the highest possible pitch."

Fleming wrote back to express his gratitude that a man of seventy-nine should take so much trouble and asked if he could quote from the letter. He also asked whether Alan Searle, who was considered an expert in such matters (he ordered pornographic material from a company called Quaintance in Phoenix, Arizona), "could send me an introduction to the people in New York who will get me into the *cinéma bleu*. It is part of the plot of my next book but only he holds the platinum key."[135]

Fleming's letter reached Maugham in Istanbul and he replied: "No, please don't use what I said about your book to advertise it. Not that I didn't mean what I said, but that I am asked all the time to write something that can be used in such a way to help some book or other and have always refused. It is obviously difficult to do that kind of thing for one person and not for another. I would not do it even for the author of the book of Genesis." Alan would, however, gain him entree to blue movies, but warned that it would have a bad effect on his morals.[136]

Maugham thought he was unknown in Turkey, but a police officer came on board their ship when it landed and said he had instructions from the chief of police to look after him. The policeman followed him everywhere, like a bodyguard. It turned out that many of his books had been pirated by the Turks, who did not subscribe to copyright laws. He was pursued by the Turkish press and said, "If hell is gratifying, this is." Alan thought Istanbul was dirty and boring, and that the few things worth seeing were in poor condition. The police escort followed him as well as Willie, which cramped his style. In Athens the king and queen asked him to lunch. Maugham took it as a compliment that they had thought of asking a number of literary persons but had decided they would rather have him all to themeslves. The king sent a car for the hour's drive out of Athens, and Maugham's arm got tired from answering the police salutes to the royal vehicle.[137]

Home in June, Maugham was invited by Churchill to have lunch at the Hotel de Paris in Monte Carlo. When he arrived with Alan, Churchill said, "I have ordered a delectable luncheon." They ate in silence. In the middle of the meal Churchill said, "I have ordered this meal for your delectation." At the end of the meal he said, "I hope you enjoyed this delectable lunch." As they left, Maugham told Alan, "I didn't enjoy it at all."[138]

When *Collier's* offered $2,000 for a two thousand-word article on having lunch with Churchill, Maugham replied with a two-word telegram: "NOTHING DOING." His attitude toward money was still paradoxical. He could turn down large sums on one hand and argue over small sums on the other. He rejected an offer from Harrap, the dictionary publishers, who wanted to use one of his stories in a reference work. "I should have thought that if they do not want a story of mine enough to pay fifteen guineas for it, they had better get a story by somebody else," he wrote his agent.[139]

In September, after the usual gregarious summer, Maugham went to Rapallo to see Max Beerbohm. Along with Bernard Berenson, who lived outside Florence, they were known as the three sages. Beerbohm said that people came to see him on the way from Berenson's to Maugham's or vice versa. He had retired to Rapallo in 1910 to enjoy a premature immortality and was now eighty-one. The less he wrote the more of a cult figure he became. He had been awarded a knighthood in 1939, even though he had once written that it was something you could buy for forty shillings. "My dear," he told Cecil Roberts, "I had two good reasons, one false and one real. I felt I might contribute some respectability to it, and as a discreet snob, give and derive pleasure." In September 1953 he was back from a Catholic rest home to which he had gone to escape the summer heat. His Villino Chiaro was two miles outside Rapallo, a cube-shaped, whitewashed villa with six rooms, a white terrace, and a backdrop of sloping hills covered with olive trees and cypresses. Max, wrinkled and diminutive, had pink cheeks and china-blue eyes. His wife, Florence, had died, and he was taken care of by Miss Elizabeth Jungman.

Another visitor was a young American writer and traveler named Wilmon Menard, who had been inspired by Maugham's stories to go to the South Seas. Maugham, sitting in the drawing room sipping a martini, reminded Menard of a mummy, disinterred after long entombment and placed into position for ancestral worship. He thought he would be perfect for the part of the Grand Lama in James Hilton's *Lost Horizon*. Maugham enjoyed reminiscing about his travels with someone who had retraced his steps, and he and Menard became friends. He approved, he said, of the Tahitian women's honest attitude toward sex. "They give themselves in venery as they might casually bestow a smile or a wreath of flowers," he said. "Quite commendable, really." It was this same sort of sexual candor that he had liked in Sue Jones, even though he had suffered from it.[140]

In October, Maugham went to London on his annual visit. His brother, aged eighty-six, had suffered a stroke and was confined to the ground floor of his house. His favorite niece, Kate Bruce, had lost her husband, Robert, a broker who had collected jade and porcelain. Maugham himself was not in the best of health: he needed a bit of patching up, having broken a toe in Corinth while, in Alan's words, he had been doing a Nijinsky, leaping from rock to rock. Also, his right hand hurt so much he could not write. When he had to sign his name a thousand times for a limited edition of *Cakes and Ale*, illustrated by Graham Sutherland, he was in terrible pain. He went to an osteopath, who fixed his toe and told him that the pain in his hand came from wastage of the muscle due to wear and tear. His body was rebelling against the demands of his profession. The osteopath told him to stop writing for three months and made him an elastic corset to wear on his hand.[141] From the Dorchester, Alan wrote Jerry Zipkin that he had scattered his heart all over Europe, and there was hardly anything left for England.[142] In December they went back to the Mauresque and spent Christmas with a lonely American soldier, recruited by Alan, as their only guest.[143]

PART VII

1954-1965

Chapter Eighteen

His outstanding merit was not the realism that gave vigour to his work, nor the beauty that transformed it, nor his graphic portraits . . . nor his poetic descriptions . . . it was his longevity. . . . But why writers should be more esteemed the older they grow, has long perplexed me. . . . When he was a young fellow in the sixties . . . his position in the world of letters was only respectable . . . He celebrated his seventieth birthday; . . . it grew evident that there had lived among us all these years a great novelist . . . At eighty he was the Grand Old Man of English Letters. This position he held till his death.

Maugham, *Cakes and Ale*

IN JANUARY 1954 Maugham's English agent, Alexander Watt & Company, sent him some eighty-year-old brandy. The wine merchant who had sold it to Watt, Anthony Berry, guaranteed that it was genuine and unrefreshed. It had worn well, as had its recipient. Maugham would be eighty on January 25. In the eleven years he still had to live he would publish two books, one of essays and one on his art collection. But in his old age he was granted the kind of veneration that is usually associated with Oriental societies. Maugham growing old was an international spectacle. No one since Dorian Gray had called so much attention to the aging process.

The media were largely responsible, recording his every activity in items such as "Maugham Ordered to Rest" and "Maugham Returns to Riviera." He was a historical curiosity, a man who had started writing in the nineteenth century and was still at it. Where so many others had fallen, he had lasted. He was a symbol of durability. Over the years he had achieved phenomenal success. According to Doubleday, four and a half million of his books had been sold in the United States. *The*

Razor's Edge alone had sold 1,367,283 copies. He had earned four million dollars with his pen. He had done it slowly, laboriously, where others had been brilliant and precocious. He had become a writer because, in the words of Ecclesiastes, "the eye is not satisfied with seeing, nor the ear filled with hearing." Something in him needed to transform experience, his and that of others, into stories. When success came, tenacity had as much to do with it as talent. He had weathered rejection slips, poor sales, and bad reviews. He had kept going with a singleness of purpose that few could match. For the most part, he had written honest books about what he knew. The motivations of his characters were grounded in psychological observation. Recurring themes in his work were a way of externalizing personal conflict. The suffering of his childhood and the death of his mother remained always with him, setting him apart from others. Maugham was not like those who, in the words of Dr. Johnson, feeling great pain, hope for ease from a change of posture. He knew there was no ease, and he was prepared to live with that knowledge. He had no certainty about his position in English literature, but he knew that he had millions of readers. The nature of his work was so well known that people spoke of a "Maugham situation." With gifts carefully tended, hard work, determination, and old age, he had reached a position of unusual eminence. Ten years earlier, in 1944, the magazine *Time* & *Tide* had invited its readers to cast votes for a British version of the Académie Française, with forty members to be chosen from among the nation's most eminent men of letters. Leading the list was G. M. Trevelyan with 80 votes, followed by George Bernard Shaw with 60 votes, and H. G. Wells and E. M. Forster with 52 votes each. Maugham and John Masefield came next, with 47 votes each.

Maugham celebrated his eightieth birthday in London, arriving on January 22. *Punch* printed a poem about him and *London Calling* put him on the cover. He cheerfully submitted to interviews. The press now looked upon him as an oracle, and he was happy to oblige. Expounding on the changed relations between the sexes, he said: "When I was a boy, you were expected to protect young girls. For instance, if you were playing lawn tennis, you would be considered a cad if you didn't lob her a high ball so she could return it easily. That made for curious relations between the sexes." A photographer asked him if he wanted the lines in his face retouched. "Certainly not," he said, "it's taken me 80 years to get those lines. Why should I allow you to remove them in two minutes?"[1] There were so many flowers in his room at the Dorchester that he remarked that Greta Garbo in her prime could have done no better. Alan grumbled, faced with the task of answering twelve hundred letters and telegrams of congratulation. *The New York Times* headline on the occasion said: "Somerset Maugham, Britain's master storyteller, began his 80th birthday with half an hour of bridge." An anonymous correspondent sent him an insurance actuarial table showing that a man his age had five years and nine months left to live.

The Garrick Club gave a birthday dinner for him. Only three other writers had been thus honored—Dickens, Thackeray, and Trollope. St. John Ervine, the playwright and theater critic, introduced Maugham, and thought that he gave a superb speech, "full of wit, humor, well-turned phrases, and surprisingly to some people but not to me, full of feeling."

Maugham had learned his speech by heart, and everything went well until he came to a passage in which he said: "I have reached the stage where I have absorbed all the philosophy I am capable of absorbing and have told all the stories I am able to tell. And I know that anything I may yet have to learn about life will be learned, not from the dusty highways and byways which I frequented in my youth, but from a comparatively secure and certainly more comfortable refuge . . . the v—" He stalled at the *v*, and the distinguished assembly sat in silence, staring hypnotized at his lower lip, which desperately sought to make the link with his upper teeth. Instead of giving up in confusion, Maugham stood perfectly still, though his fingers were trembling. After a few moments he said, "I'm just thinking of what I shall say next." Then he lapsed into silence again as ashes dropped from poised cigars and smoke drifted round the ancient pictures. "I'm sorry to keep you waiting," Maugham said, and became silent once more. Then suddenly lip and teeth connected and he came out with it: "the veranda of a luxury hotel." He finished the speech in style, remaining imperturbable throughout the ordeal, and presenting the dinner guests with a remarkable display of moral courage and self-control. When the dinner was over, instead of going home to bed, he skipped upstairs to the cardroom and played bridge until 1 A.M., when he was told to behave like an octogenarian and go home.[2]

On the day after his birthday he attended an exhibition of his manuscripts and first editions at *The Times* bookshop. His brother, Lord Maugham, was there, recovered from his stroke, and so were Liza and John Hope. Maugham arrived shortly after six, checked his hat, and was polite to the overdressed women who grimaced at him. To a young Heinemann author, T. S. Strachan, he seemed younger than his years, with brown eyes that moved like a lizard's. Alan introduced Strachan to Maugham, whose handshake was slightly damp; he said, in a tone that mixed complaint with boast, that he had gone to twenty-seven engagements in the previous three days.

"Mr. Strachan has had a novel published by Heinemann," Alan said. "Is it your first book?" Maugham asked. "My second, actually," Strachan said.

"I've been with them fifty years," Maugham said. "My advice is to find a publisher who's willing to stick to you, and stick to him."[3]

The only discordant note was a letter from one Andrew R. Witham, published in the *Evening Standard* on January 27, which said: "Somerset Maugham has made a fortune out of being a professional cynic. Nobody has been more cruel to old age than he. His savage onslaught on that really grand old man of literature, Thomas Hardy, is not easily forgotten. Yet, Maugham seems to revel in the adulation paid to him just because he is old, though when younger he satirized without mercy this lauding of the ancients."[4]

To celebrate the occasion, and as a surprise for Maugham, Heinemann commissioned the English writer Jocelyn Brooke to put together a *Festschrift*. Brooke asked some thirty British and American writers to contribute. Their replies, some evasive, some direct, give an idea of how ungrateful some of Maugham's writer friends were, and, more generally, how some of his contemporaries felt about him.

Compton Mackenzie, to whose symposium on music Maugham had cheerfully contributed in the thirties, pleaded overcommitment. So did Noel Coward, whose career Maugham had pushed by praising him and writing a preface for the American edition of *Bitter Sweet and Other Plays*. William Plomer, who had sent Maugham several of his books and received encouraging letters in reply, and who had in a review of the short-story collection *Ah King* written that Maugham's stories "are among the best now being written," said: "I'm not a great fan of his and I don't know his work well." Evelyn Waugh, who had been a guest at the Mauresque, replied with a printed card that said: "Mr. Evelyn Waugh greatly regrets that he cannot do what you so kindly suggest." Rosamond Lehmann, whose novel *A Dusty Answer* Maugham had admired, and who had been a guest at the Mauresque, where Maugham offered advice about her unhappy love affair with the poet C. Day Lewis, said: "I quite see that you do not want what you call *éloges* but I should not feel free to write critically about him under these circumstances." Vita Sackville-West, the wife of Harold Nicolson, a frequent guest at the Mauresque, said: "I don't think I had better do so, partly because I could not make it sufficiently enthusiastic for a birthday tribute, and partly because I have the reverse of admiration for his personal character. This of course is just between you and me." Peter Quennell, whom Maugham saw on the Riviera and thought of as a friend, pleaded overcommitment. The oldest friend of all, his Mediterranean neighbor Max Beerbohm, did not reply to Brooke's request.

Among those writers who were not personal friends, Elizabeth Bowen and George Painter said they were too busy. George Jean Nathan said his doctor had ordered him to forgo work. V. S. Pritchett said he had already written too much about Maugham and would only be repeating himself. Rose Macaulay said she was just off to Cyprus, adding: "I could only say that he writes extremely good stories and often very vividly, but has no style." Angus Wilson said: "I have much reverence for some of Somerset Maugham's work and for much none; but I don't think I'm at all the person to write about it." Joyce Cary said: "The trouble is that I have read almost nothing of Maugham, and haven't time to start now. From what I have read I couldn't place him at all, and shouldn't try."

The only two positive replies came from Raymond Mortimer, a friend and admirer of Maugham's, and Anthony Powell, who had written two long unsigned reviews of his books in *The Times Literary Supplement*. Mortimer promised two thousand words, "a *réchauffé* of what I have already said in reviews. But then I don't myself think that there is a great variety of things to say about Maugham. . . . A devastating paper could be written on the limitations of his taste, as revealed in an anthology he made including verse. His mind is prosaic in the extreme, though he believes that he responds to poetry. I am the last person, however, to emphasize such deficiencies—*glissez, n'appuyez pas* must be my rule, for he is a very old friend whom I regard with grateful affection."[5] Powell was apparently the only writer to finish his essay, telling Brooke that "with inconceivable agony I have managed to grind out about 3,500 words on Maugham which I enclose. If you think it unsuitable, don't hesitate to send it back. . . . I sincerely hope this is the last time I shall have to write about him."

There were so many refusals, however, that the project was scrapped. Perhaps Maugham's friends were afraid to praise him because they felt he was unpopular with critics and they might be contaminated by association. Or perhaps they felt that they could not speak honestly about him in the form of a birthday tribute. Brooke had to write the

559

people who had consented to contribute or had not yet replied. Accordingly he wrote Max Beerbohm, and received the following letter on August 2: "I would have greatly liked to pay some sort of little tribute to the great Willie Maugham, and I am so sorry your good idea has had to be abandoned."[6]

Exhausted by the celebration, and suffering from rheumatoid arthritis, Maugham returned to the Mauresque. In February his brother forwarded a letter addressed to Viscount Somerset Maugham. Upon opening it he had found that it was intended for Willie. "I know what it is going to be," Maugham wrote back. "Shakespeare and Bacon all over again. Posterity will say that as an eminent lawyer and Lord Chancellor it was impossible for you to acknowledge that you had written plays and novels under your own name, so they were produced and published under the insignificant name of your younger brother."[7]

When Lord Maugham received his younger brother's letter, he said to Robin: "I detect a distinctively unpleasant flavor about Willie's remarks. I think I shall feel obliged to make some suitable reply." He wrote: "Dear Willie, you may well be right in thinking that you write like Shakespeare. Certainly I have noticed during these last few months an adulation of your name in the more vulgar portions of the popular press. But one word of brotherly advice. Do not attempt the sonnets."[8]

In April, Ian Fleming came to stay, this time on business and without his wife. Maugham had written Anne Fleming that his book on the ten greatest novels was being published in England, revised and with a new title, *Ten Novels and Their Authors*. Fleming, who wrote the "Atticus" column for the *Sunday Times*, came to the Mauresque to request the book's serialization in his newspaper. When he arrived, Maugham told him he had been invited not to discuss serialization but to give him a brief vacation at Lord Kemsley's expense. "I have never been published in a newspaper," Maugham said, which was untrue, for he had in his youth written book reviews and sketches. "When I began I would have given anything to earn a guinea or two from the *Morning Post*. But they always turned me down. Now I don't care. I have been offered a pound a word to write for serialization in America. I have refused. As it is, I am only a glorified civil servant. With 95 per cent of my energies I work to bring in money for three governments—English, French, and American. What you would pay me would be of small concern."

"We could buy you a Renoir," Fleming said, "a small one."

"I don't want a Renoir. Anyhow it would be illegal. . . . Why should your readers of the *Sunday Times* be interested in what I have to say? Anyway, your people would hack the material about."

"We wouldn't touch a word."

They went in to lunch, and Fleming flew back the next day with a box of avocados and permission to serialize. Maugham was paid 3,000 pounds. The serial started in June and was originally scheduled to run from four to six weeks. It was heavily promoted, and circulation rose 50,000. Maugham allowed it to be extended to fifteen weeks without additional pay.[9]

He was not always so openhanded. In 1953 his friend and neighbor the Aga Khan, who had given him letters of introduction to maharajahs on his trip to India, asked Maugham for a preface to the memoirs he had just written. Maugham reluctantly obliged with several inconsequential pages, which he did not think of as the return of a favor but as a commercial transaction. On anything that touched payment for his work he was inflexible. He did not stop to think that he was being petty and graceless but wrote Watt:

> It would have been more tactful on his [the Aga's] part to show his appreciation by giving me some cuff links or pearl studs or a cigarette case, but if it is a commercial transaction, I think he should pay the proper price. I have for many years been paid a dollar a word by American magazines, and once was offered two dollars a word. The preface took me a fortnight to do and was not an easy job. If I had been commissioned to do it I would not have dreamt of undertaking it for less than $2500. I leave you to make the best arrangement you can, but I expect you to refuse quite firmly an insignificant amount.[10]

When the principle of payment by the word was not involved, however, he was often generous. The same month that he insisted on charging for his preface, he promised the Yale librarian, Donald G. Wing, one of his manuscripts, by now worth thousands of dollars, and donated the manuscript of *On a Chinese Screen*.[11]

In May he went to Venice, and then to Abano, for the rheumatism cure. Kate Bruce had asked for Annette's recipe for avocado dressing, and he replied that "Annette serves ordinary French dressing with the avocado pears—oil and vinegar, salt, pepper, and a little mustard, but what makes it different is that she adds a little chopped herb which she gathers on my hill." The principal herb, he added, was tarragon, "but avocados are horribly expensive in London; I am sure your father would say: no fortune can stand it."[12]

He heard from Robin, who said he was revising a novel in the light of his uncle's criticism. He thought it was the best thing he had done, although, he added, that was not saying much.[13] With his uncle, Robin was self-deprecating about his work. The yardstick of his literary worth was Maugham's opinion. When his novel *The Wrong People* was turned down by ten American publishers, he wrote his agent that Maugham thought it was far and away the best novel he had ever written, as though this should be sufficient to guarantee publication. When another novel, *November Reef*, was turned down, he wrote his editor at Harper, Elizabeth F. Lawrence, that Maugham had told him it was fresh and stirring.[14] Robin modeled himself on his uncle. Like him, he had a male secretary. Like him, he hoped to have three short stories made into a movie. He published in magazines in which his uncle had published, such as *Britannica and Eve*.

The cure at Abano was a success. Maugham's rheumatism was better and Alan was slim as a sapling. Back at the Mauresque early in June, Maugham found a letter from Churchill telling him he would be named a Companion of Honour in the queen's birthday honors list. Companion of Honour was an order of recent foundation, which carried no title, ranked below knighthood, and was usually given to retired generals. The honors list was announced on June 9. Maugham and Edith Sitwell were on it, along with 2,499 others, most of whom received very minor honors. The queen's secretary wrote to ask if Maugham could come to London to receive his medal. "My convenience," he replied, "is any date which suits the convenience of Her Majesty."[15] He was very proud of the honor, even though it had come late in life and was a distant second to the Order of Merit. He told friends that Companion of Honour was a very select group (it was limited to sixty-five) and that the queen had expressed the desire to give it to him privately.

In London, later that June, he went to Buckingham Palace in morning clothes and a top hat rented from Moss Bros. His appointment was at 11.45 and he had been asked to be there at 11.40. He was led through long corridors from room to room and finally a door opened and an attendant said: "Mr. Somerset Maugham, Your Majesty." He bowed and advanced and the queen shook hands with him and handed him a small leather case stamped *C.H.* Inside there was an oval gold medal attached to a red ribbon, with an inscription in blue enamel that said "Faithful in Action with Honour Clear."

Maugham thought the queen was extremely pretty, with fine eyes and skin and a charming, slight figure. She asked him to sit down, and they chatted for a quarter of an hour, after which she said, "It's been very nice to see you, Mr. Maugham." He got up and she got up, and they shook hands again, and he bowed and stepped backward, then turned to reach the door and walked out.[16] For Maugham, so great an admirer of title and position, this was one of the high points of a long career. After the ceremony he went to his niece Kate's house to show her the decoration.

The honor brought in another harvest of congratulatory letters, which Alan answered at the rate of fifty a day. He complained to Edith Sitwell that he had a permanent nasty taste in his mouth from the horrid stuff they put on the back of French postage stamps. Maugham was peeved, Alan joked, because Edith had not shared and shared alike, and nothing could convince him that he could not call himself Dame Willie.[17]

One of the letters was from Lord Beaverbrook, the Canadian-born son of a Presbyterian pastor, who had become a press lord, a lord of the realm, and a power in England. Beaverbrook, who had a villa on Cap d'Ail, would become a close friend of Maugham's in his twilight years. He wrote Maugham: "Allow me to congratulate you on the honor you have received, and I make bold to say, none more richly deserved. You add much distinction to the illustrious company whom you join."[18]

The honor put Maugham in a cheerful frame of mind. Noel Coward, who visited in July, reported that he was "merry as a grig and mellow and sweet. I would like to be certain that I shall be as entertaining and cheerful when I am rising eighty-one."[19]

When Maugham trampled the ants in the garden and reminded Alan to send for the ant man, Noel said, "Perhaps I shouldn't mention this, Willie, but there are ants in the bathroom." "Guests aren't supposed to use the bathroom," Maugham said.[20]

Cecil Roberts came to lunch and gave Maugham a copy of his latest book, *The Remarkable Young Man*, saying that he was under no compulsion to read it. "I shall read every word of it, and be consoled by all your faults," Maugham said. Roberts said he had another book coming out, which he had finished in eight weeks. "You should never tell anyone you've written a book in eight weeks," Maugham said. "People are absurd. They'll think it's no good. If you say you have taken four years, they're impressed. Well, anyone who takes four years over a book just can't write, he gets coagulated. How many hours a day do you work?" "When the tide's flowing, twelve," Roberts said. "Good God," Maugham exclaimed, "no wonder you've an ulcer. Four finishes me." He said he was still writing. "I'm a word addict and I can't shake it off."[21] He was working on a preface to a translation of the letters of Madame de Sévigné by Violet Hammersley, his childhood friend who had, like him, been born in the British Embassy in Paris in the 1870s, and with whom he had grown up in the gardens of the Champs Elysées. He did not charge her for it.

In August, Liza and John came with Liza's children by Vincent Paravicini. Nicholas at sixteen was six feet two and towered over his grandfather. Camilla promised to be a great beauty, and Maugham saw that the day was not far off when he would become a great-grandfather. He hoped that Liza would have no more children, and wrote Alanson, in the tone of the disillusioned ancient who prefers the past to the present: "I don't know why anyone should want to bring children into the world of today. Every day I congratulate myself that I was born getting on for eighty years ago and had on the whole a pretty good time; anyhow better than anyone seems to have now."[22]

It was during this visit that Maugham's feelings toward his daughter, and particularly toward his son-in-law, underwent a bizarre transformation. In order to bypass death duties he had turned the Mauresque into a corporation called the Société Civile Villa Mauresque and had put the shares in Liza's name. The papers were signed in 1954. Having done this, he began to worry that the Mauresque was no longer his and resented Liza and John for what he had given them. He felt like a guest in his own home. His annoyance focused on John, who soon noticed his father-in-law's puzzling moods. There were periods when he lapsed into complete silence and would stare hard at John with a disconcerting expression on his face. Then he would get up and go out. On one occasion John had some friends in the area and he asked if it would be all right if they came to play tennis. In order not to antagonize Maugham, he did not ask them in for drinks afterward. But Maugham complained that John was walking around as if he owned the place. As John recalled: "He was unable to bear the thought that I could have anything to do with the villa." Suddenly, in Maugham's eyes, nothing Hope could do was right. He called him "John Hopeless," complained that he was grasping, and once said, of a man with whom only a short time ago he had been on the best of terms: "He would pick a brass farthing out of a dog's turd." Liza tried to patch things up, and found her father obsessed with the idea that if she died, John would seize the house and turn him out. "Would you like a letter from him?" Liza asked. John wrote the letter, but it did not help. Maugham got more and more worked up. After 1954 he refused to repair the Mauresque, saying it was no longer his. When the roof leaked, he would not fix it. Things got so bad that for a period of several years John no longer came to the Mauresque; Liza went alone or with her children.[23]

Maugham even turned against his grandchildren. One evening Nicholas arrived at the dinner table without a dinner jacket. "I'll bet he has one when he goes to Hopetoun" (the Linlithgow estate in Scotland), Maugham said. It was in Maugham's nature to write people off, even those closest to him, for trivial offenses. Six years later, when Nick was twenty-two, Liza brought him to a dinner party for Maugham in London to fill in as an extra man. Nick, incapable of suspecting such depths of vindictiveness, went up to Maugham and said, "Hello, grandpa, it's nice to see you." Ignoring him, Maugham turned away and asked, "Who is that young man?"[24]

Alan was also upset that the Mauresque had been turned over to Liza. He worried constantly about what Maugham was leaving him and saw the family as a dangerous rival. He feared that when they had taken their share, there would be nothing left for him. Liza already had the royalties and the pictures, and now she had the Mauresque. He continued, however, to profess warm friendship for Liza. When she arrived he said, "I'm so glad you're here, dear, give me a little squeeze." He made a fuss over the children. Privately, he hated the family's visits. He felt that he was Maugham's real family, the one who bore the brunt of his moods, the one who was always present, in sickness and in health. Liza and John, he said, were only after one thing. They could never match his devotion.[25]

To protect his interests from the family Alan schemed to turn Maugham against them, passing on bits of malicious gossip to fuel his pique. Just as he had falsely told Maugham that Evelyn Waugh had spent the night in Diana Cooper's room, he now alleged that John and Liza were going around the Mauresque taking inventory. He also told Maugham that John and Liza disliked him (Alan) and would be happy to see him destitute. One night Maugham took Liza aside and said, "I hope you notice how good Alan is with the children. And yet I understand that at my death you plan to kick him out without a penny." Liza assured him that this was not so, and John told Alan, "Liza and I will see you through." When Liza left at the end of August, Alan's eyes filled with tears and he said, "You're one of my dearest friends, without you I don't know what I'd do."[26]

In September, Maugham went to Spain, and wrote Alanson that "the

Spanish are the only people left in Europe who are polite." From Spain he proceeded to England for his annual end-of-the-year trip. He complained about London prices, which had gone far beyond the reach of mortal man. The restaurants on Curzon Street had become "obscenely expensive." And yet when he went to see Alexander Frere, whom he considered "by way of being the best publisher we have in this country," he was told that the money was rolling in, with so many of his books in print, and he bought some pictures to add to his collection.[27]

In London, Maugham picked up Christopher Isherwood's new book, *The World in the Evening*, but the young man he had once considered the hope of the English novel, who had remained in California after the war to work as a screenwriter and pursue his interest in Buddhism, badly disappointed him. "Perhaps I shouldn't have felt so let down," he wrote a friend, "if I had not so greatly admired and cherished the Christopher of 20 years ago. What damage Gerald Heard did to our English literature when he induced . . . these talented writers to desert their native country for America."[28] Maugham did not stop to consider that if Heard and Isherwood had not come to America he would have been deprived of one of his best sources for material for *The Razor's Edge*.

Hearing that Robin was off to Africa, Maugham wrote to wish him bon voyage. "Don't let an angry sheik catch you in his harem and cruelly castrate you," he warned. "It would cramp your style."[29] He went to a *Daily Telegraph* party to hear the election returns. John Hope was reelected by 7,000 votes instead of the 5,000 in the previous election, but the Conservatives just scraped by.

November 30 was Churchill's eightieth birthday. He was ten months younger than Maugham. To honor the occasion, both houses of Parliament had commissioned a portrait by Graham Sutherland, who was now established as a portraitist of powerful men and women. After seeing Sutherland's Maugham, Lord Beaverbrook had asked him for a portrait in 1951. Now it was Churchill's turn. When his wife Clementine heard the news, she went to look at the portraits of Maugham and Beaverbrook. Horrified, she obtained photographs to show Churchill, saying: "Look at these. You had better say something to the committee before it's too late." Churchill looked at the photographs and said: "My God, it's the living image of Willie. And I must say, that certainly is Beaverbrook, the old scoundrel." "Yes," said his wife, "but it's his style, it's his way of looking at people that I draw your attention to, Winston." "Oh," said Churchill, "Sutherland will never see me that way."[30]

Sittings began in August, and the portrait was ready for the unveiling in Westminster Hall on November 30. Since Sutherland worked from sketches, Churchill was seeing the portrait for the first time. It showed him sitting in an armchair, with his hands clutching the ends of the armrests, his face pugnacious and warriorlike.

Churchill called it "a remarkable example of modern art," but his true feelings were otherwise.

"I don't like it," he told Maugham.

Maugham asked why.

"It doesn't make me look noble," Churchill said.

"How does it make you look?" Maugham asked.

"I look as if I was having a difficult stool," Churchill replied.[31]

At the unveiling Lord Railsham said, "It's disgusting, it's ill-mannered, it's terrible," and one critic called it "a study in lumbago." After the presentation the portrait vanished to the Churchill basement. Clementine promised her husband that it would never see the light of day. About eighteen months later she had it burned. News of the portrait's destruction was not disclosed until 1978. Sutherland called it "without question an act of vandalism."[32] When Maugham was asked what he thought of the Churchill portrait, he said, "Well, I didn't really like the one that Graham Sutherland did of me, but I think it was the very image of Churchill."[33]

In December, Maugham's American friends, Ruth Gordon and Garson Kanin, arrived in London. On Christmas day they took the Channel boat to France with Maugham and Alan. On the boat Ruth Gordon showed Maugham the money she had changed at the purser's office. Maugham turned to Alan and said, "Show them ours."

"Really?" Alan asked with surprise.

"Yes, do as I say," Maugham insisted.

Alan unlocked and opened an attaché case filled with neat stacks of hundred-dollar bills.

"Holy God," Kanin said.

"Is it safe to carry that much around?" Ruth Gordon asked.

"Certainly not," Maugham said. "It's most dangerous. There's over a hundred thousand dollars there. It might easily be lost or stolen. The train might be derailed, or the Channel boat might sink."

"Why do you do it, then?" Kanin asked.

"Because I was once trapped in the fall of France without sufficient currency in my possession, and vowed at that time that should I come through I would never again permit myself to be caught in a similar situation. Experience has taught me that American currency is usually the best coin. Had I had some at that time, I might have saved myself and my friends a good deal of difficulty and discomfort."[34]

And so the year ended with Maugham the dollar-a-word man clutching the attaché case full of hundred-dollar bills that were proof of his worth as a writer.

The next year was a quiet one, with Maugham still recovering from his eightieth-birthday celebration. Mabel and Bert Alanson came to the Mauresque in January for a small eighty-first birthday party. Maugham came down on the morning of the twenty-fifth to find the living room blazing with red carnations. He told Alanson how grateful he was for having tended his investments and made him a millionaire. He would never have been able to afford the Mauresque or his collection of pictures without him. Lady Bateman, the rich old lady who lived in Monte Carlo and never forgot his birthday, sent him a tablecloth. "How you spoil me!" Maugham wrote her. "You have got me into such extravagant ways by giving me over and over again the most beautiful things that I feel the only thing I can do is buy a Rolls Royce."[35]

The Alansons left on January 30. Alan wrote Bert that Maugham broke down in the car after saying goodbye and was so depressed in the following days that to cheer him up he filled the drawing room with carnations and said they came from the Alansons.[36]

In February, Maugham had his second opportunity in as many years to get acquainted with the queen, who, with the exception of his mother, was probably the only woman he ever admired without reservation. Gerald Kelly invited him to the annual Royal Academy dinner at Burlington House, which was to be attended by Her Majesty and the Duke of Edinburgh. The academy brought out its best silver and hung the only Michelangelo in England over the mantelpiece, flanked by two great Constables. Kelly wanted the queen to have an amusing dinner partner and asked her if he could put Maugham next to her. She said she would be too frightened. Apparently his reputation for caustic repartee had reached the palace. Kelly reassured her that he could, when he wanted to, be perfectly charming, and she agreed to take the risk. As she walked into dinner on Kelly's arm she said, "I thought Mr. Maugham lived in the south of France." Kelly replied that he did but had come to London in order to sit next to her. The queen blushed and said, "That is the prettiest compliment I have ever been paid."[37]

At the Mauresque life was less active, with fewer guests and dinner parties. At meals Maugham and Alan were often alone, and the conversation progressed in fits and starts. Alan escaped, whenever he could, to Villefranche, where the sailors were. He had a more or less steady boyfriend, an American marine he had known for two years. Alan's favorite reading was muscle magazines. Despite the opportunities, he never tried to improve himself. He lived on the Riviera but never learned to speak French. He was the companion of an excellent bridge player but never learned to play bridge. "He was a thoroughly common little man," one of his Riviera neighbors said. He did, however, take good care of Maugham, who wrote Alanson in April that he wanted to leave Alan $2,000 a year for life in addition to the other trust, into which he was paying $3,000 a year. "I want him after my death to be able to live quite comfortably," Maugham explained. "After all, he has given me many of the best years of his life."[38]

In May they went to Abano again, Maugham for his rheumatism and Alan for his lumbago, returning in June to learn that Syrie was ill. Maugham, who had seen as little of her as possible in the last twenty-eight years, although he kept up his alimony payments of 2,400 pounds a year, thought that was only natural, for she was seventy-six. On July 26 she died. Maugham had continued to detest her at a distance, and he wrote Barbara Back: "It would be hypocrisy on my part to pretend that I am deeply grieved at Syrie's death. She had me every which way from the beginning and never ceased to give me hell. Her hope, for some years, I have been told, was that she would survive me. I wonder, when she looked back, if she ever did, whether it occurred to her what a mess she had made of her life."[39]

No fair-minded person would agree that she had made a mess of her life. She had started out as "the first of the society shopkeepers" and had established herself over the years in the first rank of women decorators, the equal of Sybil Colefax, Ruby Ross Wood, and Mrs. Draper. With her all-white look, she had popularized a fashion that lasted ten years. She was famous for her all-white parties, at which she powdered her hair, stripped the leaves of lilacs and peonies so that they looked like wax flowers, and hired coal-black musicians to contrast with the whiteness of everything else. She appeared regularly in the pages of *Vogue* as an arbiter of fashion, as in this item: "Syrie Maugham's gifts are not only for decoration. She is a highly successful hostess and here are two of her favorite recipes: Pancake with Haddock; Burnt Cream."

Her circle of loyal friends included Rebecca West, Osbert Sitwell,

Lady Mendl, Beverley Nichols, Noel Coward, and Cecil Beaton. She lived a full, productive life. Also, she was a good mother, lavishing affection upon her daughter, who adored her. Liza had turned out well, married a lord, and given her four beautiful grandchildren. In her last years Syrie lived in a pleasant flat in fashionable Park Lane and continued to carry on her *métier* of decorator. She did not return Maugham's vindictiveness, took pride in his achievements, and never spoke badly of him. Godfrey Winn believed that "she went on loving him until she died. It was in her bloodstream."[40]

Her friends remembered Syrie with great fondness. Osbert Sitwell wrote in a letter to *The Times* on August 1:

> She possessed a remarkable personality and charm, both of which found expression in her voice, so characteristic in its inflexions and intonations. My mind goes back to the time many years ago when I first went to the hospitable house of Mrs. Maugham and her brilliant husband. They were always particularly kind to the young and gifted. There, in Wyndham Place, in the large beige-painted, barrel-vaulted drawing-room of this 18th-century mansion, their friends were privileged to meet all the most interesting figures connected with the world of art, literature, and the theatre in both England and America. In later years, the talent which Mrs. Maugham had always shown in the furnishing of her own home found a commercial outlet. She soon launched many fashions in interior decoration and was responsible for many schemes of adornment here and in the United States, where she was extremely well known.

Maugham could not have cared less. He had not seen her more than two or three times since their divorce.[41] He was pleased that he would no longer have to pay alimony. The coals of his resentment still smoldered. It was Syrie, he knew, who had spread the story of his homosexual liaison with Gerald Haxton through the drawing rooms of Mayfair, tearing the curtain of his respectability. When he had first met her he had been flattered by the thought that a seductive and fashionable woman wanted him. But he had never really liked her. As early as 1922, back from one of his Far Eastern excursions, he had made a note concerning a woman he called X, who can have been no one but Syrie:

> She is not only a liar, she is a mythomaniac who will invent malicious stories that have no foundation in fact and will tell them so convincingly, with such circumstantial detail, that you are almost persuaded she

believes them herself. She is grasping and will hesitate at no dishonesty to get what she wants. She is a snob and will impudently force her acquaintance on persons who she knows wish to avoid it. She is a climber, but with the paltriness of her mind is satisfied with the second rate; the secretaries of great men are her prey, not the great men themselves. She is vindictive, jealous and envious. She is a quarrelsome bully. She is vain, vulgar, and ostentatious. There is real badness in her. She is clever. She has charm. She has exquisite taste. She is generous and will spend her own money, to the last penny, as freely as she will spend other people's. She is hospitable and takes pleasure in the pleasure she gives her guests. Her emotion is easily aroused by a tale of love and she will go out of her way to relieve the distress of persons who mean nothing to her. In sickness she will show herself an admirable and devoted nurse. She is a gay and pleasant talker. Her greatest gift is her capacity for sympathy. She will listen to your troubles with genuine commiseration and with unfeigned kindliness will do everything she can to relieve them or to help you bear them. She will interest herself in all that concerns you, rejoice with you in your success and take part in the mortifications of your failure. There is a real goodness in her.[42]

In August, Maugham went to Salzburg for the music festival,[43] staying at the Hotel Winkler, but the weather was terrible, "and the place was made intolerable by strings of motor coaches full of American virgins in search of culture. One of them sat behind us at a performance of Mozart's Serenade, and through it all was scribbling away as hard as she could go. The girl next to her asked, 'What are you writing, Myrtle, a letter?' 'No,' said Myrtle, 'I'm writing my criticism of the score.' "[44]

Always fond of dispensing advice, Maugham wrote his niece Kate, after learning that her father had given his money to his children while still alive, to avoid inheritance taxes: "Spend your money on yourself my girl; let the other people fend for themselves."[45] Kate always knew how to get on her uncle's good side, a knack that her brother Robin had yet to acquire. Maugham was furious when he heard that Robin had tried to borrow money from Bert Alanson.

I hope you have not lent him any, or if you have will not lend him any more [he wrote Alanson]. He should never have asked you. He's not much good, you know. He has made a mess of pretty well everything he has tried to do, but remains convinced that he's a wonderful fellow. I don't see how he can fail to come to a sticky end and only hope that this will not happen till after his father's death. It is all a terrible pity;

he was a nice lad, with high spirits and great vivacity; he might have amounted to something if he hadn't been so self-satisfied and fond of the bottle.[46]

Home in August, Maugham learned of another death that affected him more than Syrie's, that of Mabel Alanson. He remembered meeting her for the first time with Bert, thinking that she was as beautiful a girl as he had ever seen, and wondering how on earth Bert had been clever enough to find her. He remembered a Christmas at the Mauresque when they went to the Château de Madrid for dinner and were the only ones there, and a fire was lit for them, and they all got tight.[47] The deaths of Syrie and Mabel Alanson, his contemporaries, were reminders of his own mortality.

The fall, as usual, was spent in London. Alan, as usual, had sundry ailments: lumbago, liver attacks, and bleeding piles. Maugham was besieged. "I have to walk warily," he said, "to maintain my freedom without giving offense." Alanson was still sending him food parcels, and Maugham pleaded with him to send no more, as everything was obtainable in London. The main topic of conversation was whether Princess Margaret would marry Group Captain Townsend. In November, Jerry Zipkin turned up, bubbling over with high spirits. On December 7 Gerald Kelly sold his art collection and library at Sotheby's in order to raise capital to buy the home on Gloucester Place in which he had lived for many years and from which he was now threatened with eviction. The manuscript of *The Moon and Sixpence* fetched 2,600 pounds, a record for a living author, and the buyer was Jerry Zipkin. The runner-up was Yale, and Maugham wished they had got it, for he liked to see his manuscripts in university libraries. (Zipkin's manuscript was eventually donated to the University of Texas.) Also in December, Maugham's least favorite niece, Honor Earl, visited San Francisco, and Alanson put her up. Maugham did not approve. "It is bad enough for my relations to exploit me," he wrote Alanson. "I don't at all approve of their exploiting my friends."[48] Alan told Alanson that Maugham was furious at Honor Earl foisting herself upon him. He detested her, he said, because she was pushy, and never saw her unless he couldn't help it.[49]

Maugham had patched up his quarrel with the Aga Khan, who, to thank him for the preface, invited him to Egypt. He and Alan sailed in January 1956 for Genoa and Alexandria, and he loaned the Mauresque to R. A. Butler, the Chancellor of the Exchequer, who was ex-

hausted after drawing up the budget. By January 15 they were sight-
seeing in Cairo, and on the twentieth they left for Aswan to join the
Aga Khan. Even here he was pursued by the press. He groused, but
it was flattering to have people make a fuss over him. The train trip to
Aswan was long and tiring, and the Aga Khan installed him in a suite
at the Cataract Hotel, with a terrace and a view of the Nile. They went
on a trip to the Sudan on the Aga's houseboat, and then to Luxor,
where Maugham caught bronchitis. The Aga Khan had his resident
doctor look after him. In February they were back in Cairo, where Alan
heard the welcome news that his trust fund had grown to $42,000.
Alan loved Egypt and said he had not been such a success since the age
of twelve. He found the Egyptians beautiful, and addicted to geron-
tophilism and every other kind of philism. He had, he said, become as
uninhibited as an American sailor. Maugham also enjoyed his stay but
complained about the food. The Egyptians, he said, had not learned
how to make toast.[50]

Sailing from Alexandria on February 11, they returned to the
Mauresque to find that a spring snowstorm had destroyed the garden.
Tree surgeons worked on 260 trees, cutting away the broken branches.
Maugham had not known he had so many. The central heating had
broken down, which was a serious problem since he was recovering
from bronchitis. The bronchitis resulted in a blockage of the passages
that led to the ears, and Maugham became partially deaf. He would not
become stone deaf, the specialist in Nice told him, but he would never
be able to hear as well as when he was twenty.[51]

Although no longer as productive as in his younger days, Maugham
was kept busy answering requests. Whenever he came home after a trip,
his IN basket was full. The Ceylon *Daily News* wanted twelve articles
for fifty pounds. A Japanese theatrical group wanted to put on *The
Sacred Flame* at ten dollars a performance (which led to correspondence stretching over a year on how twenty dollars should be paid in
view of taxes and currency restrictions). A Frenchman wanted to
translate *The Land of Promise* into Esperanto to demonstrate that "the
international language is perfectly suitable for literary works, both original and translated." Roland Petit wanted to direct a ballet based on
"Rain," starring Zizi Jeanmaire. Doubleday wanted to use "Lord
Mountdrago" in an anthology of good reading. The B.B.C. wanted to
print extracts from *The Moon and Sixpence* in their European bulletin.
Graham Greene wanted to include "The Hairless Mexican" in the *Spy's
Bedside Book*. Dr. Thomas Cross of the Neuropsychiatric Institute at

the University of Michigan wanted to include "Rain" in a textbook. Svenska Bokförlaget wanted to include "The Luncheon" in a Swedish school anthology. The *Ladies' Home Journal* wanted to pay five dollars for the use of one sentence from *The Summing Up*. There was no end to it.[52]

Almost as numerous were begging letters and letters from aspiring writers. Most of the former Maugham ignored, once out of curiosity adding up the sums asked for during one week; he found that the total came to nine thousand pounds.[53] The latter he always answered. He wrote Constance Maxon in Uniontown, Pennsylvania: "I don't know how to answer your question. I should have thought the only way to start a novel was to put down what you have to say. I think it is a mistake to be flowery and elaborate, and I suggest a fairly easy way of beginning is to write as though you were writing for a friend and telling him certain facts that you wanted him to know."[54]

Although he no longer wrote fiction, he was proud that his novels and short stories were still being read, whereas those of younger writers were forgotten. He wrote Félix Martí-Ibáñez in April 1956: "Today, so many of the younger novelists seem impelled to write about matters of temporary interest, and unfortunately, the critics are unanimous in praising them for this. What they don't realize is that in a year or two, their subjects, being no longer topical, their books will be unreadable. I think novelists do much better to leave science to the scientists, economics to the economists, and philosophy to the philosophers."[55]

In April the writer Ilka Chase, who was on the Riviera to do a magazine article on the forthcoming royal wedding of Prince Rainier of Monaco and Grace Kelly of Philadelphia, visited Maugham. It was tactless of him to be so spry at the age of eighty-two, she thought, as he sprinted up and down the stairs. There was a waspish satisfaction in his gaze as he watched guests huffing and puffing after him. His stammer was sometimes intense, but his conversation had the simple direct quality of his writing.[56]

Maugham, who had been invited to the wedding, asked Frere to send him his three-volume collected short stories in a leather binding to give as a present. "I think it competes very well with the Rolls Royce that the grateful people of Monte Carlo have given to the bride," he said. He insisted on paying for the books, for "there is no reason why the tottering firm of Heinemann should pay for a wedding present for the prince and his presumably chaste bride."[57]

The wedding was no fun. Maugham had to get into full evening dress at eight in the morning and sit for three hours in an icebox of a cathedral. But the lunch that followed at the palace was worth it, with tubs of caviar, mountains of foie gras, and oceans of champagne. Maugham the living legend almost upstaged the rulers of Monaco. One of the most widely reported bits of news was that his feet had been cold during the ceremony. One of the biggest pictures in the *Life* article was of him.[58]

In May, Maugham went to Paris for the five-hundredth performance of *Adorable Julia*, the adaptation of his novel *Theatre*. There was a party onstage afterward. With the royalties from this long-running comedy he bought a Rolls Royce. His chauffeur, Jean, was as pleased as he was, for it gave him prestige among his peers. In June, Maugham and Alan took the cure at Abano. The unlucky Alan had broken several ribs in a fall.

On their way back to the Mauresque they stopped outside Florence to visit Bernard Berenson, who, like Maugham, was a living legend and an object of pilgrimage. Also like Maugham, he had designed his life to shelter him from all chilling blasts. At ninety-two, he thought of himself as "a tolerated ghost in a society 'that knew not Joseph.'" He lived in I Tatti, the villa he had built, which he described as a library with living rooms attached, and thought of himself as the last true humanist of Western Europe.

Berenson was a Lithuanian Jew whose family had emigrated to Boston in 1875. He went to Harvard and returned to Europe at the age of twenty-two. His books on Italian painters established him, and he pursued a career in expertise, which led to a partnership with the London dealer Duveen. The value of an Italian painting came to depend on Berenson's seal of approval. With the proceeds of his expertise he built I Tatti, his home for the rest of his life. His reputation as a brilliant critic and conversationalist, added to the museumlike quality of his villa, made him a tourist attraction for the initiated. Those who came included Yehudi Menuhin, Walter Lippmann, Isaiah Berlin, Adlai Stevenson, Judge Learned Hand, Katherine Dunham, and now Maugham. Berenson, like Maugham, felt ambivalent about the constant stream of visitors. He wanted them and did not want them. He felt he had become a Curiosity and complained about being besieged. And yet if no one had come he would have worried about being neglected. He was looked after by his inseparable companion, Nicky Mariano (a female version of Alan), who had been with him forty years and of whom he said, "I cannot imagine life without her."

Maugham and Alan came to lunch at I Tatti on June 30. Maugham, at eighty-two, was ten years younger than his host and saw in Berenson a projection of himself in the years to come. Wrapped in a soft woolen shawl, with a little velvet cap on his head, he was a figure out of the Old Testament, an aged Hebrew patriarch. Decalcification of the bones made it difficult for him to move without pain; he had only a few good hours in the day. "To become as old as I am," he said, "is not an adventure to be recommended." He was losing interest in current events and no longer read the paper. Maugham, by comparison, was dapper in his smart Edwardian panama, and nimble in his movements as he took a seat on the terrace. The two ancients watched each other shrewdly and made discreet inquiries about health. Who would outlive the other? In his diary Berenson described Maugham thus: "Lined, wrinkled face, senile mouth, kindly expression (or is it mere resignation?). Stammered. Utterly unaffected, and no trace of playing up to his reputation. Simplicity itself."

Maugham discussed recent fiction and complained of the boredom of excessive fornication in it. Wife-swapping was not enough to keep up one's interest in a plot. One novelist he could not read was Mary McCarthy. American novelists lacked substance. After lunch Berenson took his guests on a tour of I Tatti, and decided that Maugham displayed a fantastic absence of feeling for visual art. He praised the poorest stopgap paintings. Berenson felt that Alan had better taste and more genuine interest.

A few days later Maugham and Alan came again, and this time Harold Acton was there. At lunch Berenson said that the creation of character was the hallmark of great fiction. Certain characters were so true to life that one did not think of them as coming out of a book. Maugham objected that it would be difficult to find even twenty such creations in the whole of European literature. Berenson wanted to pursue the discussion, but Maugham was tired and began to stammer. Berenson whispered to Acton, "The poor old thing's got worse."

Maugham left, and never saw Berenson again, for he died in 1959 at the age of ninety-four. In contrast to Maugham, his final years were serene. The last entry of his diary, dated April 15, 1958, said: "I remain skeptical about my personality. It really seems to have reached its present integration in the last 20 years, with the wide and far vision I now enjoy, with *tout comprendre c'est tout pardonner*, expecting little and trying to be thankful for that, the serenity for which I am now admired. But I keep hearing the Furies, and never forget them."[59]

In July and August the army of guests began arriving as usual at the Mauresque. Jane and Gerald Kelly were easy guests, because they painted all day long, and in the evening Gerald held forth until bed-time, which required no exertion from anyone else. When the Kellys left, Liza arrived with Camilla, now a very pretty fifteen, but without John. Alan dreaded their visit and wished he could go away while they were there. He continued to be ingratiating on the surface while privately complaining to friends that the family drove him to drink. He had, he said, suffered two bad liver attacks during Liza's visit and had gone on the wagon.[60]

Maugham complained about the stream of visitors to Klaus Jonas, who was setting up a Maugham exhibit at Rutgers University: "They come for a change of air or a holiday and naturally they want to be entertained. They do not realize that this is my working place and they disrupt the routine of my life. They do not know that a writer does not only write when he is at his desk, he writes all day long even though he does not put pen to paper. They leave him exhausted."[61]

Jonas' exhibit made Maugham dwell on posterity's verdict, which led to gloomy thoughts: "No one can be more conscious than I am that in a very few years after my death I may be entirely forgotten, and that all these collections of mss, typescripts and letters will be merely waste paper."[62]

Another reason for gloom was the death of close friends, which, as Dr. Johnson said, lacerates the continuity of being. Max Beerbohm, who joked that for years he had been referred to as "an interesting link with the past," died in 1956. Maugham had been to Rapallo to see him one last time, and in October, in a speech given in London to open a Heinemann exhibit, "Authors as Artists," he paid his friend of half a century this tribute:

> Was he first and foremost a writer who drew or a draughtsman who wrote? Not long before he died I spent an afternoon with him at Rapallo and we talked much of his work. He was an extremely modest man but he had a very proper sense of his own value. He knew his limitations and throughout his long life on the whole never tried to exceed them. He told me on this occasion that to write had always been a burden and a torment to him, but that to draw on the other hand had invariably been a pleasure and a relaxation. If one had asked him whether he would prefer to be remembered by his writings or his caricatures he would have passed over the question with a pleasantry; but if one had

persisted I think he would have admitted that if he were remembered at all, a matter on which he was skeptical, he would prefer to be remembered for his caricatures rather than for his books. I think he would have been right. His books are already somewhat dated. His caricatures are as fresh and lively as when they were first produced.[63]

The year ended with Maugham back at the Mauresque answering the letter of a writer named Arthur Caddick, who wanted both advice and money. "You seem to have founded your style on that of Gertrude Stein," he wrote. "To my mind, not a good model. You have certainly managed it effectively. I am not inclined to provide you with money to see you out for the next six months. From what you tell me in your letter, it seems to me that you should never have been a writer. I hope my frankness will not make you angry."[64] Caddick benefited from the correspondence, for he sold the letter for twenty-five dollars, which he used to have some dress trousers made to marry off his eldest daughter.

Christmas brought Maugham the usual haul of presents and cards, including two that pleased him from his grandsons Julian and Jeremy Hope. Liza sent him some ties, and he complimented her on her perfect taste, and his Riviera friend Lady Bateman gave him a George III solid silver sugar caster. Alan, who knew something about old silver, was sniffy about it, saying that one simply could not have silver later than George II, but Maugham liked it. He was also gratified by the beautiful year-end weather, sunny and cloudless.

In January 1957 Alan was upset to learn that Bob Tritton, who had introduced him to Maugham thirty years before, had died. Thanks to Tritton, his life had changed. But life went on, and the prospect of Jerry Zipkin's arrival cheered him up. He wrote Zipkin that he had not been well but that he was well enough to get to Villefranche when the U.S. fleet came in and do his bit toward improving Anglo-American relations. Their social life was active. Churchill had come to lunch and was in a pitiable condition. They had gone to Monte Carlo for lunch with Princess Grace, who they thought had improved Prince Rainier beyond recognition.[65]

Robin was off to India, following in his uncle's footsteps in search of material, but Maugham had given up on him and saw no future for him as a writer. "You see," he wrote Kate Bruce in February, "Robin's handicap has always been that he was not interested in people for their own sake but only for the impression he was making on them. That is why he has always surrounded himself with people he could impress. I have never forgotten a remark he made to me at Yemassee: 'There's nothing in the world I like so much as dominating a dinner table.' That's not the attitude that makes a good writer."[66]

In March, Liza came to spend a few days, again without John. Alan seemed pleased to see her and said, "Oh, I've got an evening off tonight because your father wants to have dinner with you alone." Liza told her father that she had her eye on a house on Chelsea Square, toward the purchase of which she needed 15,000 pounds. Maugham, who was in one of his better moods and seemed to have forgotten his vexation over the Mauresque, offered to advance the money. Liza could pay him back, he said, when her mother's estate was settled, which she did.[67]

One night in April, Alan heard strange noises coming from Maugham's room. Going to see what the matter was, he found Maugham rolling around in bed in agony. A doctor from Nice was there within the hour, but it took two injections of morphine to relieve the pain. He slept for twenty-four hours, and the pain did not return. It was, the doctor said, an attack of nephritis, an inflammation of the kidneys. "It's odd," Maugham said, "the things that happen to one as one gets older."[68] He thought a trip would do him good, and he left with Alan in May for a tour of Italy and Austria. The press pursued them everywhere, but it continued to please him that he was so widely known. In Badgastein he took the radioactive baths and went for walks in the woods. He thought the air was like champagne.

In July he was back at work on what he said would be his last book, another volume of essays. As he had given more farewell performances than Sarah Bernhardt, Alan took the news with a grain of salt. He was asked to parties but wrote Alanson: "I prefer to stay at home, bathe in my pool, read my books and play patience. Old age!"[69] In November there was a domestic crisis. The staff demanded a 25 percent raise. Maugham was hurt, because he had done everything to make them happy. Apparently the idea for the raise had come from the food columnist for the *Daily Telegraph*, Fannie Cradock, who had visited the Mauresque and had told Annette she deserved more pay and a new stove. When Maugham found out, he declared Miss Cradock persona non grata.[70]

Klaus Jonas, Maugham's professor friend who had launched the Center for Maugham Studies, had been in Stockholm that summer, and wrote Bert Alanson that he had learned from a confidential source in the Nobel Institute that Maugham was being considered as a candidate for the Nobel prize. "I hope and pray for a wise decision," Jonas wrote.

"In the past it has often been a disappointment to me to read the names of the people who were awarded the prize."[71] Interviewed twenty years later, however, Jonas remembered things differently:

> Maugham was unhappy that he was not taken seriously by learned institutions. Once he told me, "My greatest desire is to win the Nobel prize." Well, my wife and I used to go to Stockholm in the summer, and I got in touch with some of the leading critics there, and they told me that Maugham's writing did not fall under the criteria for the prize and that there was not the slightest chance that he would ever get it. In a way it was bad timing, because the copyright had run out on some of his early novels, which were potboilers, and a Swedish publisher had brought out a new edition of them, so that Maugham was being judged by his worst work. The Swedes told us, nothing doing. Of course I never relayed this discouraging message to Maugham.[72]

On January 25, 1958, Maugham was eighty-three. It had become a birthday tradition to fill the living room with red carnations, one for each year of his life. "I've never seen so many goddamned carnations," Maugham wrote Félix Martí-Ibáñez. "It has made me feel older than God." Churchill came to lunch, but he was a sad sight, for his mind had completely collapsed. Alan thought it was pathetic to see the end of a great man. It seemed that with each passing year someone close to Maugham died. On March 23 it was his brother, Lord Maugham, who had lived to the age of ninety-one without the benefit of Niehans treatments. He died peacefully in his sleep. "I cannot bring myself to say that I shall regret your father's death," Maugham told Kate Bruce. "He has had a long and successful life and . . . it was better that he should end it without pain or fear. These last years of his must have been dreary."[73]

When Maugham had seen him the previous fall in London, Frederic had said to him: "We must face it that both of us were endowed with very frail constitutions." According to Robin, Maugham said after his brother's death: "He was an odious man. I have met many detestable men in my life, but your father was easily the most detestable." Maugham may have said that, but the evidence shows that the brothers regarded each other with the respect due a worthy opponent. In their youth they were opposites. Frederic was popular at Dover and "won his cap" for rugby and cricket, while Willie was the unathletic outsider. At Cambridge, where he attended Trinity College on a scholarship, Frederic rowed for his college for three years and won his blue, and was president of the debating society. His younger brother stammered and did not attend a university.

Frederic gave up a promising career as a mathematician because his other college activities did not give him enough time to study, and took up the law instead. His years as a young lawyer starting out were difficult. He became forbidding and introverted, perhaps partly in reaction to the hardship of his early years. He was incapable of showing affection toward his own children, and disapproved of his brother's private life, for he had married a divorcée and lived with a male secretary. Friendly relations with such an arrogant prig cannot have been easy, and yet they were maintained. Willie confided his problems to his brother and asked him for legal advice. Frederic came repeatedly to the Mauresque, even though he had to put up with a life-style he found reprehensible. Neither brother tolerated criticism of the other from outsiders. Frederic was proud of his brother, even though Willie complained that he never had a kind word to say about his work. Willie in turn was proud of his older brother's achievements, which had been won on merit alone, without party favor. Once Willie took an American friend to the House of Lords, and, pointing to the bewigged figure of the Lord Chancellor, said, his voice rising with excitement, "That's him, that's my brother, over there."[74]

After his death, however, Maugham did not remember his brother fondly. In 1959 Mr. R. F. V. Heuston, who was writing a study of the Lord Chancellors from the late-nineteenth to the mid-twentieth century, asked Maugham for a reminiscence, and this is what Maugham replied:

> I am very much afraid that I cannot be of any help to you. My brother was a very strange, reticent and difficult man. I saw him very seldom, and if it hadn't been for my sister-in-law, his wife, I should not have seen him from year's end to year's end.
>
> I don't suppose you have ever read a novel of mine called *The Painted Veil*. I used my brother as my model for the doctor in the story.
>
> My nephew Robin can tell you much more about his father than I can, and on the whole what he tells you can be relied on. You probably know that he was very unpopular in the House of Lords, because, as one member told me, he treated the Peers as hostile witnesses.[75]

In April, Bert Alanson's brother and business partner, Lionel, died. "It must be harder for you because he owed so much to you,"

Maugham wrote Alanson. "You see, it's not so much what people do for you that attaches you to them, but what you do for them."[76] Perhaps Maugham was thinking of Gerald, whom he had done a great deal for and whose loss had diminished him. Bert, shattered by the loss of his wife and brother, was unwell.

Many persons become more good-natured as they grow older; they realize that since they cannot change the world, they might as well become resigned to it. What were once reasons for complaint become objects of contemplation. Robert Frost once said that the central problem of old age was "what to make of a diminished thing." One solution was to accept the limitations of age and exchange purpose for serenity. This was not Maugham's way. Even though he had written that old age had its pleasures, one of which was the number of things one was no longer expected to do, he grew more querulous and dissatisfied, venting daily his disappointment with life. Those who saw him noticed how deeply unhappy he was. His second childhood was as miserable as his first, and yet this unhappy man clung to life and did his utmost to prolong it. Perhaps the sight of his contemporaries dying made him determined to outlive them. Perhaps the adulation he received made it worthwhile to go on. Perhaps the rivalry with his brother made it important for him to last as long as he had. Whatever the reasons, Maugham decided it was time for Dr. Niehans again, and went to his clinic in Switzerland in May, again dragging Alan along.

Exactly twenty years before, when he was sixty-four, he had first submitted to cellular therapy. In the meantime the doctor's fame had spread. In his office there was an autographed portrait of Pope Pius XII. In 1954 the seventy-three-year-old pope had suffered an attack of hiccups that his doctors could not arrest. His Prussian-born nurse, Sister Pasqualina, told him about Niehans. And even though Niehans was a Protestant, in February 1954 he was called to the pope's summer residence at Castel Gandolfo. Pope Pius was in critical condition— vomiting, spitting up blood, and hiccuping so violently that he had to be fed intravenously. Niehans asked the nurses to turn him over on his side and massage his chest and diaphragm. The hiccups disappeared. He then gave Pius injections of deep-frozen cells. The pope recovered, and in 1955 named Niehans to the seat on the Pontifical Academy that had been held by Alexander Fleming, the discoverer of penicillin.[77]

Niehans now wore gold cuff links embossed with the keys of St. Peter, as well as the aura of a great healer. He told Maugham that the rejuvenation of the sex glands was the best protection against cancer.

Maugham and Alan once again had their buttocks filled with the thick pink fluid in the horse syringes. Niehans found Maugham in pretty good shape for a man of eighty-four but told him to be more prudent in the future. He advised him to give up smoking and drinking, but Maugham said he would not give them up for more than three months, for he had too few pleasures left in life. Alan reported that he was so full of lamb and young bull that he did not know whether to bleat or bellow. He was rejuvenated. He pouted when Maugham refused to buy toys for him. When he saw little boys in the street he wanted to go and play with them. The treatment had obviously worked, said Alan. At the same time it reminded him of Maugham's mortality and awakened old fears. What would happen when the dread day came? Protecting Maugham from those he did not want to see had made him enemies, and he was sure that the family was longing to cut his throat; he feared he would be homeless and jobless in a few hours.[78]

Noel Coward was one of the first guests at the Mauresque when Maugham returned from Switzerland on May 18. Maugham hoped to keep his rejuvenation treatments a secret, feeling rather embarrassed about the whole thing, but Coward found out and said he disapproved of Niehans because he was non-ewe.[79] Another guest, Alec Waugh, thought that his host's hale and pink-cheeked appearance seemed to provide an amulet against old age. Maugham served champagne at lunch, saying that was all he was allowed to drink, and urged Waugh to take the Niehans treatments. "When should I start having them?" Waugh asked. "Before you actually need them," Maugham said. "In your case, fairly soon." Waugh never went, for he saw in Maugham a man with a physical vigor that his mind could no longer keep up with.[80]

In May there was this item in Herb Caen's column in the *San Francisco Chronicle*: "La Triviata: New York's Doug Black, president of Doubleday & Co., checked into town this week with great news for stockbroker Bertram Alanson—who gave his invaluable collection of Maughamiana (original manuscripts, letters) to Stanford without first checking with his old friend Maugham. The good word—Maugham is 'delighted.' "[81]

The item did not mention that Alanson was dying of throat cancer. When Doug Black came to see him they had dinner at Bert's home overlooking the bay. Alanson could eat nothing and had to have a spittoon next to him. Black brought him news of Maugham, which he thought cheered him up. The next morning, May 26, the day he was to have gone to Stanford for the inauguration of his collection, Alanson died, at the age of eighty-one.[82]

Maugham had given Alanson a pair of gold cuff links on which were mounted two splendid Egyptian scarabs. Alanson willed his personal effects to his butler, Lemuel. Anne Alanson suggested to her husband Lionel, Jr., Bert Alanson's nephew, that they should buy back the scarab cuff links. When he was approached, Lemuel said, "What would I want with those ugly things?" Shortly after Alanson's death Maugham wired: "Where are the scarab cuff links?" Anne replied that Lionel, Jr., had them. Did he want them back? No, he said, he just wanted to know what had happened to them. Anne Alanson thought it was odd that Maugham's reaction to the death of one of his closest friends was to ask about a pair of cuff links he had given him many years ago.[83] But Alanson's death shocked Maugham. He considered him the last friend of his own generation.[84]

In July, Maugham was correcting the proofs on the book he said would be his last. He lamented the absence of his proofreader, Eddie Marsh, who had died in January 1953. A replacement had been proposed, a man on the *Financial Times*, but all he did was remove commas.[85] Maugham was also looking for a title for his collection of essays. He did not want anything pretentious. He thought of "Conversation Pieces" and then decided on *Points of View*.[86]

In England in November for the publication of *Points of View*, he announced that it was his last book. A publisher's note said: "And since he seems to have a way of doing what he says he is going to do, we may safely assume that with this volume of essays he will take his leave of the reading public and so put an end to a relationship that with *Liza of Lambeth* began just over sixty years ago." This "last book" included essays on the following subjects: Goethe's novels (for which he had done research in Germany); the seventeenth-century Archbishop of Canterbury John Tillotson, an early master of plain English prose; the guru he had met in India; the journals of the Goncourt brothers; Jules Renard and Paul Léautaud; and the short story. These urbane, leather-armchair discourses mixed biographical detail, personal experience, and the pronouncements of the "old party." In newspaper interviews he said he was relieved to be done with writing. "It's a wonderful thought," he said. "After 62 years I shall be free."[87] But true freedom, as he once told Godfrey Winn, was in work—and Maugham could not give it up: "Writing is the supreme solace. . . . You shut the door, and within half an hour you have completely forgotten all the petty vexations that were previously occupying your thoughts and weighing you down . . . you are a free man again and whatever the ultimate fate of your work, no one else in the world could have made a precisely similar pattern of words upon the page. It is yours and yours alone."[88]

The critics did not throw bouquets at this farewell performance. The *Spectator* on November 14 called the essays "very lazy and pale" and "full of other men's flowers." The *New Statesman* on November 15 said that Maugham's "whole literary personality is a sustained and elaborate pose, a full-dress Edwardian affair." In a more charitable vein, *The Times* on November 6 compared him to a Rolls Royce, saying that there was nothing quite like one at any stage of its existence.[89]

Maugham had been thinking about what he could leave Alan besides the trust fund that Bert Alanson had managed. Through a lawyer he informed Liza that he wanted her to give up the royalties on his works, which he had intended to leave her after his death. She voluntarily signed them away. The next time he saw her, that fall in London, Maugham said: "I hope you're not upset. After all, you are getting the pictures, and they are very valuable." But Alan, who, in the words of John Hope, ran with the hares and the hounds, told Liza, "What a fool you've been"—apparently hoping to stir up more trouble within the family. Alan's strategy was to tell Maugham damaging stories about Liza and John, and then go to Liza and John pretending to take their side against Maugham, like a pocket Iago. He was in such fear of being left in the cold that he manipulated everyone.[90]

In *Points of View* Maugham wrote that "what makes old age hard to bear is not the failing of one's faculties, mental and physical, but the burden of one's memories." In January 1959 he was eighty-five. Birthdays now reminded him of those he would not see again: Max Beerbohm, in Mrs. Steevens' garden, telling him he had no future as a playwright; Eddie Marsh, arguing over a point of grammar; Bert Alanson, on the ship to Hawaii, dapper and loquacious; his brother, complaining about small expenses that "no fortune could stand"; Gerald, so weak he had to be carried by stretcher to the hospital where he would die. So many were gone who had left tracks in his life. Each one added to the burden of memory.

Maugham also looked back on his career, evaluating his place in literature. His books were widely read, but he was out of favor with the critics. What would last? A few short stories? What did it matter, since he had done his best? He could say of himself what Johnson said of

Pope, that he never passed a fault unamended by indifference, nor quitted it by despair. In the draft of a letter to an unknown recipient he wrote:

> I have been highly praised and highly abused. On the whole I think I can truly say that I have not been unduly elated by one or unduly depressed by the other. You see, I have always written for my own pleasure. Since 1907, when I made a success with light comedies, I have been in the fortunate position of complete financial independence. If people like what I have written, I am pleased; if not, I shrug my shoulders. . . . The critic I am waiting for is the one who will explain why, with all my faults, I have been read for so many years by so many people. My stories and novels have been translated not only into all the European languages, but into Turkish, Arabic, Japanese and into several of the Indian dialects. . . . I should have thought it would interest a critic to inquire into what qualities my work must have in order to interest such vast numbers of people in so many countries. I myself haven't the smallest idea. I notice in your essay that Edmund Wilson reproaches me because I haven't what he calls a personal style so that when you read a page you know at once who the author is. That surely means that he has acquired a mannerism (Henry James, Meredith, and others). But that is just what I have tried to avoid.[91]

One of the cures to brooding about the past was travel, and Maugham in his eighties was still on the move. In April 1959 he was off to London, Munich, Badgastein, Vienna, and Venice. In London he was interviewed on the B.B.C. with Aneurin Bevan, the former Welsh coal miner who had become a leader of the Labour party and a cabinet minister. Bevan was a socialist, and Maugham said he belonged "to a party which doesn't exist. I am a radical imperialist." He said that Bevan ought to show him some sympathy since he was a member of the unemployed. "Yes," Bevan said, "the well-upholstered unemployed."[92]

Traveling was harder on Alan than on Maugham. Alan had rheumatism of the spinal cord, kidney stones, and liver attacks. He had not known that one could suffer such pain. They returned to the Mauresque to greet Liza and the family. Alan always felt unwanted when the family was there, like a stranger in the house. He wrote Jerry Zipkin that Zipkin was lucky never to have known the humiliation of dependence.[93]

In July 1959 a group of American fifth-graders wrote Maugham to ask how writers chose their subjects. "Dear fifth grade," he replied, "thank you for your charming letter. It was extremely kind of you to write to me; I was touched and much pleased. In answer to your question: writers write about things they have experienced and also a great deal about the creatures and circumstances of their imagination."[94]

Maugham was planning his first trip to the Far East in thirty years. He had been invited to Japan for the opening of a Maugham exhibit, on loan from Stanford University. He was enormously popular in Japan, where his short stories were used in university textbooks. There was a Japanese Maugham Society, with twelve hundred members, which held annual conventions and wrote studies on various aspects of his work, such as "The Moral Skeleton of W. S. Maugham." The head of the Maugham Society was a Tokyo English professor named Mutsuo Tanaka. This ardent admirer was beside himself when he learned that Maugham was arriving. He wrote Alan Searle that Maugham should meet the emperor and be decorated by him. Alan replied that this was the last thing Maugham wanted to do. He was a very old man in an indifferent state of health, rest and quiet were essential, he did not want to make speeches, become involved in official activities, or attend tiresome functions.[95]

Maugham left from Marseilles on October 6 on the French liner S.S. *Laos*. He took Jerome Weidman's new novel, *The Enemy Camp*, to read on board. A fat gentleman from Chicago came on deck with a Polaroid and asked if he could take Maugham's picture. It struck Maugham that he might be able to translate *shkutzim*, one of the Yiddish words in the book. The man from Chicago said it meant a bunch of lousy good-for-nothing gentiles.[96] That seemed a lot for one word to mean, Maugham reflected. The S.S. *Laos* stopped at Aden, Bombay, Colombo, Singapore, Saigon, Manila, Hong Kong, and Kobe. At each stop the press poured on board, and when they finally reached Yokohama, there was a crowd of several thousand waiting to greet him. Maugham was exposed to Japanese hero worship, and it did his heart good. Everywhere he went people came up as if to touch the hem of his garment. This was the writer's Olympus, where he was treated like a god. The exhibit opened in November at the Maruzen bookstore in Tokyo, Japan's largest. Maugham made a short speech, which was televised, and the pushing crowds knocked the British ambassador to the ground. While Maugham was fussed over, Alan bought Japanese sex kits for his friends and said he felt like an authority on buck teeth and bow legs.[97]

Maugham ran into Ian Fleming at the Imperial Hotel and they spent the day together. Over lunch, Fleming said, Maugham purred at his reception. Afterward they went to the Kodokan gymnasium, where fifty young men were practicing breakfalls, while in another room a group of girls obligingly staged a mock fight. On the next floor, in one vast hall, two hundred bouts were in progress. In another room a class for children between eight and ten was being conducted by a red belt, who showed a boy of ten how to use his leverage to bring down someone twice his size, while half a dozen doting mothers sat on benches and watched. This was an aspect of the East Maugham had not seen.[98]

Having arrived in Kyoto, he accepted an invitation to a geisha house. He sat on the tatami floor and watched the geishas dance the Four Seasons of the Capital in his honor. Afterward the geishas exchanged cups of rice wine with Maugham and showed him how they placed their pillows at night so as not to disarrange their complicated hairdos. When food arrived they helped him master the art of eating with chopsticks. They giggled at his efforts, and he said, "Now wait a minute, I haven't given up yet." Then holding up a tempura shrimp trapped between the chopsticks, he said, "See, there's nothing to it." When one of the geishas planted a kiss on Alan's cherubic cheek, Maugham complained that he was being left out.

When the day of departure came, Mutsuo Tanaka promised that Maugham's name would remain immortal in Japan, adding that he had provided a glorious impetus to the Maugham Society. Alan said it was the greatest triumph of Maugham's career. He himself felt like a lady-in-waiting, carrying the bouquets and the gifts. By January 25, 1960, his eighty-sixth birthday, Maugham was in Bangkok. A delegation of students poured scented water on his hands and he told an interviewer that he was an extinct volcano.

The long trip proved to be too much. The crowds and the mobbing and the being "on view" exhausted him, and when he got back to the Mauresque in March he took to his bed. The doctors diagnosed extreme fatigue. "Since then," he wrote Barbara Back, "they have been injecting my behind with one thing and another (all liquid)."[99] He also found a pile of letters three feet high, which he was going through at the rate of fifty a day. Correspondence was becoming a full-time occupation. In May, feeling rested, he went to Munich, Badgastein, and Venice.

While Maugham was touring Europe, across the Atlantic, in the pine forests of Wellfleet, Massachusetts, Edmund Wilson was again attacking him, this time in a conversation with two of his staunchest friends,

Ruth Gordon and Garson Kanin. The Kanins had come to see Wilson with Thornton Wilder, and somehow the conversation turned to Maugham. Wilson called him an overrated fraud who was interested only in money. Kanin spoke up in Maugham's defense. "Mr. Maugham is my friend," he said, "and I find it hard to sit by and hear him attacked on a personal level. Now, I know him and he's certainly not a fraud in the sense you indicate. He's a man who's devoted his life and his best efforts to his work. And, in any case, why don't we get off the subject?" Wilson went on to say that a man and his writing could not be separated. "True," Kanin said, "and I'm fond not only of Maugham but of what he writes. And so are many others." This served only to intensify Wilson's attack. It was as if Maugham's popularity and readability threatened what he stood for.[100]

In November, Maugham went to London, where he was gratified to learn that the manuscript for *Up at the Villa* had sold for nearly 1,200 pounds at an auction for the benefit of the London Library. He went to Canterbury to have lunch with Canon Shirley and announced that he wanted to give his library to the King's School. He could no longer afford to live in Cap Ferrat, he said, the Mauresque was costing him 23,000 pounds a year. He was thinking of retiring to a small house in Lausanne. Shirley said that a large room could be added to the new physics block, with its own stairway. Maugham approved, and the room was built.[101]

Alan was concerned about Maugham's health. There was nothing specific, just the fraility of old age. He was afraid Maugham was failing fast, which made him unhappy, because he loved him and could not imagine life without him.[102] And yet there were hopeful signs. He was working again, on an autobiography, which he planned to call *Looking Back*. He promised Alan the manuscript. Alan took it upon himself to discourage guests and wrote S. N. Behrman in January 1961 that Maugham was too frail now to have visitors for more than two or three days. Alan was sad and anxious about him.[103]

Maugham seemed chipper enough, however, for his eighty-seventh birthday. In one of his by now customary birthday interviews he said he had been surprised to receive a letter from Moscow with a check from the Soviet National Bank for 350 pounds. It was the tip of the iceberg of his Russian royalties. He complained that in his love affairs he had been "always the lover, never the loved," and added, "The fact is, two persons don't want to keep having intercourse indefinitely. The only way they can keep going is if one or the other has some fun on the side." Concluding the interview, he said: "You can write what you please about me. I don't give a damn what you say. I shall never read it."[104]

He had struck up a friendship with his neighbor in Cap d'Ail, Lord Beaverbrook, who had a villa called the Capponcina, where he lived with the widow of his old friend Sir James Dunn. Churchill was a frequent guest, and Beaverbrook had installed an electric chair lift in the long stairway, mainly for his benefit. Beaverbrook, who was five years younger than Churchill and Maugham, would start the chair lift and say, "Off you go, Winston, I'll see you at the top."[105]

Maugham and Beaverbrook, two old men with the habits of old men, began sending each other books and articles and pots of marmalade, delivered by their respective chauffeurs in their respective Rolls Royces. Beaverbrook sent Maugham an article on Lord French, who had commanded the British forces at the outbreak of World War I, and Maugham replied on January 23, 1961: "I read the article with a shudder. It is pretty obvious that the generals were as incompetent and self-seeking as the politicians. How on earth did they manage to win a war?" They invited each other to dinner and reminisced about both world wars. They discussed Churchill's war administration and Lloyd George's remark that of ten projects promoted by Churchill nine were dangerous and one was useful. Max explained to Willie that in August 1944 Churchill had wanted to push northward from Italy toward Vienna but the Americans insisted on invading southern France, a futile operation. Beaverbrook sent him a subscription to the *Evening Standard* and a copy of his book *Men and Power*. Maugham wrote to thank him, saying: "What seemed to me peculiarly shocking, considering that the fate of the country was in the balance, was the vanity, self-seeking, and intriguing of those VIP's, generals, admirals, MPs, ministers, and Noble Lords. What a scramble it was for office and how they clung to it." Maugham gave Beaverbrook the manuscript of his book on Spain, *Don Fernando*. Beaverbrook sent him some figs from his garden, and Maugham wrote, "We can't get figs like that in the market. They are delicious."[106]

Beaverbrook had founded an art museum in Canada and wanted Maugham to sit for a sculptor. He agreed to sit for an hour a day, wrapped in blankets, for he was recovering from the flu. When Beaverbrook showed the result to Lady Dunn, she said, "Well, the old party certainly has character." But Alan saw another side of him, and he wrote Jerry Zipkin that Maugham had taken a great fancy to will-making and wrote a new one every week, which made Alan uneasy and depressed about his future.[107] The grants to Alan in the wills were followed by the ominous phrase "if he is still in my service."

Although Alan had reduced the guests to a trickle, there was one man Maugham wanted to see, and that was Alfred Ayer, the philosopher. Ayer, the author of *Language, Truth and Logic*, was a positivist, for whom only such propositions as could be verified had meaning. There was no such thing as an immortal soul, or God, or an afterlife. Maugham had read several of his books and agreed with him in substance. He had lost his faith as a youth in Heidelberg, but with death approaching, he wanted to be reassured about the absence of an afterlife, and invited Ayer to spend a few days at the Mauresque, as a believer might have invited a priest for spiritual counsel. Maugham the nonbeliever wanted the company of Ayer the priest of agnosticism.

Ayer, an Oxford don, without the stuffiness of many of his colleagues, was a man in his forties, with a lively, expressive face and a good sense of humor. He arrived in April with his wife, an attractive young woman from Massachusetts named Dee Wells, who would later write the highly praised novel *Jane*.

Mrs. Ayer, a bit intimidated by Maugham's reputation as a crotchety old man who disliked most women, worried because her luggage was from Marks and Spencer and her gloves were soiled. She soon saw that however impressive the Mauresque was, it was not perfect. The breakfast trays did not fit the beds, and the paintings were hung so high it was hard to see them. The Marie Laurencins were in the bathroom, as a throwaway gesture to lady artists. But the service was efficient, the food was good, and meals were served at a pretty round table with crocheted tablecloths like altar cloths.

Alan was self-effacing, in the manner of a submissive wife. He struck her as a bright man who had never had the courage to strike out on his own. In Maugham she sensed a deep unhappiness and a low self-image. He deferred to Ayer, saying, "I wish I'd had your education." He kept alive the memory of those who had held power over him when he was young. His good qualities were steeped in bitterness, like olives in brine. Homosexuality, and his need to pretend ignorance of it, had contributed to the death of the heart.[108]

On the terrace before lunch, on the first day of their visit, Mrs. Ayer was served a cocktail that foamed at the top. She sat on a low wall, and Maugham said: "Where you are sitting is the exact spot where Clare Boothe Luce sat when she was here a few days ago. She told me about going to see the pope and how she lectured on Catholicism, and while she was talking about her conversion there was a lit cigarette in her hand and there was a line of ants marching along the wall and she went zip with her cigarette down the line of ants, like a dive-bomber dropping napalm." After lunch he took Mrs. Ayer to the pond and said: "I'll show you something. There are some frogs down here, in the juncture where the leaf of the plant leaves the stem. You see, they are the identical color of the plants, you must focus on their golden eyes."[109] Maugham felt a kind of kinship with the frogs, who were able to conceal their ugliness by blending with their surroundings. One day he was walking in the garden with a friend, who, spotting one of the frogs, knelt down and gently teased it with a twig. "Let it alone," Maugham ordered. "Stop doing that. Stop!" When the friend did not stop, Maugham kicked him.[110]

On the afternoon of the Ayers' visit a B.B.C. lady came to interview Maugham and said in the course of the interview, "It's much nicer to be a bit mad than boringly sane." Maugham fixed her with his lizard eyes and said, "No." He then asked Mrs. Ayer whether he had been rude, and when she said he had, he sulked and would not speak to her for several hours.

On April 15 Maugham and the Ayers were invited to dinner at Beaverbrook's. The conversation got around to an afterlife, somewhat to Freddie Ayer's dismay, for Beaverbrook was an ardent believer and Maugham was an equally ardent nonbeliever. Asked point-blank for his opinion, Ayer made the Solomon-like pronouncement that Calvinist doctrine stated that some were chosen at birth to be saved, which Beaverbrook was quite prepared to believe, since he was convinced he was one of the chosen, while Maugham did not think it mattered whether one was saved or not, since there was no afterlife.

Lady Dunn, shopping in Nice that day, had bought an eighteenth-century silver bowl with a spiral rim in a shop run by two old ladies. She had haggled over the price and was very proud of her purchase. She asked Alan, who had worked in antique stores, what he thought of it. He said it was very good. In the Rolls Royce on the way home, with Maugham sitting in the front seat lined in pearly lambskin, Alan turned to Ayer as they swayed along the *grande corniche* and asked, "Is it all right to lie?" "Why, yes," said Ayer, "I don't see how you could get through the day otherwise." "Well," said Alan, "that bowl was made circa 1923."[111]

Aside from the dinner at Beaverbrook's, evenings at the Mauresque ended early. It was more like Neuilly than the Riviera, Mrs. Ayer felt. Alan had thoughtfully stocked their room with Traveler's Companion books, and they read pornographic novels aloud to each other. One evening after dinner Maugham leaned over the back of the couch and whispered to Alan and they both vanished. Ayer remarked to his wife that there was a hint of sex in the air.[112] Thanks to the Niehans treatments, Maugham remained virile in his late eighties, and Alan proudly told his friends that his sexual services were still needed.[113]

Honors continued to be bestowed upon Maugham. In May the Royal Society of Literature created a new award, Companion of Literature, and Maugham was one of the first five to receive the scroll, along with G. M. Trevelyan, E. M. Forster, Churchill, and John Masefield. Also in May, he became the first foreigner to be made an Honorary Senator of Heidelberg, on the occasion of the five hundred and seventy-fifth anniversary of the University of Heidelberg, which he had attended as a youth of seventeen. On May 31 the Senate conferred diplomas on Maugham, two factory directors from Mannheim, and the president of the Mannheim Chamber of Commerce. Maugham was honored for "his impeccable portrayal of human character." He thought the day would never end. There were speeches by the mayor, the rector, and the chancellor. The ceremony started in the morning, and after lunch the speeches continued. It was all he could do to stay awake. When Alan took possession of the large plaque that Maugham had been awarded, the rector said: "Would you mind, when Mr. Maugham dies, returning this plaque to us? We went to great trouble with it and considerable expense. We would like to have it back as a memorial of this glorious occasion." Not knowing what to reply, Alan promised, and informed Maugham, who told him, "That is a promise I order you to break."[114] The festivities went on for several days. *Sports Illustrated* published a full-page photograph of Maugham kicking off the opening ball at a university soccer match, and the students held a beer-drinking bout in his honor.

Exhausted by the celebration, Maugham went to Venice to rest. Alan wrote Klaus Jonas that he was failing fast, and that it was horrible when he became ill in hotels away from home. "What shall I do when the dread day comes," Alan wrote Richard Cordell, "and how shall I be able to face all his horrible relations?" In this period of decline there was more interest in his work than ever. On June 24 *The Bookseller* announced that 40 million of his books had been sold worldwide. *The Times* bookshop of London had sold 300,000 copies. Sales of *The*

Razor's Edge approached 5 million. *Of Human Bondage* was the biggest seller in the Modern Library series. In Austria a student at the University of Graz, Gerhard R. Kropfitsch, wrote a doctoral dissertation on the use of demonstrative and indefinite pronouns in *Of Human Bondage.*

Returning to the Mauresque, Maugham worried about his paintings. He had been shocked by the theft of a Goya from the National Gallery. If the National Gallery, with its alarm system and guards, was not safe, what chance did he stand? A gang of art thieves was operating on the Riviera. One day the mayor of St. Jean came to see him and said: "I have never seen a house that so obviously invites robbers to enter and steal. If you want to keep your pictures you must do something about it." Maugham asked what he could do. "There's only one thing you can do, you must build a strong room and keep your pictures in it."

Maugham converted one of the guest bedrooms into a strong room, but that too was a nuisance. Whenever he went on a trip he had to send for an electrician to remove the lights and take the pictures out of their frames. He did not think it was good for the pictures. When he came home, the electrician had to put the pictures and the lights back up. It occurred to him that even if he went out to dinner he could not be sure that a thief would not make off with one or two of his pictures. Problems are amplified in the minds of the elderly, and Maugham had become obsessed about his pictures.[115]

In August, Liza came to spend ten days at the Mauresque with Camilla and her two youngest sons. John, who was once more persona grata, arrived on the last weekend of their stay. The visit was a great success despite signs that Maugham's mind was failing. Inexplicably, he would start muttering and shouting. A strange look would come into his eyes and he would start cursing and repeating, "I will show them."

When John arrived, however, he found Maugham warm and welcoming. One day, when Liza was sunning herself at the pool, he found himself alone with Maugham in the drawing room, and Maugham suddenly said: "John, I want to tell you something. I'm going to sell the pictures. I'm quite certain they'll be stolen." "Of course," Maugham added, "it will help Liza because she will be getting the money for hers." "Do you want to tell her?" Hope asked. "No, you tell her, please," Maugham replied.

John went up to the pool, finding Liza with Alan, and said, "Alan, do you know anything about this?" Alan said that he did not. Later, when Alan was alone with Liza, he told her how pleased Maugham was that John had been so reasonable and that the conversation had gone so well.[116]

A few days before the family was due to leave, Maugham took Liza, John, Camilla, and Alan out to dinner to a restaurant at Menton called Le Pirate. He was in a cheerful frame of mind, but before the dinner was over he tired, and they all left in a hurry. On the drive back to the Mauresque, Maugham sat in front next to the chauffeur, which was his practice when he did not want to make conversation. Everyone said good night and thanked him for a lovely evening, but he went upstairs without a word. Camilla asked her mother what was wrong with her grandfather. A moment later a terrible commotion was heard coming from Maugham's bedroom. Liza went up and ran into a highly agitated Alan, who was fetching a sedative. Alan explained that Maugham was having one of his attacks. He could be heard shouting at the top of his lungs: "I will show them! I'll put them back into the gutter where they belong! I'll get even with them! Sons of bitches!" The outburst lasted for half an hour. Liza made no attempt to go into his room, and Alan returned with a sedative. He told her that Maugham had been having attacks of this sort for over a year, raving about imaginary enemies, and that they were getting worse and more frequent.[117]

The next morning Maugham was cheerful and friendly, as if nothing had happened, and the day after that the family left. Liza did not get a chance to discuss the sale of the paintings with her father, but she wrote him a thank-you note from London in which she added a paragraph that said, as she remembers it: "John has told me of his discussion with you about selling the pictures. Naturally I am rather sad as I had always intended keeping some of them. However, I am sure your decision is wise and will look forward when you come to London to discussing the details of the sale." Liza took it for granted that those paintings which Maugham had bought in her name and for which she had the receipts were her property.[118]

Maugham arrived in London on his annual visit around the first of October and learned that his favorite niece, Kate Bruce, had died. He had liked her and confided in her and helped her in her ambition to be a writer, although sometimes his criticism was severe. "Your friends and family will continue telling you you're marvelous," he once wrote her, "but I do not think your gifts will ever be of use to you unless you apply to them observation enriched by experience and active, vivid, imaginative invention."[119] Her last novel, finished just before her death, was called *Roses in December*, after J. M. Barrie's words "God gave us memory so that we might have roses in December."

Two days after Maugham's arrival Liza called the Dorchester to see how he was. She spoke to Alan, who asked if he could come and see her, he had something important to tell her. Alan went round to the house on Chelsea Square and told Liza: "I have had the most terrible time with your father. He's been in a very hysterical state and it all dates back to your letter, which sent him into a rage." Alan said that when Maugham had read it he had become so angry that he threw it up into the air and said, "She has nothing to discuss with me." Liza asked Alan, who had seen the letter, whether he thought there was anything in it that could have provoked her father, and he said there was not. But, Alan added, Maugham was determined to sell the paintings as soon as he could—that December, if possible. Alan had already been to see Peter Wilson, the chairman of Sotheby's, to arrange for the sale. He told Liza that he had mentioned to Wilson that some of the pictures were hers. He advised Liza to give Maugham a week to calm down before she made any attempt to see him. Liza later learned that Maugham felt she was questioning his judgment and making a veiled demand for her share of the proceeds. Alan egged him on against Liza, and told their Cap Ferrat neighbor Rory Cameron, "He's had a letter from Liza demanding her whack."[120]

John Hope by then had done so well in his political career that he was Minister of Works, and Liza had to join him in Brighton for the Conservative party conference. Hope went to Brighton feeling that he was doing battle on two fronts, on the political front for his cabinet post and on the home front for what he felt rightly belonged to Liza.

When Liza returned from Brighton she called her father, but Alan answered the phone and said things were very difficult and Maugham refused to see her. There were things he could not say over the phone, and he went round to see her. Maugham was more hysterical than ever, Alan said. His attacks now came almost nightly. He shouted and screamed and threw water and furniture about, and Alan had to give him sedatives and could not leave him alone at night. As a result of getting very little sleep himself, Alan was a nervous wreck. Often Maugham would go to bed screaming about the sale and swearing that Liza was not going to get a penny from the pictures. In his calmer moments, however, he said he was willing to give his daughter half the proceeds from the sale of the pictures that had been bought in her name. Alan urged Liza to agree to such a settlement.[121]

Liza's response was to write her father the following letter: "Dearest Daddy, you really are making me quite miserable by refusing to see me. When I think how well we have got on, and what happy times we have had as recently as six weeks ago when you were so sweet to the children, and we all had such fun at the Mauresque, I find it all impossible to understand. How can you suddenly turn on me when I have done absolutely nothing? Please let me come and see you and don't let's have any more of this awful rift. All love, Liza."[122]

She received in reply a letter from L. A. Jacobs & Sons, solicitors, dated November 1. The letter referred to a dispute between Liza and her father and suggested that she and John should meet with the solicitors to discuss the matter. It was humiliating to Liza that her father had placed a family matter in the hands of lawyers. She returned the solicitors' letter to Maugham with a covering note that was cooler in tone. He was now "Dear Daddy" instead of "Dearest Daddy," and she wished him "love" rather than "all love." "Dear Daddy," the note said, "how could you allow me to receive a lawyer's letter referring to a dispute which we have never had either by word or letter. I cannot believe that you wish to behave like this unless something extraordinary has happened since I last saw you. Love, Liza."[123]

Three days later, on November 6, Alan called Liza and said: "Your father is standing beside me, he would like to see you for tea today, but do not mention the pictures—as far as he is concerned the whole thing is forgotten." Liza went to the Dorchester that evening and found Maugham pleasant and cheerful. In the midst of a general conversation, however, he announced that he had decided to give up the Mauresque and live in Lausanne. He told Liza that the Mauresque would be ready for her to sell by January 19, 1962.

Liza asked why he wanted to leave a home where he had been happy for more than thirty years, but Maugham would not give a reason. He was apparently more worried than ever that Liza and John would try to take the Mauresque away from him, now that he was selling the pictures in disregard of their interests. Liza said he was making a terrible mistake to move to another country at his age and she did not want to sell the Mauresque during his lifetime. Maugham replied that Lady Dunn, the widow who was living with his Riviera neighbor Lord Beaverbrook, wanted to buy the Mauresque from Liza and then give it back to him. "What an astounding suggestion," Liza exclaimed—there was absolutely no need for him to leave the Mauresque in the first place. Maugham laughed, and the conversation shifted to other matters. Alan later explained to Liza that Maugham had taken a violent dislike to the Mauresque and was determined to move away and sell its contents. Several days later Maugham left for Lausanne to be interviewed by the Swiss authorities.[124]

Once in Switzerland, however, he had second thoughts. His lawyers assured him that there was no way he could be evicted from the Mauresque, and the thought of living in Switzerland, away from the sunshine and social life of the Riviera, became less appealing. He wrote Beaverbrook from Lausanne:

> I am too old to start a new life here, and though on my death taxes would be less than they would otherwise be, I do not see why I should care. I have learned through the lawyers that the Mauresque remains absolutely mine until my death, when it will belong to my daughter. I prefer therefore to leave Switzerland as soon as possible and settle down in my house on Cap Ferrat until my demise . . . though the taxes will be a great deal more than they would be if I remained here, it will in no way inconvenience me.[125]

Beaverbrook, delighted that he was not losing a neighbor, said he was reminded of the old Scottish hymn, "Pleasant are thy courts below." By November, Beaverbrook and Maugham were finally calling each other by their Christian names. Explaining his reticence, Maugham said: "I should have liked to call you by your Christian name, but after all you were for a great many years on Christian name terms with the great ones of the earth—at least the English ones. I was afraid that you would look upon it as an impertinence if I followed their example."[126]

With the approach of the Christmas season Maugham received a great many letters that began with the word "please." He wrote a Mr. Jacob that his letter "makes me want to help, but I'm afraid I cannot do so. The scheme I have devised to help writers does not come into operation until after my death. I do what I can during my lifetime but there comes a moment when one can do no more. Incidentally, by every post demands come by the dozen for gifts, loans, guarantees, and financial assistance of every kind. I am bewildered and harassed by it all."[127]

In Switzerland, Maugham had met Georges Simenon, whose work he admired. The conversation got around to begging letters, and

Maugham mentioned a particularly touching one from a blind girl who wanted to be a writer and needed a Braille typewriter.

"Wait a minute," Simenon said, going to his files. "Oh yes, I got that one too."[128]

The year ended with Maugham finishing his autobiography. Beaverbrook wanted to serialize it in the *Sunday Express*. It contained an unflattering portrait of Syrie, full of scandalous allegations, some of them made up out of whole cloth. Alan had assured Liza, who was concerned with protecting her mother's memory, that it could never be published. In fact, however, he was the project's most enthusiastic promoter, for Maugham had assigned him the serialization rights and the copyright, and Beaverbrook said he was prepared to pay 75,000 pounds for the British Empire rights. John Junor, the editor in charge of the serialization, visited the Mauresque at the end of 1961 to discuss publication. He found Maugham obsessed with the idea that he was finished and had never been any good. "Why are you wasting your time coming to see me?" he asked. "Why don't you go after Simenon?"[129]

Maugham was having second thoughts about the sale, but Alan convinced him that it was too late to back out since all the arrangements had been made. Sensing Alan's eagerness not to lose the sale, Junor told him the *Sunday Express* could offer only 35,000 pounds, which Alan accepted, worried that the deal was slipping through his fingers. Junor returned to England in high spirits, having secured a sensational piece of writing at a saving of 40,000 pounds to his employer. Alan sent Junor photographs to illustrate the text, including the photograph of his mother that Maugham kept in his bedroom. He contributed anecdotes, such as the story of Lord Linlithgow, Liza's father-in-law, suggesting that if Willie wanted to make a marriage settlement, he might transfer part of his estate to his daughter to avoid inheritance taxes. "I also have read *King Lear*," Maugham was said to have replied.[130]

Chapter Nineteen

In most biographies it is the subject's death that is most interesting. That last inevitable step has a fascination and even a practical interest which no previous event can equal. I cannot understand why a biographer, having undertaken to give the world details of a famous man's life, should hesitate, as so often happens, to give details of his death also. . . . It imports us as much to know how great men die as to know how they live. Our lives are conditioned by outer circumstances, but our death is our own.

Maugham, *A Writer's Notebook*

MAUGHAM'S EIGHTY-EIGHTH BIRTHDAY on January 25, 1962, was a caviar-and-champagne occasion. Two Riviera friends, Lord Rothermere and Brigadier Marshall, were on hand. They talked about the Common Market. Maugham said he did not understand what it was. He blew out the candles on his cake. Alan said he was as tough as an old boiling fowl. "I was considering moving to Switzerland," Maugham told an interviewer. "There about 15% has to go to your heirs. But I decided I could not face the discomfort of Switzerland for the sake of my beneficiary. Switzerland's so dull."[1]

The sale of his paintings at Sotheby's was set for April, and Alan was busy preparing the shipment of the thirty-five best pictures to London. It nearly killed him, he complained—it took months of intrigue and bribery and corruption to get them out of France. Alan was sorry to lose the pictures after having had all the care and trouble of them. It was a sad day when the movers came to measure them for the packing cases, and you could see on the walls of the Mauresque the rectangular outlines where they had hung.[2]

The auction was scheduled for April 10. The publication of Maugham's last book, *Purely for My Pleasure*, an account of his collecting, was due to appear at the same time. In the meantime Maugham was not well. Alan took him to Switzerland for a change of air. It was terrible, he said, to watch someone you loved fading away and to be able to do nothing about it. "I have been very ill," Maugham wrote Robin, "and in the doctors' hands for some weeks. Dying is a very dull, dreary affair and my advice to you is to have nothing to do with it."[3]

He was too ill to attend the auction, and Alan went in his place. He was all excited, he said, because it was the first time since 1946 that he was going anywhere by himself. On the evening before the sale, April 9, Alan saw Liza and told her that Maugham was determined not to let her family have a penny of the proceeds. "If you press for it," Alan said, "he will break the children's trust in America." Liza said that in that case it was all the more important to hang on now. Alan, whose normal tone of voice was like the purring of a cat, lost his temper and shouted, "You're a damn fool, and I'm sure that this is all John's fault." Liza said there was no point in continuing the discussion.[4]

On April 10, outside Sotheby's on Bond Street, a line of people in evening clothes began to form, and umbrellas opened as it started to drizzle half an hour before the doors opened for the evening session. About 2,500 persons crammed into five galleries linked by closed-circuit television. The bidding was done over banks of telephones, with clerks relaying the bids from points four hundred yards apart. A hush fell over the hall as Peter Wilson, the chairman of Sotheby's, who was personally conducting the auction, made the opening announcement: "Lot number one. Roderic O'Conor's 'Still Life with Vegetables.' "

Picasso's "Death of a Harlequin," which was painted on both sides, went for $224,000 with the flicker of a white glove belonging to a woman in a blue coat, setting a record for a living artist. *"Le Polisseur,"* also known as *"Le Raboteur,"* the Toulouse-Lautrec that Maugham always asked his guests to identify, which he had bought in Liza's name for $10,000 in 1950, went to Huntington Hartford for $75,600, bidding against Lord Beaverbrook. The Gauguin door that Maugham had bought in Tahiti for a few hundred francs went for $37,400. The two Renoirs, which Maugham had bought in Liza's name in 1949 and 1950 for a total of $79,000 were knocked down for $134,000, and the Matisse which he had bought in Liza's name in 1950 for $10,000 went for $106,400. The total proceeds were $1,466,864. Alan, sitting in row N, hurried to the chairman's office to call Maugham, who said, "That's rather a lot of money for a single gentleman to get."[5]

The money was not yet his, however, for Liza, protecting what she felt to be hers for the sake of her children, sued Sotheby's in May for the proceeds of nine paintings. She claimed $648,900 of the sale's total of $1,466,864. Legally she was in a strong position, for she had the receipts to the paintings, as well as letters from her father telling her that they belonged to her, and a copy of a letter from the New York dealer Paul Rosenberg to Maugham saying, "We wish to inform you that the painting by Matisse, 'Intérieur au parquet gravé, femme assise dans un fauteuil jaune,' which your daughter, Lady John Hope, acquired from us and which has been paid in full, will be shipped by air in a week or so." Morally she and John also felt that they had a strong case, and they could think of only one reason why Maugham had turned against them: Alan's mischief-making. Liza had voluntarily given up the right to Maugham's royalties in 1958, which she presumed he would make over to Alan. In addition, Maugham had set up a trust fund for him in America. But Alan's insecurity was great, he was terrified that he would be left penniless after Maugham's death, and he came to see the family as an enemy trying to do him in. His influence over Maugham grew in these last years when he was mentally unhinged, and he used it to advance his own interests. It was not only Alan's influence, however, for there was in Maugham's nature a bitterness that made him resent his family. He once told Alan: "The trouble with those two [Liza and John] is that they're too damned happy." He did not approve of happiness, for it was beyond his reach.[6]

On May 18 Peter Wilson informed the press that Liza's suit was "a family dispute. It has nothing to do with us. When asked to sell pictures we do not ask for legal evidence that they belong to the owner. As far as we are concerned, they belong to him [Maugham]. The matter is in the hands of our solicitors."[7]

Robin sent his uncle a telegram of sympathy. "I knew of course that John Hope and Liza wanted to get the money from the sale of my pictures, but as I had never given them to Liza I did not take the matter very seriously," Maugham replied disingenuously. "In point of fact I thought their attitude was merely a bluff. . . . I shall be sorry if the lawyers come to the conclusion that the pictures belong to Liza, but it will not otherwise affect me. I shall still be able to live comfortably in the Villa Mauresque until my death."[8]

There the matter rested for the moment. Alan, whose true feelings about Liza were now in the open, wrote Jerry Zipkin that Maugham was greatly upset by the action his so-called daughter was bringing against him. It had nearly killed him, and the change in him was shocking. Alan himself was on the verge of a nervous collapse.[9] In fact, Maugham's deterioration had begun several years before Liza's action.

Alan was so worried about Maugham that he took him to the Niehans clinic that May. "I think Mr. Maugham is going insane," he confided to Niehans. "Is there anything you can do?" Niehans gave him a series of injections but could not promise results in a case of mental illness.[10]

On their way back to the Mauresque, Alan left Maugham seated on the train platform at Vevey next to an elderly lady while he struggled with the luggage, for there was a porters' strike. When he came to get Maugham, he and the lady had vanished. Alan heard someone saying "yoo-hoo" behind a column. It was Maugham, playing hide-and-seek. Alan scolded him, and the elderly lady appeared and said, "You should be gentle with that nice old man. He thinks he's Somerset Maugham."[11]

In June, Maugham was rehabilitated in the Soviet Union. An article in the *Soviet Review* said that far from being a bourgeois reactionary, his work showed hatred and contempt for the bourgeoisie. In "Rain," for instance, he showed that "religious fanaticism is merely an expression of perverted sexual urges." In other stories he showed that misery and suffering only degrade man instead of ennobling him. The theme of man escaping the bourgeois society was also to be found in such works as *The Moon and Sixpence* and "The Fall of Edward Barnard." As a result, Maugham was better than his reputation and deserved to be taken more seriously.[12]

That summer, having broken with his daughter, Maugham felt the need to see other members of his family, and invited his niece Diana Marr-Johnson and her husband Kenneth. Diana, the sister of Robin and of the deceased Kate Bruce, was a sprightly and talented woman who had written several novels. She soon realized that Maugham was suffering from senile dementia. It was painful to watch. He would tuck his arm under hers, speaking in terms of affection, and then suddenly the words would come out, as if from another mouth: "Fuck you, fuck you, fuck you." Sometimes he mistook her for Liza. Her husband would try to help him out of his chair, but he would wave him away, push himself out, and mutter, "I know what you're thinking." Once he huddled between Diana and Kenneth on the sofa, pointed at Alan, and said, "Who is that man? Don't let him hurt me." "He was," recalled Mrs. Marr-Johnson, "like Lear raving on the heath."[13]

Physically, however, he was remarkable. They saw him, at the age of eighty-eight, dive into his pool. Even mentally he continued to have his good moments. One evening they went to a restaurant in Villefranche for dinner, where a young violinist was going from table to table, and Maugham turned to Diana and said, "When that poor fellow gets up in the morning he looks at himself in the mirror and remembers that he once wanted to be a concert violinist, and now he is playing for people who don't care and aren't listening." His eyes misted over at the thought, and he thrust a wad of bank notes into the violinist's hand. "As far as I can see, he's doing quite well," Alan said.[14]

Diana thought of the time when she was president of a charity in Paddington, an old-persons' home. Maugham had asked if he might visit the place with her. He spent hours at the side of the bedridden, questioning them. What did they do during the day? How did they feel? What did they have to eat? Who came to visit them? What was old age like? Now he knew, and it was a pity that this miserable end would overshadow the rest of his life. As for her, she preferred to remember the golden days of the Mauresque, when charming and intelligent guests came to stay, enjoying the sunshine, the good food, and the conviviality. For years Willie had produced the closest thing to paradise that she had ever seen.[15]

Maugham's latest work, *Looking Back*, was due to be serialized in the fall, but when Frere saw the text, he was shocked. It seemed to him like the ravings of a lunatic. Abandoning all standards of good taste and discretion, Maugham was attacking, in the most degrading terms, a woman who was dead and could not defend herself. It was as if, preparing to die, he was determined to leave the world as he had entered it, alone and friendless. He seemed embalmed in hatred. The good moments that he had shared with his wife, their mutual joy in raising a daughter, were forgotten as the slanderous accusations poured forth. According to Maugham, Syrie was scatterbrained and snobbish, pleasure-seeking and self-absorbed, whining and selfish, dishonest, unscrupulous, and promiscuous. He did not have a single good word to say about her.

Frere decided that Heinemann could not publish *Looking Back*, and alerted Doubleday, who agreed not to publish. He went to the Mauresque that summer to tell Maugham of his decision. Frere was a friend of long standing as well as Maugham's literary executor. "You can't let a man down when he gets to the end of his life and goes raving mad," he said, explaining his decision. Maugham was furious at what he considered meddling and told Frere he no longer wanted him as executor.[16] Another reason may have been that Frere had ceased to be an executive officer of Heinemann in February 1962; he parted company with Heinemann at the end of the year. Maugham probably considered it unwise to have as his literary executor a man who might no longer be on the best of terms with his publisher.

Maugham offered the job of executor to Spencer Curtis Brown, an urbane and tactful man who had acted as the agent for his plays ever since the death of Golding Bright in 1941, and who, like Frere, had become a close personal friend, staying often at the Mauresque and seeing Maugham whenever he came to London. Spencer Curtis Brown, who also acted as the agent for *Looking Back*, was an exception to the rule that Maugham did not like tall men, for he stood well over six feet.

Alan wanted to sell the manuscript of *Looking Back* to Beaverbrook, but Maugham locked it in a bank vault and made Alan promise that it should never be published. To this day it has not been published in book form. "I imagine it is pretty tough stuff," John Junor wrote Beaverbrook. "It tells for instance why Maugham married his wife. According to Searle, it was because she was blackmailing him."[17]

Alan boasted that *Looking Back* was the most candid and ruthless autobiography ever written, not excepting the *Confessions* of Jean Jacques Rousseau. It was serialized in the *Sunday Express* in September and October 1962, with sensational headlines, such as "I begin an affair that was to last eight years," and caused a scandal. The accusations against Syrie served to deepen the rift between father and daughter. As John Hope told the press, "Recent newspaper articles by Mr. Maugham about my wife's mother, Syrie, caused my wife great distress. Since then, my wife has not written her father."[18]

John Junor, who was responsible for editing the series, defended its publication. "My God," he said, "if we'd had Shakespeare telling what happened with Anne Hathaway . . . And even if Anne Hathaway's relatives had made a fuss, we'd have had to publish. We thought the public would love it but they didn't take to it that much. The British are funny."[19]

One reader, the designer Oliver Messel, who had designed the cake for Liza's first wedding, wrote to protest: "It seems impossible to understand what Mr. Somerset Maugham hopes to achieve by writing in such a tasteless way about his dead wife," he said, "and what appears equally ignoble is the fact that it is his only child who must be hurt most by the pointless and spiteful picture he has chosen to present of a woman who is not alive and unable to defend herself."

In December a group of Syrie's friends, some of whom were also Maugham's, expressed their fondness for her memory by presenting a statuette in her name to the Victoria and Albert Museum. They included Cecil Beaton, Noel Coward, Peter Daubeny, Oliver Messel, Beverley Nichols, and Rebecca West.[20]

Noel Coward, who had been a friend of both Maugham's and Syrie's, was particularly upset when *Looking Back* was published. He said he wanted nothing more to do with Maugham and told Garson Kanin: "The man who wrote that awful slop is not the man who has been my friend for so many years. Some evil spirit has entered his body. He is dangerous, a creature to be feared and shunned."[21]

Coward channeled his indignation in the direction of what he did best, writing plays. He did to Maugham what Maugham had done to Huge Walpole in *Cakes and Ale*, but posthumously. In April 1966, four months after Maugham's death, he starred in his own play, *A Song at Twilight*. The main character, Sir Hugo Latymer, was a distinguished but secretly homosexual author who in his advanced years is brought by a former mistress some compromising letters he once wrote to a male secretary. The idea for the play, Coward said, had come to him at the time of Gerald Haxton's death in 1944, when Maugham had written him an outspoken and moving letter, but the character did not fully take shape in his mind until after the publication of *Looking Back*.

Sir Hugo Latymer, the author of best-selling novels and short stories, has become the Grand Old Man of Letters. In earlier days he had traveled to the Far East for material, "digging for treasure troves in the trusting minds of the innocent." He has been to the Niehans clinic for rejuvenation treatments. He is a crusty, disagreeable man who has always held his fellow creatures in contempt. He has missed "the knack of discovering the best in people's characters instead of the worst." He has been a homosexual all his life, but his autobiography, *The Winding River*, with its constant implications of heterosexual ardor, is "the most superlative example of sustained camouflage" ever written. In it he dismisses his secretary and traveling companion, Perry Sheldon, as "an adequate secretary." Sheldon is an alcoholic and Sir Hugo discards him.

Sir Hugo's former mistress, Carlotta, who was with Perry Sheldon when he died, has Sir Hugo's letters to him, which could incriminate him in the eyes of posterity. In the end she returns the letters while commenting that "he has never taken into account the value of kindness and the importance of compassion. He has never had the courage or the humility to face the fact that it was not whom he loved in his life that really mattered, but his own capacity for loving." The conclusion drawn is that the strain of living behind a façade destroyed Sir Hugo's capacity for true feeling. The resemblance to Maugham in every line of the text was heightened when Noel Coward made himself up to look like his old friend.

At the Mauresque in the fall of 1962 a rumor reached Maugham's ears that Liza was going to have him certified as incompetent to conduct his own affairs. There was no foundation to the rumor, but he believed it nonetheless and became obsessed with the idea that his daughter was going to have him committed. When he heard a car coming up the driveway he would say, "They're coming for me." He went to see a lawyer in Nice and asked if his daughter could have him certified. The lawyer asked if he had any other children. Maugham said he did not. The lawyer suggested that if he had an adopted child, the certification could be opposed.[22]

On December 28 the lawyer announced that Maugham had adopted his secretary, Alan Searle. A cartoon in the *Daily Mail* on the following day showed Maugham holding an infant with a face like Alan's and saying, "Nurse, he's just said dada." Alan wrote Jerry Zipkin that the beastly attacks in the press had made Maugham a broken man. His heart was filled with murder, he said, for the people who were making Maugham's last years on earth a perfect hell.[23] He wrote Klaus Jonas, however, that he was very happy about the adoption, and that his name would remain the same, he would not call himself Alan Maugham.[24] Maugham's lawyer also sued for the return of all gifts to Liza, under Article 950 of the French Code Civil, which says that gifts can be revoked if the beneficiary displays ingratitude. Liza's suit for a share in the proceeds of the Sotheby auction constituted the principal act of ingratitude.[25]

In February 1963 Liza announced that she would challenge Alan's adoption in the French courts. "It is a shock to learn that my father has adopted Mr. Searle," she said. "Her father's move is tantamount to disowning her," John Hope said. Liza's lawyers had informed her that if the adoption went through, Alan would get everything, including the Villa Mauresque.

Upon hearing the news Alan told reporters that Maugham was "a sad man who feels starved of family affection. There have been many unhappy years in his life. This is one more."[26] He took Maugham to Venice to try to forget the litigation and wrote Klaus Jonas, in the venomous tone he now reserved for Liza, that his vile so-called daughter had broken him and made his last years a misery.[27]

The adoption dispute was heard *in camera* in the Nice Palais de Justice that June. Liza, arriving to testify before Judge Bonjean, told the press: "I did not do it for financial reasons. You just cannot take being disowned sitting down. It's not only a question of our dignity and standing, but of our children." On June 12, 1963, Liza spent three hours in a Nice courtroom listening to arguments about her legitimacy. "It was a most distressing and horrifying experience," she told reporters.[28]

Maugham's lawyer argued that he should be allowed to adopt Alan because Liza was not legally his daughter. She had been born out of wedlock, in 1915, when her mother was still Mrs. Henry Wellcome. According to British law, a child born in adultery could be legitimatized only if the parents were later married in England. This had not been done. Liza's lawyer argued that since Maugham and Alan were British subjects, British adoption law should be applied.

The British press made the most of the story, with headlines such as: Why I Am Fighting the Father I Love, I Don't Need Maugham's Money, and Of Course I Am Maugham's Daughter.[29]

On July 3 the Nice court in a twenty-five-page decision ruled in Liza's favor. The adoption of Alan was void. Liza was said to be Maugham's legitimate daughter and heir on the basis of his letters to her signed "Daddy." The court argued that because both parties were British subjects, British law applied to them. British law said that a child born out of wedlock to a couple who eventually marry is legitimate. The British consul in Rome at the time of Liza's birth testified that Maugham had returned to Rome from Capri to be at Syrie's bedside. Because Maugham was a resident of France, he was subject to French inheritance laws, which hold that a legitimate child cannot be disinherited.

Liza for the moment had won. For years Maugham had had everything his way. He had surrounded himself with servants and employees who did his bidding. His publishers and agents salaamed before his sales figures. The guests at the Mauresque were court flatterers. No one dared resist his will. It was a shock when resistance came, not from an outsider but from a daughter, whose tenacity matched his own. Liza's priorities, it was clear, were toward her husband, her children, and her mother's memory. Maugham did not give up, however. He appealed the decision and waited for the judgment to be handed down by the court of appeals in Aix-en-Provence.

In June, Liza's daughter Camilla married the Greek shipping heir Bluey Mavroleon. Maugham did not go to the wedding. Alan said he had not been invited. Even if he had, he could not have attended, for his mental condition was erratic. The litigation with his daughter seemed to have accelerated a process of senility. The Niehans treatments had helped keep his body alive but could not prevent the deterioration of his mind. The curse of the rich, S. N. Behrman once said, is that they are not allowed to die.

It was a pathetic spectacle. Maugham was slowly dying, Alan wrote Behrman, and it was agony to watch a loved one fading away. In addition, there was the torment of all the dreadful lawsuits. Alan said it was not his quarrel, but he got all the knocks and the odium. The greed and callousness of the family, he asserted, were beyond belief.[30] Alan's life had become such a nightmare, he wrote Jerry Zipkin, that he was incapable of describing it. Maugham was in acute misery and rarely sensible. Alan blamed Liza. When he saw what that bitch had done to her father, he said, his heart was filled with murder. Liza, he said, went around saying that she loved her daddy and wanted to be with him, but Alan hoped she would drop dead. He was despondent over losing the adoption case, for it meant that he would lose half of what Maugham had promised him.[31]

Guests still came to the Mauresque but never knew what to expect. One day at lunch a delicious lobster salad was served by the butler on silver plates. Maugham took his plate and emptied it on the floor. "Oh, Willie, you naughty boy," Alan said. "What's wrong, Alan?" Maugham asked.[32] Alex Frere came for the last time to settle some business matters. Maugham asked him to go to dinner with him at Lady Bateman's. Alan was going to Villefranche to cruise sailors. Maugham and Frere sat across from each other in the dining room of the Hotel de Paris. The *turbot grillé sauce béarnaise* was being passed around when Maugham suddenly shouted, "Frere, you've got to get me out of this fuckin' party." "I don't think Mr. Maugham is feeling well, Lady Bateman," Frere said, and took him outside. "What do we do now?" he asked. "The chauffeur isn't coming back until eleven." "Let's go down the hill and have dinner at Rampoldi's," Maugham said. They did, and later walked back up and met the chauffeur on the steps of the Hotel de Paris.[33]

Maugham was losing both his physical and mental faculties. There was a man on the Riviera named Eric Dunstan whom he disliked, but Alan finally got him to invite Dunstan to lunch. Dunstan and Maugham chatted and chuckled, and Alan was pleased that they had patched up their grievance. After lunch, as they sipped their coffee, Maugham gave Dunstan a piercing look and said, "Tell me, whatever happened to that swine Eric Dunstan?"[34] On another occasion, Sir Malcolm Bullock, a member of Parliament, came to see Maugham with the art critic Douglas Cooper. As they walked into the drawing room Maugham popped up from behind the sofa adjusting his trousers. He had defecated on the rug, and scooped up a handful of feces like a guilty child.[35]

In October, Maugham insisted on going on his annual European jaunt. Alan took him to Munich, but it was a nightmare. Maugham's traveling days were over. When he was lucid he complained, and when he was not his behavior was unpredictable. On one of his good days he told Alan he was the best nagger since Syrie. Alan went to the Oktoberfest and got uproariously drunk.[36]

Home in November, Maugham asked to see Sam Behrman, who came to spend four days. Behrman remembered the visit as macabre. Maugham did recognize him, though, and in his best moments was delightful. Behrman asked him if he had seen Churchill. "Yes," said Maugham, "last week. If you think I'm gaga, you should see Winston." Maugham told of an American woman who had buttonholed him, saying that she recognized him from his photographs. "I was hoping that I am more attractive than my photographs," Maugham said. "Oh no, you're not," she said, "indeed you're not." Behrman was surprised one day at lunch when Maugham blurted out, "The future of literature belongs to homosexuality," for it was a subject he never discussed.

In spite of his good moments, Behrman thought, he was certainly not, as Robin Maugham insisted, in the best of health. Behrman felt sorry for Alan, who was on the verge of a nervous breakdown. On one occasion, feeling the need to get away, Alan had gone to Nice for dinner. He left at seven and returned at nine-thirty to find the house in a turmoil. Maugham had disappeared. They found him walking on one of the roads in his stockinged feet, "those murderous roads," said Behrman, "on which he might have been nipped by a car at any moment."[37]

In December, Alan wrote Sam Behrman, things were worse. He thought he would lose his own mind. Maugham's misery was pitiful to see, and with his hearing practically gone and his sight failing, life held very little for him. He could no longer read with pleasure and just sat and brooded about the past. Alan said he cursed horrible Liza Hope and her beastly husband.[38]

On January 22, 1964, three days before Maugham's ninetieth birthday, Liza's suit for her share of the Sotheby sale was settled out of court. Maugham was in no condition to appear in court, and Liza's case was too strong. The terms of the settlement were that Liza would receive $250,000 for her share of the pictures—less than half of what she had asked for—and renounce all other claims to the estate. She preferred nonetheless to settle, for she did not look forward to the prospect of dragging her mentally unwell father into court. Maugham wanted to settle, because the proceeds of the sale were in escrow pending the outcome of the suit, and he wanted to leave something to Alan before he died. A joint statement was issued: "Mr. W. S. Maugham and his daughter Lady John Hope are happy to state that all the differences between them have been settled." Maugham had to pay the legal costs. Liza's husband said, "As far as we are concerned, we won the case."

Maugham did his best to rise to the occasion of his ninetieth birthday. Godfrey Winn came to visit on the twenty-fourth and found him sitting in his favorite leather armchair, wearing his favorite velvet dinner jacket. "Good evening," he said, "are you one of Alan's friends?" Winn gave him the program of the National Theatre production of *Othello*. "I can't remember when I wrote that," Maugham said. On the twenty-fifth they went to the Château de Madrid for a birthday lunch hosted by Lady Doverdale, another wealthy Riviera woman. "Why have you changed cars?" Winn asked, pointing to the Rolls Royce. "In the past you've always used French makes of cars. You said it was more convenient for these roads, and also because you lived in France." "I know I did, Godfrey," Maugham said, "but they promise me that a Rolls is good for ten years."

"You know," Maugham said as they drove to the restaurant, "people seem to regard death as an indictable crime. They are shocked if you mention it. I wait for it now without rancor or surprise. Every morning my valet tiptoes into my rooms as though he expects to find me dead in bed—but death, like constipation, is one of the commonplaces of human existence. Why shy away from it?" Maugham was pleased at the prospect of having lunch at the most expensive restaurant on the Riviera. "We shall have fresh asparagus, baby lamb, and strawberries out of season," he said. "I am told there will be eight in the party, and do you know what it will cost our hostess, including the view? Well over fifty pounds."[39]

Maugham's good days were impossible to predict. A few days before his birthday a journalist had flown in from New York for an interview, but he left after five minutes of agonizing embarrassment. But Kenneth Allsop, who interviewed him at a later date, found him charming and articulate.

> Certainly it is true that I have never concerned myself deeply with public or political issues [Maugham told Allsop]. You see, what has influenced my life more than any other single thing has been my stammer. Had I not stammered I would probably have had the same sort of classical education as others in my class of life. Instead of becoming a wanderer on the face of the earth, I would have gone to Cambridge as my brothers did and perhaps become a don and every now and then published a dreary book about French literature. I once said to Winston Churchill, "If I had not stammered I might have gone into politics and with my knack for speaking languages, I might have become our foreign minister." He looked at me and grunted. So I became a writer.

Allsop left with this last impression of Maugham: "Illusionless, Godless, and tranquilly unperturbed by the aspect of the void, he stood in silence for a few moments, if not precisely at peace with himself, content with the expedient truce."[40]

Maugham continued to go through the motions of life, with Alan in constant attendance. He had returned to the condition of his childhood, when he was at the mercy of others. Alan had begun to wish that he would quickly slip away in his sleep. He told friends that he had become a member of the euthanasia league. He could not leave him for more than ten minutes at a time. Maugham, he said, lived in a strange world of shadows and fears.[41]

The critic Raymond Mortimer came to stay with Maugham's neighbor, Rory Cameron, Enid Kenmare's son. Mortimer said he would like to see Alan. To Cameron's amazement, Alan telephoned to say that Maugham would like to come too. He arrived, looking neat and dapper, but did not recognize Mortimer. He stared ahead of him and said nothing. At lunch there were plates of ornamental china with embossed pea pods on them, and Maugham kept picking at the pea pods with his fork. He spoke only once during lunch, to say, "I hear the king is coming down tomorrow."[42]

In April, Alan took him to Venice. The valet and the chauffeur also came along, but they proved useless. Only Alan could relieve Maugham's terrible anguish. Maugham's life was a nightmare. He was surrounded by demons and woke up screaming in the middle of the night. Alan was utterly exhausted. He was also anxious about his future. Maugham had not decided what to leave him and refused to pay for legal advice. His affairs were in a hopeless muddle. Alan was afraid that if Maugham died, Liza would grab everything. He complained to Jerry Zipkin, who told him to draw up a list of what Maugham had promised him and have him sign it. But Alan was too distracted to act.[43] Once he asked Maugham where he should go after he died. "Go into lodgings," Maugham said. Another time Maugham asked Alan what his plans for the future were. "I'll marry a rich widow," Alan said. "For God's sakes, don't," Maugham said. "You've never liked hard work, and that's the hardest job of all."[44]

In July, prompted perhaps by the death in June of the friend of his dotage, Lord Beaverbrook, at the age of eighty-five, Maugham drafted his will. He left to his daughter all the shares in the Mauresque. Alan headed the list of bequests: 50,000 pounds to Alan; 2,000 pounds to Annette, the cook; 2,000 pounds to Jean, the chauffeur; and 500 pounds each to the other servants. In addition, Alan was to get the contents of the Mauresque and all of Maugham's royalties during his lifetime, which would come to an estimated $50,000 a year. After Alan's death the royalties would go to the Royal Literary Fund.[45]

Maugham's will guaranteed Alan a comfortable future, but the present was unreal and frightening. All reason had now gone, Alan reported to Zipkin in August. Maugham lived in a state of terror; he had to be constantly reassured. Liza arrived in August to see her father —as it turned out, for the last time. John had not wanted her to go. "He's absolutely out of his mind," he told her. When Liza said she was coming, Alan warned her to "keep a piece of furniture between you. He's been violent, he attacks me." Liza thought it was horrible that her father was being talked about as if he was less than human and insisted on going. When she got there Maugham did not recognize her. He thought she was Syrie and asked, "Why don't you shut your shop?" At the same time she was amazed by his physical energy. He kept running up and down the stairs. Never had she seen such a perfect example of a fit body outliving an unfit mind.[46]

And yet he still had good days, and when he was lucid, insisted on catching up with his mail. In November he wrote a London admirer, Dora Beech: "You must forgive me if I do not ask you to come and see me when you come to the South of France. I am now a very old man—in my ninety-first year—and in poor health. I find the effort I have to make in meeting new friends is too exhausting. I am really sorry."[47] Also in November there arrived Richard Cordell, one of Maugham's last visitors. He handed Maugham a letter from S. N. Behrman. "I don't know him," Maugham said. "Why Willie," Alan said, "he's been here time after time." "No, I don't know him at all," Maugham said. Maugham still drank his cocktail before dinner and ate heartily, Cordell noted. He talked about Henry James and H. G. Wells, but recent years were a blank.

In January 1965 Alec Waugh saw Maugham in Nice. Their paths crossed as they were strolling in opposite directions along the Promenade des Anglais. Waugh was with his future wife, Virginia Sorensen, who was wearing a cape. "The wind in your cape makes you look like a bird," Maugham said. He was brisk and cheerful. It was one of his good days. Waugh wondered whether this was the last time he would see him. He hoped it was, for Maugham's sake. His faculties were failing, and life had become irrelevant.[48]

In January, Churchill died, at the age of ninety, and Maugham had his last birthday, his ninety-first, on the twenty-fifth. A photograph showed him looking out vacantly over a cake with a single candle. Churchill had been a friend for more than fifty years. Maugham had first met him before the First World War at the Allhusens' country house, Stoke Poges, where they had made a pact never to be funny at each other's expense. How distant it all seemed. There were none of his contemporaries left. Maugham was like Tennyson's Sir Bedivere: "And I, the last, go forth companionless."

Keats said that great writers lead a life of allegory. Their lives take on a larger meaning, instructive to all. In Maugham's case the allegory was that of a man who overcame his handicaps to realize his full potential. If he could do it, there was hope for everyone. The stammer that prevented him from exercising the profession of his father and grandfather, the law, contributed to his decision to become a writer. The death of his mother and his unhappy childhood gave him the material for his finest novel. He was able to convert his feeling of apartness into the writer's stance of inquisitive detachment.

His true handicap, however, was not his stammer but his essential duality. Raised in France with French as his first language, he was never able to completely identify with England and the English. He loved his mother above everyone and yet had a low opinion of women. He married and had a child but was primarily homosexual. He combined an Edwardian sense of propriety about the details of his own life with a pirate's instincts toward his literary material. He cultivated an attitude of disdain toward literary careerism but was not above flattering helpful critics. He had a low opinion of the human species but a high tolerance of human frailty.

Although strongly influenced in his youth by the pessimism of Schopenhauer, and agreeing with him that life is meaningless, he made a pact with himself to live out his allotted span as fully and productively as he could. If he was a great man, it was because of this: believing life had no meaning, he determined to make it matter. He always wanted to take things, including his own life, "to the end of the chapter." Maugham was all of these: an alienated child, a medical student, an avant-garde novelist and playwright, a bohemian in Paris, a successful West End dramatist, a London social lion, an ambulance driver on the Flanders front, a spy in Russia, a promiscuous homosexual who paid for the favors of boys in remote lands, a cuckolded husband, a host to the famous persons of his time, a World War II propagandist, the most widely read novelist since Dickens, a living legend kept alive by cellular therapy, and a senile old man who tried to disinherit his daughter and adopt his secretary.

His work redeemed him. His aim was simply to make something that gave enjoyment. As he wrote in *Points of View*:

> From prehistoric times men blessed with a creative gift have arisen who have by artistic production added adornment to the grim business of living. As anyone can see for himself by going to Crete, cups, bowls, pitchers have been decorated with patterns—not because it made them more serviceable, but because it made them more pleasing to the eye. Throughout the ages artists have found their complete satisfaction in producing works of art. If the writer of fiction can do that, he has done all that can be reasonably asked of him.

His early books were considered scandalous and did not sell, so he found a formula for commercial success on the stage. He did so well that he became known as the Grand Old Businessman of English Letters. He occupied and took pleasure in the position of most celebrated English writer. His pen earned him at least four million dollars. The writer is a man alone, without affiliation, but Maugham turned his Moorish symbol into a trademark known the world over. No one else so exemplified the profession of writer. His concern over money matters, his quarrels with publishers, his directives to agents were all a part of his ambition to control his product. There was in Maugham a supreme efficiency of performance that has rarely been seen in literature.

Success did not make him kind or magnanimous. Money in the bank did not lead to greatness of soul. The suspicion that emotional atrophy made him an artist of the second rank embittered his years of triumph. He thought that he had no illusions about people, Noel Coward said, but in fact he had little faith in the human heart. His deepest relationships were variations on the theme of subjugation. As he grew older he emanated an infinite disaffection, like a great sigh. But even in his last years when he sat ranting in the Mauresque, the prisoner of his private demons, there was something noble in his determination to see it through.

"Death is psychologically just as important as birth," Jung said. "As the arrow flies to the target, so life ends in death. . . . Shrinking away from it is something unhealthy and abnormal which robs the second half of life of its purpose." This was something Maugham instinctively understood.

In March 1965 Maugham was treated for double pneumonia. He collapsed and was taken to the hospital, and a few days later newspaper photographs showed him leaving the hospital on his way home, recovered. Now his moods alternated between self-loathing and self-pity. He would sit in a corner muttering angrily to himself and a stream of obscenities would pour from his lips. Then he would break down and sob and say that he was a horrible and evil man and that everyone who had got to know him had ended up hating him. Alan was the scapegoat, the devoted presence he could say anything to. In April, Alan wrote Zipkin that Maugham's beastliness was beyond endurance. He was shut up with a madman. If he had the courage he would commit suicide. He longed for freedom, but he could not blame Maugham for being horrible, because he did not know what he was doing.[49] In May he wrote Sam Behrman that things were unreal and horrible and he was in despair. He longed and prayed for the end to come. Maugham lived in some terrible world of his own, and at the same time longed for death and was terrified of it. Alan hoped that it would come and that he might find a little happiness in some other world, for he had found none in this.[50]

In his lucid moments Maugham worried about Alan. In early December he asked to see Romaine Brooks, a Riviera neighbor and one of his few remaining links with the past, for she had married his first lover, Ellingham Brooks. Mrs. Brooks went reluctantly, for she had heard about Maugham's condition. His stammering was such that she could not understand a word he uttered. Only when he saw her to her car and pointed his finger at her did she grasp what he was saying: "You need somebody to take care of you," and then he directed his finger toward Alan. He was bequeathing Alan to her.[51]

In December, two months short of his ninety-second birthday, the end came. On December 8 he fell in the garden and gashed a shinbone. On December 12 he tripped over a carpet before lunch and fell in front of the fireplace, cutting his head. He went to bed, awoke during the night, got out of bed, and fell again. Alan found him unconscious on the floor of his bedroom. When he picked him up, Maugham said: "Why, Alan, where have you been, I've been looking for you for months. I want to shake your hand and thank you for all that you've done for me."[52] Those were his last words. Alan took him to the Anglo-American Hospital in Nice, which had been founded in 1906 as a memorial to Queen Victoria. On December 13 he slipped into a coma. His lungs were congested, he was feverish, and his blood was not reaching his brain. On December 14 he lost his leg reflexes and was given oxygen. On December 15 he died in the hospital, but because of a French law that required autopsies for hospital deaths, he was taken back to the Mauresque in an ambulance, and Alan announced on the sixteenth that he had died at home. On the 11 o'clock C.B.S. news that night in New York the announcer said, "Life in the sky and death on earth, these stories and others, after this message." Life in the sky was about Mars, and death on earth was about Maugham.[53]

Alan had known that Maugham was dying, but he did not advise Liza of that fact until Maugham had already been dead for twenty-four hours. Maugham's instructions were that he should be cremated and that his ashes should be buried within the precincts of the King's School. He wanted no memorial service and had written: "The memorial service is an ugly feature of contemporary manners. . . . It is in fact just as much a social occasion as the cocktail party . . . The luncheon parties that follow have a peculiar savor. . . . Those present, as they sip their dry martinis, cannot help feeling a certain complacency because they are still alive."[54]

Alan placed Maugham's corpse in his bedroom, and for several days people came and paid their last respects. He had to cope with the press—which descended *en masse*—with the French authorities, and with the family in London waiting for the remains. He provided refreshment for those who came to see Maugham lying in state—gin for the English, rum for the French, and champagne for the V.I.P.s. One of the visitors stole a snuffbox. Alan spotted another, a Riviera dowager, feeling the curtains next to Maugham's bed with great concentration to see if they were lined with silk.[55]

Among the many friends of Maugham who came to the Mauresque one last time was Lord Boothby, the British political figure who had served as parliamentary secretary to Churchill in the twenties. Boothby was an old friend, who had adopted Maugham's philosophy of life, a Pyrrhic resignation to the senselessness of it, coupled with a strong resolve to see it through. In Boothby's opinion, the four Englishmen who had given more pleasure to more people than any others in the twentieth century were Charles Chaplin, Noel Coward, P. G. Wodehouse, and Maugham.

Boothby found Alan alone, calm and resigned. "In some ways," Alan told him, "your friendship with Willie was unique. . . . He was very fond of you, and always at ease. Did you notice that, when we were alone together, the stammer practically disappeared? But most important of all, he knew that you were genuinely fond of him. Not very many people were."

Maugham was upstairs in his bedroom, Alan said. He asked if Boothby would like to see him. Boothby shook his head, and when Alan asked him why, he said, "Because nothing in life looks so dead as the dead."[56]

The closest crematorium was in Marseilles, and an ambulance drove Maugham's body there on the twentieth. Attendants took the corpse and placed it in one of the ovens. An attendant said to Alan, *"Voulez-vous voir Monsieur?"* ("Would you like to see the gentleman?"). "I 'ad to 'ave a last look at 'im," Alan recalled, "and Christ if 'e didn't sit up." The heat of the oven had caused Maugham's body to double up. Alan waited two hours. An attendant arrived with a tin tray covered with ashes and two bones that had not been consumed. Alan produced a malachite jar, into which the attendant poured the ashes, but the bones would not fit. The attendant said, *"Une minute, s'il vous plaît,"* went off, came back with a hammer, and pulverized what was left of one of the masters of contemporary English fiction. The malachite jar was placed inside a small mahogany casket, which was flown to London, arriving on December 21.[57]

On December 22 the ashes were buried at the foot of the Maugham Library wall, beneath the spires of Canterbury Cathedral. There was no hymn singing, no eulogy, no religious spectacle. There was a simple procession of mourners, led by Liza (who had become Lady Glendevon in 1964, her husband having been raised to the peerage). They walked four hundred yards from the Deanery of the Green Court of the King's School to a quiet cloister, where about thirty students, who had come back from their Christmas holiday to attend the ceremony, waited in a semicircle. The interment was carried out by the Very Reverend Ian White-Thompson, Dean of Canterbury, and the Reverend Peter Newell, headmaster of the King's School. A nickel-plated plaque on the casket said: "Somerset Maugham—1874–1965." The casket was buried and wreaths were placed against the brick wall, among them "To Grandpa, Rest in Peace, Nick" and "With Love from Liza."[58] Maugham, the disbeliever in ecclesiastical ritual, was buried without ritual but on hallowed ground. Canterbury was the shrine of Thomas à Becket, murdered in 1170 in the cathedral, and the destination of Chaucer's storytelling pilgrims. It was a fitting burial place for a teller of tales.[59]

ACKNOWLEDGMENTS

Much of Maugham's correspondence remains in private hands, and I would like to thank the following persons who showed me their collections:

Elza Behrman, the widow of S. N. Behrman, who graciously allowed me to study her late husband's papers.

Ms. Verna Sabelle, editor of *MD* medical magazine, who was kind enough to show me Maugham's letters to the Spanish psychiatrist Dr. Félix Martí-Ibáñez.

Jerome Zipkin, a longtime friend of Maugham's, who kindly allowed me to study his large collection of letters.

Robert Frey, of the House of El Dieff, who graciously let me see Maugham's letters to A. S. Frere.

Mrs. Alfred E. Carlile, of Meadville, Pennsylvania, who kindly showed me Maugham's correspondence with Maria Lewis (Dillie) Fleming.

I would like to acknowledge my debt to the research libraries that hold Maugham material, whose curators and staffs were unfailingly helpful:

Warren Roberts, curator, David Farmer, assistant curator, Ellen S. Dunlap, research librarian, and John R. Payne, research librarian, Humanities Research Center, University of Texas at Austin.

Lola Szladits, curator, Henry W. and Albert A. Berg Collection, New York Public Library, Astor, Lenox, and Tilden Foundations.

Donald Gallup, curator, Beinecke Rare Book and Manuscript Library, Yale University, New Haven, Connecticut.

Florian Shasky, chief, special collections, Stanford University, Stanford, California, to whom I owe a special debt of thanks for his efforts in lifting the restriction on the Alanson collection, the single most important Maugham correspondence; and David Weber, Director of the Stanford Libraries.

Saundra Taylor, curator of manuscripts, Lilly Library, Bloomington, Indiana.

Theodore Grieder, curator, Fales Collection, New York University, New York City.

Mrs. Michael Sherman, manuscripts assistant, Princeton University, Princeton, New Jersey.

Kenneth Lohf, curator, Butler Library, Columbia University, New York City.

Houghton Library, Harvard University, Cambridge, Massachusetts.

Olin Library, Cornell University, Ithaca, New York.

House of Lords Records Office, London.

G. Hattee, librarian, and P. Pollock, archivist, the King's School, Canterbury, England.

South Caroliniana Library, University of South Carolina, Columbia, South Carolina.

Samuel A. Sizer, curator, special collections, University of Arkansas Library, Fayetteville, Arkansas.

Mary Flagg, manager of archives and special collections, University of New Brunswick, Frederiction, New Brunswick, Canada.

Carrie Singleton, collection librarian, University of Oregon, Eugene, Oregon.

Christian F. Brun, department of special collections, University of California, Santa Barbara, California.

R. Russell Maylone, curator, special collections, Northwestern University Library, Evanston, Illinois.

Holly Hall, chief, rare books and special collections, Washington University Libraries, St. Louis, Missouri.

David Mike Hamilton, assistant curator, literary manuscripts, the Huntington Library, San Marino, California.

Gratitude is expressed to the following persons who allowed themselves to be interviewed: Lord and Lady Glendevon, Kenneth and Diana Marr-Johnson, Ellen Doubleday, Kenneth D. McCormick, Raymond Mortimer, Alexander S. Frere and Mrs. Frere, Mrs. R. G. Dashwood, Raymond Marriott, Mrs. Mary Rosenblatt, Mrs. Anne Alanson Eliaser, John Junor, Wallace Harvey, S. J. Perelman, Richard A. Cordell, Spencer Curtis Brown, Sir Alfred Ayer, Lady Ayer (Dee Wells), Viscountess Norwich (Diana Cooper), Alec Waugh, Glenway Wescott, Monroe Wheeler, John Hall Wheelock, Joseph Dobrinsky, Donald Angus, Carol Brandt, Jerome Zipkin, Klaus Jonas, G. Hattee, P. Pollock, H. G. Pearson, John Foster, Major D. Neville-Willing, David Posner, and Mrs. William Kiskadden.

I am also indebted to the following for material furnished in correspondence: Rebecca West, Anthony Powell, Frank Swinnerton, David Garnett, Jerome Weidman, Cecil Beaton, Beverley Nichols, Raymond Toole Stott, Wilmon Menard, Arthur Mizener, Sir William Stephenson, Jane Sommerich, Mrs. Dorothy Howell-Thomas, Lingard Loud, and John Le Carré.

I am grateful to those who gave permission to quote from their correspondence: Anthony Powell and Raymond Mortimer, each for a letter to Jocelyn Brooke; Jerome Weidman and George Brockway, each for a letter to W. S. Maugham; and James Michener for a letter to Klaus Jonas.

This book owes a great deal to Grenville Cook, perhaps the leading Maugham expert, who was helpful not only with information but also with documents. His critique of the manuscript, which ran to more than 160 pages, saved the author from many mishaps.

Special thanks must go to Spencer Curtis Brown, the sole executor of W. Somerset Maugham's literary estate, who gave the author permission to quote from Maugham's letters and who offered many helpful suggestions concerning the manuscript.

In writing this book I had two researchers who made major contributions. Patrick O'Higgins interviewed Alan Searle and obtained from him accounts of life at the Mauresque and of Maugham's death. Jacqueline Williams, my London researcher, is someone to whom the term "creative research" applies. She developed leads of her own, and once spent six months stubbornly knocking on the Home Office door before it would open. I am very much in her debt. I would also like to thank my editor at Simon & Schuster, Nan Talese, for tirelessly guiding this book through three successive drafts, my wife, Nancy Ryan Morgan, for her valuable counsel, and Mrs. Juanita Van Wagenen for her typing.

SOURCES

Short Titles

Maugham Correspondence and Papers

Texas MSS	Humanities Research Center, University of Texas at Austin
Berg MSS	Berg Collection, New York Public Library
Indiana MSS	Lilly Library, University Libraries, Indiana University
Standford MSS	Department of Special Collections, Bender Room, Stanford University
Harvard MSS	Houghton Library, Harvard University
Fales MSS	Fales Collection, New York University
Columbia MSS	Butler Library, Columbia University
Cornell MSS	Olin Library, Cornell University
Lords MSS	Beaverbrook Papers, House of Lords Records Office, London
Arkansas MSS	University of Arkansas Library, Fayetteville, Arkansas

Works by W. Somerset Maugham

L.L.	*Liza of Lambeth* (London, 1897).
M.C.	*Mrs. Craddock* (London, 1902).
O.H.B.	*Of Human Bondage* (London, 1915).
A.	*Ashenden* (London, 1928).
C.A.	*Cakes and Ale* (London, 1930).
S.U.	*The Summing Up* (London, 1938).
R.E.	*The Razor's Edge* (London, 1944).
W.N.	*A Writer's Notebook* (London, 1949).
L.B.	*Looking Back, Show* magazine (New York: June, July, Aug. 1962).

Other Frequently Mentioned Works

R.M.	Robin Maugham, *Somerset and All the Maughams* (New York, 1966).
J.D.	Joseph Dobrinsky, *La Jeunesse de Somerset Maugham* (Paris, 1975).
W.M.	Wilmon Menard, *The Two Worlds of Somerset Maugham* (Los Angeles, 1965).
R.M.J.M.	Raymond Mander and Joe Mitchenson, *Theatrical Companion to the Plays of W. Somerset Maugham* (London, 1955).

SOURCES

R.T.S.	Raymond Toole Stott, *A Bibliography of the Works of W. Somerset Maugham* (London, 1973).
C.S.	*W. S. Maugham: An Annotated Bibliography of Writing About Him*, comp. and ed. Charles Sanders (Illinois, 1970).
B.N.	Beverley Nichols, *A Case of Human Bondage* (London, 1966).

NOTES

Preface

1. *Philadelphia Inquirer*, Nov. 17, 1957.
2. Probate Registry, Somerset House, London.
3. Alan Searle to Patrick O'Higgins.
4. S. N. Behrman to Maugham, June 2, 1952, Behrman Papers.
5. Maugham to Behrman, undated, ibid.
6. William Jackson to Behrman, Aug. 1963, ibid.
7. Behrman to Jackson, Sept. 4, 1963, ibid.
8. Behrman to Bob, Jan. 7, 1963, ibid.
9–11. Maugham to Cordell, Indiana MSS.
12. Maugham to Richard Karl Pfeiffer, 1946, Texas MSS.
13. Maugham to George Brockway, Oct. 20, 1958, Columbia MSS.
14. Brockway to Maugham, Dec. 3, 1958, ibid.
15. Maugham to Cordell, Jan. 25, 1959, Indiana MSS.
16. Karl G. Pfeiffer, *W. Somerset Maugham: A Candid Portrait* (New York, 1959).
17. Pfeiffer to Brockway, 1959, Columbia MSS.
18. R.M.

Chapter One

1. Annual Register, 1874.
2. Cynthia Gladwyn, *The Paris Embassy* (London, 1977).
3. R.M.
4. *S.U.* (London, 1938), p. 17.
5. Maugham to Paul Dottin, Oct. 1927, Texas MSS.
6. R.M.
7. Maugham to Frederic Maugham, Oct. 8, 1952, Texas MSS.
8. R.M.
9. Viscount Maugham, *At the End of the Day* (London, 1954).
10. Ibid.
11. R.M.
12. *L.B.*, *Show* magazine (June 1962), p. 63.
13. Ibid., p. 64.
14. R.M.
15. *O.H.B.* (New York, 1937), p. 4.
16. R.M.

17. *L.B.* (June 1962), p. 63.
18. R.M.

Chapter Two

1. Wallace Harvey, Whitstable historian, to author.
2. *L.B.*, *Show* magazine, (June 1962), p. 64.
3. R.M.
4. Ibid.
5. *W.N.* (New York, 1949), p. 2.
6. R.M.
7. *L.B.* (June 1962), p. 64.
8. Maugham to Joseph Dobrinsky, Feb. 16, 1961.
9. Maugham to Paul Dottin, 1937, Texas MSS.
10. Viscount Maugham, *At the End of the Day* (London, 1954).
11. Canon F. J. Shirley, "William Somerset Maugham," *The Cantuarian* (Dec. 1965).
12. I am indebted to G. Hattee and P. Pollock of the King's School for information on the real-life models for Maugham's teachers.
13. *S.U.* (London, 1938), p. 316.
14. *O.H.B.* (New York, 1937), p. 74.
15. Ronald Pearsall, *The Worm in the Bud* (New York, 1969).
16. Archives, King's School, Canterbury.
17. Ibid.
18. *L.B.* (June 1962), p. 66.
19. *S.U.*, p. 88.
20. Glenway Wescott to author.
21. *O.H.B.*, p .138.
22. *S.U.*, p. 100.
23. Hesketh Pearson, *Labby: The Life of Henry Labouchère* (London, 1936).
24. Lewis Chester, David Leitch, and Colin Simpson, *The Cleveland Street Affair* (London, 1976).
25. *O.H.B.*, p. 285.
26. Preface, *L.L.* (New York, 1936), p. v.
27. *L.B.* (June 1962), p. 66.
28. *O.H.B.*, p. 176.
29. Maugham to Dottin, Feb. 1927, Texas MSS.
30. *L.B.* (June 1962), p. 66.
31. *S.U.*, p. 63.

Chapter Three

1. E. M. McInnes, *St. Thomas' Hospital* (London, 1963).
2. Ibid.
3. *W.N.* (New York, 1949), p. 10, and *C.A.* (New York: Penguin Books, 1977), p. 116.

4. *W.N.*, p. 11, and *C.A.*, p. 112.

5. *O.H.B.* (New York, 1937), p. 292.

6. Maugham, *The Gentleman in the Parlour* (New York, 1930), p. 268.

7. *O.H.B.*, p. 290.

8. Maugham, *On a Chinese Screen* (New York, 1922), p. 173.

9. *L.B.*, *Show* magazine (June 1962), p. 66.

10. Preface, *L.L.* (New York, 1936), p. vi.

11. *W.N.*, p. 5.

12. Joseph B. Lurie, M.B., "William Somerset Maugham: An Appreciation and a Probe," *Medical Proceedings* (Johannesburg, South Africa), Jan. 16, 1965.

13. Maugham to Wentworth Huyshe, 1897, Texas MSS.

14. *R.M.*, and Grenville Cook to author.

15. *L.B.* (June 1962), p. 67.

16. Nov. 3, 1949.

17. Mrs. R. G. Dashwood to Jacqueline Williams.

18. *S.U.* (London, 1938), p. 100.

19. Ibid., p. 63.

20. *O.H.B.*, p. 443.

21. Ibid., p. 447.

22. Ibid., p. 525.

23. Ibid., p. 526.

24. Maugham, *The Land of the Blessed Virgin* (London, 1905), p. 167.

25. *W.N.*, p. 15.

26. Phyllis Grosskurth, *John Addington Symonds* (London, 1964).

27. Ibid.

28. Richard Ellman, "A Late Victorian Love Affair," *New York Review of Books*, Aug. 4, 1977.

29. H. Montgomery Hyde, *The Love That Dare Not Speak Its Name* (New York, 1970).

30. Ibid.

31. Glenway Wescott to author.

32. *B.N.* In 1961 Jeffress committed suicide after being deported from Venice.

33. Maugham, *Don Fernando* (New York, 1935), p. 246.

34. Maugham, *The Art of Fiction* (New York, 1955), p. 203.

35. Ibid.

36. Maugham, "Red," *The Maugham Reader* (New York, 1950), p. 280.

37. Maugham, *Books and You* (London, 1940), p. 66.

38. *S.U.*, p. 102.

39. Maugham to Fisher Unwin, 1896, Berg MSS.

40. Edward Garnett's reader's report, Berg MSS.

41. *W.N.*, p. 38.

42. Preface, *L.L.*, p. vii.

43. Ibid., p. viii.

44. Annual Register, London, 1897.

45. Stanley Weintraub, *Reggie* (New York, 1965).

46. H. V. Routh, *English Literature and Ideas in the 20th Century* (London, 1946).

47. Guinevere L. Griest, *Mudie's Circulating Library and the Victorian Novel*

48. *The Diary of Virginia Woolf: Vol. I: 1915–1919*, ed. Anne Olivier Bell (Bloomington: Indiana Univ. Press, 1970).
(New York, 1977).

49. Gertrude Stein, *Lectures in America* (New York, 1975).

50. G. M. Trevelyan, *History of England*, Vol. III (New York, 1953).

51. Griest, *Mudie's Circulating Library and the Victorian Novel*.

52. Trevelyan, *History of England*, Vol. III.

53. Reginald Pound, *The Strand Magazine, 1891–1950* (London, 1966).

54. P. J. Keating, *The Working Class in Victorian Fiction* (London, 1971).

55. Ibid.

56. Arthur Morrison, *A Child of the Jago*, ed. P. J. Keating (London, 1969).

57. Preface, *L.L.*, p. ix.

58. Manuscript of *S.U.*, British Museum—passage deleted from published version.

59. Stanley Unwin, *The Truth About a Publisher* (London, 1960).

60–63. Berg MSS.

64. David Garnett (Edward Garnett's son) to author.

65. Berg MSS.

66. *L.L.* contract, Yale MSS.

67. Maugham to J. B. Pinker, Texas MSS.

68. Charles Scribner Papers, Princeton University.

69. Dedicated copy of *L.L.*, Texas MSS.

70. Berg MSS.

71. *Kentish Gazette* and *Canterbury Press*, Sept. 25, 1897.

72. C.S.

73. Maugham to Paul Dottin, undated, Texas MSS.

74. Preface, *L.L.*, p. x.

75. 1924 letter from Edmund Gosse to Sidney Colvin, quoted in *The Diary of Virginia Woolf: Vol. I: 1915–1919*.

76. *W.N.*, p. 261.

77. J.D.

78. Maugham, "Looking Back on Eighty Years," *The Listener*, Jan. 28, 1954.

79. Kenneth D. McCormick to author.

80. Preface, *L.L.*, p. x.

Chapter Four

1. R.T.S.

2. Grenville Cook collection.

3. James Joyce, *Selected Letters*, ed. Richard Ellman (New York, 1975).

4. James Hepburn, *The Author's Empty Purse and the Rise of the Literary Agent* (Oxford, Eng., 1968).

5. Frederick Whyte, *William Heinemann* (London, 1928).

6. Ibid.

7. Frank Swinnerton, *An Autobiography* (New York, 1936).

8–10. Arthur Mizener, *The Saddest Story* (New York, 1971).

11. Hepburn, *The Author's Empty Purse.*

12. Maugham to Morris Colles, undated, Harvard MSS.

13. Ibid.

14. *S.U.* (London, 1938), p. 103.

15. Fisher Unwin's reader's report, Berg MSS, and contract for *The Making of a Saint*, Yale MSS.

16. John Farrar, foreword to Maugham, *The Making of a Saint* (New York, 1966).

17. Introduction, *The Making of a Saint* (New York, 1944), p. 9.

18. C.S.

19. Oct. 1898, Indiana MSS.

20. Berg MSS.

21. Maugham to Colles, Aug. 1899, Indiana MSS.

22. Maugham,*The Land of the Blessed Virgin* (New York, 1920), p. 63, and *Don Fernando* (New York, 1935), p. 2.

23. *The Land of the Blessed Virgin,* p. 125.

24. *S.U.,* p. 103.

25. *The Land of the Blessed Virgin,* p. 2.

26. *Don Fernando,* p. 59.

27. *The Land of the Blessed Virgin,* p. 33.

28. *Don Fernando,* p. 87.

29. *The Land of the Blessed Virgin,* p. 223.

30. Maugham to Colles, April 11, 1899, Harvard MSS.

31. Foreword, *O.H.B.* (New York, 1936), p. 6.

32. *Spectator,* July 7, 1961.

33. Augustus Hare, *In My Solitary Life* (London, 1905).

34. Maugham, *The Vagrant Mood* (New York, 1953), p. 15.

35. Ibid., p. 57.

36. Hare, *In My Solitary Life.*

37. Maugham to Paul Dottin, undated, Texas MSS.

38. Reginald Pound, *The Strand Magazine, 1891–1950* (London, 1966).

39. Lady St. Helier, *Memories of Fifty Years* (London, 1909).

40. Samuel Hynes, *The Edwardian Turn of Mind* (Princeton, N.J., 1968).

41. Compton Mackenzie, *My Life and Times: Octave Four* (London, 1963).

42. Maugham, preface, "A Fragment of Autobiography," *The Magician* (New York, 1956), p. viii.

43. E. F. Benson, *As We Were* (New York, 1930).

44. Maugham, *The Vagrant Mood,* p. 56.

45. *S.U.,* p. 5.

46. Ibid.

47. Christopher Hassall, *Edward Marsh* (London, 1959).

48. Osbert Sitwell, *Noble Essences* (New York, 1950).

49. Evan Charteris, *The Life and Letters of Sir Edmund Gosse* (London, 1931).

50. Maugham, *The Vagrant Mood,* p. 209.

51. Leon Edel, *Henry James: The Treacherous Years* (New York, 1969).

52. Charles Grove, *Leather Armchairs* (New York, 1963).

53. Maugham to Colles, Dec. 17, 1899, Fales MSS.

54. July 19, 1902, Indiana MSS.

55. Authors' Syndicate to Maugham, ibid.

56. Maugham, *Selected Prefaces and Introductions* (New York, 1963), p. 84.

57. Manuscript of *The Hero*, Texas MSS.

58. Maugham, *The Hero* (London, 1901), p. 148.

59. Ibid., p. 56.

60. Charles Scribner to L. W. Bangs, Nov. 7, 1899: "Both Swift and Maugham now in the hands of the Authors' Syndicate . . . so Unwin has given them up," Scribner Papers, Princeton University.

61. Maugham to Robin, April 7, 1935, Texas MSS.

62. Quoted in Anthony Curtis, *Somerset Maugham* (London, 1977).

63. Maugham, preface to Francis de Croisset, *Our Puppet Show* (New York, 1929).

64. Maugham to Robert van Gelder, Feb. 2, 1944, Princeton University.

65. *W.N.* (New York, 1949), p. 58.

66. Louise Morgan, *Writers at Work* (New York, 1931).

67. In an inscribed edition of *Mrs. Craddock* Maugham wrote: "Written when the author was five and twenty"—which would be 1899.

68. Whyte, *William Heinemann.*

69. I am indebted to Joseph Dobrinsky for the psychological analysis of *Mrs. Craddock.*

70. C.S.

71. R.M.J.M.

72. Ibid.

73. George Rowell, *The Victorian Theater* (New York, 1956).

74. Laurence Housman, *The Unexpected Years* (New York, 1936).

75. Mizener, *The Saddest Story.*

76. Violet Hunt Papers, Cornell MSS.

77. Ibid.

78. Rebecca West to author.

79. April 1943, Berg MSS.

80. Violet Hunt Papers, Cornell MSS.

81. Ibid.

82. Berg MSS.

83. Ibid.

84. 1908, ibid.

85. Violet Hunt Papers, Cornell MSS.

86. H. Montgomery Hyde, *Henry James at Home* (London, 1969).

87. Alec Waugh to author.

88. Rowell, *The Victorian Theater.*

89. Frederick T. Bason, *A Bibliography of the Writings of William Somerset Maugham* (London, 1931). This edition of the play is now a much sought-after collector's item.

90. Maugham to Golding Bright, Texas MSS.

91. Nov. 9, 1903, Yale MSS.

92. R.M.

93. Maugham, *The Collected Plays* (London, 1952), preface, I, viii.

94. Muir letter, Indiana MSS.

95. S. N. Behrman, *Portrait of Max* (New York, 1960).

96. John Pollock, "Somerset Maugham and His Work," *Quarterly Review*, No. 304 (1966).

97. Behrman, *Portrait of Max*.

98. Max Beerbohm, *Last Theaters* (London, 1970).

99. *S.U.*, p. 117.

100. Maugham to Colles, Nov. 9, 1903, Yale MSS.

101. Jan. 30, 1904, Indiana MSS.

102. R.M.J.M.

103. Margaret Webster, *The Same Only Different* (New York, 1969).

104. Louis Marlow, *Seven Friends* (London, 1953).

105. Gerald Kelly to Richard Cordell, July 22, 1959, Indiana MSS.

106. R.M.

107. Diana Marr-Johnson to author.

Chapter Five

1. Maugham to Morris Colles: Aug. 1904, Texas MSS, and Aug. 28, 1904, Indiana MSS.

2. Derek Hudson, *For Love of Painting* (London, 1975).

3. Paul Léautaud, *Journal Littéraire* (Paris, 1954).

4. *The Confessions of Aleister Crowley* (London, 1969).

5. Hudson, *For Love of Painting*.

6. *S.U.* (London, 1938), p. 63.

7. Ibid., p. 174.

8. C.S.

9. Indiana MSS.

10. July 18, 1905, ibid.

11. Yale MSS.

12. *Daily Express*, Dec. 1909.

13. *Times Literary Supplement*, May 26, 1905.

14. Maugham, preface, "A Fragment of Autobiography," *The Magician* (New York, 1956), p. ix.

15–17. Harry Philips to Joseph Dobrinsky, Sept. 16, 1966. I am indebted to Mr. Dobrinsky for showing me this letter and others from Philips.

18. Clive Bell, *Old Friends* (New York, 1957).

19. Maugham, preface, *The Magician*, p.ix.

20. Philips to Dobrinsky, 1966.

21. *Letters of Arnold Bennett*, ed. James Hepburn (London, 1966).

22. Cecil Roberts, *The Years of Promise* (London, 1968).

23. Bell, *Old Friends*.

24. Margaret Drabble, *Arnold Bennett* (London, 1974).

25. *The Journal of Arnold Bennett* (New York, 1932).

26. Ibid.

27. George Tyler, *Whatever Goes Up* (New York, 1934).
28. Hudson, *For Love of Painting*.
29. Maugham, *The Vagrant Mood* (New York, 1953), p. 235.
30. *Letters of Arnold Bennett*, ed. Hepburn.
31. Texas MSS.
32. Donald W. Buchanan, *James Wilson Morrice* (Toronto, 1936).
33. Bell, *Old Friends*.
34. Maugham, *The Magician*, p. 24.
35. *The Confessions of Aleister Crowley*.
36. Aleister Crowley Papers, Texas MSS.
37. Louis Marlow, *Seven Friends* (London, 1953).
38. Maugham, preface, *The Magician*, p. x.
39. *The Confessions of Aleister Crowley*.
40. Ibid.
41. Maugham, preface, *The Magician*, p. x.
42. Compton Mackenzie, *My Life and Times: Octave Five* (London, 1966).
43. 1905, Berg MSS.
44. Meryle Secrest, *Between Me and My Life* (New York, 1974).
45. E. F. Benson, *As We Were* (New York, 1930).
46. Secrest, *Between Me and My Life*.
47. Hudson, *For Love of Painting*.
48. Léautaud, *Journal Littéraire*.
49. Hudson, *For Love of Painting*.
50. Bell, *Old Friends*.
51. Maugham to J. B. Pinker, July 1905, Texas MSS.
52. Aug. 18, 1905, ibid.
53. Nov. 3, 1905, ibid.
54. Nov. 9, 1905, ibid.
55. Nov. 12, 1905, ibid.
56. Oct. 15, 1905, ibid.
57. Oct. 1905, ibid.
58. March 1906, Berg MSS.
59. Preface, *L.L.* (New York, 1936), p. vii.
60. C.S.
61. Preface, *L.L.*, p. vii.
62. Texas MSS.
63. Oct. 8, 1906, ibid.
64. R.T.S.
65. March 1906, Berg MSS.
66. July 3, 1906, Texas MSS.
67. *S.U.*, p. 171.
68. Robert Lorin Calder, *W. Somerset Maugham & the Quest for Freedom* (New York, 1973).
69. *L.B.*, *Show* magazine (June 1962), p. 67.
70. Ibid., p. 111.
71. *C.A.* (New York: Penguin Books, 1977), p. 188.
72. Aug. 20, 1959, Indiana MSS.

73. *A Leaf from the Yellow Book: The Correspondence of George Egerton*, ed. Terence de Vere White (London, 1958).

74. Violet Hunt Papers, Cornell MSS.

75. Ibid.

Chapter Six

1. R.M.J.M.

2. *S.U.* (London, 1938), p. 109.

3. Sept. 16, 1907, Texas MSS.

4. Maugham, *The Collected Plays* (London, 1952), preface, I, xiii.

5. R.M.

6. R.M.J.M.

7. *Letters of Max Beerbohm to Reggie Turner*, ed. Rupert Hart-Davis (London, 1960).

8. Stanley Weintraub, *Reggie* (New York, 1965).

9. Maugham,*The Vagrant Mood* (New York, 1953), p. 218.

10. Clare Boothe Luce, in seminar on Maugham, University of Southern California, 1966, published by Friends of the Libraries, U.S.C., 1966.

11. The *Observer*, Dec. 19, 1965.

12. Preface to Louis Marlow, *Two Made Their Beds* (London, 1929).

13. Clare Boothe Luce, in U.S.C. seminar on Maugham.

14. R.M.

15. Alan Searle to Patrick O'Higgins.

16. *San Francisco Chronicle*, July 1966.

17. Sept. 16, 1907, Texas MSS.

18. Yale MSS.

19. June 13, 1946, Texas MSS.

20. R.M.J.M.

21. C.S.

22. Maugham, *Strictly Personal* (New York, 1941), p. 56.

23. Maugham to Bertram Alanson, Stanford MSS.

24. Maugham to J. B. Pinker, Nov. 17, 1907, Texas MSS.

25. Isaac F. Marcosson and Daniel Frohman, *Charles Frohman, Manager and Man* (New York,1916).

26. Billie Burke, *With a Feather on My Nose* (New York, 1949).

27. Hollis Alpert, *The Barrymores* (New York, 1964).

28. R.M.J.M.

29. *The Journal of Arnold Bennett* (New York, 1932).

30. *Letters of Arnold Bennett*, ed. James Hepburn (London, 1966).

31. *S.U.*, p. 121.

32. Charles Hawtrey, *The Truth at Last*, with an introduction by Maugham (London, 1924).

33. Sewell Stokes, *Without Veils* (London, 1953).

34. Marcosson and Frohman, *Charles Frohman, Manager and Man*.

35. R.M.J.M.

36. George Bishop, *My Betters* (London, 1957).
37. R.M.J.M.
38. Sept. 20, 1908, Texas MSS.
39. Nov. 12, 1908, ibid.
40. Violet Wyndham, *The Sphinx and Her Circle* (New York, 1963).
41. Osbert Sitwell, *Noble Essences* (New York, 1950).
42. Maugham to Ada Leverson, Dec. 1908, Yale MSS.
43. Ada Leverson, *The Limit* (London, 1909).
44. Catalogue of the contents of the Villa Mauresque, Sotheby & Co., Nov. 20, 1967.
45. Maugham to Leverson, Yale MSS.
46. Ibid.
47. Cecil Beaton, *The Restless Years* (London, 1976).
48. *C.A.* (New York, 1950), p. 7.
49. Maugham, *The Vagrant Mood*, p. 250.
50. R. W. B. Lewis, *Edith Wharton* (New York, 1976).
51. Violet Hunt Papers, Cornell MSS.
52. Sept. 5, 1910, Yale MSS.
53. *S.U.*, p. 2.
54. *L.B., Show* magazine (June 1962), p. 110.
55. Ibid.
56. Alan Searle to Patrick O'Higgins.
57. Christopher Hassall, *Edward Marsh* (London, 1959).
58. *Robert Ross, Friend of Friends*, ed. Margery Ross (London, 1952).
59. R.M.J.M.
60. Maugham, *The Collected Plays*, preface, I, xv.
61. *S.U.*, p. 121.
62. Maugham to Leverson, Feb. 1909, Yale MSS.
63. Feb. 21, 1909, ibid.
64. Maugham to Pinker, Aug. 11, 1909, Texas MSS.
65. April 1909, ibid.
66. Maugham to Dion Boucicault, quoted in R.T.S.
67. George Rowell, *The Victorian Theater* (New York, 1956).
68. Jan. 28, 1909, Texas MSS.
69. Irene Vanbrugh, *To Tell My Story* (London, 1948).
70. Maugham to Golding Bright, May 20, 1909, Texas MSS.
71. Louis Marlow, *Seven Friends* (London, 1953).
72. Maugham to Bright, June 5, 1909, Texas MSS.
73. Aug. 1909, Yale MSS.
74. R.M.J.M.
75. Maugham, *Christmas Holiday* (New York, 1939), p. 311.
76. Nov. 1910, Texas MSS.
77. May 17, 1909, ibid.
78. *S.U.*, p. 123.
79. Dec. 10, 1909, Yale MSS.
80. R.M.J.M.
81. Feb. 1910, Yale MSS.

82. Vanbrugh, *To Tell My Story*.
83. R.M.J.M.

    Chapter Seven

1. Christopher Hassall, *Edward Marsh* (London, 1959).
2. Maugham to Violet Hunt, July 1910, Berg MSS.
3. Lillie Langtry, *The Days I Knew* (New York, 1925).
4. Hassall, *Edward Marsh*.
5. Samuel Hynes, *The Edwardian Turn of Mind* (Princeton, N.J., 1968).
6. Hassall, *Edward Marsh*.
7. 1917, private collection.
8. Sept. 29, 1912, private collection.
9. Sir Rupert Hart-Davis, *Hugh Walpole* (London, 1952).
10. Ibid.
11. Walpole Papers, Texas MSS.
12. Hart-Davis, *Hugh Walpole*.
13. J. B. Priestley, *Margin Released* (London, 1962).
14. *Vanity Fair* (Jan. 1920).
15. Maugham to Walpole, Texas MSS.
16. Ibid.
17. Hart-Davis, *Hugh Walpole*.
18. Maugham to Golding Bright, Oct. 16, 1909, Texas MSS.
19. Maugham to Charles Frohman, Jan. 25, 1910, Texas MSS.
20. Billie Burke, *With a Feather on My Nose* (New York, 1949).
21. John Hall Wheelock to author.
22. Ibid.
23. Eric Wollencott Barnes, *The Man Who Lived Twice* (New York, 1956).
24. Maugham speech at Morgan Library, 1950, Texas MSS.
25. Maugham to Mr. Christie, Nov. 1910, ibid.
26. Maugham, *The Vagrant Mood* (New York, 1953), p. 211.
27. Maugham to J. Beaumont Maugham, Nov. 29, 1910, Texas MSS.
28. *Tuckerton Beacon*, June 10, 1913, New York Public Library.
29. New York *Morning Telegraph*, Dec. 12, 1910, ibid.
30. New York *Dramatic Mirror*, Dec. 14, 1910, ibid.
31. Maugham to Eliot Norton, Dec. 15, 1910, Harvard MSS.
32. Texas MSS.
33. C.S.
34. Feb. 24, 1911, Yale MSS.
35. Undated, ibid.
36. 1911, private collection.
37. Grenville Cook to author.
38. Compton Mackenzie, *My Life and Times: Octave Four* (London, 1963).
39. Isaac F. Marcosson and Daniel Frohman, *Charles Frohman, Manager and Man* (New York, 1916).
40. Burke, *With a Feather on My Nose*.

41. Raymond Mander and Joe Mitchenson, *The Artist and the Theatre* (London, 1955). This anecdote may be an example of Maugham exercising artistic license at the expense of truth, for by the time the dealer had sent him a note, the bidding would probably have been over. Maugham donated his collection of theatrical paintings to the National Gallery in 1948.

42. Cecil Roberts, *Sunshine and Shadow* (London, 1972).

43. Derek Hudson, *For Love of Painting* (London, 1975).

44. *S.U.* (London, 1938), p. 196.

45. Methuen to Maugham, Berg MSS.

46. Maugham to Pinker, ibid.

47. *L.B., Show* magazine (July 1962), p. 41.

48. Books given by Maugham to the King's School, King's School archives.

49. Janet Hitchman, *They Carried the Sword* (London, 1966).

50. *L.B.* (July 1962), p. 43.

51. London *Times*, July 27, 1936.

52. Rebecca West to author.

53. *Daily Express*, Feb. 15, 1916.

54. Roberts, *Sunshine and Shadow*.

55. Reginald Pound, *Selfridge* (London, 1960).

56. *L.B.* (July 1962), p. 41.

57. Marcosson and Frohman, *Charles Frohman, Manager and Man*.

58. R.M.J.M.

59. Dec. 29, 1912, Princeton University.

60. New York *Dramatic Mirror*, Jan. 29, 1913.

61. *L.B.* (June 1962), p. 111.

62. London *Times*, April 26, 1966, and Jacqueline Williams to author.

63. Burke, *With a Feather on My Nose*.

64. Vanbrugh, *To Tell My Story*.

65. *L.B.* (July 1962), p. 42.

66. Ibid. Three years before his death Maugham told the feature editor of the *Sunday Express*, John Junor, that he always wore a contraceptive when making love to Syrie.

67. Letter, undated, private collection.

68. *L.B.* (July 1962), p. 42.

Chapter Eight

1. *L.B., Show* magazine (July 1962), p. 42.

2. E. F. Benson, *As We Were* (New York, 1930). The very particular miniature world of Lucia, a provincial social climber, found such ardent admirers as W. H. Auden, Nancy Mitford, and Noel Coward, and the Lucia novels were reissued in one volume in 1977 to critical acclaim. One reviewer, Walter Clemons of *Newsweek*, said Benson was "mildly infected with genius."

3. Compton Mackenzie, *My Life and Times: Octave Four* (London, 1963).

4. Benson, *As We Were*.

5. Ibid.

6. Mackenzie, *My Life and Times: Octave Four.*

7. James Cameron, *1914* (New York, 1959).

8. Paul Fussell, *The Great War and Modern Memory* (Oxford, Eng., 1976).

9. Cameron, *1914.*

10. Undated, private collection.

11. Desmond MacCarthy, *Experiences* (New York, 1935).

12. Desmond MacCarthy, *Memories* (New York, 1953).

13. Ibid.

14. *W.N.* (New York, 1949), p. 97.

15. Ibid., p. 93.

16. Ibid., p. 95.

17. *L.B.* (July 1962), p. 42.

18. Annual Register, London, 1914.

19. Sept. 1915, Cornell MSS.

20. Fussell, *The Great War and Modern Memory.*

21. Gerald Haxton's death certificate, New York, N.Y.

22. Alexander Frere to author.

23. Robin Maugham, *Escape from the Shadows* (New York, 1973).

24. S. N. Behrman, *People in a Diary* (Boston, 1972).

25. Undated, private collection.

26. Glenway Wescott to author.

27. Maugham, *The Collected Plays* (London, 1952), III, 21.

28. Feb. 4, 1915, private collection.

29. Isaac F. Marcosson and Daniel Frohman, *Charles Frohman, Manager and Man* (New York, 1916).

30. Undated, Texas MSS.

31. *L.B.* (July 1962), p. 43.

32. *W.N.*, p. 99.

33. Annual Register, London, 1915.

34. Lingard Loud to author.

35. *S.U.* (London, 1938), p. 196.

36. Richard A. Cordell, *Somerset Maugham: A Writer for All Seasons* (New York, 1969).

37. C.S.

38. Clare Boothe Luce, in seminar on Maugham, University of Southern California, 1966, published by Friends of the Libraries, U.S.C., 1966.

39. C.S.

40. Garson Kanin, *Remembering Mr. Maugham* (New York, 1966).

41. Maugham to Paul Dottin, Dec. 22, 1933, Texas MSS.

42. Undated, ibid.

43. *L.B.* (July 1962), p. 43.

44. Sept. 27, 1915, Cornell MSS.

45. *L.B.* (July 1962), p. 44.

46. Maugham, *The Collected Plays*, preface, III, vii.

47. R.M.J.M.

48. Court book entries for Dec. 7 and Dec. 10, 1915, Central Criminal Court, Old Bailey, London.

49. H. G. Pearson to author.

50. Maugham to Frederic Maugham, March 12, 1916, Texas MSS.

51. Sewell Stokes, *Without Veils* (London, 1953).

52. London *Times, Daily Mail,* and *Daily Chronicle,* Feb. 15, 1916.

53. Texas MSS (see n. 50, above).

54. *L.B.* (July 1962), p. 44.

55. Compton Mackenzie, *My Life and Times: Octave Six* (London, 1967).

56. Edward Knoblock, *Round the Room* (London, 1939).

57. Derek Hudson, *For Love of Painting* (London, 1975).

58. Alan Searle to Patrick O'Higgins.

59. Maugham to Mrs. Ashenden, Feb. 9, 1954, King's School archives.

60. Maugham, *Ashenden* (New York, 1951), pp. 14 ff.

61. Lady Alfred Ayer to author.

62. *L.B.,* p. 99.

63. *L.B.* (July 1962), p. 45.

64. Maugham to Leslie A. Marchand, quoted in *The Maugham Enigma,* anthology, ed. Klaus Jonas (London, 1954).

65. W.M.

66. Information on Bertram Alanson was kindly provided to the author by his niece, Mrs. Anne Alanson Eliaser, and his grandniece, Mrs. Mary Rosenblatt.

67. Behrman, *People in a Diary.*

68. *The Diaries of Sir Robert Bruce Lockhart, 1915–1938,* ed. Kenneth Young (London, 1973).

69. Undated, private collection.

70. Maugham to Alanson, Alanson collection, Stanford MSS. The Alanson collection, including the correspondence and many first editions, is at Stanford University. Until 1978 there was a restriction on the correspondence, which was lifted thanks to the efforts of Florian J. Shasky, curator of special collections, and David Weber, curator of the Stanford Libraries. The author, who is much indebted to Mr. Shasky and Mr. Weber, was the first researcher to see the collection.

71. W.M.

72. Ibid.

73. San Francisco *Call,* Jan. 24, 1939.

74–76. W.M.

77. *W.N.,* p. 112.

78. W.M.

79. *W.N.,* p. 117.

80. Jan. 30, 1917, private collection.

81. *W.N.,* p. 134.

82. Gauguin Museum, Papeete, Tahiti.

83. W.M.

84. *W.N.,* p. 137.

85. W.M.

86. C.S.

87. *San Francisco Examiner,* April 18, 1917.

88. *San Francisco Chronicle,* June 1, 1918.

89. John Hall Wheelock to author.

90. Bureau of Vital Statistics, New Jersey.
91. Kanin, *Remembering Mr. Maugham.*
92. Wescott to author.
93. *L.B.* (July 1962), p. 96.
94. B.N.
95. Cecil Beaton, *The Glass of Fashion* (New York, 1955).
96. Maugham to Miss Legatt, Feb. 7, 1927, Grenville Cook collection.
97. Donald Angus to author.
98. David Herbert, *Second Son* (London, 1972).
99. Godfrey Winn, *The Infirm Glory* (London, 1967).
100. Rebecca West to author.
101. W. B. Fowler, *British-American Relations 1917–1918: The Role of Sir William Wiseman* (Princeton, N.J., 1969).
102. Sir Rupert Hart-Davis, *Hugh Walpole* (London, 1952).
103. June 20, 1917, Texas MSS.
104. Emmanuel Victor Voska and Will Irwin, *Spy and Counter-Spy* (New York, 1940).
105. Wiseman file 91-112, Yale MSS.
106. Maugham, *Cosmopolitans* (New York, 1936), p. 28.
107. *L.B.* (July 1962), p. 49.
108. *W.N.*, p. 187.
109. *L.B.* (July 1962), p. 95.
110. Ibid.
111. Fowler, *British-American Relations 1917–1918.*
112. *W.N.*, p. 163.
113. Oct. 1917, Berg. MSS.
114. *L.B.* (July 1962), p. 95.
115. Robert Lorin Calder, *W. Somerset Maugham & the Quest for Freedom* (New York, 1973).
116. Voska and Irwin, *Spy and Counter-Spy.*
117. *L.B.* (July 1962), p. 95.

Chapter Nine

1. Maugham to Dillie Fleming, 1917, private collection.
2. 1917, Texas MSS.
3. Undated, Berg MSS.
4. *Yesterday: The Autobiography of Robert Hichens* (London, 1947).
5. *L.B., Show* magazine (July 1962), p. 95.
6. Home Office file on Gerald Haxton.
7. R.M.J.M.
8. *The Listener*, Feb. 7, 1974.
9. R.M.J.M.
10. Nov. 21, 1924, Yale MSS.
11. Jan. 1919, Texas MSS.
12. In scenes describing Strickland down and out in Marseilles, Maugham

relied on a book by Harry A. Franck, *A Vagabond Journey Round the World* (1910), in which, in a chapter entitled "A Beachcomber in Marseilles," Franck explained how impoverished travelers could find a roof and a crust of bread. Maugham acknowledged his debt to Franck in the preface to his collected works.

13. Leopold Bellak, "Somerset Maugham: A Thematic Analysis of Ten Short Stories," in *The Study of Lives*, ed. R. W. White (New York, 1963).

14. S. N. Behrman, *People in a Diary* (Boston, 1972).

15. Pola Gauguin, *My Father Paul Gauguin* (London, 1937).

16. H. T. Craven, "Tahiti from Melville to Maugham," *Bookman* (Nov. 1919).

17. C.S.

18. *W. Somerset Maugham's Introduction to English and American Literature* (New York, 1943), p. 463. However, in his introduction to *Tellers of Tales* (New York, 1939) Maugham was kinder to Miss Mansfield, writing: "I know of only two English writers who have taken the short story as seriously as it must be taken if excellence is to be achieved, Rudyard Kipling, namely, and Katherine Mansfield."

19. *L.B.* (July 1962), p. 96.

20. June 1, 1919, Texas MSS.

21. Compton Mackenzie, *My Life and Times: Octave Five* (London, 1966).

22. R.M.J.M. In America it was produced as *Too Many Husbands*, and was twice made into movies: in 1940 with Jean Arthur, Fred MacMurray, and Melvyn Douglas; and in 1955 as a musical with Betty Grable, Jack Lemmon, and Gower Champion.

23. *W.N.* (New York, 1949), p. 190.

24. Jan. 3, 1920, private collection.

25. Ibid.

26. Maugham, *On a Chinese Screen* (New York, 1922), p. 16.

27. Ibid., p. 141.

28. Maugham to Golding Bright, Jan. 12, 1920, Texas MSS.

29. Harold Acton, *More Memoirs of an Esthete* (London, 1970).

30. March 1920, Texas MSS.

31. Godfrey Winn, *The Positive Hour* (London, 1960).

32. Maugham, *On a Chinese Screen*, p. 106.

33. Maugham, *The Gentleman in the Parlour* (New York, 1930), p. 49.

34. R.M.J.M.

35. C.S.

36. Kevin Brownlow, *The Parade's Over* (New York, 1968).

37. *North American Review* (May 1921).

38. Edward Knoblock, *Round the Room* (London, 1939).

39. *W.N.*, p. 199.

40. Maugham to Bert Alanson, Feb. 26, 1921, Stanford MSS.

41. Maugham, *Books and You* (London, 1940), p. 89, and Maugham to Knoblock, March 19, 1921, Berg MSS.

42. Aug. 17, 1921, Berg MSS.

43. Victor Purcell, *The Memoirs of a Malayan Official* (London, 1965).

44. Ibid.

45. Maugham, *The Gentleman in the Parlour*, pp. 47 and 54.

46. Ibid., p. 47.

47. Norman Sherry, "How Murder on the Veranda Inspired Somerset Maugham," *Observer*, Feb. 22, 1976.

48. Introductions to television broadcasts of Maugham short stories, Texas MSS.

49. R.M.J.M.

50. J. C. Trewin, *The Gay Twenties* (London, 1958).

51. Maugham to Alanson, April 25, 1921, Stanford MSS.

52. Maugham to Alanson, ibid., *W.N.*, p. 204.

Chapter Ten

1. Maugham to Bert Alanson, Aug. 23, 1921, Stanford MSS.

2. "Extreme happiness, separated from extreme despair by a trembling leaf, is that not life?"

3. Manuscript of *The Trembling of a Leaf*, Stanford MSS.; the manuscript was given by Maugham to Bert Alanson in 1947 "in memory of a long friendship."

4. Richard A. Cordell, *Somerset Maugham: A Writer for All Seasons* (New York, 1969).

5. C.S.

6. Michener to Klaus Jonas, Feb. 13, 1952, Texas MSS.

7. *The Listener*, Dec. 23, 1965.

8. Nov. 18, 1921, Stanford MSS.

9. Dwight Taylor, article in *Vogue*, Sept. 1, 1953.

10. Mark Schorer, *Sinclair Lewis* (New York, 1961).

11. Yale MSS.

12. Texas MSS.

13. C. R. W. Nevinson, *Paint and Prejudice* (New York, 1938).

14. S. N. Behrman, *People in a Diary* (Boston, 1972).

15. Maugham to S. N. Behrman, June 23, 1951, private collection.

16. Louise Morgan, *Writers at Work* (New York, 1931).

17. Basil Dean, *Seven Ages* (London, 1970).

18. Maugham, *The Collected Plays* (London, 1952), preface, III, x.

19. C.S.

20. Maugham to Alanson, July 25, 1922, Stanford MSS.

21. Maugham, preface, *The Travel Books* (London, 1955), p. viii.

22. *Sunday Express* file, Oct. 1922.

23. C.S.

24. *Britannia and Eve*, a monthly journal for men and women (July and Aug. 1929).

25. Wilmon Menard to author.

26. Nov. 10, 1922, Yale MSS.

27. Maugham, *The Gentleman in the Parlour* (New York, 1930), p. 182.

28. R.M.J.M.

29. C.S.

30. March 1923, Yale MSS.

31. Maugham, *The Gentleman in the Parlour*, p. 280.
32. Jack Hines, article in *New York Times* Book Review, June 17, 1923.
33. May 23, 1923, Stanford MSS.
34. *Sunday Express* files, June 7, 1923.
35. Frank Swinnerton, *My Autobiography* (London, 1937).
36. Arnold Bennett, *Letters to His Nephew* (New York, 1935).
37. Cecil Roberts,*The Bright Twenties* (London, 1970).
38. Selections from *Vanity Fair* (1960).
39. *L.B., Show* magazine (July 1962), p. 98.
40. Bennett, *Letters to His Nephew*.
41. Aug. 21, 1923, Stanford MSS.
42. R.M.J.M.
43. Maugham to Alanson, Oct. 6, 1923, Stanford MSS.
44, 45. Maugham to Alanson, Oct. 25, 1923, ibid.
46. Karl G. Pfeiffer, *W. Somerset Maugham: A Candid Portrait* (New York, 1959.
47. R.M.J.M.
48. Maugham to Alanson, Jan. 14, 1924, Stanford MSS.
49. March 3, 1924, Fales MSS.
50. *Everybody's Book of the Queen's Doll's House*, ed. A. C. Benson (London, 1924).

Chapter Eleven

1. Basil Dean, *Seven Ages* (London, 1970).
2. Maugham to Bert Alanson, Oct. 1, 1924, Stanford MSS.
3. Bruce Kellner, *Carl Van Vechten and the Irreverent Decades* (Oklahoma, 1968).
4. Maugham to Carl Van Vechten, Oct. 7, 1924, Berg MSS.
5. *The Collected Letters of D. H. Lawrence* (New York, 1926).
6. Ibid.
7. Frieda Lawrence, *Not I, but the Wind* (New York, 1934).
8. *The Collected Letters of D. H. Lawrence*.
9. Ibid.
10. *W. Somerset Maugham's Introduction to English and American Literature* (New York, 1943), p. 241.
11. Maugham to Forshaw, May 19, 1962, Texas MSS.
12. Oct. 1924, Berg MSS.
13. Alan Searle to Patrick O'Higgins.
14. Nov. 21, 1924, Yale MSS.
15. Feb. 1, 1925, Berg MSS.
16. Maugham, *The Painted Veil* (London, 1925), p. 26.
17. May 17, 1925, Stanford MSS.
18. C.S.
19. Michael Holroyd, *Lytton Strachey* (London, 1967–68).
20. Cornelius Weygandt, *A Century of the English Novel* (New York, 1925).

21. Tallulah Bankhead, *Tallulah: My Autobiography* (New York, 1952).

22. Dean, *Seven Ages*.

23. May 17, 1925, Stanford MSS.

24. Bankhead, *Tallulah: My Autobiography*.

25. Dean, *Seven Ages*.

26. Maugham to James Rumsey, June 12, 1925, Yale MSS.

27. May 17, 1925, Stanford MSS.

28. L.B., *Show* magazine (July 1962), p. 98.

29. Beverley Nichols, *Are They the Same at Home?* (New York, 1927).

30. Beverley Nichols, *A Case of Human Bondage* (London, 1966).

31. Nov. 1925, Berg MSS.

32–34. Maugham to Alanson, July 9, 1925, Stanford MSS.

35. June 19, 1924, ibid.

36. Maugham to Ellingham Brooks, Oct. 3, 1925, Texas MSS.

37. Maugham to Charles Hanson Towne, Sept. 25, 1925, Yale MSS.

38. Nov. 23, 1925, ibid.

39. R.M.J.M.

40. *William Somerset Maugham, Novelist, Essayist, Dramatist*, with an essay by Charles Hanson Towne (Doran, 1925).

41. Maugham to Alanson, March 15, 1926, Stanford MSS.

42. L.B. (July 1962), p. 100.

43. Roderick Cameron, *The Golden Riviera* (London, 1975).

44. L.B. (July 1962), p. 100.

45. April 1927, Yale MSS.

46. George Doran, *Chronicles of Barabbas* (New York, 1935), and In Memoriam booklet for Nelson Doubleday, 1949.

47. Maugham to Edward Knoblock, March 27, 1926, Berg MSS.

48. May 20, 1926, Stanford MSS.

49. *The Diaries of Sir Henry Channon*, ed. Robert Rhodes James (London, 1967).

50. *The Journal of Arnold Bennett* (New York, 1932).

51. R.M.J.M.

52. July 1, 1926, Texas MSS.

53. London *Times*, June 14, 1951.

54. Sotheby's catalogue, sale of the contents of the Villa Mauresque, Nov. 20, 1967.

55. B.N.

56. C.S.

57. In an inscribed copy of *The Casuarina Tree* Maugham wrote: "No one knows anything about his own work, but they say 'The Outstation' is my best story."

58. C.S.

59. Oct. 29, 1926, Berg MSS.

60. Maugham to Alanson, Oct. 11, 1926, Stanford MSS.

61. L.B. (July 1962), p. 100.

62. Kellner, *Carl Van Vechten and the Irreverent Decades*.

63. Hollis Alpert, *The Barrymores* (New York, 1964).

64. R.M.J.M.

65. Aug. 24, 1935, Yale MSS.

66. Sept. 10, 1935, ibid.

67. Maugham to Miss Moseley, Nov. 24, 1926, Fales MSS.

68. *L.B.* (July 1962), p. 100.

69. Sewell Stokes, *Without Veils* (London, 1953).

70. R.M.J.M.

71. Maugham to Paul Dottin, Feb. 1927, Texas MSS.

72. R.M.J.M., and Dean, *Seven Ages*.

73. Arnold Bennett, *Letters to His Nephew* (New York, 1935).

74. *L.B.* (July 1962), p. 100.

75. R.M.J.M. *The Constant Wife* was revived twice in London—in 1937 and 1946—both times unsuccessfully. A third revival in 1973 did a bit better, largely because of the star, Ingrid Bergman, and the director, John Gielgud. Surely the strangest performance of *The Constant Wife* was Miss Bergman's when she took the play on tour in the United States. She broke her foot on a street in Los Angeles and played the part in a wheelchair, rolling herself offstage at the end of the third act to join her lover for a trip to Europe. In 1929 Famous Players bought the film rights for $25,000, and it was made into a movie called *Charming Sinners*, with Ruth Chatterton, Clive Brook, and William Powell.

76. *The Journal of Arnold Bennett.*

77. Lady Glendevon to author.

Chapter Twelve

1. Maugham, *Strictly Personal* (New York, 1941), p. 137.

2. Ibid., p. 56

3. Alan Searle to Patrick O'Higgins.

4. *L.B., Show* magazine (July 1962), p. 100.

5. *Daily Express* file.

6. Ruth Gordon, *My Side* (New York, 1976), and Lord and Lady Glendevon to author.

7. Aug. 1, 1927, Stanford MSS.

8. Anthony Powell, *Infants of the Spring* (New York, 1976).

9. Anthony Powell to author.

10. Maugham, *Strictly Personal*, p. 23.

11. *Daily Express* file.

12. Kenneth McCormick to author.

13. Searle to O'Higgins.

14. George Doran, *Chronicles of Barabbas* (New York, 1935).

15. Maugham to Max Beerbohm, Feb. 1928, Berg MSS.

16. Searle to O'Higgins.

17. May 20, 1939, Texas MSS.

18. David Cornwell (John Le Carré) to author.

19. Alec Waugh to author.

20. Alexander Frere to author.

21. Glenway Wescott to author.
22. Godfrey Winn, *The Infirm Glory* (London, 1967).
23. Aug. 6, 1928, Stanford MSS.
24. Anthony Curtis, *Somerset Maugham* (London, 1977).
25. Winn, *The Infirm Glory*.
26. Ibid.
27. *The Letters of Alexander Woollcott* (New York, 1944).
28. Ruth Gordon, *Myself Among Others* (New York, 1971).
29. *S.U.* (London, 1938), p. 159.
30. R.M.J.M.
31. Oct. 31, 1929, Texas MSS.
32. Winn, *The Infirm Glory*.
33. Arnold Bennett, *Letters to His Nephew* (New York, 1935).
34. April 2, 1929, Berg MSS.
35. April 29, 1929, Texas MSS.
36. May 16, 1929, ibid.
37. May 20, 1929, ibid.
38. Maugham to Bert Alanson, Oct. 31, 1930, Stanford MSS.
39. Undated, Yale MSS.
40. Pino Orioli, *Memoirs of a Bookseller* (London, 1938).
41. E. F. Benson, *As We Were* (New York, 1930).
42. Compton Mackenzie to Grenville Cook, Indiana MSS.
43. Bennett, *Letters to His Nephew*.
44. Cole Lesley, *Remembered Laughter: The Life of Noel Coward* (New York, 1976).
45. Searle to O'Higgins.
46. Lesley, *Remembered Laughter*.
47. Nov. 20, 1929, Texas MSS.
48. Dec. 1929, Indiana MSS.
49. Fred Bason manuscript dated Jan.–Feb. 1966, Indiana MSS.
50. Bason to Cook, Indiana MSS. Bason told Grenville Cook that it was his mother who had warned him about Maugham. Cook says that Bason's recollections were "a grab-bag of truth and falsehood," and that if he had been invited to the Mauresque he would have gone.
51. Bason to Cook, ibid.
52. Oct. 13, 1931, Indiana MSS.
53. Nov. 13, 1931, ibid.
54. Bason to Cook, undated, ibid.
55. Maugham to Bason, Sept. 30, 1935, ibid.
56. May 4, 1936, ibid.
57. May 11, 1936, ibid.
58. Sept. 22, 1943, ibid.
59. Sept. 1946, Texas MSS.
60. Bason manuscript, dated Jan.–Feb. 1966, Indiana MSS. Grenville Cook, who knew Bason well, thinks he made up this story, and that his shabby appearance would have barred him from admission to an expensive hotel. The story does, however, seem consistent with what we know about Maugham.

61. Jan. 2, 1930, Indiana MSS.

62. Basil Dean, *Mind's Eye* (London, 1977).

63. *A Leaf from the Yellow Book: The Correspondence of George Egerton*, ed. Terence de Vere White (London, 1958).

64. *Daily Express* file, 1930.

65. Derek Patmore, *Private History* (London, 1960).

66. Handwritten manuscript by Derek Patmore (London, June 1970), Indiana MSS.

67. Maugham, *The Vagrant Mood* (New York, 1953), p. 245.

68. Ibid., p. 223.

69. Maugham to Barbara Back, May 25, 1930, Texas MSS.

70. 1930, Yale MSS.

71. June 13, 1930, Arkansas MSS.

72. June 25, 1930, Texas MSS.

Chapter Thirteen

1. Annual Register, 1930.

2. Sir William Rothenstein, *Men and Memories* (New York, 1940).

3. Maugham to Paul Dottin, Jan. 1, 1931, Texas MSS.

4. *C.A.* (New York, 1950), p. 9. Maugham was not the only writer who thought Walpole was a fraud. E. M. Forster wrote in his diary on Oct. 15, 1910: "No other age can have produced such a mannikin of letters. He is the impact of commerce, or rather advertisement, upon belles lettres."

5. Hugh Walpole, *The English Novel* (London, 1925).

6. Alexander Frere to author.

7. New York *Herald Tribune*, Dec. 16, 1965.

8. Frere to author.

9. In the United States, Ray Long, the editor of *Cosmopolitan*, said he could not serialize it because it had no climaxes, but Charles Hanson Towne, Maugham's former agent and now an editor of *Harper's Bazaar*, ran it from March through July 1930.

10. Walpole had accepted the chairmanship on Oct. 26, 1928, and the first Book Society choice was published in April 1929.

11. Sir Rupert Hart-Davis, *Hugh Walpole* (London, 1952).

12. Frere to author.

13. Hart-Davis, *Hugh Walpole*.

14. Undated, Texas MSS.

15. Hart-Davis, *Hugh Walpole*.

16. Robert Lorin Calder, *W. S. Maugham & the Quest for Freedom* (New York, 1973).

17. A. Riposte, *Gin and Bitters* (New York, 1931).

18. C.S.

19. Hart-Davis, *Hugh Walpole*.

20. April 20, 1931, Texas MSS.

21. May 14, 1931, ibid.

22. July 15, 1931, Arkansas MSS.

23. London *Times*, Oct. 6, 1931.

24. Anthony Curtis, *Somerset Maugham* (London, 1977).

25. Berg MSS.

26. *C.A.* (New York: Penguin Books, 1977), p. 10.

27. Ibid., p. 104.

28. Allen B. Brown, "The Originals for the Characters in Cakes and Ale," *Papers of the Michigan Academy of Science, Arts and Letters*, Vol. XLV (Ann Arbor, 1960).

29. Jan. 1, 1931, Texas MSS.

30. Michael Holroyd, *Lytton Strachey* (London, 1967–68).

31. David Garnett to author.

32. Frere to author.

33. Frank Swinnerton, *Figures in the Foreground* (London, 1963).

34. C.S.

35. Maugham to Elizabeth Douglas, April 5, 1929, South Caroliniana Library, Columbia, S.C.

36. Desmond MacCarthy, *Humanities* (Oxford, Eng., 1954).

37. R.M.J.M.

38. Maugham to Barbara Back, Dec. 1930, Texas MSS.

39. Frere to author.

40. Cecil Roberts, *The Bright Twenties* (London, 1970).

41. Reginald Pound, *Arnold Bennett* (New York, 1953).

42. Maugham to Gladys Cooper, June 9, 1931, University of Southern California Library, Los Angeles, Ca.

43. Maugham to Cooper, Aug. 13, 1931, ibid.

44. Maugham to Back, June 1931, Texas MSS.

45. Maugham to Back, July 18, 1931, ibid.

46. Ibid.

47. Maugham to Kate Mary, July 1931, Berg MSS.

48. Maugham to Back, July 18, 1931, Texas MSS.

49. April 24, 1931, Stanford MSS.

50. Alec Waugh, *A Year to Remember* (London, 1971).

51. Alec Waugh to author.

52. Maugham to Cooper, Sept. 23, 1931, University of Southern California Library, Los Angeles, Ca.

53. Oct. 13, 1931, Texas MSS.

54. Cyril Connolly to Tony James, B.B.C. radio, May 10, 1970.

55. C.S.

56. Michael Swan, *Ilex and Olive* (London, 1949).

57. Fales MSS.

58. Maugham to Back, April 1932, Texas MSS.

59. Curtis, *Somerset Maugham*.

60. Kenneth and Diana Marr-Johnson to author.

61. Maugham, *The Collected Plays* (London, 1952), preface, III, xv.

62. R.M.J.M.

63. Roberts, *The Bright Twenties*.

64. Klaus Jonas, *The Gentleman from Cap Ferrat* (New Haven, Conn.: Center of Maugham Studies, 1956).

65. Maugham, *The Narrow Corner* (London, 1932), p. 296.

66. C.S.

67. P. N. Furbank, *E. M. Forster*, Vol. II (London, 1978).

68. *Daily Express* file.

69. L.B., *Show* magazine (Aug. 1962), p. 99.

70. Maugham to Fred Bason, March 4, 1933, Texas MSS.

71. March 11, 1933, ibid.

72. Maugham to Bert Alanson, May 30, 1933, Stanford MSS.

73. Hamilton Basso, Maugham profile, *The New Yorker* (1943).

74. *The Diaries of Sir Robert Bruce Lockhart, 1915–1938*, ed. Kenneth Young (London, 1973).

75. 1933, Texas MSS.

76. Frere to author.

77. Maugham to Back, June 1933, Texas MSS.

78. Maugham to Back, July 1933, ibid.

79. R.M.J.M.

80. Ronald Hayman, *John Gielgud* (London, 1971).

81. James Agate, *Ego I* (London, 1935).

82. Leslie Rees, "A Meeting with Somerset Maugham," *Meanjin Quarterly* (Summer 1967).

83. *A Leaf from the Yellow Book: The Correspondence of George Egerton*, ed. Terence de Vere White (London, 1958).

84. Maugham, *Ah King* (London, 1933).

85. C.S.

86. *W.N.* (New York, 1949), p. 253.

87. Maugham to Back, Oct. 1933, Texas MSS.

Chapter Fourteen

1. G. B. Stern, *And Did He Stop and Speak to You?* (London, 1936).

2. G. B. Stern, "Somerset Maugham Comes of Age," *John O'London's Weekly*, Jan. 22, 1954; Alec Waugh to author.

3. Alan Searle to Patrick O'Higgins.

4. *Film Weekly*, March 29, 1935.

5. Glenway Wescott, *Images of Truth* (New York, 1963).

6. Klaus Jonas, *The Gentleman from Cap Ferrat* (New Haven, Conn.: Center of Maugham Studies, 1956).

7. *Daily Express* files.

8. *O.H.B.* (New York, 1937), p. 73.

9. Karl G. Pfeiffer, *W. Somerset Maugham: A Candid Portrait* (New York, 1959).

10. Richard A. Cordell, *Somerset Maugham: A Writer for All Seasons* (New York, 1969).

11. *S.U.* (London, 1938), p. 221.

12. *Sixty-Five* (publicity brochure, published by Doubleday, New York, 1939).

13. Aug. 1934.

14. *Collected Essays of George Orwell*, Vol. II (London, 1968).

15. Maugham to Alexander Woollcott, Feb. 12 and March 14, 1934, Harvard MSS.

16. April 29, 1934, Stanford MSS.

17. Daphne Fielding, *Those Remarkable Cunards* (New York, 1968), and Cecil Roberts, *Sunshine and Shadow* (London, 1972).

18. *Bookman* symposium, Texas MSS.

19. Compton Mackenzie, *My Life and Times: Octave Six* (London, 1967).

20. Rumsey to Golding Bright, July 24, 1934, Indiana MSS.

21. Maugham to Barbara Back, June 16, 1934, Texas MSS.

22. Maugham to Ivor Back, June 1934, ibid.

23. June 4, 1934, ibid.

24. Robin Maugham, *Escape from the Shadows* (New York, 1973).

25. Dec. 23, 1933, Texas MSS.

26. Robin Maugham, *Escape from the Shadows*.

27. Aug. 8, 1934, Texas MSS.

28. Sept. 19, 1934, Berg MSS.

29. Library of Congress MSS.

30. Maugham to Back, undated, 1934.

31. *The Diaries of Sir Robert Bruce Lockhart, 1915–1938*, ed. Kenneth Young (London, 1973).

32. Norman and Jeanne Mackenzie, *H. G. Wells* (London, 1973).

33. Searle to O'Higgins.

34. Jan. 1935, Texas MSS.

35. The material on Edward Marsh is drawn from "Eddie Marsh, Sketches for a Composite Literary Portrait of Sir Edward Marsh, K.C.V.O.," comp. by Christopher Hassall and Denis Mathews, pub. by Lund Humphries for the Contemporary Art Society (London, 1953), and Christopher Hassall, *Edward Marsh* (London, 1959).

36. Hassall, *Edward Marsh*.

37. Feb. 9, 1935, Texas MSS.

38. C.S.

39. Hassall, *Edward Marsh*.

40. C.S.

41. *The Diaries of Sir Henry Channon*, ed. Robert Rhodes James (London, 1967).

42. *The Diaries of Sir Robert Bruce Lockhart, 1915–1938*.

43. George Bishop, *My Betters* (London, 1953).

44. July 13, 1935, Texas MSS.

45. Maugham to Marie Meloney, July 24, 1935, Columbia MSS.

46. Maugham newspaper file in Lincoln Center Library, New York City.

47. Gerald Haxton to Carl Van Vechten, 1935, Texas MSS.

48. *W.N.* (New York, 1949), p, 266.

49. Maugham to Back, 1936, Texas MSS.

50. *W.N.*, p. 270.

51. Maugham to Back, 1936, Texas MSS.

52. Maugham, "A Man With a Conscience," in *The Mixture as Before* (New York, 1940), p. 28.

53. Feb. 21, 1936, Texas MSS.

54. C.S.

55. Cordell, *Somerset Maugham: A Writer for All Seasons.*

56. March 30, 1936, Texas MSS.

57. Maugham to Van Vechten, May 19, 1936, Berg MSS.

58. *New York Times* and *Daily Express*, July 25, 1936.

59. Garson Kanin, *Remembering Mr. Maugham* (New York, 1966).

60. Maugham to Bert Alanson, Aug. 26, 1936, Stanford MSS.

61. Maugham to Robin, Aug. 21, 1936.

62. Maugham, "Why and How I Collected," *New York Times Magazine*, April 1, 1962.

63. Robin Maugham, *Escape from the Shadows.*

64. Maugham correspondence with PEN Club, Texas MSS.

65. Maugham, *The Vagrant Mood* (New York, 1953), p. 222.

66. Norman and Jeanne Mackenzie, *The Time Traveller: The Life of H. G. Wells* (London, 1973).

67. Harold Nicolson, *Diaries and Letters* (New York, 1966).

68. J. MacLaren-Ross, *Memories of the Forties* (London, 1965).

69. James Agate, *Ego III* (London, 1938).

70. Maugham to Alanson, Nov. 1, 1936, Stanford MSS.

71–73. King's School archives.

74. Sir Rupert Hart-Davis, *Hugh Walpole* (London, 1952).

75. Hassall, *Edward Marsh.*

76. Name omitted by the editor of the Lockhart diaries.

77. *The Diaries of Sir Robert Bruce Lockhart, 1915–1938.*

78. Maugham, *Theatre* (London, 1937).

79. *S.U.*, p. 44.

80. C.S.

81. Agate, *Ego III.*

82. March 1937, Texas MSS.

83. Maugham to Back, March 25, 1937, ibid.

84. Ruth Gordon, *Myself Among Others* (New York, 1971).

85. Whitsunday 1937, Texas MSS.

86. Maugham to Kate Mary, May 10, 1937, Berg MSS.

87. Maugham to Alanson, May 16 and Oct. 13, 1937, Stanford MSS.

88. July 1937, Texas MSS.

89. July 3, 1937, Stanford MSS.

90. Maugham to Back, June 1937, Texas MSS.

91. Cecil Roberts, *The Bright Twenties* (London, 1970).

92. Aug. 4, 1937, Indiana MSS.

93. Aug. 22, 1937, Harvard MSS.

94. Maugham to Back, Sept. 1937, Texas MSS.

95. Maugham to Frank Swinnerton, 1933, Arkansas MSS.

96. May 19 and Sept. 10, 1937, ibid.

97. Oct. 1937, Berg MSS.

98. Maugham to Frank Swinnerton, Oct. 26, 1937, Arkansas MSS.

99. *The Diaries of Sir Robert Bruce Lockhart, 1915-1938*.

100. C.S.

101. Maugham to Karl Pfeiffer, Feb. 26, 1938, Texas MSS.

102. Maugham, *Strictly Personal* (New York, 1941), p. 10.

103. Maugham to Sir William Rothenstein, Jan. 11, 1938, Harvard MSS.

104. *W.N.*, p. 297.

105. Ibid., p. 304.

106. Maugham to Swinnerton, Jan. 25, 1938, Arkansas MSS.

107. Mercedes de Acosta, *Here Lies the Heart* (New York, 1960).

108. *W.N.*, p. 302.

109. De Acosta, *Here Lies the Heart*.

110. *W.N.*, p. 303.

111. De Acosta, *Here Lies the Heart*. A few weeks after Maugham's visit, Mercedes de Acosta, a Spanish-born artist, visited the Bhagavan and heard that a famous English novelist had fainted in his presence. She asked his name, but they did not know how to pronounce it. One of the disciples retired and came back with "Somerset Maugham" written on a piece of paper.

112. *W.N.*, p. 280.

113. Maugham, foreword, *The Memoirs of Aga Khan* (New York, 1954).

114. Feb. 26, 1938, Texas MSS.

115. *W.N.*, p. 285.

116. March 15, 1938, Stanford MSS.

117. Lord Glendevon to author.

118. Maugham to Back, March 26, 1938, Texas MSS.

Chapter Fifteen

1. C.S.

2. G.B. Stern, *And Did He Stop and Speak to You?* (London, 1936).

3. *S.U.* (London, 1938), p. 317.

4. Christopher Hassall, *Edward Marsh* (London, 1959).

5. Maugham to Edward Marsh, 1938, Berg MSS.

6. Stanley Weintraub, *Reggie* (New York, 1965).

7. May 13, 1938, Stanford MSS.

8. Maugham to Hermon Ould, 1938, Texas MSS.

9. May 6, 1938, Berg MSS.

10. Maugham to Kate Mary, June 16, 1938, ibid.

11. June 15, Yale MSS.

12. Harold Nicolson, *Diaries and Letters* (New York, 1966).

13. Ibid.

14. Godfrey Winn, *The Infirm Glory* (London, 1967).

15. Karl G. Pfeiffer, *W. Somerset Maugham: A Candid Portrait* (New York, 1959).

16. Raymond Mortimer to author.

17. Duchess of Sermoneta, *Sparkle Distant Worlds* (London, 1946).

18. Maugham to Robin, Sept. 8, 1938, Texas MSS.
19. Alan Searle to Patrick O'Higgins.
20. Patrick M. McGrady, *The Youth Doctors* (New York, 1968).
21. Niehans file, *New York Times*.
22. Searle to O'Higgins.
23. Maugham to Barbara Back, Sept. 14, 1938, Texas MSS.
24. Maugham to Bert Alanson, Oct. 23, 1938, Stanford MSS.
25. Stern, *And Did He Stop and Speak to You?*
26. S. N. Behrman, *People in a Diary* (Boston, 1972).
27. Christopher Isherwood, *Christopher and His Kind* (New York, 1976).
28. Michael Swan, *Ilex and Olive* (London, 1949).
29. Maugham to Frank Swinnerton, Jan. 2, 1939, Arkansas MSS.
30. Oct. 23, 1938, Stanford MSS.
31. Maugham to G. B. Stern, Nov. 10, 1938, Texas MSS.
32. R.M.
33. Robin Maugham, *Conversations with Willie* (London, 1978).
34. Maugham, *Christmas Holiday* (London, 1939), p. 77.
35. Glenway Wescott, *Images of Truth* (New York, 1962).
36. C.S.
37. Maugham file, Lincoln Center library, New York City.
38. Feb. 11, 1939, Texas MSS.
39. Feb. 25, 1939, Stanford MSS.
40. Maugham file, Lincoln Center library, New York City.
41. March 18, 1939, Texas MSS.
42. Maugham to Back, April 23, 1939, ibid.
43. Kenneth McCormick to author.
44. Maugham, *Strictly Personal* (New York, 1941), p. 8.
45. May 5, 1939, Texas MSS.
46. June 12, 1939, Stanford MSS.
47. Glenway Wescott to author.
48. Maugham, *Strictly Personal*, p. 20.
49. Ibid., p. 21.
50. Horace de Carbuccia, "Adieu à Mon Ami Anglais," *Gringoire*, Nov. 7, 1941.
51. Maugham to Alanson, Oct. 1940, Stanford MSS.
52. Robin to Alanson, Oct. 18, 1939, ibid.
53. Oct. 7, 1939, Texas MSS.
54. Sept. 28, 1939, ibid.
55. Sept. 25, 1939, Stanford MSS.
56. Oct. 21, 1939, ibid.
57. Maugham, *France at War* (London, 1940), p. 12.
58. Maugham, *Strictly Personal*, p. 101. Maugham described his encounter in Nancy with an English newspaper columnist whom he called George Potter, who had written a promising first novel, played first-class tennis and bridge, had been invited to the Mauresque to work on his second novel, and was the highest-paid journalist in England. This was so obviously Godfrey Winn that the chapter concerning him was deleted in the English edition of *Strictly Personal*, brought out by Heinemann in March 1942, because of the publisher's fear of a libel action.

59. Nov. 18, 1939, Stanford MSS.
60. Maugham, *France at War*, p. 1.
61. C.S.
62. Jan. 31, 1940, Yale MSS.
63. Nov. 22, 1939, Texas MSS.
64. Maugham to Robin, Jan. 2, 1940, ibid.
65. Maugham, *Strictly Personal*, p. 134.
66. Nicolson, *Diaries and Letters*.
67. Lady Glendevon to author.
68. Maugham to Wilmon Menard.
69. Maugham, *Strictly Personal*, p. 181.
70. Edith Sitwell, *Selected Letters* (New York, 1970).
71. Aug. 19, 1940, Stanford MSS.
72. Aug. 1940, Indiana MSS.
73. Maugham, *Strictly Personal*, p. 249.
74. Vincent Sheean, *Between the Thunder and the Sun* (New York, 1951).
75. Maugham, *Strictly Personal*, p. 242.
76. Sheean, *Between the Thunder and the Sun*.
77. Maugham to Colonel Thomson, March 6, 1949, Texas MSS.
78. Sept. 1940, ibid.
79. Raymond Marriott to author.
80. Wescott to author.
81. Swan, *Ilex and Olive*.

Chapter Sixteen

1. *New York Post*, Oct. 9, 1940.
2. Biographical sketch by Ellen Doubleday, New York, Doubleday Publishers, 1955.
3. Ibid.
4. *New York Post*, May 31, 1944.
5. Maugham to Karl Pfeiffer, Oct. 25, 1940.
6. Peter Daubeny, *My Life in the Theater* (London, 1971).
7. Maugham to Margot Hill, Dec. 12, 1940, Fales MSS.
8. *New York Post*, Nov. 1940.
9. Ellen Doubleday to author.
10. Dec. 1940, Texas MSS.
11. Mrs. Kiskadden to author; Lady Glendevon to author.
12. Maugham-Behrman correspondence, courtesy Elza Behrman.
13. S. N. Behrman, *People in a Diary* (Boston, 1972).
14. Cecil Roberts, *Sunshine and Shadow* (London, 1972).
15. Jerome Weidman to author.
16. Gerald Haxton to Louis Legrand, Dec. 1940, Stanford MSS.
17. Typescript of speech, Texas MSS.
18. Ruth Gordon, *Myself Among Others* (New York, 1971).
19. Texas MSS.

20. "Writers at Work," *The Paris Review Interviews*, First Series (New York, 1967).

21. Maugham, introduction, *The Portable Dorothy Parker* (New York: Viking Press, 1944), p. 13.

22. Maugham to Kate Mary, March 17, 1941, Berg MSS.

23. Wilmon Menard, "Maugham in Hollywood," *Michigan Quarterly Review* (Summer 1968).

24. Feb. 4, 1941, Texas MSS.

25. Sept. 29, 1941, ibid.

26. Maugham to Margot Hill, March 1, 1941, Fales MSS.

27. Maugham to Kate Mary, March 17, 1941, Berg MSS.

28. Ibid.

29. Maugham to Robin, May 23, 1941, Texas MSS.

30. Maugham, *Up at the Villa* (New York, 1941), p. 33.

31. Ibid., p. 52.

32. Glenway Wescott to author.

33. Haxton to Legrand, June 1941, Stanford MSS.

34. Lady Glendevon to author.

35. June 1941, Berg MSS.

36. Maugham to G. B. Stern, June 1941, Texas MSS.

37. Maugham to Pfeiffer, July 1941, ibid.

38. Sybille Bedford, *Aldous Huxley* (New York, 1974).

39. Edmund Wilson, *Classics and Commercials* (New York, 1958).

40. Christopher Isherwood, *Exhumations* (New York, 1966).

41. Arthur Koestler, *The Yogi and the Commissar* (London, 1945).

42. June 12, 1941, Berg MSS.

43. Bedford, *Aldous Huxley*.

44. July 1941, Texas MSS.

45. Karl G. Pfeiffer, *W. Somerset Maugham: A Candid Portrait* (New York, 1959).

46. Menard, "Maugham in Hollywood."

47. Aug. 8, 1941, Stanford MSS.

48. Maugham to Pfeiffer, undated, Texas MSS.

49. Maugham to Pfeiffer, Feb. 26, 1938, ibid.

50. Pfeiffer, *W. Somerset Maugham: A Candid Portrait*.

51. Sept. 16, 1941, Texas MSS.

52. Kenneth McCormick to author.

53. George Morrill, *Snow, Stars, and Wild Honey* (New York, 1955).

54. Maugham to Marie Meloney, Nov. 12, 1941, Columbia MSS.

55. Maugham business papers, Indiana MSS.

56. Pfeiffer, *W. Somerset Maugham: A Candid Portrait*.

57. April 1943, Berg MSS.

58. Maugham to "Muzzi," undated, South Caroliniana Library.

59. Biographical sketch by Ellen Doubleday.

60. Patrick M. McGrady, *The Youth Doctors* (New York, 1968).

61. Maugham to Pfeiffer, Jan. 30, 1942, Texas MSS.

62. Jan. 1942, ibid.

63–65. Wescott to author.

66. Maugham to Robin, 1941, Texas MSS.

67. Sir William Stevenson to author.

68. Maugham to Bert Alanson, March 24, 1942, Stanford MSS.

69. July 1941, Texas MSS.

70. Norman Mailer, "Our Man at Harvard," *Esquire* (April 1977).

71. Maugham to Pfeiffer, April 27, 1942, Texas MSS.

72. June 4, 1942, ibid.

73. Alanson Papers, Stanford MSS.

74. Maugham to Alanson, Nov. 25, 1942, ibid.

75. C.S.

76. Maugham file, Lincoln Center library, New York City.

77. *W. Somerset Maugham's Introduction to English and American Literature* (New York, 1943), p. 15.

78. Sept. 15, 1942, Texas MSS.

79. Jerome Zipkin to author.

80. *The Letters of Alexander Woollcott*, eds. Beatrice Kaufman and Joseph Hennessey (New York, 1944).

81. Zipkin to author.

82. Maugham to Margot Hill, Dec. 14, 1942, Fales MSS.

83. Maugham to Lord Maugham, 1943, Berg MSS.

84. John Keats, *You Might as Well Live: The Life and Times of Dorothy Parker* (New York, 1970).

85. Feb. 14, 1943, Columbia MSS.

86. Maugham to Lord Maugham, April 12, 1943, Berg MSS.

87. Oct. 6, 1943, Texas MSS.

88–90. David Posner to author.

91. Maugham to Lord Maugham, June 10, 1943, Berg MSS.

92. Pfeiffer, *W. Somerset Maugham: A Candid Portrait*.

93. Maugham to Pfeiffer, May 12, 1943, Texas MSS.

94. Maugham to Barbara Back, July 1943, ibid.

95. Maugham to André David, August 4, 1943, ibid.

96. Maugham to Back, July 1943, ibid.

97. Maugham to Alanson, Oct. 29, 1943, Stanford MSS.

98. Nov. 24, 1943, Texas MSS.

99. July 1943, ibid.

100. Jan. 25, 1944, ibid.

101. Oct. 6, 1943, ibid.

102. Posner to author.

103. Ibid.

104. Maugham to Pfeiffer, Jan. 12, 1944, Texas MSS.

105. Maugham, unpublished text, "For Tammie," Indiana MSS.

106. *W.N.* (New York, 1949), p. 352.

107. Ibid., p. 357.

108. Jan. 31, 1944, Berg MSS.

109. *The Diaries of Sir Henry Channon*, ed. Robert Rhodes James (London, 1967).

110. Maugham, *The Razor's Edge* (New York, 1944), p. 188.
111. Ibid., p. 258.
112. C.S.
113. Cyril Connolly, *The Condemned Playground* (London, 1945).
114. Isherwood, *Exhumations.*
115. *Letters of John Cowper Powys to Louis Wilkinson* (London, 1958).
116. Maugham to Edward Marsh, June 1944, Berg MSS.
117. Maugham to Alanson, May 16, 1944, Stanford MSS.
118. Wescott to author.
119. Maugham to Marsh, June 1944, Berg MSS.
120. *The Diaries of Sir Henry Channon.*
121. June 26, 1944, Texas MSS.
122. June 26, 1944, ibid.
123. Maugham to Back, July 10, 1944, ibid.
124. July 1, 1944, ibid.
125. Maugham to Back, July 10, 1944, ibid.
126. Maugham to Alanson, Aug. 1, 1944, Stanford MSS.
127. Maugham to Alanson, Aug. 14, 1944, ibid.
128. Aug. 15, 1944, Texas MSS.
129. Sept. 1944, Berg MSS.
130. Wescott to author; Behrman, *People in a Diary.*
131. Oct. 3, 1944, Texas MSS.
132. Maugham to Robin, Oct. 2, 1944, ibid.
133. Dec. 6, 1944, ibid.
134. Alan Searle to Patrick O'Higgins.
135. Wescott to author.
136. Ibid.
137. Roberts, *Sunshine and Shadow.*
138. R.M.
139. Robin Maugham, *Escape from the Shadows* (New York, 1973).
140. Ibid.
141. Maugham to Kate Mary, May 19, 1945, Berg MSS.
142. May 17, 1945, ibid.
143. Maugham to Back, May 1945, Texas MSS.
144. Gavin Lambert, *On Cukor* (New York, 1972).
145. Maugham, *Purely for My Pleasure* (London, 1962), p. 17.
146. Menard, "Maugham in Hollywood."
147. Anne Baxter, *Intermission* (New York, 1976).
148. Oct. 1945, Texas MSS.
149. Maugham to Alexander Frere, Sept. 4, 1945, House of El Dieff.
150. Behrman, *People in a Diary.*
151. Nov. 20, 1945, Texas MSS.
152. June 1949, courtesy Verna Sabelle.
153. Nov. 28, 1945, courtesy Verna Sabelle.
154. Feb. 23, 1945, Texas MSS.
155. Maugham to Pfeiffer, Dec. 22, 1945, ibid.
156. Wescott to author.

157. Searle to O'Higgins.
158. Posner to author.
159. Raymond Marriott to author.
160. Zipkin to author.
161. Behrman, *People in a Diary*.
162. Mrs. Dorothy Howell-Thomas to Jacqueline Williams.
163. Jan. 22, 1946, Stanford MSS.
164. Behrman, *People in a Diary*.
165. April 1946, Texas MSS.
166. April 1946, ibid.
167. Feb. 1946, Berg MSS.
168. Maugham, introduction to Charles H. Goren, *The Standard Book of Bidding* (New York, 1944).
169. Charles H. Goren, *Sports Illustrated*, Jan. 17, 1966.
170. Maugham to Alanson, May 21, 1946, Stanford MSS.
171. Address by Luther H. Evans, Texas MSS.
172. Speech by Maugham, ibid.
173. C.S.
174. Ibid.
175. Wilson, *Classics and Commercials*.
176. *S.U.* (London, 1938), p. 221.
177. Behrman, *People in a Diary*.

Chapter Seventeen

1. Michael Swan, *Ilex and Olive* (London, 1949).
2. June 13, 1946, Texas MSS.
3. Harold Nicolson to Louis Legrand, Stanford MSS.
4. David Posner to author.
5. Maugham to Marsh, July 8, 1946.
6. Alexander Frere to author. Waugh's version of the story, as noted in his diary, was slightly different: "Tea with Frank [Pakenham, Lord in Waiting to the king] at the House of Lords. An old lord whose name I didn't hear sat with us. Frank said I was a writer. 'My young brother wrote a book the other day which sold a million copies.' It was Lord Maugham."
7. C.S.
8. James Agate, *Ego IX* (London, 1948).
9. S. N. Behrman, *Jane* (New York, 1947), and *People in a Diary* (Boston, 1972).
10. Oct. 2, 1946, Stanford MSS.
11. Peter Daubeny, *My Life in the Theatre* (London, 1971).
12. Behrman, *People in a Diary*.
13. Dec. 20, 1946, Stanford MSS.
14. Maugham to Lady Glendevon, Feb. 1947, courtesy Lord and Lady Glendevon.
15. Undated, Texas MSS.

16. March 1947, House of El Dieff.

17. March 29, 1956, Washington University Libraries, St. Louis, Mo.

18. London *Times*, April 17, 1947.

19. Maugham to a Mr. [or Miss] Adams, Oct. 28, 1947, Texas MSS.

20. July 1947, Indiana MSS.

21. July 6, 1947, ibid.

22. Maugham, "The Author Excuses Himself," *Creatures of Circumstance* (New York, 1948), p. 4.

23. Introductions by Maugham to television broadcasts of his short stories, Texas MSS.

24. Lady Glendevon to author.

25. Aug. 21, 1947, Stanford MSS.

26. Maugham to Bert Alanson, Sept. 8, 1947, ibid.

27. Alan Searle to Patrick O'Higgins.

28. *The Diaries of Sir Henry Channon,* ed. Robert Rhodes James (London, 1967).

29. Nov. 1947, House of El Dieff.

30. Maugham business correspondence, Indiana MSS.

31. Dec. 14, 1947, Texas MSS.

32. Maugham to Alanson, Dec. 23, 1947, Stanford MSS.

33. Jan. 13, 1948, Indiana MSS.

34. Raymond Marriott to author.

35. Undated, Berg MSS.

36. Undated, ibid.

37. Maugham to Roger Senhouse, March 20, 1948, Stanford MSS.

38. Douglas Cooper, *Graham Sutherland* (London, 1961).

39. Maugham to Alanson, May 13, 1948, Stanford MSS.

40. Searle to Alanson, June 20, 1948, ibid.

41. Maugham to Lady Bateman, June 1948, Yale MSS.

42. Lord Glendevon to author.

43. Ibid.

44. Frere to author.

45. Maugham, *Catalina* (London, 1948), p. 96.

46. C.S.

47. Sept. 10, 1948, Yale MSS.

48. Maugham to Félix Martí-Ibáñez, Aug. 1948, courtesy Verna Sabelle.

49. Maugham, *The Art of Fiction* (New York, 1955), p. 236.

50. Jacques Chambrun to Maugham, March 1949, Indiana MSS.

51. Green to Chambrun, April 1949, ibid.

52. Maugham to Anthony Darnborough, Nov. 16, 1948, Berg MSS.

53. MD magazine (Aug. 1962).

54. Maugham to A. P. Watt, Jan. 19, 1949, Berg MSS.

55. Kenneth McCormick to author.

56. Nelson Doubleday memorial booklet, Texas MSS.

57. Maugham to Robin, March 17, 1949, ibid.

58. O'Higgins to author.

59. Maugham to Alanson, Feb. 1949, Stanford MSS.

60. MD magazine (Aug. 1962).
61. Catalogue, *Portraits by Graham Sutherland*, National Portrait Gallery, 1977.
62. Cecil Roberts, *Sunshine and Shadow* (London, 1972).
63. June 24, 1949, Indiana MSS.
64. June 29, 1949, ibid.
65. June 24, 1949, ibid.
66. Maugham to Chambrun, undated, ibid.
67. July 1, 1949, Berg MSS.
68. Aug. 23, 1949, Stanford MSS.
69. Jerome Zipkin to author.
70. Aug. 23, 1949, Stanford MSS.
71. Aug. 14, 1949, courtesy Elza Behrman.
72. Sept. 1949, courtesy Elza Behrman.
73. C.S.
74. Ibid.
75. *W.N.* (New York, 1949), p. 13.
76. Derek Hudson, *For Love of Painting* (London, 1975).
77. Nov. 22, 1949, courtesy Elza Behrman.
78. Nov. 13, 1949, Stanford MSS.
79. Maugham to Alanson, Jan. 13, 1950, ibid.
80. Dec. 20, 1949, Glendevon papers.
81. Cecil Roberts, *One Year of My Life* (London, 1952).
82. Maugham to Robin, Feb. 3, 1950.
83. Maugham to Bennett Cerf, Jan. 16, 1950, Columbia MSS.
84. Maugham to Frere, March 3, 1950, House of El Dieff.
85. Maugham to Alanson, March 14, 1950, Stanford MSS.
86. From a speech given by Maugham at the opening ceremony of the Windmill Press Extension on June 24, 1952, Texas MSS.
87. *The Diaries of Sir Henry Channon.*
88. Viscountess Norwich to author.
89. O'Higgins to author.
90. Aug. 1950, Columbia MSS.
91. Aug. 22, 1950, ibid.
92. Meryle Secrest, *Between Me and My Life* (New York, 1974).
93. Maugham to Alanson, June 24, 1950, Stanford MSS.
94. Oct. 1950, Columbia MSS.
95. Library of Congress speech, Oct. 1950, Texas MSS.
96. Institute of Arts and Letters speech, Oct. 1950, Columbia MSS.
97. Glenway Wescott to author.
98. Morgan Library speech, Oct. 1950, Texas MSS.
99. Irwin Edman to Maugham, Oct. 30, 1950, Columbia MSS.
100. Edman to Maugham, Nov. 1950, ibid.
101. Frere to author.
102. Nov. 7, 1950, Stanford MSS.
103. Edman to Maugham, Nov. 1950, Columbia MSS.
104. *The Diaries of Sir Henry Channon.*
105. Maugham to Alanson, Dec. 22 and 25, 1950, Stanford MSS.

106. Maugham to Kate Mary, Jan. 18, 1951, Berg MSS.
107. Maugham speech at Royal Academy, Texas MSS.
108. Maugham to Alanson, May 11, 1951, Stanford MSS.
109. Maugham, *Purely for my Pleasure* (London, 1962), p. 6.
110. Major Neville Willing to author.
111. July 29, 1951, Texas MSS.
112. Maugham to Lady Glendevon, Jan. 1952, Glendevon papers.
113. Maugham to Lady Glendevon, Jan. 1952, ibid.
114. Maugham to Barbara Back, Texas MSS.
115. Feb. 26, 1952, Texas MSS.
116. Maugham to Alanson, Jan. 29, 1952, Stanford MSS.
117. Viscountess Norwich to author.
118. Maugham to Lady Glendevon, Glendevon papers.
119. March 24, 1952, Stanford MSS.
120. May 2, 1952, Berg MSS.
121. Watt files, Berg MSS.
122. Wescott to author.
123. Searle to Klaus Jonas, July 1952, Texas MSS.
124. June 25, 1952, Stanford MSS.
125. Maugham to Daniel Longwood, Aug. 13, 1952, Columbia MSS.
126. Maugham to Alanson, Sept. 27, 1952, Stanford MSS.
127. Jan. 13, 1950, Texas MSS.
128. Frank McShane, *Raymond Chandler* (New York, 1976).
129. Oct. 13, 1952, Stanford MSS.
130. Nov. 1952, courtesy Elza Behrman.
131. Nov. 1952, courtesy Elza Behrman.
132. Canon F. J. Shirley, "William Somerset Maugham," *The Cantuarian* (Dec. 1965).
133. Ibid.
134. Searle to Alanson, Jan. 29, 1953, Stanford MSS.
135. Pearson, *The Life of Ian Fleming*.
136. Ibid.
137. Maugham to Alanson, April 1953, Stanford MSS.
138. Searle to O'Higgins.
139. Maugham to Watt, June 1953, Berg MSS.
140. W.M.
141. Maugham to Alanson, Oct. 30, 1953, Stanford MSS.
142. Nov. 1953, courtesy Jerome Zipkin.
143. Maugham to Alanson, Dec. 26, 1953, Stanford MSS.

Chapter Eighteen

1. Maugham to Bert Alanson, Jan. 1954, Stanford MSS.
2. St. John Ervine to Church, Feb. 19, 1954, Texas MSS.
3. Account by T. S. Strachan, Texas MSS.
4. London *Times* file.

5. Raymond Mortimer, in a letter to the author, said he would like to add: "I keenly admire a number of his books."

6. Jocelyn Brooke Papers, Stanford MSS.

7. Maugham to Lord Maugham, Feb. 4, 1954, Texas MSS.

8. R.M.

9. John Pearson, *The Life of Ian Fleming* (London, 1966).

10. April 1, 1954, Berg MSS.

11. Maugham to Donald Wing, April 27, 1954, Yale MSS.

12. May 2, 1954, Berg MSS.

13. May 28, 1954, Texas MSS.

14. Robin in letters to agent and editor, 1962, Columbia MSS.

15. Maugham to Lady Bateman, June 1954, Yale MSS.

16. Maugham to Alanson, June 1954, Stanford MSS.

17. Alan Searle to Edith Sitwell, June 28, 1954, Texas MSS.

18. June 10, 1954, House of Lords library.

19. Cole Lesley, *Remember Laughter: The Life of Noel Coward* (New York, 1976).

20. Leonard Lyons, *New York Post*, July 27, 1954.

21. Cecil Roberts, *Sunshine and Shadow* (London, 1972).

22. June 11, 1954, Stanford MSS.

23. Lord and Lady Glendevon to author.

24. Ibid.

25. Searle to Klaus Jonas, Aug. 6, 1954, Texas MSS.

26. Lord Glendevon to author.

27. Maugham to Alanson, Nov. 23, 1954, Stanford MSS.

28. Jonathan Fryer, *Isherwood* (New York, 1978).

29. Dec. 22, 1954, Texas MSS.

30. Clare Boothe Luce, in seminar on Maugham, University of Southern California, 1966, published by Friends of the Libraries, U.S.C., 1966.

31. Searle to O'Higgins.

32. Sutherland file, *New York Times*.

33. Clare Boothe Luce, in U.S.C. seminar on Maugham.

34. Garson Kanin, *Remembering Mr. Maugham* (New York, 1966).

35. Maugham to Lady Bateman, Jan. 1955, Yale MSS.

36. Feb. 8, 1955, Stanford MSS.

37. Gerald Kelly to Alanson, April 8, 1955, ibid.

38. Maugham to Alanson, April 8, 1955, ibid.

39. Aug. 11, 1955, Texas MSS.

40. Godfrey Winn, *The Positive Hour* (London, 1960).

41. Maugham to Alanson, April 22, 1955, Stanford MSS.

42. *W.N.* (New York, 1949), p. 196.

43. Maugham to Alanson, July 28, 1955, Stanford MSS.

44. Maugham to S. N. Behrman, Sept. 1955, courtesy Elza Behrman.

45. Aug. 1955, Berg MSS.

46. July 28, 1955, Stanford MSS.

47. Maugham to Alanson, July 16, 1955, ibid.

48. Oct. 1955, ibid.

49. Searle to Alanson, Dec. 13, 1955, ibid.
50. Maugham to Alanson, Dec. 18, 1955, and Jan. 15 and Feb. 1956, ibid.
51. Maugham to Alanson, March 13, 1956, ibid.
52. Watt collection, Berg MSS.
53. Maugham to Alanson, April 5, 1954, Stanford MSS.
54. June 18, 1956, Harvard MSS.
55. April 1956, courtesy Verna Sabelle.
56. Ilka Chase, *The Carthaginian Rose* (New York, 1961).
57. Maugham to Alexander Frere, April 1956, courtesy House of El Dieff.
58. Maugham to Alanson, April 22, 1956.
59. Bernard Berenson, *Sunset and Twilight* (New York, 1963), and Harold Acton, *More Memoirs of an Esthete* (New York, 1970).
60. Searle to Alanson, July 18, 1956, Stanford MSS.
61. Maugham to Jonas, Aug. 1956, Yale MSS.
62. Ibid.
63. Maugham speech at Army and Navy Stores, Oct. 15, 1956, Texas MSS.
64. Dec. 24, 1956, Texas MSS.
65. Searle to Jerome Zipkin, Jan. 1957, courtesy Jerome Zipkin.
66. Feb. 2, 1957, Berg MSS.
67. Lord and Lady Glendevon to author.
68. Maugham to Alanson, April 19, 1957, Stanford MSS.
69. July 26, 1957, ibid.
70. Searle to O'Higgins.
71. Oct. 8, 1957, Stanford MSS.
72. Jonas to author.
73. March 1958, Berg MSS.
74. Searle to O'Higgins.
75. R. F. V. Heuston, *Lives of the Lord Chancellors, 1885–1940* (Oxford, Eng., 1964).
76. April 1958, Stanford MSS.
77. Patrick M. McGrady, *The Youth Doctors* (New York, 1968).
78. Searle to Alanson, May 18, 1958, Stanford MSS.
79. Searle to O'Higgins.
80. Alec Waugh to author.
81. *San Francisco Chronicle* file.
82. Anne Alanson Eliaser to author.
83. Ibid.
84. Maugham to Terry Bender, June 10, 1958, Stanford MSS.
85. Maugham to Frere, July 9, 1958, House of El Dieff.
86. Maugham to Raymond Toole Stott, April 12, 1957, University of Santa Barbara MSS.
87. *Daily Express*, Oct. 4, 1958.
88. Winn, *The Positive Hour*.
89. C.S.
90. Lord and Lady Glendevon to author.
91. Undated, Texas MSS.
92. Maugham file, Lincoln Center library, New York City.

93. Searle to Zipkin, May and Aug. 1959, courtesy Jerome Zipkin.

94. July 21, 1959, Fales MSS.

95. Searle to Mutsuo Tanaka, undated, Texas MSS.

96. Maugham to Jerome Weidman, Oct. 1959, ibid.

97. Searle to Zipkin, Nov. 10, 1959, courtesy Jerome Zipkin.

98. Ian Fleming, *Thrilling Cities* (New York, 1964).

99. May 4, 1960, Texas MSS.

100. Kanin, *Remembering Mr. Maugham.*

101. Canon F. J. Shirley, "William Somerset Maugham," *The Cantuarian* (Dec. 1965).

102. Searle to Jonas, Sept. 6, 1960, Texas MSS.

103. Searle to Behrman, Jan. 19, 1961, courtesy Elza Behrman.

104. *Look* magazine, Jan. 5, 1961.

105. A. J. P. Taylor, *Beaverbrook* (London, 1972).

106. Beaverbrook Papers, House of Lords library.

107. Feb. 1961, courtesy Jerome Zipkin.

108. Lady Alfred Ayer to author.

109. Ibid.

110. Glenway Wescott to author.

111. Lady Ayer to author.

112. Ibid.

113. Searle to O'Higgins.

114. S. N. Behrman, *People in a Diary* (Boston, 1972).

115. Maugham, "Why and How I Collected," *New York Times Magazine,* April 1, 1962.

116–118. Lord and Lady Glendevon to author.

119. Maugham to Kate Mary, 1932, Berg MSS.

120. Lord and Lady Glendevon to author.

121. Ibid.

122. Lady Glendevon to Maugham, Oct. 1961, Glendevon papers.

123. Lady Glendevon to Maugham, Nov. 3, 1961, ibid.

124. Lord and Lady Glendevon to author.

125. Maugham to Lord Beaverbrook, Nov. 1961, House of Lords library.

126. Maugham to Lord Beaverbrook, Nov. 1961, ibid.

127. Dec. 5, 1961, Fales MSS.

128. Searle to O'Higgins.

129. John Junor to author.

130. Beaverbrook Papers, House of Lords library.

Chapter Nineteen

1. *Daily Express* file.

2. Alan Searle to Jerome Zipkin, Feb. 1962, courtesy Jerome Zipkin.

3. March 1962, Texas MSS.

4. Lord and Lady Glendevon to author.

5. *Daily Express* file.

6. Lord and Lady Glendevon to author.
7. *Daily Express* file.
8. Maugham to Robin, May 1962, Texas MSS.
9. May 1962, courtesy Jerome Zipkin.
10. Searle to Patrick O'Higgins.
11. Ibid.
12. C.S.
13–15. Diana and Kenneth Marr-Johnson to author.
16. Alexander Frere to author.
17. Beaverbrook Papers, House of Lords library.
18. *Daily Express* file.
19. John Junor to author.
20. *Daily Express* File.
21. Sheridan Morley, *A Talent to Amuse* (New York, 1975).
22. Frere to author.
23. Jan. 1963, courtesy Jerome Zipkin.
24. Jan. 1963, Texas MSS.
25. *Daily Express* file.
26. Ibid.
27. April 1963, Texas MSS.
28. *Daily Express* file.
29. Ibid.
30. July 26, 1963, courtesy Elza Behrman.
31. Aug. 21, 1963, courtesy Jerome Zipkin.
32. Searle to O'Higgins.
33. Frere to author.
34. Searle to O'Higgins.
35. Ibid.
36. Searle to Klaus Jonas, Nov. 15, 1963, Texas MSS.
37. Behrman to Richard Cordell, Nov. 29, 1963, courtesy Elza Behrman.
38. Dec. 8, 1963, courtesy Elza Behrman.
39. Godfrey Winn, *The Infirm Glory* (London, 1967).
40. Kenneth Allsop, *Books and Bookmen* (May 1966).
41. Searle to Zipkin, March 15, 1964, courtesy Jerome Zipkin.
42. Raymond Mortimer to author.
43. Searle to Zipkin, May 15 and June 25, 1964, courtesy Jerome Zipkin.
44. Searle to O'Higgins.
45. Probate Registry, Somerset House, London.
46. Lady Glendevon to author.
47. Nov. 2, 1964, Indiana MSS.
48. Alec Waugh to author.
49. April 1965, courtesy Jerome Zipkin.
50. May 1965, courtesy Elza Behrman.
51. Romaine Brooks to Winifred Bryher, Dec. 26, 1965, courtesy Barbara Guest.
52. Searle to O'Higgins.
53. *Daily Express* file.
54. L.B., *Show* magazine (June 1962), p. 63.

55. Searle to O'Higgins.
56. Lord Boothby, *Recollections of a Rebel* (London, 1978).
57. Searle to O'Higgins.
58. *Daily Express* file.
59. In 1966 Lady Glendevon went to Nice and formally renounced her share of her father's estate, holding to her end of their out-of-court agreement. The Mauresque was hers, and Maugham, before he became hostile, had often urged her to keep it and live in it, but that was out of the question, and she put it up for sale. Visiting the villa for the last time, she was surprised to see what a thorough job Alan had done of cleaning the place out. There was not a removable object left inside the house. The light fixtures had been pulled off the walls, and even the door handles were gone. The venerable firm of Knight, Frank & Rutley, which had sold the Mauresque to Maugham in 1926 for $48,500, put it up for sale once again, advertising it as "an opportunity to acquire one of the most beautiful and famous properties on the Riviera . . . for 40 years the home of Mr. Somerset Maugham." The asking price was more than one million dollars. It remained on the market until 1969, when an American real estate promoter bought it for $730,000 and broke it up into lots.

Alan sold the villa's contents at auction at Sotheby's in November 1967 for a total of about $75,000. Scattered in all directions were the objects and furniture Maugham had brought back from his travels, the large wood carving of the Chinese goddess of mercy, Kuan Yin, the Thai Buddha, the West African statuettes, the Greek icons, the bust of Voltaire, and the Spanish desks. The antique Spanish table Maugham used as a writing desk was bought by Godfrey Winn for 550 pounds. The articles Maugham despised would henceforth be composed on the desk on which *Cakes and Ale* and *The Summing Up* had been written. "I shall sit at *the* desk every day when I am in London," Winn wrote in a magazine article, "and it will give me not only encouragement and confidence, because of its literary associations, but also a sense of tradition."

Alan moved to a pleasant mezzanine flat at 30 avenue de Grande Bretagne, in Monte Carlo, with off-white walls and sage-green carpets. It was furnished with a few of Maugham's things that he had kept. There were damask curtains, "handwoven in Lyons," Alan said, and Tiepolo drawings, and Maugham's favorite sofa, and Maugham's books in a locked glass-fronted cupboard. Alan was in a pathetic state. He was glad that Maugham had died, but he felt lost and bewildered. In August 1968 he wrote Richard Cordell that he was in a black, black depression, and missed Maugham more every day of his life. He suffered from chronic depression, influenza, asthma, bronchitis, and Parkinson's disease. At one point he decided to take shock treatments, but S. N. Behrman convinced him not to. He felt that Maugham's friends had dropped him, that they were against him because he had profited from his death. In fact, he complained, he was broke. It took years to settle the estate, and he borrowed from his friends. Jerry Zipkin loaned him $8,000. It developed that Maugham, through careless handling and poor advice, had made a mess of his affairs, and there was not enough left in the English estate to pay Alan's legacy of 50,000 pounds. Alan survived by selling his remaining books and treasures. He had lost the desire to live, he wrote his friends, and suffered from an indescribable loneliness. In 1966 he became engaged to Isabelle Darley, the wealthy widow of a Hussar colonel, who lived in the same block of flats. She was lonely and Alan brought her out. She took him to Darley Hall, in Yorkshire, with its glorious gardens. Alan liked gardening. They decided to get married and buy a villa. But Alan leaked the news to the *Daily Express*, and Mrs. Darley was so angry that she broke off the engagement.

As he began collecting his inheritance, including Maugham's royalties and his American trust, Alan traveled to the places where he had been with Maugham, where the hotel concierges knew him—London, Venice, Munich, Badgastein. Occasionally he went to Los Angeles to stay with the pendulous-lipped and sagging-jowled George Cukor, on Cordell Drive, where he became known as the man who came to breakfast, lunch, and dinner. Alan, Cukor said, traveled with one suitcase filled with pornography and the other filled with cuff links. People used to say of Cukor, "George gives luncheons for the *beau monde* and in the evening the naughty boys come and eat the leftovers." The naughty boys were still summoned to provide amusement for Alan during his visits. Aside from the naughty boys, his greatest pleasure was dining in expensive restaurants, where he made a habit of overtipping, the affluent man's form of ingratiation. Poor health was his lot, and the Parkinson's disease got so bad that he was unable to shave or dress himself and had to take a valet with him on trips. In addition, he developed a tumor on his tongue, a piece of which was surgically removed.

In the fall of 1976 the seventy-two-year-old Searle was in Beverly Hills, where he ran into Patrick O'Higgins, whose visit to the Mauresque had been cut short when he stayed out all night. Alan was twice his former size but had the Niehans look, unlined, pink-cheeked, and cherubic. He wore white trousers, a blazer, an Eton tie, and black-and-white oxfords. O'Higgins asked him how he was. "Oh, I'm very tired, quite exhausted," Alan said. "Why are you wearing an Eton tie?" "It reassures me." "Are you happy in Monte Carlo?" "No, I loathe it." "Why don't you move?" "I'm too lazy." They had lunch and Alan drank three martinis. "I've taken to drink," he said. "I'm lonely. I have no friends to speak of. I miss Willie."

THE WORKS OF W. SOMERSET MAUGHAM

These are listed according to the year of publication or performance; not included are collected editions, anthologies in which Maugham appeared or which he compiled, and articles and stories not published in book form.

1897   *Liza of Lambeth* (novel)
1898   *The Making of a Saint* (novel)
1899   *Orientations* (short stories)
1901   *The Hero* (novel)
1902   *Marriages Are Made in Heaven* (play)
　　　 Mrs. Craddock (novel)
1903   *A Man of Honour* (play)
1904   *Mademoiselle Zampa* (play)
　　　 The Merry-Go-Round (novel)
1905   *The Land of the Blessed Virgin* (travel book)
1906   *The Bishop's Apron* (novel)
1907   *Lady Frederick* (play)
　　　 The Explorer (novel)
1908   *The Explorer* (play)
　　　 Mrs. Dot (play)
　　　 Jack Straw (play)
　　　 The Magician (novel)
1909   *Penelope* (play)
　　　 The Noble Spaniard (play)
　　　 Smith (play)
1910   *The Tenth Man* (play)
　　　 Grace (play)
1911   *Loaves and Fishes* (play)
1913   *The Perfect Gentleman* (play)
　　　 The Land of Promise (play)
1915   *Of Human Bondage* (novel)
1916   *Caroline* (play)
1917   *Our Betters* (play)
1918   *Love in a Cottage* (play)

1919   *The Moon and Sixpence* (novel)
       Caesar's Wife (play)
       Home and Beauty (play)

1920   *The Unknown* (play)

1921   *The Circle* (play)
       The Trembling of a Leaf (short stories)

1922   *East of Suez* (play)
       On a Chinese Screen (travel book)

1923   *The Camel's Back* (play)

1925   *The Painted Veil* (novel)

1926   *The Constant Wife* (play)
       The Casuarina Tree (short stories)

1927   *The Letter* (play)

1928   *The Sacred Flame* (play)
       Ashenden (short stories)

1930   *The Breadwinner* (play)
       The Gentleman in the Parlour (travel book)
       Cakes and Ale (novel)

1931   *Six Stories Written in the First Person Singular* (short stories)

1932   *For Services Rendered* (play)
       The Narrow Corner (novel)

1933   *The Mask and the Face* (play)
       Ah King (short stories)
       Sheppey (play)

1935   *Don Fernando* (travel book)

1936   *Cosmopolitans* (short stories)

1937   *Theatre* (novel)

1938   *The Summing Up* (autobiographical essay)

1939   *Christmas Holiday* (novel)

1940   *France at War* (reportage)
       Books and You (essays)
       The Mixture as Before (short stories)

1941   *Up at the Villa* (novel)
       Strictly Personal (reminiscences)

1942   *The Hour Before the Dawn* (novel)

1944   *The Razor's Edge* (novel)

1946   *Then and Now* (novel)

1947   *Creatures of Circumstance* (short stories)

1948   *Catalina* (novel)

1948 *Great Novelists and Their Novels* (essays)
1949 *A Writer's Notebook* (excerpts from the author's notebooks)
1952 *The Vagrant Mood* (essays)
1958 *Points of View* (essays)
1962 *Purely for My Pleasure* (reminiscences)

PHOTO CREDITS

copyright 1940, 1941 by W. S. Maugham, by permission of Doubleday & Co., Inc., and A. P. Watt Ltd. and William Heinemann Ltd.

The Summing Up, W. S. Maugham, copyright 1938 by W. S. Maugham. Used by permission of Doubleday & Co., Inc., and A. P. Watt Ltd. and William Heinemann Ltd.

Sunset and Twilight, Bernard Berenson, by permission of Harcourt Brace Jovanovich, Inc.

Sunshine and Shadow, Cecil Roberts, by permission of Hodder & Stoughton Ltd.

The Time Traveller: The Life of H. G. Wells, Norman and Jeanne MacKenzie, by permission of Weidenfeld (Publishers) Ltd.

The Truth About a Publisher, Sir Stanley Unwin, by permission of George Allen & Unwin Ltd.

The Two Worlds of Somerset Maugham, by permission of Wilmon Menard.

The Vagrant Mood, W. S. Maugham, copyright 1949, 1950, 1952 by W. S. Maugham, copyright 1933 by Doubleday & Co., Inc., copyright 1940 by the Curtis Publishing Co., by permission of Doubleday, and A. P. Watt Ltd.

Whatever Goes Up, George Tyler, by permission of The Bobbs-Merrill Co., Inc.

William Heinemann, Frederick Whyte, by permission of Jonathan Cape Ltd.

With a Feather on My Nose, Billie Burke, by permission of Appleton-Century-Crofts.

Without Veils, Sewell Stokes, by permission of Sewell Stokes.

Writers at Work, Louise Morgan, by permission of Louise Morgan and Chatto and Windus Ltd.

W. Somerset Maugham: A Candid Portrait, Karl G. Pfeiffer, pub. by W. W. Norton & Co., Inc., 1959, by permission of McIntosh & Otis, Inc.

The Youth Doctors, Patrick M. McGrady, by permission of Julian Bach Literary Agency, Inc.

All possible care has been taken in tracing the ownership of copyrighted material used in this book and in making acknowledgment for its use. If any owner has not been acknowledged, the publishers apologize and will be glad of the opportunity to rectify the error.

INDEX

ABOUT THE AUTHOR

TED MORGAN, a Pulitzer Prize-winning author and journalist, began doing research on Somerset Maugham five years ago and his diligence has uncovered information about the elusive English writer that has for years been kept from public view. Mr. Morgan lives in New York.

Outstanding Paperback Books from the Touchstone Library